ADDITIONAL PRAISE FOR *EXCEPTIONAL AMERICA*

"Mugambi Jouet traveled from Paris, France, to Houston, Texas, as a college freshman and has been trying to make sense of the American experience ever since. The result is a richly textured account of the forces that make the United States unlike anywhere else in the world."

—JUNE CARBONE, Robina Chair in Law, Science, and Technology, University of Minnesota Law School, and coauthor of *Red Families v. Blue Families*

"Using a comparative perspective, and seeking to place American values in a larger context, Mugambi Jouet provides perspectives on the pervasive culture war that divides Americans."

—NAOMI CAHN, Harold H. Greene Professor of Law, George Washington University Law School, and coauthor of *Red Families v. Blue Families*

"*Exceptional America* is a seminal work written by a French author from a comparative framework. It is an eye-opening presentation of America's contradictions, highly relevant in contemporary politics and a must-read for policy makers."

—PASHAURA SINGH, Chair, Department of Religious Studies, University of California, Riverside

Exceptional America

Exceptional America

WHAT DIVIDES AMERICANS
FROM THE WORLD
AND FROM EACH OTHER

Mugambi Jouet

UNIVERSITY OF CALIFORNIA PRESS

University of California Press, one of the most distinguished university presses in the United States, enriches lives around the world by advancing scholarship in the humanities, social sciences, and natural sciences. Its activities are supported by the UC Press Foundation and by philanthropic contributions from individuals and institutions. For more information, visit www.ucpress.edu.

University of California Press
Oakland, California

Library of Congress Cataloging-in-Publication Data

Names: Jouet, Mugambi, 1981– author.
Title: Exceptional America : what separates Americans from the world and
    from each other / Mugambi Jouet.
Description: Oakland, California : University of California Press, [2017] |
    Includes bibliographical references and index.
Identifiers: LCCN 2016046909 | ISBN 9780520293298 (cloth : alk. paper) |
    ISBN 9780520966468 (eBook)
Subjects: LCSH: Exceptionalism—United States. | National characteristics,
    American. | United States—Social policy. | United States—Economic
    policy. | United States—Politics and government—21st century.
Classification: LCC E169.12 .J68 2017 | DDC 973—dc23
LC record available at https://lccn.loc.gov/2016046909

Manufactured in the United States of America

25 24 23 22 21 20 19 18 17
10 9 8 7 6 5 4 3 2 1

It is impossible to understand a country without seeing how it varies from others. Those who know only one country know no country.

Seymour Martin Lipset

CONTENTS

PREFACE

On November 9, 2016, a puzzled world woke up to a new face of America. How could Donald Trump follow Barack Obama into the White House? Experts were stunned.

I began writing this book several years before the election, and it went to press shortly afterward. I also did not expect Trump to defeat Hillary Clinton, insofar as polls predicted her victory. I was nonetheless skeptical of the conventional wisdom that Trump hardly reflected the views of the Republican Party or most ordinary American conservatives. My research instead suggested that the difference between Trump and the G.O.P. establishment was often one of style, rhetoric, and temperament. While he built his platform on conspiracy theories about Obama's forged U.S. birth certificate and other spectacularly fact-free claims, scores of Americans were already convinced that climate change and the theory of evolution are myths. Some of Trump's campaign promises, such as barring Muslims from entering America, surely went beyond what contemporary leaders had called for. But it was not as if he had suddenly brought bigotry back to America after the civil rights movement of the 1960s ended it once and for all. Yes, Trump's incendiary declarations demonstrated reservations about democracy and the rule of law, yet many citizens and prominent politicians had come to embrace torture and indefinite detention without trial at Guantánamo.

My thesis was that conservative America has become an outlier in the Western world because of its growing radicalization over the past three decades. Four peculiar mindsets especially stood out: profound anti-intellectualism, fervent Christian fundamentalism, a visceral suspicion of government, and racial resentment. This nexus has fostered an exceptionally hard-line and anti-rational ideology, which culminated in Trump's election, although it has much older roots in the birth of modern democracy in the United States. It is therefore my hope that this book will humanize Trump voters by tracing their ideology to the fabric of America, including its history, culture, politics, law, economics, religion, and race relations.

Longstanding features of American exceptionalism have shaped the nation's intensifying polarization, from an egalitarian spirit to a tradition of religious liberty and a remarkable demographic diversity. These traits can manifest themselves in inspiring, contradictory, and destructive ways. They ultimately led to the presidency of a man whose movement has cast a shadow over the principles of democracy and human rights that America helped spread throughout the world.

Introduction

I exit the subway and walk past the Flatiron Building toward the Manhattan state appellate court, crossing elegant Madison Square Park on the way. Escaping the city's bustling corners on a weekday afternoon, quiet parkgoers sit pensively by the water fountain or chat lightheartedly on the lawn. But now is not the time for dawdling, as I am about to argue a criminal case before a panel of five judges.

It is 2009 and I am a public defender, namely a human rights lawyer defending poor people who cannot afford an attorney. My colleagues and I represent the most underprivileged members of society in a broad range of criminal cases, from homicides to petty drug offenses—an uphill battle at a time when America has the world's top incarceration rate. Over 2.2 million people live behind bars in "the land of the free."[1] America has 5 percent of the global population and 25 percent of its prisoners.[2] It is also among the countries that execute the most people, alongside authoritarian regimes such as China, Iran, Saudi Arabia, and North Korea. No other Western democracy still resorts to the death penalty, which has been abolished by two-thirds of all countries in law or practice.[3] Capital punishment is primarily a Southern phenomenon but harsh justice is not limited to red states. Judges in New York routinely inflict draconian prison terms regardless of mitigating circumstances.

Upon arriving at the courthouse I am greeted by my client's mother, who asks me whether the judges are likely to overturn her son's conviction for selling a small quantity of drugs. I explain that there is no basis to challenge his guilty plea, though the judges have the discretion to reduce his six-year sentence. Despite her resilience, she has little hope after witnessing the toll of the "War on Drugs" on her neighborhood. The young Afro-Latino man I defend is among the multitude of destitute New Yorkers incarcerated in distant rural counties whose economies heavily revolve around the prison-industrial complex.[4] I previously visited my client in an austere upstate prison, but the judges will never have to look him in the eye. Unlike for trial proceedings, prisoners have no right to attend the appellate arguments that seal their fates.

I sit down and gaze around while several other cases are heard. A remarkable feat of architecture, the Manhattan state appellate courtroom is decorated with Renaissance-inspired murals.[5] The salient figure is Lady Justice waiting to render her noble judgment. "In God we trust" is engraved above the judges' bench. Yet a peculiar brand of justice is meted out here every day.

The five judges in black robes finally grant me seven minutes to present my case. That is a fairly long time by the court's standards. Once I was afforded barely five minutes to argue in an attempted murder case.

"May it please the court. Mugambi Jouet, appearing on behalf of Hector Merced."[6]

I am defending an American citizen by relying on American law even though I am not American by birth. I have always wondered whether judges can tell my background. My accent is sometimes hard to place, as I grew up in Paris in a bilingual environment.

I urge the judges to find that the two years that my client has already served in prison are sufficient for a mere fifteen-dollar drug sale, as it would be senseless to force him to spend four more years behind bars, away from his family. The judges are uninterested in my references to studies showing that lengthy prison terms for nonviolent offenders are ineffective in reducing crime and costly to taxpayers. They are likewise unfazed by my appeal to the humane principle of rehabilitation.

As expected, a judge eventually asks me a familiar question: "Your client is serving six years in prison. Under the law, couldn't he have received up to twelve years for this crime?"

That habitual question epitomizes how superficial the debate over criminal justice has become in modern America. One might imagine that in Manhattan—the cosmopolitan center of the nation's intellectual, cultural, and artistic life—appellate judges would be inquisitive about the latest studies in criminology or prisoners' prospects for rehabilitation in the age of mass incarceration.[7] Nevertheless, local judges, whether Democratic or Republican appointees, often embrace the "tough on crime" ideology or fear appearing "soft on crime."

I readily concede the judge's point for strategic reasons but press on. Six years behind bars is excessive for a relatively minor drug offense. The judges' notion of what constitutes an excessive sentence has been skewed by the ruthless penal laws now commonplace in America. If the maximum sentence for a drug sale is twelve years, then six years in prison can seem lenient. The court will issue its official decision in a few weeks, although the outcome is predictable. My client will spend six years in a grim cellblock in the name of justice. In Europe, he might have served a few months in prison.

· · ·

Seven years later, the dehumanizing justice system I fought against as a public defender finally received more public attention. After declaring her candidacy for the 2016 presidential race, Hillary Clinton raised eyebrows by denouncing the "tough on crime" policies that once helped her husband win the White House. The spotlight had turned to criminal justice after police killings of unarmed black men led to peaceful and violent protests in Ferguson, Baltimore, and beyond. Clinton promised that as president she would not only strive to stop police brutality but also "end the era of mass incarceration" and fight "institutional racism." Americans ultimately chose as their president a man advocating a harsher penal system. Casting himself as "the Law and Order Candidate," Donald Trump vowed to make America safe from threatening undocumented immigrants and inner-city thugs.

However, mass incarceration reveals far more about America than persistent discrimination or the difficulty of finding common ground for genuine reform.[8] Figure 1 illustrates how American justice is on the fringe of contemporary Western civilization.

"One can judge a society by its prisons." This timeless observation attributed to Albert Camus, the French novelist and philosopher, evokes Fyodor Dostoyevsky's earlier reference to nineteenth-century Russia: "The degree of civilization in a society can be judged by entering its prisons."[9] Indeed, one can learn much about a society from whether it recognizes that even people convicted of serious crimes should be treated with dignity and compassion. When future generations look back on modern America, they may see its inhumane justice system as the embodiment of disturbing trends. In the words of Bryan Stevenson, a prominent attorney who has devoted his life to defending vulnerable Americans, "you judge the character of [societies] not by how they treat their rich and the powerful and the privileged but by how

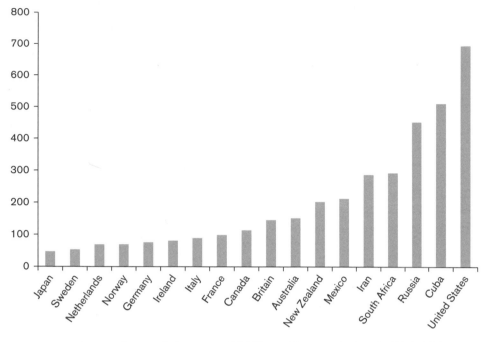

FIGURE 1. Incarceration rates (prisoners per 100,000 people). SOURCE: Institute for Criminal Policy Research, "World Prison Brief" (2016).

they treat the poor, the condemned, the incarcerated. Because it's in that nexus that we actually begin to understand truly profound things about who we are."[10]

The degeneration of American justice embodies American exceptionalism. Readers may pause to ask: "American exceptionalism? Isn't that the belief that America is a superior country chosen by God to enlighten the world?" No, it is not. Or not really.

While the word "exceptional" can imply greatness or superiority, the concept originally referred to how America is "exceptional" in the sense of "unique," "different," "unusual," "extraordinary," or "peculiar." Put differently, "American exceptionalism" means that America is an exception compared to other countries, for better or worse.[11] We will see in Chapter 1 how Republican leaders misleadingly redefined this concept as "American superiority," then used it as a rhetorical weapon against Obama by relentlessly accusing him of lacking faith in "American exceptionalism." In their view, the unpatriotic Obama precipitated the nation's decline by seeking to transform it into Europe with his "socialist" and "un-American" agenda. These accusations matched the spread of conspiracy theories claiming that Obama is not truly American because he has a forged U.S. birth certificate and is a closeted Islamist. The partisan redefinition of "American exceptionalism" obscured its original meaning and why it matters today.

Throughout this book I turn on its head the popular belief that American exceptionalism means that America is a "shining city upon a hill" picked by God to be a beacon of light to the world. Major features of American exceptionalism are instead sources of serious conflict and injustice that could spell American decline. Ironically, scores of Americans equate "exceptionalism" with their nation's superiority when it might be its Achilles heel—a self-destructive vicious circle threatening admirable dimensions of American society. Compared to other Western democracies, modern America has the worst degree of wealth inequality and the worst human rights record. Even though American exceptionalism has both positive and negative dimensions, some of its troubling features have intensified in recent decades. This book describes how Americans are now profoundly divided over their core values and what path their country should take. The people who pay the greatest price for these social problems are usually the most vulnerable members of society. The struggling poor, working class, and middle class. Women. LGBTQ people. Racial and ethnic minorities. Immigrants. Prisoners.

The United States' extraordinary polarization is partly explainable by peculiar dimensions of contemporary American conservatism: virulent anti-intellectualism, visceral anti-governmentalism, and fervent Christian fundamentalism. They foster an uncompromising, hardline ideology that impedes rational decision-making and problem-solving. Data on voting patterns confirm that the G.O.P. has moved "sharply to the right" in recent decades, though the Democratic Party's leftward shift has been more modest.[12] Donald Trump's victory in the 2016 election may have been unexpected, but his rise should have surprised no one. Contrary to conventional wisdom in the run-up to the vote, Trump's views on many issues are similar to those of the Republican establishment, as exemplified by how both have supported reintroducing torture into Western civilization[13] and insisted that climate change is a myth.[14] Evidence further indicates that mainstream politicians have long incited animosity toward minorities with "dog whistles," racially coded language recognizable by sympathizers.[15] Trump did so more openly. His actions as president might not always match his vitriolic campaign rhetoric, which often lacked coherence. In any event, Trumpism is a product of conservative America's peculiar ideological evolution.

Intriguingly, America and other Western nations are moving apart and closer at the same time. While liberal America is mainly evolving in the same direction as the rest of the West, conservative America has become an outlier because of its unusual ideology. Liberal America's worldview is not simply vastly different from the worldview in conservative America but also closer to the dominant worldview elsewhere in the Western world: Europe, Canada, Australia, and New Zealand.* Tellingly, universal health care is broadly supported by both liberals and conservatives in all Western nations except America, where Republicans persistently denounce the evils of "socialized medicine." In other words, "conservatism" tends to have a deeply different meaning in America than other Western nations.

The growing radicalism of American conservatism is not the only source of the nation's intense polarization. Singular dimensions of U.S. history, politics, law, culture, religion, and race relations have shaped the views of conservative and liberal citizens by leading to peculiar ways of approaching a wide range of issues. On one hand, crippling polarization could foster America's decline, including its ability to tackle fundamental problems at home and its credibility as a global leader. On the other hand, modern America's acute social conflicts and injustices appear to be part of a historical cycle, as they have old roots even as they take on new forms.

Alexis de Tocqueville's classic *Democracy in America* remains the most insightful book on the roots of American exceptionalism. Traveling through the young nation in the 1830s, the Frenchman remarked that Americans could live in different worlds given the hierarchy between whites and blacks, as well as the divide between North and South. However, he published his essay almost two centuries ago, before the Civil War and other major developments. Among later generations of comparatists, Seymour Martin Lipset stands out for noting that "the American Creed can be described in five terms: liberty, egalitarianism, individualism, populism, and laissez-faire." [16] But America has also changed in the nearly two decades since the publication of his magnum opus, *American Exceptionalism: A Double-Edged Sword*.

This book aims to go further than traditional explanations of American exceptionalism focusing mainly on how America as a whole compares to other nations. I argue that American exceptionalism is not only what divides

* The definition of "the West" used in this book does not include Latin American nations because of differences in history, culture, and economic development. Russia and various other former Soviet bloc countries, such as Belarus, are also not considered Western, although some Eastern European nations are gradually aligning with the West.

Americans from the world—it is also what divides Americans from each other. Compared to other Westerners, Americans are far more polarized over fundamental questions regarding the purpose of government, socioeconomic equality, the literal veracity of the Bible, sexual morality, science, human rights, and foreign policy. As a result, America is torn apart by conflicts and injustices existing nowhere else or to nowhere near the same extent in the modern Western world.

The first chapter begins by examining the history and meaning of American exceptionalism. This storied concept became a recurrent topic in recent years as Republican politicians turned it into a rhetorical weapon to impugn Obama's patriotism. Meanwhile, intensifying social polarization emerged as a major dimension of American exceptionalism's true meaning. The already huge rift between conservative and liberal America during the George W. Bush presidency worsened during the Obama era,[17] when Congress reached its worst degree of partisan polarization since the post–Civil War Reconstruction period.[18] Throughout the Bush and Obama years, America faced a series of grave crises. "The War on Terror." Hurricane Katrina. The financial collapse and Great Recession. Health care reform. The government shutdown. Climate change. Ferguson. Criminal justice reform. The list goes on, from the clashes over gay rights and Planned Parenthood to the incendiary rhetoric and violence at Trump rallies. Polarization shows little sign of abating during his presidency.

Chapter 2 considers the exceptional weight of anti-intellectualism in parts of America. This peculiar mindset is animated by outright skepticism of education, leading to "a cult of ignorance."[19] Anti-intellectualism has exacerbated the polarization of American society by precluding a rational debate on nearly every single political issue. The Bush administration's debunked justifications to invade Iraq[20] were followed by the normalization of propaganda during the Obama era, as numerous politicians routinely made absurd claims about his "fake" birth certificate and "covert Muslim faith," the perils of "socialized medicine," the creation of "death panels," the "myth" of climate change, the "tyranny" of the federal government, radical tax hikes that never occurred,[21] the treasonous Benghazi plot, and other canards. Trump's ludicrous rhetoric was merely the tip of the iceberg.

Much like other peculiar mindsets that might spell American decline, anti-intellectualism was ironically shaped by positive dimensions of U.S. history. We will see that it stems from an unusual conception of equality rooted in America's heritage as the first modern democracy to emerge from the

Enlightenment. As Tocqueville observed in the 1830s, the birth of modern democracy in the United States generally led to a greater "equality of conditions" among white men there than in Europe.[22] A pitfall of this progress was the rise of a populist creed viewing knowledge as little more than a badge of elitism of the pseudoaristocracy, because all one needs is "common sense."[23] Anti-intellectualism proved particularly influential in the South, the poorest region of the country. By encouraging irrationality, gullibility, and skepticism of education, the profound anti-intellectualism in parts of America has facilitated disinformation—false information deliberately spread to manipulate public opinion. By contrast, the evolution of democracy in Western Europe was less shaped by the conflation of egalitarianism and anti-intellectualism. While political extremism in contemporary Europe is troubling, it is less mainstream and more focused on immigration—the main target of far-right European parties. Disinformation has a far less important role in Europe than in America today, unlike in the era of European fascism, Nazism, and communism.

Interestingly, anti-intellectualism in America coexists with a vibrant intellectual life, exemplified by its outstanding universities, which may be the best in the world. In criminology and other fields, American scholars are widely esteemed by their peers abroad. Nevertheless, laws and policies are less likely to be crafted in consultation with experts in America than in other Western democracies.[24] The eggheads' knowledge is commonly deemed futile in the United States. The surge of its prison population to world-record levels would probably not have occurred but for the weight of the oversimplistic perspective behind slogans like "Tough on crime," "Zero tolerance," "You do the crime, you do the time," and "Lock people up and throw away the key."

The next two chapters explore the extraordinary role of religion in shaping American exceptionalism. Chapter 3 explains why organized religion remains highly influential in America at a time when it frequently inspires indifference, skepticism, or suspicion in other developed nations. I call into question the conventional view of an America divided between believers and nonbelievers. In reality, the divide is mainly *among* people of faith, since nonbelievers are a limited, albeit rapidly growing, group of Americans. Roughly four in ten Americans gravitate toward Christian fundamentalism—an ultratraditional faith practically nonexistent in other modern Western nations. A similar proportion of Americans share liberal-moderate faiths. Chapter 4 analyzes the "culture wars" over faith, sex, and gender. In almost no other developed country are issues such as abortion, contraception, homosexuality, and sexual education as controversial as in America. However, the political impact of Christian fundamentalism is not narrowly limited to religious issues. By fostering anti-intellectual, retrograde, black-and-white, and authoritarian mindsets, Christian fundamentalism also influences how millions of Americans think about education, science, climate change, economics, crime, foreign policy, war, and more. This sheds light on why many religious traditionalists flocked to Trump's movement regardless of his evident irreligiosity and unabashed vulgarity.

Like anti-intellectualism, religious radicalism paradoxically stems from admirable aspects of American history. The relative separation of church and state since the United States' founding spared Americans the long history of religious warfare and clerical domination that Europeans once suffered. This is among the factors behind the comparatively limited skepticism toward organized religion in America, which has largely enabled Christian fundamentalism to thrive despite its radical theology. Around 40 percent of Americans, a huge minority, are creationists, who deem that God made humans in their present form ten thousand years ago.[25] The same proportion expects Jesus to return by 2050.[26] Legions are persuaded that apocalyptic biblical prophecies are relevant to U.S. foreign policy in the Middle East.[27] But a peculiar conception of religious freedom that equates questioning dogma with intolerance has recurrently shielded fundamentalist theology from critical analysis in America.

The following chapters turn to wealth inequality, which is much sharper in America than in other Western nations. Chapter 5 describes how it has evolved from a relatively middle-class society into a winner-take-all economy since the 1980s. Chapter 6 considers why millions of ordinary Americans vote against their economic interest. Several factors help explain this puzzling dimension of U.S. politics: myopia molded by anti-intellectualism; the role of racial divisions in hindering economic solidarity; the relationship between Christian fundamentalism and market fundamentalism; and unbridled faith in the American Dream, fostering the conviction that any hardworking citizen can become affluent without government assistance.

The prison system provides a revealing window into this aspect of American exceptionalism. The surge of wealth inequality in America since the 1980s has paralleled the mass imprisonment of poor people, although the concentration of wealth in the hands of the richest 1 percent of Americans has received greater attention than the plight of the 1 percent of American adults behind bars.[28] Tighter control on the poor via a stringent penal system has coincided with greater "liberty" for the rich,[29] as symbolized by the Supreme Court's *Citizens United* decision allowing moneyed interests to spend unlimited sums on political campaigns.[30] Penal systems are often mirror images of socioeconomic systems. Statistical research indicates that the more unequal a country is, the likelier it is to imprison people.[31]

In addition to being the Western nation with the sharpest wealth inequality, America is the only one without a universal health care system. Prison is therefore the sole place where certain Americans can receive public health care. In recent years, a number of desperate people have deliberately gotten arrested to receive shelter and medical care in prison. For example, Rickie Lawrence Gardner, a forty-nine-year-old white man, staged a bank robbery in Moulton, Alabama, since he preferred heading to prison rather than face homelessness after being on the verge of losing his job because of a leg injury. "His is the first bank robbery I've ever worked where the robber was waiting outside the bank for the police to turn himself in," the local police chief said.[32]

The full story of American exceptionalism cannot be told without looking more specifically at the disturbing evolution of the nation's penal laws, which I do in Chapter 7. This is an area where the stark divide between American ideals and reality hits home powerfully. Modern American justice is astoundingly harsh. The nation not only has virtually the highest incarceration rate worldwide, but is also the sole Western democracy to retain the death penalty. American justice is further characterized by pervasive discrimination and other degrading practices. It was not always so, as foreign observers once saw American justice as enlightened.

Police shootings are far more common in America than in other Western democracies, a tragedy influenced by racial animus. Strikingly, British civilians are one hundred times less likely to be shot by police. Most British police officers do not even carry a gun.[33] Of course, another reason why U.S. police officers are more trigger happy is that more criminals are armed in America. Nearly one gun is available to each American on average—a world record. Yemen is a distant second in the number of guns per capita.[34] The obsession with guns among numerous Americans and die-hard groups such as the National Rifle Association epitomizes the visceral suspicion of government in much of the country. The right to bear arms is not merely envisioned as a way to defend oneself from criminals—it is equally envisioned as a way to defend oneself from the government. In this view, armed patriots might well be the last line of defense when the federal government goes one step too far in violating the American people's "liberty."[35] The extraordinarily lax gun control shaped by this far-right ideology is a major reason why America has the highest murder rate and the most gun violence in the West. Americans are generally three to five times likelier to be murdered than Europeans.[36]

Still, America does not have an exceptionally ruthless justice system because it has an exceptionally high crime rate. Homicides aside, its crime levels are comparable to those of other Western nations.[37] The degrading punishments routinely inflicted on American prisoners instead reflect a peculiar view of human dignity. Illustratively, the Supreme Court held that the incredibly long sentences imposed under California's "three-strikes law" are not "cruel and unusual" under the Eighth Amendment of the U.S. Constitution. The court therefore upheld the fifty-year-to-life sentence of a man who had shoplifted videotapes worth only $153, since he had prior convictions for petty theft, burglary, and transporting marijuana.[38] America further stands apart from other Western democracies by relying on solitary confinement for lengthy periods, regardless of the enormous mental harm it causes. A United Nations expert on torture denounced these practices, pointing to two American prisoners who spent over four decades alone in tiny cells.[39] The U.N. Human Rights Committee has additionally expressed concern about the U.S. practice of shackling pregnant prisoners even while they give birth.[40] Perhaps one may see progress in the fact that, since a 2005 Supreme Court case decided by a 5–4 vote, it is no longer constitutional to execute juveniles in America.[41] But America remains essentially the only country to sentence teenagers to life imprisonment.[42]

Other fundamental human rights issues are also extremely divisive in America. The Bush administration's creation of the Guantánamo camp stood for the proposition that terrorists have no human rights—and that it is therefore acceptable to torture and detain them forever without trial. Although many citizens condemned such practices as "un-American," this treatment was not as much a deviation from contemporary American values as they thought, since it fit within the notion that criminals' lives are worthless. America's self-defeating "War on Terror" recalls its "War on Crime" in how both emphasize striking hard at offenders, downplaying root social causes behind their actions, and dismissing humanitarian concerns.[43]

America considers itself "the leader of the free world," yet it regularly violates international human rights standards. Paradoxically, the human rights movement that came to life after World War II was partly led by Americans, including Eleanor Roosevelt.[44] Her vision of universal human rights bore more fruit abroad than at home. References to "human rights" are rare in the

U.S. legal and political debate. In modern America, "human rights" often evoke foreign problems like abuses in Third World dictatorships.[45]

This brings us to the last chapter, examining America's singular relationship to the world. The United States has long been far more inclined than other Western democracies to defy norms of diplomacy, international law, and human rights deemed against its interests. Americans are thus quite divided over key aspects of U.S. foreign policy, as shown by radically different perspectives on the invasion of Iraq, Guantánamo, and torture. These attitudes reflect diverse facets of exceptionalism, such as America's superpower status, its relative geographic isolation, and the idea that God chose it to lead the world.

Insularity helps explain why America often stands alone among developed nations in pursuing the numerous counterproductive policies discussed throughout this book. Studies show that Americans are generally less knowledgeable than other Westerners about foreign countries.[46] They also travel less internationally, as nearly two hundred million do not have passports,[47] in the image of Sarah Palin, who had left North America only once before becoming the 2008 Republican vice-presidential candidate.[48]

Insularity is a curious state of mind in a country that considerably influences the world culturally, economically, geopolitically, and militarily. Yet a tension between globalism and isolationism has long existed in the United States. Millions of Americans are well traveled and sincerely interested in foreign cultures. American universities have some of the finest international programs of all academic institutions worldwide. In the end, America is a land of immigrants. While millions are uninquisitive about the countries from which their ancestors came, America's global citizens are mindful that their country now lags behind other industrialized nations in areas like criminal justice, health care, and human rights.

In sum, this book explores the intriguing relationship between different dimensions of American exceptionalism. Even though no chapter is specifically devoted to race and immigration, they are recurrent themes. Next to other Western democracies, America has historically had a far bigger proportion of racial and ethnic minorities, which now constitute 38 percent of its population.[49] Racism has therefore played a bigger role in shaping American attitudes. That may be counterintuitive at first. After all, America has been more successful at integrating immigrants than European nations in a number of ways. It was the first Western democracy tolerant enough to choose a person of color as its leader. Obama's election was a source of inspiration to millions of people worldwide, as he came to embody the idea that "anything is possible in America."

The flip side is that America's extraordinary diversity has had troubling consequences by hindering socioeconomic solidarity. For instance, scores of Americans believe that most beneficiaries of universal health care would be minorities on welfare, who should work harder instead of expecting a "handout." Such stereotypes are among the reasons why the Republican base virulently opposed the Obama administration's health care reform. In reality, millions of Americans who would benefit from universal health care are white and employed.[50]

By contrast, few Europeans think of universal health care as a program primarily for racial minorities or even poor people. Race has had less influence in molding attitudes toward inequality in Europe than in America. This may again seem hard to believe, given the growing sway of far-right European political parties, not to mention discrimination against Muslims, blacks, and other minorities on the Old Continent. The difference is probably due not to lower racism but rather to the fact that there were few people of color in Europe until recent decades, when a surge of immigration from Africa, Asia, the Middle East, Caribbean islands, and beyond increased their proportion.* European institutions like national health insurance were created before their arrival. Similarly, European attitudes toward social justice were framed long before the current immigration crisis, as illustrated by the creation of the European Court of Human Rights in 1959. Simply put, part of the reason why white Europeans are more inclined than white Americans to think that depriving people of health care or executing prisoners is an affront to human dignity is that these attitudes largely originated at a time when nearly all Europeans were white. Conversely, race has always been an issue in America, thereby coloring attitudes toward inequality and human dignity.

In our journey through America we will see that it incarnates progress in countless ways but is also a nation of stark contradictions. Why does a country that prizes "liberty" so dearly have virtually the highest incarceration rate in the entire world? Why is America the only Western country to retain the death penalty, even though its people are the most suspicious of the authority of "big government" over their lives? How could the first Western nation to

---

* The Holocaust is a powerful reminder that scapegoating and persecution are not new problems in Europe, although groups such as Jews and Roma have historically constituted smaller shares of the European population than blacks and other minorities in the United States.

elect a person of color as its head of state suffer from institutional racism? Why is anti-intellectualism so prevalent in the United States, considering the quality of its universities and the impressive contributions of Americans to human thought? Why has Christian fundamentalism remained so prominent in one of the countries that spearheaded the advent of science, the sexual revolution, and other modern developments? How does one explain the insularity of many Americans given their country's influential role on the global stage? And why do myriad Americans vote against their self-interest by opposing sensible reforms in an age of staggering inequality?

. . .

The adrenaline from my court argument slowly wears off as I head back to my office, a few blocks from the World Trade Center's ruins. I linger around the workplace. Gotham's nightlife beckons but I am not in the mood to socialize. I am alone with my thoughts as I decide to walk by the Hudson River.

Drifting along the waterfront toward the southern tip of Manhattan, I eventually find a quiet bench in Battery Park. The Statue of Liberty, which left France's shores in 1885, stands on the horizon, carrying its celebrated message from the Jewish poet Emma Lazarus: "Give me your tired, your poor, your huddled masses yearning to breathe free." I wonder whether my client will stay in prison. My mind begins to wander as I reflect on the path that led me here.

My roots are American in a sense, as my French mother and Kenyan father met in New York when they were international students at Columbia University. Their backgrounds could hardly have been more different. My father was born in the rural village of Kangeta to illiterate parents who never attended school, since British colonial authorities sharply limited access to education for African children. The Kenyan government did not do much better following independence in 1963, although determination and good fortune enabled my father to attend college in Nairobi before pursuing his studies in America. My mother, on the other hand, is from Brittany, the Celtic region of France. Leaving her comfort zone, she spent years living in America, Ivory Coast, and Kenya.

Unlike Barack Obama, I was actually born in Kenya. I then moved to Paris with my mother after my parents separated when I was three years old. Their short-lived marriage left me, their only child, between worlds: France-Kenya, Europe-Africa, white-black. Growing up a few minutes from the

Eiffel Tower, I received a French upbringing at home while attending a bilingual French-English international school.

I first set foot in America in the summer of 1989, at the age of eight, to visit my father, who had become a professor at UCLA. A summer in sunny Los Angeles provided all the youthful excitement I could handle, including visits to Universal Studios and other amusement parks. My fascination with America had begun. During my childhood I returned to California and visited additional parts of the country. Attending college in America seemed inevitable, as I was eager to broaden my horizons and gain independence. My parents encouraged me to do so because they held U.S. universities in high regard. I finally chose Rice University in Houston, since it was a reputable institution in another world, Texas, a state I had yet to discover. I arrived there ready to embrace its people and certainly had the opportunity to do so, as a large share of my fellow students were from Texas and neighboring Southern states.

Houston bears little resemblance to European cities. Urban sprawl. No subway system. The consequent need to drive almost everywhere. The proliferation of strip malls. On the upside, Rice University's agreeable campus blended elegant architecture with green areas. NASA's fantastic space station was only a short drive away.

Compared to the French, Americans are generally more informal and outgoing with strangers, perhaps even more so in states like Texas, where people pride themselves on Southern hospitality. It was not uncommon for a stranger to greet me with a smile as I strolled around campus, something I did not experience when pursuing my graduate studies in New York and Chicago. Southerners are reputed to be anti-French, but my Gallic origins usually generated warm reactions. Anti-French attitudes in America typically arise over foreign policy disagreements, such as France's opposition to the Bush administration's war on Iraq. However, I no longer lived in Texas by the time America invaded Iraq, so no Texan had a chance to offer me a helping of "freedom fries" or "freedom toast."

Living in Texas was nonetheless a culture shock, as I saw things I had never witnessed in France. People who said grace before meals, rejected the theory of evolution, and preached abstinence until marriage. People who invoked their Christian faith to support the death penalty—"an eye for an eye"—and interpreted "Thou shalt not kill" as a license to execute prisoners. People who were content to lack universal health care because it would be a great leap toward the "tyranny of socialized medicine" in other industrialized nations. And middle-class persons who never left their country except maybe to visit Cancún, a sanitized version of Mexico for U.S. tourists.

Originally a frontier land, Texas enjoyed independence for nearly a decade after seceding from Mexico in 1836. The Lone Star State joined the United States in 1845, although it tends to regard itself as a land of mavericks. In twenty-first-century Texas, the governor can proudly give the following response on being asked whether secession is an option: "We've got a great union. There's absolutely no reason to dissolve it. But if Washington continues to thumb their nose at the American people, you know, who knows what might come out of that?" These cavalier remarks were made by the former governor—and aspiring president of the United States—Rick Perry at a Tea Party rally. Of course, the South had already tried to secede, and the U.S. Civil War cost approximately six hundred thousand lives.

George W. Bush was serving his second term as governor when I arrived in Texas, but I did not yet know who he was. While W. was convinced that God wanted him to become president,[51] not all Texans felt the same way. Still, many of my Texan friends and acquaintances who struck me as intensely religious and quite conservative happened to be Democrats. As the political scientist John Kingdon has noted, "The center in American politics is considerably to the right of the center in the politics of other industrialized countries."[52] That is particularly true in Southern states like Texas, where Democrats are typically well to the right of mainstream European conservatives.

Living in Texas planted the first seed of this book in my mind. Why is the South so different from both Europe and the rest of America? When asked this question, people tend to respond that Southerners are more conservative, religious, skeptical of education, and distrustful of government. But why is that the case? After all, conservatives in Europe widely accept the theory of evolution and universal health care, whereas such ideas are often anathema to American conservatives, especially in the South.

When I moved to New York, it sometimes felt like I was in a different country from Texas and that I had taken a step closer to Paris. New Yorkers seemed to have more in common with Europeans than with Southerners in terms of their worldviews. I saw the same pattern while living and traveling in other blue states. On multiple fundamental issues, such as evolution, abortion, universal health care, or the "War on Terror," talking with a New Yorker, Bostonian, Chicagoan, or San Franciscan was not far removed from talking to an average person on the Old Continent. Upon later visiting

Canada, Australia, and New Zealand, as well as researching the nature of their political debates, I again noticed that people there were closer to U.S. liberals than to U.S. conservatives in their worldviews. That planted the second seed leading me to write this book. The hardline conservatism in red states is unusual elsewhere in the modern Western world, except for attitudes toward immigration, which have grown more reactionary in many Western countries.

Even as the contrast between conservative America and the rest of the West became clearer, certain features of American society as a whole struck me as peculiar. One of them was the exceptionally harsh criminal punishments described above. Though New York justice is less draconian than Texan justice, both are drastically more punitive than justice elsewhere in the West. On closer examination, American prisons seemed to be a microcosm of American society. That was the final seed of the book's genesis. The most vulnerable members of society, including prisoners, frequently pay the worst price for national crises.

This book is based primarily on multidisciplinary academic research encompassing law, history, sociology, political science, policy analysis, and economics. My focus is deliberately broad. Academic studies and news stories about American society tend to address issues piecemeal while overlooking the interrelationship between them. I aim to connect the dots here.

Seeking inspiration from Tocqueville, who blended an objective analysis of American society with a narrative of his experiences as a French traveler, I complement qualitative and quantitative evidence with my observations as an insider-outsider in modern America. Born in Kenya, raised in France, I eventually spent years in diverse regions of the United States. I was steeped in Bible Belt life during my college days, helped destitute Houstonians search for employment at the Urban League, visited evangelical and Mormon churches, spent Christmas with friends in New England, represented indigent prisoners in Manhattan, met with men on Alabama's death row, and witnessed innumerable other facets of American society. Europeans who relocate to the United States are not usually well integrated. They stay in communities of expats or international students. That was not my case. From blue to red states, I lived almost only among Americans, some of whom did not realize my foreign background, as I have an Americanized accent.

Other life experiences sparked my interest in comparative studies. After being a Manhattan public defender, I moved to The Hague, Netherlands, to serve as a judicial clerk at the United Nations war crimes tribunal for

Yugoslavia, which allowed me to discover Dutch society. I previously studied abroad in Mexico, immersing myself in its culture and acquiring Spanish fluency. I have visited multiple other countries, from Peru to Japan and India, often as a low-budget backpacker mingling with locals. Comparing America to other nations finally became the focus of my research at Stanford University.

I bring to this book my lifelong admiration of American society and my concern about how certain dimensions of American exceptionalism harm both the United States and the world. Above all, it is an effort to understand America. There is no ultimate answer to what makes it a unique country, but the book aims to identify multiple pieces of the puzzle. American exceptionalism has a wide range of interrelated dimensions shaped by fascinating historical, political, legal, economic, social, cultural, religious, and racial factors. These features can be perceived in a positive or a negative light. Some may be strengths, others sources of decline or injustice. At the very least, American exceptionalism leaves no one indifferent.

ONE

———

One Nation, Divisible

Living in red and blue states, I was always struck by how stars and stripes appear on nearly every corner in "the land of the free." By the same token, "The Star-Spangled Banner" is sung before virtually each sporting event, and schoolchildren are commonly expected to pledge allegiance to the flag. From Texas to New York, Chicago, and the Bay Area, legions of Americans follow such rituals calling on people to worship their country. If the rituals' meaning must sometimes be inferred, the nation's leaders are usually more straightforward. Both Democratic and Republican politicians regularly proclaim that America is the greatest country in history and a nation picked by God to enlighten the world.

In most other democracies, flags hang mainly on government buildings. People rarely wave them, except on national holidays or when a national team competes in a major event like the World Cup or Olympics. Anthems are also generally reserved for national holidays or competitions involving national teams, not ordinary sporting events between high schools, universities, or professional clubs. While the majority of Americans take ubiquitous flag waving and anthem singing for granted, the Pledge of Allegiance has become fairly controversial, although that is largely because it refers to America as a "nation under God," a concern for secularists. The very idea of urging children to pledge allegiance has not proved remotely as divisive.

National chauvinism has evolved into a religion in America, where around 80 percent of the public agrees that "the U.S. has a unique character that makes it the greatest country in the world." [1] Americans are typically convinced that their nation's superiority was bestowed by the Almighty, as 62 percent deem that "God has granted America a special role in human history." [2]

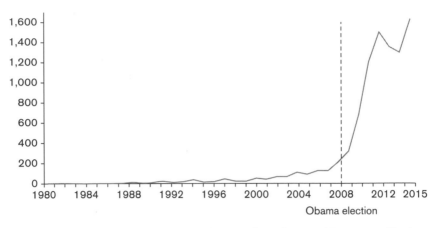

FIGURE 2. Mentions of "American exceptionalism" in U.S. media, 1980–2015. SOURCE: Westlaw.

Faith in the inherent greatness of the United States is often described as "American exceptionalism." Figure 2 shows how references to "American exceptionalism" skyrocketed in the media after Barack Obama entered the White House in 2009,[3] as Republican leaders constantly invoked the phrase to impugn his patriotism. From Mitt Romney to John Boehner, Jeb Bush, Marco Rubio, Ted Cruz, and Donald Trump, the G.O.P. brass insisted that Obama does not believe in "American exceptionalism" and aimed to turn the United States into "socialist" Europe or, at best, Canada. Yet it was not simply Obama's policies that were allegedly un-American. The Republicans' focus on defending "American exceptionalism" paralleled an explosion of conspiracy theories claiming that Obama was secretly born in Kenya, lacks a valid U.S. birth certificate, and is a covert Muslim with jihadist sympathies.

However, American exceptionalism does not necessarily mean what most people think. As the phrase became a recurrent talking point during the Obama presidency, few people paused to consider its original definition. Until being hijacked by politicians in recent years, the concept of American exceptionalism was primarily used by academics to identify America as an *exception* compared to other countries, especially Western nations. A more capitalistic economy lacking universal health care, more punitive penal system coexisting with lax gun control, and more unilateral foreign policy are among the aspects of American exceptionalism that academics have explored.

While many Americans equate "exceptionalism" with their country's inherent superiority, certain dimensions of American exceptionalism may contribute to its decline. One of them is the worsening division of American society under the presidencies of George W. Bush, Barack Obama, and Donald Trump. Conservative and liberal Americans have grown further and further apart in their worldviews, values, and factual understandings.

Both the polarization of American society and American exceptionalism have received extensive media coverage for nearly a decade. But journalists and academics have largely overlooked the interrelationship between these two major issues by analyzing them separately. The intense polarization of American society is actually a key dimension of American exceptionalism. In no other Western nation are people so divided over fundamental questions about the role of government, access to health care, wealth inequality, financial regulation, climate change, science, sexual propriety, reproductive rights, the literal truth of the Bible, warfare, and human rights. This acute polarization has led to a gridlock with profound consequences for American society and the world.

THE STORIED LIFE OF AMERICAN EXCEPTIONALISM

"For a transitory enchanted moment man must have held his breath in the presence of this continent, compelled into an aesthetic contemplation he neither understood nor desired, face to face for the last time in history with something commensurate to his capacity for wonder." Drawn from the conclusion of *The Great Gatsby,* F. Scott Fitzgerald's stirring homage to America echoes longstanding ideas about the "New World."

The Europeans who colonized North America were persuaded that they had settled a unique world. America was not simply a remote continent with exotic sceneries and "strange" Indian "heathens." Many Europeans perceived America as a land with a special destiny awaiting the arrival of its rightful owners, who would mold it into an ideal society.[4]

The Founding Fathers shared this conviction. "America was designed by Providence for the Theatre, on which Man was to make his true figure, on which science, Virtue, Liberty, Happiness and Glory were to exist in Peace," John Adams wrote.[5] Once thirteen colonies defying the British Empire, the United States became a continent-size country as following generations settled westward and thwarted rival claims to territory by Indian tribes and the British, French, Spanish, and Mexicans. "Manifest Destiny," a phrase coined in 1845, refers to the United States' expansion across North America in the name of progress and liberty. As the historian Anders Stephanson explained,

"Manifest Destiny" evoked "God's chosen people in the Promised Land" in a "reenactment of the Exodus narrative." The faithful widely thought that the United States' creation and growth fulfilled biblical prophecies. While certain citizens called into question expansionism and the violence it could entail, the notion that America is a special country pursuing a divinely chosen path had not merely been ingrained by then. It was also already a way of justifying political actions, however inspiring or troubling they might be.[6]

America the Exception

To countless people nowadays, "American exceptionalism" evokes an inherent superiority hallowed by God—the same sentiment shared by colonists convinced that their takeover of Indian land was God's plan, Founding Fathers confident that Providence was on their side, and later generations trusting in America's Manifest Destiny.

Yet the initial description of America as an "exceptional" country has mostly been traced to a foreigner who did not use the term in this sense, namely Alexis de Tocqueville. The nineteenth-century Frenchman's epic journey through America led him to describe it as uniquely different from Europe. "The position of the Americans is therefore quite exceptional, and it may be believed that no democratic people will ever be placed in a similar one," he wrote in one of his many observations.[7] Tocqueville is frequently remembered as an admirer of the United States. He indeed praised Americans for their trailblazing democratic institutions, sense of civic duty, industriousness, and spirit of innovation. Nevertheless, he criticized Americans on other grounds, including their common support for slavery, mistreatment of Indians, and materialism. When describing America as an "exceptional" country, Tocqueville meant that it is an exception—a singular nation, not an inherently superior one.

Tocqueville apparently never used the precise phrase "American exceptionalism," and scholars have ironically attributed its coinage to communists critical of America. Jay Lovestone, the leader of the U.S. Communist Party, used the phrase in the 1920s to argue that communism would evolve differently in the United States than elsewhere because of the country's special conditions, a thesis he called "American exceptionalism." Lovestone's view drew the ire of none other than Joseph Stalin, who condemned it as heresy deviating from Marxism's universal laws. After a tense meeting in Moscow, the Soviet dictator threatened Lovestone and had him detained until he narrowly escaped with the help of a Latvian contact. Lovestone was subsequently expelled from the Communist Party.[8]

By the 1950s, "American exceptionalism" was mainly a descriptive concept used by academics to refer to the social traits that make America an exception compared to other countries.[9] As American exceptionalism developed into a significant topic of research in history, politics, law, sociology, economics, and other fields, academics advanced diverse theories about what makes America unique and whether such features are positive or not.[10] For instance, the absence of universal health care in America may be admirable or problematic, depending on one's values. The same thing can be said about its retention of the death penalty, its immense military budget, and beyond.

In sum, "exceptionalism" has not historically meant "greatness." Two decades ago, the social scientist Seymour Martin Lipset already expressed concern about this misconception: "When Tocqueville or other 'foreign traveler' writers or social scientists have used the term 'exceptional' to describe the United States, they have not meant, as some critics of the concept assume, that America is better than other countries or has a superior culture. Rather, they have simply been suggesting that it is qualitatively different, that it is an outlier."[11]

However, the distortion of the concept reached unprecedented levels during the Obama years, as Republican politicians recurrently blasted him for repudiating "American exceptionalism." The media and rank-and-file citizens thus also came to readily conflate "American exceptionalism" with a conviction in American superiority. Even prominent journalists like Glenn Greenwald, who disclosed classified National Security Agency files handed to him by Edward Snowden, have overlooked the phrase's original meaning. Greenwald therefore denounced "belief in objective U.S. superiority, this myth of American exceptionalism," thereby accepting the redefinition of the concept by the G.O.P.[12]

An Anti-Obama Slogan and Dog Whistle

Expressing faith in America's superiority has long been a theme of U.S. politics. God made America "a shining city upon a hill," Ronald Reagan famously said, combining words from the Puritan colonist John Winthrop and the lyrics of "America the Beautiful."[13] While politicians of all stripes have proclaimed similar ideas throughout history, Figure 2 demonstrates that Republicans did not systematically use the expression "American exceptionalism" until Obama was elected.

At the 2015 Conservative Political Action Conference—a major stop for prospective presidential candidates—the Fox News pundit Sean Hannity asked Jeb Bush his thoughts on exceptionalism. "I do believe in American exceptionalism," Bush responded, unlike Obama, who "is disrespecting our history and the extraordinary nature of our country." The third scion of the Bush family aiming to be president added that the post-Obama era must begin with "restoring a love of our country."

Rudolph Giuliani, New York's ex-mayor, was more explicit. "I do not believe that the president loves America," he asserted, as Obama does not think "we're the most exceptional country in the world." Giuliani's tirade came in a speech encouraging Wisconsin Governor Scott Walker to run for president. Asked if he agreed that Obama does not love America, Walker answered: "I don't really know what his opinions are on that one way or another."

Ted Cruz later declared his candidacy in a speech emphasizing that "American exceptionalism" has made the United States "a clarion voice for freedom in the world, a shining city on a hill"—a promise Obama had purportedly betrayed. Marco Rubio followed suit by saying he would run for president "because I believe our very identity as an exceptional nation is at stake." Donald Trump concurred, underlining that "maybe my biggest beef with Obama is his view that there's nothing special or exceptional in America—that we're no different than any other country" and that "America would be better off if we acted more like European socialist countries." [14]

The 2012 Republican presidential candidates sang the same tune. Mitt Romney insisted that, unlike Obama, he believes in "American exceptionalism," by which he meant that America is "the greatest nation in the history of the world and a force for good." According to Romney, Obama "thinks America's just another nation" and wants it to become "a European-style entitlement society." John Sununu, the cochair of Romney's campaign, added that Obama should "learn how to be an American." Rick Santorum agreed that Obama "doesn't believe America is exceptional" and aimed to "impose some sort of European socialism." Newt Gingrich published a campaign book, *A Nation like No Other: Why American Exceptionalism Matters,* making the same points.

The evolution of the Republican platform is also striking. From 1856 to 2008, the party's official platforms never used the expression "American exceptionalism" or even the adjective "exceptional" to describe the country.[15] By contrast, the final section of the 2012 Republican platform, lambasting the Obama presidency, was titled "American Exceptionalism." [16] The 2016 platform was more straightforward. The first line of its preamble stressed: "We believe in American exceptionalism."[17]

In practice, protecting the country's "exceptional" character meant embracing the G.O.P. program of massive tax cuts, sweeping deregulation, and religious ultratraditionalism. "American exceptionalism is the product of unlimited freedom," Texas Governor Rick Perry argued. "And there is nothing troubling our nation today that cannot be solved by the rebirth of freedom." The redefinition of "American exceptionalism" as freedom from "big government" and "Euro-style socialism" especially galvanized Tea Party supporters.

Obama had supposedly abandoned "American exceptionalism" by implementing stimulus measures and improving financial regulation following the gravest economic and financial crises since the Great Depression. Worse, he had profoundly threatened the liberty of the American people with a radical socialist takeover of everyone's health care—by passing a moderate reform derived from Republican plans that were once considered market friendly and limited in scope. Few Americans are aware that the policy misleadingly labeled "Obamacare" was advanced by Richard Nixon and the Heritage Foundation before being instituted in Massachusetts by Romney when he was its governor.[18] Republican leaders set these facts aside as part of a strategy depicting Obama as a dangerous radical. Around 41 percent of Republican citizens were indeed persuaded that Obama "wants to use an economic collapse or terrorist attack as an excuse to take dictatorial powers."[19]

Instead of trumpeting U.S. superiority, Obama was allegedly busy "apologizing" to the world because of his uneasiness with America's superpower status. Taking umbrage at Obama's "apology tour," Romney argued that America is a quasi-perfect country. "I will never, ever apologize for America," he insisted. But this frequent Republican talking point was a straw man. Obama had never "apologized" for America.[20] Rather, he had struck a conciliatory tone with the international community and the Muslim world in the aftermath of George W. Bush's widely unpopular foreign policy. The Bush administration's unilateralism, invasion of Iraq, approval of torture, attempt to detain any terrorism suspect forever without trial at Guantánamo, and other human rights abuses had greatly tarnished America's international reputation, hindering its capacity to lead by example.*

---

* We will see in Chapter 8 that the Obama administration eventually institutionalized certain controversial Bush-era counterterrorism policies.

Above all, the Republicans' focus on "American exceptionalism" was premised on the idea that Obama denied America's specialness. In fact, he had long proclaimed that Americans are a unique people, such as by affirming that America is "a light to the world" and "the greatest nation on Earth." But the G.O.P. shed doubt on Obama's conviction by exploiting his nuanced language. When Obama was asked his opinion on American exceptionalism, he responded: "I believe in American exceptionalism, just as I suspect that the Brits believe in British exceptionalism and the Greeks believe in Greek exceptionalism." He then added that America has a special culture and plays an "extraordinary role in leading the world." Various pundits quoted solely the first part of the answer as proof of his lack of patriotism.[21] Much of the Republican base was even persuaded that Obama is not really American but rather a covert Muslim with a forged U.S. birth certificate.[22]

Paradoxically, Trump criticized establishment Republicans for talking about "American exceptionalism," describing it as national chauvinism,[23] although he ran an ultranationalistic campaign and himself accused Obama of not believing that America is "exceptional."[24] This epitomized Trump's tendency to systematically take self-contradictory positions throughout his campaign. Hillary Clinton reacted by denouncing Trump for not believing in "American exceptionalism,"[25] mirroring the Republicans' attacks on Obama, who likewise tried to co-opt the phrase. "My entire career has been a testimony to American exceptionalism," Obama previously emphasized.

Naturally, the meaning of words can change over time. But the conflation of "American exceptionalism" with "American superiority" during Obama's presidency did not occur through a natural process of linguistic evolution. It was a political strategy that led American exceptionalism to become a major topic following the election of the first black president, a man with a foreign-sounding name. For decades, mainstream politicians have used dog whistles—coded racial rhetoric—to stir hostility against minorities. The evolution of "American exceptionalism" into an anti-Obama rallying cry with nativist overtones evoked Republican leaders' appeals to "states' rights" to rouse whites resenting the end of segregation.[26]

While Trump mostly abandoned dog whistles for an overtly nativist campaign, his slogan "Make America Great Again" echoed the Republican establishment's calls to restore the golden age of "American exceptionalism," whose ideals Obama had betrayed. Trump's conspiracy-mongering about Obama's birthplace and Islamism also expanded on the Republican establishment's repeated assertions about Obama's un-American values. These were not the only ways that the Republican establishment provided fertile ground for Trumpism.

Why did Obama's presidency prove so divisive? This question relates to the original meaning of exceptionalism—America is an *exception* within the Western world partly because its conservatives and liberals are far more divided than other Westerners over their core values. Problems that have long been essentially resolved in almost all other Western nations, such as health care and abortion, are therefore explosive issues in America. Social divisions have always existed in America, but partisan polarization has surged in recent decades, as Figure 3 shows, making the country quasi-ungovernable at times.

In 2004, Obama famously declared that "there is not a liberal America and a conservative America—there is the United States of America." In reality, that assertion was less a fact than an aspiration, wishful thinking, or a political strategy based on a theme of unity. The dominant worldview in liberal America is not only vastly different from the one in conservative America. It is also often closer to the dominant worldview elsewhere in the Western world: Europe, Canada, Australia, and New Zealand.

Living in Different Worlds

Pundits routinely identify partisan gerrymandering as a leading cause of polarization,[27] although the evidence for this claim appears thin.[28] Blaming polarization largely on Republican-led gerrymandering suggests that it is an artificial situation caused by political gamesmanship. This account minimizes the genuinely different worldviews separating modern American conservatives and liberals.

Obama hoped to unify the nation and practically usher in a postpartisan age following the clashes of the Bush presidency. The precise opposite occurred. Since the post–Civil War Reconstruction era, Congress was never as polarized as during the Obama presidency, according to a sophisticated statistical study.[29] Irreconcilable views about the purpose of government have kept Democratic and Republican leaders from finding common ground on nearly every single issue. A crippling shutdown of the federal government ensued in 2013, which again set America apart from other Western nations, whose

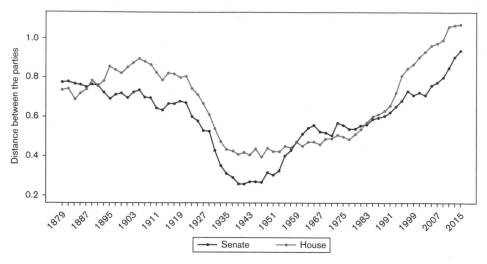

FIGURE 3. Party polarization in Congress, 1879–2015, based on roll call voting records. SOURCE: Nolan McCarty, Keith Poole, and Howard Rosenthal (MIT Press; voteview.com).

governments face virtually no risk of shutdown.[30] In 2016, after Justice Antonin Scalia died, Republican senators categorically refused to consider any replacement that Obama might propose for the Supreme Court. Like federal institutions, "state legislatures are becoming significantly more polarized."[31]

While Obama was reelected with a wide margin of Electoral College votes, 332 to 206, he won barely 51 percent of the popular vote. His contest against Romney was tighter than it seemed and featured two very distinct conceptions of what America should be. Obama's reelection utterly dismayed the millions of conservatives who identified him as a dangerous "socialist" bent on America's economic and moral decline. This situation was reminiscent of George W. Bush's reelection in 2004, which deeply appalled most liberals.

The gulf between conservative and liberal America worsened in the 2016 campaign, given the starkly different values defended by Hillary Clinton and Donald Trump, if not Ted Cruz or Paul Ryan. Clinton won the popular vote by approximately three million ballots.[32] Trump won the Electoral College comfortably, 304–227 votes, notwithstanding his endless stream of extremist, megalomaniac, racist, sexist, vulgar, and baseless statements. "I could stand in the middle of Fifth Avenue and shoot somebody and I wouldn't lose any voters," Trump boasted in early 2016. A few weeks later he tweeted a quote from Benito Mussolini—whose Fascist regime fought against America in World War II—insisting that it was "a very good quote" and "I know who said it." [33] He also repeatedly praised Vladimir Putin, the Russian dictator. In the run-up to the vote, Trump alleged that it would be "rigged" and suggested that he might not accept the democratic process: "I will totally accept the results—if I win." Even though he is not a traditional fascist in Mussolini's mold, his campaign had neofascist dimensions. Robert Paxton, an expert on the history of fascism, observed that "Trump shows a rather alarming willingness to use fascist themes and fascist styles." [34] But Paxton and several other experts described Trump as more of a far-right populist. [35]

It may come as no surprise that the divide is partly regional. Republicans from the most conservative regions of the country, the South and Midwest, are generally more conservative than Republicans from the most liberal regions, the Northeast and West Coast. By the same token, Democrats from liberal regions are more liberal than Democrats from conservative regions. What people usually overlook, however, is that the intensity of America's regional divide is exceptional. There are obviously rather liberal and conservative regions in other Western nations, but their citizens are not sharply divided over such basic issues as whether people should have a right to medical treatment.

Besides, the extraordinary polarization of American society is not merely between blue and red states, as a major partisan rift has occurred nationwide. Republican leaders in blue states typically join their counterparts in red states in defending hardline positions on essentially all issues. It is revealing that the New Yorker Trump proved popular not only among Southern or Midwestern conservatives. Rudolph Giuliani and Chris Christie, who respectively served as the mayor of New York and the governor of New Jersey, vehemently supported his extremist campaign.

Of course, Trump feuded with establishment Republicans, some of whom found the specter of his presidency fearful. The party's two prior presidential candidates notably urged voters to reject him. Mitt Romney labeled Trump a dangerous "phony." Yet he had gladly welcomed Trump's endorsement in his 2012 campaign—regardless of how Trump spouted bigoted conspiracy theories about Obama's forged birth certificate. John McCain equally criticized Trump, although McCain contributed to the degeneration of the political debate by catapulting Sarah Palin onto the national stage. His decision to pick her as his running mate in 2008 aimed to energize the Republican base rather than appeal to moderates. [36]

According to conventional wisdom, hardline conservatism is basically limited to Trump or the Republican base, whereas the Republican establishment is moderate. In reality, the G.O.P. establishment has long defended policies that are objectively far right by either U.S. historical standards or international standards. The rise of the Tea Party movement skewed perceptions by making hardline establishment conservatives like George W. Bush and John Boehner seem center right in comparison. Indeed, when the implacable Freedom Caucus succeeded in ousting Boehner as the Speaker of the House in 2015, various commentators depicted this as a rift between the "conservative" and "moderate" wings of the G.O.P. The same narrative emerged when then–House majority leader Eric Cantor unexpectedly lost his congressional seat to Dave Brat, a primary challenger who painted Cantor as a pusillanimous conservative. However, neither Boehner nor Cantor are moderates. Both played an active role in fomenting the radicalism of the Republican base after Obama's election, such as by denouncing his "socialist" "takeover of health care,"[37] which was actually modeled on Republican plans.[38] As we will see, insurance under Obama's limited reform was still primarily provided by private companies, and twenty-seven million people in the United States were projected to remain uninsured following its implementation.[39] It was not a radical reform.

Nevertheless, Boehner painted "Obamacare" as "Armageddon" and a "monstrosity" that would "ruin" America. "Your government is disrespecting you, your family, your job, your children," he proclaimed at a 2010 rally prior to becoming Speaker. "Your government is out of control. Do you have to accept it? Do you have to take it?" Boehner answered his own questions: "Hell no, you don't!" Interviewed on *60 Minutes,* he was literally in tears when explaining his desire for children to continue to "have a shot at the American Dream" in the Obama era. Boehner was not merely pandering to the Tea Party, given that he had already taken radical stances back in the 1990s, as when he led a drive to abolish the Department of Education and helped Newt Gingrich craft the "Contract with America."[40] Asked about the need for "compromise" after the G.O.P. reclaimed the House in 2010, Boehner stated, "I reject the word." While he was relatively more measured than the Freedom Caucus elements who sought his resignation, he fanned the flames that eventually brought about his downfall.

Criticism of this trend has often taken the form of "both-sides-ism" blaming extremists on each side for political gridlock. After suggesting that the ideologies of the Republican Party and the Obama administration were comparable, proponents of both-sides-ism argued that the rise of Donald Trump's and Bernie Sanders's anti-establishment campaigns proved that America has become a "land of extremes." In fact, Trump and Sanders are not mirror images. Several of Sanders's key proposals, such as universal health care, are broadly accepted by both the left and the right in other industrialized nations. Simply put, universal health care is not the equivalent of Trump's call to ban Muslims from America. And even though Sanders misrepresented or sugarcoated some of his plans, his rhetoric was incomparable to Trump's systematic disinformation and bigotry.

The agendas of Trump and the Republican establishment were more similar than many commentators realized. To be sure, Trump seemed marginally more moderate than traditional Republicans on certain economic issues, as when he expressed support for Social Security. Leaving his populist rhetoric aside, Trump's policies may worsen wealth inequality, from his vow to repeal "Obamacare" to his tax plan favoring the richest of the rich.[41] In addition to economics, Trump and establishment Republicans took comparable stances on the alleged myth of climate change, the need to use torture in the "War on Terror," and other major issues, as we will see in later chapters. What commonly set Trump apart was rhetoric, style, and temperament. He unequivocally proved far less mentally stable, educated, thoughtful, and qualified to be president than Romney or various other traditional Republicans. But the ideological evolution of the Republican establishment contributed to Trump's rise.

Statistical analysis of voting patterns in Congress confirms that since the 1960s "the Republican Party has moved sharply to the right while the Democratic Party has moved, if not quite as dramatically, to the left."[42] Another major study concluded that "Republicans in the North and South have moved sharply to the right," "moderate Democrats in the South have been replaced by Republicans," and the remaining Democrats "are somewhat more liberal" than 1960s Democrats on economic issues.[43] Both-sides-ism is a false narrative, as the G.O.P. has a demonstrably more hardline ideology.[44]

The main disagreement among experts is about whether the polarization of elected officials truly reflects the public's views.[45] Certain political scientists doubt that American citizens are intensely polarized. The most prominent advocate of this perspective is the political scientist Morris Fiorina, who argues that partisan polarization is basically an elite phenomenon limited to politicians and activists. According to Fiorina, most Americans hold moderate or ambivalent views, although professional campaigners are convinced that mobilizing a base with extreme views is crucial to winning elections—a self-fulfilling prophecy if it turns moderates away from politics. From this angle, it appears that much of the public votes for hardline candidates because there is little alternative under the two-party system.[46] Evidence indeed suggests that conservative politicians are likelier than liberal ones to overestimate public support for their agenda, which may partly explain why the modern G.O.P. takes hardline positions.[47] Still, its stances are not so far removed from the public's values that it fails to attract substantial support.[48] The average voter has also become more engaged and partisan over time, regardless of how politics repulses some people.[49] The most politically active citizens seem the most polarized.[50]

A wide and growing body of evidence suggests that America is profoundly polarized by ideology, race, religion, and other factors. "Liberal Republicans and conservative Democrats" are now "almost extinct," as Alan Abramowitz describes in a book questioning Fiorina's theory of elite polarization.[51] While Fiorina is undoubtedly correct that politicians play a significant role in polarization, the public is responsible too. Ordinary conservative and liberal citizens appear increasingly consistent in adopting partisan positions on all major issues.[52] If politicians' views accurately reflect the public's views, it is because voters want politicians to represent *their* policy preferences—not some moderate mix of conservative and liberal views.[53]

What else accounts for how polarization between Democrats and Republicans in Congress is the strongest since Americans fought over slavery?[54] One factor is partisan realignment, as the parties have homogenized in recent decades after long being hodgepodges of conservatives and liberals.[55] The Democratic Party notably enjoyed support among white segregationists who belonged to Franklin Delano Roosevelt's New Deal coalition. But the South gradually became Republican once the Democrats backed the civil rights movement in the 1960s. The religious right's subsequent resurgence exacerbated the Democrats' difficulties in the Bible Belt. However, "southern realignment does not fully account for the increase in polarization. The Republican Party became much more conservative across all regions of the United States."[56]

The G.O.P.'s growing radicalism has thus been a key factor in polarization, as contemporary conservative citizens "take extremely conservative positions on nearly all issues,"[57] hindering the chance of compromise with Democrats. Illustratively, 82 percent of consistent U.S. liberals believe in making compromises, next to barely 32 percent of consistent U.S. conservatives.[58] But both sides tend to see opponents' actions as illegitimate. A social study even concluded that "partisan animus in the American public exceeds racial hostility,"[59] a remarkable finding given persistent racial animus.

The relative popularity of Trump's unabashedly bigoted campaign only worsened racial tensions after the Ferguson crisis and other police shootings triggered the emergence of the Black Lives Matter movement. Race relations in the last year of Obama's presidency were perceived as the worst in more than two decades according to polling data.[60] The receptiveness of many whites to Trump's message that they are losing their country is consistent with data showing that whites think that anti-white racism is now worse than anti-black racism.[61] Trump lauded white supporters who assaulted black protestors at his rallies, characterized undocumented Mexican immigrants as "criminals" and "rapists," tweeted an anti-Semitic image of Hillary Clinton next to a Star of David, and broke new ground in modern America by insisting that all members of a religious group be barred from the country. A full 36 percent of Americans, including 59 percent of Republicans, agreed with his call to ban Muslims.[62]

Xenophobia is not a new problem in the United States, as shown by the notorious Chinese Exclusion Act of 1882 and past opposition to immigration from Ireland, Italy, and other parts of Europe, not to forget hostility toward Jewish émigrés. But the animosity, fear, and resentment of modern white nativists is tied to a new development: whites might no longer be the majority of a diversifying U.S. population by 2050.[63]

Religion is just as explosive an issue as race in America, given its "culture wars" over abortion, gay rights, and beyond. The religious right spurred state legislatures to pass a record number of abortion restrictions during Obama's presidency.[64] The partisan divide on abortion and religion has widened in recent decades.[65] Overall, whites who never attend church are drastically likelier to vote Democratic than whites who attend church weekly, especially evangelicals.[66]

Fiorina remains skeptical about polarization due to "culture wars," which he describes as issues leaving the public ambivalent. Data from the historic 2008 election that won Obama the White House indeed show that 93 percent of voters considered the economy "extremely" or "very" important to their vote. More than 80 percent felt the same way about Iraq, health care, and education. Fewer voters, 50 and 36 percent respectively, had the same opinion about abortion and gay rights. Such figures lead Fiorina to conclude that abortion and homosexuality are marginal questions.[67] In my view, however, these statistics show that a considerable share of the public, between half and a third, finds them highly important.[68] At a minimum, culture war issues are extremely contentious in America by international standards. We will see in Chapter 4 that few people in other Western nations embrace the ultratraditional morality representing a major side of America's culture wars.

Moreover, Americans are intensely divided along partisan lines on economic issues, as exemplified by conflicting attitudes toward Obama's health care reform.[69] Diverging economic perspectives relate to worsening wealth inequality since the 1980s. Neighborhoods are significantly segregated by class and race,[70] which affects children's life outcomes.[71] Some people have no option but to live in certain neighborhoods—others choose to live in bubbles of like-minded individuals[72] and follow ever more influential hyperpartisan media, such as Fox News or, to a lesser extent, MSNBC.[73] Meanwhile, the intensifying blue state–red state fracture appears to have decreased the number of swing states in presidential elections.[74] The sway of lobbying by moneyed interests has played a role in this trend by distorting the democratic process. A strong historical correlation exists between polarization and wealth inequality.[75]

Last but not least, clashes over the role that America should play as the only global superpower contribute to social polarization. Americans were bitterly divided about the Bush administration's use of torture, its aim to detain alleged terrorists forever without trial, and its catastrophic invasion of Iraq on grounds later revealed to be false. The Obama administration's relatively distinct approach to foreign policy proved divisive too. We will return to this issue in depth in the book's final chapter.

Polarization does not mean that there are no independents or citizens who do not fall squarely within the categories of "liberal America" and "conservative America." People's beliefs cannot be perfectly categorized. Rather, the point is that conservative and liberal Americans increasingly live in different worlds shaped by profoundly different values.

Oceans Apart

Nowadays the basic worldview in liberal America is not only highly different from the one in conservative America but also generally *closer* to the dominant worldview in other Western nations when it comes to religion, government, and foreign policy. Sure, liberal and conservative Americans share a common culture, from the same language to traditional heritage and popular entertainment. For instance, New Englanders and Southerners may feel a special bond when they hear "The Star-Spangled Banner" before watching the Super Bowl. Yet their values tend to diverge considerably on fundamental questions.

The list of issues below indicates that liberal Americans are often closer to other Westerners than to conservative Americans in their thinking. Naturally, this broad picture should not obscure key nuances. Americans are on the whole more skeptical than other Westerners of "big government."[76] Few U.S. liberals want European-style welfare states or tax rates. Nevertheless, given the tremendous hostility to universal health care in conservative America, liberal Americans are manifestly closer to Europeans and other Westerners in accepting the idea of state-funded health care for everyone. Indeed, numerous Democrats wanted Obama's health care reform to go further, by creating a "public option" insurance plan or a single-payer system, whereas Republicans categorically opposed expanding access to health care.[77] Besides, well-informed Americans know that Europe has far lower health care costs, partly due to pricing regulations that barely exist in America's profit-driven medical system. The claim that "America cannot afford universal health care" rests on a false premise.

Beyond health care, various examples suggest that Republicans stand apart from other Westerners on many basic economic issues. Following the disastrous 2008 financial crisis, Republicans oddly grew more hostile to financial regulation. Disregarding how deregulation and Wall Street's recklessness had contributed heavily to the financial meltdown, Republicans chiefly blamed the crisis on government overregulation, as we will see in Chapter 5. Similarly, in the aftermath of the massive BP oil spill in the Gulf of Mexico in 2010, the G.O.P. backed legislation that would have weakened regulation of offshore drilling.[78] These peculiar stances reflect the considerable influence of a radical ideology among U.S. conservatives: free-market fundamentalism. As described by Joseph Stiglitz, a winner of the Nobel Prize in Economics, market fundamentalists believe that virtually all economic problems stem from "big government," regulation, and taxes.[79] Their staunch opposition to environmental laws is exacerbated by skepticism about climatology and modern science. Like U.S. liberals, most other Westerners take drastically more moderate or progressive positions on such issues.

The religiosity of Americans would seem to disprove the notion that U.S. liberals are closer to fellow Westerners than to U.S. conservatives.[80] Faith certainly has a far greater sociopolitical role in the United States than in other industrialized nations. Only a small, albeit growing, share of Americans do not believe in God.[81] However, Americans are intensely

ISSUES ON WHICH U.S. LIBERALS ARE GENERALLY
CLOSER TO OTHER WESTERNERS THAN TO
U.S. CONSERVATIVES

- Universal health care
- Financial regulation
- Environmental regulation
- Climate change
- Opposition to substantial tax cuts for millionaires
- Opposition to unlimited corporate or tycoon spending on elections
- Perception of Trump and Tea Party as extreme/far right
- Perception of U.S. religious right as extreme/far right
- Rejection of literal interpretation of Bible
- Acceptance of theory of evolution
- Skepticism of biblical prophecies
- Support for a discretionary right to abortion
- Support for broad access to contraception
- Rejection of abstinence-only sexual education
- Tolerance of homosexuality
- Opposition to indefinite detention without trial at Guantánamo
- Opposition to torture
- Opposition to the invasion of Iraq
- Support for the United Nations and international law

divided between fundamentalist and liberal-moderate conceptions of Christianity. Fundamentalist Christians tend to interpret the Bible word for word, reject the theory of evolution in favor of a literal understanding of Genesis, deem apocalyptic biblical prophecies relevant to U.S. foreign policy in the Middle East, support abstinence-only sexual education, oppose state funding for contraception, condemn abortion, and find homosexuality unacceptable. Chapters 3 and 4 make the case that this ultratraditional form of

Christianity is widespread in conservative America but not in liberal America or other Western countries.

Criminal justice is perhaps the biggest exception to the trend, as the attitudes of liberal Americans are decidedly closer to those of conservative Americans than to those of fellow Westerners on this question. American justice is harshest in the Deep South, but sentences in blue states remain extremely punitive by international standards. Democratic leaders commonly embrace the death penalty in principle and tend to express concerns only about its administration, such as racial discrimination or the risk of executing innocents. Other Westerners are more inclined to consider executions a moral affront to human dignity.[82] Draconian prison terms are also routinely inflicted in blue states. Still, Republicans show a greater appetite for the most extreme punishments, such as executing juveniles or the mentally retarded—practices abolished in controversial Supreme Court decisions scorned by conservative judges like Antonin Scalia.[83]

While we will explore other nuances, the gist of the argument holds true: conservative America stands out within the modern Western world in numerous ways. In other words, the issue is not whether Democrats are trying to turn America into Europe, as Republicans have charged. Rather, it is that liberal America is closer to Europe and other parts of the West than to conservative America on many of its political, social, and moral values. To a large extent, it is conservative America that is an exception in the modern Western world, since it is dominated by peculiar mindsets that have little to no weight elsewhere, including virulent anti-intellectualism, visceral anti-governmentalism, and fervent Christian fundamentalism. Because of their hardline ideological stances, U.S. conservatives are frequently unable to see eye to eye with U.S. liberals, whose views are moderate by Western standards.

That is not to say that polarization is unique to America. Divisions exist in all countries. What distinguishes America from other Western nations is that its polarization not only is more intense but also concerns very fundamental matters on which there is a general consensus elsewhere in the West. As a result, the U.S. political and social debate focuses on issues like whether people should have a right to medical treatment; whether tycoons, corporations, and lobbies should be allowed to donate unlimited sums to political campaigns; whether financial and environmental regulations should be utterly eviscerated; whether global warming is a hoax; whether evolution or creationism should be taught in public schools; whether women should have a discretionary right to abortion; whether public health insurance should cover contraception; whether abstinence-only sexual education should be required; whether people should have an unbridled right to bear arms; whether to have mass incarceration; whether to inflict life sentences on juveniles; whether to abolish the death penalty; whether to torture alleged terrorists and detain them forever without trial; whether to respect or defy international human rights treaties; whether to embrace diplomacy or a unilateral foreign policy; whether strife in the Middle East fulfills apocalyptic biblical prophecies; and whether shutting down the government is an acceptable response to seemingly unresolvable conflict. People elsewhere in the modern Western world may have vigorous and acrimonious disagreements, yet these are not the kinds of basic issues that usually divide them.[84]

Immigration is an exception, since it has become a divisive issue in America, Europe, and other parts of the West. Nativist movements have played a leading role in efforts to dismantle the European Union and return to an age with no open borders or international institutions. However, the rise of bigoted far-right parties in Europe should not eclipse how its mainstream parties have been moving in the same direction on numerous core issues.[85] Again, my point is not that Europeans have a consensus about all political matters but that the issues dividing them are less fundamental than those dividing Americans.

That is why Europeans, who closely follow U.S. presidential elections, have overwhelmingly supported Hillary Clinton, Barack Obama, and John Kerry over Donald Trump, Mitt Romney, John McCain, and George W. Bush in their bids for the White House. According to a 2012 poll of around 7,500 people in Britain, Denmark, France, Germany, Norway, and Sweden, an astounding 90 percent of Europeans would have voted for Obama over Romney.[86] This confirms that even European right-wingers have far more affinities with U.S. liberals than with U.S. conservatives, whose views come across as peculiar and extreme in the modern Western world. Amusingly, the British Parliament actually debated whether to ban Trump from visiting the United Kingdom.

In various ways, the gulf is between conservative America and not merely the rest of the West—but the rest of the world. A poll conducted in forty-five countries covering nearly three-quarters of the global population found massive support for Clinton over Trump. Russians were alone in saying they would have voted for Trump.[87] This is not a new development. The vast majority of countries worldwide welcomed, if not celebrated, Obama's election in 2008.[88] That was partly an adverse reaction to George W. Bush's foreign policy. Obama's charisma had additionally swept the international community off its feet. The son of a white American mother and a black Kenyan father, the nation's first African-American president represented the rise of a more equal and open-minded America—the side of the country that much of the world admires.

Obama's efforts to expand access to health care against categorical Republican opposition were again revealing. In addition to other Western democracies, most nations worldwide have either established universal health care or aspire to. For example, Japan has had a top-notch universal health care system for decades.[89] South Korea established one in 1989.[90] Taiwan did so in 1994 following a bipartisan reform movement at around the same time as Republicans torpedoed Bill and Hillary Clinton's health care reform.[91] Mexico is on its way toward establishing universal health care.[92] South Africa has taken steps in that direction too. The constitution it ratified after apartheid is viewed as a model for its human rights provisions, which are partly guiding aspirations to address enduring inequality. The South African Constitution notably provides that "everyone has the right to have access to . . . health care services, including reproductive health care."[93]

For all these reasons, it was not solely liberal Americans who were stunned as an increasingly radical G.O.P. heatedly denounced the "tyranny" of "Obamacare" and other moderate reforms by the Obama administration. Both liberals and conservatives in other Western democracies—not to mention scores of people in Africa, Asia, Latin America, and beyond—were struck by the magnitude of the ideological backlash against the Obama administration in conservative America. In all likelihood, the international community will strongly favor the Democratic opposition over Donald Trump throughout his presidency.

Exceptionalism and Decline

The Republicans' partisan redefinition of "American exceptionalism" was evidently a political strategy. But persistent claims about Obama's lack of faith in the nation's greatness and his aim to transform America into lowly Europe reflected broader concerns about American decadence. Around 71 percent of Americans are convinced that the United States' global standing is declining,[94] and 54 percent think that it is facing the start of a long-term decline when it will lose its place as the world's leading country.[95]

Certain developments may indeed be interpreted as signs of American decline. Soaring wealth inequality. The surge of the U.S. incarceration rate to world-record levels. Presidents claiming the authority to detain any alleged terrorist forever without judicial review, which would have been unthinkable on September 10, 2001. The Bush administration's reintroduction of torture as an official practice in Western civilization. Republican promises to bring back torture after Obama discontinued its use. The regression of Republican leadership from thoughtful moderates like Dwight Eisenhower to the demagogue Donald Trump. And so on.

Another interpretation could be that America has made tremendous progress. The election of a black president appeared impossible a generation ago. Despite continuing discrimination, LGBTQ people have taken strides toward equality, culminating in the hard-won right to same-sex marriage—again, an unthinkable step one or two decades earlier.

However, many of these trends may be interpreted as historical cycles rather than as American decline or progress.[96] Periods of soaring wealth inequality are far from unprecedented. Because of the dismantlement of the New Deal model beginning in the 1980s, wealth in America is essentially as unequally distributed now as it was in the 1920s prior to the Great Depression.[97] The senseless Iraq War evokes the Vietnam War. Human rights abuses, social injustices, and racial discrimination have recurred throughout American history, alongside periods of social progress. The ignoramus Trump is only the most glaring example of the longstanding anti-intellectual subculture discussed in the next chapter. The intransigence of today's Christian fundamentalists recalls prior cultural battles.

Polarization has made America a particularly difficult country to govern, yet that is an old problem too. Compared to other democracies, the U.S. political system is exceptionally fragmented, due to the combination of federalism and the separation of powers, which greatly hamper the national government's ability to implement systemic reforms.[98] This challenge is compounded by the Senate's adoption of a filibuster rule that permits the stonewalling of legislation unless a supermajority of sixty senators agree to support it. Both parties have historically resorted to the filibuster, but its use reached record levels during Obama's presidency because of the G.O.P.'s systematic obstructionism.[99] Elsewhere in the democratic world, legislation can normally be passed by a simple majority vote. Similarly, other nations can ratify international treaties by a simple majority vote, whereas the U.S. Constitution requires two-thirds of the Senate to do so. The Senate has never ratified an international human rights treaty when it had fewer than fifty-five Democratic members.[100] In sum, these supermajoritarian institutional devices preclude majority rule, thereby empowering minorities of Republican hardliners to block reforms and international treaties.

The Electoral College further hinders democracy. Like Hillary Clinton, Al Gore won the popular vote in a crucial election but never became president, since he lost the Electoral College. The outcome of the 2000 presidential contest might have been different if the Supreme Court had not seemingly handed the election to George W. Bush by halting the Florida ballot recount. It would not have come down to that in nearly all other democracies, because they lack electoral colleges. America's unusual voting system is a vestige of an oppressive era. Back in the eighteenth century, Southern states feared that a direct presidential election would lead them to be outvoted, as they had fewer eligible white voters than Northern states. The resulting compromise was an electoral college under which Southern states received votes proportional to three-fifths of their sizable slave populations, in addition to those for their free populations.[101] The fact that America still employs an anachronistic electoral system largely created to accommodate slavery exemplifies a broader issue. It is often said that America is a young nation, but it is also an old democracy. It has the oldest written national constitution in use anywhere in the world, which has been a mixed blessing by fostering both stability and immobilism.

Yet institutional peculiarities only go so far in explaining political gridlock in modern America. For instance, the political scientist David Mayhew has noted that "if majority rule is in principle the preferred standard, conditions may be bad in the Senate today but weren't they even worse in the past?" The threshold to defeat a filibuster was "an even higher two-thirds vote between 1917 and 1975 (that would mean 67 senators today, not 60)."[102] Major systemic reforms were nonetheless achieved during the New Deal era, when a relative bipartisan consensus supported a more equitable economic model.

While peculiar institutions enable hardliners to use obstructionist tactics or exercise excessive leverage over policy-making, the fundamental issue remains why they wish to do so. We saw earlier that the main reason for the acute polarization of modern American society is the Republican Party's shift toward the far right in recent decades. Republican leaders insist that America is declining because it is becoming less exceptional, due to the toll of Obama's "un-American" and "socialist" presidency. In fact, America remains very exceptional, and certain features of American exceptionalism may contribute to its decline. These features are mainly concentrated in conservative America: profound anti-intellectualism, visceral anti-governmentalism, and Christian fundamentalism. They foster a purist, far-right ideology that is hostile to compromise and impedes rational decision-making and problem-solving.

Additional evidence suggests that the peculiar ideology of contemporary U.S. conservatives plays a greater role than peculiar U.S. institutions in shaping American society. Indeed, the fact that legislatures in other Western democracies can adopt national reforms by a simple majority vote would theoretically make it easier for their conservatives to abolish national health insurance or abortion. But such radical policies are hardly on the conservative agenda in other Western nations. Universal health care is broadly accepted there across the left and right. Abortion also tends to be broadly accepted in other Western democracies, except for a few countries, including Ireland, Poland, Spain, and Portugal. For example, we will see in Chapter 4 that although France's legalization of abortion in 1975 was a fierce battle, French conservatives largely moved on within a decade and now widely support abortion rights. By contrast, American conservatives are far less inclined to move on from the social and economic battles that they have lost. Some have been eager to relitigate them for years and years. Trump was elected partly by vowing to repeal "Obamacare" and appoint Supreme Court justices who will reverse *Roe v. Wade*, the landmark 1973 decision that recognized a constitutional right to abortion. That is because the conception of "conservatism" tends to be far less moderate and far more ideological in America—notwithstanding the growing power of fringe far-right parties or the hardening rhetoric of certain mainstream right-wing parties in Europe.

America is not alone in struggling nowadays. Democracy has yet to fulfill its promise in much of the world. However, there was a time when America was among the countries paving the way toward progress.

TWO

From the American Enlightenment
to Anti-Intellectualism

"How stupid are the people of Iowa?" In what would have been a surreal moment to anyone unfamiliar with his diatribes, Donald Trump asked this condescending question when campaigning in Iowa. The uncultured billionaire turned reality TV star was shocked that some Iowans believed the "crap" from Ben Carson, one of his rivals in the Republican primary.[1] Trump eventually lost the Iowa caucus, finishing second to Ted Cruz, but went on to win the presidency. Fact-checkers found that these Republicans were far likelier than Democrats to routinely make blatantly false claims about the evils of "Obamacare," the "myth" of climate change, the "threat" of immigration, and beyond.[2] They also often got away with it, as the Republican base proved highly receptive to their rhetoric. After all, Trump had been a main promoter of the canard about Obama's fake birth certificate. His question about Iowans seemed to mirror what many concerned people were asking themselves about the latest generation of Republican leaders: "How stupid are the Americans who vote for such politicians?"

The answer is that stupidity has very little to do with it. At most, stupidity is a symptom of a peculiar subculture rooted in American exceptionalism. The Founding Fathers were learned men of the Enlightenment who deemed that government requires educated citizens. But the emergence of modern democracy in America fostered a populist attitude perceiving education as little more than a sign of elitism. Legions of Americans became convinced that cultivating one's mind is both unnecessary and pretentious, as "common sense" is supposedly enough to make money and understand politics. In the words of Isaac Asimov, "a cult of ignorance" in America has promoted "the false notion that democracy means that 'my ignorance is just as good as your knowledge.'"[3] Numerous politicians have shared or exploited this attitude by

43

peddling outlandish propaganda and conspiracy theories, an increasingly easy feat with the explosion of mass media. American society cannot be understood without considering that curious mindset, as it shapes the views of millions on diverse issues explored in this book, from the economy to health care, wealth inequality, climate change, criminal justice, foreign policy, and religion. Notwithstanding this cult of ignorance, generations of American thinkers, scientists, writers, and artists have made immense contributions to the life of the mind, exemplifying the United States' age-old contradictions.

MIND PUZZLE

One of the greatest culture shocks I experienced as a Parisian living in the South was witnessing peculiar attitudes toward education. I vividly recall a freshman history course at Rice University where few students participated in group discussions. A classmate named Greg stood out as an exception, yet I soon realized that he had feigned interest in the subject. One day after class, he proudly told me that he asked questions only so the professor would give him a good grade and that he was not in the least interested in the course. Perhaps that was how Greg really felt, or perhaps he lied because he did not want to be perceived as an intellectual or a nerd. Unlike Greg, a student-athlete and stereotypical jock, my friend Trevor was an ordinary student diligently preparing for medical school. But he too seemed solely interested in education insofar as it had a practical purpose. I once encouraged Trevor to take a history class that I found fascinating. He understandably replied that he had no time to do so, given his scientific course load. I therefore suggested that he watch a brief documentary on the subject in his spare time. To my surprise, he squarely said that he saw no point in learning about history.[4]

Greg and Trevor definitely did not represent all Rice students, many of whom had genuine intellectual curiosity. Still, these two students' attitudes reflected the weight of anti-intellectualism in American society. The most ordinary form of anti-intellectualism is simply indifference to the cultivation of one's mind, especially when it appears to have no practical value. Anti-intellectualism can also entail "a suspicion of too much learning,"[5] a downright hostility toward intellectuals, or a kind of anti-rationalism. Such attitudes undoubtedly exist in Europe, yet anti-intellectualism is both blunter and more influential in the United States.

Growing up in Paris, I rarely heard people unabashedly denigrate the value of education, as I sometimes did later in Texas, which was particularly dumbfounding since I had moved to America largely because of my exalted image of its universities. While I was impressed by the excellent quality of education at Rice, a fair number of students displayed limited thirst for knowledge. My culture shock had nothing to do with finding Southerners "dumb," as some Northerners stereotype them. Many of those I met were highly intelligent and well educated, like Trevor, the aspiring medical student and Democrat, who did not fit the reductive image of anti-intellectualism as Trumpism or Palinism. Besides, I soon found that anti-intellectualism is not limited to the South. How could this mindset be so common in a nation known for its stable political institutions, state-of-the-art technology, and top-notch universities?

I increasingly mulled over that question when witnessing the role of anti-intellectualism in U.S. politics. As George W. Bush made his way from the Texas Governor's Mansion to the White House, I made my way through college in Texas. Tellingly, Bush was unaware of the historic sectarian tensions between Iraqi Shiites and Sunnis that contributed to the spread of war in the Middle East and, ultimately, the metastasis of ISIS. In the run-up to his invasion of Iraq, Bush had met with Iraqi-Americans to discuss the potential repercussions of destabilizing the country by toppling Saddam Hussein. They then noticed that W. was unfamiliar with the terms "Shiite" and "Sunni."[6] This is hardly an isolated example of the mindset of a president who cast himself as a man of action animated by disdain for education. "I don't spend a lot of time thinking about myself, about why I do things," Bush admitted, saying his approach to diplomacy was "not very analytical."

As his presidency came to a close, America saw the rise of Sarah Palin, an even less thoughtful figure. Palin was never as popular as Bush once was, and some believe that she cost John McCain the presidency. She nonetheless asserted herself as an influential voice appreciated by a significant minority of the electorate, notably strident supporters of the emerging Tea Party movement. This trend facilitated the spread of conspiracy theories about Obama's forged birth certificate and Islamism, a "socialist" takeover, "death panels," the "hoax" of global warming, phantom tax hikes, and countless other canards. Next, much of the world was baffled by the gaffes and displays of ignorance of most of the 2012 Republican presidential candidates. The highlights of their race to the bottom included Texas Governor Rick Perry forgetting the name of a key federal agency he wanted to eliminate, and the tycoon

Herman Cain not knowing that China has had nuclear weapons for decades. Irrational fears of everything from the alleged menace of "Obamacare" to Ebola played a role in the G.O.P.'s decisive victory in the 2014 midterm elections. The debate degenerated further as the 2016 election kicked into gear with the tirades of Donald Trump, Ted Cruz, and Ben Carson.

These politicians' critics regularly attribute their mindsets to idiocy, as Bill Clinton did when contending that Republicans had created an environment where "you can't be authentic unless you've got a single-digit I.Q." But the answer to the puzzle lies elsewhere. America's exceptional history helps explain why certain politicians draw support partly by boasting their ignorance in a country with no shortage of bright minds.

THE ROOTS OF ANTI-INTELLECTUALISM

Ironically, anti-intellectualism largely stems from a positive value in American society: equality. Alexis de Tocqueville, who visited America in 1831 to study the world's first modern democracy, famously found a higher degree of equality there than in Europe. "Amongst the novel objects that attracted my attention during my stay in the United States," he noted, "nothing struck me more forcibly than the general equality of conditions."[7] From his vantage point as a Frenchman, Tocqueville believed that democracy was an equalizing influence in America, whereas Europe's monarchical, aristocratic, and feudal systems had fostered greater social stratification. Suffrage in the United States indeed was the widest in the world in the early nineteenth century.[8] Economic data confirm that white Americans enjoyed more income equality than Western Europeans when the United States was founded.[9] Numerous Americans of limited schooling then prospered as merchants, artisans, and farmers.[10]

Naturally, nineteenth-century notions of democracy and equality were very restrictive by modern standards. Slavery remained in part of the country. Free blacks, Native Americans, and women were also denied equal rights. Significant inequalities of wealth existed, even among white males.[11] Nevertheless, egalitarian ideals animated the America that Tocqueville explored.[12]

Winner-take-all capitalism has made twenty-first-century America far more unequal than Europe,[13] yet back in the eighteenth and nineteenth centuries various European observers shared Tocqueville's impression about the value of equality in America. Adam Smith, the Scottish philosopher, wrote that "there is more equality . . . among the English colonists than among the inhabitants of the mother country." J. Hector St. John de Crèvecœur, a French-born American colonist, remarked that "the rich and poor" were "not so far removed from each other" in America as in Europe. Thomas Paine, who emigrated from England and went on to become a Founding Father of the United States, likewise felt that America was a land of unparalleled equality.[14] These circumstances had far-reaching ramifications.

A Suspicion of Education

In *Anti-Intellectualism in American Life,* Richard Hofstadter analyzed how egalitarian ideas led generations of Americans to grow wary of the influence of the privileged elite, the pseudoaristocracy, and what they construed as its symbols, including *education.* Such attitudes existed in all regions of the country but became especially prevalent in the Deep South, where people had the highest levels of poverty and the lowest levels of education. Even though disadvantaged whites widely supported the racial caste system, they resented their low social status relative to more privileged and educated whites, particularly the Northern elite. A peculiar conception of education took hold as the popular mind often associated learning with elitism.

Nineteenth-century Americans commonly believed that "too much learning might set one citizen above another and violate the very democratic ideals that education was supposed to foster," as Susan Jacoby has explained.[15] The general public was inclined to support the creation of free elementary education programs, yet many concurrently disdained "high culture" and perceived university education as little more than a privilege serving to maintain the elite's power. Academic education was frequently seen as not only pointless but also detrimental to practical tasks by encumbering the mind with abstract distractions. Learning for its own sake was considered a pastime of the idle pseudoaristocracy.[16] Tocqueville observed that Americans appeared solely concerned with the aspects of their trade having "an immediate practical application." [17] Science primarily served to please the body rather than the mind, and practicality was more important than "beauty," which was expected to be "useful." [18] Tocqueville concluded, exaggeratedly, that "no class" in America valued "intellectual pleasures" or "the labors of the intellect." [19]

This attitude rested partly on the misconception that a person is either a thinker or a doer and that those who think or know too much are incapable of acting. Cultured men were sometimes depicted as effeminate and lacking virility. "As popular democracy gained strength and confidence," Hofstadter wrote, "it reinforced the widespread belief in the superiority of inborn, intuitive, folkish wisdom over the cultivated, over-sophisticated, and self-interested knowledge of the literati and well-to-do." [20]

Nowadays the relative popularity of uncultured politicians is frequently seen as modern decadence, although they embody a longstanding mindset. When Sarah Palin mocks Obama by saying, "We need a commander in chief, not a professor of constitutional law giving us a lecture," or when the magnate Herman Cain adds, "We need a leader, not a reader," they are echoing historical stereotypes about inept intellectuals whose minds are dimmed by useless knowledge.

A Twist of Irony

It is intriguing that a nation born of the Enlightenment has offered fertile ground for anti-intellectualism. The Founding Fathers aspired to rescue history from Europe's political and moral failures by creating a system combining individual liberty, religious freedom, and wise government. [21] The birth of the United States represented the beginning of a momentous experiment in democracy that preceded the French Revolution of 1789. The American experiences of illustrious Frenchmen—the Marquis de Lafayette, Crèvecœur, and Tocqueville—led them to view the United States as a country where humankind had made great strides. America was not a utopia, yet it was praiseworthy. The Marquis de Condorcet, a leading French philosopher, did not travel overseas but wrote that, because of the American Revolution, people no longer had to learn about the rights of men from philosophy—they could now learn from "the example of a great people." [22] These men were not alone in admiring the Founding Fathers, as many European thinkers shared this sentiment, [23] despite the emergence of anti-Americanism. [24] The Americans had not passively realized "European ideals in the drama of the American Revolution"—they had made their own imprint on human thought. [25]

A trailblazing, republican form of government had been created in the New World, enshrined in the Declaration of Independence and the U.S. Constitution. The latter became a model for the constitutions of other countries. Of course, the new American republic's egalitarian ideals were far from fulfilled, due to glaring contradictions ranging from the persecution of Native Americans to the cruelties of slavery and the oligarchy of propertied white males. But European nations were guilty of comparable abuses, especially colonial powers such as Britain, France, Portugal, Spain, and the Netherlands.

The founding of the United States coincided with the American Enlightenment, an age of intellectual vitality.[26] The Founding Fathers were well-read, highly cultivated polymaths, some of whom were even remarkably versed in science, like Benjamin Franklin and Thomas Jefferson. The exceptionally brilliant Franklin made groundbreaking discoveries in electricity, meteorology, and oceanography, as when he charted the Gulf Stream. The Founders embraced the Enlightenment's celebration of reason. James Madison illustratively declared that "it is the reason, alone, of the public, that ought to control and regulate the government. The passions ought to be controlled and regulated by the government." [27] Political pamphlets had a broad readership, as the literacy rate for adult males in New England then may have surpassed England's. In particular, Thomas Paine's *Common Sense* sold 120,000 copies in three months, a phenomenal number for the time.[28]

The origins of the United States in the Enlightenment may have led to the conclusion that it would blossom into a country animated by a broad consensus on the value of education, intellect, and reason. But the rise of a populistic conception of democracy tied to anti-intellectualism restrained the spread of these ideals. The emergence of a populistic conception of religion seeing education as an obstacle to faith—a dominant trait of American evangelicalism—also fostered anti-intellectualism, as we will see in Chapter 3.

Oddly enough, the modern leaders most inclined to passionately invoke the Founding Fathers typically have an anti-intellectual bent. John Boehner, the former Speaker of the House, repeatedly accused Obama and the Democrats of unpatriotically ignoring the framers. "This is my copy of the Constitution," Boehner defiantly proclaimed at a rally, "and I'm going to stand here with the Founding Fathers, who wrote in the preamble: 'We hold these truths to be self-evident, that all men are created equal, that they are endowed by their creator with certain unalienable rights including life, liberty and the pursuit of happiness.'" Boehner apparently did not know that these words come from the 1776 Declaration of Independence, not the Constitution, which was created more than a decade later.

The general public's grasp of elementary history is not more impressive. Only 58 percent of Americans know that it was in 1776 that their nation declared independence. One in four also does not know from which country it seceded (Great Britain).[29] One in three is unable to name any of the three branches of government (executive, legislative, judicial). Only 38 percent can name all three.[30] *Newsweek* had one thousand Americans take the civic education exam that immigrants must pass to become U.S. citizens—38 percent failed.[31] Such ignorance is condoned, if not encouraged, by prominent politicians. Consider how Boehner proudly affirmed that being the Speaker of the House requires no higher education: "Trust me—all the skills I learned growing up are the skills I need to do my job." And Donald Trump became president despite never having served in government and being proudly ignorant of basic policy-making.

Anti-Intellectualism across the Atlantic

While Americans have tended to stress the practical value of education, Western Europeans have been more inclined to emphasize its intrinsic value. The democratization of French society was notably expected to gradually broaden the masses' access to the joys and benefits of culture and higher learning. Ideally, a good French citizen should acquire *culture générale*—a broad body of knowledge—even though many do not, because of scant intellectual curiosity or limited educational opportunities. Conversely, in parts of America, democracy was expected to usher in a more equal epoch, when cultivating one's mind would finally be recognized as pretentious and futile elitism. The weight of these contrary civic ideals in America and Europe was relative, not absolute, but they help explain the fairly divergent attitudes toward intellectual curiosity existing to this day on each side of the Atlantic.

In contemporary Western Europe, a broad education is not merely considered important for the sake of cultivating one's mind—it is expected to enable people to adequately participate in the political process. These ideals have likewise long existed in America. Yet the influence of anti-intellectualism in parts of society has fostered an opposite perspective: education is not particularly useful to political participation, because all one needs is "common sense." In the end, equality of education may be achieved by promoting the best education for everyone or by ensuring that no one is "too educated." The former proposition has had more sway in Europe, and the latter has greatly shaped the populist psyche in America.

Scorn of education has relatively limited weight in twenty-first-century Western Europe. That was not always the case, as anti-intellectual attitudes were prevalent in nineteenth-century France, according to the observations of Jean-Marie Déguignet (1834–1905), who was raised in a destitute peasant family in Brittany. A self-educated freethinker, he joined the French army in search of a better wage, which took him around the world on various military campaigns. He ultimately returned to farmwork in Brittany and commented at length on the superstition, ignorance, and backward-mindedness of its impoverished rural inhabitants. The latter resented Déguignet's education, republicanism, and anti-clericalism. They mocked him for introducing modern agricultural techniques to his farm in spite of his unparalleled success.[32]

Déguignet's account shows a France quite removed from its famous philosophers and writers. Ordinary French people lacked educational opportunities and sometimes felt disdain and resentment toward the learned. Those sentiments gradually abated as commoners gained greater access to public education and France became a more equal society.[33] Resentment of social inequality and the domination of elites still exists in modern France but seldom encompasses an outright denigration of education. A revealing exception nowadays is the case of marginalized French ghettos, where certain poor, minority, and immigrant youths are inclined to scorn education as a privilege of well-to-do whites. Henry Louis Gates made comparable observations about the plight of underprivileged African-American youths, some of whom believe that "speaking standard English, getting straight A's, or even visiting the Smithsonian" amounts to "acting white."[34] One can see in both countries related forms of anti-intellectualism spurred by resentment of racism and socioeconomic inequality. However, education simultaneously became what Ta-Nehisi Coates called "a profound act of auto-liberation"[35] for other members of disempowered minority groups in America and France. Leaders like Frederick Douglass, Malcolm X, and Aimé Césaire were well aware that slaves and colonized people were widely barred access to education—a threat to all forms of oppression.

We therefore cannot forget periods in not too distant European history when education and reflection faced aggressive repression. The rise of Nazism, fascism, and communism were largely spurred by propaganda that promoted a black-and-white worldview and violently discouraged critical thinking. While the Allied democracies also resorted to propaganda, theirs did not reach the level of the Axis powers, the Soviet Union, Vichy France, or Franco's Spain. Political extremism often has an intensely anti-intellectual bent. We will return to this issue later in this chapter when examining how, during the Obama presidency, America's anti-intellectual subculture helped foster demagoguery of a magnitude rarely witnessed in modern Western democracies.

The fiercest anti-intellectualism in American society is a staple of the far right, but as we have seen, the mindset transcends the conservative-liberal divide. The problem is frequently blamed on the poor quality of public schools, yet it largely stems from a peculiar conception of education rooted in America's exceptional history.

I have cited various polls showing that a significant share of Americans, including college graduates, lack elementary civic or historical knowledge. Other polls suggest the same. For example, nearly half of U.S. Protestants are unaware that Martin Luther inspired the Protestant Reformation.[36] A comparative study similarly found that Americans were less likely than Europeans to know who the Taliban are, despite the fact that U.S. forces led the invasion of Afghanistan following the 9/11 attacks on America.[37] Consider another example from Susan Jacoby, the American author. On September 11, 2001, she was in Manhattan among other civilians shocked after the terrorist attacks. Two of them were businessmen in expensive attire. "This feels just like Pearl Harbor must have," one said. The other responded: "Pearl Harbor? What's that?" "It's when the Vietnamese bombed one of our harbors and started the Vietnam War," the first man explained.[38]

Even though no one knows everything, this degree of ignorance is staggering, especially among the well-to-do in the world's only superpower. Why does anti-intellectualism persist, given that American universities have been among the very best worldwide for decades? And how does one square this circumstance with America's countless contributions to science, literature, art, and other vast dimensions of human thought? These questions point to one of the greatest contradictions of modern American society: a vibrant intellectual world coexists with the crassest anti-intellectualism.

The Qualities and Peculiarities of American Education

In the nineteenth century, America emerged on the world stage as the country whose population had the most years of formal education. From New England to rural Iowa, Americans were global pioneers in gradually instituting free public education at all stages: elementary school, middle school, high school, and university. European nations generally did so later than America, as certain European experts then deemed the U.S. model "wasteful" in schooling so many people, including girls in a relatively gender-neutral system. European nations usually tested children to determine those suited to receive more than an elementary education, thereby favoring the well-to-do and the ruling class.[39] The American South nonetheless lagged in this area, as its segregated schools denied education to blacks, and even Southern whites were less likely to be schooled than Northern whites.[40] Still, for decades America had a major global lead in school enrollment and graduation levels. This lead had decreased by the 1980s, which also saw the start of worsening wealth inequality. America's educational advantage has now largely evaporated next to multiple industrialized nations that have established rather egalitarian school systems. As Claudia Goldin and Lawrence Katz conclude in their comparative study, "the United States is no longer the first in the world in high school and college graduation rates and lags considerably in K–12 quality indicators."[41]

Even as America made impressive strides in providing mass public education by the twentieth century, a suspicion of deeper learning and reflection remained, prompting Hofstadter to remark that "American education can be praised, not to say defended, on many counts; but I believe that it is the only educational system in the world vital segments of which have fallen into the hands of people who joyfully and militantly proclaim their hostility to intellect."[42] Hofstadter published his research in 1963, but the suspicion he described may have subsequently intensified because of the resurgent religious right movement, which exacerbated resentment of secular public schools among Christian fundamentalists.[43] The latter have denounced public education for promoting "liberal" ideas and calling into question ultratraditional beliefs, such as by teaching the theory of evolution instead of creationism.

Despite the popular tendency to value narrow, practical training, American universities commonly strive to impart a wide body of knowledge about the world. Undergraduate education is less specialized in the United States than in many other countries. The possibility to choose multiple electives enables one to simultaneously study fields as varied as history, political science, anthropology, and astronomy. Moreover, American universities are front-runners in producing scholarly and scientific research. Numerous top European academics have relocated to the United States. In particular, French professors teaching in America normally consider that greater rewards for talent, industriousness, and innovation can be found there. Interestingly, many deem U.S. universities more intellectually stimulating than French ones, which they find rigid, bureaucratic, and averse to change.

Of course, U.S. universities possess vastly superior resources with which to fund research and attract top academics by offering them hefty salaries that are typically two or three times higher than those in France.[44] These resources partly come from exorbitant tuition, leading a significant proportion of U.S. students to graduate with considerable debt from academic loans.[45]

Although America is a global leader in providing quality university education, the limited thirst for knowledge of many students has undercut this effort. Leading politicians, sometimes marginally cultured, have likewise downplayed the importance of being learned and suggested that it dims one's judgment. As the governor of California, Ronald Reagan tellingly deplored that the state's public universities were "subsidizing intellectual curiosity," shocking professors who retorted that this was their very mission. Rick Santorum later went further in contending that Barack Obama was guilty of "snobbery" for setting the goal of a college education for all Americans. Other leaders, such as John McCain[46] and John Boehner,[47] proposed eliminating the federal Department of Education as superfluous "big government." As we will now see, a suspicion of "too much" education can even be found among certain graduates of America's best universities.

Studying Abroad in America

Two contradictions immediately struck my mind as I attended college in Texas. While I admired the outstanding quality of American university education, I was baffled by the lack of intellectual curiosity of various students.

My professors at Rice University were undisputed experts in their fields. Though not a model student, I found most of my classes genuinely interesting. I befriended Dr. Bob O'Dell, my astronomy professor, who was formerly a chief scientist for the Hubble Space Telescope and took me on a private tour of Houston's NASA station. We stayed in touch following my graduation, and Bob regularly impressed me with his vast knowledge of the humanities and literature in addition to science. Millions of people have been exposed to his research, as the acclaimed TV program *Cosmos: A Spacetime Odyssey* featured wondrous images of the universe captured by the Hubble Telescope. Campus life could also be highly intellectual stimulating. Student groups organized cultural events. Prominent scholars gave lectures. Nelson Mandela even came to campus in 1999 to give a moving speech about his life struggles.

Scores of Rice students took a vivid interest in learning. One of them was Corey, a charming Midwestern conservative who regularly approached professors after class to ask more questions about his favorite subjects. He availed himself of the broad range of opportunities at Rice, from serving in student government to volunteering at a research center. Eager to broaden his horizons, he traveled to several continents and sometimes practiced his Spanish with me and fellow students outside class. Myriad other students had a broad range of interests, such as budding anthropologists, authors, and activists for social change. In 1999, Rice organized a public service trip to Haiti in which I participated. The students in the group had diverse origins, but all showed a broad interest in tackling social problems and discovering the local culture.

The fact that many students were inquisitive was not surprising at a selective institution. The presence of students who had anti-intellectual mindsets despite being well accomplished was far more unexpected. They seemingly saw college merely as a practical way of getting a good job, as well as a place to have fun in the meantime. That category included Greg, the jock who feared being perceived as an intellectual, and Trevor, the smart aspiring medical student who unabashedly said he had no interest in learning about history. Rice students were not an exception in this regard but similar to various alumni of other top colleges I have met over the years.

An unsettling experience made me realize that certain students effectively ignored or frowned on those who tried to raise important issues. A representative of the Nigerian government had been invited for an event at Rice's public policy center. The subject came up when I had lunch with several students, including Edna, a Nigerian foreign student eager to meet the diplomat. Given that the Nigerian regime was extremely authoritarian and corrupt, I asked Edna if she had qualms about fraternizing with its representative. She downplayed the regime's abuses. I then inquired about her thoughts on the notorious case of Ken Saro-Wiwa, the peaceful activist whom Nigerian authorities executed in 1995.* Edna pointedly dismissed that case as trivial. I pressed on about how the Nigerian government had hanged Saro-Wiwa after a sham trial. Annoyed, she argued that the unfairness of the trial was a mere allegation: "That's *their* story." As we talked for several minutes, we were seated at a small table with three or four American friends, white and black. All of them stayed silent, utterly uninterested in the conversation, unfazed

* Saro-Wiwa led a protest movement in the Niger Delta, where the Nigerian government, along with Shell, extracts oil from the lands of local tribes. The region is highly polluted because of reckless extraction and remains destitute, as much of the oil revenue goes to corrupt government officials and Shell instead of being invested there.

by Edna's defense of brutal authoritarianism, and insular in outlook. I suspected that I might have bothered everyone by trying to engage in a serious political discussion. The following week, I found myself again seated with Edna. I ventured to ask if she had had a chance to reflect on Saro-Wiwa's execution. Her response was scathing: "Saro-Wiwa was just a little journalist!" The other students at our table were unperturbed, continuing to eat their meals in a mental stupor. Of course, they may not have reacted because they wanted to avoid a confrontation. Perhaps they also did not want to sound politically incorrect. What I sensed, however, was profound apathy.

The sociologist Nina Eliasoph documented the relative prevalence of such attitudes in American society. While interacting with various social groups as part of a study, she observed that political conversations were rare, including among volunteers and activists. Social analysis aroused little interest and supposedly lacked practical value. Eliasoph concluded that a social dynamic leads certain Americans not simply to be apathetic but to deliberately avoid meaningful conversations by mingling in superficial ways and ignoring those who try to raise serious issues.[48]

Indifference toward knowledge or reflection is obviously not unique to America. Some may consider Europe the mecca of Western culture, but it would be wrong to assume that the vast majority of its people are vividly interested in art, literature, history, or politics. The average European may be more inquisitive than the average American because of the stronger influence of anti-intellectualism in the United States, although the difference goes only so far. However, a greater lack of intellectual curiosity is palpable among the most educated Americans next to their European counterparts.

The contradictions of American education that I observed in college were also noticeable when I attended the Northwestern University School of Law in Chicago. Much like at Rice, I was impressed by the faculty at Northwestern and found most classes captivating. Various students contributed to intellectual life on campus by organizing well-attended events where experts debated topical issues, such as the war on Iraq, campaign finance reform, and gay marriage. There was no clear distinction between inquisitive students along left-right, Democratic-Republican lines. While Northwestern was a largely liberal environment, I befriended students of all stripes, including libertarians and evangelicals with whom I enjoyed debating legal, political, and social issues. We rarely agreed but did learn from one another's perspectives.

On the other hand, certain law students felt lukewarm about learning for its own sake. Some were exasperated by the Socratic method: when a professor asks a student to give his or her opinion on a legal problem and the student's answers are followed by more questions from the professor or counter-arguments from other students. Such prolonged classroom discussions, these students charged, did not provide "the answers." They just wanted to know "what the law is" and what to say in their final exams. Of course, complex legal questions have no single answer but rather competing answers based on different analytical frameworks, policy preferences, and moral values.

These students almost systematically preferred small talk. A few even resented the label "intellectual." I recall a dumbfounding experience with a studious classmate who had received an academic distinction. When I unsuspectingly used the detestable term to compliment her, she erupted, "I'm *not* an intellectual!" I had just insulted her. The term has become politically charged and is sometimes associated with the "liberal elite." But this student was a liberal. While most of our fellow students probably would not have taken umbrage at being called intellectuals, and a number might have defined themselves that way, her virulent reaction was intriguing.

To a greater extent than in other Western nations, peer pressure leads Americans to believe that they should not appear "too smart" if they want to be popular. A recurrent theme in American movies and TV series is the tale of the intelligent and socially awkward high school student struggling in a conformist environment dominated by dumb jocks and bullies. Such stories reveal social tensions.

American Intellectual Life

Anti-intellectualism has not fully eradicated the spirit of the American Enlightenment, as generations of citizens have continued to make immense contributions to thought and culture. They could hardly be summarized in an entire book, but diverse examples demonstrate how a vibrant intellectual life has coexisted in America alongside anti-intellectualism—a powerful reminder that it is a nation of fascinating contradictions.

America has produced a host of brilliant authors, such as Henry David Thoreau, Emily Dickinson, Mark Twain, F. Scott Fitzgerald, Ernest Hemingway, John Steinbeck, Richard Wright, Sylvia Plath, Langston Hughes, Tennessee Williams, James Baldwin, Harper Lee, J. D. Salinger, Toni Morrison, Robert Pirsig, Jon Krakauer, Jared Diamond, and Carl Sagan. Art critics esteem American painters like James Whistler, Georgia O'Keefe, Edward Hopper, Andy Warhol, Jasper Johns, Keith Haring, and

Jean-Michel Basquiat. In the musical realm, the composers George Gershwin, Samuel Barber, and Aaron Copland have crafted masterpieces. Americans have otherwise greatly shaped, if not invented, various modern musical genres, including jazz, rock, and rap. The virtuosity of John Coltrane is undeniable, the folk songs of Bob Dylan are compelling, countless rappers fuse activism with rhythm, and Yo-Yo Ma's eclectic tunes, from Appalachian to Silk Road music, embody the cosmopolitan side of America.

The list of American accomplishments goes on. Thomas Edison was one of the greatest inventors in history. Architecture and design are indebted to the contributions of Frank Lloyd Wright and Frank Gehry, among others. Americans have been instrumental in the advancement of modern science, which enabled them to send the first people to the moon. American academics have provided insightful perspectives on innumerable issues. Global culture has long been patronized by American philanthropists and promoted by institutions like the Smithsonian and the New York Philharmonic. America has produced excellent films, although Hollywood's commercialism has at times hindered its creativity. Leading U.S. newspapers, magazines, and public radio programs are on a par with their equivalents in Europe. Last but not least, millions worldwide have turned to diverse American icons for inspiration, from Thomas Jefferson to Benjamin Franklin, John F. Kennedy, Martin Luther King, Malcolm X, Cesar Chavez, Margaret Sanger, and Harvey Milk.

While anti-Americans perceive the United States as a haven of ignorance, its contributions to human thought since independence rival those of Europe. The antidote to anti-intellectualism in American life lies not in imitating Europe but in drawing on the United States' own intellectual tradition. "We have been afraid to think," John Adams wrote prior to the American Revolution. "Let us dare to read, think, speak and write." [49]

Are TV, the Internet, and Social Media to Blame?

The elevation of Donald Trump, a superficial reality TV star, to the status of U.S. president marks a cultural crisis in Western civilization. Social critics have long expressed concern about how modern popular culture exacerbates intellectual apathy. From America to France, scores spend most of their free time glued to their TV sets and read few or no books each year. [50] Given that social pressure against cultivating one's mind is not as significant in Europe as in America, something else may be at work.

TV, the internet, and other mass media have come to play a dominant role in people's lives at the dawn of the twenty-first century. While they have facilitated access to information, mass media can concurrently numb the mind, considering how legions watch little besides sports, shallow sitcoms, formulaic films, and reality TV. Social media has likewise been a boon for busybodies and cranks, who got an efficient means of sharing gossip and conspiracy theories. That said, modern popular culture and mass entertainment are not necessarily mindless. One can find analytical news coverage and insightful documentaries on TV or online. *The Simpsons, South Park,* and various other programs stand out for their witty social satire. Thoughtfulness can also be found in other series, from *Mad Men* to *Band of Brothers* and *Lost.*

Assuming TV and the internet are what we choose to make of them, the question becomes why certain people massively gravitate toward their most superficial dimensions. On one level, some prefer light entertainment to concentrating on more complex issues, which can be understandable after a stressful day at work or school. On another level, mass media can mold the collective imagination with shallow messages. But as we ponder mass media's negative dimensions, we should be wary of idealizing the past. "The vast amount of time most Americans spend with television is appalling," the sociologist David Riesman bewailed more than half a century ago, "but the pre-TV alternatives, such as driving aimlessly about, sitting vacantly, attending sports events, or playing canasta, are hardly more 'real' or less appalling." [51]

If mass media has led the citizenry further into a mental stupor, it may help explain *indifference* to the life of the mind. The contrast between America and Europe is only relative in this regard. What sets America apart is an influential subculture animated by *disdain* of intellectual pursuits. In the end, some may argue that this is a nonissue because the value attributed to intellect is a matter of preference. Given that different people and societies value different things, is there really any harm in not valuing inquisitiveness, reflection, and knowledge? Such a position would overlook how anti-intellectualism can shape a country's political culture in far from innocuous ways.

THE RISE OF THE ANTI-INTELLECTUAL POLITICIAN

The rise of know-nothing politicians like George W. Bush, Sarah Palin, and Donald Trump cannot simply be equated with American decline, as they are heirs to a long tradition of anti-intellectualism. While the Founding Fathers were learned men of the Enlightenment, intellect soon became a relative liability in the nation's politics. Thomas Jefferson's opponents branded him a Francophile philosopher whose mind was unfit for practical tasks because of its preoccupation with abstract and theoretical questions. The now familiar attack was repeated against John Quincy Adams, whom Andrew Jackson and his supporters accused of being a scholar rather than a man of action and common sense. As president, Adams wanted the government to promote science and culture, an aspiration his adversaries ridiculed. Adams could write but Jackson could fight, it was said. Adams conversely saw Jackson as "a savage who can scarcely spell his own name." Jackson, an "untutored genius" to his admirers, won the presidency in 1828, thwarting Adams's bid for reelection and leading the country toward a more populist form of democracy.[52]

Educated politicians have had to prove that they are not just thinkers but doers, the latter trait being the preferable one. Some have tried to connect with the common man by emphasizing their military or athletic experience or by using plain language and tough talk to promote an image of folksiness and virility. Theodore Roosevelt was esteemed for his work as a naturalist, writer, and president of the American Historical Association, yet his experience as a soldier, hunter, and boxer dispelled doubts about his manliness.[53] Adlai Stevenson, the Democratic candidate in the 1952 presidential election, was handicapped by his learnedness, an "ivory tower." His victorious opponent, Dwight Eisenhower, was admired as a military hero and equally benefited from what many saw as his concrete knowledge of the world next to the bookish Stevenson.[54] Eisenhower's secretary recalled that he was "deathly afraid of being considered highbrow." But one of Eisenhower's speechwriters observed that he had a greater ability with the English language than anyone else the speechwriter had known and was an "absolute pedant" in private, although much of the public had come to think of the president as someone "who had no concept of the English language, no interest in it."[55] Eisenhower, undoubtedly highly intelligent, may have sought to appear less intellectual than he actually was. One of Richard Nixon's speechwriters likewise described Nixon as "an intellectual who pretended not to be."[56]

Eisenhower and Nixon were fairly moderate conservatives, but extreme voices, from Senator Joseph McCarthy to the John Birch Society, were especially scathing in denigrating intellectuals and associating them with communists. The election of John F. Kennedy in 1961, however, suggested that anti-intellectualism was retreating. Kennedy's intelligence and sophistication contributed to his popularity, and he appeared comfortable exuding these qualities. Still, his image as a World War II hero tempered doubts that his erudition would translate into weakness.[57] Perhaps only a pessimist could then have expected that anti-intellectualism would remain a major dimension of U.S. politics at the dawn of the twenty-first century.

In light of a privileged background that gave him the best educational opportunities, George W. Bush could only have been an anti-intellectual by choice. After getting admitted to Yale based on his connections, Bush graduated with mediocre results.[58] He later became a multimillionaire businessman. Yet the two-term president painted himself as an average Joe, "the kind of guy you can have a beer with," a political strategy facilitated by his scant intellectual curiosity. Spectacularly inarticulate, Bush multiplied peculiar declarations like "Too many ob-gyns aren't able to practice their love with women all across the country" and "Rarely is the question asked: is our children learning?" Entirely overlooking World War II, he told a Tokyo audience that "for a century and a half now, America and Japan have formed one of the great and enduring alliances of modern times." Bush's misstatements about the Iraq War were either comical or revealing: "You know, one of the hardest parts of my job is to connect Iraq to the War on Terror." "I am surprised, frankly, at the amount of distrust that exists in [Washington D.C.]. And I'm sorry it's the case, and I'll work hard to try to elevate it." "[Our enemies] never stop thinking about new ways to harm our country and our people, and neither do we." Speaking about his upcoming memoir, Bush announced: "When the history of this administration is written at least there's an authoritarian voice saying exactly what happened."

Bush's worldview made no room for nuance. He defended a black-and-white morality, labeled his critics unpatriotic, and warned that "either you're with us or you're with the terrorists." Paul O'Neill, his secretary of the Treasury, remarked that Bush was strikingly uninterested in debating policy ideas.[59] As Tony Blair stated, "George had immense simplicity in how he saw the world."[60]

Bush surrounded himself mainly with people who thought like him. John DiIulio, a conservative political scientist, resigned from a senior post in his administration after eight months, expressing dismay at what he had witnessed: "I heard many, many staff discussions, but not three meaningful, substantive policy discussions. . . . On social policy and related issues, the lack of even basic policy knowledge, and the only casual interest in knowing more, was somewhat breathtaking . . . Senior and junior [staff] consistently talked and acted as if the height of political sophistication consisted in reducing every issue to its simplest, black-and-white terms for public consumption, then steering legislative initiatives or policy proposals as far right as possible."[61]

Studies suggest that scores of Bush's supporters shared his thoughtlessness. Consider the public response to W.'s signature policies, the "Bush tax cuts" and the Iraq War, both of which had lasting consequences for the U.S. economy and global order. First, the Bush administration's 2001 and 2003 tax cuts were among the largest in American history, but surveys found that a full 40 percent of the public had not even thought about the issue. Among those who had formed an opinion, support for the tax cuts was very high, despite the fact that they aimed to benefit a minority of wealthy citizens. Middle-class and working-class Americans received a tiny tax cut in comparison and were disproportionately disadvantaged by consequent limitations on spending for services such as education and health care. Larry Bartels, a political scientist, noted other startling incoherencies in the public's views: "Most of the people who recognized and regretted the fact that economic inequality [had] been increasing nevertheless supported President Bush's tax cuts. People who wanted to spend more money on a variety of government programs were *more* likely to support tax cuts." Public support for Bush's tax cuts was lower among well-informed citizens.[62]

Second, the Bush administration easily manipulated most of the public into embracing a reckless invasion of Iraq with predictably grave human and financial costs. Not only was the administration's rationale dubious—a preemptive war, an easy victory—but it was rooted in false assertions about weapons of mass destruction and Saddam Hussein's alliance with Al-Qaeda. Roughly half of Americans still think that invading Iraq was the right decision, notwithstanding the fact that experts debunked Bush's justifications for the war long ago. That proportion has not dropped since the surge of ISIS—a repercussion of toppling Hussein's largely secular dictatorship. If anything, Americans appear less likely to regret invading Iraq since ISIS has gained ground there.[63]

However, the tendency to dumb down presidential rhetoric did not start with Bush. A study by Elvin Lim indicates that presidential speeches have become linguistically and substantively simpler since the early 1800s. Nixon exacerbated the trend in 1969 when he separated speechwriting and policy-making into two separate departments in his administration. Subsequent presidents maintained this arrangement, which prioritizes style over substance. In addition, earlier generations of speechwriters had greater academic training and important policy-making responsibilities. Their current counterparts specialize in speechwriting only, further explaining why presidential addresses have become, in Lim's words, "increasingly devoid of policy substance, simplistic, and sloganistic."[64] Beyond the presidency, that pattern is apparent in U.S. politics as a whole. For example, TV campaign ads do little more than broadcast slogans, sound bites, emotional appeals, personal attacks, or downright propaganda.

By promoting an anti-intellectual form of politics for decades, mainstream politicians in both the Democratic and the Republican Parties paved the way for the Tea Party's rise and Trump's election in 2016. Ironically, Obama's decisive electoral victory in 2008 was interpreted as the dawn of a more rational age. Bush had been repudiated, and Palin, the G.O.P.'s rising star, had been ridiculed for her peculiar statements during the campaign. The president was now a worldly intellectual whose résumé included the presidency of the *Harvard Law Review* and a law professorship at the University of Chicago. Obama's distinctions, together with the high hopes accompanying his election, may have led his supporters to grow overly optimistic in expecting anti-intellectualism to abate in political life.

DISINFORMING THE MASSES

Demagogues and extremists around the world have historically been fiercely anti-intellectual. Whether they are on the left or the right, their rhetoric thrives on ignorance, fear, emotion, and prejudice. One of their primary tactics is disinformation: the deliberate spread of false information to manipulate public opinion. Disinformation goes further than misinformation—information that is merely incorrect—as it is a shrewd political strategy.

In an authoritarian regime, disinformation can work by controlling all information, censoring dissent, and tolerating only official versions of history. Disinformation must operate differently in a democratic society like the United States, where information and ideas can circulate quite freely. It then largely relies on repeating falsehoods to make people believe them. Concurrently, disinformation leads people to disbelieve facts by distorting them, claiming that they are myths, or denigrating their sources, such as scientists or the "liberal media." The weight of anti-intellectualism in America has therefore facilitated disinformation by fostering irrationality, gullibility, and skepticism of education. This helps explain why conspiracy theories and blatant deception came to play a major role in the Obama years as an increasingly far-right opposition resorted to propaganda on a scale unmatched in contemporary Western democracies.

A Covert Muslim with a Forged Birth Certificate

John McCain and Sarah Palin campaigned for the White House to the tune of "Who is the real Barack Obama?" and effectively encouraged conspiracy theorists convinced that he was secretly born in Kenya. That would supposedly mean that Obama was unlawfully elected, because of the constitutional requirement that the president be "a natural born citizen." [65] Of course, Obama was born in Hawaii. In an effort to put the issue to rest, he disclosed his birth certificate, which public officials authenticated. Undeterred, the "birthers" either disputed the certificate's validity or maintained that Obama had never produced a certificate. "What I don't know is why the president can't produce a birth certificate," Representative Roy Blunt of Missouri illustratively said. A year into his presidency, 8 percent of Democrats and a full 45 percent of Republicans were convinced that Obama "was not born in the United States and so is not eligible to be President." [66]

Along came reports that growing numbers of Islamophobes falsely identified Obama as a Muslim, some of whom may have recalled the McCain-Palin campaign's claim that Obama was "palling around with terrorists." Obama's estranged Kenyan father was raised a moderate Muslim but became an atheist, and his American mother was spiritual but not religious. [67] Although Obama spent part of his childhood in Indonesia, a predominantly Muslim nation, his Christian faith had been well publicized. Around a quarter of Americans still came to identify him as a Muslim. [68] Rumors about Obama being a closet Muslim become so viral that he opted not to visit Amritsar's Golden Temple, a Sikh holy site, during his state visit to India. [69] Obama would have had to wear a turban inside the temple, and his administration was concerned that a picture of him turbaned would fuel conspiracy theories over his supposed Islamic faith. There was apparently little hope that the public would know that Muslims do not typically wear turbans or that Sikhism is a different religion from Islam.

"Take our country back!" became a Tea Party slogan. That exhortation implied not only that Obama's agenda was un-American but also that he was essentially a foreigner. Various politicians promoted this idea, such as Mike Huckabee and Herman Cain, who both asserted that Obama was raised in

Kenya, a claim reflecting either startling ignorance or brazen deception. It was subsequently revealed that in a crucial Supreme Court case aiming to torpedo "Obamacare," *King v. Burwell,* one of the plaintiffs had proclaimed that Obama is the "anti-Christ" and was elected by getting "his Muslim people to vote for him." No less than 54 percent of Republicans thought that "deep down" Obama believes in Islam.[70]

The Republican leadership generally refused to condemn such conspiracy theories and stated that Obama's birthplace and religion are matters of personal opinion, not matters of fact. Boehner was asked on *Meet the Press* whether he had a "responsibility to stand up to that kind of ignorance" within his party. "It's not my job to tell the American people what to think," the Speaker of the House objected before pressing on about why the public should reject Obama's policies. Rick Santorum also employed this standard defense, protesting that he had no duty to correct a supporter who told him that Obama is an "avowed Muslim" and not "legally" President. "I'm doing my best to get him out of the government," Santorum had instead assured her. Romney proceeded to campaign for president with Donald Trump's backing, noting that the huckster was entitled to promote birther canards.

By the time of the 2016 election, more than six in ten Trump supporters thought that Obama is a foreign-born Muslim.[71] When Obama visited a mosque to promote tolerance, Trump said, "Maybe he feels comfortable there." After the gruesome terrorist strike at an Orlando gay nightclub, Trump implied that Obama is a jihadist sympathizer: "We're led by a man that either is not tough, not smart, or he's got something else in mind." He later argued that Obama is "the founder of ISIS." Ted Cruz too tried to capitalize on fear by insisting that Obama is "the world's leading financier of radical Islamic terrorism" because of his nuclear deal with Iran. Cruz made Frank Gaffney—a conspiracy theorist who claims that Obama is a Muslim—one of his campaign advisers. Likewise, Wisconsin Governor Scott Walker squarely answered "I don't know," when asked if Obama is a Christian. In the final weeks of the campaign, Trump sought to appear more presidential by grudgingly admitting that Obama was born in America while accusing Hillary Clinton of starting the birther movement.

The union of anti-intellectualism and bigotry turned pure sophistry into a major national issue. Elevating a black man to the presidency—to boot, one with an alien-sounding name—made certain people uneasy. It represented something foreign, un-American. Fear of rebuke made it hard to express such ideas openly, but the prejudiced could more easily make a "constitutional" claim that Obama is not a "natural born citizen." In addition to an illegitimate president, a forged birth certificate would make Obama an undocumented immigrant—a member of the vilified group that Trump and many others want deported. The hoax about Obama's Muslim faith went further in insinuating jihadism.

This controversy epitomizes American society's contradictions. A large share of the public was open-minded enough to support the election of a black president. No Western country had, until then, ever had a head of state who happened to be a person of color. Conversely, much of the opposition doubted that Obama was even American in the first place. Yet while no more than a solid minority of Americans believed absurd theories about the president's identity, far more people were prepared to accept false allegations about his policies.

The Alleged Evils of "Socialized Medicine"

Fistfights, arrests, and hospitalizations occurred in several cities as Americans clashed over Obama's health care reform.[72] Even as more than fifty million U.S. residents had no medical insurance,[73] twenty-five million were critically underinsured,[74] and scores of people were ruined by medical bills or denied care—sometimes with fatal consequences—Republican leaders roused much of the public against reform. Turning the world upside down, they claimed that America offered excellent access to treatment as part of the world's "best" health care system[75] and that instituting universal health care would lead to callous "rationing."

Exemplifying the relentless propaganda of "Obamacare" opponents, Rick Santorum claimed that "in socialized-medicine countries" disabled children "don't survive," because they "are not given the treatment that other children are given." "Care is rationed, and it's rationed by government agencies who decide which lives are valuable and should be cared for," Santorum said. "They just simply refuse care. It's just too expensive." Sarah Palin similarly warned that "Obamacare" would include "death panels" of bureaucrats who would decide who should live or die, based on their "level of productivity in society," because of the outrageous cost of "socialized medicine." In fact, countries with universal care have far lower medical costs than America and generally achieve better or equal health levels,[76] as Chapter 5 explains in greater detail.

Republicans nonetheless favored the status quo and stressed that "Obamacare" was a "government takeover" of health care, heeding the advice of a strategist who said this would make the reform sound like a "coup" by a "dictator."[77] In reality, the law did not create a single-payer system or even include a reasonably priced "public option" (i.e., government-run) insurance plan to compete against private companies. Rather, it copied past Republican proposals under which for-profit companies would still be the primary insurance providers.[78] Obama's limited reform included a controversial mandate to purchase health insurance—once embraced by Nixon, Romney, and the Heritage Foundation—but it was no more a "government takeover" than are laws requiring drivers to purchase car insurance.[79]

The shortcoming of Obama's reform, the Affordable Care Act, was that it introduced insufficient regulation, not too much. An estimated twenty-seven million people were expected to stay uninsured following the law's full implementation.[80] Another thirty-one million were direly underinsured as of 2014.[81] The law equally failed to regulate the uniquely steep pricing of medical drugs and treatment in America's profit-driven health care system. In other developed nations, legal regulations and ethical norms strictly limit profiteering from people's medical problems.[82] Regardless of its drawbacks, the Affordable Care Act improved access to health insurance for millions of Americans, such as by finally preventing insurance companies from denying coverage to people with preexisting medical conditions—a virtually unthinkable practice elsewhere in the developed world. However, the G.O.P. falsely maintained that "Obamacare" caused a drop in the number of insured Americans.[83]

Not a single Republican member of Congress voted for health care reform, whereas around half of Republicans in Congress voted to create Medicare back in 1965.[84] "Obamacare" proved extraordinarily divisive, yet much of the public was ignorant of its most basic provisions. An astonishing 52 percent of Americans wrongly thought it included a new, government-run insurance plan, and 41 percent were unaware that it prohibited insurance companies from denying coverage because of preexisting medical conditions.[85] Even among Americans reporting that they or someone in their household had a preexisting condition, 39 percent were unaware that the law prohibited insurance companies from denying them coverage.[86] Unscrupulous politicians exploited and promoted such misconceptions, precluding rational debate on a key issue that utterly poisoned the Obama presidency. Trump ultimately won the 2016 election in no small part by lambasting "Obamacare." As this book went to press, he emphasized that getting rid of it would be a priority after he entered the White House.

Faced with health care reform and other Democratic policies, Republican leaders claimed that the Obama presidency was bringing America to the brink of collapse and toward an authoritarian "socialist" regime. Extreme statements ran the gamut. John Boehner declared that "Obamacare" is a "monstrosity" that will "ruin" America. Mike Huckabee said that "Lenin and Stalin would love" this law. Newt Gingrich affirmed that Obama's "secular-socialist machine represents as great a threat to America as Nazi Germany or the Soviet Union once did." Ted Cruz vowed that surrendering to Obama would be like saying "Accept the Nazis." Ben Carson concurred that Obama's rule evoked "Nazi Germany" and added that "Obamacare" is "the worst thing that has happened in this nation since slavery."

Substantial proportions of Republicans were indeed prepared to believe that Obama "wants to use an economic collapse or terrorist attack as an excuse to take dictatorial powers" (41 percent), is "anti-American" (41 percent), "is doing many of the things Hitler did" (38 percent), and "may be the Anti-Christ" (24 percent).[87] Chain e-mails spreading conspiracy theories were far likelier to target Obama and the Democrats than Republicans.[88] Conservative politicians had long advanced ludicrous claims, and the public had caught on. Leftist conspiracy theories, like the nonsense that Bush orchestrated 9/11, never had remotely the same influence on Democrats.

Far-right pundits helped normalize disinformation. In particular, Glenn Beck swore that scheming leftists have been pushing America toward totalitarianism. Among an endless list of accusations, he frantically warned that radicals prepared to kill 10 percent of the U.S. population had infiltrated the federal government. Beck even contended that "Obamacare" includes health insurance for pet dogs. Liberals and moderate conservatives find him repulsive, yet he is popular among the Republican base. Fox News broadcast Beck's lunatic show for three years but denied that the network has a far-right perspective. According to Roger Ailes, who founded Fox News and headed it for twenty years, it is rather National Public Radio that is a "Nazi" organization.

Fox News is the leading cable news channel, with twice as many prime-time viewers as CNN or MSNBC.[89] Data indicate that Fox News is both the most trusted and the most distrusted media outlet in America, given the conflicting reactions it evokes on the right and the left. Notwithstanding the rise of MSNBC as an alternative, liberal partisan station, conservatives are far likelier to identify Fox News as their most trusted media outlet than liberals are to identify MSNBC as theirs,[90] reflecting Fox News' dominance in conservative America. While it cannot be said that Fox News viewers are always the least informed citizens,[91] research shows that they are particularly ill informed on key issues such as climate change, health care reform, and the Iraq War compared to citizens whose primary source of information is MSNBC or more traditional media outlets. For instance, a survey found "a negative association between Fox News viewership and acceptance of global warming, even after controlling for numerous potential confounding factors." [92]

The sway of fringe media outlets reached another level during the 2016 presidential race. Trump appointed the disreputable Stephen Bannon as the director of his campaign. Until then, Bannon had headed *Breitbart News,* a website known for its extreme-right ideology, conspiracy-mongering, and bigotry. After winning the election, Trump intended to make Bannon his chief White House strategist.[93] In addition to alt-right news outlets, Trump masterfully used Twitter and other social media to spread his propaganda. More to the point, he chronically denigrated the traditional media, all while benefiting from the extensive airtime it gave to his deliberately provocative campaign.

The diminishing influence of traditional media is tied to America's shift toward an increasingly capitalistic economic system. "Since the 1980s, commercial broadcasting has been almost entirely deregulated, meaning that American news organizations are essentially entrepreneurial actors which strive to maximize profit" to a greater extent than media in other Western democracies, where thoughtful public-broadcasting TV channels typically have a far bigger audience.[94] Traditional American media outlets struggled to consistently provide "hard news" as they lost viewers to competing outlets emphasizing "soft news," including such questionable topics as the lives of frivolous celebrities and sensationalized crime stories. Although millions of Europeans are ill informed, a thorough comparative study concluded that "Americans are significantly less informed about public affairs than Europeans," partly because U.S. news programming "is aimed at entertainment more than education." [95]

The normalization of far-right news outlets is tied to an ideological evolution as well. Reactionary pundits whose propaganda is disseminated on TV, talk radio, or social media are now far from the fringe. As we have seen, a significant share of the electorate and political leadership was convinced that the Obama administration led the country toward a leftist dictatorship. Richard Hofstadter is again instructive, here for his essay "The Paranoid Style in American Politics," which describes the prevalence of a mindset characterized by "heated exaggeration, suspiciousness, and conspiratorial fantasy" that "could create a political climate in which the rational pursuit of our well-being and safety would become impossible" even if those sharing this mindset did not win the White House.[96] Hofstadter was writing with the problems of the 1950s and 1960s in mind—McCarthyism, Bircherism, Goldwaterism, religious fundamentalism—but his observations are applicable to modern times.

"The paranoid style" is more than a mindset. It is also a political strategy. Republican leaders galvanized much of the country by hysterically asserting that Obama had radically raised taxes on entering office, although his economic stimulus plan cut income taxes for 95 percent of working families.[97] Despite their obsession with excessive taxation, barely 2 percent of Tea Party supporters knew that taxes had decreased, and a whopping 44 percent thought Obama had raised taxes.[98] Contrary to popular belief, income tax rates in modern America have not escalated toward all-time highs. The tax rate for the top income bracket was 35 percent during Obama's first term, the same as under George W. Bush. As Figure 4 shows, it was 50 percent during most of Reagan's presidency in the eighties and more than 90 percent under Eisenhower in the fifties. The rate modestly rose to 39.6 percent at the outset of Obama's second term.[99] The Affordable Care Act further included a tax raise of 3.8 percent on top capital incomes and 0.9 percent on top labor incomes.[100] Rush Limbaugh nonetheless affirmed that "Obamacare" was "the largest tax increase in the history of the world." Ted Cruz added that it was "the biggest job-killer in this country" and had forced millions into joblessness, even as the unemployment rate dropped. Jeb Bush agreed that "Obamacare" was "the greatest job suppressor in the so-called recovery." Donald Trump floated the idea that the true unemployment rate might be as high as "42 percent."

The rabid fear of "socialism" among the conservative base encouraged congressional Republicans in their refusal to compromise with the Obama administration. Brinksmanship ultimately led certain Republican leaders to precipitate the shutdown of the federal government in late 2013. In a spectacular feat of demagogy, Cruz and other hardliners most responsible for the shutdown then joined protests by World War II veterans denouncing the closure of war memorials due to the shutdown.

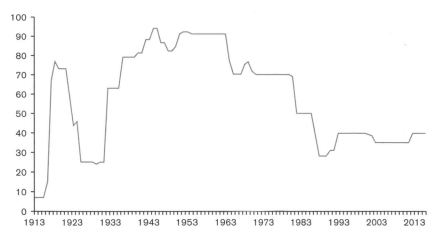

FIGURE 4. Top marginal individual income tax rate (percent), 1913–2016. SOURCE: Tax Policy Center.

Disinformation about the Obama administration's policies had clear beneficiaries: the richest of the rich, most of whom oppose improved regulation and a more equal economic system at a time when America has by far the worst degree of wealth inequality in the West. We will further see in Chapter 5 how moneyed interests aggressively backed claims about Obama's "tyranny" via lobbying and campaign donations.

The "Hoax" of Climate Change

In late 2015, 195 nations reached a landmark agreement in Paris to fight climate change. But the Republican Party would have none of that, as it denounced Obama for backing the Paris Agreement. Like health care, climate change is a far more controversial issue in America than in other Western countries. To legions of U.S. conservatives, it is "junk science" concocted by scheming, know-it-all scientists, an attitude steeped in anti-intellectualism and irrational conspiracy theories. By contrast, a relative consensus on the issue exists across both the left and the right in Europe, where conservatives are drastically less inclined to embrace the disbelief of science fueling both climate change denial and creationism among the U.S. right wing.[101]

As a result, the international community partly crafted the Paris Agreement mechanism to circumvent two dimensions of American exceptionalism. First, the G.O.P. adamantly opposed the deal because of its peculiar ideology. Second, America is virtually the only country where treaties cannot be ratified by a simple majority vote.[102] Instead, the Constitution requires the agreement of two-thirds of the Senate—a higher threshold than needed to defeat a filibuster.[103] In a bitterly gridlocked Senate, finding a supermajority to ratify a climate change treaty was a nonstarter. As a successful deal required America's cooperation, the Paris Agreement has limited binding provisions. The Obama administration essentially considered it a nonbinding executive accord—not a treaty up for ratification.[104] This would enable a Democratic president to comply with the deal, just as a Republican might not. The future of the Paris Agreement hangs in the balance, as few Republican politicians accept climatic science.[105]

Because America is the leading global economy, Republicans have had a disproportional impact on the planet by scuttling previous agreements on climate change. Despite its reservations, the Clinton administration signed the Kyoto Protocol, a failed prior treaty on climate change. But the Senate never ratified it, and George W. Bush refused to push the matter further. His head treaty negotiator admitted to pseudoscience-touting oil lobbyists that Bush "rejected Kyoto in part based on input from you." [106] Canada withdrew from the treaty in 2011, arguing that it harmed its ability to compete economically with America, which never adhered to the treaty.[107] Certain countries likewise backed away from the Copenhagen Accord, another failed treaty, after pointing to U.S. lawmakers' refusal to adopt binding limits on greenhouse gas emissions.[108] Unfazed, the Republican Party inserted the following clause in its 2016 platform: "We reject the agendas of both the Kyoto Protocol and the Paris Agreement, which represent only the personal commitments of their signatories; no such agreement can be binding upon the United States until it is submitted to and ratified by the Senate." [109]

The G.O.P. does not merely oppose reforms to curb climate change—it aims to eviscerate existing policies by barring the Environmental Protection Agency from continuing to regulate greenhouse gas emissions.[110] The "conspiratorial fantasy" evoked by Hofstadter animates the party's top brass. James Inhofe, anointed the Chair of the Senate's environmental committee, is convinced that global warming is a "hoax" invented by the United Nations to stifle the U.S. economy with environmental regulations. In a cartoonish antic, Inhofe threw a snowball on the Senate floor to "prove" that global warming is nonsense. Ralph Hall, whom Republicans made the Chair of the House's committee on science, claimed that global warming is a hoax by scientists looking for funding. "I just don't think we oughta mind 'em," he said. "I'm really more fearful of freezing. And I don't have any science to prove that." Lamar Smith, who replaced Hall as the Chair, led a witch hunt against federal scientists accused of doctoring data on climate change. Skepticism of climatic science is particularly common among hardline evangelicals.[111] Tellingly, the global warming deniers Mary Fallin and Rick Perry, then the governors of Oklahoma and Texas, respectively, encouraged their states' residents to "pray for rain" to stop droughts and wildfires. In sum, Donald Trump was far from alone in promoting the idea that climate change is a "hoax." [112]

Corporate interests exacerbate skepticism of climatic science by spending billions to lobby against environmental laws. In the 2012 election cycle alone, the oil and gas industries donated more than $86 million to federal candidates, 88 percent of which went to Republicans.[113] As Upton Sinclair observed, "It is difficult to get a man to understand something, when his salary depends upon his not understanding it." [114] Because of their close ties with lobbyists, these politicians promote pseudoscientific studies funded by polluting industries that deny evidence of climate change. That tactic would be far less effective if they were unable to exploit the profound ignorance and anti-rationalism of millions of Americans.

The bold anti-intellectualism and cynicism of the modern G.O.P. on environmental issues is a regression from the days of Richard Nixon, under whom the Clean Air Act passed with bipartisan support. Not a single senator and only one representative voted against the bill, an unimaginable feat in contemporary America. But the pendulum might finally swing back, as polls suggest that a growing share of Republican citizens are concerned about climate change.[115] For the time being, however, climate change skeptics remain extremely influential in America. As soon as Obama entered the Paris Agreement, his administration's corresponding environmental plan became entangled in domestic legal and political challenges that were unresolved at the time of writing.[116] Eliminating America's participation in the international accord, as Trump said he would on the campaign trail, could have disastrous environmental repercussions.

A Loss for Democracy

Far-right populism played a decisive role in thwarting Obama's agenda. His administration barely passed its health care and financial reforms on party-line votes.* Once the Democrats lost their filibuster-proof sixty-seat majority

---

* No Republican member of Congress voted for health care reform. Only three senators and three House representatives in the party voted for financial reform.

in the Senate, Obama was largely unable to govern because the Republicans categorically blocked all his major initiatives, such as his jobs bill. Obama's presidency may have disappointed his supporters, but it marked, above all, a great loss for democracy.

Anti-intellectual populism could foster American decline, as it impedes rational decision-making and problem-solving. It also contributes to polarization by tilting conservative America to the far right, thereby hindering the possibility of compromise with liberal America. The latter has not made an equivalent shift to the far left,[117] as its views generally range from center left to center right in the Western world's political spectrum. It is contemporary Republicans who stand out, not only by international standards but by U.S. historical standards too. "Rockefeller Republicans," "liberal Republicans," and "moderate Republicans" hardly exist anymore.[118]

These developments led Mike Lofgren to quit his position as a congressional Republican operative and lament that his party was "becoming less and less like a traditional political party in a representative democracy and becoming more like an apocalyptic cult, or one of the intensely ideological authoritarian parties of 20th century Europe."[119] The Republican establishment's ideology was mostly behind that trend, which worsened with the Tea Party and Trump movements. It is particularly revealing that Trump and Vladimir Putin have enthusiastically praised each other. Trump notably insisted that, unlike Obama, the Russian dictator is a real "leader," regardless of his regime's violent crackdown on journalists and political opponents, not to mention his invasion of Ukraine. Trump was further acclaimed by European extremists such as Geert Wilders, the leader of the Dutch far right, who attended the 2016 Republican National Convention and was generally warmly received.[120]

This does not mean that the Democratic Party is a model of integrity. Fact-checkers have rated numerous statements of the Obama administration as either false or half-truths. For example, in an effort to build support for reform, Obama notoriously argued: "If you like your health care plan, you can keep it." That could not have been true for various reasons, including that his reform aimed to bar insurance plans failing to meet certain benchmarks. Even though Obama blatantly distorted the truth, only around two million people ultimately had their plans canceled. As the policy analyst Jon Gabel underlined, that number is similar to what "the normal churn" of the private insurance market produces, and "these cancellations affected less than one percent of persons holding comprehensive private insurance."[121] Many of the

TABLE 1 Accuracy of statements by U.S. politicians

	False or "Pants on fire" claims (%)	Mostly false claims (%)	Half-true claims (%)	True and mostly true claims (%)
Ben Carson	57	25	11	7
Donald Trump	51	19	15	15
Ted Cruz	35	30	13	22
John Boehner	35	19	16	31
Barack Obama	14	12	27	48
Hillary Clinton	12	14	24	51
Bernie Sanders	11	17	21	51
Jeb Bush	9	22	22	48

SOURCE: PolitiFact, November 14, 2016.

people who protested losing their old plan did not realize that it did not protect them well. In the end, virtually no one "lost" insurance, as alternatives replaced subpar plans.[122] However, America still has the worst health insurance system in the industrialized world, notwithstanding the fact that some Democrats touted "Obamacare" as a huge success. Bernie Sanders was not among them, yet he too made dubious claims when campaigning for president, such as promising to achieve a fantastic economic growth rate of 5.3 percent.[123]

That being noted, few Democrats have displayed an indifference to facts comparable to that of the countless Republicans who levied outlandish allegations about Obama's counterfeit birth certificate and secret Muslim faith, the "tyranny" of his "out of control" government, the evils of "socialized medicine," phantom tax hikes, the "hoax" of climate change, the treasonous Benghazi conspiracy, and more. Data show not only that Republican voters were significantly less inclined than Democratic voters to trust experts, but also that Republican leaders were much more willing than Democrats to make false or ludicrous claims.[124] Table 1 summarizes the findings of PolitiFact, a nonpartisan fact-checking group. We see that the likes of Trump, Carson, and Cruz used extremely deceptive rhetoric. Boehner, who played a leading role in the Republican establishment's opposition to Obama, was far closer to them in his falsehoods than to Democratic leaders and Jeb Bush. If anything, this table does not reflect the full extent of disinformation from the Republican establishment, given its consistently misleading rhetoric about key issues such as global warming and "Obamacare." This environment provided fertile ground for Trump's systematic disinformation. Fact-checkers who set out to follow his declarations for five days on the campaign trail strikingly found that he made eighty-seven false statements during that period.[125] Liberal and conservative America have come to hold increasingly irreconcilable worldviews, grounded in both different values and different factual understandings.

HOW EXCEPTIONAL IS THIS TREND?

Needless to say, political extremism, demagogy, and ignorance are not unique to America. These pitfalls of electoral politics exist, to a greater or lesser extent, in all democracies. In particular, European politics can be a dismal spectacle.

Regardless of whether the United Kingdom's departure from the European Union was a positive or a negative step, ignorance, disinformation, and anti-immigrant propaganda clouded the 2016 referendum on "Brexit." After the British voted to leave, their most Googled questions were "What does it mean to leave the EU?," "What is the EU?," and "Which countries are in the EU?"[126]

The French political debate is not more thoughtful. Nicolas Sarkozy, who held the French presidency from 2007 to 2012, was faulted for his uncultured manner. "Oh, I am not an intellectual!" he insisted. "I am a practical person."[127] Although Sarkozy is not as uncultured as, say, George W. Bush, his words recall a premise of American anti-intellectualism: too much learning hinders common sense. Known for his close ties to France's jet set and his taste for luxury, the man dubbed *Président Bling-Bling* sought to challenge the French political and intellectual elite. His platform combined promises of innovative reforms with a nativist theme and an oversimplistic tough-on-crime stance. Sarkozy routinely made grand proposals that he did not follow up on, such as *la république irréprochable* (the unfulfilled promise that his administration would be free from ethical scandals), *le Plan Marshall des banlieues* (a never implemented program to revitalize poor suburbs), *la discrimination positive* (a never undertaken affirmative action program), and *la politique de civilisation* (a concept snatched from the sociologist Edgar Morin, whose call for a more equal social system was contrary to Sarkozy's policies).[128] A divisive figure, Sarkozy seemed overly preoccupied with promoting his image. Public debate worsened during his tenure, as he was charged with debasing the presidency with his short temper and unbecoming behavior. The most humorous or inexcusable antic, depending on one's point of view, may have been his outburst of *"Casse-toi, pauvre con"* ("Beat it, jerk") to a bystander who refused to shake his hand.[129]

Sarkozy's main contribution to French political life was normalizing anti-immigrant scapegoating in a failed effort to co-opt supporters of the National Front (*Front National,* or FN), France's extreme-right party. The FN's founders included supporters of Marshal Philippe Pétain, who led the local collaboration with the Third Reich during its occupation of France.[130] Jean-Marie Le Pen, the FN's leading founder, is known for his staunch opposition to immigration, legal or illegal, but especially colored. He equally distinguishes himself as a Nazi sympathizer and anti-Semite. In his view, the Nazi occupation of France "was not particularly inhumane," and the Holocaust is merely a "detail" of history. The FN is now led by his more charismatic daughter, Marine Le Pen, an arriviste who ousted her father from his own party. The parricide gave the FN a more mainstream look appealing to both extremists and naïve voters.[131] A cynical strategist, she secured a 9 million euro loan for the FN from a Russian bank tied to Putin's brutal regime, which she admires.[132] While a vote for the FN is essentially a neofascist vote, the French sometimes describe it euphemistically as a "protest vote" against the establishment. Many ordinary people formerly construed their support for Hitler or Mussolini as a protest against the establishment too. The French left also has radical elements, such as Jean-Luc Mélenchon, who argues that Cuba is not a dictatorship. Yet it is not the far left but the far-right FN that has drawn popular support in recent decades. This trend was exacerbated by the mediocre record of François Hollande of the center-left Socialist Party, who was elected president in 2012. His prime minister, Manuel Valls, notably evoked Bush when declaring that seeking "cultural or sociological explanations" for terrorism is condoning it.

Other examples of demagogy and extremism abound in modern Europe. Politicians such as Silvio Berlusconi, Viktor Orbán, Nigel Farage, Geert Wilders, Jörg Haider, and Norbert Hofer come to mind. The continent struggles with its own set of grave problems and the growing influence of far-right anti-immigrant parties. Europe's case shows that America is not alone in being affected by reactionary forces. A lack of insightful leaders is not what distinguishes America either. The likes of Obama, the Clintons, the Kennedys, Eisenhower, Truman, Franklin Roosevelt, and Theodore Roosevelt have proved no less thoughtful than their European counterparts, to whom they have often compared favorably.

One might therefore ask if America is truly exceptional in this area. After all, the main reasons for political extremism in contemporary Europe may appear similar to those in America at first glance. First, there is hostility toward (legal or illegal) immigrants, who are accused of taking away precious jobs and resources while committing crimes and making no effort to respect European customs—a concern at times animated by Islamophobia.* Second, there is resentment of the bureaucratic establishment, including the European Union, as ordinary people struggle in a time of economic stagnation. Both concerns are intertwined because the European Union has promoted open borders, which xenophobes hate. These factors foster the rise of leaders who scapegoat immigrants, defy the establishment, and call for dismantling the European Union. These two forms of extremism exist in America too, given the animosity toward Muslim and Latino immigrants, not to mention resentment of the establishment, particularly Washington insiders.

Yet extremism has other driving forces in America that are much rarer elsewhere in the West. Three interrelated ideologies stand out: virulent anti-intellectualism, visceral anti-governmentalism, and fervent Christian fundamentalism. As discussed throughout this book, they are major dimensions of American exceptionalism that profoundly intensify demagogy. That nearly half of Republicans could consider Obama a Muslim[133] with a fake birth certificate[134] evidences this trend. Such conspiracy theories do not have as much traction or political influence in other Western nations. That universal health care, which is broadly accepted by the right and the left in the rest of the West, could be widely identified with Machiavellian totalitarianism in conservative America further demonstrates that it is an outlier.

Extremism is more of a fringe phenomenon in Europe so far, leaving aside exceptions such as Hungary, where the far right was in power at the time of writing. Other prominent far-right parties, like France's National Front and the Netherlands' Party for Freedom, generally receive around 15 to 25 percent of the vote.[135] They focus mainly on immigration, not universal health care, financial deregulation, or abortion, for instance.[136] Moreover, far-right parties have less clout in various other European nations. By contrast, the Republican Party is a mainstream party—a leading party in a two-party system—that was already heavily influenced by extremist leaders and a reac-

* Many of the people they consider "immigrants" are actually second- or third-generation citizens.

tionary base adopting hardline positions on virtually every single issue well before Trump's rise.[137]

Because demagogy has a noxious effect on the political debate, its prevalence in America has powerfully contributed to social polarization. A crop of extraordinarily anti-intellectual leaders, who would usually be relegated to the fringe in other Western democracies, are regularly able to attain top offices. Resorting to an astounding degree of disinformation, they exploit their supporters' ignorance, skepticism of education, and irrationality.

America seems to have evolved into what the political scientist Francis Fukuyama describes as a "post-truth society."[138] Millions of citizens are unable or unwilling to accept simple facts. Naked propaganda has been normalized on mass and social media. Donald Trump not only engaged in relentless disinformation and conspiracy-mongering to win the presidency. He additionally tended to systematically take self-contradictory positions, thereby enabling his supporters to hear what they wanted to hear.[139] Trump's rhetoric evoked what George Orwell called "doublethink" in the dystopia of *1984*: "the power of holding two contradictory beliefs in one's mind simultaneously, and accepting both of them." The doublethinking authoritarian in Orwell's novel "knows that he is playing tricks with reality; but by the exercise of *doublethink* he also satisfies himself that reality is not violated."[140] America is a democracy, not Orwell's dystopia, although this image captures how Trump did not merely deceive others. He may even have deceived himself to rationalize his own fabrications.

THREE

The Exceptional Influence of Christian Fundamentalism

"There is no country in the world where the Christian religion retains a greater influence over the souls of men," the Frenchman Alexis de Tocqueville wrote after visiting America in the 1830s.[1] Two centuries later—in an age when Christianity generally inspires indifference, skepticism, or suspicion in other Westerners—nonbelievers remain a limited minority of the U.S. population that is frequently perceived as immoral, radical, or un-American.[2]

Like Tocqueville, I was struck by the weight of religion in America after moving from Paris to attend college in Texas, a pillar of the Bible Belt. While Jesus was almost nowhere to be seen in France, I discovered that myriad Americans had "a personal relationship" with him.[3] The recurrent displays of faith by both Democratic and Republican politicians, the pious invocations at presidential inaugurations, and other signs suggested that America is indeed "one nation under God," as in the Pledge of Allegiance. However, living in more secular regions of the country led me to conclude that faith is at least as great a source of division as of unity in American society. Its religious divide is typically thought of as a conflict between religious and non-religious citizens. In reality, it is mainly *among* people of faith. Seventy percent of Americans identify as Christian,[4] but their churches are often at odds on basic issues, such as whether the Bible should be interpreted literally.

A series of social changes since the eighteenth century have had profound implications for American religion: the spread of evangelicalism, the rise of modern science, the liberalization of social mores, and the increasing secularization of government. These developments split American Christianity into two main currents. One encompasses liberal and moderate Christians, who are relatively tolerant, try to combine religion with modernity, and do not usually interpret the Bible literally. Their views are not distinctively American, as this approach to religion is common among people of faith elsewhere in the West. The opposite current is Christian fundamentalism, an absolutist form of faith characterized by biblical literalism, anti-intellectualism, ultratraditionalism, and deep reservations about science, including the theory of evolution. Conservative America is the sole part of the modern Western world where Christian fundamentalism is widespread. Some may object to the term "fundamentalism," yet it is more accurate than "conservatism," since millions of religious conservatives in Europe, Canada, Australia, and New Zealand do not typically interpret scripture literally, denigrate education, or resist modernity as fundamentalists do. If approximately four in ten Americans lean toward fundamentalism, a similar proportion share liberal and moderate forms of faith.[5] Meanwhile, the ranks of secular-minded and nonreligiously affiliated Americans are growing, although millions among the unchurched still believe in God.[6]

Why is faith so intense in America? Part of the answer lies in the fact that the relative separation of church and state in the United States since its founding spared Americans the history of religious strife and oppression that Europeans once endured. Americans are thus far less suspicious of organized religions, which many see as benign means of worship, not social institutions. Paradoxically, various Founding Fathers were skeptical of Christian dogma. But modern-day Americans widely celebrate faith over reflection while approaching religion as practical self-help. Levels of religious literacy are low. In twenty-first-century America, most Christians are prepared to believe in Jesus's prophesied return,[7] yet half do not know who Martin Luther was.[8] Even though Americans are sharply divided by their faiths, there is little public debate on theology.[9] The political manifestations of Christian fundamentalism—especially anti-abortion, anti-contraception, anti-gay, and anti-scientific attitudes—tend to anger nonfundamentalists, but it is often taboo to question the religious beliefs shaping these views, such as the notion that the Bible is inerrant divine revelation. Challenging dogma is regularly conflated with opposing religious freedom. All of these factors have enabled religious extremism to thrive, with grave consequences for America and, at times, the rest of the world. Ironically, millions of Americans lean toward Christian fundamentalism when the United States is battling Islamic fundamentalists in the "War on Terror."

Because faith is quite shielded from scrutiny in America, people commonly overlook how the social influence of Christian fundamentalism extends beyond religion, as it can mold an anti-intellectual, black-and-white, and authoritarian ideology. We will see that this helps explain why legions of evangelicals joined Donald Trump's movement irrespective of his irreligiosity, profanity, and libertinage.

FROM THE ENLIGHTENMENT TO FUNDAMENTALISM

The sway of religious fundamentalism in modern America is intriguing, given that the nation was born of Enlightenment ideas. Leading Founding Fathers shared views that would seem radically irreligious nowadays. However, the more rational approaches to faith that emerged during the American Enlightenment were offset by the rise of evangelicalism, which fostered an anti-intellectual and dogmatic understanding of faith. American Christianity ultimately split into the fundamentalist and liberal-moderate currents that remain antagonistic today.

The Religious Enlightenment and the Founding Fathers

The Enlightenment marked a shift toward forms of religion giving more room to reason and liberty of thought, and less room to dogmatism, superstition, and authority. This movement had diverse currents, ranging from moderate to radical. Certain philosophers aimed to refine Christian theology. Others embraced deism and shunned Christianity. Some prized skepticism above all.[10] Yet this revolution of thought went only so far in America, despite its standing as the nation where Enlightenment ideals of political liberty led to the birth of modern democracy. Christianity remained prevalent in America as the religious Enlightenment made progress in eighteenth- and nineteenth-century Europe.[11] Still, the religious Enlightenment had a remarkable influence on key Founding Fathers.

Deism, a form of monotheism emphasizing rationality, was particularly influential among American thinkers of the founding era.[12] Deists usually respected Jesus's precepts but tended to oppose the Christian religion and its claims about divine revelation. They argued that whatever was immoral, irrational, or contradictory in the Bible could not truly come from God. Deists were disproportionately found in Virginia's upper class, the intellectual capital of Philadelphia, and New England, notably Vermont.[13]

The most prominent deist may have been Thomas Jefferson, who famously crafted his own version of the Bible by removing descriptions of supernatural events and other passages that he regarded as irrational or forged. Jefferson considered Jesus a magnificent moral teacher but argued that his "pseudo followers" had filled scripture with "a groundwork of vulgar ignorance, of things impossible, of superstitions, fanaticisms and fabrications."[14] To Jefferson, the virgin birth, the divinity of Jesus, the Trinity, and divine revelation were all social constructs.[15] Orthodox Christians were appalled by the spread of deistic beliefs at the University of Virginia, which Jefferson founded, prompting efforts to strengthen Christianity's influence there after his death.[16] In fact, Jefferson's private correspondence would probably scandalize most modern Americans: "Among the sayings and discourses imputed to [Jesus] by his biographers, I find many passages of fine imagination, correct morality, and of the most lovely benevolence; and others, again, of so much ignorance, so much absurdity, so much untruth, charlatanism and imposture, as to pronounce it impossible that such contradictions should have proceeded from the same Being. I separate, therefore, the gold from the dross; restore to Him the former, and leave the latter to the stupidity of some, and roguery of others of His disciples."[17]

In Jefferson's opinion, the Holy Trinity was nothing more than "hocus-pocus" and "abracadabra."[18] As for the Book of Revelation's apocalyptic prophecies, which roughly half of twenty-first-century Americans believe in,[19] they were "the ravings of a maniac, no more worthy nor capable of explanation than the incoherences of our nightly dreams."[20] His anti-clericalism led him to conclude that priests live on "duperies" and "dread the advance of science as witches do the approach of daylight."[21]

Benjamin Franklin also believed in a supreme being who ought to be worshiped, yet found various aspects of religion irrational. On one hand, he thought that the soul is immortal and that people would be rewarded for good conduct in the afterlife. On the other hand, he was skeptical of Christian dogma. Franklin viewed Jesus's morals as "the best" but had "doubts as to his divinity" and thought that his doctrines had "received various corrupt changes."[22] Franklin felt that people could "live a virtuous life without the assistance afforded by religion," although the "weak and ignorant" need religion to be virtuous.[23]

Other Founding Fathers shared comparable views. John Adams, a Unitarian Christian whose faith resembled rational deism,[24] wrote that "the question before the human race is, whether the God of nature shall govern the world by his own laws, or whether priests and kings shall rule it by fictitious miracles?"[25] James Madison likewise sought to blend religion with reason and enjoyed reading the skeptic Voltaire, among other philosophers.[26] Alexander Hamilton was disturbed by religious fanaticism and superstition, as well as atheism. He apparently evolved from deism to a renewed interest in orthodox Christianity in his last years.[27] Thomas Paine's criticism of Christianity was particularly iconoclastic, drawing the scorn of Adams and other peers.[28] In *The Age of Reason,* Paine praised Jesus but called the Bible a "book of lies, wickedness, and blasphemy" that "served to corrupt and brutalize mankind."[29]

George Washington's faith is perhaps the most ambiguous because of his lack of definite statement on the issue. Evangelicals have long tried to reinvent this quintessential American icon as one of their own. Historical research suggests that Washington was not an orthodox Christian but held moderate views shaped by both Christian and deist beliefs.[30]

In the end, these Founding Fathers' relative religious skepticism did not reflect the creed of the average citizen. America remained solidly Christian throughout the Enlightenment.[31] Certain founders, such as Samuel Adams, Elias Boudinot, John Jay, and Patrick Henry, held orthodox Christian views.[32] Unlike in Europe, deism made only limited progress in America and had essentially disappeared by the 1830s. It was commonly denounced as a cult of reason aiming to supplant Christianity and create a radical new social order. Some saw it as a kind of atheism, although by definition, deists are not atheists. As deism and religious skepticism were influential in France at the time, Americans, like Jefferson, who gravitated toward these ideas faced accusations of atheistic Francophilia.[33]

As Tocqueville wrote, "in political matters, there was not a country in the world where the boldest doctrines of the philosophes of the eighteenth century were more applied than in America; only the anti-religious doctrines of the French* were never able to make headway there."[34] That is partly because Americans never experienced the long history of religious control that the French and other Europeans endured, which meant that irreligion did not readily go hand in hand with revolutionary ideals of freedom in the United States.

The Rise of Evangelicalism

While leading Founding Fathers vigorously questioned Christian dogma, politicians in twenty-first-century America are widely expected to believe in

---

* French philosophes like Voltaire and Diderot were far from alone in promoting skepticism of organized religion, as illustrated by the influential writings of Baruch Spinoza and David Hume, who were respectively Dutch and Scottish.

the trustworthiness, if not the literal truth, of scripture. That is largely because modern American religion was shaped far less by the Enlightenment ideas of the Founding Fathers than by the spread of evangelicalism in the eighteenth and nineteenth centuries in momentous stages known as the Great Awakenings.[35]

In that epoch the traditional American clergy lost touch with the common people because of its perceived formalism and austerity. This favored the rise of a populist alternative, namely "revivalist" evangelical preachers, who used unconventional methods to gather large followings. Revivalists gave lively sermons to emotional and boisterous crowds, dramatically urging people to embrace Jesus so their souls could be saved. They celebrated faith as a kind of self-help. Their rather theatrical and entertaining performances allowed little room for an intellectual understanding of religion.

Evangelical revivalists frequently believed that people do not need to read any books except the Bible. The influential preacher Dwight Moody (1837–99) denigrated all education lacking a religious purpose: "I would rather have zeal without knowledge; and there is a good deal of knowledge without zeal." "I have one rule about books," he stressed. "I do not read any book, unless it will help me to understand *the* book." [36] Not all revivalists belittled the value of education. Yet many were suspicious of intellect, not simply because of anti-elitism but also because they saw education as a corrupting influence that would lead people to question religion.

By contrast, the learned clergy believed that the Bible could not be properly interpreted without scholarship and that education should encompass nonreligious topics. While the traditional Puritan clergy had contributed to the development of New England's intellectual life, the revivalist ideology was rooted in the conviction that any person could reach God without using clergy as intermediaries, an idea analogous to the Protestant Reformation's rebellion against the Catholic clergy's claim over the Bible.

Revivalism spread throughout the country but had the most appeal in the relatively poor rural areas and frontier lands of the South and Midwest, where the educated clergy lacked a significant presence. Harsher living conditions made people more receptive to evangelical sermons emphasizing straightforward and consoling themes of struggle, sin, repentance, forgiveness, and redemption.[37]

The American Enlightenment once downplayed religious dogma, but evangelicalism did the opposite. American Christianity started to favor faith and emotion over education and reflection. Dogmatism was increasingly defended as true faith. An anti-intellectual conception of religion grew in parallel with the anti-intellectual conception of democracy and education described in Chapter 2. Religious and secular life became marked by a common emphasis on practicality and disdain for refined ideas.[38] To this day, the most rabid anti-intellectual populists are typically Christian fundamentalists, in the image of Sarah Palin.

The Split of American Protestantism

Evangelical revivalism was not the only factor in the spread of Christian fundamentalism in America, as it was also a reaction to the challenges that modernity posed to traditional religion. The term "fundamentalist" derives from booklets called *The Fundamentals,* published in the 1910s in defense of the "fundamentals" of Christianity against modern and liberal influences.

In the nineteenth century, scientific breakthroughs called many accepted beliefs into question. The Scottish geologist Charles Lyell theorized that slow geological forces had shaped the earth over extremely long periods of time. His findings helped change the conception of the planet's age and formation. Lyell was a model to Charles Darwin, whose theory of evolution likewise rests on the notion of minute changes over ages. Before Darwin published *On the Origin of Species* in 1859, Genesis was often treated as recorded history. Religious contemporaries faulted him for removing God from our understanding of the world. But Darwin explained that he had only reported his findings: "With respect to the theological view of the question; this is always painful to me. I am bewildered. I had no intention to write atheistically." Darwin did not say much about religion and considered evolution "quite compatible with the belief in a God." He described himself as agnostic and thought the question of God's existence "beyond the scope of man's intellect."[39]

American fundamentalists responded by seeking to forbid the teaching of evolution. These efforts precipitated the famous Scopes "Monkey Trial" in 1925, when a Tennessee high school teacher was prosecuted for teaching the theory. The trial received extensive national media coverage that led millions of U.S. citizens to identify fundamentalists as backward provincial elements.[40] Additional difficulties beset fundamentalists. Scholarly research on the Bible increasingly challenged its historical accounts, as well as its textual errors and discrepancies.[41] Freudianism and modern psychology contributed to shaping a secular perception of the mind. Within a generation, religious considerations disappeared from vast areas of American thought and academic life.[42] Some felt that religion had become anachronistic.

For the many more Americans who retained religious beliefs, social change demanded the reconciliation of religion and modernity. The cultural transformations of the late nineteenth and early twentieth centuries created a crisis in American Protestantism, leading it to split into two major lines. Liberal and moderate Protestants were willing to adapt their religious beliefs to modern knowledge. They did not insist that the Bible was literally true. Conversely, conservative Protestants defended "the fundamentals" of the faith and clung to traditional doctrines. The following declaration summarizes their stance: "Fundamentalism is a protest against that rationalistic interpretation of Christianity which seeks to discredit supernaturalism. This rationalism, when full grown, scorns the miracles of the Old Testament, sets aside the virgin birth of our Lord as a thing unbelievable, laughs at the credulity of those who accept many of the New Testament miracles, reduces the resurrection of our Lord to the fact that death did not end his existence, and sweeps away the promises of his second coming as an idle dream. . . . In robbing Christianity of its supernatural content, [modernists] are undermining the very foundations of our holy religion." [43]

Numerous conservatives ended up leaving mainline Protestant denominations. Conservative theology gradually became associated with conservative politics, and liberal theology with liberal politics, although in past times many evangelicals had been involved in progressive reform movements, such as the abolition of slavery.[44] Besides the social changes precipitated by modern knowledge, massive immigration of Catholic, Jewish, and unchurched Europeans, often deemed undesirable groups, contributed to the fundamentalists' urge to defend the nation's "true" faith.[45]

In an influential 1922 sermon, Harry Emerson Fosdick, a liberal evangelical pastor based in Manhattan, accused fundamentalists of aiming "to drive out of the evangelical churches men and women of liberal opinions." To Fosdick, fundamentalists were hostile to science and accepted only thinking that "brings you to certain specified, predetermined conclusions." "A great mass of new knowledge has come into man's possession—new knowledge about the physical universe, its origin, its forces, its laws," he explained, "and new knowledge, also, about other religions and the strangely similar ways in which men's faiths and religious practices have developed everywhere." Fosdick argued that the Christian faith does not require a belief in the literal truth of the Bible, the virgin birth, or the Second Coming of Christ—its meaning is broader than that.[46] He thus wrote in favor of teaching Darwin's theory of evolution, denouncing creationists as proponents of "medievalism" who discredit the Bible by misrepresenting it as "an authoritative textbook in science."[47] As Fosdick saw it, "the new knowledge and the old faith had to be blended in a new combination," a process that fundamentalists resisted and liberal Christians accepted.[48] These social changes did not separate U.S. Protestants into two absolutely distinct groups, as some stood between the fundamentalist and modernist camps.[49] But Fosdick's words are emblematic of a religious divide that persists in America.

A growing regional divide matched the split of American Protestantism. Few people realize that fundamentalist theology was partly developed in the North in the late nineteenth and early twentieth centuries. Illustratively, the Princeton Theological Seminary played a significant role in framing the doctrine of biblical inerrancy. Major religious conferences held in the North also promoted faith in apocalyptic prophecies.[50] However, liberal and moderate forms of Christianity mostly carried the day in the North, as on the West Coast, whereas the South and Midwest gravitated heavily toward fundamentalism, sometimes denigrating liberal theology as a wicked Yankee influence.[51]

UNITED AND DIVIDED BY GOD

Religion continues to be a source of both unity and polarization in America, where an extraordinary diversity of Christian denominations bitterly disagree over what the Bible says and what Jesus would do. Citizens without a formal religious affiliation are a fast-growing group, but many still believe in God, prayer, life after death, and supernatural blessings.[52] Modern America is therefore largely divided between Christian fundamentalism and moderate-to-liberal faiths. In comparison, the religious contrast in most other Western countries pits moderate-to-liberal believers against a vast number of nonbelievers. Christian fundamentalism is either absent from or significantly less influential in Europe, Canada, Australia, and New Zealand, where religion is seldom a source of controversy. Islam stands out as an exception because it is an object of intolerance in these parts of the West, as in America.

Unlike other modern Western countries, America has an important evangelical movement, which tilts much of the nation toward religious ultratraditionalism. During most of the past two decades, more than 40 percent of

TABLE 2 Religious affiliations in America by percentage of population

Evangelical Protestant	25.4
Mainline Protestant	14.7
Historically black Protestant*	6.5
Catholic	20.8
Mormon	1.6
Jehovah's Witness	0.8
Other Christian	0.9
Jewish	1.9
Muslim	0.9
Buddhist	0.7
Hindu	0.7
Other	1.8
Unaffiliated	22.8
"Don't know"	0.6

SOURCE: Pew, "America's Changing Religious Landscape" (2015).

*Many of these churches are also evangelical.

Americans have described themselves as either evangelical or born-again Christians.[53] Though most born-agains are evangelicals, not all are. Certain Catholics and Mormons, among others, identify as born-again.[54] Charismatism, another radical Christian current, is relatively common in America.[55] Charismatics believe in faith healing, prophesizing, and speaking in tongues—speaking spontaneously in an unknown language (or gibberish), interpreted for divine messages. Born-agains and charismatics lean toward fundamentalism because of their usual conviction that the Bible is literally true.

These categories are malleable, as 42 percent of Americans do not belong to their childhood faith. Aside from the growing ranks of unchurched citizens, this trend reflects how Americans convert to other denominations quite regularly. Conversions especially benefit evangelical churches aiming to turn lapsed Christians into born-agains, as they gain more adherents than they lose, unlike struggling mainline Protestant churches.[56]

The diversity of America's religious landscape, shown in Table 2, should not obscure the quasi-consensus on the existence of God. Approximately 80 percent of Americans believe in God, and another 12 percent believe in a universal spirit. Only 6 percent believe in neither, as Table 3 indicates.[57] By

TABLE 3 Faith in various countries by percentage of population

	Belief in God	Belief in a spirit or life force	Belief in neither
United States	80	12	6
Australia	49	11	24
Czechia	16	44	37
Denmark	28	47	24
France	27	27	40
Germany	44	25	27
Ireland	70	20	7
Italy	74	20	6
Netherlands	28	39	30
Poland	79	14	5
Portugal	70	15	12
Spain	59	20	19
Sweden	18	45	34
United Kingdom	37	33	25
European Union average	51	26	20
Turkey	94	1	1

SOURCES: "Religion | Gallup Historical Trends" (2010); European Commission, "Eurobarometer: Biotechnology," October 2010; Nielsen, "Faith in Australia," December 16, 2009.

contrast, skepticism of religion is ordinary in the rest of the West.[58] When they do believe in a higher power, other Westerners are far less likely than Americans to believe in a definite, personal God rather than a vague spirit or life force.

Seven in ten Americans nonetheless think that religion "is losing its influence" in the United States.[59] Antonin Scalia, the late Supreme Court justice, exemplified that conviction when declaring that "the Devil" is "a real person" who is engaged in "getting people not to believe in him or in God" nowadays. The share of Americans without a religious affiliation indeed rose from 16.1 to 22.8 percent between 2007 and 2014.[60] While they lead increasingly secular lifestyles, 61 percent of the unaffiliated believe in God, despite their lukewarmness toward organized religion.[61] Likewise, the conventional notion that younger Americans are flocking to atheism is doubtful. A full 86 percent of eighteen- to thirty-three-year-olds believe in God.[62] But younger Americans are significantly more skeptical of religion than average, not to mention less churchgoing and fundamentalist-minded.[63]

Around 40 percent of Americans report attending religious services on a weekly basis.[64] Even though social pressure leads people to exaggerate their church attendance, the actual rate in America is undoubtedly high.[65] Organized religion is prevalent in only a few Western countries besides the United States, such as Ireland, Italy, and Poland. And America is the only one where fundamentalist forms of Christianity are widespread.

I witnessed these immense contrasts firsthand as an international student in Texas. To be sure, religion had limited weight at Rice University, my undergraduate alma mater, as most students ranged from moderately devout to nonreligious. I still befriended a number of pious evangelicals, many of whom were Democrats, notwithstanding their social conservatism. They practiced their faith privately and without proselytizing. While moderate by Southern standards, they were extremely religious next to both Europeans and Americans from the Northeast. They considered Jesus their "Lord and Savior," said grace before meals, routinely read scripture, and went to church every Sunday—practices that were quite foreign to me as a nonreligious Frenchman. I respected their faith but was struck by how, despite their intelligence and education, dogma had shaped their entire lives. Disbelieving in God was not merely a cardinal sin in their eyes—it was not even an option if one wanted to lead a moral and meaningful life.

The religious fervor I observed in the South differed widely from the rather soft Catholicism I was accustomed to in France. Throughout my childhood I sporadically attended mass. At twelve years old, I chose to immerse myself more fully in Catholicism by attending religious classes for a year at my local parish, a few blocks from the Eiffel Tower. I was left unconvinced. Religion no longer played a role in my life by the time I arrived in Houston, but I remained spiritual and open to learning about my Texan friends' faiths. On a dozen occasions, curiosity led me to attend services at various evangelical churches in Houston, joining friends or visiting by myself. The congregations were either overwhelmingly white or overwhelmingly black, as is the case in much of American social life, where interactions between racial groups go only so far. But having a Kenyan father and a French mother, I felt comfortable entering both black and white churches.

I vividly recall an eloquent African-American preacher giving a moving sermon about how, as a child, he was once stuck in a city late at night with no money to take the bus back home. Scared, he proceeded to pray for God's help. He suddenly remembered that he had a coin in his pocket. A few moments later, he found another coin on the street, completing his bus fare.

As his congregation listened attentively, he then proclaimed: "There are no coincidences in the lives of God-loving people!" The faithful cheered and I clapped along. On further reflection, I found that the preacher had drawn sweeping conclusions from a patently mundane event. What he and his congregation saw as unmistakable divine assistance was hard to reconcile with the fact that millions of innocents succumb to violence and disease despite pleading for God's help.

This is not an isolated example, as American Christians commonly see divine signs in trivial events—a belief that would puzzle most European Christians. Consider the case of Francis Collins, the prominent U.S. scientist who led the Human Genome Project. Collins used to be an atheist but was eventually tempted to become a Christian. He demanded a sign from God. It came when Collins went hiking one day and stumbled upon a frozen waterfall formed into three parts. Taking it as a revelation of the Trinity, he converted to Christianity.[66] One is left to wonder if Collins would have converted to another religion if the waterfall had been frozen into any other number of parts with a sacred significance, such as the Five Pillars of Islam.

Comparative studies show that when it comes to religiosity, America often has more in common with poor, developing countries than with other industrialized nations.[67] This illustrates American religious exceptionalism. We will now take a closer look at the most peculiar and anachronistic aspects of faith in modern America before considering why Americans remain so attracted to religion.

Creationist Zeal

In 2002, Mike Pence, the future U.S. vice president, gave an eloquent speech calling into question Darwin's theory of evolution. Then a Congressman from Indiana, Pence declared on the House floor that evolution had never been "proven by the fossil record" and was merely a "theory," not a "fact." Emphasizing that people are God's creation, he advocated "teaching other theories of the origin of species," especially "intelligent design." Pence further predicted that "someday scientists will come to see that only the theory of intelligent design provides even a remotely rational explanation for the known universe."[68] That is unlikely to occur, however, as experts have easily identified intelligent design as a pseudoscientific creationist theory. In 2005, a federal district court found that a Pennsylvania school board's attempt to depict intelligent design as nonreligious biological education was a "sham." [69] The court held that teaching intelligent design in public schools violates the separation of church and state.

America is the only Western nation with a substantial share of creationists.[70] Around 42 percent of Americans think that "God created human beings pretty much in their present form at one time within the last 10,000 years or so." [71] More Americans believe in angels (68 percent), the soul's survival after death (64 percent), hell (58 percent), and the Devil (58 percent) than in evolution (47 percent), ghosts being close challengers (42 percent).[72]

People typically think of evolution as a source of polarization between secularists and fundamentalists, yet it sharply divides Christians too. Most U.S. evangelicals reject the theory, unlike most U.S. Catholics and mainline Protestants,[73] whose clerical leaders generally recognize evolution but believe that God has guided the process. It may come as no surprise that the fairly open-minded Pope Francis of Argentina accepts evolution. What is more revealing is that his predecessor, Pope Benedict XVI, a conservative German cleric, lambasted creationists for depicting evolution and faith as mutually exclusive. "This contrast is an absurdity, because there are many scientific tests in favor of evolution, which appears as a reality that we must see and enriches our understanding of life and being," Benedict stressed.[74]

While the roots of the modern creationist movement are American, it has also emerged internationally because of proselytization. In New Zealand, the Discovery Institute and the local branch of Focus on the Family—American fundamentalist groups—distributed heaps of unsolicited creationist materials to public schools.[75] Creationism has made some progress in other countries, such as the United Kingdom.[76] These developments prompted the Council of Europe to declare that creationism was spreading after having long been "an almost exclusively American phenomenon." The council urged European schools not to teach creationism, which it depicted as "religious extremism closely linked to extreme right-wing political movements" that denigrate science and aim "to replace democracy by theocracy." [77]

The U.S. Supreme Court has barred efforts to teach creationism in public schools in light of the separation of church and state. But resilient fundamentalists have sought to circumvent the law by promoting intelligent design as "science." Because fundamentalists believe that it offers a more spiritually desirable worldview than evolution, they insist that creationism must be factually accurate. The creationist movement therefore aims to have intelligent design taught as an alternative to evolution before ultimately replacing it in the curriculum.[78] A large share of Americans embrace this goal: four in ten support teaching creationism instead of evolution in public schools, and six in ten are amenable to teaching creationism alongside evolution.[79] Disinformation fuels the creationist movement, as fundamentalists claim there is no consensus among scientists about evolution. Illustratively, former Representative Michele Bachmann contended that "there are hundreds and hundreds of scientists, many of them holding Nobel Prizes, who believe in intelligent design," a blatant falsehood. Around a third of Americans think that many scientists harbor serious doubts about evolution.[80]

Nevertheless, it would be misleading to simply conclude that creationism is prevalent in the United States. Liberal America widely accepts evolution, like the rest of the Western world. It is conservative America that stands out for embracing creationism.

The Apocalypse Cometh

In a last-ditch effort to persuade the French president Jacques Chirac to support his invasion of Iraq, George W. Bush told him that "biblical prophecies are being fulfilled" and that "Gog and Magog are at work in the Middle East," a reference to an apocalyptic conflict between good and evil that Ronald Reagan also mentioned during the Cold War. "This confrontation," Bush claimed, "is willed by God, who wants to use this conflict to erase his people's enemies before a New Age begins." Bush's literal interpretation of scripture appalled Chirac, a barely religious French conservative, and strengthened his resolve to defy Bush by opposing the Iraq War.[81]

Following his presidency, Bush was the keynote speaker at a fund-raiser for the Messianic Jewish Bible Institute, a group aiming to convert Jews to Christianity. Its broader objective is to "restore" Israel to bring about the Second Coming of Christ.[82] Evangelicals widely believe that the return of the Jews to Israel is a precondition of Jesus's prophesied return. Around 35 percent of Americans hold this view, and another 18 percent are unsure about whether it might be true.[83] Behind the religious right's seemingly unconditional support for Israel lie ideas about its destruction during the epic battles of the Apocalypse and a conception of Israelis as pawns serving to hasten Jesus's return.* Indeed, Christian fundamentalists often think that Jews will be sent

* Other factors also shape steadfast support for Israel among U.S. conservatives. For instance, many identify with its struggle against terrorism, which they commonly associate with the Palestinian cause as a whole.

to hell on doomsday, along with all non-Christians, unless they finally accept Jesus's divinity.[84]

Chirac was not alone in his incredulous reaction to Bush's religious rationalizations for invading Iraq.[85] The revelation that religion partly influenced the war shocked scores of liberal Americans, just like Europeans, Canadians, Australians, and New Zealanders. They were notably dumbfounded when Bush answered, "There is a higher father that I appeal to," when asked if he had consulted with his father about the war. Such beliefs were arguably less shocking to conservative Americans, as Bush's claims did not come out of nowhere. It is common for evangelical politicians to declare that God guides their policies or told them to run for office.[86] Belief in an impending Apocalypse, intertwined with the image of a vengeful God, is ordinary too. Six in ten Americans think that the prophecies in the Bible's Book of Revelation will come true, meaning that the world will end when Jesus returns to "rapture" Christians to heaven and send others to hell.[87] Four in ten also expect Jesus to return by 2050.[88]

This brand of apocalypticism is rooted in the doctrine of premillennial dispensationalism, which holds that the moral decline of civilization and the Jews' return to the holy land will precipitate the Second Coming of Christ. Fundamentalists believe that several omens point to the End of Days: the creation of the state of Israel, strife in the Middle East, clashes with Islamic terrorists, the decreasing influence of religion, and the abandonment of traditional morality signaled by trends like gay marriage. These convictions combine great pessimism about the state of the world with great optimism about Jesus's return.

Numerous Americans therefore interpret global events in light of apocalyptic prophecies. A year after September 11, 2001, nearly a quarter were convinced that the Bible had predicted the terrorist strikes.[89] The reverends Jerry Falwell and Pat Robertson claimed that the attacks were divine retribution for the ways of "abortionists," "pagans," "feminists," "gays," and those "who have tried to secularize America." Although most Americans find these views offensive, both preachers had significant influence in their careers. Reagan even relied on Falwell to help mobilize his base.[90]

Similarly, various religious conservatives suggested that Hurricane Katrina was divine punishment for New Orleans's hedonism and tolerance of LGBTQ people.[91] These views are, again, far from extraordinary. Approximately 49 percent of Americans agree that "the severity of recent natural disasters is evidence of what the Bible calls 'the end times.'"[92]

Biblical prophecies already led earlier generations of Americans to see signs of the end of times. Some colonists interpreted their War of Independence against the British as such an omen. The French Revolution and Napoléon's rise led to more eschatological predictions. People of all stripes saw apocalyptic signs in the carnage of World Wars I and II. Certain evangelicals even viewed the 1991 Gulf War as an omen.[93] The arrival of the year 2000 supposedly marked the end of times—a purely ethnocentric notion, since the Gregorian calendar is only one of multiple calendars used by diverse civilizations throughout history. To Bush and millions of Americans, the "War on Terror" again signaled a looming doomsday.[94]

The historical context in which the Bible's Book of Revelation was written suggests that it may have been a metaphor for events of the first century CE surrounding the Roman Empire's rule. Christians have nonetheless interpreted Revelation for two thousand years as if it applied to current events and described an imminent Apocalypse.[95] Nowadays, however, America is one of the few remaining parts of the developed world where belief in biblical prophecies is both widespread and intense. Yet faith in apocalyptic prophecies is not evenly distributed nationwide. The fact that much of conservative America takes biblical prophecies with the utmost seriousness while much of liberal America finds that absurd further demonstrates their largely irreconcilable worldviews.

Religious Illiteracy

As Bart Ehrman describes in *Jesus, Interrupted,* millions of devout Americans remain in the dark about what biblical scholars have revealed for centuries. The average person tends to read the Bible in sequence or pick passages here and there for inspiration, unlike scholars who examine the textual, factual, and theological discrepancies in scripture.

It is no secret that the apostles' Gospels were written not by them but by unknown authors who inherited their accounts from a malleable oral tradition decades after Jesus's time.[96] Significant contradictions therefore exist between the Gospels of John, Luke, Mark, and Matthew regarding Jesus's genealogy, birth, teachings, last supper, trial, crucifixion, last words, and resurrection. For example, the idea that Jesus was born to a virgin is found only in Matthew and Luke. And these two Gospels trace Jesus's lineage through Joseph, even though they would have had no blood relation, since Jesus was reportedly born to the Virgin Mary, whose lineage is not given. Besides, Matthew and Luke both provide different lineages for Joseph.[97]

Naturally, there may be mythological and allegorical value to biblical stories reflecting ancient civilizations' efforts to explain the world based on the knowledge at their disposal. While a historical understanding of scripture is compatible with faith, it is irreconcilable with a fundamentalist mindset. In the eyes of fundamentalists, the Bible *must* be literally true because God would not have given us a flawed text.

Certain Americans deliberately reject information contradicting their religious beliefs, yet many simply lack elementary religious education. The first comprehensive survey on the issue found that atheists and agnostics had greater knowledge of religion than the devout.[98] It revealed that only 47 percent of Protestants and 42 percent of Catholics know that Martin Luther was the main figure behind the Protestant Reformation, compared to 68 percent of agnostics and atheists. In addition, more than half of Americans are unaware that the Koran is the Islamic holy book and that Ramadan is the Islamic holy month. No more than 65 percent can identify Zeus as the supreme divinity in Greek mythology. Barely 62 percent realize that most people in India are Hindus. Only 47 percent know that the Dalai Lama is Buddhist. Surely, all human beings have gaps in their knowledge, although miseducation of this magnitude is remarkable. In the words of Stephen Prothero, the author of *Religious Literacy,* a substantial proportion of Americans are both "deeply religious and profoundly ignorant about religion."[99]

A DISTINCTIVE APPROACH TO FAITH

Why are so many Americans drawn to religion in the first place? The uncanny appeal of faith in the United States is epitomized by the Jesus Movement, an evangelical current within the hippie counterculture of the sixties and seventies. Known as the Jesus People, its followers sought to fuse evangelical dogma with hippie skepticism of conventional ideas. These Christian radicals "believed in a love that their elders preached but did not follow," while embracing the hippie struggle against "the establishment and the Vietnam War," as Tanya Luhrmann writes in her book on modern evangelicals.[100] Jesus People could be indistinguishable from fellow hippies, and some used drugs to attain psychedelic spiritual states. Their movement contributed to the rise of Christian rock music, which equally benefited from Bob Dylan's controversial conversion to evangelicalism. Jesus People aimed to reinvent Christianity because they could not bring themselves to abandon religion despite their radicalism.

One regularly sees similar patterns when talking to ordinary Americans or following the news. American LGBTQ Catholics press the pope to recognize their rights—and reconsider the church's longstanding sexism and prudishness.[101] A "black Mormon feminist" aims to reform the Mormon Church, whose history of racism and patriarchy is well documented.[102] These examples reflect a broader trend. The history of American religion, like perhaps all religion, is one of constant reinvention. African-Americans co-opted Christianity as a gospel of resilient hope even though it served to rationalize their enslavement. Quakers redefined as a pacifist creed a faith that others used to justify wars of conquest. Fundamentalist and modernist Protestants split into opposite currents. Today new generations redefine what God wants as social circumstances change. However, the trend has not been identical on the Old Continent. Since the Enlightenment, Europeans have redefined Christianity but have also been more willing to let go of religion.

Social pressure to be religious partly explains Christianity's popularity in America. Yet it appears to stem mainly from a tendency to envision religions as benign means of worship, self-help, and fellowship rather than as human-made institutions, as is often the case in Europe. Dogma is thus commonly absolved from critical thinking in America, which allows organized religions to thrive regardless of how peculiar their views may be.

A Moral Society Needs Religion

Nearly two centuries ago, Tocqueville made a revealing observation after traveling from France to the United States: "I stop the first American whom I meet . . . and I ask him if he believes religion to be useful to the stability of laws and to the good order of society; he answers me without hesitation that a civilized society, but above all a free society, cannot subsist without religion. . . . Those least versed in the science of government know that at least." [103]

Tocqueville remains insightful, as lacking a religious faith is still unacceptable in numerous American communities. Atheism and agnosticism are regularly associated with extremism, immorality, and nihilism in the United States.[104] Those who admit to not believing in God risk being ostracized by their peers, particularly in conservative areas.[105]

These circumstances do more than encourage people to be devout—they entice people to show that they are, thereby creating a strong social norm of religiosity. A Danish expat interviewed as part of a comparative study was astonished by what he witnessed on moving to California. Faith is a private matter in Denmark, as is largely the case throughout Europe, but in America multitudes have bumper stickers with messages about God. Morten, the Dane, wondered: "Are they saying this because they want other people to see that they are [so religious]?" He described how he casually asked an acquaintance whether he went to church. "No, but I study the Bible at home," the man replied. Morten sensed that "he thought he had to say that—that he was embarrassed for not going to church." Morten was likewise shocked by how U.S. politicians, from George W. Bush to Hillary Clinton, made sure to tell voters that they believe in God.[106]

Virtually no Democratic or Republican politician has ever accepted the label "nonbeliever." A full 43 percent of Americans would not vote for a qualified presidential candidate who happened to be an atheist—a remarkably higher proportion than for a Catholic (5 percent), a Jew (6 percent), a Mormon (18 percent), or a Muslim (40 percent).[107] Social pressure therefore encourages U.S. politicians of all stripes to invoke God regularly. In turn, religious rhetoric from the nation's leaders helps normalize religiosity and dissuade skepticism, irrespective of whether such public displays of faith are heartfelt or contrived. Politicians' religious rhetoric turns off some Americans, yet we will see in the next chapter that millions welcome displays of faith, which supposedly enable them to relate to their leaders on a personal level.

The religious right and certain religious moderates like ex-senator Joe Lieberman warn that an irreligious society would be chaotic, depraved, full of crime, and filled with selfish, empty-feeling people.[108] Phil Zuckerman, an American sociologist, sought to test this theory by moving to Denmark and Sweden, two of the world's least religious countries. He found scores of irreligious people leading moral, loving, and satisfying lives. The nonnegligible share of Danes and Swedes who believe in God or subscribe to Christianity are far closer to rational deism than to dogmatism. Almost no one considers the Bible literally true. People observe certain Christian rites, such as baptizing their children or getting married in church, more out of custom than faith. Politicians basically do not discuss their religious views. Despite their secularism, Denmark and Sweden are highly prosperous nations with high levels of well-being and low crime levels.[109]

In America, accepting modern knowledge, science, and social mores has often meant adopting liberal or moderate forms of faith. Elsewhere in the West, accepting these dimensions of modernity has often meant abandoning religion altogether. Religious skepticism there has not been mostly limited to progressive circles, unlike in America. Numerous European conservatives, for instance, harbor viewpoints that would be labeled archliberal in America, such as the notion that biblical accounts are only "stories." While faith has not disappeared from Europe, Canada, Australia, or New Zealand, few of the people who remain religious there lean toward Christian fundamentalism.

Certain Americans fear that their country may follow other nations into a postreligious age, although that seems unlikely in the immediate future. While religion is not as dominant in America in the twenty-first century as in prior centuries, it retains considerable weight. In fact, merely 22 percent of Americans want organized religion to have less social influence. The rest want it to have either equal or greater influence.[110]

From Self-Help and Fellowship to Indoctrination

Notwithstanding social pressure to be religious, scores of Americans are genuinely attracted to organized religion. But many are not initially drawn to its theological, moral, or spiritual dimensions. People commonly join fundamentalist churches for the same reason that others join moderate or liberal churches: religion is often seen as a means of self-help and fellowship in America.[111] People are told that faith will offer solace and help them succeed in their careers, that the Bible will provide concrete dos and don'ts, and that a supportive church community will give them a meaningful social life. This approach to religion is illustrated by one of the conclusions in Luhrmann's anthropological study of evangelicals: "Their faith is practical, not philosophical."[112]

Over the years I have met diverse American evangelicals, Catholics, and Mormons drawn to organized religion by the notion that it would give them a sense of purpose, a belief system, a supportive community, and comfort. They wanted more than what secular morality, education, social activities, friendships, and romantic relationships had to offer.

A landmark study found that joining hardline churches can be especially rewarding.[113] If not taken past a certain threshold, strictness and even adherence to eccentric beliefs can enhance fellowship by screening out individuals who lack devotion. This stimulates participation for those who remain, enriching their experience. In general, the more distinctive a church is, the more its members attend services—like Mormons and Jehovah's Witnesses, for example.

In other words, the primary reason for joining a religious community is not necessarily whether its assertions about God and the universe are true. People who belong to evangelical churches may not have thoroughly examined whether the Bible is inerrant, just as Catholics may not have fully considered whether the pope has special knowledge of God. Acquiring such dogmatic beliefs is commonly a by-product of joining a church where one hopes to find fellowship, structure, and self-help. Churchgoers in other Western countries may be drawn to organized religion for the same reasons. But American churches are likelier to indoctrinate their members with fundamentalist ideas.

I debated religion with my friend Judy, a cheerful Democrat raised in a left-leaning family in California. In search of religious fellowship and guidance after graduating from college, she decided to join an evangelical church. It turned out to be a fundamentalist one. Judy was taught that homosexuality and any form of premarital sex are grave sins. She learned about creationism and was convinced that scientists regularly forge fossils to fabricate evidence of evolution. Judy was also trained to proselytize. In our conversations she demonstrated the ability to present her case in a constructive way that might have persuaded ill-informed or ambivalent people. Her main argument was that the universe must have a God because life could not exist on earth if it were at a slightly different distance from the sun. She likewise asserted that neither a cell nor a full organism has been proved to evolve. Judy therefore concluded that Genesis must be literally true. Based on her reasoning, one could equally conclude that ancient Greek mythology or the Koran must be absolutely true. But Judy was just repeating her church's teachings.

Legions similarly enter fundamentalist churches seeking a self-help system, emotional fulfillment, a sense of belonging, and spirituality. They then embrace a narrow yet all-encompassing ideology, proclaim the literal truth of ancient scripture, promote creationism, extol intolerance, and defy reason.

Those whom Richard Hofstadter described as "men of emotional power or manipulative skill" commonly play a role in that process.[114] The fundamentalist preacher Rick Warren rose to fame with his bestseller *The Purpose Driven Life,* a self-help religious book. Preachers like Warren encourage their followers to build "a personal relationship with God." This evangelical aspiration is far more than a metaphor. It rests on the conviction that one can literally talk and interact with God on a routine basis. Luhrmann's anthropological research led her to meet numerous evangelicals who "were invited to put out a second cup of coffee for God while they prayed, to go for a walk with God, to go on a date with God, to snuggle with God, to imagine that they're sitting on a bench in the park and God's arm is around their shoulders, and they're kind of talking about their respective days."[115] Luhrmann found that the evangelicals she studied approached religion as a "self-help" means of feeling content and confident. Alongside this process of emotional fulfillment, Warren and other fundamentalist preachers encourage churchgoers to interpret the Bible literally, reject evolution, endorse abstinence-only sexual education, and condemn abortion, gay rights, and stem-cell research.[116]

How Secular Government Helped Religion

Americans have fewer historical reasons than Europeans to be wary of organized religion, which helps explain the stronger dogmatism found in the United States. The official establishment of religion in premodern Europe fostered mistrust. European clergy were frequently considered corrupt and oppressive allies of authoritarian monarchs who claimed to be divinely chosen. Because of the union of church and state, challenging one's government could imply challenging the authority of intertwined religious institutions and vice versa. Even though millions of Europeans remained faithful Christians, these conditions helped build awareness on the Old Continent that the Catholic Church, Anglican Church, and other churches are partly sociopolitical institutions. Meanwhile, members of Europe's persecuted Christian denominations sought refuge in America.

This is not to say that early American colonists necessarily embraced religious liberty. The Puritans fled religious persecution in England but enforced religious orthodoxy in their Massachusetts Bay Colony, leading to clashes with Quakers, Baptists, and other dissenters, some of whom were expelled. Strikingly, between 1659 and 1661, Puritan authorities hung four Quakers for their unorthodox religious views.[117] Colonies under the yoke of the Anglican Church likewise enjoyed limited freedom of worship. Quakers were comparatively tolerant and stood out for their pacifism.[118] It is therefore a myth that early colonists, especially the Pilgrims and the Puritans,* established

---

* People often conflate these two groups despite key differences. In broad terms, the Puritans sought to reform the Church of England, whereas the Pilgrims were separatists who aimed to leave it altogether.

religious liberty in America. The Founding Fathers deserve more credit for doing so a century later, as they deliberately avoided establishing a national religion in the U.S. Constitution of 1787.[119] We will return to the history of secular American government in the next chapter. At this stage, it is important to grasp how greater religious liberty helped organized religion spread in America.

The comparative absence of coercive, state-established religion in the United States since its founding spared Americans the religious strife and clerical domination that Europeans once faced.* Early generations of Americans further tended to define themselves as the opposite of Europeans, whom they faulted for repressing religious freedom.[120] These circumstances enabled democracy and Christianity to grow in relative harmony in the United States. "In France," Tocqueville wrote in the 1830s, "I had almost always seen the spirit of religion and the spirit of freedom pursuing courses diametrically opposed to each other; but in America I found that they were intimately united, and that they reigned in common over the same country."[121]

Unlike in America, the struggle for democracy in Europe was partly predicated on ending the dominance of clerical institutions over society. The relative separation of church and state in the United States meant that Americans who opposed their government did not necessarily become critical or skeptical of religion, as many Europeans did. Religion in America was thus able to prosper in an independent sphere where it was quite shielded from scrutiny.[122]

Religious conflict has obviously not been fully absent from U.S. history. Nativist riots against Catholic immigrants occurred in the nineteenth century. Jews, Muslims, Hindus, Sikhs, and other minorities have also faced discrimination. Moreover, modern-day liberal and conservative Americans are polarized by diverging conceptions of Christianity. Nevertheless, the average American tends to regard religious faith with a presumption of goodness. By contrast, the average European is more inclined to view all organized religions with at least some suspicion. When debating religion with Americans, I regularly felt that the first question on their minds was: "If a religion makes someone happy, who am I to question it?" Europeans seem more disposed to consider: "Is this religion true?" In the eyes of countless

---

* We will see in the next chapter that churches were officially established in several states at the time of the founding, although the separation of church and state nationwide was generally stronger than in Europe.

Europeans, religions are human-made institutions serving as means of political, social, and gender control, bolstered by dubious supernatural claims. Americans are more inclined to regard religions as personal matters of worship, self-help, or fellowship, thereby enabling Christian fundamentalists to promote radical ideas while facing limited opposition.

A Peculiar View of Religious Freedom

Several prominent American writers mounted a protest when the PEN American Center presented its Freedom of Expression Courage Award to *Charlie Hebdo* after jihadists tragically massacred its cartoonists for publishing caricatures of Muhammad.[123] The French satirical newspaper's critics argue that it capitalizes on bigotry in a society where discrimination against Muslims is undoubtedly common. Its defenders respond that barely 7 percent of its headlines from 2005 to 2015 focused on Islam, as *Charlie Hebdo* has satirized multiple other targets, from the Catholic Church to a wide array of politicians.[124]

However, another aspect of the issue was mostly overlooked: it is far less socially acceptable to criticize religion in America than in France, whether mockingly or constructively. This helps explain why Americans are likelier to perceive caricatures of Muhammad as discrimination or hate speech. Few people grasp that such cartoons are, at least to an extent, the fruit of anti-Christian attitudes that spread during the Enlightenment and eventually fostered greater skepticism toward all faiths in Europe than in America.

There is a remarkable taboo against questioning religious beliefs in the United States. Tellingly, Christian fundamentalism leaves millions of Americans unfazed despite its extremist theology. Barely 26 percent have an "unfavorable impression" of "Christian fundamentalist religions," while 35 percent have a favorable one. A third have no opinion on the matter.[125] Liberal and moderate Americans generally oppose the fundamentalist agenda on issues like abortion, gay rights, and evolution. But many consider it inappropriate to question fundamentalist *religious* beliefs. Paradoxically, it is difficult to undermine the political manifestations of fundamentalism without challenging its underlying religious dogma, such as the notion that the Bible is inerrant.

The taboo against questioning even hardline dogma is palpable in the stances of politicians and the media. During Bill Clinton's presidency, the head of the Southern Baptist Convention asked him: "I just want an answer, not a political answer. A straight yes [or] no answer. Do you believe the Bible is literally true or not?" Clinton responded: "Pastor, I think it is completely true. But I don't think you or I or anyone else on earth is smart enough to understand it." [126] Answering no might have been political suicide. Much of the media has displayed a similar reluctance to question fundamentalist theology. CNN and Fox News, for example, have devoted nonanalytical coverage to biblical prophecies and claims that strife in the Middle East signals the Apocalypse.[127]

Of course, exceptions exist. Certain journalists have critically analyzed the faiths of politicians like Bush, Palin, Romney, and Obama. Richard Dawkins's *The God Delusion,* Sam Harris's *The End of Faith,* and other atheist treatises were bestsellers in America. Bill Maher and various other U.S. comedians mock religion. Humorous television shows, such as *The Simpsons, Family Guy,* and *South Park,* have parodied the religious right. On an episode of *The West Wing,* the U.S. president sarcastically asked a Bible-toting fundamentalist whether he should sell his daughter into slavery because the Bible licenses that behavior (Exodus 21:7–8). Unsurprisingly, the episode concluded with a religion-friendly balancing act in which the main characters sequentially repeated "God bless America" with conviction.[128]

The taboo against applying critical thinking to religion rests on a peculiar conception of religious freedom. It is widely thought that challenging religious beliefs amounts to challenging the right to believe in them, a profound misconception. Freedom of religion is obviously a basic human right. Yet respecting people's faiths does not preclude skepticism. Religious freedom encompasses the rights to criticize, analyze, and debate faith. These are largely the fruit of Enlightenment ideas that arose in response to theocratic governments that repressed not only religious minorities but also iconoclastic philosophers and anyone who doubted religion.

From the Protestant Reformation to the Enlightenment, innumerable historic events would never have occurred if religion had been exempt from critical thought. Christianity itself would not exist. Indeed, the argument that questioning religion is intolerance is hard to square with the views of the founders of leading religions. Abraham, Moses, Jesus, Muhammad, Martin Luther, and the Mormon prophet Joseph Smith did not preach "Believe anything you want—all religions are great." In fact, they could be critical of other faiths, from "primitive" polytheism to rival forms of monotheism.

America's general reluctance to analyze religion is epitomized by the scant attention devoted to Mormon theology as the nation came close to awarding the presidency to Mitt Romney, whose entire life has been steeped in Mormonism. Long considered a fringe movement, the Mormon Church has made efforts to enter the mainstream in recent decades. It abandoned the racist policy that barred blacks from its priesthood until 1978, as well as various sexist rites,[129] although it remains a highly patriarchal institution. Romney's 2012 presidential race led the media to focus on whether his faith could cost him votes and on the political and social values of Mormons, who constitute barely 2 percent of Americans. But the media and the public widely declined to scrutinize the alleged revelations of Joseph Smith (1805–44), the founder of the faith, even though they are the religion's very premises and more than 90 percent of Mormons believe in them.[130]

Smith, a treasure hunter, claimed that an angel called Moroni led him to ancient golden plates buried in upstate New York. According to Smith, they revealed that Native Americans are of Jewish origin and were visited by Jesus after his crucifixion. Smith said that the plates were written in an unknown language, "reformed Egyptian," which he translated into the Book of Mormon by using supernatural seer stones that he placed at the bottom of a hat. The angel later took the plates away. Smith gained a following as a prophet that eventually enabled him to polygamously marry around thirty women, including ten who were already married to other men. Smith assured them that marrying him would have spiritual rewards. He did not believe that whites and blacks should marry, however, despite opposing slavery.[131] Fleeing religious persecution from hostile contemporaries, Smith and his followers reached the American hinterland, where he received another revelation: the Garden of Eden was once in what is now Jackson County, Missouri.

Mormon theology is noticeably America-centric: the Garden of Eden was in America, Jesus came to America, the greatest prophet since Jesus was an American, and so forth. If a Dutch person were to say that the Garden of Eden was near Rotterdam, that Jesus visited the Netherlands, and that the greatest prophet since Jesus was Dutch, the Dutch and other Europeans would widely dismiss such assertions as chauvinistic nonsense. Expressing such skepticism is often deemed unacceptable on the other side of the Atlantic in the twenty-first century.

Eight in ten Americans indicated that Romney's Mormon faith should not be a major reason to support or oppose his presidential candidacy.[132] What could be viewed as exemplary tolerance may also be interpreted otherwise. Only half of the U.S. public knows who Joseph Smith was.[133] Many Americans know little about Mormonism beyond the idea that it involves polygamy,[134] a practice that the Mormon Church has long repudiated and that only marginal elements carry on. If people decline to question Mormon beliefs without caring to learn about their very basics, is that truly a reflection of tolerance? Could it instead be a sign of indifference or an unwillingness to analyze religion?

Most Americans have "faith in faith."[135] They celebrate it but are frequently indifferent to the meaning of underlying religious beliefs. That sentiment is captured by President Eisenhower's statement that "our form of government has no sense unless it is founded in a deeply felt religious faith, and I don't care what it is."

The taboo against examining Mormon beliefs is remarkable, given that Smith's account raises elementary factual issues besides there being no proof of the golden plates' existence. For example, linguists dispute his key assertion about the existence of a "reformed Egyptian" language, Egyptologists ridiculed his interpretation of hieroglyphics,[136] and archeologists and anthropologists find no support for his claim that Native Americans descend from Israelites—they instead find the Book of Mormon rife with anachronisms. Yet a broader apprehension may dissuade people from skepticism. Questioning whether Smith received divine revelations could open the door to doubting the revelations of Moses, Jesus, Muhammad, and other figures.

While Mormons faced persecution in the nineteenth century, they are now fortunately accepted as members of American society. Refusing to question organized religion is far preferable to intolerance. But tolerance is compatible with critical thinking. People with distinct religious views can still form sincere friendships and constructively debate religion, which is the greatest form of tolerance. No beliefs, whether religious or irreligious, conservative or liberal, should be deemed beyond analysis or discussion. Mormon friends with whom I debated Smith's revelations once invited me to attend church services with them. I gladly did so. It was a moving human experience that enabled me to learn more about their world.

There is ultimately no valid reason why America could not have a good president who happened to be a moderate Mormon. Church members have made valuable contributions to society, such as Marriner Eccles, who served as the chair of the Federal Reserve during the New Deal. The Constitution rightly bars a religious test for office. However, this clause should not be used as a shield while religious rhetoric is used as a sword. Romney downplayed his Mormonism, but like many politicians of both parties, he recurrently invoked God to try to obtain votes. Romney notably affirmed that the country's sharp wealth inequality is a nonissue and that focusing on it "is entirely inconsistent with the concept of one nation under God."

The progress of Mormonism in America reflects a major social dynamic. New religions often face public rebuke and outright skepticism, as Mormonism did in the nineteenth century. Its case shows that, with resilience and a sophisticated public relations strategy, a new religion can cross a tipping point in how outsiders perceive it. As the religion becomes more established, it gains respectability in the public eye so that questioning its beliefs is less acceptable.

Around the time when Romney was preparing his presidential race, the journalist Lawrence Wright obtained the military records of L. Ron Hubbard (1911–86), the founder of the Church of Scientology—an authoritarian and secretive religion accused of abusing and financially exploiting its members. The records disproved Hubbard's claims about having graduated from college, having received certain medals for military service, and having been gravely wounded during World War II—injuries he allegedly healed with Scientologist techniques. The Church of Scientology possessed different, forged versions of Hubbard's records.[137] In other words, as with Smith, some of Hubbard's most important claims are demonstrably false. Another parallel can be drawn between these men. Smith was a treasure hunter who said he received revelations from ancient golden plates discovered with an angel's guidance. Hubbard was a science-fiction writer who professedly received revelations that the earth formerly belonged to a galactic confederation under the domination of aliens.

Scientologists claim that questioning their beliefs amounts to bigotry, although it is more socially acceptable in contemporary America to criticize (or mock as "science fiction") their beliefs than those of more established faiths, from Catholicism to Mormonism. Yet if Scientology becomes more transparent, waters down some of its practices, and improves its public image, it might someday become a mainstream religion, gain social influence, and be shielded from criticism. Thus far, Scientology is mostly known for appealing to celebrities like Tom Cruise and John Travolta. They largely approach Scientology as a self-help system meant to provide focus, fellowship, and well-being.[138] Perhaps one day America will have key political leaders of Scientologist faith.

This chapter has described how ordinary, kind, and educated people can gravitate toward religious fundamentalism. While fundamentalists are sometimes demonized, this oversimplistic perspective ignores the historical and social roots of their faith.

Even though ample evidence indicates that Christian fundamentalism has considerably more weight in America than in other Western nations, polls may not fully gauge nuances in intensity of belief.[139] Among the Americans who report to pollsters that the Bible is literally true, there are scores of pious individuals but also some who are not extremely religious, have not thought much about the matter, and reiterate conventional ideas about the good book's noble truths. Their answers may be more attributable to conformism, limited reflection, or a lack of information than to a downright fundamentalist ideology. But insofar as such answers may be simply reflexive, they still reflect a bent toward dogmatism over skepticism. In addition, not all people who intensely believe in the literal truth of the Bible are hardline militants in the image of reverends Pat Robertson and Jerry Falwell. In fact, ultraconservative evangelical leaders receive disproportional media attention compared to moderate and liberal ones.[140]

Nevertheless, the influence of religious fundamentalism on American society should not be underestimated. Religious beliefs help frame one's worldview, moral code, and conception of existence. Fundamentalism therefore has significant repercussions in shaping how millions of people think.

First, it encourages people to embrace irrationality and anti-intellectualism with open arms. Fundamentalists combine extraordinary gullibility concerning religious dogma with extraordinary skepticism of science, history, and other knowledge contradicting biblical inerrancy. Indeed, disbelieving this evidence is a litmus test of their faith. Their anti-rationalism fosters a great degree of credulity, especially relative to nonfundamentalist believers and the irreligious. That mindset is not limited to religion, as fundamentalists are particularly receptive to political disinformation, such as claims about the evils of "socialized medicine" or the "myth" of global warming.

Second, fundamentalism is an inherently retrograde ideology. Ambiguous scriptures written by human beings ages ago are taken as infallible divine dictates about how we should live after the Enlightenment, the progress of democracy and human rights, and the rise of science. By idealizing ancient times, fundamentalists seek to lead civilization backward.

Third, fundamentalism fosters a rigid, narrow, black-and-white worldview. Whereas liberal and moderate forms of religion give more room to discernment, fundamentalists often think in absolutes. They are likelier to categorically oppose abortion, contraception, homosexuality, and premarital sex, on the grounds that these are simply immoral. When it comes to crime, they usually value harsh retribution over rehabilitation, forgiveness, and redemption. Fundamentalist-leaning denominations, including the Southern Baptist Convention, Assemblies of God, and Lutheran Church–Missouri Synod, favor biblical literalism, deny the evolution of species, and tend to strongly support the death penalty. Conversely, the nonfundamentalist Catholic Church, Episcopal Church, Presbyterian Church, United Methodist Church, and United Church of Christ generally reject biblical literalism, accept evolution, and oppose the death penalty.[141] In short, fundamentalist churches see limited value in compassion, unlike nonfundamentalist ones. Naturally, not all members of a denomination endorse its stance on issues such as the death penalty, although church teachings are not irrelevant.

Fourth, fundamentalism fosters an authoritarian mindset. Fundamentalists imagine God not as a figure of unconditional love but rather as a dictatorial one prepared to lavishly reward those who obey his commandments and to subject others to eternal damnation. Authoritarian approaches to faith translate into other aspects of life. Fundamentalists are particularly inclined to embrace militarism and downplay the values of peace, democracy, and human rights. A relationship also exists between their authoritarian religious model and the patriarchal family model they commonly defend, which rests on the authority of the man as the head of the household. Statistical studies confirm that, on average, evangelicals are more authoritarian than mainline Protestants, Catholics, Jews, or nonbelievers.[142]

Fifth, fundamentalism seeks to blur or undo the separation of church and state. When people are persuaded that they hold God-given absolute truths, they may try to bring government under the fold of religion to counter the perceived moral decadence of secular life. Fundamentalism thus plays a role in shaping public policy.

Sixth, Christian fundamentalism is a dangerous ideology for America and the world. Many fundamentalists believe that God made the earth for humankind and therefore would not let climate change occur.[143] An Indiana Tea Party activist illustratively emphasized that global warming is "a flat-out lie" because the Bible says that God "made this earth for us to utilize." A fellow Tea Partier concurred: "I cannot help but believe the Lord placed a lot of minerals in our country and it's not there to destroy us." [144] Similarly, James Inhofe, whom the G.O.P. made the chair of the Senate's environmental committee, cited scripture as evidence that climate change is a "hoax." "'As long as the earth remains there will be seed time and harvest, cold and heat, winter and summer, day and night,'" Inhofe said, quoting Genesis 8:22. "God's still up there. The arrogance of people to think that we, human beings, would be able to change what he is doing in the climate is to me outrageous." John Shimkus, a member of a key House committee on energy, likewise dismissed the danger of climate change by citing "infallible" biblical prophecies: "The earth will end only when God declares it's time to be over. Man will not destroy this earth. [It] will not be destroyed by a flood." Rick Santorum, the former senator and presidential candidate, added that efforts to curb global warming reflect "a phony theology" that is not "based on the Bible."

Fundamentalism is also dangerous because it shapes attitudes toward warfare. We saw earlier that millions of Americans are persuaded that strife in the Middle East is an omen of the Apocalypse and that George W. Bush believed his invasion of Iraq fulfilled a biblical prophecy. Another influential president believed in prophecies. In 1971, then–California governor Ronald Reagan stated: "For the first time ever, everything is in place for the battle of Armageddon and the Second Coming of Christ. . . . Ezekiel says that fire and brimstone will be rained upon the enemies of God's people. That must mean that they'll be destroyed by nuclear weapons. They exist now, and they never did in the past." Trying to fit ancient prophecies into the modern world, Reagan thought that Armageddon would consist of a nuclear war against the Soviet Union, the evil, godless empire, sparked by an incident in the Middle East.[145] (Biblical literalism additionally led Reagan to proclaim that evolution is "theory only," unlike creationism, which he said ought to be taught in public schools.)[146]

As president, Reagan became amenable to negotiating with the Soviets for nuclear disarmament. Notwithstanding his pragmatism in the face of a potential nuclear holocaust, he included Reverend Jerry Falwell in National Security Council briefings on the Cold War.[147] That is Falwell the fundamentalist preacher, who later declared that the 9/11 attacks were a divine punishment;[148] that the Anti-Christ was a Jew already present on earth as of 1999, because of Jesus's impending return, which Falwell expected to occur by 2009;[149] and that pornography leads God to chastise people with problems like oil crises.[150] Because Falwell and his Moral Majority group were an important part of Reagan's base, Reagan recruited him to speak out against the proposed freeze on nuclear weapons. Falwell claimed that advocates of nuclear freeze had ties to the Kremlin.[151]

In sum, Christian fundamentalism fosters anti-intellectual, retrograde, black-and-white, authoritarian, and dangerous mindsets. These are also among Donald Trump's traits, shedding light on why he appealed to millions of evangelicals despite his impieties. In the 2016 election, Trump won the votes of white evangelical/born-again Christians by 81 to 16 percent against Hillary Clinton.[152] Tellingly, the evangelicals who denounced Trump usually embraced the evangelical Ted Cruz, another demagogue with similar ideological traits.[153] Recall that Hofstadter described long ago how certain religious ultratraditionalists are drawn to "men of emotional power or manipulative skill." [154] The fact that evangelical support for the irreligious Trump commonly puzzled ordinary citizens and experts alike epitomizes the exceedingly narrow understanding of religion in much of American society. Religions are not mere means of worship, as they can profoundly mold people's minds.

We will see in following chapters that Christian fundamentalism influences other aspects of modern America, from attitudes toward economics to social policy, criminal justice, and foreign affairs. Fundamentalism may lead to American decline, as it fosters a purist, uncompromising, far-right ideology that impedes rational decision-making and problem-solving. While its influence is strongest in conservative America, it has repercussions for the nation as a whole, particularly since one of the two main parties is under the sway of the religious right. For years, numerous Republican leaders have been fundamentalist or fundamentalist-leaning, such as Ronald Reagan, George W. Bush, Tom DeLay, Mike Huckabee, Sarah Palin, Rick Santorum, Michele Bachmann, Rick Perry, Scott Walker, Sam Brownback, Ben Carson, Marco Rubio, and Ted Cruz, to name only a few. Moreover, most state-level G.O.P. organizations are "under the effective control of the religious right." [155] These circumstances exemplify the considerable political implications of religious beliefs.

FOUR

The Culture Wars of Faith, Sex, and Gender

As a college student in Texas, I encountered a conception of morality that I had never witnessed in France. As I did not limit my friendships to liberal circles, I interacted with many evangelicals who held ideas entirely foreign to me. In their eyes, abortion was one of the greatest evils the world had ever known, premarital sex was sinful, and unmarried couples who "shacked up" together were dissolute. Naturally, not all Southerners share these values, although they are ordinary in the Bible Belt. When I later lived in New York, Chicago, and the Bay Area, I felt that attitudes toward these issues there were closer to those in Western Europe.

In almost no other Western country are questions of faith, sex, and gender as controversial as in America. The "culture wars" over such issues reflect sharply different understandings of religion, secularism, sexuality, gender roles, and the family. A modernist worldview essentially prevails in liberal America, where people hold moderate religious beliefs or none at all. Modernists largely support the separation of church and state, reproductive rights, and gay rights. On the other hand, an ultratraditionalist worldview is commonplace in conservative America, where people lean toward Christian fundamentalism. Ultratraditionalists generally take a dim view of secular government, abortion, contraception, homosexuality, and sexual education unless it teaches abstinence only. While modernists tend to favor gender equality over patriarchy, ultratraditionalists typically believe that the man should be the head of the household.

Of course, millions of Americans do not fall neatly within the modernist or traditionalist camps. Some blend opposite views, like following orthodox evangelical precepts except for supporting gay marriage because of the conviction that people should have equal rights under the law. Others do not practice what they preach, such as encouraging abstinence until marriage but not abstaining themselves. The modernist and traditionalist categories are nonetheless helpful to understand America's culture wars.

It might seem obvious that values vary greatly between the Northeast and West Coast, where Democrats are more liberal and Republicans less conservative, and the South and Midwest, where Republicans are more conservative and Democrats less liberal. However, people often overlook the fact that a regional divide of that magnitude hardly exists in most other Western nations. When one leaves Amsterdam or Paris for provincial regions of the Netherlands or France, for example, one may meet more conservative people. But one does not enter a world where people widely wish to teach creationism and abstinence-only sexual education in public schools, as in the U.S. Bible Belt. Even if one takes into account pockets of blue in red states and vice versa, America's regional divide is striking.

Overall, the modernist worldview shared by liberal Americans is the norm in nearly all other Western nations. Few Europeans, Canadians, Australians, or New Zealanders share the ultratraditional morality found in both conservative America and much of the developing world. Yet, the United States' culture wars may eventually fade, given the growing ranks of unchurched young Americans who are highly tolerant and opposed to ultratraditionalism.[1] For the time being, the conflict rages on, as the G.O.P. remains largely under the religious right's domination and citizens without a religious affiliation have become a third of Democrats.[2]

THE CULTURAL BATTLES OF THE OBAMA YEARS

At first glance, traditionalists seem to have accomplished little during the Obama years. Abortion remained legal and the LGBTQ movement enjoyed a series of victories culminating in the Supreme Court decision recognizing same-sex marriage as a constitutional right. But the religious right profoundly shaped the Republican agenda in a bitter battle against the Democratic Party over hot-button issues, evoking the words of George Washington: "Religious controversies are always productive of more acrimony and irreconcilable hatreds than those which spring from any other cause."[3]

In 2012, Richard Mourdock, a Republican senatorial candidate, provoked a storm by arguing that pregnancy from rape is "a gift from God" and that abortion should not be tolerated. Republican Representative Todd Akin distinguished himself too by claiming that "if it's a legitimate rape, the female body has ways to try to shut that whole thing down"—a pseudoscientific way of rationalizing his opposition to abortion even in rape cases. Akin was then a member of the House Committee on Science. The G.O.P.'s evolution into "the anti-science party" was further reflected by the ideology of Representative Ralph Hall, the committee's former chair, who asserted that there is no point in trying to stem global warming, because "I don't think we can control what God controls." Representative Paul Broun, who also served on the science committee, affirmed, "I don't believe that the earth's but about 9,000 years old. I believe it was created in six days as we know them. That's what the Bible says." "All that stuff I was taught about evolution and embryology and the big bang theory, all that is lies straight from the pit of Hell," Broun stressed. Members of the Senate's science committee expressed similar ideas. Senator James Inhofe, its chair, insisted that human-caused climate change is impossible because God controls the climate. The presidential candidate Marco Rubio, another Senate science committee member, declared that earth's age is a "mystery," even though scientists agree it is around 4.5 billion years old—unlike "young earth" creationists, who claim it is a few thousand years old. Rubio added that it is impossible to know if God created the planet in seven days or not. He later retracted his remarks.

Certain Republicans voiced their profound disagreement, but these statements did not reflect fringe mindsets. The G.O.P. hardly recognizes human-caused climate change.[4] Its official platforms have recurrently called for a ban on abortion via constitutional amendment, without exceptions for rape, incest, or danger to the life of the mother.[5] Its 2016 platform referred to "abortion" thirty-two times and "God" sixteen times, on top of endorsing "the public display of the Ten Commandments" in government buildings. It went on to "condemn" the Supreme Court decision holding that gay marriage is a constitutional right. The Democratic Party took opposite stances.

State legislatures passed abortion restrictions in record numbers between 2011 and 2014.[6] For instance, Virginia state legislators backed a law that would have forced women seeking an abortion to undergo an invasive vaginal ultrasound to compel them to see the fetus. The law was passed after a compromise replaced the vaginal ultrasound with a mandatory abdominal ultrasound. The Supreme Court subsequently overturned a Texas law that deliberately forced around half of the state's abortion clinics to close by imposing highly burdensome and unnecessary administrative regulations.[7] Americans equally fought over whether "Obamacare" should compel employers with religious objections to cover contraception under their insurance plans. The Supreme Court ultimately ruled in favor of family-owned Christian businesses in its *Hobby Lobby* decision—one of the most controversial cases in recent history.[8] In a separate battle, Republicans relentlessly tried to block all federal funding for Planned Parenthood, a major provider of contraception, HIV tests, cancer screenings, and other health services for women.* Like multiple Republican leaders, Jeb Bush nonetheless assured his supporters that Planned Parenthood is "not actually doing women's health issues."

Meanwhile, Congress narrowly voted to end "Don't ask, don't tell," a policy resembling those of developing nations and theocracies that ban gays from serving in their militaries.[9] Gay marriage was an even more contentious issue, despite rising support for marriage equality. After the landmark Supreme Court decision holding that states cannot ban same-sex marriage, certain states adopted "religious freedom laws" allowing "Christian businesses" to discriminate against gay customers. Georgia's Republican governor opted to veto such a bill in light of public pressure and the threat of losing business investments.

The first politician to declare his candidacy for the 2016 presidential election, Ted Cruz, made his announcement at Liberty University, a bastion of Christian fundamentalism founded by Reverend Jerry Falwell. Donald Trump, once avowedly "very pro-choice," stated that women who abort should be punished. Trump sought to improve his religious bona fides by picking Mike Pence as his vice president. A fervent Christian and longstanding culture warrior, Pence notably believes that a woman's primary roles should be mother and homemaker.[10]

Religious moralizing likewise played a role in the 2012 presidential race. Rick Santorum, the runner-up in the Republican primaries, stressed that contraception is "not okay," because "it's a license to do things in a sexual realm that is counter to how things are supposed to be." He added that America is falling prey to "Satan." Santorum's reactionarism partly obscured the fact that Mitt Romney, his victorious adversary in the primaries, had urged pregnant women not to get abortions when he was a Mormon bishop. As the governor of Massachusetts, Romney later vetoed a law that would have made the "morning-after pill" available over the counter and required

---

* Planned Parenthood also offers abortions but has long been barred from using federal funds for that purpose.

hospitals to offer it to rape victims. The state legislature overrode his veto by a landslide.[11] Romney otherwise took fairly tolerant positions on abortion and gay rights when he was a politician in Massachusetts, which he renounced when running for president, drawing praise from the Republican base. The base's hostility to reproductive rights was epitomized by how Rush Limbaugh, the truculent talk show host, labeled a young woman a "slut," "prostitute," and "feminazi" for demanding that students' health care cover contraception.

Social scientists offer competing theories about the culture wars. According to James Davidson Hunter, Americans with a liberal-modernist worldview reject fixed moral standards in favor of learning from experience and social context. Conversely, those of conservative-traditionalist bents emphasize deference to "transcendent authority," based on inflexible conceptions of religion or tradition.[12] Morris Fiorina instead argues that no "culture wars" truly exist in America, as people usually hold moderate or ambivalent views on these issues. He does not dispute that the conflict matters to politicians and activists but deems that it "never had much of a mass base."[13] The role of politicians and activists in the culture wars is indeed significant, yet it is not extraordinary. As in other democracies, elected officials, political parties, interest groups, and the media influence public opinion in the United States. This influence does not mean that the public lacks agency.

Research by Alan Abramowitz suggests that the culture wars are not narrowly limited to elites or activists, as numerous citizens are far from ambivalent about the hot-button issues that have gained political importance since the 1970s, especially abortion and gay rights. Data indicate that religious beliefs now "are stronger predictors of party affiliation and candidate preference than characteristics traditionally associated with partisan orientations such as social class and union membership." To Abramowitz, the polarization of politicians accurately reflects the electorate's polarization.[14] Providing historical perspective, fellow political scientist Marc Hetherington estimates that the polarization of modern-day Americans on gay rights is statistically similar to the polarization over civil rights in the 1960s, although race has been a more pivotal political issue.[15]

At the very least, culture war issues are extremely divisive in America by comparative standards. Few people elsewhere in the modern Western world defend the ultratraditional morality representing a major side of America's cultural battles. What explains this intense divide? We will see that it is the sum of many dimensions of American exceptionalism.

Ironically, even though the vast majority of Americans are devout Christians, religion divides them far more than Europeans. We saw in Chapter 3 that around four in ten Americans share liberal or moderate forms of faith, while a similar proportion lean toward fundamentalism. In particular, evangelicals are likelier to condemn abortion and gay marriage, as well as identify with the G.O.P., than either mainline Protestants or Catholics.[16]

Polarization between evangelical and mainline Protestants partly reflects the split of U.S. Protestantism discussed in Chapter 3. Differences between evangelicals and Catholics are more subtle. Despite rejecting creationism and strict biblical literalism, the Catholic Church remains a highly conservative institution. It does not approve of condoms or other means of "artificial" contraception, such as the pill, even for married couples. The U.S. Conference of Catholic Bishops has distributed a "fact sheet" contending that contraception does not decrease unwanted pregnancies.[17] The church denounces homosexuality and abortion too. It excommunicated Sister Margaret McBride, an administrator at Saint Joseph's Hospital in Phoenix, because she approved an abortion for a woman who risked death by continuing her pregnancy. The hospital was stripped of its affiliation with the Catholic diocese after backing Sister Margaret.[18] The church also made clear that anyone who ordains a woman as a priest will be excommunicated along with the woman.[19] "There may be a legitimate diversity of opinion even among Catholics about waging war and applying the death penalty, but not, however, with regard to abortion," the future Pope Benedict XVI warned.[20] Since then, Pope Francis has promoted a more inclusive perspective but few substantive changes.

Yet numerous Catholics in America (and beyond) oppose church teachings on abortion, contraception, and homosexuality.[21] When it comes to difficult moral questions, 73 percent of U.S. Catholics rely "a great deal" on "their own conscience," while merely 21 percent look to church teachings.[22] Just as there are modernist Catholics, certain evangelicals lean toward modernism. Dozens of evangelical leaders defied orthodoxy by signing a letter supporting gay marriage.[23] They included Reverend Richard Cizik, whose tolerance led him to be fired as the chief lobbyist for the National Association of Evangelicals. Cizik underlines that younger evangelicals are likelier to embrace gay rights.[24]

In other words, the modernist-traditionalist divide also exists *within* religious denominations. Conservative U.S. Catholics have notably joined most evangelicals in defending religious traditionalism in recent decades. The end of the Protestant-Catholic divide as a source of conflict in America made this development possible. Many nineteenth-century Protestants resented the influx of Catholic immigrants, because of xenophobia, class differences, and competition for jobs. Popular conspiracy theories warned of the Vatican's takeover of America.[25] As recently as the 1960s, an alliance of Catholics and evangelicals would have been difficult to imagine.[26] John F. Kennedy, America's first Catholic president, had to rebuff fears about his loyalty to the Vatican by declaring: "I believe in an America where the separation of church and state is absolute."

Suspicion of Catholicism has faded among Protestants, although abortion has become a big issue and evangelicals have lauded the Vatican's opposition to the procedure.[27] Evangelicals remain the leading force behind the religious right, yet it now includes prominent Catholic Republicans such as Jeb Bush, Rick Santorum, and Sam Brownback. The Supreme Court justices Antonin Scalia and Clarence Thomas, both staunch Catholics, drew the religious right's praise for opposing abortion and gay rights in their decisions. But it is not conservatives alone who transcend denominations. In the image of Protestants like Hillary Clinton or Catholics like Joe Biden and Justice Sonia Sotomayor, religious liberals of all stripes—some of whom are hardly church-going—have joined the growing share of irreligious Americans defending modernism and secular government.

WHETHER TO SEPARATE CHURCH AND STATE

On the surface, the separation of church and state seems to have always been stronger in America than in Europe. The United States has never had an official national religion since gaining independence in the eighteenth century, but Anglicanism remains the mother country's official faith in the twenty-first century.[28] Twenty-six Church of England bishops sit in the House of Lords as a matter of law. Crucifixes are displayed in Italian public schools. Other practices call secularism into question, such as tax funding for churches in various European nations.[29] By contrast, France lacks an official church and is among the countries where state secularism, there known as *laïcité*, is particularly intransigent. It encompasses contentious measures like banning religious attire, especially Muslim headscarves, in public schools. Exceptions still exist, as in Alsace and Lorraine, where the French government pays priests' salaries because these were German territories when *laïcité* became French law.

Nevertheless, religion has far more political clout in modern America than in Europe. We saw in Chapter 3 that most Europeans lead highly secular lives, and their politicians tend to treat faith as a private matter, regardless of the presence of official churches. Illustratively, the rhetoric of the German chancellor Angela Merkel is quite secular, even though her party is the Christian Democratic Union, whose theological views are very moderate compared to those of the U.S. religious right. Overall, both Democratic and Republican politicians are far likelier than European politicians to invoke God, base their agendas on religion, proclaim that their nation is fulfilling a divinely chosen destiny, or assert that God told them to run for office.

The Trials and Tribulations of Secularism

References to God abound in American public life. Children in public schools are asked to recite the Pledge of Allegiance, describing their country as "one nation under God," a passage added during the Cold War to differentiate America from the Soviet "godless empire." Elected officials are commonly sworn into office while touching a Bible. The Senate and the House both begin their sessions with prayers. Each has its own chaplain. Prayers are delivered at presidential inaugurations. Even the Supreme Court, which has issued controversial decisions enforcing the separation of church and state, begins its proceedings with "God save the United States and this Honorable Court."

However, traditionalists are concerned that America is turning its back on its Christian roots. This has allegedly led to moral decadence, as exemplified by the legalization of abortion and gay marriage. Roy Moore, a leading voice of the religious right who has served as the chief justice of Alabama's Supreme Court,[30] stressed that "separation of church and state never was meant to separate God and government." Moore is convinced that the Ten Commandments are the foundation of American law.

In fact, the U.S. Constitution mentions neither God nor Christianity but for the indication that it was written "in the year of our Lord" 1787. That is unsurprising, given that many Founding Fathers were not orthodox Christians. The Constitution explicitly precludes a religious test for office. The phrase "separation of church and state" appears nowhere in its text, yet the First Amendment states that "Congress shall make no law respecting an establishment of religion." The 1776 Declaration of Independence mentions

God, but it is not a constitutional or statutory text and was written by Thomas Jefferson, a rational deist known for his anti-clericalism. The expression "separation of church and state" has been traced to him.[31] His fellow Founding Father John Adams wrote that the U.S. government was created "merely by the use of reason and the senses." "It will never be pretended," Adams vowed, that the founders "were in any degree under the inspiration of Heaven."[32] The 1796 Treaty of Tripoli, which Adams signed, provides that "the government of the United States of America is not in any sense founded on the Christian religion."[33]

While the religious right falsely claims that the Constitution is based on biblical principles, the secular left also engages in revisionism by claiming that the Founding Fathers wanted an absolute separation of church and state. In reality, legislative sessions commonly began with public prayers in the era of the framers, as they still do today. In the early years of the republic, taxes funded churches in certain states, whereas Virginia notably forbade that practice, due to the efforts of Jefferson and Madison.[34] There was no clear consensus among the Founding Fathers about what "establishment of religion" means under the First Amendment.*

Nineteenth-century U.S. public schools had children read the King James Bible, a Protestant text, and figure out its meaning without clerical assistance. Catholics, who were growing in number because of European immigration, criticized such "nonsectarian" moral instruction as Protestantism in disguise. The Catholic Church used a different version of the Bible and insisted that scripture must be interpreted by its clergy. Proposals to discontinue Bible reading in public schools were rejected and led to anti-Catholic nativist riots. Only a minority of Catholics managed to send their children to private Catholic schools. Most had little choice but to accept public schools and their Protestant teachings.[35] Students were exposed to other orthodox beliefs in the process. Popular textbooks in the nineteenth and early twentieth centuries included lessons on the importance of prayer, "the goodness of God," religion as "the only basis of society," and the Bible as "the best of classics."[36]

In the early 1960s, the Supreme Court ultimately disallowed official prayers and religious teachings in public schools, emphasizing that laws must

---

* The Supreme Court did not apply the First Amendment, along with most of the Bill of Rights, to state governments before the twentieth century. The amendment previously concerned only actions by the federal government.

have "a secular legislative purpose and a primary effect that neither advances nor inhibits religion."[37] It thus seems inconsistent that the Supreme Court has not disallowed the mention of "God" in the Pledge of Allegiance recited by public school children, "In God we trust" on the dollar, and public prayers before legislative sessions and presidential inaugurations.[38] Behind this contradiction lie the assumptions that essentially everyone believes in God and that nonbelievers are somehow un-American. These celebrations of monotheism also set aside the views of citizens from other traditions, such as Hindus, Buddhists, and Native Americans. In 2014, the Supreme Court further disregarded minorities by authorizing official Christian prayers at government assemblies over objections from Jewish and atheist citizens in a case from a small town in New York.[39]

The government's generic promotion of God may seem innocuous, but it entails promoting certain religious beliefs over others, which is technically what the justices forbid. Their convoluted First Amendment jurisprudence may be an attempt to accommodate public opinion. As many as nine in ten Americans want to keep "God" in the pledge and on the dollar.[40] Eight in ten support official prayers at government assemblies.[41] A clear majority of 57 percent even opposes the half-century-old ban on official prayers in public schools.[42]

Wanting More God in Government

The Supreme Court's First Amendment jurisprudence has not dismayed only the secular left. Traditionalists applauded Justice Scalia for emphatically dissenting in various decisions expanding the separation of church and state.[43] Expressing his personal views in an article, Scalia said he took comfort in how U.S. politicians frequently mention God and how references to God appear on the dollar and in the Pledge of Allegiance. According to him, government "derives its moral authority from God" and Americans "are a religious people, whose institutions presuppose a Supreme Being." The well-traveled justice denounced "secular Europe" and the "tendency of democracy to obscure the divine authority behind government."[44]

Scalia and other traditionalists have sought to undermine secularism by mischaracterizing it as an atheistic concept—a far-reaching conflation, because atheists are deeply unpopular in much of America. Secular government does not require nonbelieving citizens. Millions of religious Americans oppose policies shaped by fundamentalism, such as teaching creationism or abstinence-only education. For instance, Reverend Barry W. Lynn of the United Church of Christ has led Americans United for Separation of Church and State.

When asked to explain how America was created as a "Christian nation," traditionalists can have difficulty answering except in vague terms, although some contend that the Ten Commandments are a cornerstone of American government.[45] In 2001, Roy Moore used his authority as the chief justice of the Alabama Supreme Court to place a 2.6-ton Ten Commandments monument in the court building. A judicial ethics panel eventually removed him from office after he defiantly rejected a federal court order to remove the monument because it violated the First Amendment. While many liberals ridiculed Moore as a backward Bible-toter, traditionalists celebrated him as a heroic martyr.[46] He lost his subsequent bid for Alabama governor but was reelected as the chief justice of the Alabama Supreme Court in 2012. Moore was again suspended in 2016, for instructing state judges to disregard the U.S. Supreme Court decision recognizing a constitutional right to same-sex marriage.

Nevertheless, only the most hardline activists aspire to build a full-blown theocracy. Numerous evangelicals feel lukewarm about proselytization. Even those convinced that all Americans should share Christian values can simultaneously say that people should be free to live as they wish.[47] Seventy percent of evangelicals state that "the best thing to do when someone disagrees with you about religion" is to "try to understand the person's beliefs and agree to disagree."[48] Still, if most traditionalists do not aspire to end the separation of church and state, they often aim to blur it. And in their view, God has much to say about the rights of women and gays.

CLASHING OVER SEX AND GENDER ROLES

America's endless culture wars over gender roles, sexual propriety, and "family values" can mostly be traced to the peculiar stances of ultratraditionalists. While patriarchy, sexism, and homophobia definitely remain common on the Old Continent,[49] they have far less impact there in shaping public policy, because European religious conservatives are much less radical than their American counterparts, besides constituting a smaller share of the population. The distinct worldview of U.S. ultratraditionalists was epitomized by President George W. Bush's insistence that America form an alliance with

Iran and other authoritarian Islamic states at the United Nations in an effort to block international standards on reproductive and gay rights.[50] Other Western countries generally took opposite positions at the U.N., as the Obama administration later did.[51]

From Patriarchy to Feminism

America was among the first countries to legalize female suffrage, with the Nineteenth Amendment's ratification in 1920. While it did not enable all women citizens to vote—black women living under Jim Crow were deprived of that right until the 1960s—American suffragettes were pioneers. New Zealand had paved the way by granting female suffrage in 1893, which several American states and territories also did in the late 1800s.[52] By contrast, France and Italy did not recognize women's right to vote until 1944 and 1945, respectively. America was later one of the nations where the sexual revolution of the 1960s had the greatest impact. Generations of American feminists have inspired women abroad. American scientists largely invented the birth-control pill, which allowed women to make strides toward autonomy and sexual liberation.[53] Nonetheless, twenty-first-century America is among the developed countries where women's rights are the most fiercely contested.

American traditionalists are concerned that social emancipation harms the family by leading women to value their education and careers over their duties as wives and mothers. In the 1970s, activists came close to passing an Equal Rights Amendment (ERA) to the U.S. Constitution, which would have barred discrimination on the basis of gender. But the ERA movement faced great opposition from both male and female conservatives, such as Phyllis Schlafly, who swore it would wreck family cohesion—an argument previously used to oppose women's voting rights. They also worried that it would eventually guarantee rights to abortion and gay marriage.[54]

William Rehnquist, who went on to become the chief justice of the Supreme Court, wrote in a 1970 Justice Department memo that the ERA would result in "the sharp reduction in importance of the family unit, with the eventual elimination of that unit by no means improbable." In his view, the ERA movement had "a virtually fanatical desire to obscure not only legal differentiation between men and women, but insofar as possible, physical distinctions between the sexes." Rehnquist blamed ERA supporters for challenging "the traditional difference between men and women in the family unit" and "woman's traditionally different role in this regard."[55] On Rehnquist's death, George W. Bush appointed John Roberts to lead the court. Like Rehnquist, Roberts had expressed patriarchal views and fought the ERA. During his time in the Reagan administration, Roberts questioned "the purported gender gap" and "whether encouraging homemakers to become lawyers contributes to the common good." He also opposed abortion rights and supported school prayer.[56]

The ERA was never ratified. Additionally, America is the sole Western democracy that has not ratified the U.N. Convention on the Elimination of All Forms of Discrimination against Women—a major international human rights treaty—chiefly because of the opposition of traditionalists fearful that it would bolster reproductive rights.

In principle, traditionalists commonly believe that the husband should head the household. In practice, however, their marriages often revolve around mutual decision-making, not strict male authoritarianism.[57] But patriarchal assumptions remain ingrained, as reflected in the words of an evangelical woman describing her relationship with her husband: "Just because he's the head doesn't mean that he's the boss. He's not the boss. He's just there to answer for situations. To be the strong leader, the responsible person. To depend on."[58] The same contradiction stands out in the words of the evangelical politician Michele Bachmann. "My husband is the head of the household," and "We're equals," she said before admitting that "if it came down to it, I'd probably let him have the last word." Bachmann also told a church audience that the Bible requires her to be "submissive" to her husband. Mike Huckabee, another influential evangelical politician, once led a massive marriage vow ceremony where thousands of women promised to "submit" to their husbands.[59] Representative Steve Pearce of New Mexico similarly wrote in his memoirs that husbands must "lead" and wives "submit." Certain biblical passages indeed urge women to be submissive, such as 1 Corinthians 14 and 1 Timothy 2. Historical research suggests that these were forgeries added to the Bible at later stages of antiquity,[60] although fundamentalists insist that scripture is inerrant. Regardless of the reliability of scripture, patriarchy is embedded in Christian imagery, as illustrated by masculine terms like "Heavenly Father" and "Lord."

Yet religion does not tell the whole story. Research by Naomi Cahn and June Carbone shows that sharply different family models have evolved in America. Blue states gravitate toward a modern model, deferring family formation until both partners have reached emotional maturity and financial independence. It is not considered responsible to have children before obtaining a college or graduate degree and professional experience—or at least the latter if one cannot attend university. Contraception is widely embraced and sexuality is a private matter. Conversely, an ultratraditional family model prevails in red states, as well as blue state communities that are particularly religious and rural. Americans in these areas marry and have children at younger ages, hindering their ability to invest in higher education and thus placing them at an economic disadvantage. Earlier marriages also contribute to higher divorce rates. Further, by encouraging abstinence until marriage while frowning on contraception, red families wind up with higher teenage pregnancy rates.[61]

The modern family model is the product of vast social changes in America and the rest of the West. Broader access to contraception, especially the birth-control pill, has made it easier for women to defer childbearing until after acquiring a university education and professional experience. Throughout the 1960s, the percentage of women students in professional schools was extremely low: 10 percent in medicine, 4 percent in law, and 3 percent in business. These numbers had respectively surged to 30, 36, and 28 percent by 1980.[62] Today, women have nearly reached parity with men in medicine and law but lag behind in business. And they are now the majority of all doctoral and master's degree recipients.[63] Despite a persistent gender gap and glass ceiling in America, women have achieved greater independence because of the liberalization of social mores.

If modernists consider patriarchy to be on the wrong side of history, it cannot be anachronistic to traditionalists vowing to defend eternal values.[64] Some traditionalists argue that opposition to abortion is the truest feminism because bearing children is women's special role.[65] Sarah Palin, for example, invoked "feminism" a dozen times in a 2010 speech urging voters to oppose pro-choice candidates. "Our prominent woman sisterhood is telling these young women that they are strong enough to deal with [pregnancy]," the self-dubbed "Mama Grizzly" declared. Palin made clear that she would outlaw abortion and publicly funded contraception if she could. In her 2016 presidential campaign, the multimillionaire executive Carly Fiorina advanced a comparable agenda, which would have denied to many poor and middle-class women the economic opportunities she had enjoyed.

Meanwhile, Donald Trump ran a relatively popular campaign partly built on machismo. He notably suggested that Fiorina's looks made her unelectable and that a journalist who asked him a challenging question was menstruating. In the final stages of the 2016 race, certain Americans were shocked by the release of a 2005 video in which Trump boasted about groping women without their consent, although the future president had a lengthy history of misogynistic and callous statements.

The Interminable Abortion War

Abortion in early stages of pregnancy was relatively tolerated in both Europe and America until being gradually criminalized in the nineteenth century. Women continued to obtain illegal abortions, often performed with hazardous methods. Thousands died.[66] Fast-forward to the early twenty-first century, and America remains one of the few Western nations where a battle over abortion is still being fought.[67]

In 1973, the Supreme Court's *Roe v. Wade* decision held that women have a constitutional right to abortion. The ruling received limited attention at first but eventually provoked a backlash that contributed to the resurgence of Christian fundamentalism and the shift of the Republican Party to the far right.[68] Abortion opponents charged that *Roe* was an endorsement of baby killing by liberal "judicial activists." Few contemporary Republican politicians support the right to elective abortion, sometimes known as "abortion on demand." John McCain, the archetypical moderate Republican, has stressed that abortion should be banned except in cases of rape, incest or threat to the life of the mother.[69] The G.O.P. has been unable to reverse *Roe* thus far, as several Republican Supreme Court appointees—Sandra Day O'Connor, Anthony Kennedy, and David Souter—voted to uphold abortion rights. But the religious right wants to relitigate the issue and, if it loses again, keep litigating until kingdom come.

Abortion intensely divides America because people view it as a moral issue but for sharply different reasons. Social liberals think that abortion is a fundamental right grounded in liberty and privacy. They consider it a responsible option to avoid forcing women to give birth when they are unwilling or unprepared to have children. To the contrary, social conservatives believe that teaching women responsibility requires them to follow through with pregnancies resulting from their immoral sexual choices. The anti-abortion stance holds that life begins at conception and that a fetus is a full human life—abortion is consequently murder. The abortion-rights stance is that a fetus is a potential life and that women should have the choice of whether to carry a pregnancy to term.[70]

The legalization of abortion by the French Parliament in 1975 was hotly contested too. "I had not imagined that I would become the object of such hatred," said Simone Veil, the law's main architect as the health minister. Certain legislators accused Veil—a Jewish survivor of Holocaust death camps—of "choosing another genocide" and throwing fetuses in "gas chambers."[71] France's lengthy history of abortion restrictions had been shaped not only by social conservatism but also by a natalist policy identifying abortion as a national security threat, especially from the 1870s to 1940s. French leaders then asserted that the country's small population and comparatively low birthrate next to neighboring Germany hindered its ability to raise a large army. However, French conservatives had largely moved on by the late 1970s, as few wished to relitigate the issue. Social mores have evolved, and abortion is no longer a significant issue in France four decades later.[72] In fact, it is covered by the national health care system. A fringe effort to end public funding of abortion in 2014 lost by a 142–7 vote after drawing virtually no support from French right-wing legislators.[73] Yet American conservatives have hardly moved on, as exemplified by the record number of abortion restrictions that state legislatures passed during the Obama presidency. These state restrictions cannot constitutionally abolish abortion, but they aim to make it difficult or quasi-impossible to obtain.[74]

As in France, abortion is broadly accepted elsewhere in Europe, except in a few nations. Because of the weight of Catholicism, Ireland and Poland do not allow elective abortion. Portugal legalized it in 2007 after a referendum backed it by more than 59 percent. Spain also did so in 2010, under a socialist government, but the subsequent election of a right-wing government led to a heated debate over its agenda to reban abortion except in cases of rape or threat to the mother's health.[75] Again, these countries are exceptions, and most Europeans who have moral reservations about abortion rarely feel as strongly about it as Americans, a large number of whom make it a central consideration in their votes.[76] Although abortion remains fairly divisive in Portugal, for example, the intensity and political importance of the U.S. anti-abortion movement surprised Beatriz Padilla, a Portuguese expert on gender issues, who found that in America "many fundamentalists are involved in the debate" and "it's always about the fetus and never about the women."[77]

America technically provides a very broad right to abortion, as it is among fewer than ten countries worldwide allowing elective abortion after five months of pregnancy. Other Western nations generally limit this to the first trimester of pregnancy.[78] Nevertheless, American women can face greater hurdles to obtain abortions in practice. The federal government and most states notably bar public funding for elective abortion, unlike numerous Western governments.[79] On the other hand, the laws of European nations commonly create other obstacles to abortion, from mandatory waiting periods to counseling about alternatives.[80] Such regulations exist on a state-by-state basis in the United States, not nationwide.[81] They tend to be less controversial in Europe than in America, whose pro-choice movement strongly condemns them as attempts to dissuade women from exercising their absolute right to abortion. While the stance of American pro-choice activists may seem uncompromising, contextual differences are important. Restrictions on abortion in countries like France are not moves toward outlawing elective abortion as a whole. By contrast, the U.S. pro-life movement makes no secret of its goal to use such restrictions as stepping stones toward eliminating all elective abortions.

Barely 15 percent of Americans oppose abortion when the woman's health is endangered, although 22 percent oppose it in rape cases and 46 percent if the child would be physically impaired.[82] But the crucial battle is over abortion motivated by personal reasons. Four in ten think that it should be illegal if a woman is poor and cannot afford more children, is unmarried and does not want to marry the father, or is married and does not want any more children.[83] Overall, Americans are basically evenly split in identifying as either "pro-choice" or "pro-life."[84]

Ironically, many Americans who identify as "pro-life" categorically support the death penalty, have limited reservations about warfare, and oppose state-funded health care for the needy, including children. This contradiction further suggests that what the U.S. anti-abortion movement rationalizes as a fight for life is largely a defense of patriarchy and ultratraditionalism.

Moralizing Sex

In addition to condemning abortion, millions of Americans stand out in the modern Western world for opposing state-funded contraception and backing abstinence-only sexual education. The United States is simultaneously home to a continuing sexual revolution.

Paradoxically, the strict opposition to premarital sex often advocated in conservative America comes across to Europeans as unbelievably prudish, while the openness of dating mores in much of liberal America can strike even the French as excessively permissive. Indeed, if attitudes toward sexuality in conservative America are among the most traditional in the West, attitudes in liberal America are perhaps the freest. Europeans are more inclined to think that a couple is in a boyfriend-girlfriend relationship after they have kissed or slept together. Once two people have started dating, it is usually considered wrong for either to go out with anyone else. Modern American couples are mostly unburdened by these expectations until they have been dating for some time. It is quite acceptable to date other people unless a formal commitment has been made.[85] The sexual openness found in liberal America reflects pragmatism toward relationships, allowing people to forgo a commitment until they feel truly compatible with a partner.

However, the tension between sexual openness and prudishness in American society can lead to ambivalence, if not pathological behavior. Practices like males "slut-shaming" teenage girls or young women for being sexually open[86] appear more pervasive in America than in countries such as the Netherlands, where gender roles are more equal and sexual freedom is better accepted.[87] The sexism behind "slut-shaming" reflects the idealization of female virginity, a longstanding dimension of patriarchy alongside double standards tolerating or glorifying male promiscuity.[88] These social tensions may be among the root causes of an emerging federal bureaucracy requiring U.S. universities to regulate "social norms around sex and relationships" so broadly as to punish "sexual behavior that is not sexual violence or harassment."[89] According to the Harvard law professors Jacob Gersen and Jeannie Suk, this "sex bureaucracy" aims to stamp out "impersonal sex" by promoting traditional, monogamous sex as the only morally acceptable or even legally permissible choice. Students may thus face suspension or expulsion for engaging in fully consensual "hookups" if their partner later files a complaint that may stem from regrets caused by the stigma associated with sexual liberation.[90] Leaving aside consensual intercourse, troubling reports about a rape "epidemic" on university campuses[91] likewise raise profound social questions about the tensions between patriarchy, sexism, sexual liberation, and sexual oppression.

American traditionalists typically identify the 1960s as the time when sexual morality came under threat, thanks to libertine youths and hippie rebels. In reality, the liberalization of social mores was a gradual process over generations. By the 1920s, sex was already a common theme in movies and tabloids. "Along with this change in the popular culture came the virtual collapse of communal enforcement of standards of personal behavior," the historian George Marsden writes. "Women smoked in public, did not always cover

TABLE 4 American public opinion on the morality of premarital sex between a man and a woman (percentage of population)

	Wrong	Only sometimes wrong	Not wrong
1972	45	24	26
2012	26	15	56

NOTE: The table's first category merges answers for "always wrong" and "almost always wrong."

SOURCE: NORC at the University of Chicago, "Final Report: Trends in Public Attitudes about Sexual Morality" (2013).

their knees (even in church), and refused to follow the domestic examples of their mothers. Dancing, which had long been a taboo for many Protestants, now was an integral part of social acceptability in the age of the flapper. While some church leaders simply conceded the issue and even brought dancing into church youth group meetings, others were horrified."[92]

Despite lingering social tensions, most Americans no longer have prudish ideas about sex. Table 4 shows that more than twice as many people in 2012 as in 1972 thought that premarital sex is simply "not wrong." Still, the proportion that found premarital sex "wrong" remained substantial at 26 percent. Another poll indicates that a third of Americans consider premarital sex immoral.[93] Obama's plan to have businesses cover their employees' contraception proved controversial, since traditionalists felt the government had licensed sexual immorality. The alternative of publicly funded contraception for everyone, as in Europe,[94] would have been even more controversial.

If attitudes toward sex are more traditional in red states than in blue states, the divide is not absolute. Living in Texas, I met numerous evangelicals who said that one should remain a virgin until marriage. Some stayed chaste. Others engaged in foreplay or intercourse anyway. Those who did so could feel remorseful because they had "misbehaved." More-liberal Texans had no qualms about premarital sex and regularly spent the night at their partner's home. There was not much difference between them and liberal Northerners in their dating lives, although Texans were more inclined to think that moving in with their partner before marriage would be wrong.

Americans are likelier to get married than other Westerners, and they do so at younger ages.[95] Growing numbers of young Americans cohabit out of wedlock,[96] yet America still feels uneasy about this, as reflected in the general expectation that politicians be married. When running for president, Hillary

Clinton strikingly began her Twitter biography with traditional gender roles: "Wife, mom, grandma, women+kids advocate, FLOTUS, Senator, SecState, hair icon, pantsuit aficionado, 2016 presidential candidate."

In comparison, Julia Gillard became the Australian prime minister in 2010 despite having a male life partner to whom she was not married. And she did not have children. Either of these facts would be almost unthinkable for a prominent U.S. politician. Similarly, Ségolène Royal, the runner-up in the 2007 French presidential election, cohabitated and had four children with her partner, François Hollande, another politician. Hollande was elected president in 2012. By then he had a different female partner, to whom he was also not married. None of this was a secret or an issue in the elections. Most French people hardly care about politicians' private lives or sexuality.[97] The French press is loath to report on politicians' extramarital affairs, because these are deemed private matters. Steamy intrigues may fill the pages of tabloids but have virtually no bearing on elections. By contrast, concerns over American politicians' private lives spurred impeachment proceedings against Bill Clinton, among innumerable "sex scandals." When Nikki Haley ran for South Carolina governor in 2010, two unscrupulous men accused her of having had extramarital affairs with them. Haley, who won the election, vowed to resign if the allegations were proved.[98] The public was left to wonder if the claims were true. Few seemingly thought, "Who cares?"

Social conservatives claim that sexual open-mindedness threatens "family values," thereby suggesting that social liberals do not love their families. Once people have children, promoting familial stability may indeed be laudable, as parental separation can harm children. Yet blaming high divorce rates on liberal values overlooks the fact that blue states enjoy more-stable marriages than red states.[99] Notwithstanding its moralism, the Bible Belt largely accounts for why America has the highest rate of unintended teenage pregnancy in the industrialized world.[100] The states with the highest teenage birthrates are in the South and Midwest, the nation's poorest regions. Over 95 percent of sexually active American women will use contraception in their lives, but poor women with inadequate insurance cannot always afford the pill or an abortion. They are also likelier to receive abstinence-only sexual education.[101]

If adolescent sex is commonly "dramatized" in America, it is often "normalized" in Europe. European teens are much likelier to use the pill, which is generally state-funded.[102] When their teenage child has a steady boyfriend or girlfriend, for example, many Dutch parents will let the couple spend the night together at home, knowing they will probably have sex. This enables the parents to stay connected to the emotional lives of their children, who are not forced into secretive sexual activity. This approach reflects the "need to adjust the moral rules governing sexual life to real behavior." The opposite has occurred in America, especially in traditionalist communities, where "No sex!" or "Not under my roof!" is the typical attitude.[103]

The U.S. federal government spent $1.5 billion on abstinence-only programs between 1997 and 2009. The Bush administration more than doubled their budget.[104] Abstinence-only programs are sometimes run by activists lacking public health credentials. They do not discuss safe sex or birth control except to peddle disinformation on failure rates.[105] Using condoms has "little to no benefit," as one curriculum put it.[106] The Government Accountability Office found that, despite the common inaccuracies in abstinence-only education, the Bush administration never reviewed many of its grantees' materials for scientific accuracy.[107]

Bush tellingly placed Pam Stenzel, an abstinence educator, on a Department of Health and Human Services task force. At the 2003 Reclaiming America for Christ conference, Stenzel was less circumspect than the Bush administration about the goals of abstinence-only education, as she openly admitted that it "doesn't matter" whether the policy works, because people must "answer to God." In her words, unplanned pregnancies and sexually transmitted diseases (STDs) are "not the enemy." It is, rather, the "stinking, filthy, dirty, rotten sin" of premarital sex.[108]

Comprehensive sexual education does not license sex, since it encompasses arguments for both abstinence and contraception.[109] Unsurprisingly, teens who receive abstinence-only education are likelier to face unplanned pregnancies and STDs. Studies of evangelical teenagers show that only the most devout, roughly a quarter, abstain from sexual activity to a greater degree than other teens. For various reasons, including class differences, evangelicals on average lose their virginity at younger ages than members of religions with more flexible attitudes toward sex. The vast majority of evangelicals have sex before marriage, and their rate of nonmarital sex is at least as high as that of everyone else.[110] The failure of abstinence-only education is epitomized by how Sarah Palin's then seventeen-year-old, unmarried daughter, Bristol, became pregnant while her mother was campaigning for the vice presidency.

Following his election as president, Barack Obama aimed to end federal support for abstinence-only education, but Republican legislators managed to include $250 million for it in the budget.[111] The G.O.P. also seeks to eviscerate Title X of the Public Health Service Act, which provides federal funding for contraception, STD prevention, and cancer screenings. Family planning was not always a hot-button issue. Title X passed with strong bipartisan consensus in 1970 under Richard Nixon.[112]

The Broader Implications of Gay Rights

The rapid progress of gay rights in America is striking. From having almost no legal protections a few decades ago, LGBTQ people are now increasingly treated as equals. The Supreme Court's 2015 decision in *Obergefell v. Hodges,* which held that banning gay marriage is unconstitutional, might suggest an end to this conflict. Yet it was a deeply controversial 5–4 decision, and it is too early to tell if opponents will refuse to move on, as with abortion. "Unfortunately, people of faith can take no comfort in the treatment they receive from the majority today," Chief Justice Roberts wrote in dissent. Justice Scalia agreed and later declared in a speech that *Obergefell* was an "extreme" decision "contrary to the religious beliefs of many of our citizens." Senator Marco Rubio likewise insisted that "God's rules always win" and that believers should "ignore" Supreme Court decisions conflicting with their faith.

The clash over gay rights is an extension of the conflict between traditional patriarchy and the more egalitarian gender system of modern times. Patriarchy seeks to affirm unambiguous gender roles: men are expected to be "masculine" and women to be "feminine." Homosexuality inherently challenges traditional patriarchy, because men seemingly assume a "feminine" identity and women a "masculine" one.[113] Homosexuality consequently threatens the religious right's conception of the family, which is fundamentally patriarchal. Because traditionalists also tend to equate sexuality with procreation, at least in principle, they commonly find homosexuality taboo. These are among the reasons why they describe gay marriage as an assault on the family and an effort to destroy society. What may sound like hyperbole is true from the point of view of patriarchal traditionalists.

Traditionalists do not want the definition of marriage to become a matter of secular government policy, despite how civil marriage without religious ceremony long preexisted gay marriage. In their eyes, desecrating the "sanctity of marriage" would be the last straw in abandoning "family values," namely the patriarchal family model. Illustratively, the official platform of the Republican Party's Texas branch stated for years that "homosexuality tears at the fabric of society and contributes to the breakdown of the family."

That clause was replaced in 2014 with an endorsement of "therapy" seeking to straighten gays. The broader implications of gay rights help explain why traditionalists hailed Kim Davis, a Kentucky county clerk, as a martyr after her short stint in jail for refusing to issue marriage licenses to gays, in defiance of the Supreme Court.

American evangelicals are much less tolerant of homosexuality than either mainline Protestants or Catholics.[114] Some emphasize that the Bible calls homosexuality an "abomination" in Leviticus 20:13,[115] although those who say so normally disregard passages that they find anachronistic, absurd, or revolting. Leviticus 20:10 calls for the execution of adulterers. Leviticus 11 states that eating pork, lobster, crab, shrimp, oysters, or various other animals is an "abomination" too. Leviticus 19:19 forbids planting different crops in the same fields or wearing garments made from different materials. Deuteronomy 13 teaches that if a child proselytizes for another god, the parent must kill the child. Even fundamentalists do not follow the Bible to the letter. Conversely, American liberals often take God out of the equation by regarding marriage primarily as an expression of love and commitment. Because of their greater tolerance, they usually do not see a valid reason why gay couples cannot be responsible partners or parents.[116]

Of course, homophobia does not stem solely from traditional conceptions of religion or the family. It can equally reflect animosity or uneasiness toward those who seem different. The taboo can range from "a defensive attitude that responds to a perceived threat to the boundaries of the self" to "an unexamined echo of attitudes that [people] have unreflectively learned and internalized." [117]

Opposition to gay marriage is surely not unique to America. At the time of writing, it was legal in only around twenty countries. The considerable contrasts found within America are more remarkable. When the U.S. Episcopal Church became one of the first major churches worldwide to elect an openly gay bishop, Gene Robinson, he faced such an onslaught of calumnies and threats that he wore a bulletproof vest under his robe during his consecration ceremony in New Hampshire. On one hand, Americans have largely spearheaded the global movement for gay rights, whose icons include the activist Harvey Milk. Certain blue states like Massachusetts, Vermont, and Washington, were among the world's trailblazing jurisdictions in recognizing gay marriage. On the other hand, the leaders of various other states have endorsed the criminalization of homosexuality, as is now the case in much of the developing world. Indeed, many traditionalists were appalled when the Supreme Court held in 2003 that consensual sex between men cannot be criminalized.

That decision, *Lawrence v. Texas,* concerned a virtually never enforced Texas law under which two men were convicted of sodomy. By a 6–3 vote, the court held that the law violated fundamental liberty and was discriminatory. Justice Scalia wrote a sharp dissent joined by Justices Thomas and Rehnquist.* "Many Americans do not want persons who openly engage in homosexual conduct as partners in their business, as scoutmasters for their children, as teachers in their children's schools, or as boarders in their home," Scalia underlined.

The most comparable European case was decided more than three decades earlier, when the European Court of Human Rights held that homosexual relations could not be penalized.[118] The Supreme Court's majority in *Lawrence* cited this precedent for its persuasive value—it is obviously not binding on U.S. courts—thereby offending conservatives who protested that America has nothing to learn from foreign courts.[119] President Bush subsequently pushed an unsuccessful constitutional amendment to ban gay marriage.

After *Lawrence,* Americans were quite evenly divided on whether consensual gay sex between adults should be legal or not.[120] By 2016, the proportion saying that it should be legal had reached 68 percent, a modest majority for a question concerning basic privacy and equality.[121] The shift on gay marriage is more impressive. Only 35 percent of Americans supported it in 2001. That number had surged to 55 percent by 2016. But profound divisions remain, as 70 percent of Democrats favor gay marriage, compared to 33 percent of Republicans.[122]

The protests in Paris against France's legalization of gay marriage in 2013 show that this remains a hot-button issue in many Western countries. But opposition to gay rights has been more uncompromising in America. French conservatives who oppose gay marriage have generally accepted gay civil unions, which were legalized in 1999 following a divisive debate. Conversely, multiple blue and red American states passed laws banning both gay marriage and civil unions. These bans are no longer constitutional, because of the Supreme Court's *Obergefell* decision.

Another battle illustrates the extraordinary divide over gay rights in America. In 2011, Democrats managed to repeal "Don't ask, don't tell"

---

* Recall that Rehnquist had opposed the Equal Rights Amendment in the name of traditional gender roles in the 1970 memo discussed above.

(DADT), a policy that the Clinton administration adopted in 1993. Clinton had promised to stop excluding gays from the military, yet certain members of Congress opposed his efforts, leading to a compromise under which enlisting persons would not be asked about their sexual orientation. But DADT remained a discriminatory policy and resulted in more than thirteen thousand people being discharged from the armed forces for homosexual conduct.[123]

By the time Obama was president, America stood alone in the West in continuing to ban openly gay people from the military, a policy characteristic of authoritarian and theocratic regimes.[124] At least seven in ten Americans then favored integrating gays into the military, including a majority of Democrats and Republicans.[125] Prominent military figures, such as General David Petraeus and Admiral Mike Mullen, publicly supported ending DADT. The Pentagon conducted a study finding that a large majority of troops would be comfortable with repeal.[126] Nevertheless, only eight Republican senators and fifteen Republican representatives voted to end the discriminatory policy, illustrating how G.O.P. officials almost uniformly embrace the religious right's views. After all, it was John McCain, one of the most moderate Republicans of modern times, who led the opposition to repeal. Ignoring contrary evidence from the Pentagon study, he claimed that this would endanger American troops. McCain was visibly angry on the Senate floor when DADT was repealed. It was "a very sad day," he said.[127]

Gay rights are exceptionally controversial in America because they relate to multiple aspects of the culture wars, including the religious divide, sexual liberty, the clash between ultratraditional and modern conceptions of the family, the tension between patriarchy and equal gender roles, and the separation of church and state. Like the rest of the West, liberal America has been evolving toward modern norms of tolerance on these issues while conservative America has resisted this process. Even though conservatives in other Western nations can be quite traditional-minded, they rarely embrace the wide range of radical stances that many Republicans defend, such as criminalizing homosexuality or excluding gays from the military.

In Britain, then–prime minister David Cameron and his Conservative Party–led coalition spearheaded efforts to legalize gay marriage, frustrating certain British conservatives and clergy members. "I don't support gay marriage despite being a conservative," Cameron declared. "I support gay marriage because I am a conservative." This decision was partly strategic, as it aimed to woo moderates and young voters. But it also epitomizes how the

British right wing is generally closer to Democrats than to Republicans. In the run-up to the United Kingdom's legalization of gay marriage in 2013, there were twelve openly gay members of Parliament from the Conservative Party, more than from all the other parties combined.[128]

A poll of five Western nations found the United States the least tolerant on homosexuality. Sixty percent of Americans felt that society should accept homosexuality, a far lower proportion than of people in Spain (91 percent), Germany (87 percent), France (86 percent), or Britain (81 percent).[129] The views of Republicans mainly account for this disparity, once again showing that conservative America is an outlier in the West.

The divide over gay marriage in America initially led Obama to declare that his faith made him oppose it. Back in 2004, he stressed that "tradition and my religious beliefs say that marriage is something sanctified between a man and a woman."[130] He said substantially the same thing during a 2008 campaign debate, adding that marriage is "a sacred union" where "God's in the mix."[131] Once polls showed growing support for gay marriage, however, Obama affirmed that his views were "evolving," and he endorsed it toward the end of his first term. Despite his prior statements, he had long been sympathetic to gay rights and openly acknowledged his gay supporters in his 2008 electoral victory speech. Yet if Obama's past claims that his faith made him oppose gay marriage were calculations, that raises the question of whether they were attempts to exploit religion for political gain. This leads us to the final part of this chapter.

USING GOD

Something more than the culture wars is at work behind all the talk about God and moral values in American politics, namely the strategic use of religion by politicians of all stripes. Not only is it more common for politicians to appeal to faith in America than in essentially all other developed countries, but there are also reasons to believe that many Americans are oblivious to how this is a political strategy.

George W. Bush cultivated the image of a born-again Christian and credited Jesus with solving the alcohol problem he faced before becoming the governor of Texas. "I believe God wants me to run for president," he once told a preacher. Bush later denied feeling a divine calling. "Did God want me to be president?" he pondered. "I don't know. My relationship is on a personal basis trying to become as closer [*sic*] to the Almighty as I possibly can." At the same time, W. could not help betraying the belief that God guided his presidency. "There is calm in the Oval Office. People say, 'But how do you know that it's because of prayer? . . . It's just a crutch.' For me, it's not a crutch," he said. "For me it's the realization of a power of a universal God and recognition that the God came manifested in human [*sic*] and then died for our sins." Summarizing how faith had benefited his life, Bush said, "It gave me strength and understanding. There is love, universal love."[132]

Such declarations would be unthinkable in practically all other Western countries, where people would probably interpret them as phony demagogy. Of course, Bush's God talk dismayed certain Americans. Some were particularly offended by his claim that God guided the decision to invade Iraq. Bush nonetheless convinced numerous supporters that he was a compassionate man of faith. After his presidency ended, a strikingly vain remark suggested that his pious rhetoric may have been contrived. "Eight years [as president] was awesome, and I was famous and I was powerful. But I have no desire for fame and power anymore," he admitted.

Religious rhetoric is commonly assumed to be a Republican tactic, yet Democrats also use it to bolster their agenda. Obama did not reject the influence of religion in government—he approached it differently than his predecessor. Obama mentioned "God" five times in his first inauguration speech. "Let it be said [that] with eyes fixed on the horizon and God's grace upon us, we carried forth that great gift of freedom and delivered it safely to future generations," he proclaimed. The inescapable suggestion was that God supported Obama's inauguration.

It is one thing for private citizens or religious leaders to invoke God to support their views. It is another for politicians to do so. Religious rhetoric by public officials does not technically violate the First Amendment, but is incompatible with the spirit of secular government. If God exists, how does one define God? And what does God want from us? Throughout history there have been countless answers to these questions among Christians alone, not to mention other groups. Both society and religion suffer when politicians speak on these questions for their own gain and that of their party.

Most Americans do not share this view, as they want politicians to express faith in God, which notably allows voters to see if they can personally relate to their leaders. Barely 27 percent of Americans consider that there is "too much" religious rhetoric from politicians. The vast majority deem that there is either not enough or just enough of it.[133] Relatively few Americans identify politicians' expressions of faith as strategic efforts to increase their popularity. This obliviousness reflects the presumption of goodness associated with religion in America, as described in Chapter 3.

Since the United States' founding, politicians have mentioned God, offered prayers, quoted scripture, and argued that America has a divinely chosen destiny. But the infusion of religion into politics has surged in recent decades. In 1953, in the midst of the Cold War against the atheistic Soviet Union, Dwight Eisenhower became the first president to be baptized in office. He also instituted prayers at cabinet meetings, promoted nondenominational faith in a broadcast called *Back to God,* and lauded Congress for passing a resolution making "In God we trust" the official U.S. motto.[134]

However, as David Domke and Kevin Coe document in *The God Strategy,* Eisenhower and other presidents of the 1940s to 1970s used religious rhetoric less systematically than their successors. For example, immediately after Pearl Harbor, Franklin Roosevelt spoke to the nation once and invoked God a single time. In contrast, following the September 11 attacks, Bush addressed the nation thrice and invoked God more than twenty times. In 1947, after an electoral defeat led his Democratic Party to lose control of both chambers of Congress, Harry Truman's State of the Union speech placed moderate emphasis on faith. Bill Clinton adopted a different approach in his 1995 State of the Union address following the Democrats' loss in midterm elections. Clinton then used religious symbolism forty-nine times, such as by declaring, "We are the keepers of a sacred trust." [135]

The religious right's radicalization was a key factor in this development. The G.O.P. tried to capitalize on this movement early on, as when Richard Nixon denounced the liberal excesses of the sixties. But the Watergate scandal ultimately forced him to resign and favored the election of Jimmy Carter, an evangelical Democrat. Yet conservative evangelicals were utterly disappointed with Carter's presidency, given his relative support for secularism and abortion rights, not to mention their concerns about his economic and foreign policies. Ronald Reagan crushed Carter in the 1980 election and was reelected by a landslide. A large proportion of evangelicals and other social conservatives backed Reagan, who had no qualms about condemning abortion, making public displays of faith, or catering to hardline fundamentalists like Reverend Jerry Falwell.[136]

Reagan's success helped change the standards of acceptability of religious speech and symbolism. Prior presidents had referred to God regularly in their national addresses, but Figure 5 shows that Reagan made this a quasi-

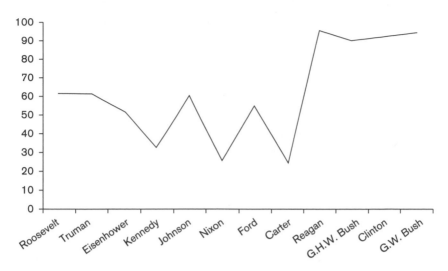

FIGURE 5. Percentage of national presidential speeches invoking God. SOURCE: David Domke and Kevin Coe, *The God Strategy* (Oxford University Press, 2010). The study was completed before Obama's presidency.

systematic practice, as he did so 96 percent of the time. His successors followed suit. Reagan was also the first president to regularly say "God bless America," an expression that all his successors adopted. It had been employed only once before in a national presidential speech, by Nixon.[137]

The God strategy can backfire. To become a U.S. senator in 2004, Obama had to defeat the Republican Alan Keyes, who campaigned on a socially conservative platform—a curious strategy in a blue state like Illinois. "Christ would not vote for Barack Obama," Keyes said with the assurance that he himself would have gotten Jesus's vote. Obama predictably won by a wide margin, yet Keyes refused to congratulate him, instead calling the future president "evil" because of his tolerance of abortion and gays.

When used more cleverly, religion can be a powerful weapon. Politicians who decline to speak about their faith do so at their own risk, as John Kerry observed when reflecting on his failed presidential race against George W. Bush: "Despite this New Englander's past reticence of talking publicly about my faith, I learned that if I didn't fill in the picture myself, others would draw the caricature for me. I will never let that happen again." [138] Even moderate use of the God strategy might not do. Obama regularly used religious rhetoric but faced criticism for not being sufficiently public about his Christian faith, besides conspiracy theories about being Muslim.

Hillary Clinton took notice. Gearing up for her 2016 presidential race, she claimed that the Bible was the book that had the "biggest influence" on her thinking. Her rival Bernie Sanders represented the rise of the religiously unaffiliated, as he admitted that faith played a limited role in his life. He was nonetheless an exception, as most candidates boasted about their faith. "Father God, please, keep this awakening going," Ted Cruz tellingly proclaimed at a rally. Donald Trump could not credibly claim to be devout, but many evangelicals gave him the benefit of the doubt or identified with his agenda, as demonstrated by the endorsement of Reverend Jerry Falwell Jr.[139]

Other Western leaders typically treat religion as a private matter and do not face nearly as much pressure to display their faith. Again, consider how Julia Gillard became the head of government in Australia regardless of her atheism, a feat hard to imagine in modern America. When asked if she believed in God, she was unequivocal. "No, I don't.... I'm not a religious person.... I'm not going to pretend a faith I don't feel," Gillard answered, distancing herself from opponents who used an Aussie version of the God strategy.[140] But U.S. politicians are far likelier than their counterparts in the West to feel religious faith, regardless of whether they exploit it for political gain. A study suggests that members of Congress are even more religious than the average citizen. Only one member of the 114th Congress was religiously unaffiliated, compared with around 20 percent of Americans.[141]

It goes without saying that the omnipresence of religion in U.S. politics mirrors the nation's religiosity. Yet the sword cuts both ways. Elected officials promote religion by invoking God or publicly displaying their faiths, which exacerbates the culture wars by legitimizing the infusion of religion into politics. The culture wars reflect not only genuine cultural divisions but also a political strategy. These cultural divisions intensify the political game and vice versa, further pitting Americans against one another. However, they are at least as polarized over economic issues,[142] as we will see in the next two chapters.

FIVE

Between Democracy and Plutocracy

Wealth inequality is more acute in America than in other Western nations.[1] The bulk of U.S. income growth since the 1980s has gone to the richest of the rich.[2] America further stands out as the only industrialized nation without universal health care, leading myriad citizens to face tremendous medical and financial hardship. America has objectively been evolving toward a plutocracy—a society largely governed by the rich—as its political system is considerably influenced by campaign donations and lobbying from tycoons, corporations, and Wall Street. The already significant role of money in U.S. politics reached another level following the Supreme Court's 2010 decision in *Citizens United v. Federal Election Commission,* which significantly curtailed campaign finance regulations.

But America once was on the same path as nations with more equal economic systems. It developed from a land of stark wealth inequality in the 1920s into an increasingly middle-class society after Franklin Roosevelt launched the New Deal in the 1930s.[3] FDR's agenda involved greater wealth redistribution, higher taxes on the affluent, fairer labor conditions, and other reforms to improve the lives of ordinary people. A relative consensus emerged among both Democrats and Republicans about the merits of the New Deal model, which lasted until the 1980s, when anti-government hardliners grew influential. Ronald Reagan associated the New Deal with "fascism" and his heirs followed suit.[4] Wealth inequality surged as the G.O.P. adopted a near-categorical stance against taxation, regulation, and public assistance. This helped tilt the Democratic Party's economic agenda to the right. Bill Clinton was persuaded that "the era of big government" was fortunately over and that financial deregulation was needed, helping pave the way for the disastrous 2008 financial crisis. Wealth in America is essentially as unequally distributed now as in the 1920s, before the New Deal.[5]

The Obama presidency was marked by gridlock on virtually every economic issue, as partisan polarization in Congress reached record levels.[6] The huge ideological divide between the parties continued throughout the 2016 election. Despite bitter disagreements, Hillary Clinton and Bernie Sanders jointly called for the government to tackle wealth inequality and preserve, if not expand, public health care. In contrast, all the Republican presidential candidates aimed to eviscerate "Obamacare" and make the U.S. economy more capitalistic. At times, Donald Trump blurred party lines and distanced himself from the "small government" platforms of fellow Republicans, as when he suggested support for Social Security and regulating the cost of pharmaceutical drugs. He nonetheless repeatedly painted the image of a haywire federal government ruining America with taxes and worthless government programs. Alongside the repeal of "Obamacare," Trump notably proposed colossal tax cuts for the rich and said that attempts to reduce wealth inequality were "class warfare."[7] However, Democrats and Republicans were not always so far apart.

Toward a New Social Contract

We saw in Chapter 2 that relative economic equality existed in the United States' early years, particularly among white men. But the nation's industrialization concentrated the fruits of growth in a few hands by the 1920s.[8] Because of a purist ideology, conservatives in that epoch were commonly persuaded that taxation, regulation, and income redistribution were hardly compatible with capitalism.[9] If they failed to block legislation seeking to assist ordinary people, they could regularly count on the Supreme Court to invalidate it. The court then adhered to a narrow interpretation of the Constitution that led it to find various economic regulations unconstitutional, including statutes that aimed to curtail unsafe working conditions and child labor.[10] Writing in dissent, Justice Oliver Wendell Holmes argued that the majority's reasoning reflected "an economic theory which a large part of the country does not entertain."[11]

The Progressive movement was ultimately able to implement significant reforms in the late nineteenth and early twentieth centuries, such as the creation of the federal income tax, anti-corruption initiatives, and measures to rein in monopolies and trusts. But partisans of unregulated capitalism continued to oppose efforts to reduce the nation's immense wealth inequality. The time was ripe for social change when the Wall Street crash of 1929 and the subsequent Great Depression undermined the establishment and facilitated Franklin Delano Roosevelt's election.[12] Even though the New Deal was essentially limited to FDR's age, it became the cornerstone of a broader economic model that remained in place until the 1980s.

FDR wanted the federal government to play a more active role in fighting the economic crisis and bettering the lives of ordinary Americans. Beside public work projects aiming to create jobs, the New Deal encompassed assistance to the poor and improved labor conditions. Workers notably gained the right to unionize, as well as minimum wage and maximum hour protections.[13] Despite coming from an extremely privileged family, FDR also substantially raised taxes on the rich.[14]

Roosevelt went on to propose a "Second Bill of Rights" guaranteeing an adequate wage, a decent home, a good education, and proper health care. It was left unrealized but exemplified his vision. "I have never believed that with our capitalistic system people have to be poor," FDR said. "I think it is an outrage that we should permit hundreds and hundreds of thousands of people to be ill clad, to live in miserable homes, not to have enough to eat; not to be able to send their children to school for the only reason that they are poor." [15] Yet Roosevelt was not a naïve idealist, as his reforms partly aimed to co-opt leftist opponents and prevent social unrest.[16]

The New Deal would hardly have been possible if the Supreme Court had not stopped blocking reforms that ran against its ideology of laissez-faire economics. In 1937, Roosevelt threatened to have Congress pass a dubious constitutional amendment raising the number of justices from nine to fifteen. It would have allowed him to pack the court with loyalists—a serious challenge to the separation of powers. His proposal was defeated, but certain historians believe that it pressured some justices to stop striking down New Deal legislation. Others argue that the court's jurisprudence had started to evolve before the court-packing controversy began, as the justices minded their growing unpopularity.[17] At any rate, several justices died or resigned during FDR's twelve-year presidency,* so that by his death in 1945 he had appointed seven of the then-serving nine justices.[18] The court largely refrained from reviewing economic regulations for decades afterward.

---

* After FDR died, the Twenty-Second Amendment's ratification limited presidents to two elected terms.

A growing bipartisan consensus pointed toward a social contract under which the government had to ensure the American people's basic well-being. Much of the Republican Party had initially opposed the New Deal, although many conservatives came to accept its popular reforms. "Should any political party attempt to abolish social security, unemployment insurance, and eliminate labor laws and farm programs, you would not hear of that party again in our political history. There is a tiny splinter group, of course, that believes you can do these things. . . . Their number is negligible and they are stupid," Dwight Eisenhower privately wrote about hardliners within his party.[19] Richard Nixon, the next Republican president, agreed to a tax increase, a significant expansion of Social Security, the establishment of a national food stamp program, and the creation of the Environmental Protection Agency. He also tried to introduce a national health insurance system.[20] "I am now a Keynesian in economics," Nixon remarkably declared.

In that era, taxes on the wealthy were significantly higher than they had been in the 1920s or were after the New Deal model increasingly fell into disfavor beginning in the 1980s. U.S. tax rates then even topped those in Europe. Under Eisenhower, the top marginal tax rate illustratively was over 90 percent. That did not preclude growth, as America enjoyed prosperity in the decades following World War II.[21] Among other factors, the war contributed to reducing wealth inequality by shrinking the fortunes of capital owners who were heavily taxed to fund the hostilities.[22]

However, America did not move toward universal health care, partly because of an accident of history. FDR had instituted wage controls during World War II that did not apply to health insurance. Labor unions therefore saw it as a precious, nontaxable benefit and were not necessarily enthusiastic about the government establishing health insurance, which became closely tied to Americans' jobs. This path dependence was compounded by mistrust of "socialized medicine," foreshadowing reactions to "Obamacare." Fearmongering by the American Medical Association played a key role in torpedoing Harry Truman's 1949 plan for national health insurance.[23] Medicare was finally created in 1965, under the Democrat Lyndon Johnson, to provide government-funded health insurance to the elderly. Certain Republicans denounced it as a step toward communism. In 1961, Ronald Reagan notably declared that Medicare threatened "the continuation of our free enterprise system" and would lead to a leftist dictatorship: "Behind it will come other federal programs that will invade every area of freedom [until] we will wake to find that we have socialism." Nevertheless, approximately half of Republicans in Congress voted for Medicare, reflecting the bipartisanship of the times.[24]

Roosevelt's vision of solidarity had its limitations, as his agenda hardly encompassed abolishing racial segregation. The Democratic Party then consisted of a coalition including white Southerners who staunchly supported Jim Crow. Yet the civil rights icons Charles Hamilton Houston and Thurgood Marshall spearheaded legal challenges culminating in the Supreme Court's 1954 decision in *Brown v. Board of Education,* which officially ended segregation by rejecting its deceitful rationale: "separate but equal." The decision was barely enforced, however, until mass protests spurred Congress to enact civil rights legislation a decade later. The movement opened new doors for African-Americans, although segregation and discrimination persisted more insidiously. This was not an idyllic time, but it seemed that, like other Western nations, America was evolving toward a relatively equal socioeconomic system.

No More "Fascism"

The hardline branch of the Republican Party grew more influential in the 1980s. Reagan, who led this trend, claimed that "fascism was really the basis for the New Deal."[25] Once president, he condemned "big government," pushed for huge tax cuts, and backed corporate efforts to disempower labor unions. America's unionization rate had been higher than those of Canada, France, and Italy in the 1950s,[26] yet the nation's rightward shift led to a significant drop in union membership, thereby hindering working people from resisting policies favoring the wealthy.[27]

The G.O.P. would have had greater difficulty defending winner-take-all economics if the South had not become solidly Republican, partly due to resentment over desegregation. Until Lyndon Johnson signed civil rights legislation in the 1960s, the Democratic Party had enjoyed extensive influence in the South, the poorest region of the nation, which disproportionately benefited from the New Deal. But the New Deal coalition gradually collapsed as Southern whites largely abandoned the Democratic Party.[28] We will see in the next chapter that Reagan and other conservatives capitalized on white resentment by infusing their criticism of "big government" with racially coded rhetoric about lazy blacks living on welfare.

The Republican Party's evolution helped change the U.S. political debate and tilt the left to the right. Democrats of yesteryear had been bolder in

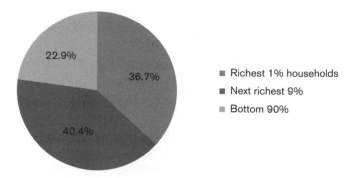

FIGURE 6. Distribution of net worth in the United States. SOURCE: Edward N. Wolff, "Household Wealth Trends in the United States, 1962–2013" (National Bureau of Economic Research Working Paper, 2014), 49.

fighting inequality. In addition to the New Deal, FDR proposed his "Second Bill of Rights," and Johnson launched a "War on Poverty." Modern Democratic presidents have stayed clear of such sweeping initiatives. The closest thing to them was the Obama administration's limited health care reform—a program based on past Republican plans[29] that modern Republicans identify as "radical socialism."

As a result, the vast majority of U.S. income growth since the 1980s has gone to the wealthiest citizens, while the income of ordinary people has stagnated or risen modestly.[30] Nowadays, the richest 1 percent of U.S. households possess 37 percent of the nation's net worth and the next richest 9 percent another 40 percent. Figure 6 shows that the bottom 90 percent—a category including the middle class, the working class, and the poor—own only 23 percent.[31] The primary beneficiaries of this evolution have been corporate executives and financiers, who are the majority of the richest 1 percent.[32] Tellingly, the six Walmart heirs are worth as much as the bottom 41 percent of U.S. families combined.[33] Wealth inequality would be even worse but for the fact that American women are likelier to be employed now than they were a generation ago, which has increased household income.[34]

Contrary to what some commentators claim, the main gap is not between people with advanced degrees or technological skills and those without them, but rather between the richest of the rich and everyone else.[35] The dramatic escalation in corporate executive pay epitomizes winner-take-all economics. In 1965, the CEOs of the top 350 U.S. firms earned around twenty times as much as the average worker. By 2014, they earned three hundred times as much.[36] The Home Depot CEO Bob Nardelli got a $210 million severance package as the company's stock prices fell, exemplifying unabashed self-dealing by the corporate elite.[37] The presidential candidate Carly Fiorina similarly received a golden parachute of more than $42 million on being fired as Hewlett-Packard's CEO.[38] No empirical relationship exists between massive executive pay, company performance, and individual competence. Surging executive pay is largely traceable to a shift in cultural norms. Huge tax breaks for the rich since the Reagan revolution have encouraged executives to demand higher pay, the bulk of which previously would have gone directly to the government in taxes. Members of compensation committees that set executive pay are mostly drawn from the corporate elite and share its values.[39]

The struggling middle class has received some attention from politicians, yet it has minimal political clout next to the wealthy. The destitute tend to be ignored entirely.[40] The degree of extreme poverty in America is among the worst of wealthy nations.[41] America has long been the world's leading economy, though other Westerners are likelier to share the fruits of growth.[42] Various nations also experienced rises in inequality in past decades, but they were both more modest and alleviated by stronger efforts to reduce inequality.[43] The exorbitant cost of health care in America's for-profit medical system has further wiped out income gains of ordinary families.[44] Additionally, America's higher degree of inequality closely correlates with worse health and social problems, as Figure 7 demonstrates. This picture reflects a historic reversal. Income inequality was more acute in Europe than in America in the early twentieth century.[45]

Despite soaring inequality since the 1980s, surveys indicate that conservatives were more than twice as likely as liberals to deny the fact that wealth inequality had risen.[46] This finding further suggests that a factual divide has powerfully contributed to the polarization of American society.

Some expected social change when Barack Obama was elected and reelected president after consistently vowing to tackle wealth inequality. His eight years in the White House, however, did not spell the end of winner-take-all economics. After inheriting a catastrophic economic situation from the Bush administration, Obama focused primarily on rebooting the economic system, not fundamentally rethinking it. A whopping 58 percent of the income gains from the 2009–14 economic recovery went to the richest 1 percent.[47] Perhaps most important, Obama was unable to find common ground with the Republican opposition. Notwithstanding certain similarities in

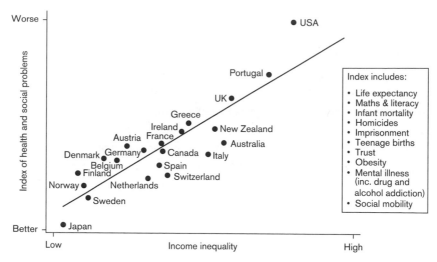

FIGURE 7. Correlation of health and social problems with income inequality. SOURCE: Richard Wilkinson and Kate Pickett, *The Spirit Level* (Bloomsbury, 2009).

both parties' economic programs, the modern Republican Party's radical anti-government ideology led it to systematically oppose Obama's moderate agenda and resort to a degree of obstructionism essentially unprecedented in U.S. history.[48]

THE IMPACT OF MARKET FUNDAMENTALISM

By the time of the Obama presidency, the G.O.P.'s radical branch was not simply influential—it controlled the party. Around 95 percent of the Republicans in Congress signed a pledge to never raise taxes under any circumstances,[49] an initiative of Grover Norquist, a libertarian ideologue who aims to reduce government "to the size where we can drown it in the bathtub." At a debate during the 2012 Republican presidential primaries, all eight candidates memorably said that they would reject a hypothetical deficit-cutting deal with ten times the amount of spending cuts as tax increases. By the same token, nearly all Republican leaders remained adamantly opposed to increasing regulation after the 2008 financial crisis brought the U.S. and global economies near breakdown. Following the disastrous BP oil spill in the Gulf of Mexico, Republican leaders equally pushed for legislation that would have made regulation of offshore drilling weaker than it was before the spill.[50]

That intransigence reflected the triumph of a peculiar ideology: free-market fundamentalism. According to Joseph Stiglitz, a winner of the Nobel Prize in Economics, this ideology assumes that "markets are self-correcting and that society can rely on the self-interested behavior of market participants to ensure that everything works honestly and properly—let alone works in a way that benefits all." [51] Market fundamentalism has shaped policies that concentrated wealth at the top in both the pre–New Deal and modern eras, contradicting the notion that wealth "trickles down" to the masses. In any case, market fundamentalists believe that wealth redistribution is illegitimate. This conviction intensified with the rise of the Tea Party, whose activists advanced views in the vein of "government is for the post office, and to defend our country, and maybe for the roads. That's all." [52]

Right-wing think tanks have had an important role in promoting the idea that regulation, taxes, and public assistance cause nearly all economic problems. Since the 1980s, the billionaire Koch brothers alone donated well over $100 million to seemingly independent groups defending their radical anti-government ideology and personal financial interests. This strategy "weaponized philanthropy" by enabling them to receive substantial tax breaks for giving money to such "nonprofit organizations" that otherwise would have gone to the government as tax revenue. [53]

Many Republican politicians likewise promoted this ideology, but not all practiced what they preached. Some who denounced Obama's economic stimulus as a wasteful "big government" program used stimulus money to assist their own states. [54] They included Paul Ryan, the Speaker of the House, who has a history of seeking public funding for his Wisconsin district while advocating libertarianism. [55] Similarly, Representative Michele Bachmann's vigorous opposition to public assistance programs for the poor was hard to square with her affluent family's collection of around $240,000 in federal farm subsidies. [56] In other words, stances that appear to be ideologically driven may instead be posturing. We will now take a closer look at this intriguing dimension of American exceptionalism.

Into Plutocracy

Roughly half of Americans doubt that wealth inequality is a serious problem. [57] This helps explain why the G.O.P. nominated Mitt Romney, a businessman with a net worth of at least $255 million, as its 2012 presidential candidate. Echoing stereotypes about destitute people living comfortably on welfare,

Romney declared: "I'm not concerned about the very poor. We have a safety net there." During a primary debate, Romney casually challenged another candidate to a $10,000 bet in the way that an ordinary person would have offered a $10 bet. Romney said that the $360,000 he had lately made from public speaking engagements was "not very much" money. In his view, focusing on wealth inequality "is entirely inconsistent with the concept of one nation under God," as it should be discussed only "in quiet rooms," if at all. Four years later, Romney practically looked like the incarnation of capitalism with a human face next to Donald Trump, who became the party's standard-bearer. Trump routinely bragged about his opulence and embodied dog-eat-dog capitalism with exploitative practices, illustrated by his for-profit Trump University.[58]

Meanwhile, Hillary Clinton blasted Wall Street despite taking millions from it in campaign contributions. The Clintons equally made more than $153 million in speaking fees from 2001 to 2015, including at least $7.7 million from banks.[59] Hillary sought to rationalize these practices by claiming that they were "dead broke" after Bill left the White House. As she set her own eyes on the presidency, Hillary also received six-figure fees for speeches at colleges. That money partly went to the philanthropic Clinton Foundation, but it could have helped students crushed by steep tuition.[60] Bill also received more than $17 million for serving as the "honorary chancellor" of a for-profit college.[61] However, the Clintons defended policies that would raise their own taxes, unlike Trump or Romney.

America's evolution into a plutocracy is further reflected by the growing wealth of Congress members. Between 1984 and 2009, the median net worth of a House member jumped from $280,000 to $725,000 in inflation-adjusted dollars, excluding home equity. American families saw theirs decline from $20,600 to $20,500 during that period.[62] By 2014 and for the first time in history, most Congress members were millionaires.[63]

Moneyed interests have additionally grown more influential in recent decades, partly due to the revolving door between lobbying and government. Lobbying is a key reason why pharmaceutical drugs are far costlier in America than in other Western democracies. Representative Billy Tauzin, who chaired the House committee regulating the pharmaceutical industry, left office in 2005 for a lucrative position as the CEO of the industry's top lobbying group.[64] Before becoming a lobbyist for the industry that he was supposed to regulate, he helped pass a law establishing the first Medicare prescription drug benefit for seniors. This legislation was highly profitable for drug companies because of an arrangement prohibiting the federal government from negotiating lower prices for medication. Tauzin later played an instrumental role in ensuring that Obama's health care reform would not regulate drug prices, unlike universal health care systems. The administration struck a deal with the pharmaceutical industry, which essentially agreed to back "Obamacare" in exchange for obtaining millions of new customers who would keep paying exorbitant prices for medication.[65]

The leverage of lobbyists in American government may seem like naked corruption, yet it is perfectly lawful. The law has evolved from being an ineffective bulwark against moneyed interests to giving them nearly free rein. Over the vigorous dissent of four justices, the Supreme Court eviscerated campaign finance regulations in its 2010 *Citizens United* decision. The court's conservative majority held that corporations and unions should be able to donate unlimited sums as long as they are not given "directly" to candidates, their parties, or their campaigns. Subsequent decisions extended this ruling to donations by individuals.[66] The justices thus enabled tycoons and big corporations to donate unlimited sums to candidates via third-party groups known as Super PACs (political action committees). The court's claim that so-called "independent expenditures" to Super PACs are "not coordinated with a candidate" was difficult to reconcile with the fact that former staff members of both Obama and Romney came to head their respective Super PACs. The Democratic Party nonetheless opposed the *Citizens United* decision, unlike the Republican leaders who filed amicus briefs supporting it.[67]

After the justices opened the floodgates, "independent expenditures" soared from around $147 million in the 2008 election to over $1 billion in the 2012 election.[68] Sheldon Adelson, a reactionary casino mogul, spent at least $98 million in the latter cycle.[69] Anonymous donors secretly gave hundreds of millions.[70] While the court has so far not abolished "base limits"—the maximum amount a donor may directly give to a candidate—they can now be circumvented by donating to Super PACs.

Justice Anthony Kennedy wrote that unlimited donations to Super PACs "do not give rise to corruption or the appearance of corruption" and "will not cause the electorate to lose faith in our democracy."[71] Opinion polls strongly suggest otherwise. Long before *Citizens United,* scores of Americans already believed that campaign donations have a corrupting influence.[72] The court's decision exacerbated that mistrust. In an ensuing case striking down more campaign finance regulations, Chief Justice Roberts still repeated that donating a fortune to get "political access" to elected officials cannot be seen as "corruption."[73]

This has led to a debate about whether the justices cannot grasp the considerable role of money in U.S. politics from their ivory tower.[74] According to the court's conservatives, more "speech," meaning more campaign donations by corporations or tycoons, makes society more democratic. Its definition of "corruption" is essentially limited to bribery. That is not so much a naïve view as one reflecting a particular ideology. As Roberts emphasized, it is unacceptable for the government to try to "level the playing field."[75] From this angle, equality means allowing all citizens to freely compete by donating as much money as they can to influence politicians. It does not matter if a millionaire can donate more than millions of citizens put together. For market fundamentalists, a society functions best without government intervention. Naturally, an economic system tailored to benefit the affluent is not really a free market. Nor can a system where special interests actively influence government truly be laissez-faire.

In the end, spending does not always change the result of an election. Jeb Bush did not win the 2016 Republican primary, despite having the most Super PAC money.[76] Hillary Clinton's huge fundraising advantage over Donald Trump could not lead her to victory.[77] However, regardless of who wins a particular race, money can heavily shape the political agenda by ensuring that the interests of the rich are a central part of the debate. They would not donate otherwise.

A key statistical study of 1,779 policy issues found that average citizens have minimal political influence compared to economic elites and special interest groups. Unsurprisingly, the demands of "business-oriented groups are *negatively* related to the average citizen's wishes." The study's conclusion was unequivocal: "When a majority of citizens disagrees with economic elites or with organized interests, they generally lose."[78]

The Wall Street Economy

Conservative America's reaction to the 2008 financial crisis reflects the extent to which it has become an outlier in the Western world. One might have thought that the crisis would lead more Republicans to acknowledge the need for financial regulation and for reforms to curb the nation's stark wealth inequality. Instead, the Republican establishment grew even more hostile to regulation and egalitarian policies. This period also marked the rise of the Tea Party, just as financial crises have historically fostered far-right movements and intensified polarization.[79]

The 2008 financial crisis was precipitated by a bubble that led housing prices to be artificially inflated. This led numerous people to borrow money by mortgaging their homes. Agencies commonly loaned money at usurious rates to unsophisticated low-income persons who took risky mortgages.[80] James Theckston, a regional vice president for Chase Bank in southern Florida, described how executives earned a commission seven times higher for subprime loans than for prime ones. That encouraged them to seek borrowers with limited education, no prior mortgage experience, or no English fluency.[81] Certain subprime mortgages had variable interest rates that were low at first but sharply rose over time, thereby precluding borrowers from repaying them. They offered little protection if houses lost value or homeowners lost their jobs. Regulations in various other countries bar such risky mortgages.[82]

Mortgage lenders frequently sold these loans to financial institutions, which combined them with other loans into securities and resold them to investors. These practices largely aimed to maximize short-term profits for Wall Street institutions, with little regard for the interests of their clients or society.[83] When the housing bubble burst and home prices fell, legions were ruined and lost their homes. And financial institutions that had heavily invested in mortgage-based securities were devastated. Ratings agencies could have stemmed the growth of toxic financial instruments. They instead ratified them. Federal authorities equally declined to adopt measures to limit predatory lending.[84]

The crisis was the worst financial collapse since the Wall Street crash of 1929, which had seemingly been lost to history. The growing popularity of laissez-faire economics in the 1990s had led the Clinton administration and both political parties to back sweeping financial deregulation at the bidding of lobbyists. What was good for Wall Street was deemed good for the economy. Reforms included terminating the separation of commercial from investment banking under the 1933 Glass-Steagall Act. This New Deal measure had aimed to preclude the risky speculation that contributed to the Great Depression. Partisans of laissez-faire believed it was obsolete. But deregulation led to riskier investments, sharply heightened leverage, and increased domination of the financial system by a few big banks.[85]

During the 2008 financial meltdown, a member of the House Committee on Oversight and Government Reform asked Alan Greenspan—the former chair of the Federal Reserve and an advocate of minimally regulated markets—whether his "ideology" had led to poor decision-making. "Yes, I've found a flaw," he answered euphemistically. "I don't know how significant or permanent it is." Greenspan appeared stunned that Wall Street could not police itself: "Those of us who have looked to the self-interest of lending institutions to protect shareholders' equity, myself included, are in a state of shocked disbelief." Numerous other U.S. regulators remained skeptical of or hostile toward regulation even after the crisis ravaged the global economy. Spencer Bachus, the Republican chair of the House Committee on Financial Services, was explicit: "In Washington, the view is that the banks are to be regulated, and my view is that Washington and the regulators are there to serve the banks."

Republican leaders attributed the crisis mainly to irresponsible low-income borrowers, as well as Freddie Mac and Fannie Mae, government-sponsored mortgage lenders. In Marco Rubio's words, "big government" was to blame: "This idea—that our problems were caused by a government that was too small—it's just not true. In fact, a major cause of our recent downturn was a housing crisis created by reckless government policies." To the contrary, government-sponsored lending agencies and regulations were not the primary causes of the crisis. Paul Krugman, a Nobel Prize in Economics laureate, stressed that "private lenders actually made the vast majority of subprime loans" and "only one of the top 25 subprime lenders was subject to the regulations in question."[86] Besides, the rationale behind public policies promoting homeownership for poor people was to encourage stable, affordable possession. Predatory lending and toxic instruments instead entailed "putting someone in a home for a few months and then tossing him out after having stripped him of his life savings," as Joseph Stiglitz, another Nobel Prize winner, emphasized.[87]

The bipartisan bailout of Wall Street in the Bush administration's final months proved unpopular. The banks repaid the rescue funds with interest,[88] yet people wondered why the government had rescued rich bankers from their gambles while millions were deprived of public assistance as they struggled financially or lost their homes. The refusal to prosecute bankers for fraud additionally stood in sharp contrast to the harshness of American justice toward the poor.

Once elected president, Obama warned bank CEOs that he would be "the only thing between you and the pitchforks." Despite criticizing the banks' recklessness, he kept fairly close ties to Wall Street figures, such as Larry Summers, an engineer of financial deregulation under Clinton. Obama made Summers his top economic adviser and would plausibly have named him the chair of the Federal Reserve but for protests from his base. Obama ultimately opted for Janet Yellen, a moderate economist known for questioning unregulated markets. Congress also passed legislation that put a wider range of financial companies under federal oversight, regulated instruments like credit derivatives, founded the Consumer Financial Protection Bureau, and instituted the Volcker rule—a measure akin to the repealed Glass-Steagall Act.[89]

If American decline stems from gridlock in the face of grave national problems, it was exemplified by the aftermath of the financial crisis. This was a wake-up call for liberals who realized that the Clinton administration's financial deregulation was a mistake and that the bulk of wealth created by Wall Street flows into few hands. Conversely, the G.O.P. reacted by calling for more deregulation and more tax cuts for the wealthiest citizens. Only three Republican senators and three Republican representatives voted for the Obama administration's financial reform, known as the Dodd-Frank Act. All of the 2012 and 2016 Republican presidential candidates vowed to repeal it, notwithstanding the fact that reform hardly crippled Wall Street, which continued to enjoy record profits.[90] Summarizing the consensus among the party, Representative Pete Sessions declared that the relatively modest reform was "about diminishing the free-enterprise system" and "creating larger government that will encroach upon every single one of us and ultimately crush us." Mitt Romney agreed that financial regulators were "gargoyles." Various prominent financiers equated the Obama administration's economic program with the policies of Adolf Hitler or Mao Zedong.[91] These peculiar reactions epitomized the exceptional influence of market fundamentalism in conservative America. In the age of globalization, the U.S.-born financial crisis had negative economic repercussions abroad, but conservatives in other Western democracies seldom reacted by calling for barebones financial regulation.

The Absence of Universal Health Care

America is the only developed country without a genuine universal health care system.[92] Paradoxically, its system is the most expensive in the industrialized world yet offers the least coverage to the public. Prior to Obama's controversial health care reform, almost fifty-one million Americans lacked medical insurance and twenty-five million were seriously underinsured.[93] The reform expanded access to health care, but approximately twenty-seven million people were expected to stay uninsured after its implementation.[94] High deductibles for coverage purchased on the new insurance exchanges still saddle people with hefty out-of-pocket costs.[95] And thirty-one million people were dangerously underinsured as of 2014.[96] Trump vowed to repeal the law upon entering office. As the book went to press it was unclear what alternative, if any, he would propose.

Unlike in other Western nations, health care in America is largely considered a for-profit business instead of a public service and a fundamental human right. Tellingly, the CEO of the University of Pittsburgh Medical Center makes more than $6 million per year.[97] And this is a "nonprofit" hospital. By some estimates, the medical industry's profit margins exceed those of the financial sector.[98] Steven Brill, an investigative reporter, uncovered multiple examples of price gouging, including $283 for a basic X-ray worth only $20, a $30,000 profit on the sale of an implantable device, $15,000 for lab tests worth a few hundred dollars, a cancer drug sold for $13,700 at a 400 percent profit margin, and a person being charged $21,000 for a three-hour hospital visit.[99] Costs for insured people are lower, because insurance companies negotiate discounts, although hospitals still make vast profits after that process. Costly hospital bills in turn encourage insurance companies to charge expensive premiums. In the jargon of U.S. insurance companies, paying for a client's treatment is a "loss" because it reduces profits.[100]

Inadequate health insurance has put myriad Americans one major illness or injury away from ruin. A study found that medical expenses were a leading cause of 62 percent of U.S. bankruptcies in 2007. Most of the bankrupted were not poor but middle-class people who had attended college and owned homes. Three-quarters had health insurance yet were direly underinsured. Average out-of-pockets costs were $17,943.[101] While this study might have overstated its conclusions,[102] medical bankruptcy is "an extreme example of a much broader phenomenon," namely medical debt.[103]

In other industrialized nations, people do not face bankruptcy or considerable debt because of medical bills.[104] Ruthless price gouging is practically impossible there in light of regulations on the costs of drugs and treatment, not to mention ethical norms frowning on profiteering from medical problems. For instance, the average cost of an MRI is $1,080 in America, $599 in Germany, and $281 in France.[105] America spent more than $280 billion on prescription drugs in 2012. It could have saved around $94 billion if it had paid what other countries do for the same drugs. This system is sometimes defended on the ground that huge financial incentives inspire groundbreaking research, yet only a limited segment of the pharmaceutical industry's revenues goes toward research.[106]

The U.S. medical system's singular lack of transparency facilitates profiteering. A researcher who called more than one hundred hospitals to ask about the cost of a hip replacement found that barely half of them would offer an estimate in advance. Prices also varied arbitrarily from $11,100 to $125,798 among those willing to provide information.[107]

Ironically, the Affordable Care Act went only so far in making care more affordable, because it lacked adequate measures to regulate pricing. The medical industry spent over $4 billion on lobbying between 2008 and late 2016.[108] It thus "steered the debate from why bills are so high to who should pay them," as Brill describes.[109] Under Obama's reform, for-profit insurance companies received scores of new clients who got government subsidies to cover overpriced services.

It may seem counterintuitive that other industrialized countries can have lower health care costs while insuring everyone, but they do, as Figure 8 shows. Universal health care is not "free," as some people claim, although regulations ensure far lower costs than those in the United States' profit-oriented system. Instituting universal health care could raise each American's disposable income by 8 percent of the gross domestic product.[110] America has among the highest rates of death from treatable medical problems in the West.[111] It also does poorly on other indicators, such as infant mortality, life expectancy, and survival of major diseases. Exceptions exist, as America ranks well in the rate of survival of breast cancer, for example.[112] But the big picture is clear: the U.S. health care system is plagued by problems that exist nowhere else in the West or to nowhere near the same extent there. Even wealthy Americans, who are generally well off, are not healthier than their European counterparts.[113]

Nevertheless, approximately half of Americans are persuaded that their country has "the best" health care system worldwide.[114] That poll finding came before the 2010 reform barred insurance companies from denying coverage to people with preexisting medical conditions. This conviction in American superiority signals not only chauvinism but also insularity, as much of the U.S. public knows little about other nations' health care systems.

We saw in Chapter 2 that opponents of reform exploited this ignorance by resorting to extraordinary propaganda. Leading politicians compared "Obamacare" to the tyranny of Nazi Germany or the U.S.S.R. Likening it to despicable foreign medical systems was another recurrent theme. "It's the

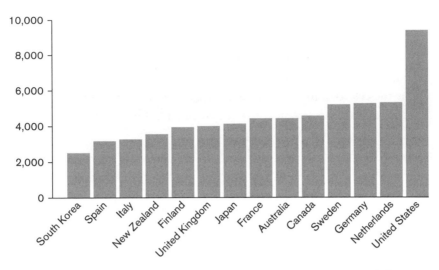

10,000

8,000

6,000

4,000

2,000

0

South Korea · Spain · Italy · New Zealand · Finland · United Kingdom · Japan · France · Australia · Canada · Sweden · Germany · Netherlands · United States

FIGURE 8. Annual health spending per capita (U.S. dollars with purchasing power parity). SOURCE: Organisation for Economic Co-operation and Development (2015).

Europeanization of America, and that's the worst thing that could possibly happen to our country," Senator Orrin Hatch said as the reform passed. Representative Michele Bachmann warned that those who criticized public health insurance would be blacklisted and denied treatment, as she contended was the case in Japan.[115] The Republican base paid attention. Before the bill passed, Senator Arlen Specter illustratively faced a hostile crowd at a town hall in Lebanon, Pennsylvania, where he was told: "We don't want this country to turn into Russia," "God is going to stand before you, and he's going to judge you," "It says plainly right there they want to limit the type of care elderly can get," and "They are talking about killing people." [116]

Meanwhile, many Democrats wanted "Obamacare" to go further by creating a single-payer health care system, thereby exacerbating the partisan divide. Bernie Sanders ran a fairly popular presidential campaign in 2016 by demanding "Medicare for all" and emphasizing that all other industrialized nations have universal health care. Medicare is less expensive than for-profit insurance policies, which have higher administrative costs because of marketing, claim reviews, and more.[117] Medicare is also less expensive because the U.S. government has the power to negotiate lower costs from medical providers, like other industrialized countries do. But it would be cheaper if lobbyists had not managed to preclude Medicare from negotiating lower drug prices, as previously discussed. That being said, Sanders probably lowballed his plan's cost and tax burden.[118] The price tag of "Medicare for all" could indeed prove exorbitant, unless the cost of medical services in America was substantially lower. This would mean rethinking profit-based health care. In any event, Sanders's "democratic socialist" agenda stood little chance in Congress.

Republicans frequently insist that neither "Obamacare" nor "Medicare for all" is necessary since, in Mitt Romney's words, "we don't have people that become ill, who die in their apartment because they don't have insurance." While hospitals are obliged to treat people facing certain emergencies, such treatment can be prohibitively expensive.[119] Besides, multiple serious conditions do not qualify as "emergencies." Nor does routine or preventive care. The claim that emergency rooms are sufficient defies logic. If this were true, why would anyone bother to obtain medical insurance or visit a doctor? Surely the politicians who make this claim all have health insurance. According to a comprehensive study, uninsured people have a higher risk of death, even after accounting for socioeconomic factors. Up to forty-five thousand annual deaths in America were attributable to lack of health insurance before Obama's reform.[120] Breast cancer, for instance, tends to be detected later in uninsured women.[121]

Opponents of reform further claim that in countries with "socialized medicine," people wait an eternity to receive care because of "rationing." In reality, many of these countries offer quicker access to care and more choice than America, where "in-network" lists of doctors or the requirement that an insurance company preauthorize an expense can limit access to treatment.[122] Only certain universal health care systems have relatively long waiting lists. "Canada and Britain limit the number of specialists and operating rooms in the system to save money, with the result that patients wait weeks or months for nonemergency care," a comparative study noted. "But other nations—Germany, France, Sweden, Denmark—perform better than the United States on standard measures such as 'Waiting time to see a specialist' and 'Waiting time for elective surgery.'" [123]

Contrary to other myths, overbearing governments do not control everything in nations with universal health care, which instead rely heavily on the private sector to pay for or provide treatment. This misconception is due to the common conflation of "single-payer system" with "universal health care." A single-payer system essentially exists in Britain, where the government pays for nearly all treatment via taxation. But numerous industrialized nations do not have a single-payer system, as they fund treatment through diverse combinations of government insurance, nonprofit insurance companies, and out-of-pocket costs. In addition, their doctors are generally private practitioners—as is also the case in Britain's system.[124]

Irrational fears about "socialized medicine" partly reflect the exceptional role of money in U.S. politics. By the summer of 2012, approximately $69 million had been spent on ads supporting the Obama administration's health care reform. More than three times as much, $235 million, had been spent on ads attacking it. Among opponents of the law were uninsured people who had been convinced that it would limit access to care and that America simply "can't afford" to insure more people.[125]

It is no secret that the G.O.P. resisted "Obamacare." What is more striking is that well before it passed, many Republicans argued that overregulation causes America's health care problems. Consider Ronald Reagan's thoughts on national health insurance: "I'm opposed. There is no health care crisis in America. Most of the problems we have today with the increasing cost of medical care have been caused by government intervening in the health scene." [126] Similarly, Paul Ryan, the Speaker of the House, claimed that Obama's "takeover" of health care would harm a system that was "already heavily burdened, manipulated, and distorted by government spending and regulation."

Market fundamentalists promote a utopian dream: a purely private health care system, with minimal government intervention, that would serve the public good. What about the people who would remain uninsured or critically underinsured? (Namely, seventy-five million Americans before Obama's health care reform.)[127] No worries, Michele Bachmann and other prominent lawmakers declared, charity would somehow take care of exorbitant medical bills.[128] Senator Tom Coburn added that seniors were better off before Medicare was enacted in 1965. According to him, communities came together to provide adequate medical help to most. Doctors and hospitals were not always paid, he said, but they sometimes accepted chickens or baked goods in exchange for their services.[129]

The Economic Failures of Modern Democracy

America does not have a monopoly on wealth inequality. The vast ghettoes and sizable homeless populations found in both Paris and New York evoke the recurrent failure of modern democracy to deliver economic justice on each side of the Atlantic. The life of the middle class is not trouble free either on the Old Continent, where wealth has become very unevenly distributed too.[130]

People often attribute Europe's economic woes to overbearing governments. Businesses in France and neighboring countries complain that the cost of labor has spiked because of high taxes. This problem may be compounded by inflexible labor regulations that can make it difficult to lay off workers in periods of economic downturn or when they are underperforming. Certain companies consequently refuse to risk hiring new workers at a high cost, which may contribute to rather high unemployment rates. An attempt in France to address these concerns by reforming labor regulations led to mass protests in 2016. Some opponents of the reform rejected it categorically, whereas others argued that it might work in theory but is one-sided in practice. In their view, the reform will lead to layoffs, the spread of precarious, low-paying jobs, and more inequality.[131] Its long-term effects were unclear at the time of writing.

Generous public assistance programs have factored in Europe's substantial deficit and debt levels. The cost of universal health care is not negligible, although it is not the cause of Europe's struggles, as it has far lower medical expenditures than America. Rather, European governments spend significant sums on pensions, subsidies, poverty relief, and additional services.[132]

European economies face serious challenges, but according to the renowned French economist Thomas Piketty, the U.S. gross domestic product (GDP) per capita did not grow "any more rapidly" than those of Germany, France, Denmark, or Sweden between 1980 and 2010.[133] More recent data indicate that the Eurozone economy was far more affected than America by various shocks since 2008, from the U.S.-born subprime crisis to the mismanagement of the euro currency. The Obama administration responded to these situations with more budgetary flexibility than European nations that adopted "austerity measures," meaning steep cuts in public spending, and other counterproductive policies precipitating what Piketty called a "lost decade" of economic growth for Europe.[134]

The GDP per capita in America stands above those of almost all European nations. As of 2015 only Norway and Switzerland had higher GDPs per capita than America, while Denmark and Sweden* lagged slightly behind.[135] But GDP per capita is an average measure that does not account for wealth inequality or well-being. In addition to lacking universal health care, America is the lone industrialized country that does not guarantee workers paid

* Norway and Switzerland are not EU members. Denmark and Sweden are part of the EU but have not joined the euro monetary union.

vacation or paid maternity leave.[136] Put otherwise, the average American does not necessarily enjoy a better quality of life than fellow Westerners, as the United States' winner-take-all system has concentrated the benefits of its economic power in the hands of the most privileged.

A PECULIAR CONCEPTION OF DEMOCRACY

If conservative Americans generally stand out in the West for embracing market fundamentalism, the economic values of liberal Americans are rather similar to those of other Westerners in supporting universal health care, relative wealth equality, and meaningful regulation. Granted, Democratic economic policies have historically been further to the right than those of other left-wing parties in the West.[137] But whether at the center left or the center right, Democrats' economic values have been comparable to those of leading liberal and conservative parties in Europe, Canada, Australia, and New Zealand. By contrast, the contemporary Republican economic agenda is radical by Western standards.

These circumstances reflect the peculiar nature of politics in America, where "conservative" does not mean the same thing as elsewhere in the West. At first glance, conservatives in other Western nations may appear to share similar values with modern-day Republicans. They too have deep reservations about the welfare state, overtaxation, and overregulation. Nevertheless, European conservative leaders like Theresa May, Angela Merkel, and Nicolas Sarkozy widely support universal health care. They are equally amenable to sensible financial and environmental regulations. Contemporary Republicans tend to condemn such moderation, which runs contrary to the ideological purity of market fundamentalism.

Recurrent allegations that Obama is a dangerous "socialist" rarely gave way to rational debate about what the term means. While the rise of Bernie Sanders, a proud "democratic socialist," reflected a measure of change, "socialism" largely remains taboo in America. This is partly because it is a double entendre. On one hand, it can refer to communism, as exemplified by the name of the defunct Union of Soviet Socialist Republics. On the other hand, "socialism" may also refer to "social democracy," which is sharply different from a communist dictatorship. Karl Marx and Friedrich Engels argued that communism "may be summed up in the single sentence: Abolition of private property." [138] Communists have sought to do away with the market altogether to build utopian societies, by force if necessary, where "a new man" would somehow come into existence. Conversely, most social democrats recognize the value of private property and a market economy in which personal profit is an incentive. But they believe that unbridled capitalism can lead to severe inequality, recklessness, and other market failures. They consequently aim to steer the market to serve the greater good.

The American social scientist Seymour Martin Lipset emphasized that two of the European figures most associated with the emergence of social democracy in the late nineteenth century were conservatives: Otto von Bismarck of Germany and Benjamin Disraeli of the United Kingdom. "They represented the rural and aristocratic elements, sectors which disdained capitalism, disliked the bourgeoisie, and rejected materialistic values. Their politics reflected the values of *noblesse oblige,* the obligation of the leaders of society and the economy to protect the less fortunate," Lipset wrote.[139] The aristocracy has mostly lost political power in modern Europe, though conservative leaders still believe that the government has a duty to ensure the public's basic well-being. Conservatives in Canada, Australia, and New Zealand are prone to share this conviction. So are liberals in these countries and in the United States. As a result, the overwhelming majority of Westerners consider universal health care a *pillar of democracy.*

Conservative Americans are the main exception, as many gravitate toward an ideology on the fringe of modern Western civilization because of a visceral suspicion of government.[140] In their eyes, universal health care is the *antithesis of democracy,* since it threatens individual liberty. From the 1950s to 1980s, Republicans were more inclined to recognize that the government has a responsibility to provide for the public's well-being. But the government's foremost duty is now primarily seen as getting out of the way, as one of Reagan's quips suggests: "The nine most terrifying words in the English language are 'I'm from the government and I'm here to help.'" Individualism has come to trump nearly all other values.

Tea Party protestors, some of whom are affluent,[141] defended unbridled individualism the most stridently. At a rally in Columbus, Ohio, several insulted an elderly man holding a sign indicating that he backed health care reform because he had Parkinson's disease. A Tea Partier pointedly told him: "If you're looking for a handout, you're in the wrong part of town. Nothing for free. You have to work for everything you get." Another Tea Partier threw dollar bills at the ailing man while yelling: "I'll decide when to give you money!" The crowd additionally called the man a "communist."[142] Tea

Partiers likewise heckled supporters of health care reform at various town halls, including a wheelchair-bound woman and a woman who explained that her young, pregnant daughter-in-law had died and lost her unborn child because she lacked insurance.[143]

Such reactions reflect not only a lack of empathy but also a misconceived sense of individualism. People cannot fulfill their life goals if they are beset by medical problems and exorbitant bills. Universal health care does not negate individualism—it helps enable it.[144] "Necessitous men are not free men," as Franklin Roosevelt stressed.

The tendency to overlook the greater good is further embodied in the *Citizens United* decision and its progeny, which have permitted unlimited spending on political campaigns in the name of individual "freedom of speech." This kind of individualism empowers only the handful of individuals who can donate enormous sums to political campaigns, ignoring the innumerable individuals who cannot. American conservatives have generally dismissed this concern by stating that society must treat all individuals equally, without regard to income differences. Under that Orwellian conception of democracy, all citizens are equal but some are more equal than others.

Narrow individualism similarly shaped reactions to the 2008 financial crisis. We saw that mortgage-lending agencies issued loans at usurious rates to unsophisticated people, many of whom were ruined and lost their homes when the housing bubble burst. Numerous American conservatives nonetheless argued that poor people had only themselves to blame for irresponsibly taking unaffordable mortgages. They were disinclined to blame mortgage lenders or Wall Street for engaging in predatory lending and risky investments on a colossal scale. This stance reflects the idea that investors have no duty to act in a socially responsible manner or with the interests of others in mind.

Hostility to basic gun control also echoes unbridled individualism. Because of incredibly lax regulations, America has by far the highest rate of gun violence in the West.[145] But the Second Amendment's fiercest supporters focus solely on their individual right to bear arms, regardless of social costs. In their peculiar view, gun control is a slippery slope toward the end of all liberties. Consider how Larry Pratt, the director of Gun Owners of America, portrayed citizens who support gun control: "They are coming for our freedom, for our money, for our kids, for our property. They are coming for everything because they are a bunch of socialists."

However, a significant exception to conservative America's staunch individualism stands out: morals legislation. Chapter 4 describes the wide support for policies based on ultratraditional values among modern Republicans. For example, Paul Ryan casts himself as a libertarian devoted to ending government control, yet he wants the government to prevent women from having abortions.[146] Criminal justice presents another contradiction, as conservative Americans commonly have a narrow conception of prisoners' individual rights, as we will see in Chapter 7.

The radical conception of individualism in modern conservative America should not obscure the positive role that individualism has played in history. Enlightenment thinkers called for expanding individual liberty against state and clerical authorities. The Western democracies that emerged from the Enlightenment beginning in the eighteenth century—the first of which was the United States—were based on individual rights. In contrast, communist regimes have seldom recognized individual rights, under the pretense that the individual's perspective is encompassed by the collective perspective, which has paradoxically been defined by a handful of individuals exercising dictatorial powers.

Even though individualism is indispensable to democracy, it is a double-edged sword because it can threaten democracy if taken too far. A democratic government must strive to protect the individual and the greater good. A society that provides primarily for the well-being of a minority of privileged individuals might be democratic in a narrow, procedural sense but not in substance.

SIX

Millions Standing against Their Own Economic Interest

Living in Manhattan, I discussed politics with Robert, a friendly white working-class neighbor who toiled long hours for such a measly salary that he had trouble paying rent. Priding himself on being a "Ronald Reagan fiscal conservative," he believed that America "cannot afford" universal health care, even though he had limited medical insurance. He seemed unaware that nations with universal health care have drastically lower medical costs than America. As the 2008 Obama-McCain presidential race unfolded, Robert was on the fence about which candidate's policies would most help him. At any rate, he was fixated on whether Obama might have forged his birth certificate. Overall, Robert resented his relative poverty and fiercely distrusted politicians. "They don't care about guys like me," he insisted. Like countless ordinary Americans, he protested his low economic status in a way that helped perpetuate it.

The Dutch philosopher Baruch Spinoza wrote that people can be led to "fight for their servitude as if they were fighting for their own deliverance." [1] That observation seems applicable to modern-day America, where millions of common people stand against their own economic interest by defending policies that heavily benefit the richest of the rich.

Insofar as Donald Trump's election was a revolt of struggling working-class and middle-class whites, it epitomized this peculiar phenomenon. Trump is not a small-business owner, social democrat, or altruistic person. He is a billionaire who campaigned on a platform of massive tax cuts that would primarily favor the affluent.[2] He is the head of a shifty business empire that has a history of refusing to pay its employees and contractors, has used a phony "charity" for self-dealing, has operated an exploitative and fraudulent for-profit "university," and has mostly manufactured its products in China and other developing countries—yet who ran for president on an anti-trade agenda promising to aid plain folk.[3] To boot, legions flocked to Trump as he relentlessly vowed to repeal "Obamacare," a program that was intended to help them—and that would have helped them more if not for adamant obstructionism from his party.

The G.O.P.'s shift toward winner-take-all economics beginning in the 1980s might not have been possible if numerous nonaffluent citizens had stopped voting Republican. But "weakness of pressure from the left is [also] one of the main reasons that the United States has less ambitious domestic programs and a smaller public sector than is found in other industrialized countries," as the political scientist John Kingdon wrote.[4] This aspect of American exceptionalism is not new. Seymour Martin Lipset underlined that "the United States had a lower rate of taxation, a less developed welfare state, and many fewer government-owned industries than other industrialized nations" well before Ronald Reagan became president.[5]

Given that sharp wealth inequality and the lack of universal health care harm not just the poor but also the middle class—the vast majority of the U.S. population—why do so many ordinary Americans vote against their own economic interest? This chapter considers various pieces of the puzzle: myopia fostered by anti-intellectualism; the relationship between religious fundamentalism and market fundamentalism; racial divisions hindering economic solidarity; and unbridled faith in the American Dream leading people to think that anyone can become affluent without government assistance.

MYOPIA

Contrary to conventional wisdom, voting preferences in America are not all backwards. The poor are likelier to vote Democrat. That is a regular finding in political science studies,[6] and it again seemed true in the 2016 election. Hillary Clinton won the vote of citizens with an annual income below $30,000 by 13 points over Trump. The vote of the wealthy was split rather evenly between both candidates, contradicting the notion that Trump's support narrowly came from the working class. The tally is nonetheless striking if we factor race into the equation. Trump won the vote of whites without a college degree by 39 points.[7]

Voting against one's economic interest did not begin with Trumpism. A comprehensive study of presidential elections between 1976 and 2004 found that Republican candidates received a large share of the white vote in all economic categories: low income (49 percent), middle income (56 percent), and upper income (63 percent). Support for the G.O.P. among nonwealthy whites was somewhat counterbalanced by the tendency of racial and ethnic minorities to vote Democrat.[8] Other data confirm this general pattern. In 2012, 35 percent of all voters making less than $30,000 per year backed Mitt Romney.[9] In 2004, a considerable minority of the destitute voted for George W. Bush, namely 36 percent of voters making less than $15,000.[10]

Voting against one's pocketbook can go the other way, as a sizable proportion of the well-to-do have historically voted Democrat, partly due to a sense of solidarity with poorer Americans. But what is more remarkable is the Republican Party's ability to consistently draw significant support from ordinary citizens even as its policies have increasingly catered to the wealthy few. Many nonwealthy people also vote for conservative parties in other Western nations,[11] yet "conservative" does not mean the same thing there as in America. The modern G.O.P. is far more supportive of winner-take-all economics.

Scholars have long observed that Americans are quite complacent about stark wealth inequality.[12] While other Westerners are more concerned about the income gap in their countries,[13] around half of Americans think that the United States "would be better off if we worried less about how equal people are."[14] This lack of concern partly reflects unawareness of the magnitude of wealth inequality in modern America. The typical American thinks that the CEO of a Fortune 500 company makes about $1 million a year, when the median is more than $10 million.[15] People in other countries also underestimate earnings at the top, but to a far lesser extent.[16]

Data indicate that the more conservative Americans are, the less likely they are to recognize that wealth inequality has risen in the United States in recent decades.[17] The weight of anti-intellectualism helps explain this situation, as people who deprecate education and rational analysis are more disposed to vote against their own interest. Recall the public's response to the Bush tax cuts discussed in Chapter 2. Most of the citizens who were concerned about worsening inequality supported the huge tax cuts, even though they primarily benefited the wealthy. A landmark study by Larry Bartels, a political scientist, concluded that Americans' opinions commonly reflect "rather simple-minded—and sometimes misguided—considerations of self-interest stemming from their views about their own tax burdens."[18]

Paradoxically, taxation and regulation are most fiercely resisted in the states where people most benefit from them. The staunchly conservative states of the South and Midwest receive more federal money than they pay in federal taxes, whereas the rather liberal states of the Northeast and West Coast receive less than they pay.[19] Democratic states effectively subsidize Republican states, which are poorer and lag behind in areas such as health and education. As the political scientist Andrew Gelman wrote, "The richest segment of Connecticutians is only barely more likely to vote Republican than the poorest Mississipians."[20]

A multitude of working-class and middle-class citizens thus flocked to the Tea Party, demanding a barebones federal government that would disproportionately harm the states where the movement enjoyed the most support. Business elites stood behind this supposedly anti-elitist revolt. "Grassroots" Tea Party rallies were partly funded by moneyed interests, such as the billionaire Koch brothers. Major corporations like Pfizer, Lockheed Martin, JPMorgan Chase, Dow Chemical, and Rolls-Royce have been represented on the board of the U.S. Chamber of Commerce, a lobby that Tea Party activists enthusiastically embraced.[21] Much of the poor South subsequently became Trump Country.[22]

Apart from the pompous billionaire, politicians who stem from the business elite commonly try to hide their identity by claiming to be ordinary people. John Boehner, for instance, said that he headed a "small business" before being elected to Congress. His wife stressed that the Boehners were "just normal, average people." In reality, Boehner made millions while running a marketing firm. Similarly, in his prime-time speech accepting the 2012 Republican presidential nomination, Mitt Romney said, "When I was thirty-seven, I helped to start a small company." This was Bain Capital, which had $37 million in funds. Paul Ryan, the Speaker of the House, hails from a rich family. He nonetheless suggested that he had struggled to fulfill the American Dream: "When I was growing up, when I was flipping burgers at McDonald's, . . . washing dishes, or waiting tables, I never thought of myself as stuck in some station in life."[23] Champions of the business elite tend to misrepresent not only their identities but also their policies, such as by affirming that huge tax cuts for the rich will help "working families" or that repealing "Obamacare" will improve access to health care.

The mix of disinformation and peculiar mindsets has led some ordinary Americans to go exceptionally far in fighting against their own good. A retired Boston police officer interviewed at a Tea Party rally condemned the idea that America should have universal health care: "My little girl, when she was three, she got real sick. Had to be in intensive care for ten days. Had to have a tracheotomy. I had shit for insurance. The hospital sent me a bill. Ten thousand dollars. I got a second job; I sent the hospital one hundred bucks a week. That was the right thing to do." The man claimed that Obama's efforts to broaden access to health care were plain "wrong." "If people want something," he argued, "they have to work for it."[24] His anger was misdirected toward alleged loafers who depend on "big government," rather than against profiteering by the medical industry. He had become active in a movement defending a system that put his daughter's life at risk.

Likewise, the plaintiffs in *King v. Burwell*, an unsuccessful Supreme Court challenge to health care reform, were mainly low-income whites who probably benefited from the law despite claiming that it harmed them. Some were so poor that they were exempt from the modest tax penalty imposed on people who refuse to obtain health insurance. One plaintiff apparently did not grasp that her lawsuit could have led millions to lose health insurance. "I don't want things to be more difficult for people," she told a journalist. "I don't like the idea of throwing people off their health insurance." Two other plaintiffs had previously faced $8,500 in out-of-pocket medical costs, which had contributed to their filing for bankruptcy after their company collapsed during the financial crisis of 2008. Another plaintiff called Obama the "anti-Christ" and said that "his Muslim people" elected him.[25]

Of course, other Americans have protested in favor of greater equality. The Occupy Wall Street movement gained traction in 2011 by demanding a fairer economy and denouncing "the 1 percent." Bernie Sanders's relatively popular 2016 presidential campaign echoed the same concerns. But neither had as much influence on the Democratic Party as the Tea Party did on the G.O.P.[26] Besides, similar egalitarian movements exist elsewhere in the West. The Tea Party incarnated American exceptionalism, since no other modern Western country has had an influential movement advocating extreme anti-governmentalism and leading scores of ordinary people to vote against their own good while helping millionaires.[27]

Fewer Americans might vote against their own economic interest if they realized the magnitude of wealth inequality in America next to other industrialized nations. "The masses never revolt of their own accord, and they never revolt merely because they are oppressed," George Orwell wrote in his pessimistic novel *1984*. "Indeed, so long as they are not permitted to have standards of comparison, they never even become aware that they are oppressed."[28]

In *What's the Matter with Kansas?*, Thomas Frank argued that many working-class whites vote Republican because of the party's ultratraditional stances on culture war issues such as abortion and gay rights, thereby enabling the G.O.P. to implement economic policies favoring the rich. However, Frank's theory did not seem to square with the data, which show that most voters are more concerned about economics than about culture war issues.[29] On average, the rich also care more than the working class about the culture wars, perhaps because voters are more inclined to focus on social issues once they are financially secure.[30] In response to Frank's 2004 bestseller, the political scientist Larry Bartels presented compelling data showing that working-class whites had not abandoned the Democratic Party. Still, the data indicated that half of them voted Republican in presidential elections between 1976 and 2004, the period of his study.[31] *What's the Matter with Kansas?* is more persuasive if we think of the culture wars as one of several reasons why certain working-class Americans vote Republican. Even if these citizens are a minority of the public, they can influence the outcome of elections.[32]

Most of the debate over the role of religion in U.S. elections seems to revolve around the question that Frank's theory raises: how much do the culture wars matter to voters? People generally overlook another way in which faith may influence political decision-making: religious convictions can mold people's worldviews. Earlier chapters describe how roughly four in ten Americans gravitate toward biblical literalism and other aspects of religious fundamentalism—a form of Christianity nearly absent elsewhere in the modern Western world. Christian fundamentalism fosters anti-intellectual, black-and-white, and authoritarian mindsets. This influence is not limited to culture war issues, as Christian fundamentalism can also shape how people think about the economy.

How Religious Fundamentalism and Market Fundamentalism Overlap

Both religious fundamentalism and market fundamentalism emphasize ideological purity.[33] Religious fundamentalists have an unbending faith in the literal veracity of the Bible and consequently dispute all conflicting science, from the theory of evolution to the Big Bang. By the same token, market fundamentalists dispute facts that call into question strict laissez-faire economics. The catastrophic 2008 financial crisis and ensuing Great Recession did not change their conviction that markets can adequately regulate themselves without government intervention.[34] Since their radical views do not square with reality, fundamentalists commonly make up their own facts by resorting to disinformation and conspiracy theories. Religious fundamentalists claim that the theory of evolution is a "fraud" and that many scientists believe in creationism.[35] Market fundamentalists likewise resort to glaring misrepresentations, such as claiming that overregulation caused the financial meltdown or denouncing the evils of "socialized medicine."

Fundamentalists are usually oblivious to the social costs of ideological purity. This is reflected not merely in indifference toward soaring wealth inequality or the plight of people without medical insurance. They have fought efforts to curb global warming regardless of the consequences. In any event, most reject climatic science. Some market fundamentalists, particularly Tea Party activists, would rather see the federal government shut down than allow it to operate with a budget not encompassing drastic tax and spending cuts.[36] Religious fundamentalists have displayed an equivalent indifference to the social costs of their ideology. Given their conviction that premarital sex is a grave sin, they have promoted abstinence-only sexual education while seeking to eviscerate reproductive rights. These attitudes help explain why America leads the industrialized world in the rate of unintended teenage pregnancies.[37]

Religious fundamentalism and market fundamentalism do not merely parallel each other. These two ideologies often overlap. Christian fundamentalists typically hold hardline views on economic issues.[38] The Tea Party movement is primarily known for its denunciation of "big government," but many of its activists also condemned abortion and gay rights in the name of religion. A study indicates that, after being a Republican, expecting religion to play a prominent role in politics was the strongest predictor of Tea Party support.[39] Moreover, Tea Partiers are significantly likelier than the average voter to be biblical literalists.[40]

Millions of American conservatives think that "dependence on a secular state" threatens "personal virtue."[41] In the words of Jim DeMint, who left the Senate to head the Heritage Foundation, "You can't be a fiscal conservative and not be a social conservative." He aspires to abolish the federal income tax and the IRS.[42] DeMint also thinks that gays and unmarried pregnant women should be barred from teaching in public schools.[43] He once skipped a conference because a gay rights group was invited.[44] "We've been told we need a truce on social issues," former Representative Michele Bachmann concurred, "and I would highly disagree with that because social conservatism is fiscal conservatism."[45] Bachmann, who has accused Obama of being a "socialist," believes that to be gay is "part of Satan."[46] She runs a Christian counseling clinic where people "cure" homosexuality through prayer.[47] Bachmann embraces traditional patriarchy, as she thinks that "God" wants women to be "submissive" to their husbands. She also declared that "God" told her to run for office.[48]

"The long-standing divide between economic, pro-business conservatives and social conservatives has blurred," according to a Pew survey. Contemporary American conservatives commonly "take extremely conservative positions on nearly all issues."[49] The union of fiscal conservatism and religious conservatism is not always coherent. It has led the G.O.P. to try to block federal funding to Planned Parenthood while ignoring the relationship between family planning and economic prosperity. Unintended pregnancies cost taxpayers roughly $21 billion per year.[50] Meanwhile, millions of federal dollars have been spent on abstinence-only sexual education, a counterproductive policy. The odd relationship between market and religious fundamentalism is epitomized by how legions want to compel underprivileged women to bear children but usually reject the notion that society should provide for these children.

Conservative America is essentially the only part of the modern Western world where religious fundamentalism and market fundamentalism have colossal weight. This peculiar nexus of ideological purity provides the context for the observation of the Nobel Prize–winning economist Joseph Stiglitz, who wrote that "many American conservatives, but far fewer [people elsewhere] in the developing world," share a "fundamentalist" faith in "unfettered markets."[51]

The Religious Right's Economic Agenda

The politicians who have steered the Republican Party toward market fundamentalism starting in the 1980s have largely been religious hardliners. We previously saw that Presidents Ronald Reagan and George W. Bush were devout evangelicals. Numerous other Republican leaders have similarly shared a quasi-absolutist faith in both the market and religion.

Tom DeLay of Texas, who served as the House majority leader, declared that God chose him to promote "a biblical worldview." He argued that the

Columbine High School shooting occurred "because our school systems teach our children that they are nothing but glorified apes who have evolutionized out of some primordial mud." Like DeLay, Bill Frist of Tennessee, the former Senate majority leader, was involved in the religious right movement.[52] These leaders embraced hardline economic policies. So did Rick Santorum, who attained the chairmanship of the Republican Senate Caucus and later campaigned for president by proclaiming: "People underestimate me, people underestimate what God can do." "I almost threw up" were the words he used to describe his reaction to JFK's famous speech on the separation of church and state. Claiming that Voltaire would agree with him, Santorum argued that barring the teaching of creationism in public schools stands against the Enlightenment and would "thwart scientific progress." His vitriol about Obama's "socialist" and "Marxist" policies was just as extreme.

David Brat said, "God acted through people on my behalf," after he managed the unprecedented feat of unseating a House majority leader in a primary election, Eric Cantor of Virginia, a fellow Republican. Brat has called for a system that would "synthesize Christianity and capitalism" and has warned of the rise of a Hitler-like ruler if Christians do not embrace strict laissez-faire economics. Other key figures of the modern Republican Party have suggested that they embody God's will, such as Scott Walker, who tweeted, "Philippians 4:13"—namely "I can do all things through [Christ,] who strengthens me." Walker sparked intense protests as the governor of Wisconsin by implementing sweeping tax and budget cuts, as well as drastic anti-union measures. He is a member of Meadowbrook Church in Wauwatosa, whose statement of faith lists belief in biblical inerrancy and the prophesied Second Coming of Christ.[53] Sam Brownback, the governor of Kansas, launched another ambitious experiment in barebones government and massive tax cuts in his state. He is also an ultratraditionalist.[54]

Several leading 2016 presidential candidates were hardliners in matters of economics and religion. After winning the Iowa caucus, Ted Cruz argued that constitutional rights come from God, which suggests that he is a divine messenger, since he often expounds on his interpretation of constitutional rights. Marco Rubio contended that "God's rules" should trump Supreme Court decisions. Ben Carson, a devout Seventh-day Adventist, was scarcely more moderate. Mike Pence, who came across as Donald Trump's more rational running mate, is a proponent of "intelligent design," the pseudoscientific creationist theory.[55] All of them have relentlessly denounced the threats of "Obamacare" and "big government."

Sarah Palin's faith equally deserves attention, given her far-right economic views. In 1996, after becoming the mayor of Wasilla, a small Alaskan town, she sought to ban from the public library books promoting tolerance of homosexuality. A creationist, Palin also insisted in a private conversation that humans and dinosaurs "coexisted on an Earth created 6,000 years ago." [56] She compared voting for her to putting things "in God's hands."

Glenn Beck, whose influential punditry blends conspiracy theories and far-right economics, is a hardline Mormon.* He thinks that the theory of evolution is "ridiculous," just like climate change. "I haven't seen a half monkey–half person yet," Beck quipped. Apocalyptic biblical prophecies have received serious attention on his shows. He once suggested that doomsday would occur on August 22, 2006.[57] As authoritarians do not always see eye to eye, Beck has clashed with his rival pundit Stephen Bannon, the former head of the alt-right *Breitbart News* who became Trump's campaign director. Bannon may not be an ordinary religious traditionalist, but he has criticized secularism and called for returning to a supposed golden age when capitalism and Christianity operated in unison.[58]

The far-right intellectual Dinesh D'Souza received attention after contending that Obama incarnates his father, whom Obama barely knew. "The U.S. is being ruled according to the dreams of a Luo tribesman of the 1950s," D'Souza claimed. "This philandering, inebriated African socialist, who raged against the world for denying him the realization of his anticolonial ambitions, is now setting the nation's agenda through the reincarnation of his dreams in his son." D'Souza is also a fervent born-again Christian who has sternly denounced secularism, feminism, abortion, contraception, homosexuality, and sexual education. He charged that America's "cultural left" was responsible for the 9/11 terrorist strikes because its immorality provoked anger in the Muslim world and Al-Qaeda's attack.[59]

Many other Republican leaders combine hardline religious and economic views, including Mike Huckabee, Rick Perry, Bobby Jindal, and Herman Cain. Even some of the ostensibly religiously moderate G.O.P. leaders tend to hold hardline convictions. Paul Ryan usually avoids strident religious rhetoric and is mainly known for his libertarianism. Still, his staunch Catholicism has led him to oppose abortion even in rape or incest cases.[60] He equally supported a constitutional amendment against gay marriage and

* Needless to say, moderate Mormons have rejected Beck's views as unrepresentative of their faith.

voted against ending "Don't ask, don't tell." But Ryan's moral values seem moderate next to those of fellow Republicans such as former senator Tom Coburn, who declared, "I favor the death penalty for abortionists." Coburn additionally thinks that "Obamacare" will "Sovietize the American healthcare system." He embraced the federal government's shutdown and suggested that defaulting on the national debt could be "a wonderful experiment."

In sum, a substantial share of politicians and pundits who have driven the uncompromising modern Republican economic agenda happen to be religious hardliners, if not downright Christian fundamentalists. This trend is likewise found among the public, as rank-and-file conservatives have increasingly adopted hardline attitudes toward both religion and economics since the 1980s.[61] Of course, a correlation between religious fundamentalism and market fundamentalism does not prove a causality. But a relationship arguably exists between these rigid fundamentalisms, which reinforce each other because of the ideological similarities discussed above.

Christian fundamentalists are certainly not the only people who have played a role in tilting the G.O.P. to the far right on economic issues. Wall Street financiers and other business elites, some of whom are not socially conservative or even religious, frequently defend winner-take-all economics. The irreligious Donald Trump stems from this world. Moreover, not all religious fundamentalists embrace strict laissez-faire economics. For instance, Pentecostals are marginally more liberal than other evangelicals with regard to assistance for the needy.[62] More to the point, African-American evangelicals in the Deep South commonly hold traditional religious views but vote Democrat and favor egalitarian economic policies. Nevertheless, the relationship between far-right attitudes toward religion and toward the economy is palpable in the contemporary G.O.P. The phenomenon is not new. In the 1950s, for example, the iconic reverend Billy Graham praised big business while condemning "socialism," government regulations, and labor unions.[63] Yet the G.O.P. has grown more radical on both religious and economic issues since then.

Winner-take-all economics seems incompatible with Jesus's message of compassion and charity for the poor. According to Matthew 6:24, Jesus said, "You cannot serve God and wealth." In Matthew 19:23, he added that "it will be hard for a rich person to enter the kingdom of heaven." But recall that if roughly four in ten Americans lean toward religious fundamentalism, a comparable proportion share liberal or moderate faiths. Jimmy Carter, a liberal evangelical, has been particularly critical of the fundamentalists' take on economics. "If you are a wealthy white man, then you are naturally inclined to think that the poor are inferior and don't deserve your first consideration," he said. "This builds up a sense of prejudice and alienation that permeates the Christian right these days."[64]

The relationship between Christian fundamentalism and market fundamentalism is not inherent. In an earlier age, partisans of unbridled markets included social Darwinists who claimed that regulating the economy and assisting the needy violated the laws of nature. They co-opted the theory of evolution to justify the "survival of the fittest," namely the wealthiest members of society. Their staunchest opponent was William Jennings Bryan (1860–1925), the three-time Democratic presidential candidate now primarily remembered for condemning evolution in the "Scopes Monkey Trial," where a Tennessee professor was prosecuted for teaching the heretical theory.[65] Bryan was not merely a biblical literalist. He had a far more progressive agenda than most of his contemporaries, distinguishing himself as "an early proponent of women's suffrage, railroad regulation, the federal income tax, opposition to capital punishment, a federal department of labor, campaign fund disclosure, state initiative and referendum, and vigorous enforcement of antitrust law."[66] The tide has turned, however, as the modern-day conservatives least likely to accept the theory of evolution are among those likeliest to champion a contemporary social Darwinism, rooted in the belief that the rich simply deserve their wealth and the poor deserve their poverty. This mindset is related to the American Dream, a national ideal that may be a greater source of division than of unity.

HOW FAITH IN THE AMERICAN DREAM
DRIVES THE NATION FURTHER APART

Millions of Americans fervently believe that what makes their country exceptional is the possibility of becoming wealthy through personal effort and without government assistance.[67] This conception of the American Dream rests on the image of America as a beacon of freedom, a land of unrivaled opportunity, a classless country unhindered by the aristocratic, feudal, or class divisions that have impeded Europe's progress. America is the nation where self-made men and women can succeed, where people can rise from rags to riches, where the poor can pull themselves up by their own bootstraps. Such idealism fosters the notion that the government is fundamentally a meddler, a nuisance, a usurper in a blessed, free country that can mostly do without it.

In reality, modern-day America stands out not as an equal meritocracy but as the developed nation with the sharpest inequality. It is not the possibility of realizing the American Dream that makes America exceptional—it is the prevalence of this *belief,* especially among conservatives. Faith in the American Dream often serves to rationalize the nation's stark inequality. If one assumes that virtually any hardworking person can become affluent in America, one is likely to conclude that it is wrong for the government to reduce wealth inequality, assist the needy, or establish universal health care. This conviction reinforces myopia by downplaying systemic factors of wealth inequality and focusing almost exclusively on personal traits, such as one's work ethic.

The Dream and the Reality

Contrary to popular belief, intergenerational mobility is lower in contemporary America than in various nations with economic systems that are more social democratic. The mobility of children is tied to their parents' achievements more closely in America than in multiple countries, including Canada, Denmark, Finland, France, Germany, Norway, and Sweden.[68] Within America, economic mobility is lowest in the South, the region where market fundamentalism is strongest. A statistical study concluded that "nine states, all in the South, have consistently lower upward and higher downward mobility compared to the nation as a whole." With the exception of Utah, the eight states with better-than-average economic mobility were Democratic-leaning and in the North.[69]

Nevertheless, Republican leaders promote the belief that America enjoys the greatest economic mobility because its system is the most capitalistic. Consider Paul Ryan's arguments in a 2011 speech at the Heritage Foundation. "Class is not a fixed destination in this country," he said. "We are an upwardly mobile society with a lot of income movement between income groups." Ryan contrasted America with Europe, where "top-heavy welfare states have replaced the traditional aristocracies, and masses of the long-term unemployed are locked into the new lower class." Rick Santorum went further, arguing that the term "middle class" is "Marxism talk," since "there are no classes in America." Echoing the same theme, Matt Kibbe, a Tea Party leader, declared that "the difference between Europe and America, and why America is so great, is that Europe has haves and have-nots."[70]

While ardent faith in the American Dream is rooted more in chauvinism than in fact, there was indeed a time when America was a place of exceptional social mobility. Many Europeans were able to improve their lot by migrating to America in the sixteenth through nineteenth centuries, notably because vast expanses of fertile land were available or seized from Native Americans. In the eyes of early colonists, American land was waiting in an unoccupied and uncultivated state for "a good people to populate it," as Indian "heathens" had no valid property rights.[71] Access to land was of consequence in an epoch when agriculture played a major economic role. Cultivating crops could result in significant profit or at least provide for a family's well-being. Colonists managed to acquire landholdings far larger than they could have dreamed of in Europe, where vast expanses of land were hardly there for the taking or were off limits to commoners because of feudalism. Overall, it seemed that hard work had greater rewards in America, which came across as an "exceptionally fluid and mobile" society.[72]

"What impressed observers most about the societies of colonial British America," the historian Jack Greene noted, "was the fact that the entire top of the European status order was missing."[73] Europe was then under the control of monarchies characterized by rigid aristocratic and feudal systems. The contrast became even more significant when the United States attained independence and established the first modern democracy. As Tocqueville and other travelers found, nineteenth-century America stood out for the unusual degree of equality found among white men there. Modern economic studies confirm their observations.[74]

Yet the unparalleled opportunities found in preindustrial America declined in the nineteenth century. Agriculture gradually diminished in importance and the value of farmland dropped while industrial, financial, and real estate capital expanded. The early fruits of capitalism largely flowed into the hands of a new gilded class. Ordinary people who aimed to rise up the social ladder faced a different challenge than colonists who became small landowners.[75] Moreover, the comparatively high social mobility in America's early days was also due to the fact that it lacked the feudal systems that kept people down in Europe (except for African-Americans, who lived under a caste system). But Europe evolved too, ultimately establishing social democracies that made twentieth- and twenty-first-century Europe more equal than America in many ways. In other words, the ideal of the American Dream is partly rooted in two anachronisms: an America and a Europe that no longer exist.

Even in America's early days, the success of certain colonists was not simply the product of hard work. Fertile land was often forcibly taken from Native Americans, many of whom were massacred or died from European diseases to which they had no biological immunity.[76] The economy relied on the brutality of African slavery. Scores of white men struggled in indentured servitude or other forms of poverty. And women were disempowered in a firmly patriarchal society. These circumstances profoundly contradicted the notion that anyone could succeed with ambition alone.

The American Dream has always represented what is possible, not necessarily what is plausible. It is symbolized by self-made men who made fortunes despite humble beginnings and little formal education. Cornelius Vanderbilt (1794–1877), for instance, started working at eleven years old on the New York waterfront and ultimately became a billionaire in the steamboat and railroad industries. But self-made men (and women) are exceptions. One may even doubt whether any person can be genuinely "self-made." Economic success depends, to an extent, on factors beyond our control. Behind stories of self-made men one frequently finds auspicious social circumstances, not to mention supportive associates. Government is also influential in enabling private activity, such as by enforcing contracts and building infrastructure.[77]

Of course, hard work and determination can greatly contribute to individual success. The stories of self-made men can be inspiring in celebrating these values. They are more questionable when presented as proof of the claim that acute inequality does not truly exist because anyone can become rich merely by working hard. In America, as in any country, the affluent have commonly enjoyed a variety of advantages. Donald Trump did not become a billionaire because he is a billion times more intelligent and hardworking than the average person. His father was extraordinarily rich. People who rise from dire poverty to tremendous wealth are few and far between. The American Dream makes the exception the rule and the rule the exception.

A Divisive National Ideal

In times of crisis, a country often turns to its national ideals in the hope that they will provide guidance and common ground. Yet invoking the American Dream has hardly attenuated the United States' polarization, because the views of Democrats and Republicans largely rest on incompatible premises. When it comes to fulfilling the American Dream, they respectively see the government as either a helper or an obstacle.

To Democrats, the American Dream is an aspiration that the government must help realize via meaningful regulations, public assistance programs, and wealth redistribution. Citing Theodore and Franklin Roosevelt's policies, Barack Obama called for such government intervention while affirming that worsening inequality "gives [the] lie to the promise that's at the very heart of America: that this is a place where you can make it if you try."[78]

Conversely, to many Republicans the American Dream is far more than an aspiration. It is a factual proposition: America is an equal meritocracy where every hardworking person can become rich without government assistance. Seventy-seven percent of Republicans believe that "everyone has an equal opportunity to succeed in America," compared to 35 percent of Democrats.[79] Republicans typically consider that people are likelier to rise up the social ladder in an economy rendered more efficient by the elimination of virtually all regulation, taxes, and public assistance. As Ted Cruz said, "Government control hurts those trying to achieve the American Dream." Donald Trump agreed that Obama's vow to reduce wealth inequality was "class warfare."[80]

While conservatives long denied that wealth inequality had risen in America,[81] the majority now recognize that fact.[82] Most are nonetheless persuaded that the way to reduce poverty is to cut assistance programs to the poor and lower taxes on the rich, to encourage economic growth. Liberals believe the opposite.[83] How to realize the American Dream may seem an intractable matter of opinion, yet the evidence suggests that strict laissez-faire hinders economic mobility, which is higher in nations with systems that are more social democratic. However, the conviction that all hard workers would become rich if the government simply got out of the way is ideological and usually unshakable.

The American Dream is, almost by definition, a myth. A dream is not reality. Exalted faith in this ideal can distort one's perspective. The more one treats it as a factual proposition, the more one believes that those who fail to succeed have only themselves to blame. Despite enjoying a life of fabulous privilege since birth, George W. Bush had no doubt that the destitute can pull themselves up by their bootstraps, as he proclaimed that people "who work hard and make the right decisions can achieve anything they want in America." From this standpoint, redistributing wealth is unnecessary—fairness instead requires that the rich receive generous tax cuts. Similarly, there is no need for universal health care—the millions of uninsured Americans could obtain proper health care for themselves if they worked harder. Nor is there a need to regulate campaign financing to limit lobbying by moneyed interests—lobbying is fair competition in an equal arena. Those who can give the most money to politicians deserve the most influence because they earned their fortunes simply through their own efforts.

The American right traces most of the country's economic problems to the New Deal era, which spoiled the fruits of meritocracy by fostering dependence on "big government." This view of history is embodied in "A Roadmap for America's Future," a policy initiative by Paul Ryan: "Until [the creation of the welfare state], Americans were known and admired everywhere for their hopeful determination to assume responsibility for the quality of their own lives; to rely on their own work and initiative; and to improve opportunities for their children to prosper in the future. But over time, Americans have been lured into viewing government—more than themselves, their families, their communities, their faith—as their main source of support. . . . The trend drains individual initiative and personal responsibility."

This narrative is recurrent. Note how Chris Christie explained American decadence: "I think it's really simple. It's because government's now telling [people], 'Stop dreaming, stop striving, we'll take care of you.' We're turning into a paternalistic entitlement society." He added that anyone can succeed all alone in America: "When the American people no longer believe that this a place where *only* their willingness to work hard and to act with honor and integrity and ingenuity determines their success in life, then we'll have a bunch of people sittin' on a couch waiting for their next government check." Senator Rand Paul, who prides himself as a wonk, likewise downplayed wealth inequality, by asserting that it is simply "due to some people working harder and selling more things." Mitt Romney even disparaged nothing less than "47 percent" of all Americans for being "dependent upon government." "I'll never convince them that they should take personal responsibility and care for their lives," he insisted.*

Of course, some people are indeed lazy and irresponsible. But the case of the working poor belies the stereotype that the impoverished are, by and large, idle welfare recipients.[84] Besides, it is not the poor alone who are in a

---

* Romney was referring to the 47 percent of people who did not pay income taxes in 2011, which he ludicrously equated with the Democratic electorate. First, these "47 percent" include not only the destitute but also students and the elderly who do not pay income taxes because of their low income. Second, many of them pay other taxes, such as payroll taxes. Third, some do not pay income taxes because of tax cuts advocated by Republicans. Fourth, many of these "47 percent" vote Republican.

tough predicament, as the income of the middle class has stagnated or slightly increased for decades while the bulk of income growth has gone to the wealthiest citizens.[85] Attributing systemic inequality to sloth implies that only the rich are hardworking. To be sure, Republicans are not alone in denouncing the indolence of the masses. For example, Nicolas Sarkozy, the French conservative leader, argued that on Labor Day the French should celebrate people who "really work" rather than loafers on public assistance. Yet he and other leading European conservatives support universal health care and have a much more moderate economic agenda than contemporary Republicans.

Living in a Dream

Belief in the American Dream does not serve only to rationalize inequality. It can also have a positive social influence by inspiring ambition. The prospect of fulfilling the American Dream can be a source of hope for the poor, immigrants, or the struggling middle class. But such idealism can hinder realism if taken too far. A large share of people with modest incomes believe they will realize the American Dream. More than one in three citizens with an annual income under $25,000 expect to do so. Further, 44 percent of those making $25,000 to $50,000 share this belief.[86] These findings are remarkable in light of the relatively limited economic mobility in modern America.

Many destitute Americans aspire to make it out of their current situation without questioning the economic system. In *Nickel and Dimed,* Barbara Ehrenreich described her experience working with an impoverished maid who saw no problem with cleaning lavish mansions for a pittance. "All I can think of is like, wow, I'd like to have this stuff someday," the maid said. "It motivates me and I don't feel the slightest resentment because, you know, it's my goal to get to where they are." Ehrenreich, a writer, had conducted a social experiment by taking on the kinds of lowly jobs the working poor live on. Despite pinching pennies, she could barely subsist on the roughly $7 an hour she earned toiling as a maid, waitress, nursing-home aide, and Walmart associate. Nonetheless, she saw that only a small fraction of the working poor truly resented their miserable predicament and were interested in doing something to change it, such as unionizing.[87] David Shipler made a similar observation in his study of America's working poor: "Rarely are they infuriated by their conditions, and when their anger surfaces, it is often misdirected against their spouses, their children, or their co-workers. They do not usually blame their bosses, their government, their country, or the hierarchy of wealth, as they reasonably could. They often blame themselves, and they are sometimes right to do so."[88]

Again, not all ordinary Americans are politically apathetic or eager to vote against their own interest.[89] Numerous working-class and middle-class citizens want the government to reduce wealth inequality and provide meaningful public assistance programs. The economic downturn of the Bush and Obama years led scores of Americans to grow pessimistic about their chances of becoming affluent. Half of the public thinks that the main reason why some people are rich is because they have had more advantages. A similar share believes that the main reason why some people are poor was circumstances beyond their control.[90] Many Americans thus doubt that they live in a meritocracy. But unbridled faith in the American Dream remains influential in shaping the worldview of a significant part of the population.

Seymour Martin Lipset emphasized that America's lack of an "aristocratic or feudal past" has made its citizens "less class conscious" than Europeans.[91] However, voting patterns might be more marked by social class in modern America than in Europe.[92] In other words, America has a class-based society even though legions think it is essentially the only country without social classes.

DIVIDED BY COLOR

Myriad Americans are persuaded that poor people have only themselves to blame for their predicament. Beyond the ideology behind the American Dream, this perspective is frequently rooted in racial and ethnic stereotypes. A sizable share of Americans equate "big government" with little more than a system of handouts to people of color who do not want to work.

America has historically been the Western nation with by far the highest proportion of racial and ethnic minorities. This has hindered economic solidarity by separating ordinary Americans into distinct communities. Generations of white labor unions illustratively were either ambivalent about or hostile toward embracing black, Latino, and Asian workers.[93] Such divisions have been less influential in shaping economic attitudes in other Western countries, which had few, if any, people of color until the surge of immigration following World War II. Today the proportion of minorities in America still dwarfs those in European nations.

In the last chapter we saw that it would have been more difficult for the G.O.P. to defend winner-take-all economics if the South had not become solidly Republican partly because of resentment toward racial desegregation beginning in the 1960s. But the backlash against racial integration was not limited to Southerners convinced that integration violated "states' rights." Slavery and segregation were abolished earlier in the North, although integration had been limited in practice. Attempts to remedy this problem by busing white and black children to public schools in other neighborhoods were frequently resented and even led to violent protests in Boston in the 1970s. Meanwhile, affirmative action policies contributed to the growth of the African-American middle class yet solidified the impression of certain voters that the Democratic Party had done too much to help blacks. Reagan, the father of the modern G.O.P., fomented this resentment by insinuating that lazy blacks on welfare were heavily responsible for the country's economic problems,[94] proclaiming his support for "states' rights," and saying that the government has no business fighting discrimination: "If an individual wants to discriminate against Negroes or others in selling or renting his house, it is his right to do so."[95]

Two chairs of the Republican National Committee, Michael Steele and Ken Mehlman, ultimately admitted that, for over forty years, the G.O.P. pursued a "Southern Strategy" seeking the vote of whites hostile to racial progress. The party tried to "benefit politically from racial polarization," as Mehlman apologetically acknowledged in 2005.[96] They appear to be exceptions. Other Republicans have typically been outraged by the notion that racism has shaped their party's ideology or strategy in the postsegregation era. After all, the G.O.P. has not used explicitly racist language like the segregationists of yesteryear. But that is precisely because the Southern Strategy epitomized dog whistle politics—coded language targeting people at a conscious or subconscious level. The strategy involves "three basic moves," as the legal scholar Ian Haney López explains: "a punch that jabs race into the conversation through thinly veiled references to threatening nonwhites," "a parry that slaps away charges of racial pandering, often by emphasizing the lack of any direct reference to a racial group or any use of an epithet," and "a kick that savages the critic for opportunistically alleging racial victimization."[97]

Lee Atwater, a prominent Republican operative behind the Southern Strategy, perfected this game. As he stated in a 1981 off-the-record interview that was republished with his name after his death, "You start out in 1954 by saying, 'Nigger, nigger, nigger.' By 1968 you can't say 'nigger'—that hurts you, backfires. So you say stuff like, uh, forced busing, states' rights, and all that stuff, and you're getting so abstract." [98]

As market fundamentalism grew increasingly influential beginning with the Reagan revolution, government assistance was commonly framed in racially coded terms. For instance, a "welfare state" technically describes a government that provides for the public's well-being in key areas, such as education, health care, housing, and retirement. However, "welfare" has become one of the most racially charged words in America, as to some it conjures the image of shiftless blacks happy to depend on government handouts. In reality, people "on welfare" have never exceeded approximately 5 percent of the U.S. population, and they now constitute around 2 percent. Besides, blacks are a minority of welfare recipients, and abuse is not as widespread as politicians profess. [99]

Various Republicans thus sought to obstruct Barack Obama's economic program by equating it with black America's supposed culture of welfare, crime, and anti-white racism. Pat Buchanan alleged that "Obama is a drug dealer of welfare" who "wants permanent dependency." Senator Tom Coburn agreed that Obama wanted to "create dependency because it worked so well for him." "As an African-American male," Coburn claimed, Obama had received "tremendous advantage from a lot of these programs" on his agenda. Michele Bachmann compared "Obamacare" to "crack cocaine." Rush Limbaugh described Obama's health care reform as "a civil rights bill" and "reparations" for slavery. Representative Mo Brooks equated Obama's agenda with "a war on whites." Glenn Beck asserted that Obama "has a deep-seated hatred for white people or the white culture" and is "a racist." A full 42 percent of Republicans shared Beck's view that Obama is "a racist." [100] Sarah Palin concurred that Obama aspired to take America "back to days before the Civil War," to a time "when we were in different classes based on income, based on color of skin." A sophisticated statistical study confirms that these are not fringe views, as most white Americans now believe that anti-white racism is worse than anti-black racism. [101]

Donald Trump capitalized on this resentment. After being an early proponent of conspiracy theories about Obama's birth certificate, he campaigned for president on a bigoted and anti-immigration platform. Incited by his incendiary rhetoric, his supporters assaulted minorities in various incidents. After a white man punched a black protestor at a rally, Trump said, "That's what we need a little bit more of." Trump even expressed ambivalence about disavowing Ku Klux Klan supporters.

The Republican establishment occasionally distanced itself from Trump's campaign, although its dog whistles have long conveyed comparable messages more politely. Jeb Bush, perhaps the most moderate candidate in the 2016 Republican primary, notably reiterated that Democrats win the black vote by saying, "Get in line, we'll take care of you with free stuff."

Other establishment Republicans made similar claims in the 2012 presidential race. Newt Gingrich declared that "the African-American community should demand paychecks and not be satisfied with food stamps." Rick Santorum likewise conflated African-Americans with welfare cheats, insisting, "I don't want to make black people's lives better by giving them somebody else's money." Moreover, Mitt Romney falsely claimed that Obama wanted to "gut welfare reform" by ending work requirements. After losing the election, Romney attributed the outcome to the "gifts" that Obama had handed out to his base, "especially the African-American community, the Hispanic community and young people."

To a lesser degree, Jimmy Carter, Bill Clinton, and other Democrats also used dog whistles to rally white voters and co-opt the Southern Strategy.[102] In her 2008 primary contest against Obama, Hillary Clinton remarkably argued that she had "a much broader base," given her popularity among "whites." "Obama's support among working, hardworking Americans, white Americans, is weakening," she stressed, implying that blacks are averse to work.

Notwithstanding Obama's election and reelection, dog whistle politics particularly helped the G.O.P. galvanize its base to obstruct the first black president's agenda. The emergence of the Tea Party movement, often described as a revolt of fiscal conservatives fed up with "big government," had a palpable racial dimension. Tellingly, 52 percent of Tea Partiers deemed that too much had been made of black people's problems, compared to 28 percent of the general public.[103] Another study concluded that Tea Partiers "are overwhelmingly white, but even compared to other white Republicans, they had a low regard for immigrants and blacks long before Barack Obama was president, and they still do." [104]

Othering People

In the United States, recipients of public assistance are commonly stereotyped as blacks and Latinos. On one hand, it is true that these minorities disproportionately receive public assistance, because they are poorer on average. While society regards education as an equalizer, the net worth of black college graduates is ten times lower than that of white college graduates.[105] Institutional and individual racism heavily contribute to this stark disparity. When identically qualified minorities and whites apply for the same jobs, for instance, the former are less likely to be interviewed or hired.[106] On the other hand, minorities do not have a monopoly on economic hardship. Around 42 percent of all low-income families are white, whereas 30 percent are Latino and 22 percent are black.[107] As a result, many low-income whites receive public assistance.

In addition to racial stereotypes, attitudes toward the welfare state in America have been influenced by the misconception that it exists only to help the poor. In fact, the middle class has greatly benefited from a broad range of public assistance programs. In what appears to be cognitive dissonance, numerous citizens who benefit from the U.S. welfare state are willfully blind to that fact. Almost six in ten Americans say they have never "used a government social program." It turns out that 94 percent of those who denied doing so had availed themselves of at least one program. In particular, around 40 percent of the people who had received benefits from Medicare, Social Security, Pell Grants, the GI Bill, or unemployment subsidies claimed they had never used a government program. People who identified as "liberal" were far likelier than those who identified as "conservative" to admit to having used a government program,[108] recalling the factual divide between liberal and conservative America. A significant share of those who think they have not benefited from government assistance are, in all likelihood, working-class and middle-class whites who deem that the welfare state exists not for them but for other people. There is little doubt that these "others" are mainly envisioned as lazy blacks or Latinos on welfare.

Public assistance at the peak of the New Deal was less seen in racial terms, as people generally grasped that most of its beneficiaries were white.[109] That was partly because pro-segregation Southern Democrats had sufficient leverage to ensure that economic reforms were implemented discriminatorily. For example, professions that made up the majority of the black labor force, such as farmworker and maid, were deliberately excluded from legislation establishing modern unions, minimum wages, and maximum work hours, as well as from Social Security until the 1950s. Benefits granted to veterans under the GI Bill were likewise administered discriminatorily. The New Deal consequently was much more helpful to whites than to blacks in the attainment of middle-class status.[110]

The civil rights movement of the 1960s, which initially focused on racial discrimination, eventually broadened its message by calling for economic rights for poor Americans of all colors. This led Martin Luther King Jr. to fall into disfavor with some white civil rights supporters, who did not agree with his interracial message of socioeconomic justice, not to mention his outspoken opposition to the Vietnam War.

But for racial and ethnic divisions, Americans would be likelier to embrace the welfare state and a universal health care system. Southern states with large black populations, such as Alabama, Louisiana, and Mississippi, vote solidly Republican in presidential elections despite being among the poorest states nationwide. That is partly because certain white Southerners associate the Democrats with policies assisting African-Americans, which exacerbates their suspicion of "big government." A revealing study indicates that states with large black populations have more-limited poverty assistance programs than other states. A strong correlation exists between racial homogeneity and support for wealth redistribution.[111]

Such divisions have been less influential in hindering economic solidarity in Europe. Few white Europeans assume that the welfare state exists mainly to assist racial minorities. Universal health care is widely accepted there, and documented immigrants normally have full access to it. That is fundamentally not because there is less racism in Europe but because of distinct historical circumstances.

Western European welfare states, which emerged in the nineteenth century, aimed to assist downtrodden members of society. Aside from oppressed groups like Jews and Roma, underprivileged Europeans were mostly white Christians. Enslaved or colonized people of color under the domination of Europeans predominantly lived in remote continents: Africa, Asia, Oceania, and the Americas. Racial minorities formed only a tiny segment of Western Europe's population until the post–World War II surge in immigration from former colonies. European welfare states were thus largely conceived before their populations became less homogenous.[112]

Nowadays, even far-right European parties such as France's *Front National* do not denounce the welfare state per se, which they describe as an important service that should be for "citizens" only.[113] (Again, many of the "immigrants" they want to get rid of are second- or third-generation citizens of color.) The logic of the modern European far right is analogous to National Socialism, the Nazi doctrine, minus its extreme violence and militarism, as it rests on the following idea: "We take care of our own but not others."

By contrast, the G.O.P. is categorically opposed to universal health care for a host of reasons, including racial stereotypes. Scores of white U.S. conservatives incorrectly perceived "Obamacare" as a handout to blacks and Latinos, even though millions of its beneficiaries were white.[114] Unlike in Europe, race has almost always been in the background when people in America have contemplated economic issues.

Much of the American public has nonetheless grown highly tolerant. People of color are present in spheres of power and influence to a greater extent in modern America than in other Western nations, as epitomized by Obama's election. Racial and ethnic divisions may therefore eventually diminish as obstacles to economic solidarity. Still, the nation's outstanding diversity has disturbed the popular psyche. As the ever insightful Richard Hofstadter observed back in the 1960s, "We boast of 'the melting pot,' but we are not quite sure what it is that will remain when we have been melted down."[115]

ATYPICAL INSTITUTIONS AND APATHETIC VOTERS

While acute wealth inequality in America partly stems from the peculiar cultural and historical factors discussed so far, distinctive institutions have also helped cement the status quo. We saw in Chapter 1 that federalism, the separation of powers, the Senate filibuster, and the Electoral College hinder simple majority rule, unlike in other Western democracies. These atypical U.S. institutions can empower a minority of legislators, primarily Republican hardliners, to obstruct reforms that would benefit most Americans. More to the point, Donald Trump and George W. Bush became president despite losing the popular vote.

Yet such institutional factors are probably not the main reason why modern America's economic system is highly unequal. After all, a relatively bipartisan consensus about the legitimacy of a more equal economic system emerged around the New Deal. The ideological nexus shaping a visceral suspicion of government therefore appears critical to understanding modern America's evolution into a winner-take-all economy.

If poor, working-class, and middle-class Americans resolutely supported a "new New Deal," it might become a reality, given their overwhelming voting power. This brings us to the question of voter turnout, which is not a singularly American problem. In many democracies, a large share of the electorate does not vote and is deeply apathetic. But voter turnout still tends to be lower in America than in other Western nations.[116] Illustratively, turnout was 58 percent in the 2012 U.S. presidential election, compared to 80 percent in the French presidential election the same year.[117]

Poor turnout in America reflects not only apathy or the undemocratic inconvenience of having to vote on a weekday but also the potential impact of atypical institutions. Because of the Electoral College, some citizens may see little point in casting a ballot in states where a clear majority will vote either Democrat or Republican, say Massachusetts or Texas. They might be more motivated to vote in a direct presidential election, where every vote would count.[118] Besides, why should Florida, Ohio, and a few other swing states decide America's fate? And why should unrepresentative states such as Iowa and New Hampshire have disproportional leverage in elections by kick-starting the primary and caucus season?

Despite the shortcomings of democracy, voting is not futile. Lack of turnout among working-class and middle-class citizens helps explain why modern America is so unequal. Failing to vote is a good way to ensure that one's interests will be overlooked.

SEVEN

Mass Incarceration, Executions, and Gun Violence in "the Land of the Free"

Before serving as a defense lawyer for indigent New Yorkers, I represented juveniles in Chicago while attending law school at Northwestern University. Under the guidance of astute professors who had forgone lucrative careers in business to fight for justice, my classmates and I defended Alberto, a fifteen-year-old Latino teenager accused of several violent felonies. He faced decades in prison. I had a chance to forge a bond with Alberto as I visited him in detention. His empty eyes were always filled with despair as he tried to grasp that he might spend his entire life locked up for the misdeeds of his youth. After grueling litigation in which prosecutors painted him as a callous predator, Alberto fortunately received a fairly moderate sentence, due to the zealous pro bono representation of Northwestern's Legal Clinic. But many American teenagers wind up serving life sentences. Other Western democracies consider life sentences for juveniles blatant human rights violations. If this is how the U.S. penal system treats children, one can imagine the punishments it metes out to adults.

The lyrics of "The Star-Spangled Banner" describe America as "the land of the free." Its people are indeed among those who most passionately invoke "liberty." So why is America the country most willing to incarcerate human beings? And why is it the sole Western democracy to still conduct executions, even though its people are the most suspicious of the government's authority over their lives?

The U.S. criminal justice system is a microcosm of American exceptionalism. The draconian sentences inflicted on racial minorities and the poor, including low-income whites, reflect the nation's profound inequalities. Unbridled individualism encourages numerous Americans to ignore root social causes of crime, from poverty to failing schools and lax gun control. In their view, offenders are merely "bad people," who must "take responsibility" for their actions. Anti-intellectualism bolsters this oversimplistic mindset, as both ordinary citizens and public officials commonly deem criminology, sociology, economics, psychology, and psychiatry irrelevant to understanding criminal behavior. The black-and-white morality of Christian fundamentalism, particularly in the Bible Belt, reinforces the tendency to view offenders as little more than evildoers. And the extraordinary role of demagogy in U.S. politics exacerbates all of these factors. Politicians, judges, and prosecutors often get elected by fomenting fear and vowing to be "tough on crime." As a result, American justice strongly emphasizes harsh retribution, not rehabilitation or prevention. Paradoxically, draconian punishments have not made America safer than countries with "lenient" policies. It has by far the highest murder rate in the West and the most gun violence.[1] Meanwhile, indifferent or defiant attitudes toward human rights shed light on the normalization of dehumanizing practices in the United States.

Contrary to other aspects of American exceptionalism explored in this book, criminal justice is an area where both U.S. conservatives and U.S. liberals are outliers in the modern Western world. Executions are concentrated in the South, but prison terms in red and blue states alike are draconian by international standards. No single factor can explain this phenomenon. A poisonous cocktail blending multiple peculiar ingredients has led modern America to have a justice system in name only.

THE DEGENERATION OF AMERICAN JUSTICE

Alexis de Tocqueville, who thoroughly studied American prisons in the 1830s, wrote that "in no country is criminal justice administered with more mildness than in the United States."[2] Illustratively, Michigan and Wisconsin permanently abolished capital punishment as early as 1846 and 1853, respectively, well before Western European countries, which generally did so in the twentieth century. There was never a golden age of criminal justice in America, as lynchings and chain gangs demonstrate,[3] but it once was comparatively advanced.

Few observers today would make the same observation as Tocqueville, who advised France to adopt elements of American justice.[4] To modern experts in the United States and abroad, American justice is now largely a model of disastrous policies to avoid. Because of the rise of mass incarceration, America has approximately 25 percent of the world's prisoners despite having 5 percent of the world's population.[5]

Figure 1 (see page 4) shows that America incarcerates around five times as many people as Britain, seven times as many as France, Ireland, and Italy, and ten times as many as Scandinavian countries like Norway and Sweden. Naturally, some American states are more punitive than others. Those with the highest incarceration rates are in the South and Midwest, including Louisiana, Texas, and Oklahoma. Nevertheless, even the states with the lowest incarceration rates, such as Maine and Massachusetts, are far more inclined than other Western democracies to lock people up.[6] In some ways, American prison terms are harsh even compared to those in dictatorships like Cuba or Iran.[7]

As of 2016, the U.S. incarceration rate had technically been surpassed by the Seychelles—a tiny African archipelago with a troubling human rights record.[8] But since the rate represents the number of prisoners per 100,000 people and the population of the Seychelles is 90,000, that means it has barely 800 prisoners, compared to over 2.2 million in America.[9]

The same crimes are punished drastically more severely in America than in other Western nations. Sentences for violent crimes are generally five to ten times longer in America than in France, for example.[10] A substantial proportion of U.S. prisoners serve lengthy terms for relatively minor offenses like burglary or selling $15 worth of drugs. People locked up for nonviolent crimes represent around half of state prisoners.[11] In addition to shorter sentences, European authorities are likelier to rely on alternatives to incarceration, including community-based rehabilitation programs, probation, and fines.[12] Political and legal authority are much more decentralized in America's federal system, rendering policy-making less coherent than in European nations. Data suggest that local American prosecutors, who enjoy extensive discretion, played a particularly important role in driving mass incarceration for decades, given their growing willingness to file felony charges.[13]

America does not have an extraordinarily repressive justice system because it has an extraordinarily high crime rate. Its murder rate is by far the highest in the West, but its rates for other crimes are ordinary.[14] America's incarceration rate was comparable to those of European nations until the 1970s.[15] Mass incarceration stems from the emergence of peculiar attitudes toward crime. The notion that both serious and minor offenders need to be eliminated from society or cast away for a long time gained ground in the 1980s as American justice regressed dramatically.

The evolution of American law in the 1960s did not suggest that the country was on the path to building the most ruthless penal system in the history of modern democracy. Under Chief Justice Earl Warren, the Supreme Court concluded that penal practices routinely ran afoul of the Constitution. In *Mapp v. Ohio* (1961), it held that evidence seized by the police in unconstitutional searches cannot be admitted at trial. Until then, what is known as the exclusionary rule had not covered the actions of state governments, only federal authorities. The rationale was deterring police misconduct, at the possible price of acquitting the guilty. In reality, relatively few people have gone free because of this rule. Motions to suppress evidence are difficult to win, since the defendant's word is pitted against that of a police officer, more conservative justices carved out various exceptions to the rule in later decades, and the police can circumvent legal challenges by easily obtaining search warrants from pliant judges in a nonadversarial process.[16] Still, *Mapp* became a cornerstone of constitutional law, as did the Warren Court's subsequent decision in *Brady v. Maryland* (1963), which held that law enforcement cannot keep secret "any evidence favorable to an accused," since this could notably result in the conviction of an innocent.

The Warren Court went one step further by holding in *Miranda v. Arizona* (1966) that the police must give the now famous warnings to suspects before interrogating them: "You have the right to remain silent. Anything you say can be used against you. You have the right to an attorney. If you cannot afford an attorney, one will be provided for you."* Consequently, a confession by an unwarned defendant might no longer be admissible at trial. In practice, however, *Miranda* changed little. Most defendants waive their right to remain silent because they naïvely think they can talk their way out of accusations or because police goad them into talking. Those who invoke their *Miranda* rights are typically recidivists or well-to-do defendants who understand how the law works. Besides, the justices also carved out various exceptions to this rule over time.[17] *Miranda* nonetheless remarkably held that incommunicado interrogations are "destructive of human dignity" and serve "no purpose other than to subjugate the individual to the will of his examiner" through "intimidation."

---

* The warnings need not follow this precise wording.

Among other key reforms, the Warren Court ruled in *Gideon v. Wainwright* (1963) that states must provide lawyers to criminal defendants who cannot afford them. It unanimously held that "lawyers in criminal courts are necessities, not luxuries." Many indigent defendants previously had no lawyers at all. The Warren Court additionally revolutionized juvenile justice by holding in *In re Gault* (1967) that children cannot be locked up without constitutional due process. The Warren Court did not focus solely on criminal justice, of course, as *Brown v. Board of Education* (1954) was among its seminal decisions. To this day, it is considered the most liberal Supreme Court in history.

The Warren Court's decisions led to a backlash, as certain conservatives felt it went too far in expanding the rights of black people and criminals.[18] That resentment reflected broader concern about social change in the 1960s, a decade that contributed profoundly to the polarization of America. To many liberals, this period marked achievements toward greater equality and fairness: the civil rights movement, the sexual revolution, anti-war protests, and other challenges to the establishment. But the sixties also gave rise to a counter-counterculture among those hostile to the liberalization of society.[19] Dubbed the "Silent Majority," they had no sympathy for prisoners, black militants, feminists, or anti-war protestors. In their view, a Supreme Court run amok had violated "states' rights" by acting as an unelected liberal legislature. The deep-seated suspicion of "judicial activism" among Republicans can largely be traced to this period.

Beginning in the Nixon presidency, the Supreme Court has been staffed by increasingly conservative justices, some of whom made no secret of their hostility to Earl Warren's court. That evolution paralleled the rise of the so-called tough on crime movement as Supreme Courts headed by Chief Justices Warren Burger, William Rehnquist, and John Roberts rubber-stamped draconian punishments that the Warren Court would probably have found unconstitutional.

No Mercy

America's state prison population surged by more than 700 percent from the 1970s to the 2010s.[20] That partly reflected a "massive and incontestable" rise in crime from the 1960s to the 1980s,[21] although the prison population explosion is explained more by how America responded to crime than by crime itself.[22] Mass incarceration represented not merely a shift toward draconian sentences but also a radically different way of thinking about crime.

While rehabilitation had become a driving principle of American justice by the 1960s, it was mostly abandoned in the following decades, as David Garland describes in *The Culture of Control*. Conservative critics charged that criminology was a field tainted by liberal assumptions, because rehabilitation does not work.[23] The rehabilitative model did not cause the spike in crime, but it could entail a lack of pragmatism by discounting "occasional, opportunistic, rationally motivated offending," since it "spoke to no particular pathology and offered no opportunity for expert treatment or correctional reform." Despite its imperfections, the rehabilitative model grasped the influence of social circumstances on criminal behavior. Its repudiation was synonymous with a shift toward an oversimplistic conception of crime: bad people doing bad things. Policy-making became animated by a "zero-sum" attitude whereby "the offender's gain is the victim's loss, and being 'for' victims automatically means being tough on offenders."[24]

Meanwhile, the Supreme Court abdicated its duty to review "cruel and unusual punishments" under the Eighth Amendment by interpreting it so narrowly as to practically eliminate it from the Constitution.[25] The justices thus licensed "three-strikes laws" inflicting extremely long prison terms on recidivists with three felony convictions of any gravity. In 1980, they upheld Texas's three-strikes law and affirmed the life sentence of a man convicted of credit card fraud, forging a check, and obtaining money under false pretenses—nonviolent property offenses worth less than $230 in total.[26] The court revisited the issue in 2003 and upheld California's three-strikes law. The defendant in that case received a fifty-year-to-life sentence for shoplifting videotapes worth $153, as he already had convictions for theft, burglary, and marijuana transportation.[27] That decision was authored by Sandra Day O'Connor, who was then considered a moderate or centrist justice. Furthermore, in an influential precedent upholding a life sentence for cocaine possession, the court explicitly held that the Eighth Amendment does not require that a prison sentence be "proportional" to the crime.[28]

Those three cases were decided by 5–4 margins by conservative justices who rationalized their votes as deferring to states' rights to run their justice systems as they wished. Because of such precedents, prisoners serving obscenely long sentences had no constitutional recourse. The court's logic could be read between the lines: "If people want merciless justice, let them have it."

During a 1988 presidential campaign debate, a journalist asked the Democratic candidate Michael Dukakis if he would hypothetically support executing a man who had raped and murdered Dukakis's wife. "No," the candidate calmly responded, "I think you know that I've opposed the death penalty during all of my life." Dukakis's answer may have helped cost him the election against George H. W. Bush, as critics impugned his unwillingness to kill in vengeance as a character flaw.

If politicians fear being similarly called "soft on crime," it is partly because news coverage in America is often sensationalized, as reporters tend to favor shock value.[29] News coverage of crime escalated in the 1990s even as crime dropped, thereby giving the impression that society was increasingly dangerous. Blacks and Latinos were likelier than whites to be portrayed as social predators.[30]

Politicians tried to capitalize on fear. The 1996 Democratic platform thus adopted an approach to crime that earlier Democrats had condemned. "Today's Democratic Party believes the first responsibility of government is law and order," the platform stated, reflecting the view of the Clinton administration. However, in 1972 the Democrats had declared that the Nixon administration's "law and order" approach justified "repression and political persecution." By the same token, the 1972 Democratic platform vowed to "abolish capital punishment," depicting it as "an ineffective deterrent to crime, unequally applied and cruel and excessive." By 1996 the Democrats were instead boasting of having made the death penalty applicable for more crimes.[31]

In 1992, when then–Arkansas governor Bill Clinton was out of state campaigning for the presidency, he returned to Arkansas to signal support for its execution of a seriously mentally impaired black prisoner.[32] Clinton later declared, "No one can say I'm soft on crime."[33] George W. Bush equally sought to burnish his presidential credentials by emphasizing his satisfaction with Texas's 152 executions during his tenure as governor, despite his avowed "compassionate conservatism." As for Obama, he said that the death penalty "does little to deter crime," though he supports it in cases "so heinous, so beyond the pale, that the community is justified in expressing the full measure of its outrage." In fact, that rationale is likely to justify executions in virtually all murder cases—any deliberate homicide is an understandable source of outrage. Obama's phrasing is also misleading because "the full measure" of outrage would be not simply death but also torture or mutilation, as in executions of yesteryear. Upon viewing executions by lethal injection, certain victims' relatives express frustration that the prisoner did not suffer enough.[34] Politicians indulge such ideas when they bow to calls to kill prisoners.

Hillary Clinton embraced the push for increased executions and draconian prison terms in the 1990s. Far from a passive First Lady, she was a respected policy adviser whose opinion mattered. She notably supported the harsh 1994 federal crime bill by citing pseudoscientific and racially coded studies about juveniles. "They are not just gangs of kids anymore," she warned. "They are often the kinds of kids that are called 'super-predators.' No conscience, no empathy."[35] Multiple experts denounced the "teenage super-predator" theory as a myth. Its chief proponent, the political scientist John DiIulio, later disavowed his research as juvenile crime dropped considerably, counter to his predictions of a teenage crime onslaught.* To his credit, DiIulio tried to undo his damage by calling for reform. It was too late for countless children. New state laws facilitated the transfer of adolescents to criminal court, where they were prosecuted as adults and received unforgiving sentences.[36] Figure 9 shows that the gulf in incarceration rates between America and other Western democracies nowadays is even worse for children than for adults.

The greater responsiveness of American officials to calls for ruthless justice contributed to this extraordinary repressiveness. America is essentially the sole country worldwide with elected judges and prosecutors.† Their counterparts abroad are either political appointees or career civil servants.[37] Nonelected judges and prosecutors enjoy more independence, as they are fairly insulated from calls to crack down on crime if they want to stay in office. But even ordinary elected politicians in Europe have been far less inclined than their American counterparts to embrace ruthless justice. There has been a movement to make sentences harsher in Europe, yet it has focused on violent crimes. Europe has seen no push to make sentences extremely harsh for all offenders as in America.[38] Different racial dynamics and attitudes toward human rights partly explain why European politicians appear

---

* As we saw in Chapter 2, DiIulio later joined the George W. Bush administration but left after a few months because he found that it devoted insufficient attention to rigorous policy analysis.

† In the federal system and certain states, judges and prosecutors are appointed, not elected.

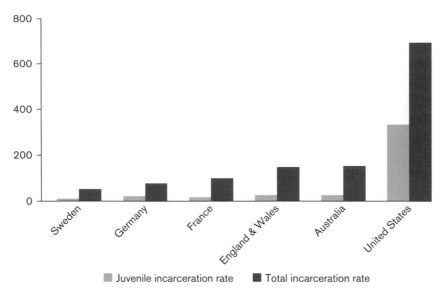

800

600

400

200

0

Sweden   Germany   France   England & Wales   Australia   United States

■ Juvenile incarceration rate   ■ Total incarceration rate

FIGURE 9. Incarceration rates (prisoners per 100,000 people). SOURCES: Institute for Criminal Policy Research, "World Prison Brief" (2016) (total rate); Neal Hazel, "Cross-National Comparison of Youth Justice," Youth Justice Board for England and Wales (2008) (juvenile rate).

more responsible than U.S. politicians in refusing to heed calls for degrading punishments, as we will see below.

Nevertheless, it would be misleading to imagine U.S. officials passively responding to public pressure for retribution. Certain politicians, judges, and prosecutors are elected precisely by fomenting hysteria, such as by promising to get "tough on crime" and denigrating their adversaries as "soft on crime." Some run televised ads boasting about the number of people locked up or executed during their tenure.[39] Without demagogy by politicians and misleading media coverage, the public would probably have been less inclined to embrace the "tough on crime" movement.

Indeed, much of the public does not fully grasp that draconian punishments are routinely imposed in their name and on their behalf. Practicing law in Manhattan from 2006 to 2009, I tried to get a sense of the picture. Whenever friends and acquaintances asked me what I did for a living, I said that I was a public defender and usually mentioned that America practically has the top incarceration rate worldwide. Few were aware of that fact, even though the people I questioned in my informal survey were predominantly university educated and included lawyers. Many grasped that U.S. sentencing laws are punitive, especially for drug crimes. But almost no one knew how repressive they are compared to other democracies. I recall a conversation with a student at a top law school who aspired to be a prosecutor but had absolutely no idea that America was such an outlier. She was frankly surprised when I described the harshness of U.S. prison sentences.

Deference to the public's actual or supposed demands for ruthless justice has eclipsed the views of experts, most of whom have long underlined that excessive prison terms do not deter crime, are costly to taxpayers, and can hinder rehabilitation or exacerbate prisoners' mental problems. The subculture of anti-intellectualism examined in Chapter 2 helps to explain why experts have less input on penal policies in America than in other Western democracies.[40] When I argued cases before the Manhattan state appellate court, I cited studies showing that imposing lengthy prison terms on relatively minor offenders is counterproductive. The judges tended to treat such studies as if they were totally irrelevant. When they asked me questions during my presentations, they seemed to care only about whether defendants would get their just deserts. There was typically no discussion of their prospects for rehabilitation or mitigating circumstances. When it was the prosecutors' turn to defend the sentence, judges almost never asked them to justify how a lengthy stay in prison would serve justice and be in society's best interest. The prosecutors' presentations, which the judges generally found persuasive, depicted defendants as simply bad people who should spend a long time in prison without making excuses. Prosecutors would add that there was no basis for protest, since in most cases an even longer sentence could have been legally imposed, such as twenty years instead of fourteen. Whether the judges were Democratic or Republican appointees, asking them to reduce a sentence, even by a year, frequently felt like talking to a brick wall.

In sum, it is not the average person on the street who is primarily responsible for the degeneration of American justice but rather people in positions of power who have abdicated the important responsibilities coming with public office. Simple-minded mottos like "Tough on crime," "Zero tolerance," "You do the crime, you do the time," "Adult time for adult crime," "Lock them up and throw away the key," "An eye for an eye," and "Just deserts" sometimes reflect the views of the public—but they also summarize the attitudes of many public officials.

"Increasingly, Republicans are talking about helping ex-prisoners find housing, drug treatment, mental-health counseling, job training and education. They're also reconsidering some of the more punitive sentencing laws for drug possession." This quotation is from a 2006 news article.[41] Talk about a growing bipartisan consensus for criminal justice reform has continued since then, yet little has changed. In 2006, America had more than 2.2 million prisoners.[42] A decade later it still did.[43] Its incarceration rate has slightly decreased relative to the growth in the U.S. population. This reduction has also been stronger for blacks than for whites.[44] America's incarceration rate nonetheless remains enormous next to those of other Western democracies. Both Democrats and Republicans have failed to tackle the problem.

At the outset, the federal government has restricted authority in this area, regardless of Hillary Clinton's promise to fight mass incarceration if she were elected president. Federal prisons hold a small minority of all inmates. The rest are in state prisons or county jails. The federal government can certainly provide incentives for reform, such as by funding state prisoner rehabilitation or reentry programs. But profound change will probably have to happen at the state and local level.

Some states have taken laudable steps. California, New York, and New Jersey significantly reduced their prison populations while seeing their crime rates decline faster than the national average.[45] In 2012, California voters approved a ballot initiative to scale back the state's three-strikes law. The previous year, the Supreme Court had ordered California to decrease its dramatically overcrowded prison population because "depriv[ing] prisoners of basic sustenance, including adequate medical care, is incompatible with the concept of human dignity."[46] As of early 2016, Governor Jerry Brown had granted parole to approximately 2,300 lifers convicted of murder and about 450 lifers convicted of lesser offenses. California had then reduced its prison population by 44 percent since 2006.[47] How far this effort will go is uncertain. Even if crime declines or remains steady, some parolees will unavoidably recidivate. That could lead to a backlash.

In any case, ending mass incarceration will take much more than what has been done so far. Many liberals apparently think that legalizing marijuana will go a long way toward solving the problem. To be sure, a whopping 620,000 people were arrested in America for mere marijuana possession— not sale—in 2014.[48] Still, people locked up for drug offenses constitute barely a quarter of the prison population. Half of all state prisoners are serving time for violent crimes.[49] The debate on ending mass incarceration has essentially focused on petty offenders, although the notion that anyone who commits a violent crime should be removed from society for decades contributed to the prison buildup. The real question is not whether someone has been convicted of a violent or a nonviolent crime but whether the sentence fits the crime. Aside from raising humanitarian questions, draconian sentences are hardly necessary for public safety. It is well established that crime drops considerably with age, for various reasons including that the last parts of the brain to evolve relate to impulse control.[50] A twenty-year-old who commits a serious assault may no longer be a threat to society after spending a decade in prison, especially if he receives meaningful rehabilitation. Yet once draconian laws are in place, it is exceedingly challenging to scale them back. Politicians fear being labeled "soft on crime" or being blamed for the consequences if crime were to spike after reform.

The misconception that mass incarceration made America safer is another obstacle to reform.[51] After complacently watching Hillary Clinton distance herself from his "tough on crime" policies throughout her 2016 campaign, Bill Clinton seemed to reveal what he really thought when he vehemently responded to Black Lives Matter activists who interrupted one of his speeches to criticize his 1994 crime bill. "Because of that bill we had a 25-year low in crime, a 33-year low in the murder rate, and because of that and the background-check law, we had a 46-year low in deaths of people by gun violence!" His supporters cheered. But experts dispute these claims as either baseless or grossly exaggerated. Crime began to drop before that federal law's passage, and criminal justice is primarily handled at the state or local level.[52] It is also doubtful that the 1994 crime bill greatly contributed to mass incarceration, regardless of how it ratcheted up federal penalties. Mass incarceration started well before the law's passage.[53] The Clintons still bolstered the "tough on crime" movement with their hardline stances and irresponsible rhetoric.

Few social scientists think that mass incarceration was the main cause of the significant drop in crime since the 1990s. Experts have identified various other factors, from a changing economy to revamped policing tactics, different social circumstances, and beyond.[54] The bottom line is that experts do not fully understand the reasons for fluctuations in crime.[55] And even if mass incarceration contributed to reducing crime, low crime levels can undoubtedly be attained by different means. No other Western democracy has adopted the ultrapunitive policies characterizing American justice. Despite this repressiveness, Americans are generally three to five times more liable to be murdered than other Westerners.[56]

At first glance, there appears to be broad support to end mass incarceration. Some 69 percent of voters say it is important to reduce America's prison population, including 81 percent of Democrats and 54 percent of Republicans. Moreover, 58 percent believe this would "help communities by saving taxpayer dollars that can be reinvested into preventing crime and rehabilitating prisoners."[57] Seventy-seven percent favor ending mandatory minimum sentences in all cases, to give judges "the flexibility to determine sentences based on the facts of each case." Opposition to draconian sentences seems strongest for minor drug offenses, as barely 25 percent of Americans would back a mandatory ten-year sentence for a drug dealer selling narcotics on the street, compared to 68 percent for a drug kingpin.[58]

The evolution of the parties' platforms is also encouraging. The 2016 Republican platform urged improved rehabilitation, alternatives to incarceration, and "restorative justice."[59] The Democratic platform supported "ending mass incarceration" and "systemic racism." It equally vowed to "abolish the death penalty" because it is "cruel and unusual."[60] Various prosecutors nationwide have additionally been elected by embracing reform, demanding more humane sentences for underprivileged minorities, and promising to swiftly prosecute police brutality. Perhaps the most memorable prosecutorial race saw Mark Gonzalez—a longtime defense attorney with "Not Guilty" tattooed across his chest—unseat a prominent district attorney in Nueces County, Texas.[61]

However, growing public concern and improved media coverage about harsh justice should not obscure the fact that scores of Americans still find their penal system neither excessively punitive nor discriminatory. Even though the United States has world-record imprisonment levels, only 51 percent of Americans think there are too many people in prison.[62] A vast proportion, 47 percent, think that "in most cases" it is "a waste of time and money" to try to rehabilitate adults convicted of violent crimes. And 36 percent, a big minority, feel the same way about nonviolent adult prisoners.[63] Besides, a majority of the electorate is direly misinformed, as exemplified by how, year after year, people mistakenly think that crime is rising,[64] which can temper support for reform.

Unlike minorities, most whites think the justice system "treats people of all races equally," in the face of massive evidence to the contrary.[65] Whites, especially conservatives, are also likelier to think that police shootings of unarmed black men are isolated incidents that do not reflect racism or profiling.[66] Remarkably, Donald Trump baselessly asserted in his presidential campaign that blacks kill 81 percent of white homicide victims. The actual figure is 15 percent—it is whites who kill 82 percent of white homicide victims.[67] Interracial crime is less common than people realize. Data indicate that whites overestimate the share of crime by blacks and Latinos. They likewise overestimate the share of white victims.[68] Fear of colored predators has hindered reform. Trump's nativist campaign also brought "tough on crime" rhetoric back toward the center of the political debate. Misleadingly depicting Obama's America as a chaotic nation falling prey to "illegal immigrants" and like-minded black thugs, Trump cast himself as "the Law and Order Candidate" when accepting the presidential nomination at the 2016 Republican Convention.

For all of these reasons, ending mass incarceration remains a tall order. It is particularly striking that much of the debate has focused on whether mass incarceration is too expensive rather than inhumane. Without a moral evolution, most Americans might find that mass incarceration is worth its financial cost if crime spikes or if the price of running prisons drops because of technological automatization in the future.

A WINDOW INTO AMERICAN SOCIETY

America's shift toward mass incarceration cannot be explained merely by growing conservatism, hysteria over crime, and the weight of anti-intellectualism over policy-making. A justice system has broad functions beyond law enforcement, as it is an extension of society's overarching values. We will now see that the U.S. penal system embodies key aspects of American exceptionalism: a thorny history of racism, sharp wealth inequality, religious traditionalism, and a peculiar conception of democracy that discounts human rights. These are all obstacles to genuine and lasting criminal justice reform, which may ultimately depend on more Americans reconsidering how they think about race, class, religion, and democracy.

Racial Discrimination

Minorities are extremely overrepresented in the U.S. penal system. Blacks constitute 13 percent of the U.S. population but around 36 percent of state and federal prisoners. Latinos are 17 percent of the population yet 22 percent of prisoners.[69] Discrimination is present at each stage of the legal process. Minorities who commit the same offenses as whites are likelier to be arrested, charged, convicted, and mercilessly sentenced.[70]

In *The New Jim Crow,* Michelle Alexander argued that mass incarceration has replaced segregation as a means of controlling blacks. Ex-prisoners are commonly denied the rights to vote and serve on juries, like blacks under racial segregation. Moreover, they are frequently unable to obtain work, housing, or public benefits, because of their criminal records. They thus become permanent second-class citizens. Alexander traces the mass incarceration of African-Americans primarily to the "War on Drugs," which enabled authorities to gain control over underprivileged blacks by harshly repressing petty drug offenses, such as possessing a tiny quantity of marijuana, crack, or cocaine for sale or personal use.[71] While studies show that people of all colors use and sell drugs at similar rates, law enforcement has strongly focused on drug offenses by blacks. This disparity is not explainable by the notion that blacks are more inclined to sell drugs outdoors and can be more easily apprehended there—research suggests that police tend to ignore open-air drug markets with white dealers in white neighborhoods.[72] Rather than pursue, say, white college students or yuppies who consume drugs, police instead target black people in ghettos. Black drug users are treated as dangerous thugs, whereas whites are perceived as benign, recreational users. Local police forces were given millions of dollars in federal funding to wage the "War on Drugs," a major incentive.[73] By attributing mass incarceration largely to the "War on Drugs," however, Alexander may have underestimated the fact that drug offenders are a minority of all prisoners, many of whom are locked up for violent crimes.[74]

Irrespective of the nature of the crime, racism has undoubtedly contributed to ruthless justice. Psychological studies show that whites are more inclined to consciously or subconsciously support harsh punishments if they perceive offenders as blacks. Fear of crime is also greater when offenders are identified as blacks.[75] And the "blacker" offenders are perceived to be, based on African features, the more they are perceived to deserve the death penalty.[76] Evidence of racism in the administration of capital punishment corroborates psychological research.[77] Modern executions have roots in the tradition of vigilante justice, as a high correlation exists between a state's number of executions and its past number of lynchings. No less than 88 percent of lynchings occurred in the South, the region most likely to execute today. Three in four lynching victims were black.[78]

In *McCleskey v. Kemp,* a 1987 case, anti–death penalty advocates brought compelling evidence of discrimination in Georgia.[79] An intricate statistical study demonstrated that, all other factors being equal, blacks who killed whites were likelier to receive a death sentence. The Supreme Court's most conservative members were unfazed. During oral arguments, Justice Antonin Scalia derisively asked: "What if you do a statistical study that shows beyond question that people who are naturally *shifty-eyed* are to a disproportionate extent convicted in criminal cases? Does that make the criminal process unlawful?" John Charles Boger, who represented the black death row prisoner, responded by pointing to the obvious: "This is not some sort of statistical fluke or aberration. We have a century-old pattern in the state of Georgia of animosity [toward blacks]."[80] Scalia and four other justices nonetheless chose to analyze discrimination out of its social context, including in cases from Southern states with a long history of slavery, segregation, and lynchings.

McCleskey, a 5–4 decision, held that Georgia's capital punishment system was fully constitutional. It largely closed the door to statistical evidence as a means of challenging systemic discrimination in sentencing under the Eighth Amendment of the U.S. Constitution. The majority reasoned that a defendant must prove intentional discrimination in his or her own case—an almost impossible standard without considering systemic patterns. Its opinion expressed concern about opening the door to other claims of systemic discrimination. In a memorable dissent, Justice William Brennan denounced this "fear of too much justice."

Some state courts and legislatures have been more receptive to statistical evidence of racial discrimination in sentencing. The Connecticut Supreme Court remarkably acknowledged that the death penalty "inevitably open[s] the door to impermissible racial and ethnic biases."[81] This was a key factor in its 2015 decision holding that executions violate the Connecticut state constitution. The state legislature had abolished capital punishment in 2012, and the court held that this reform retroactively barred people remaining on death row from being executed. Empirical evidence of racial bias and other endemic problems played a significant role in both the legislative and court proceedings.[82] That being noted, abolition was a vigorous battle in Connecticut, whose death penalty proponents vehemently denied racial bias.

Alongside blacks, Latinos face harsh sentences and stigma, regardless of their citizenship, because the immigration debate has been increasingly criminalized. Donald Trump urged the deportation of all Mexican "illegals," describing them as "criminals" and "rapists." Rush Limbaugh similarly affirmed that undocumented Mexicans are "a renegade, potential criminal element" that is "unwilling to work." Both said aloud what many think in private. In fact, the U.S. economy could scarcely function without undocumented people, as the overwhelming majority come to America to work hard and lift their families out of poverty. Research strongly suggests that deporting undocumented immigrants, including those with criminal records, has led to "no meaningful reductions" in the crime rate.[83] That is partly because they appear to have a lower crime rate than native-born Americans. Ironically, acculturation to American society might foster criminal conduct, as second-generation citizens are more drawn to criminal activity than first-generation immigrants.[84]

Yet racism is hardly the sole reason for the harshness of American justice, as some argue. Racism in America long predated the shift toward draconian prison terms in recent decades.[85] Besides, it is difficult to claim that Americans are considerably more racist than Europeans, and that this accounts for the exceptional repressiveness of American law. Minorities and immigrants are also highly overrepresented among prisoners in countries like France, Germany, the Netherlands, and the United Kingdom.[86]

What sets America apart in this area, however, is that it has historically been the Western nation with by far the biggest proportion of racial minorities, as discussed earlier. Racism is thus more entrenched in American institutions than in European ones. After all, discrimination in modern Europe has not encompassed subjecting minorities to mass incarceration and the death penalty. Furthermore, America is essentially the lone democracy that strips former convicts of their right to vote.[87] Around 7.7 percent of African-Americans cannot vote as a result.[88] In European countries, even current prisoners can generally vote.[89]

Racism may have played a lesser role in shaping European attitudes toward criminal punishment because there were relatively few people of color in Europe until the surge of immigration in the post–World War II era. The European Court of Human Rights, which has helped bar the kinds of dehumanizing punishments routinely inflicted in America, was created in 1959, when Europe's population was far more homogenous than it is today. We saw in Chapter 6 that social democracy in Western Europe, which began to develop in the late nineteenth century, aspired to lift up downtrodden members of society, who were historically white Christians. Conversely, in the United States, people in the bottom rungs of society have always included a large minority of blacks, with whom many whites have had difficulty identifying. The legal historian James Whitman suggested that "what must drive continental European sensibilities is the natural identification that most Europeans are able to feel with their low-status ancestors. *We were all,* most of them can say, *once at the bottom.* It is precisely the nature of American slaveholding that we Americans were not all once at the bottom; most Americans do not by any means identify with African slaves."[90] According to Whitman, this is a key reason why justice is far less humane in America than in Europe.

But race's role is complicated. James Forman, a law professor and former public defender, stressed that legions of African-Americans supported the ultrapunitive laws leading to mass incarceration and more executions.[91] The surge in crime from the 1960s to the 1980s helps explain their support, as it disproportionately harmed blacks. These are among the critiques that Forman levels at Alexander's "New Jim Crow" theory despite acknowledging its outstanding contributions to explaining mass incarceration. Forman notably emphasizes that few blacks supported Jim Crow segregation, unlike the "tough on crime" movement. Other experts have underlined that blacks also wanted the government to address root social causes of crime, from poverty to jobs failing to pay a living wage and subpar schools. These calls fell on deaf ears as whites focused almost exclusively on punitiveness.[92]

Race is ultimately best understood as one of various factors making modern American justice exceptionally harsh. My personal skepticism toward the claim that racism alone explains the problem stems from my time in Texas, where I was struck by how several of my black Democratic friends adamantly supported the death penalty in principle. Others condemned executions as inherently inhumane, echoing the stances of Martin Luther King, Frederick Douglass, and Thurgood Marshall. The black community is not homogenous. In particular, it is revealing that a significant segment of African-Americans seem primarily concerned with capital punishment's discriminatory application, mirroring the declarations of innumerable Democratic politicians who never suggest that executions are inhumane per se.

Whatever the reason, the sensibilities of Americans of all colors often differ from those of other Westerners—Europeans, Canadians, Australians, New Zealanders—whose penal systems are far more humane. This is a key reason why recognizing racism in America's justice system would not necessarily mean abolishing the death penalty or draconian prison terms. To some Americans, the solution to discrimination is ensuring that harsh justice is inflicted "equally" on people of all races. In practice, this would entail executing and locking up more whites rather than abandoning dehumanizing punishments altogether.

This logic contributed to mass incarceration. In the 1970s and 1980s, some advocates of penal reform felt that judges favored white and well-to-do offenders because they had too much discretion at sentencing. With partisans of harsher justice, they backed the creation of mandatory minimum sentences leaving judges little or no discretion to consider mitigating circumstances.* Avowed efforts to make the law more equal therefore led sentences to ratchet up.[93] That did not help minorities who disproportionately received ruthless sentences. It did not eliminate systemic discrimination either. Additional evidence suggests that nonracist justice may not mean humane justice. Even in predominantly white prisons in heavily white states such as Idaho, white prisoners commonly face inhumane treatment.[94]

Thinking of harsh justice solely in racial terms further disregards the facts that a third of state and federal prisoners are white and that around 55 percent of executed prisoners since 1976 have been white.[95] These are not negligible proportions. Promoting the misconception that virtually all prisoners are people of color may help perpetuate the stereotype that blacks and Latinos are criminals. Whites commit crimes too. Moreover, the misconception that almost only minorities face harsh punishment may hinder the ability of certain whites to identify with prisoners and lead them to think that the real solution to mass incarceration is for minorities to "fix their communities" rather than expect leniency. Psychological research shows that support for penal reform increases the more whites perceive prisoners as fellow whites—and decreases the more they perceive them as blacks.[96] One can draw a parallel with how racism exacerbates wealth inequality, as previous chapters describe. Just as many white Americans oppose wealth redistribution and universal health care because they wrongly think these policies would mainly assist minorities, many whites are lukewarm to penal reform because they assume it would help primarily minorities. Profound criminal justice reform will probably require a multiracial movement recognizing racial discrimination along with other injustices in the penal system.[97]

---

* That factor has gone only so far. In many cases, judges retained extensive discretion, and some have routinely inflicted draconian sentences well above the minimum.

The Other 1 Percent

Regardless of skin color, those who are locked up and executed in America usually have one thing in common: they are poor. The historic surge in wealth inequality in America since the 1980s coincided with the mass incarceration of poor people on an unprecedented scale. Strikingly, 1 percent of American adults came to be locked up while income growth flowed into the pockets of the richest 1 percent of Americans.[98] As the courts endorsed tighter control of the poor via ultrapunitive sentencing laws, they simultaneously favored greater "liberty" for the rich with increasingly business-friendly decisions.[99] Partisans of winner-take-all economics often dismissed compassion for the poor, as exemplified by how George F. Will ridiculed concerns about mass incarceration being inhumane, unjustified, or racially discriminatory. "Liberalism likes victimization narratives and the related assumption that individuals are blank slates on which 'society' writes," Will stressed. "Hence liberals locate the cause of crime in flawed social conditions that liberalism supposedly can fix."[100]

Criminal justice systems largely reflect economic systems.[101] It is no coincidence that penal practices are the most humane in Scandinavian nations, known for their high degree of economic solidarity. In a society marked by sharp wealth inequality like modern America, the penal system can come to embody the notion that those on the bottom rungs of society are nuisances, if not parasites.[102] Within America, states with higher levels of wealth inequality are more inclined to imprison people and retain capital punishment. That is also true at the international level: the more unequal a country is, the likelier it is to imprison people.[103] Richard Wilkinson and Kate Pickett describe these findings in their groundbreaking study *The Spirit Level:* "In societies with greater inequality, where the social distances between people are greater, where attitudes of 'us and them' are more entrenched and where lack of trust and fear of crime are rife, public and policy makers alike are more willing to imprison people and adopt punitive attitudes towards the 'criminal elements' of society."[104]

Americans are likelier than other Westerners to deem that criminals have nobody but themselves to blame, and less likely to empathize with them as fellow members of society headed down the wrong road. This mindset relates to the attitudes toward wealth inequality analyzed in Chapter 6, especially the notion that any hardworking citizen can realize the American Dream without any government assistance. The Americans most opposed to assisting the poor are those most supportive of harsh sentences. Illustratively, a study indicates "an extremely strong relationship between supporting capital punishment and opposing welfare." [105]

America spends less than other Western nations on public assistance programs yet considerable sums to lock up its citizens. In the 1980s, during a period of growing wealth inequality, public spending on prisons increased six times as fast as spending on education.[106] America spends around $80 billion per year on corrections.[107] Locking up poor people has become a lucrative business. Private prison corporations like the Corrections Corporation of America and the Geo Group have annual revenues of more than $1 billion apiece.[108]

The perceived worthlessness of the poor is epitomized by the unwillingness to provide them with adequate lawyers. Even in capital cases, court-appointed lawyers often receive scant financial compensation—sometimes below minimum wage if one takes into account the combination of low legal fees and the endless hours needed to prepare a capital defense.[109] After serving twenty years on the Supreme Court, Justice Sandra Day O'Connor stated: "Perhaps it's time to look at minimum standards for appointed counsel in death cases and adequate compensation for appointed counsel when they are used." [110] "People who are well represented at trial do not get the death penalty," Justice Ruth Bader Ginsburg also said in a speech. "I have yet to see a death case among the dozens coming to the Supreme Court on eve-of-execution stay applications in which the defendant was well represented at trial." [111]

Certain lawyers who represent the poor are truly committed, but systematically underfunding the defense means that many will be inexperienced, incompetent, unmotivated, or overworked while coping with insufficient resources. Well-to-do judges, prosecutors, and politicians would never tolerate such a poor caliber of defense for themselves if they risked spending one day in jail.

Divine Retribution

On the day I graduated from law school at Northwestern University, I had an unforgettable conversation with a classmate's mother. After I mentioned that capital punishment was among my areas of interest, the middle-aged white lady politely said she was pro–death penalty. I mentioned that given the number of homicides in America, executing every single murderer might mean putting to death more than ten thousand people per year. "As they should be," she emphatically answered. "An eye for an eye and a tooth for a tooth." Her response was probably not shaped by bigotry, since she was the parent of an interracial child. But it might have been influenced by religion.

We saw in prior chapters that religion evolved differently in the United States than in other Western nations, leading approximately four in ten Americans to gravitate toward Christian fundamentalism. By fostering a black-and-white worldview, fundamentalism encourages people to see prisoners as evildoers deserving retribution. By contrast, liberal and moderate forms of religion have a more nuanced understanding of criminal behavior and place more emphasis on rehabilitation. Fundamentalist-leaning denominations, such as the Southern Baptist Convention, Assemblies of God, and Lutheran Church–Missouri Synod, tend to strongly support the death penalty. On the other hand, the nonfundamentalist Catholic Church, Episcopal Church, Presbyterian Church, United Methodist Church, and United Church of Christ stand against the death penalty, as do the Quakers.[112]

Consider the official statement on the death penalty by the Assemblies of God, a Pentecostal denomination.[113] While noting that not all its members support capital punishment, the statement underlines that most do: "This consensus grows out of a common interpretation that the Old Testament sanctions capital punishment, and nothing in the New Testament negates maximum punishment as society's means of dealing effectively with serious crimes." The statement goes on to suggest that life imprisonment is an unsatisfactory alternative because "the cost of such lifetime maintenance and the number of criminals needing incarceration are genuine concerns for a society that is already heavily taxed." This argument is rooted in a glaring factual error. The death penalty has a higher financial cost than life without parole because the legal process in capital cases is extremely expensive, as we will see later in this chapter. That falsehood reflects the anti-intellectualism of fundamentalist churches, which contest basic facts on the theory of evolution, earth's age, climate change, the effectiveness of abstinence-only sexual education, and other issues. Although it makes a passing reference to "the sacredness of human life (of the criminal as well as of the victim)," the church suggests that a tax cut has greater value than a person's life.

The Assemblies of God's statement further omits any discussion of compassion, forgiveness, rehabilitation, or social factors behind crime, which it depicts solely as "heinous," "despicable," "outrageous," and "irresponsible" conduct. While the statement briefly notes "the power of God to transform even the most violent sinners," it immediately adds that this "must be balanced with the obligation of government to protect its citizens." In other words, even people who have attained redemption can be executed in the interest of law and order. Finally, the statement describes executions as "retribution or repayment to victims or society." There is no suggestion that killing is simply wrong.

It is common for Americans to argue that their Christian faith calls for the death penalty, such as by saying, "An eye for an eye." [114] This tit-for-tat mindset seems contrary to the teachings of Jesus, who reportedly said in the Sermon on the Mount: "You have heard that it was said, 'An eye for an eye and a tooth for a tooth.' But I say to you, Do not resist an evildoer. But if anyone strikes you on the right cheek, turn the other also" (Matthew 5:38–39). "An eye for an eye" is one of the few precepts from the Hebrew Bible that the New Testament explicitly rejects, yet few believers know that.[115] It is hard to reconcile support for executions and other draconian punishments with Jesus's call to "love your enemies" (Matthew 5:44). Jesus is ultimately crucified next to two "criminals," one of whom tells him, "Remember me when you come into your kingdom," to which Jesus responds, "Today you will be with me in Paradise" (Luke 23:42–43).* Given that Jesus apparently did not probe whether the prisoner felt remorse for his crime, his words suggest unconditional compassion.

In other biblical passages, Jesus seems to embrace the Old Testament principle of executing people who curse and fail to honor their parents (Matthew 15:3–6; Mark 7:9–10). As Bart Ehrman and other scholars have noted, contradictory passages abound in the Bible.[116] One cannot be certain about what Jesus would think of capital punishment if he were alive today. Still, the crucifixion of Jesus—the most famous victim of the death penalty—seems to exemplify the cruelty of executions.

The late justice Antonin Scalia, who was revered by the religious right, offered a distinct understanding of Christianity. A staunch supporter of capital punishment, he even dissented in rulings abolishing it for juveniles and the mentally retarded.[117] He also wrote an essay claiming that executions are divinely ordained. In his opinion, "the more Christian a country is the *less* likely it is to regard the death penalty as immoral." Scalia argued that,

---

* The Gospels of John, Mark, and Matthew provide different accounts of the crucifixion.

unlike people in nations that have abolished capital punishment, Americans "are more inclined to understand, as St. Paul did, that government carries the sword as 'the minister of God,' to 'execute wrath' upon the evildoer." "I attribute [this difference] to the fact that, for the believing Christian, death is no big deal," he stressed.[118]

"Death is no big deal" to Christians? Are most Christians somehow unafraid of death because of their belief in an afterlife? Are we to infer that Christians take executions more lightly and are justified in doing so? In fact, millions of Christians condemn executions. That is the position of the Catholic Church, of which Scalia was a member.

Scalia aimed to distinguish himself from the liberal "judicial activists" he accused of imposing their moral values on the public. He therefore began his essay by emphasizing that his own values had no bearing on how he ruled in capital cases, an incredible assertion. It is impossible for judges to wholly dissociate themselves from their worldviews when on the bench. Scalia's essay indeed states, "I could not take part in [the death penalty] process if I believed what was being done to be immoral," contradicting his disclaimer.

According to Scalia, the strongest justification for an execution is that the "evildoer" morally "deserves" it. In his view, recognizing social factors behind crime negates "free will" and means "there is little sense in assigning blame." From this standpoint, criminology, sociology, economics, psychology, and psychiatry have nothing to teach us about the complexities of criminal behavior—crime is simply a matter of sinful people doing evil things.

This approach to faith can intensify moral support for retribution among the Americans leaning toward religious traditionalism. However, we must recall that different religious beliefs polarize American Christians. Attitudes on punishment reflect this divide, as liberal and moderate believers support more humane policies. Not only do nonfundamentalist churches oppose the death penalty, but certain evangelicals have been at the forefront of criminal justice reform. William Stuntz, the great American criminal law professor, was a moderate evangelical.[119] Evangelicals, mainline Protestants, Catholics, Jews, Muslims, and other people of faith run prisoner rehabilitation programs.[120] Numerous American secularists oppose ruthless punishments too. All of these Americans demanding a fairer justice system should not be forgotten, even as I focus in this chapter on those whose peculiar mindsets have led the United States to adopt exceptionally harsh punishments.

Whether a person may be executed or imprisoned for life for a crime committed as a child would seem to many foreign observers a question that only a fascist regime would debate—or perhaps a society where people commonly share the peculiar conception of democracy described in previous chapters. Unlike in other Western democracies, the concepts of "human rights" and "human dignity" do not figure prominently in U.S. notions of law and morality. In practice, people often forfeit their humanity by committing a crime in America, as dehumanizing treatment is ordinary once one becomes a prisoner.

It was not before 2005 that the Supreme Court decided, in a Missouri case, that the death penalty cannot be inflicted on juveniles.[121] There was no consensus on the matter. Missouri defended the juvenile's death sentence to the end, and four justices dissented. Americans can no longer be executed for crimes committed before they are deemed mature enough to vote or buy a beer. But they can still be imprisoned for the rest of their lives. America is now virtually the only country worldwide to sentence adolescents to life in prison without the possibility of parole.[122] An estimated twenty-five hundred people in America are serving such sentences for crimes committed before turning eighteen, usually homicides.[123]

When Arkansas defended before the Supreme Court a sentence of life without parole for a fourteen-year-old convicted of murder, the state's lawyer argued that "the punishment for this crime reinforces the sanctity of human life." Given that empathy for the victim of a crime and empathy for the culprit are not mutually exclusive, what is most striking about Arkansas's approach is that it negated the value of the teenager's life. It was simply a nonfactor. As Justice Ginsburg told Arkansas's lawyer, "You're making a fourteen-year-old a throwaway person," who "will die in prison without any hope."[124]

The Supreme Court declined to abolish life without parole for juveniles under the Eighth Amendment's bar on "cruel and unusual punishments," although it limited its scope in two key decisions. In 2010, the court held that life without parole cannot be imposed on juveniles in nonmurder cases.[125] In 2012, it added that this cannot be a mandatory sentence for a murder by a juvenile.[126] Sentencing teenagers to life without parole thus remains constitutional, so long as it is not an automatic penalty for murder. Besides, sentencing teenagers to regular life sentences (with the option of parole) or extremely long prison terms (say twenty to fifty years) remains perfectly lawful. While these two decisions were significant, given the justices' habitual hands-off attitude toward draconian punishments, there was no consensus about children's basic rights, as the cases were respectively decided by 6–3 and 5–4 votes. The fact that contemporary Americans are debating whether children should be among those who may be put to death or permanently incarcerated reflects the United States' position on the fringe of modern Western civilization.

People often ask: "How did America change in recent decades to adopt such harsh justice?" What they usually overlook is that other Western democracies also changed during that period by strengthening their human rights standards, which largely preclude the degrading practices that have become routine in modern America. We will see in the next chapter that America was frequently the lone Western democracy that refused to adopt international human rights treaties spearheaded by the United Nations in the post–World War II era. This period also marked the creation of the European Court of Human Rights and multiple domestic human rights commissions throughout the West.[127]

This does not mean that other Western nations' justice systems are exemplary. For instance, France has regularly subjected prisoners to abusive, naked strip searches, which led to its condemnation by the European Court of Human Rights.[128] Prison overcrowding and harsh living conditions are likewise notorious problems in France, whose prisons are heavily filled with racial and ethnic minorities, including underprivileged Muslims.[129] Despite dubbing itself "*le pays des droits de l'homme*" (nothing less than "*the* country of human rights"), France has a poor human rights record compared to various other European nations. Still, its incarceration rate is seven times lower than America's.[130]

No other modern Western democracy resorts to American practices such as mass incarceration, the death penalty, the merciless treatment of juveniles, placing prisoners for years in solitary confinement,[131] or shackling female prisoners while they give birth.[132] Experts commonly see America as a systematic human rights violator in criminal justice.

Tellingly, the detention of alleged terrorists at Guantánamo represents an extension of the notion that people forfeit their humanity by committing a grave crime. To be sure, Guantánamo went far beyond the U.S. penal system, since the camp's creation stood for the proposition that alleged terrorists can be tortured and detained forever without trial. But Guantánamo also stood for the proposition that the worst of the worst criminals have no human rights. It appalled scores of Americans, yet numerous others wondered what the big deal was about. That may be because Guantánamo fit within the preexisting notion that criminals' lives have no value. It is revealing that the worst abuses there occurred under the watch of the most fiercely pro–death penalty president in modern U.S. history. George W. Bush's ability to run for the presidency as a "compassionate conservative" after 152 prisoners were put to death during his time as the governor of Texas epitomizes the worthlessness of prisoners' lives to a significant share of the public.

To Americans, "human rights" generally evoke foreign problems, not domestic ones. Americans instead normally refer to concepts like "civil rights" or "due process" when talking about problems at home. But this is not just a semantic difference. "Human rights" place emphasis on protecting human dignity. Notwithstanding the growing importance of "dignity" in Supreme Court decisions,[133] this principle still has far less weight in America than in other Western nations.[134]

That is a regression, given that Americans, led by Eleanor Roosevelt, played a central role in drafting the Universal Declaration of Human Rights after World War II.[135] It is not a binding treaty but a cornerstone of modern human rights standards, although it is less respected in modern America than in other democracies. Any American lawyer or politician citing it nowadays would risk ridicule.

Human rights skeptics argue that America is more "democratic" than other Western nations whose elected officials are less inclined to heed their citizens' calls for merciless justice. In particular, the abolition of the death penalty in Europe, Canada, Australia, and New Zealand in the face of relative popular support has been criticized as contrary to democracy—an alleged reflection of elitist leaders' preferences. Indeed, differences in public opinion go only so far in explaining why America is the only Western nation to retain capital punishment. Between 50 and 60 percent of Americans, depending on the data, favor the death penalty for murder.[136] Solid majorities supported it in various European nations around the time of abolition. While the United Kingdom abolished capital punishment in 1965, a 1975 poll indicated 82 percent support for its reintroduction.[137] But support has declined over time. In 2015, the British public's support for the death penalty dipped slightly below 50 percent for the first time on record.[138] The trend is comparable in France, where 52 percent want to bring back capital punishment—a less socially acceptable view than at the time of abolition.[139]

Reservations are stronger in Scandinavia. Only a third of Swedes support the death penalty, for example.[140]

However, democracy is not limited to simple majority rule, since it encompasses individual rights. This principle is more readily acknowledged when Americans think about constitutional protections for racial and ethnic minorities, gays, and women against discrimination supported by a majority of citizens.[141] Constitutional rights trump the majority's will. The same rationale should guide politicians and judges approaching prisoners' rights. The fundamental question is not whether the death penalty, draconian prison terms, or other sentencing practices are popular. Rather, it is whether they are just and humane.

At first glance, that seems to be the analysis called for by the Eighth Amendment's ban on "cruel and unusual punishments." But defining "cruel" is problematic. The Supreme Court has held that its meaning is not fixed in time, as it must reflect "evolving standards of decency," [142] although the justices have often disagreed about these standards. The Eighth Amendment ultimately may not have a particular meaning besides the one that the Supreme Court chooses, as the Constitution's text is amenable to multiple interpretations and the justices have extensive discretion, even when considering their general duty to follow precedents. From this angle, the question becomes why many justices have chosen to interpret the Constitution in a way that treats humanitarian concerns as virtually irrelevant, unlike courts in other Western democracies. Their agency does not exist in a vacuum. Diverse dimensions of American exceptionalism shape judicial decisions, from distinctive institutions to historical circumstances, social dynamics, and cultural sensibilities.

Killing Justice

A closer look at the death penalty can tell us a lot about American sensibilities. The United States is the only Western democracy retaining capital punishment. It is also among the countries that execute the most people worldwide, alongside dictatorships like China, North Korea, Iran, Saudi Arabia, and Yemen.[143] More than fourteen hundred people have been executed in America since the Supreme Court reauthorized capital punishment in 1976 after abolishing it in 1972 on the ground that it was applied arbitrarily and discriminatorily.[144] These problems have remained pervasive despite the adoption of new procedures aiming to make the death penalty "fair."

TABLE 5 Number of executions by U.S. region from 1976 to November 14, 2016

South	1,172
Midwest	178
West	85
Northeast	4
Texas alone	538
Total	1,439

SOURCE: Death Penalty Information Center.

Meanwhile, it has been abolished in law or in practice by more than two-thirds of all countries and is increasingly recognized as a violation of international human rights standards.[145]

Capital punishment is very unevenly applied in the United States. Table 5 shows that the vast majority of executions are conducted in conservative America, especially Southern states. Texas alone has executed over five hundred people since 1976, more than a third of all other states combined. By contrast, we see in Table 6 that nineteen states have abolished the death penalty, most being in the North and Democratic leaning. Abolition has made remarkable progress in the past decade. Disparities are huge within states too. Around 52 percent of executions since 1976 stem from merely 2 percent of counties nationwide.[146]

The distinguished National Research Council of the National Academies has found no compelling evidence that capital punishment deters crime more than prison does.[147] Besides, America has a far higher murder rate than other Western nations, even though they all have abolished the death penalty. Within America, states without it have lower murder rates than states retaining it.[148]

In response, it is often said that society should save money by killing prisoners rather than pay to imprison them for the rest of their lives—a claim resting on a false premise. Life imprisonment is far less expensive than the death penalty for various reasons, including the longer trial and appellate process in capital cases.[149] For instance, California spends $184 million more on death penalty cases annually than it would if capital punishment had been abolished.[150] Some have thus called for abbreviating legal proceedings in capital cases to save money, notwithstanding the fact that more than 150 innocents have so far been exonerated after being sentenced to die—

TABLE 6 American states and federal district without the death penalty

	Year of abolition		Year of abolition
Alaska	1957	Minnesota	1911
Connecticut	2012	New Jersey	2007
Delaware	2016	New Mexico	2009
Hawaii	1957	New York	2007
Illinois	2011	North Dakota	1973
Iowa	1965	Rhode Island	1984
Maine	1887	Vermont	1964
Maryland	2013	Washington DC	1981
Massachusetts	1984	West Virginia	1965
Michigan	1846	Wisconsin	1853

SOURCE: Death Penalty Information Center.

sometimes after spending years on death row desperately contesting their guilt.[151] Misidentifications, coerced confessions, the withholding of exculpatory evidence by police or prosecutors, and incompetent defense lawyers are among the main reasons for wrongful convictions.[152] "If statistics are any indication," Justice O'Connor admitted, "the system may well be allowing some innocent defendants to be executed." [153] That problem is inherent to the death penalty, an irreversible punishment requiring flawless justice. Nevertheless, 53 percent of Americans think it is "applied fairly." [154]

When it comes to capital punishment, America has more in common with the dictatorships with which it leads the world in executions than with democratic societies. A dictatorship is prepared to mistakenly execute some innocents to continue executing guilty people. By contrast, nearly all modern democracies have found it preferable to abandon the death penalty altogether rather than risk executing a single innocent person. Leaving innocence aside, a society's attitude toward executing the *guilty* is even more revealing. After all, recognizing that innocents should not be executed is a low benchmark of humanity.

While death sentences and executions have decreased in America since the 1990s,[155] this seems primarily due to growing concern over administrative problems such as financial cost, racial bias, and the risk of executing innocents. Talking to American death penalty opponents in both blue and red states, I have regularly been struck to hear things in the vein of "I have no moral problem with executing murderers, but I'm not comfortable with the way the system is run, so we should probably get rid of it." The movement against capital punishment has not necessarily been matched by a moral evolution.[156]

For strategic or moral reasons, U.S. death penalty opponents tend to avoid suggesting that executions are inherently inhumane. Illustratively, in a 2015 capital case about lethal injection protocols, Justices Ruth Bader Ginsburg and Stephen Breyer issued an influential dissenting opinion urging legal advocates to bring a broader challenge to the death penalty's constitutionality. Their lengthy opinion lists almost every imaginable argument against the death penalty—except the very idea that killing prisoners is inhumane.[157]

Conversely, opposition to the death penalty in other Western democracies is largely rooted in the idea that executions inherently violate human dignity, as they entail unnecessarily killing prisoners. Indeed, it is hardly possible to support executing a prisoner without first dehumanizing him or her to remove the misgivings that we normally have about killing. Prisoners' troubling upbringings or mental health problems are often disregarded. They are reduced to their worst act or imagined as little more than monsters. They must die.

Capital punishment negates the principle of rehabilitation and the possibility of redemption. The lengthy period between a death sentence and an execution, usually well over a decade,[158] means that prisoners have frequently changed by the time they are put to death. Examples abound of prisoners who engaged in introspection, repented, and educated themselves while on death row but were still executed.[159] Consider the last words of Napoleon Beazley, a black man executed by Texas at twenty-five years old for a murder perpetrated at seventeen: "The act I committed to put me here was not just heinous, it was senseless. But the person that committed that act is no longer here—I am."

Of course, not all killers feel remorse after causing victims and their loved ones tremendous hardship. This is a key argument used to justify the death penalty: "Remorseless people who heinously murder innocents don't deserve to live." In other words, most people approach the death penalty by focusing on the *offender*.

But the death penalty says far more about the *executioner* than about the executed person. People commonly expect the government to execute people in their name and on their behalf without ever coming face-to-face with that act. Those who support the death penalty in the abstract might not be prepared to execute people themselves if they had to. How many citizens would be willing to strap human beings to a gurney, inject poison into their veins, and not find satisfaction until their death? Confronting this reality might raise reservations in those who romanticize the death penalty. The French Enlightenment philosopher Denis Diderot wrote that "our virtues depend on the sensations we receive." He argued that people would prefer killing a human being at a distance to slaughtering with their own hands the animal they would eat for dinner.[160]

However, history demonstrates that many people are capable of killing in cold blood under certain circumstances. The genocides of World War II, Cambodia, Rwanda, Yugoslavia, and beyond were extraordinary atrocities committed largely by ordinary persons. Scores of people who favor executions might thus be prepared to conduct them in person, especially since the process has been sanitized in modern America. Means of putting prisoners to death have evolved from the gallows, rifle squad, gas chamber, and electric chair to lethal injection. This forcible euthanasia has led to agonizing pain in various botched executions. Yet it is often considered the most "civilized" method. Ronald Reagan compared it to putting down an animal. "Being a former farmer and horse raiser, I know what it's like to eliminate an injured horse by shooting him. Now you call the veterinarian and the vet gives it a shot and the horse goes to sleep—that's it," Reagan said before suggesting that America should adopt "more humane methods" of executing human beings.[161]

There are reasons to be skeptical when people deem prisoners so worthless that they should be killed—and simultaneously declare that they really care about not causing them pain. The search for painless methods of execution is not animated by empathy. Rather, it reflects society's efforts to ease its qualms about killing incapacitated persons.[162] This ambivalence may also explain why most death row prisoners are never executed and languish behind bars until dying from "natural causes."[163]

Support for the death penalty is obviously not unique to America. Numerous people elsewhere in the West favor it despite its abolition, as noted above. What distinguishes America is "the intensity with which people identify with the death penalty rather than . . . the proportion of respondents who express support," as Franklin Zimring underlined in a comparative study.[164] Expressing support for capital punishment is unlikely to mean the same thing in Sweden as in Texas. The third of Swedes who favor the death penalty would plausibly back it in a narrower range of cases.[165] By contrast, if rhetoric from politicians and ordinary citizens is any indication, a fair number of Southerners approach the death penalty in cut-and-dried terms: you kill someone, we kill you, end of story. Living in Texas, I once debated the issue with friends at a Houston restaurant. Overhearing our conversation, a stranger at a nearby table saw fit to interject. "I understand what you're saying," she said amicably, "but I think that if somebody kills someone we should do exactly the same thing to them."

What about murder victims' loved ones? Most will support execution, and we should honor their wish, one might argue. Since the 1990s, executions in America have been increasingly defended on the ground that killing murderers will provide "closure." [166] In fact, seeking the death penalty can prolong loved ones' suffering, because court proceedings in capital cases take years to end.[167] Capital punishment has nonetheless come to be seen as "a service program for homicide survivors," as Zimring describes it. That is partly why people who are otherwise extremely wary of "big government" can feel comfortable with government executions.[168]

However, not all victims are pro–death penalty. Martin Luther King notably denounced capital punishment, and his wife Coretta Scott King reemphasized this conviction after his assassination: "An evil deed is not redeemed by an evil deed of retaliation. Justice is never advanced in the taking of a human life. Morality is never upheld by a legalized murder." Similarly, the group Murder Victims' Families for Reconciliation brings together people who oppose capital punishment despite having lost parents, children, and spouses to murder. In their view, a society cannot show that killing is wrong by vengefully killing people.[169]

While it is widely assumed that victims' loved ones are entitled to see perpetrators executed, that is hardly how the system works.[170] Around fourteen thousand homicides currently occur each year in America but only several dozen executions.[171] The death penalty is sought in only a fraction of murder cases, for reasons distinct from the gravity of the crime, including prosecutors' temperaments, whether they or judges are seeking reelection, whether counties have sufficient funds to try death cases, the degree of news attention cases have received, and the races of victims and defendants.[172] As Justice Potter Stewart famously wrote, being sentenced to death is as arbitrary as "being struck by lightning." [173] Nevertheless, whether the death penalty is sought is often interpreted as a judgment on the social worth of the victim, leading some loved ones to feel "cheated" if a murderer is not put to death.[174] Empathy for victims and empathy for prisoners are commonly seen as mutually exclusive.

In 2004, I attended a protest vigil outside a Georgia prison where a man was executed for a horrible crime—raping and murdering his two-year-old niece.[175] Fifty feet away from the protestors stood people who came to support the execution, including the victim's loved ones. Some of them stared at us angrily. They misinterpreted our stance as a sign that we condoned the crime. As the scheduled execution time arrived, a fellow protestor solemnly rang a bell and said: "We are here to mourn the victim and the man who will be executed tonight." Moments later, an ambulance drove out of the prison. Inside lay the man who had just been put to death. The victim's loved ones then started singing:

> Amazing Grace, how sweet the sound,
> That saved a wretch like me.
> I once was lost but now am found,
> Was blind, but now I see . . .

"Liberty," Guns, and Prisons

Killing seems more socially acceptable in the United States than in other Western nations. Intense support for executions among millions of Americans is matched by uncanny gun violence and gun toting. That is the final ingredient of the cocktail poisoning American justice.[176]

A striking contrast exists between the radical deprivation of liberty via mass incarceration and the unbridled liberty to own guns in America. To an extent, mass incarceration is a reaction to violent crime and the fear of it, both of which partly stem from the right to bear arms under the Second Amendment. Any other country with as much tragic gun violence as America would most likely have repealed that amendment long ago. In fact, only nine countries have had a right to bear arms in their constitutions since 1789. By 2013, the United States, Mexico, and Guatemala were the sole ones left—and the United States construed this right considerably more broadly. The other nations had eliminated it from their constitutions.[177] While few Americans would support repealing the Second Amendment, many demand better gun control. But this has proved impossible because of dimensions of American exceptionalism discussed in prior chapters, from the clout of moneyed interests to radical anti-governmentalism.

Americans are about ten to twenty times likelier than other Westerners to be killed by firearms, as Figure 10 illustrates.[178] This is a key reason why the U.S. murder rate is the highest in the West. Around 67 percent of murders in America are perpetrated with firearms.[179] The number of guns per capita in America has doubled since 1968. Approximately 310 million guns are now in the hands of U.S. civilians.[180] Forty-three percent of American house-

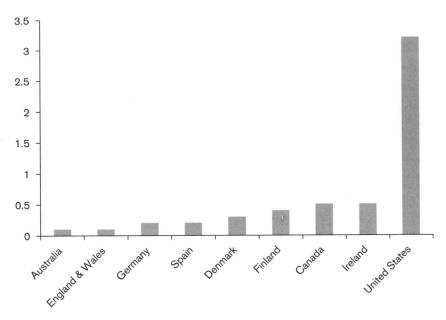

FIGURE 10. Homicides by firearm per 100,000 people. SOURCE: U.N. Office on Drugs and Crime (2009 and 2010 data).

holds report owning a gun—some own several, others none.[181] It is simple to obtain weapons illegally in America, such as on the street or via a "straw" purchase, whereby an intermediary buys a gun for someone who could not pass a background check.[182] But what is most striking is how easily one can legally obtain guns. In multiple states, people can purchase firearms at gun shows without any background check or questions asked.[183] State regulations barring people from buying more than one gun per month pass for significant control. Jerry Brown, California's Democratic governor, vetoed such a provision because he felt it went too far.[184] Virginia had one but repealed it.[185] It later adopted a law allowing people to carry concealed weapons in bars or restaurants where alcohol is served. That occurred after the 2007 carnage at Virginia Tech cost thirty-three lives.[186] The shooter had acquired his guns legally.[187] So had the man who used semiautomatic rifles to massacre the audience in a movie theater in Aurora, Colorado.[188] And the man who killed six people and gravely wounded Representative Gabrielle Giffords in Tucson, Arizona.[189] Even people with a criminal record or a history of mental illness are commonly authorized to buy guns.[190]

Stricter gun control is a major reason why other Western nations have far less gun violence. There are also wrongdoers and deranged people there, but it is harder for them to lay their hands on guns. However, regulations would go only so far in limiting access to guns in America, because it has a world-record number in circulation.[191]

To die-hard partisans of gun rights, there is no relationship between easy access to guns and murders perpetrated with guns. They believe the opposite: more guns make society safer. Numerous politicians therefore oppose basic gun control, back right-to-carry laws, and idealize vigilantism.[192] According to Wayne LaPierre, the head of the National Rifle Association, "the only thing that stops a bad guy with a gun is a good guy with a gun." The NRA is much more popular than its critics realize, as more than half of Americans view it favorably.[193] The NRA spends roughly ten times more on lobbying than all gun control groups combined.[194]

The Second Amendment reads: "A well regulated militia, being necessary to the security of a free State, the right of the people to keep and bear arms, shall not be infringed." Today, conservative and liberal scholars disagree about whether that refers to an individual right to bear arms or a collective right of states to maintain armed militias like the National Guard.[195] Since the 1970s, the NRA has been instrumental in pushing the individualist view, which historically was the minority position.[196] In a 1991 interview, the former chief justice Warren Burger argued that the NRA's interpretation of the Second Amendment was "one of the greatest pieces of fraud, I repeat the word 'fraud,' on the American public by special-interest groups that I have ever seen in my lifetime." Yet the Supreme Court ultimately embraced the NRA's stance in a 2008 decision that further weakened gun control. Dismissing the "well regulated militia" clause, the court's conservative major-ity held by a 5–4 vote that the Second Amendment provides an individual right to possess a firearm.[197] Assuming that the amendment indeed confers such a private right, it is an anachronistic remnant of the revolutionary era.

Fifty-one percent of Americans remained opposed to banning semiauto-matic weapons even after an insane man massacred twenty children and six adults at an elementary school in Newtown, Connecticut.[198] The main reforms later proposed by the Obama administration—background checks at gun shows and bans on assault weapons—were backed by most of the public but failed in Congress.[199] At any rate, the effort's limitations were clear when Vice President Joe Biden urged people to "buy a shotgun" instead of an assault rifle.

The romanticized notion of being able to lead an insurrection against Washington's despotism is a motivating factor for the Second Amendment's fiercest partisans. Sharron Angle, the Nevada Republican who lost a close senatorial race in 2010, identified "Second Amendment remedies" as a recourse against "a tyrannical government." In 2016, gun-toting men took over federal land in Oregon. One died in a standoff with government forces. Twenty-nine percent of Americans, including 44 percent of Republicans, believe that "in the next few years an armed revolution might be necessary in order to protect our liberties."[200]

The obsession with guns reflects a broader subculture of violence. Modern-day Americans are more inclined on average than other Westerners to embrace military force.[201] Even considering the greater risk of criminals being armed in America, its legal system gives the police extensive discretion to kill suspects.[202] In the first twenty-four days of 2015, more people were fatally shot by American police than by police in England and Wales combined over the prior twenty-four years.[203] Certain U.S. politicians emphasize their capacity for violence, such as then-senator Tom Coburn, who declared that "it's just a good thing I can't pack a gun on the Senate floor," to take care of its "elitists" and "cowards," or then–Texas governor Rick Perry, who described himself as "the kind of guy who goes jogging in the morning, packing a Ruger .380 with laser sights and loaded with hollow-point bullets, and shoots a coyote that is threatening his daughter's dog." Perry was cheered at a Republican presidential campaign debate when he said he had no regrets about the 234 prisoners who had been executed during his tenure as Texas governor.[204] Donald Trump's supporters acclaimed him as he vowed to assassinate both terrorists and their families.[205] Like many of his fellow Republicans, he also promised to bring back the Bush administration's torture methods. Trump encouraged mob violence at his rallies too.

American society already had a reputation for violence by the nineteenth century, as dueling or brawling to defend one's honor was relatively common. Alexander Hamilton, the distinguished Founding Father, was mortally wounded in a duel. In the run-up to the Civil War, the South Carolina representative Preston Brooks notoriously used his cane to assault the Massachusetts senator Charles Sumner on the Senate floor. During his journey through the South in the early 1830s, Tocqueville inquired about whether "people in Alabama are as accustomed to violence as is said." His interlocutor, a young lawyer, unequivocally agreed: "Yes, there's no one here who doesn't carry weapons under his clothes. At the slightest quarrel he'll have a knife or a pistol in his hand." The lawyer had several deep scars from his habitual fighting.[206]

At the dawn of the twenty-first century, weapons are deadlier than ever, yet half of Americans think that ordinary citizens should have access to semi-automatic rifles resembling those used by military troops.[207] To a degree, lethal violence in America is what economists call a negative externality, namely an indirect social cost of lax gun control. To some, that is a small price to pay for the "liberty" to clench a gun.

EIGHT

America and the World

America's decision to invade Iraq in 2003 has had far-reaching repercussions. It exacerbated the instability of the Middle East by spurring the rise of ISIS, the ruthless jihadist group that conquered part of Iraq and Syria. ISIS went on to organize or inspire terrorist strikes in the West, which bolstered demagogues playing on fear and Islamophobia. This ultimately contributed to the election of Donald Trump in the United States and strengthened far-right European parties.

In the early stages of the 2016 U.S. presidential race, two candidates struggled to explain their past support for the fateful invasion. Hillary Clinton admitted that her senatorial vote for it was a mistake based on faulty intelligence that Saddam Hussein had weapons of mass destruction (WMDs), had forged an alliance with Al-Qaeda, and was involved in the terrorist attacks of September 11, 2001. Jeb Bush likewise evoked intelligence failures but was loath to recognize that his brother's invasion was a blunder. The debate subsequently focused on whether describing the war as a "mistake" was accurate, given evidence suggesting that the George W. Bush administration had overstated intelligence to justify an invasion driven by perceived geopolitical interests.

Other parts of the equation received little to no attention. We saw in Chapter 2 that the incurious Bush did not know about the historic sectarian tensions between Iraqi Shiites and Sunnis, which contributed to Iraq's destabilization after America toppled Hussein.[1] Bush also tried to persuade French President Jacques Chirac to back the invasion by claiming that it fulfilled biblical prophecies.[2] As Bush predicted that U.S. soldiers would be widely welcomed as liberators, only 41 percent of Americans were aware that most people worldwide strongly condemned the invasion.[3] People with a modicum of knowledge about the Middle East were otherwise puzzled by Bush's conflation of Hussein, a largely secular Arab dictator, and Al-Qaeda, an Islamist terrorist group. Hussein's regime had a record of repressing Islamists.[4] Certain governments, especially those of France and Germany, opposed the war by disputing the intelligence that Bush advanced.[5] They were dismissed as cowards trying to appease Saddam as "old Europe" had once appeased Hitler.[6]

Anti-intellectualism, Christian fundamentalism, and insularity help explain why Bush persuaded a substantial share of Americans to support a war that changed the course of history. These factors have received less attention than other aspects of American exceptionalism influencing U.S. foreign policy, such as its tendency to exempt itself from international law and human rights standards.

However, the "War on Terror" proved intensely controversial, as millions of Americans were appalled by the Bush administration's actions. Clashes over the role that the United States should play as the only global superpower have contributed to the polarization of American society. Other Westerners seldom face such disagreements. That is because their countries are not just far less powerful than America but also less polarized over these issues. A relative consensus exists nowadays among Europeans, Canadians, Australians, and New Zealanders about warfare and basic human rights.[7] The same cannot be said about Americans. Yet it is again the views of American conservatives that are most exceptional. American liberals generally agree with other Westerners that torture is unjustifiable, Guantánamo is troubling, international courts have more benefits than costs, and the 2003 invasion of Iraq was a mistake. In contrast, many American conservatives continued to defend the Iraq War even after it became evident that Hussein did not have WMDs or an alliance with Al-Qaeda.[8] While some American conservatives have denounced torture and Guantánamo, they have been more inclined than liberals to embrace these practices. No less than 79 percent of self-identified U.S. conservatives believe America should continue to operate the Guantánamo detention camp, compared to 33 percent of liberals.[9] Around 61 percent of Republicans think that torture is justifiable, next to 40 percent of Democrats.[10] American conservatives have additionally played a crucial role in keeping the United States from adhering to international law, as Republican senators have historically led efforts to block the ratification of multiple treaties.[11]

Foreign policy differences between Democrats and Republicans are not absolute. Barack Obama opposed the Iraq War and announced an end to torture but, as we will see, pursued other aspects of Bush's "War on Terror" and sometimes took them further. Nevertheless, Donald Trump was elected president after painting Obama as a weak leader, threatening to use military force more aggressively, openly defying the international community, promising to reinstate torture, and planning to end America's participation in the Paris Agreement—the landmark 2015 international accord against climate change that Obama had firmly supported.

Experts commonly analyze foreign affairs by focusing closely on international law, policy-making, and geopolitics. In this chapter I take a different approach, beginning with American cultural peculiarities and then offering a theory of how this social context helps shape attitudes toward foreign policy and international law. These two approaches are not incompatible, yet the latter can shed light on the neglected roots of America's exceptional relationship to the world.

RIVAL WORLDVIEWS

Living in Texas, I regularly saw on TV a recruitment commercial for the U.S. Marines titled "Contest of Honor." [12] It featured a man slaying a hideous fire monster in a coliseum while spectators cheered. The man then transformed into a uniformed marine. The message was clear: U.S. soldiers are the incarnation of good, the nation's enemies are simply evil, and people are expected to cheer for war. But what is perhaps most remarkable about this video is that it was created before September 11, 2001. It symbolizes the longstanding influence of a self-righteous, black-and-white worldview in American society that only grew stronger once the "War on Terror" began.

In the age of mass media, a video montage gone viral embodies a rival worldview. Named "Where the Hell Is Matt?," it features a globe-trotting American joyfully performing a dance routine with locals in dozens of countries worldwide. [13] This compelling performance reflects a belief in reaching out to other cultures, and it is revealing that an American, Matt Harding, took the initiative of realizing it.

These two videos illustrate two conflicting worldviews. Even though Americans have long been influential on the global stage, some have maintained an insular mentality comparable to the one that reinforced the nation's isolationist foreign policy between the First and Second World Wars. Millions of Americans rarely or never travel abroad and have sparse knowledge of foreign nations. Parochial and chauvinistic mindsets are typically matched by fierce suspicion of diplomacy, the United Nations, and international law. The Americans who share this outlook are prepared to embrace a deeply unilateral foreign policy if it appears to serve U.S. interests. They have limited qualms about military force or the clout of the military-industrial complex. While this worldview is prevalent among Republicans, in Europe it can be found almost only among supporters of extreme-right, nationalist parties nowadays.

America's global citizens tend to see the world differently. These citizens have traveled internationally, are eager to learn about foreign cultures, and have made parts of the United States highly cosmopolitan. One frequently comes across such Americans when traveling in Europe, Africa, Asia, or Latin America. They want America to assert its influence through diplomatic cooperation with the international community. They are wary of military force. Their approach to international affairs is comparable to those of most other Westerners.

Naturally, these two camps are not all-encompassing, as numerous Americans are neither parochial chauvinists nor global citizens. But these social tensions exist and stem from key dimensions of American exceptionalism.

Patriotism and Nationalism

Eight in ten Americans agree that "the U.S. has a unique character that makes it the greatest country in the world." [14] Politicians of both parties recurrently emphasize faith in American superiority. Barack Obama declared that America is the "greatest nation on Earth" and "a light to the world." His rival Mitt Romney described it similarly: "The greatest nation in the history of the world and a force for good." As the journalist Scott Shane observed, modern-day Americans demand from their leaders "constant reassurance that their country, their achievements and their values are extraordinary." [15]

This is not a new development. Leo Damrosch, an American scholar, noted that nineteenth-century European travelers were "exasperated by the Americans' tendency to boast about their country and to extort compliments from visitors." Along with flattering observations about the United States, Alexis de Tocqueville wrote that "the people here seem to me to be stinking with national conceit." [16] He added that "no pains have been spared to convince the inhabitants of the United States that they constitute the only religious, enlightened, and free people." [17]

Americans do not have a monopoly on national chauvinism. Charles de Gaulle and other Gallic leaders, for instance, have historically promoted a sublime image of France. A study asked people in various countries whether they agreed that "our people are not perfect, but our culture is superior to others." The proportion of Americans who agreed (49 percent) was similar to those of Germans (47 percent) and Spaniards (44 percent). A significant, albeit lower, share of British (32 percent) and French (27 percent) people also did.[18] Yet polls can fail to account for intensity of belief. One reason why chauvinism is more intense in the United States is that Americans are both far more religious than Europeans and far likelier to think that their country's greatness has been bestowed by God. Six in ten believe that "God has granted America a special role in human history."[19] Such ideas were fairly common in European countries in the age of their colonial empires. But few Europeans would seriously claim nowadays that God has made their country superior to others. U.S. politicians routinely proclaim "God bless America," which comes across as arrogant navel-gazing to foreigners. If a benevolent God exists, it should bless all countries.

A comparative study confirms that Americans are particularly proud of their nationality. They also appear more self-righteous than other Westerners in claiming the authority to act militarily regardless of opposition from the international community.[20] Consider this declaration by Mitt Romney: "God did not create this country to be a nation of followers. America is not destined to be one of several equally balanced global powers." Such rhetoric is ordinary in America. In European countries, only far-right, anti-immigration parties express their sense of national superiority so bluntly, and they usually do not bring God into the picture.

Americans rarely call this kind of rhetoric by its name: *nationalism*. At most, critics fault the politicians who speak that way for their excessive "patriotism." But patriotism (loving one's country) is different from nationalism (believing that it is superior). Nationalism is a complex phenomenon often animated by the notion that a country should either dominate others or isolate itself from the rest of the world. Both tendencies are palpable in American nationalism, given the draw of imperialism and insularity.

The roots of American nationalism can largely be traced to the revolutionary era. The Founding Fathers widely believed that they had created an ideal country blessed by Providence that would stand apart from the corrupt outside world.[21] Thomas Jefferson warned that "an American coming to Europe for education, loses in his knowledge, in his morals, in his health, in his habits, and in his happiness." [22]

Faith that America is fulfilling a divinely chosen destiny suggests that atrocities in its history, from the extermination or expulsion of Native Americans to the enslavement of Africans, were part of God's plan. That is indeed what European colonists and their American descendants usually thought. The Indians' military defeats and losses of land were interpreted as signs that God was not on their side. The viruses that decimated them were considered another godsend. In the words of John Archdale, a British colonial official, "unusual Sicknesses" sent by God thinned the indigenous population "to make room for the English" and pave the way for "introducing a Civilized State" in America.[23] Similarly, African slavery was rationalized as a way to civilize and Christianize savages.

The canonization of the Founding Fathers evokes the spirit of nationalism, which is buoyed by an unbridled veneration of national heroes. For example, one of Ronald Reagan's speeches would have us forget that when America was founded, slavery existed and only propertied white males could vote: "In this country of ours took place the greatest revolution that has ever taken place in the world's history; the only true revolution. Every other revolution simply exchanged one set of rulers for another. But here, for the first time in all the thousands of years of man's relations to man, a little group of men, the Founding Fathers, for the first time, established the idea that you and I had within ourselves the God-given right and ability to determine our own destiny."

The tendency to minimize past wrongs is obviously not unique to Americans. Many Europeans downplay shameful aspects of their history, such as the practice of slavery or the atrocities that their colonial empires committed. Gérard Longuet, a prominent French conservative politician, tellingly made a forearm jerk—a variant of the middle finger—during a 2012 TV interview to show what he thought of Algeria's demand for "an honest acknowledgment of the crimes perpetrated by French colonialism." Longuet later asserted that "France need not be ashamed of its presence in Algeria during colonization."[24] Because of a mix of denial and ignorance, scores of French people do not recognize the realities of colonialism: invading a foreign land, exploiting its population and resources, violently repressing dissent, all while claiming that one is civilizing primitive people, if not inferior races. The rise of far-right European political parties has bolstered the idealization of colonialism, as they aim to return to a supposedly idyllic time when whites were in power. Donald Trump's campaign had a similar message.

Beside the fact that the G.O.P. is a mainstream party, unlike European far-right parties, nationalism is particularly common in America because it is promoted on a daily basis: U.S. flags are ubiquitous, the national anthem is sung at everyday sporting events, and schoolchildren recite the Pledge of Allegiance. Such rituals, which hardly exist in other Western democracies, encourage people to think that loving one's country means regularly singing its praises and having unquestioning allegiance to it.

The Worldly and the Insular

"No man is an island, entire of itself," wrote the poet John Donne, yet America can come across as a nation disconnected from the rest of the world. At a time when America has been facing Islamist terrorism, has led wars in Afghanistan and Iraq, and has long been heavily involved in the Muslim world, half of Americans do not know what the Koran or Ramadan are.[25] This exemplifies a remarkable contradiction: America actively influences the world but much of its population knows very little about things beyond its borders. While multiple factors and interests shape U.S. foreign policy, it cannot be understood outside this social context.

Ironically, as a global superpower America would seem to be the precise opposite of an insular country. The intense polarization of liberal and conservative Americans sheds light on this paradox, as it tends to mirror the divide between worldly and insular citizens. Two figures embody this social divide. Barack Obama is the exemplar of a global citizen because of his mixed American and Kenyan background, not to forget his partial upbringing in Indonesia. Conversely, Sarah Palin, the archetype of parochial reactionarism, did not obtain a passport before 2006. She had left North America only once when she became the 2008 Republican vice presidential candidate.[26] Just 30 percent of Americans have a passport, compared to approximately 50 percent of Australians, 60 percent of Canadians, 75 percent of New Zealanders, and 80 percent of the British.[27] Naturally, some Americans do not travel internationally because they are poor. But scores of middle-class people are also disinclined to do so. Additionally, some of the Americans who do travel internationally go only to tourist resorts like Cancún. Of an estimated sixty-one million international trips originating in the United States in 2009, about half were to either Mexico or Canada.[28] The point is not that

Americans as a whole are insular—many travel abroad—but that they are more likely than other Westerners to share that trait.

One of the reasons why Americans travel less is that they have fewer vacation days. Besides, there is much to visit within America, including fascinating cities, national parks, ski resorts, beaches, and deserts. Further, the United States is relatively isolated geographically as a continent-size country situated between two oceans and with only two immediate neighbors.

Living in different regions of America, I met a fair number of university-educated people who had limited knowledge of the world. Some thought that Indians, Iranians, and Turks are Arabs. One college student did not know that Britain is an island. Others were unaware of the existence of several foreign countries, including Kazakhstan, Mauritania, and Slovenia. A Latvian woman I met in New York asked me, with a concerned look, if I knew of Latvia. I said I did. She sighed in relief and explained that many New Yorkers had never heard of her country. By the same token, a Lithuanian acquaintance residing in a Virginian suburb of Washington, D.C., became accustomed to saying that she was from Russia, because most of the Americans she met had never heard of Lithuania.

Rick Shenkman, a U.S. academic, made a comparable observation when describing his discussion with a young American he met aboard a train from Paris to Amsterdam: "[He] had graduated from college and was now considering medical school. He had received good grades in school. He was articulate. And he was anything but poor, as was clear from the fact that he was spending the summer tooling around Europe. But when the subject involved history, he was stumped. When the conversation turned to Joseph Stalin, he had to ask who Stalin was." [29]

Polls confirm that a sizable segment of Americans know little about world history, including events that involved America. Forty percent are unaware of who America fought in World War II.[30] Thirty percent do not know what the Holocaust was.[31] In 1980, during the Cold War, 38 percent of Americans thought that the Soviet Union was part of the North Atlantic Treaty Organization (NATO), an anti-Soviet alliance.[32] A comparative study found that Americans know far less than Brits, Danes, and Finns about basic aspects of international affairs, as Table 7 indicates. Americans were less likely to correctly identify the Taliban, even though the United States led the invasion of Afghanistan after the 9/11 attacks on American soil. Similarly, fewer Americans could identify the Kyoto Accords as a treaty on climate change, Kofi Annan as the United Nations secretary-general, or

TABLE 7 Percentage of correct answers to international affairs questions

Topic	United States	United Kingdom	Denmark	Finland
Taliban	58	75	68	76
Kyoto Accords	37	60	81	84
Kofi Annan	49	82	91	95
Slobodan Milošević	33	58	78	72

SOURCE: Shanto Iyengar, James Curran, and Anker Brink Lund, "Media Systems, Public Knowledge and Democracy," *European Journal of Communication* 24, no. 1 (2009): 5–29.

Slobodan Milošević as the Serbian leader against whom America and other countries went to war. A later study again concluded that "the knowledge gap between the Americans and the Europeans was huge" on international news.[33]

Even America's closest allies sometimes come across as obscure foreign lands. Professor Charles Lockhart of Texas Christian University, an expert in comparative politics, was "frequently surprised by how sketchy the understandings of intelligent, well-educated Americans are of the most fundamental differences between politics in the United States and in societies relatively well-known to Americans such as the United Kingdom or Canada."[34] Chauvinism and ignorance of foreign countries usually go hand in hand. John Kingdon, who taught at the University of Michigan, noticed that students generally entered his classes with the conviction that America is simply "the best" despite having "very little knowledge" of other countries.[35]

Yet numerous American universities have top-notch international programs for students eager to broaden their horizons. And the cosmopolitan environment at certain American universities is the antithesis of insularity. My personal experiences studying and teaching in American universities were overwhelmingly positive. Faculty and students aware of my French and Kenyan roots were warm and welcoming regardless of whether their academic fields had an international dimension. Few seemed to share the ultra-chauvinistic perspective trumpeted by various politicians. This may be because America's universities often lean to the left of the political spectrum. Comparably, the views of the French extreme right have limited traction at French universities.

The parochialism of many U.S. politicians is nonetheless striking. George W. Bush declared that "Africa is a nation that suffers from incredible disease," echoing the misconception that Africa is a homogeneous country rather than a diverse continent. Likewise, the presidential candidate and tycoon Herman Cain said he wanted to prevent China from acquiring nuclear weapons, although it had already been a nuclear power for half a century. It is no coincidence that such politicians lean toward Christian fundamentalism, as those who most fervently believe that God made America "the best" may have scant interest in the rest of the world.

Basic knowledge of foreign nations easily disproves certain claims at the heart of the U.S. political debate, as we have seen throughout this book. If politicians and the public were better informed, for instance, they might not claim that countries with universal health care have much higher medical costs. The precise opposite is true. Well-traveled Americans are far less inclined to accept propaganda about the evils of "socialized medicine." The political divide on this issue is remarkable as well. In the abstract, both Republicans and Democrats affirm that America is the world's best country.[36] In practice, however, Democrats appear less chauvinistic. Prior to Obama's health care reform, 68 percent of Republicans thought that the U.S. health care system was "the best" worldwide, compared to 32 percent of Democrats.[37] Most Democrats want America to join the rest of the developed world in establishing universal health care. Republicans are adamantly against it.[38]

Whether America has anything to learn from other countries has become a divisive matter in its courtrooms. References to international human rights standards in Supreme Court decisions abolishing the death penalty for juveniles and the mentally retarded scandalized both dissenting justices and Republican politicians.[39] In the age of globalization, it is common for courts in democratic nations to evaluate foreign legal practices when deciding intricate or novel issues.[40] But this tends to divide conservative and liberal Americans. During the Supreme Court confirmation hearings for Elena Kagan—an Obama appointee and former dean of Harvard Law School—a Republican senator took offense at Harvard's requirement that students take a course in international law. Another Republican senator voiced concern that citizens "could turn to foreign law to get good ideas."[41] Kagan responded that foreign law can be instructive, a point that would be uncontroversial elsewhere in the West.

As America has the world's oldest written constitution, foreign countries have regularly turned to it for inspiration, given its numerous wise principles of government. Yet certain Americans favor a one-sided approach. They are content to have America serve as a model abroad but believe that it has nothing to learn from foreign laws, as they regard the U.S. Constitution as a sacrosanct text. This attitude is common among proponents of "originalism," a doctrine holding that the Constitution's meaning cannot evolve over time—irrespective of unforeseeable developments, changing values, or the profound disagreements among the framers themselves over how to interpret the Constitution. The historian Joseph Ellis suggested that this doctrine is rooted in the belief that the Founding Fathers were miraculously "permitted a glimpse of the eternal verities and then embalmed their insights in the document." "Any professional historian proposing such an interpretation today would be laughed off the stage," Ellis observed. "We might call it the Immaculate Conception theory of jurisprudence." [42]

In sum, Americans are quite divided in their global outlooks, although those who share deeply nationalistic and insular mindsets especially stand out in the West nowadays. These citizens have played a major role in shaping the "War on Terror," with grave consequences for America and the world.

THE VICIOUS CIRCLES OF U.S. FOREIGN POLICY

Even considering that America was emotionally vulnerable to calls for retribution after 9/11, the ease with which the Bush administration manipulated most of the public is remarkable. Nearly all Republicans and around half of Democrats supported the 2003 invasion of Iraq, which was widely unpopular throughout the world. Support decreased among Democrats as the plan turned into a fiasco and as it became clear that Saddam Hussein neither had ties to Al-Qaeda nor WMDs—notwithstanding Dick Cheney's assertion that Hussein "has, in fact, reconstituted nuclear weapons." But Republican support for the war remained steadfast. Three years after the invasion, 80 percent of Republicans continued to back the Iraq War. Barely 20 percent of Democrats still did. [43] Statistical research shows that the partisan divide was much deeper over the Iraq War than over the Vietnam War. [44] As of 2015, merely 31 percent of Republicans recognized that invading Iraq was a mistake, compared to 68 percent of Democrats. Overall, only 51 percent of all Americans deemed the Iraq War a mistake. [45] These findings are striking because the Bush administration's 2003 invasion of Iraq predictably exacerbated terrorism well before the emergence of ISIS, as Robert Pape and James Feldman emphasized in a statistical study published in 2010:

Far from declining, anti-American-inspired terrorism—particularly suicide terrorism—is more frequent today than before 9/11 and even before the invasion of Iraq. In the 24-year period from 1980 to 2003, there were just under 350 suicide terrorist attacks around the world—of which fewer than 15% could reasonably be considered directed against Americans. By contrast, in the six years from 2004 to 2009, the world has witnessed over 1,833 suicide attacks—of which 92% are anti-American in origin.... The more we've gone over there, the more they've wanted to come over here—and the absence of another 9/11 is due more to extensive American domestic security measures, immigration controls, intelligence, and pure luck than to lack of intent or planning by our enemies.[46]

Multiple jihadist plots were envisioned as retaliation for the invasion of Iraq, including the 2004 Madrid and 2005 London terrorist bombings.[47] Similarly, the two French jihadists who killed *Charlie Hebdo* cartoonists in January 2015 were partly radicalized by the U.S. invasion of Iraq and the mistreatment of Muslims by American personnel at Abu Ghraib.[48]

Naturally, the global crisis of terrorism cannot be pinned simply on the Bush administration. We will see below that Obama's foreign policy also was counterproductive. European leaders such as François Hollande, the French president, deserve blame too. Although France opposed the 2003 invasion of Iraq, it joined the American-led coalition against ISIS in Iraq in 2014, which led ISIS to identify France as a prime target.[49] Among other factors, the 2015 Paris attacks can be traced to the shortcomings of France's counterterrorism services and the marginalization of underprivileged French Muslims, some of whom have become jihadists. Nevertheless, legions of ISIS members come from privileged socioeconomic backgrounds or countries where Muslims are a majority, thereby demonstrating that the troubling discrimination against European Muslims is hardly the sole reason behind the rise of ISIS.[50] This complex phenomenon lacks a single explanation and has, of course, also been influenced by the Middle East's internal dynamics, including the Syrian Civil War. Even after taking these nuances into account, there is no doubt that the Bush administration's war on Iraq profoundly worsened global terrorism. Why did most Americans readily believe in 2003, as many still do, that invading Iraq was the right decision?

Good versus Evil

If the United States incarnates good in this world to numerous Americans, the flip side is that the nation's enemies can come to represent evil. This may not seem remarkable at first. After all, the people of any country tend to view themselves positively and their enemies negatively. But what sets America apart in the modern democratic world is the impact of a black-and-white moralism encapsulated in George W. Bush's farewell speech: "I have often spoken to you about good and evil. This has made some uncomfortable. But good and evil are present in this world, and between the two there can be no compromise." The tendency to see the world in dualistic terms of good versus evil is especially palpable among Americans with nationalistic and insular mindsets. It heavily influenced U.S. foreign policy and the "War on Terror" during the Bush presidency.

Shortly after the 9/11 attacks, a cleric in the Lutheran Church–Missouri Synod, a fundamentalist denomination, told Bush that he was "a servant of God called for such a time like this." Bush answered, "I accept this responsibility." Bush also gave a speech at the National Cathedral in Washington declaring that America's "responsibility" is to "rid the world of evil." [51] Like a comic book character, he set out to fight an "Axis of Evil," warning, "Either you're with us or you're with the terrorists." In his eyes, America was "chosen by God and commissioned by history to be a model to the world."

The best-selling author Joel Rosenberg, a proponent of apocalyptic prophecies, was invited to speak at a White House Bible study. He met with various congressional leaders and national security officials to advise them on biblical prophecies purportedly relevant to U.S. foreign policy.[52] Rosenberg said he did not meet with Bush during this visit, although Bush himself claimed that a divine signal inspired his "crusade" against Islamic terrorism. "I was praying for strength to do the Lord's will," he explained after invading Iraq.[53] Asked whether he had consulted his father about the war, Bush famously answered: "There is a higher father that I appeal to." He tried to persuade French President Jacques Chirac to support his invasion of Iraq by arguing that it fulfilled biblical prophecies about an apocalyptic conflict between good and evil that would precede the Messiah's return. Bush's exegesis baffled Chirac.[54] Bush likewise invoked God when trying to convince King Abdullah II of Jordan to back the invasion.[55] Bush's spiritual acumen also supposedly gave him insight into the mind of Vladimir Putin, Russia's cynical dictator. "I looked the man in the eye. I found him to be very straightforward and trustworthy," Bush said. "I was able to get a sense of his soul."

The religious rhetoric surrounding the Iraq campaign made some soldiers uneasy. A marine reported that "it was frowned upon" to opt out of chapel and prayer sessions. Chaplains came into bunkers and said, "Bow your heads and pray." Base personnel received a daily prayer by email. The marine had difficulty coping with the fact that troops had "killed a lot of people" during her first tour of duty. When she asked for help, she was sent to a chaplain, even though she did not believe in God.[56] Trijicon, a weapons manufacturer with a $660 million military contract, took it upon itself to engrave biblical references on rifles used by U.S. soldiers in Afghanistan and Iraq. It stopped doing so after a public outcry led military leaders to object to the inscriptions.[57]

The fascination of Christian fundamentalists with an apocalyptic conflict in the Middle East was not new. The presidential notes of George H. W. Bush indicate that the prominent evangelical preacher Billy Graham, who was close to the Bushes, supported the 1991 Gulf War and thought that Hussein was the "anti-Christ."[58] Still, Bush the elder was religiously moderate next to his son, who appointed General William Boykin to head the hunt for Osama bin Laden. An outspoken evangelical, Boykin asserted that America was leading "the army of God" in a fight against "Satan."[59]

To an extent, the "War on Terror" devolved into a conflict between fundamentalist conceptions of Islam and Christianity. The infusion of religion into warfare had gone full circle when the Navy SEAL who killed bin Laden in Pakistan proclaimed that he had done so "for God and for country." Bin Laden's death occurred during a mission authorized by Obama, who had stood against Bush's invasion of Iraq. It is noteworthy that Vice President Joe Biden, a moderate Catholic, anxiously clenched a rosary when following the bin Laden mission from the White House. Biden suggested that those in attendance go to mass after the mission.[60] Yet faith did not significantly influence the Obama administration's foreign policy, as opposed to the Bush administration.

Self-righteousness buoyed by faith particularly helps explain why Bush and much of the American public thought that U.S. troops would be broadly acclaimed as liberators in Iraq. Americans commonly envisioned themselves as "the good guys," who would get rid of Saddam, "the bad guy." A predictable insurgency was not anticipated. Nor was the fact that invading a Muslim country on questionable grounds and against strong opposition from the international community would exacerbate the resentment and anti-Americanism that contribute to terrorism.[61] Standard counterinsurgency strategy, which stresses measured force and efforts to gain the trust of the local population, was mostly ignored in Iraq under Bush. American troops emphasized force in dealing with both actual and suspected insurgents. This led to abuse that was not limited to the Abu Ghraib scandal. A significant number of

Iraqi civilians were humiliated, threatened, beaten up, baselessly detained, or otherwise mistreated by U.S. troops, ruining the efforts of American soldiers who honestly tried to help Iraqis.[62] It was not before several years into the war that various officers, including General David Petraeus, finally led a shift toward standard counterinsurgency strategy.[63] Its premise is straightforward: excessive force is counterproductive, alienating locals and spurring resistance. That dynamic may seem evident. However, people with a moralistic perspective are disinclined to consider social factors behind terrorism because they tend to identify their enemies as simply "evil."

Self-righteousness has also shaped U.S. attitudes toward Iran, which Bush included in the "Axis of Evil." The popular perception of Iran as plainly evil disregards the fact that its Islamist regime was preceded by a pro-American dictatorship led by the Shah, a secular monarch who amassed a fortune through corruption while the multitude struggled. Back in 1953, America, Britain, and the Shah conspired to depose Mohammed Mosaddeq, Iran's democratically elected prime minister, who was faulted for nationalizing Iran's oil production.[64] Yet the Shah's dictatorship and America's meddling in Iranian affairs helped radicalize the elements who led Iran's Islamic Revolution in 1979, who have themselves promoted a Manichean view of America as "The Great Satan."

People may disagree over whether it is wiser not to interfere in foreign states or to support "the lesser of two evils" when hostile factions exist within a country. America has often preferred the latter course. Indeed, what largely drives U.S. foreign policy is not virtue but realpolitik—a geostrategy based on raw calculations of a nation's perceived best interest. Realpolitik negates idealistic and humane considerations unless they are politically advantageous, such as by improving a nation's image.

Hence, America chooses which dictators are good or bad depending on whether they serve its interests. Saddam Hussein was depicted as an evil tyrant who oppressed his own people. President Hosni Mubarak of Egypt was praised as a solid U.S. ally even though he ruled with an iron fist. Iran is faulted for its authoritarianism, Islamist extremism, and oppression of women, yet Saudi Arabia has historically been one of America's closest allies despite sharing these traits. Naturally, realpolitik and its double standards are hardly unique to America. Britain, France, and other countries have likewise backed ruthless regimes sympathetic to their interests. But the cynicism of realpolitik coexists with an exceptionally moralistic bent in U.S. foreign policy.

At first glance, realpolitik seems incompatible with the notion that God has made America a force for good, since, by definition, supporting "the lesser of two evils" means supporting evil. Self-righteous rhetoric can be a smoke screen for ulterior motives. The Bush administration certainly would not have invaded Iraq simply out of religious conviction or to altruistically spread democracy in the Middle East, as neoconservatives claimed. However, moralism is not solely a pretext in U.S. foreign policy, given that it can also shape policy decisions and serve to rationalize contradictions. It is comforting to believe that America is waging a battle for good against evil when one is faced with countless civilian deaths in Afghanistan and Iraq, the use of torture, the abuses of pro-American dictatorships, and other consequences of realpolitik.

Interest in black gold was more readily acknowledged in the First Gulf War, precipitated by Hussein's 1990 invasion of Kuwait. Colin Powell then wrote that "since the free flow of oil from the Persian Gulf was as crucial to us as blood pumping through an artery, Iraqi and Iranian threats to Kuwaiti oil tankers would be met."[65] In contrast, American partisans of the 2003 invasion of Iraq were generally duplicitous or in self-denial about oil. Tony Blair, who defied British public opinion by thrusting the United Kingdom into the war, was somewhat franker when questioned by a British commission. "I think it is at least arguable that [Hussein] was a threat and that, had we taken that decision to leave him there with the intent, with an oil price, not of $25, but of $100 a barrel, he would have had the intent, he would have had the financial means and we would have lost our nerve," Blair said.[66] The former prime minister's statement epitomizes not only the speculation behind this preemptive war but also the notion that Westerners are entitled to obtain oil from developing countries at a satisfactory price. Imagine the leader of a poor nation claiming that invading America or Europe is justified because their technology is too expensive.

Overall, the Bush administration's intelligence on Iraq was blatantly false.[67] It is unclear whether it deliberately advanced false intelligence or recklessly used unreliable intelligence while ignoring contrary information.[68] In any event, it undoubtedly persuaded itself that toppling Hussein was imperative because of perceived national security and geopolitical interests. Paul O'Neill, who attended National Security Council meetings as the Treasury secretary, reported that ten days after Bush's inauguration—long before 9/11—the administration began discussing how to effect regime change in Iraq, occupy it militarily, and secure access to its oil. After 9/11, Bush took war on Iraq as a foregone conclusion.[69] Powell and George Tenet, who respectively served as Bush's secretary of state and CIA director, acknowledged that the war was hardly debated.[70] Notes taken by Donald Rumsfeld's aides indicate that within hours of the 9/11 attacks, the defense secretary was considering whether to "hit SH [Saddam Hussein] at same time—not only UBL [Usama bin Laden]."[71]

Lieutenant-General Gregory Newbold, then the director of operations for the Joint Chiefs of Staff, recalled that a large fraction of the military leadership was taken aback by the Bush administration's agenda. "I can't tell you how many senior officers said to me, 'What in the hell are we doing?'" "They just didn't understand," he said. "'Why Iraq? Why now?'" Newbold chose to retire because of his opposition to the war.[72] Dissent was nonetheless markedly limited, given the enormity of the Bush administration's actions.

Drawing Peculiar Lessons from History

The lessons that Americans have drawn or not drawn from history have often set them apart from other Westerners. They help explain why America boldly invaded Iraq against considerable opposition from the international community, thereby worsening strife in the Middle East.

America emerged from the Cold War as the world's sole superpower. The collapse of the Soviet bloc confirmed the United States' sense of moral superiority. The atheism of communist regimes and their repression of religion strengthened the notion that America is a divinely chosen country. To many Americans, Ronald Reagan brought down the Soviet Union by bravely standing against communism and forcing the Russians into an arms race they could not keep up with.

While America was indeed an important bulwark against Russian imperialism, the Soviet bloc's collapse largely stemmed from longstanding internal problems.[73] Communist economies failed to create wealth, as illustrated by the stark differences in living standards between the U.S.S.R. and the United States or between East and West Germany. Moreover, the oppression of communism spurred recurrent protests, which ultimately were somewhat tolerated—some would even say encouraged—by Mikhail Gorbachev. Pope John Paul II and dissidents such as Andrey Sakharov, Aleksandr Solzhenitsyn, Václav Havel, and Lech Wałęsa also had an influential historical role in rousing people against communism. Nevertheless, the popular image of Reagan single-handedly defeating the atheist Soviet empire, like Saint George slew the dragon, fostered confidence in the United States' ability to prevail against evil.

America's decisive victory in World War II likewise shaped that perspective. References to World War II were therefore frequent in the run-up to the 2003 invasion of Iraq. The Bush administration and its supporters depicted the war's most influential adversaries, French President Jacques Chirac and German Chancellor Gerhard Schröder, as naïve and pusillanimous pacifists who recalled the "old Europe" that had tried to appease Hitler. On the other hand, Tony Blair, Silvio Berlusconi, and José María Aznar—respectively the British, Italian, and Spanish prime ministers—were lauded for embodying a "new Europe," given their support for invading Iraq, notwithstanding the fact that most of their citizens condemned the war. Even though the invasion of Iraq was widely unpopular worldwide, 56 percent of Americans thought that global opinion either favored the war or was evenly divided.[74] Americans eager to invade Iraq mainly equated opposition with the pesky French, prompting irritated hawks to spill out their supplies of French wine.

The epithet "old Europe" evoked the naïveté and ineptitude of the British and French governments of the 1930s, which had indeed failed to grasp the threat that Hitler posed. The French leadership was especially reprehensible, as its poor strategy caused France to suffer a quick and humiliating defeat to the Third Reich. A visit to the D-Day beaches and the local U.S. military cemetery in Normandy provides a compelling reminder of the sacrifice that Americans made in liberating Europe. America was, by far, the main reason the Allies won the war. Yet the Bush administration's suggestion that America took the initiative in combating Nazism while cowardly Europeans refused to fight was historical revisionism. America was ambivalent about entering World War II and did not do so until after Japan's attack on Pearl Harbor on December 7, 1941, well after the war started in 1939.

The denunciation of "old Europe" in 2003 resonated with nationalistic Americans partly because many had drawn lessons from World War II distinct from those of Europeans, who experienced the conflict quite differently. While the war was hardly fought on American soil, it ravaged Europe. Additionally, the outcome confirmed America's military and economic superiority. The British and French never regained their global power and soon lost their colonial empires. The toll of the war was even worse for Germany. World War II was the culmination of centuries of warfare in Europe, and it helped persuade Europeans that they must live together peacefully—an aspiration that motivated the creation of the European Union.

Naturally, European reservations about warfare are far from categorical. Following World War II, certain European states tried to brutally crush armed independence movements in their colonies, such as France in Madagascar, Indochina, and Algeria; the Netherlands in Indonesia; and the United Kingdom in Kenya. (Several other colonies attained independence through fairly peaceful processes.) European nations have further been involved in NATO operations, including in Afghanistan following 9/11.

Still, a comparative study confirms that modern Americans are more supportive than other Westerners of military force. Americans express the strongest support for the right to preemptively attack a foreign nation, as well as the lowest support for the idea that countries should gain U.N. approval before using military force.[75] The more powerful a country is, the more military victory may be plausible in its eyes. From that standpoint, it is unsurprising that war seems a more attractive means of conflict resolution to Americans than to Europeans. However, most of the major wars fought by America since World War II have shown the limits of military power. The Korean War ended in stalemate and the Vietnam War in defeat. At this time it appears that the Afghan War will end in stalemate. The invasion of Iraq was either a Pyrrhic victory or a defeat, considering that it contributed to the rise and spread of ISIS. The Iraq War left nearly forty-five hundred Americans dead and many more suffering from physical or mental wounds. The number of Iraqi deaths directly or indirectly caused by the war is harder to estimate but appears to be approximately half a million.[76]

In particular, the invasion of Iraq was comparable to the Vietnam debacle, as both were unnecessary wars with considerable human and financial costs that profoundly damaged America's global standing. Four decades after the Vietnam War, Vietnam remains a one-party communist state. It is hard to believe that the existence of communism in that remote country has significantly threatened the United States, even though 58,000 Americans died in this conflict, not to mention 1 to 3.8 million Vietnamese (sources differ).[77] The prediction that the fall of Vietnam would have a domino effect, leading multiple other countries to become communist, was never realized. The historian Arthur Schlesinger Jr. doubted that most Americans had learned anything from this conflict. "[In Vietnam] we suffered military defeat—fighting an unwinnable war against a country about which we knew nothing and in which we had no vital interests at stake," he lamented, "but to repeat the same experiment thirty years later in Iraq is a strong argument for a case of national stupidity."[78] Indeed, America being deathly afraid of Iraq was like an elephant fearing a mouse. Yet insular-minded citizens were swayed by the Bush administration's disinformation, from nonexistent WMDs to the notion that there was no difference between the secular tyrant Saddam Hussein and Al-Qaeda jihadists, who were actually enemies. Hussein had long persecuted jihadists. Bush lumped them all together.[79]

Remarkably, the "War on Terror" was also defended on the ground that it would protect America's "freedom." The wars in Afghanistan and Iraq were respectively named Operation Enduring Freedom and Operation Iraqi Freedom. French fries and French toast were rebaptized "freedom fries" and "freedom toast." U.S. troops were said to be fighting in Iraq and Afghanistan so that Americans could continue to be "free"—a peculiar contention, given that terrorists do not genuinely aspire to turn America into an Islamist dictatorship. Their main goal has instead been to expunge American influence from the Muslim world in order to establish theocracies there.[80] The invasion of Iraq could therefore have been defended on the ground that it protected Americans' safety, albeit unconvincingly, since Iraq had nothing to do with 9/11. But to say that Americans were fighting for their own freedom was absurd. So was the claim that the primary reason to invade Iraq was to bring freedom to its people.[81]

Unilateralism

The Bush administration's invasion of Iraq violated international law, as U.N. Secretary-General Kofi Annan underlined, reflecting the consensus among legal experts.[82] Similarly, its decision to torture presumed terrorists blatantly violated international human rights standards and the U.N. Convention against Torture, which America ratified in 1994. (Torture also violates domestic U.S. law.) Bush further asserted the power to detain alleged terrorists forever without trial, another flagrant international human rights violation. Such unilateralism did not begin with his administration, as America has long stood out among modern Western democracies for refusing to follow norms of diplomacy and international law that it deems against its interests.

For generations, the United States has been involved in creating international laws and institutions while exempting itself from their jurisdiction, mainly because of the opposition of conservatives.[83] The first major episode in this pattern occurred in the aftermath of World War I, when President Woodrow Wilson proposed a League of Nations to help resolve conflicts diplomatically and avoid warfare. The League of Nations was eventually founded, but America never joined it, as the Senate refused to heed Wilson's call to ratify the treaty.

Given its failure to prevent the carnage of World War II and other conflicts, the League of Nations was deemed ineffective and replaced by the United Nations, which was founded with active American support. This time America rejected isolationism and immediately became a member of the U.N., whose headquarters are in New York. While the League of Nations was considered a paper tiger, the U.N. has broader ability to authorize peacekeeping operations. However, its charter ensures that no U.N. troops will be dispatched without the consent of the United States, the United Kingdom, France, China, and Russia. These five countries are permanent members of the U.N. Security Council, authorized to veto any of its resolutions. The U.N. is sometimes described as an obstacle to U.S. power, but America has significant power within the organization because of its veto. In addition, Americans are quite well represented among U.N. staff members. The United States is also the organization's biggest financial contributor. Whereas America's absence profoundly undermined the League of Nations' mission, its involvement in the U.N. has helped build it into a respectable, albeit imperfect, organization.

The days when America embraced hardline isolationism seem gone, yet its superpower status has allowed it to defy norms of diplomacy and international law. In particular, the U.N. has spearheaded several human rights treaties that America has refused to ratify, matching the stances of dictatorships like Iran, Saudi Arabia, Syria, China, and North Korea. All other Western democracies basically support human rights treaties.[84] America considers itself "the leader of the free world," but its hostility to international law weakens its ability to credibly lead by example, a crucial dimension of "soft power."[85]

This aspect of American exceptionalism reflects the conservative-liberal divide. Mainly due to the efforts of Democrats, America has played an active role in developing international laws and institutions, while Republicans, especially Southern and Midwestern conservatives, have recurrently ensured that it would not fall under their jurisdiction. The Senate has never ratified an international human rights treaty when Democrats held fewer than fifty-five seats (though some were ratified under Republican presidents).[86]

Racism was an early driving factor in resistance to international human rights. Southern segregationists initially opposed ratifying the U.N. Genocide Convention and the U.N. Covenant on Civil and Political Rights because they feared these treaties would bar lynching African-Americans or restricting them to second-class citizenship. America finally ratified them in 1988 and 1992, respectively, decades after their enactment.[87]

To this day, America has refused to ratify other major treaties. Religious traditionalists notably blocked the ratification of the U.N. Convention on the Elimination of All Forms of Discrimination against Women. They contend that it would license abortion, which the convention does not provide a right to. Similarly, America never ratified the Convention on the Rights of the Child, because opponents dubiously claimed that it would bolster children's abortion rights and eviscerate U.S. parental laws, especially regarding homeschooling, a concern for evangelicals opposed to secular public schools. But this convention would indeed prohibit the death penalty or life imprisonment for juveniles—a nonstarter for advocates of merciless sentences. Every nation worldwide has ratified that treaty, except America.

Beyond racism and social conservatism, realpolitik has motivated Americans hostile to international law. John Bolton, a far-right ideologue, argued that "it is a big mistake for us to grant any validity to international law, even when it may seem in our short-term interest to do so, because, over the long term, the goal of those who think that international law really means anything, are those who want to constrict the United States." Bolton suggested that America should be the only permanent member of the U.N. Security Council. "There is no United Nations," he declared. "There is an international community that occasionally can be led by the only real power left in the world, and that's the United States." Bolton is not a fringe figure. George W. Bush made him America's ambassador to the United Nations, albeit via a recess appointment, to circumvent a filibuster by Democrats appalled by the prospect of giving this key diplomatic position to the man who said that the U.N. is so worthless that "if [its headquarters] lost ten stories, it wouldn't make a bit of difference."

In practice, most U.S. diplomats have taken a more nuanced approach to international law than Bolton's scorched-earth rhetoric suggests. This was apparent when I worked in The Hague, Netherlands, as a judicial clerk for the U.N. International Criminal Tribunal for the Former Yugoslavia (ICTY), the court that tried Serbia's ex-president Slobodan Milošević and other alleged war criminals. On one hand, the ICTY was created in 1993 with U.S. support and employs many Americans. On the other hand, America has declined to join the International Criminal Court (ICC), another court in The Hague. What explains this double standard? The ICTY focuses solely on Balkan war criminals, but the ICC is a permanent court that might try Americans someday, such as for abuses in the "War on Terror."

My American colleagues at the ICTY, who were progressive and well-traveled, considered this double standard shameful.

The ICC was created in 2002 to try people for mass atrocities, especially genocide, crimes against humanity, and other war crimes. It is the first and only permanent court of its kind. The Clinton administration had reservations about the ICC's jurisdiction over Americans but eventually signed the treaty establishing the court. The Senate never ratified it. George W. Bush subsequently withdrew America's signature on the ground that no international court should ever prosecute an American. His administration even passed legislation empowering America to invade The Hague if a U.S. soldier ever came into the court's custody.[88]

The rival perspectives of the men who conducted the ICC signature protocol epitomize the partisan divide over international law. David Scheffer, a diplomat who devoted his career to promoting international human rights and stopping mass atrocities, proudly signed the ICC treaty on behalf of Clinton after helping to negotiate its terms when serving as the U.S. Ambassador-at-Large for War Crimes Issues. Scheffer was later a law professor of mine at Northwestern University, and his enthusiasm for international human rights was palpable, just like his respect for foreign cultures. However, Bush had Bolton "unsign" the treaty. Bolton called this act the "happiest moment" of his career, to Scheffer's dismay.

If America were to join the ICC, this would technically empower its prosecutor to pursue Americans suspected of war crimes. Yet the ICC has "complementary jurisdiction," meaning that it could intervene only if America failed to prosecute its own war criminals. For example, the ICC could not try rogue American soldiers who were convicted by U.S. authorities for murdering and abusing Iraqis and Afghans. However, it could charge members of the Bush administration who authorized torture, since they never faced domestic prosecution. The Obama administration declined to re-sign the ICC treaty and announced that it would simply have a cooperative relationship with the court. Given the nature of both the Bush and Obama administrations' actions in the "War on Terror," from Bush's use of torture to Obama's reliance on drone strikes with significant collateral damage, it is unsurprising that they refused to have the ICC scrutinize their actions.

Even if Obama had backed the ICC treaty, the Senate would not have ratified it. The U.S. Constitution is atypical in requiring two-thirds of the Senate to ratify a treaty—an even higher threshold than the sixty votes needed to defeat a filibuster. Legislators can ratify a treaty by a simple majority vote in essentially all other democracies.[89] This peculiarity enables a minority of Americans—mainly hardline Republicans—to exempt the United States from international law.

Perceived geopolitical interests have also dissuaded America from recognizing other international courts. It accepts the jurisdiction of the International Court of Justice only on a case-by-case basis.[90] This institution was established in 1945 to decide disputes between countries. America does not recognize the Inter-American Court of Human Rights, an arm of the Organization of American States. But the refusal to join the ICC has particularly undermined America's moral credibility and global efforts to punish mass atrocities. America likewise set a bad example by failing to ratify the Kyoto Protocol and the Copenhagen Accord, two treaties aiming to curb climate change. The future of the subsequent Paris Agreement on climate change partly depends on the outcome of America's internal conflicts, as Democrats have vowed to support it, while Republicans have expressed opposition.

VARIATIONS ON A THEME

In 2009, Barack Obama received the Nobel Peace Prize "for his extraordinary efforts to strengthen international diplomacy and cooperation between peoples." The Norwegian Nobel Committee's press release struck a decidedly positive tone: "Only very rarely has a person to the same extent as Obama captured the world's attention and given its people hope for a better future." He had become highly popular internationally in no small part because he was perceived as the antithesis of Bush.

Obama thus received the Nobel Peace Prize at the start of his first term and before he had done anything to concretely advance peace. In fact, he accomplished little on the matter during his presidency. He intensified the war in Afghanistan; sharply increased drone attacks, notwithstanding their high civilian toll; failed to close Guantánamo; refused to prosecute Bush administration officials who had licensed torture; declined to push for America's membership in the ICC; and maintained U.S. support to various dictatorships, from Egypt to Saudi Arabia and Yemen.

That raises the question of whether Obama rejected merely Bush's abrasive rhetoric without truly changing his policies. To his credit, on his first day in office, Obama signed an executive order to close Guantánamo within a year. But neither Democratic nor Republican lawmakers wanted its detainees brought to America for trial or continued detention. The Senate notably voted 90–6 to block funding that Obama requested to close the camp.[91] He still pursued efforts to try to transfer prisoners away from Guantánamo.[92]

Obama put an end to waterboarding and other torture methods but declined to prosecute Bush administration officials for authorizing their use. A climate of impunity now prevails. George W. Bush and Dick Cheney proudly admitted to authorizing waterboarding. Many other Republicans openly advocate a return to "enhanced interrogation techniques," a euphemism for torture. Aside from figures like John McCain—a former prisoner of war who was tortured in Vietnam—numerous prominent Republicans support torture, including Mitt Romney, Mitch McConnell, Marco Rubio, Ted Cruz, and Donald Trump.[93] Roughly half of the American public finds torture justifiable, although we saw above that support is stronger among conservatives.[94]

America might therefore have become even more polarized if Obama had taken the step of prosecuting his predecessor. Obama instead adopted a conciliatory attitude toward Bush, whom he invited to lead, along with Bill Clinton, a fund-raising project for victims of the 2010 Haiti earthquake. This sign of goodwill got Obama nothing from his Republican opponents, who remained categorically opposed to all his proposals.

Despite denouncing profligate spending on "big government," Republicans accused Obama of underfunding the military. During the 2012 presidential race, Obama responded by promising a raise while boasting that "military spending has gone up every single year that I've been in office."[95] Indeed, both parties have sought to maximize American power by engaging in a perpetual arms race and projecting a worldwide military presence. The United States leads the world in both military spending and deployment, by far. As Figure 11 shows, its military budget is 36 percent of the world's total. America spends as much on its military as the next eight countries combined, all of which are U.S. allies except for China and Russia, which are not technically its enemies. Further, America had approximately 900 military bases or offices in 148 countries worldwide as of 2011, a colossal deployment even considering that 56 of those countries had fewer than 10 staff members on active duty.[96]

The public tends to accept politicians' claims about the need for massive military spending, as only a third of Americans deem current levels

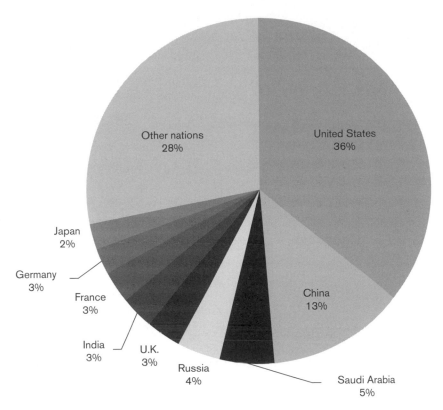

Other nations
28%

United States
36%

Japan
2%

Germany
3%

France
3%

India
3%

U.K.
3%

Russia
4%

Saudi Arabia
5%

China
13%

FIGURE 11. Percentage of global military spending. SOURCE: Stockholm International Peace Research Institute (2016).

excessive.[97] The country has not heeded President Dwight Eisenhower's warning about "the acquisition of unwarranted influence, whether sought or unsought, by the military-industrial complex," which he depicted as a threat to democracy. The five-star general added that outsize military spending could help make a country insolvent.[98]

Foreign policy is an area where presidents have significant leeway to act as they see fit, as their authority is less circumscribed there than in domestic policy-making. That was undoubtedly tempting to a president like Obama, whom a hostile Congress stymied for most of his tenure. Tellingly, his administration asserted the legal authority to detain alleged terrorists forever at Guantánamo despite promising that it did not intend to do so. It even created a procedural framework to manage their prolonged detention.[99] The

Obama administration also asserted that habeas corpus protections do not apply to those held in Bagram, Afghanistan, whom it claimed could be detained indefinitely without judicial review.[100]

While Obama denounced Bush's surveillance methods, he backed the National Security Agency's dragnet collection of millions of internet and telephone records under the PRISM program. Obama duplicitously defended PRISM as "transparent," [101] although it came to light only because of a whistle-blower, Edward Snowden. Obama later claimed that "there is no spying on Americans." European nations have likewise expanded spying operations and other practices jeopardizing the rule of law, as exemplified by France's dragnet police searches and arrests with minimal judicial oversight following several terrorist strikes in Paris. At this stage, however, the U.S. surveillance apparatus appears to go beyond those of all other Western democracies.

With regard to warfare, Obama carried on Bush's foreign policy and even took it further in some areas. During his first presidential campaign, Obama strategically stressed his longstanding opposition to the increasingly unpopular Iraq War. He equally sought to project toughness by vowing to step up the war in Afghanistan, depicting it as the true battle against terrorism, which Bush had neglected. Once president, Obama indeed withdrew U.S. troops from Iraq and boosted their ranks in Afghanistan. But he simultaneously announced their planned withdrawal from the latter, revealing his ambivalence. According to the military historian Andrew Bacevich, Obama did not believe in the Afghan War and intensified it only for political reasons, whereas Bush believed that America could bring "freedom" to Afghanistan. "Who is more deserving of contempt?" Bacevich asked. "The commander-in-chief who sends young Americans to die for a cause, however misguided, in which he sincerely believes? Or the commander-in-chief who sends young Americans to die for a cause in which he manifestly does not believe and yet refuses to forsake?" [102]

It seems unrealistic to expect to turn Afghanistan into a modern democracy and reliable American ally through little more than force. An impoverished rural country with a hostile landscape, it is home to an intricate traditionalist society. Dubbed "the graveyard of empires," it essentially proved indomitable by the British colonial empire and the Soviet Union.[103] America scarcely managed to pacify the country after toppling the ruthless Taliban regime, which had enabled Al-Qaeda to orchestrate 9/11 from Afghanistan. The Taliban regrouped as a resistance force that has only grown stronger. In 2015, Obama finally halted the withdrawal of U.S. troops from Afghanistan and indefinitely prolonged America's role in a fifteen-year conflict that had already cost more than $65 billion.[104]

The war in Afghanistan dragged on partly because the Bush and Obama administrations tried to either decidedly crush the elusive Taliban or kill them all. Yet killed Taliban are regularly replaced by relatives, peers, or jihadists from foreign countries eager to avenge them.[105] The Taliban has further drawn recruits among Afghans who resent the U.S. military presence. While the vast majority of Afghan civilian casualties have come at the Taliban's hands, the relatively significant collateral damage in U.S. operations has also fostered animosity.[106] Mistrust of America is exacerbated by its support to the highly corrupt Afghan government, from which certain officials and soldiers have defected to the Taliban.[107]

Moreover, Obama relied on drones to kill alleged terrorists to a far greater extent than Bush.[108] Because of its tendency to count only U.S. casualties of war,[109] America's concern over drone strikes has mostly centered on whether it is constitutional to use them to assassinate U.S. citizens accused of terrorism, such as Anwar al-Awlaki, a cleric killed by a drone in Yemen. Less attention has been paid to the predicament of foreigners killed by drone strikes. A 2012 study indicated that, in Pakistan, U.S. drones had killed between 2,562 and 3,325 people, including between 474 and 881 civilians, since 2004. "High-level" terrorists were merely 2 percent of those killed.[110] Another study found that several attacks in Yemen by U.S. drones and other aerial weapons killed 82 people, including at least 57 civilians. Inhabitants of targeted regions commonly live in fear of being instantaneously struck by U.S. drones.[111] Terrorists mention drone strikes in recruitment efforts.[112]

Given that America's actions generate terrorists even as they eliminate others, the "War on Terror" has turned into an endless struggle. Terrorism and jihadism are ideologies that cannot be eradicated mainly by violence, which predictably begets more violence. Peter Neumann, an expert on terrorism, emphasized that jihadists aim to "inspire overreaction" from Western governments in order to radicalize more jihadists.[113] But the moralistic perspective described above leads numerous Americans to perceive terrorists and Taliban as simply "bad guys." The preferred solution is then to try to kill them all so that only "good guys" are left.

Obama's overreliance on force may have reflected a desire to placate opponents who depicted him as "soft" on terrorism. Such criticism did not abate even after he authorized bin Laden's assassination. Denouncing Obama's pusillanimity, Donald Trump vowed to assassinate both terrorists and their families. This would be a war crime, yet his supporters cheered him on.[114] Ted Cruz called for "carpet-bombing" the entire area occupied by ISIS, which would cause huge civilian casualties. Even more moderate Republican leaders echoed these views. Asked whether America should negotiate with the Taliban to end the war in Afghanistan, Mitt Romney answered: "These people have declared war on us. They've killed Americans. We go anywhere they are, and we kill them."

The Obama administration's foreign policy exemplified how American exceptionalism can lead to path dependence. The blank check that Congress, the courts, and most of the public generally gave the Bush administration to conduct the "War on Terror" after 9/11 sent America on a path that it may have great difficulty abandoning. Some of Bush's autocratic measures became more institutionalized under Obama, who defended them in court.[115] During his first presidential campaign, however, Obama had given this answer when asked what he would do if elected: "Guantánamo, that's easy. Close down Guantánamo. Restore habeas corpus. Say no to renditions. Say no to wireless wiretaps." "We are gonna lead by example, by maintaining the highest standards of civil liberties and human rights," Obama insisted. "No more ignoring the law when it is inconvenient. That is not who we are."[116] Obama ultimately found some of his predecessor's methods convenient. So will his successor, Donald Trump, who will enjoy the executive power and massive surveillance apparatus at his disposal.

Conclusion

America is undoubtedly an exceptional country, in every sense of the word. If "exceptional" is taken to mean "great," it is a fitting description, given the nation's impressive achievements since the American Enlightenment. The birth of modern democracy in the United States in the late eighteenth century became a model for the world. Naturally, the understanding of democracy then was extremely narrow by today's standards, considering slavery, the restriction of the franchise to white male landowners, and other injustices. America nonetheless began as a land of progress, and subsequent generations built on that heritage to lead their country forward.

In the twenty-first century, America still stands out as a global leader in diverse areas, although it remains a land of contradictions. The outcome of the 2016 presidential election epitomizes the cycle of progress and reactionarism that has driven American history. The United States went from being the first modern Western nation to elect a person of color as its head of state to being the first one to elect a far-right anti-immigration populist.* Obama's election reflected the open-mindedness of millions of Americans. Conversely, much of the country suspected that the U.S. president was not truly American. Donald Trump painted himself as the antithesis of Obama by stoking fear about the first black president's purported jihadist sympathies and forged U.S. birth certificate, which would make Obama an undocumented immigrant as well as an illegitimate president.

Other glaring contradictions epitomize tensions at the heart of American society. American women were pioneers in fighting for gender equality, yet

---

* The election of Viktor Orbán in Hungary is the main modern precedent, insofar as this former Soviet bloc country is now part of the West.

patriarchal ultratraditionalists retain extraordinary influence in American society. The United States is one of the Western nations where LGBTQ people have made the greatest strides toward equality—and the one where homophobic legal measures have been the fiercest in recent decades.[1] Americans make outstanding contributions to science and technology, as exemplified by the dramatic landing of the *Curiosity* rover on Mars in 2012. But around 40 percent of Americans obstinately reject the theory of evolution and believe in anachronistic biblical prophecies.[2]

Because of the lack of consensus between U.S. conservatives and liberals on very fundamental issues, America stands out as the Western country where certain social problems are the most acute. It is the one with the worst degree of wealth inequality. The sole one without universal health care. The one where moneyed interests have the strongest lobbying and electoral influence. The one where conspiracy theories about climate change and other issues have the most sway. The one where basic reproductive rights are the most relentlessly challenged. The one whose criminal justice system is the most inhumane. The one with the worst gun violence. The one that openly reintroduced torture into Western civilization. The one that paved the way for detaining alleged terrorists indefinitely without trial. And the one that led the 2003 invasion of Iraq on dubious grounds, further destabilizing the Middle East, predictably exacerbating terrorism, and contributing to the rise of ISIS.[3]

Where does Trumpism fit in this picture? Throughout this book we have seen that the Republican Party's growing radicalization over the past three decades has fostered an exceptionally hardline and anti-rational ideology. Four peculiar mindsets central to this ideological evolution helped enable Trump's movement: profound anti-intellectualism, fervent Christian fundamentalism, a visceral suspicion of government, and racial resentment. The first three are considerably more intense in conservative America than elsewhere in the West in light of diverse dimensions of American exceptionalism. Racial animus is hardly limited to America, although its ideological weight there stems from another facet of American exceptionalism: the United States has historically been the Western nation with by far the biggest proportion of racial and ethnic minorities. This has led attitudes toward socioeconomic rights and human dignity to be more racialized in America. In other words, each of these four peculiar mindsets has itself been shaped by interrelated aspects of American exceptionalism, if not path dependence traceable to the nation's singular circumstances.

These circumstances have been obscured by the Republican establishment's redefinition of "American exceptionalism" as an anti-Obama catchphrase with nativist overtones. Creating fertile ground for Trump's "Make America Great Again" movement, Republican leaders spent years accusing Obama of betraying "American exceptionalism" and turning his back on the Founding Fathers. In reality, "exceptionalism" has historically referred to how America is an *exception*. It is objectively different from other countries. These differences are not necessarily positive, and some may precipitate American decline.

In the early days of the American republic, Alexis de Tocqueville joined multiple foreign observers in praising its people. "Americans are hardly more virtuous than others, but they are more enlightened (I speak of the masses) than any other people I know," the Frenchman concluded. "The mass of those with a grasp of public affairs, a knowledge of laws and precedents, a feeling for the well-understood interests of the nation, and an ability to understand them, is greater there than in any other place on earth."[4]

Today, one may reverse Tocqueville's observation. Because of the extraordinary weight of anti-intellectualism and unbridled individualism in vast segments of modern America, its people are arguably the least informed of all Westerners and the likeliest to ignore the greater good, such as by opposing universal health care, financial and environmental regulation, or basic gun control as matters of ideological principle.

EXCEPTIONAL NO MORE?

"The irresponsible rhetoric of our president, who has used the pulpit of the presidency to divide us by race and color, has made America a more dangerous environment for everyone." One might assume that this was a statement by a Trump critic. These are instead Trump's own words denouncing Obama upon accepting the 2016 Republican presidential nomination. Of course, Trump had long engaged in explicit race-baiting, mobilizing nativists and white supremacists like no other major politician in modern U.S. history. A wave of hate crimes occurred during his campaign and after his election.[5] To boot, Trump savaged all of his critics, from fellow Republicans to a disabled reporter,[6] although his campaign called for an end to bullying.[7] In the Orwellian world of Trumpism, doublethink and role reversals are ubiquitous—a reality TV star plays with reality.

It is too early to tell whether Trumpism will normalize itself. The U.S. demographic group that is the most staunchly conservative on average, white males, is decreasing in the face of immigration and higher birthrates for minorities. For the first time ever, in 2013 more minority than white babies were born in America.[8] The Latino population increased by 43 percent between 2000 and 2010—four times faster than the general U.S. population.[9] Latinos now represent around 16 percent of the U.S. population, compared to 13 percent for African-Americans, previously the largest minority group. The Asian population also grew by more than 43 percent during that period, reaching nearly 6 percent overall, another fairly large minority.[10] Community-based socializing and groupthink remain strong among both minorities and whites. Around a quarter of whites still oppose a family member marrying a black person.[11] But the number of children born to parents of different racial or ethnic groups is increasing.[12]

America's diversifying population may weaken the clout of staunchly conservative voters, as racial and ethnic minorities are rather liberal on average. Barack Obama was elected partly because he won the vote of minorities by a landslide. Hillary Clinton fared slightly worse than he did among minorities but enjoyed a sizable advantage over Trump. As a result, Republican leaders have long backed efforts to make it harder for minorities to vote or register to do so. This cynical strategy is rationalized as an effort to fight rampant voter fraud—another baseless conspiracy theory.[13] A thorough investigation of voter impersonation found barely thirty-one incidents out of a billion votes cast.[14]

Certain whites who formerly voted for Obama decided to vote for Trump, exemplifying how racial attitudes are not black-and-white. Data indicate that the public's image of blacks and Latinos deteriorated during the Obama years.[15] Human beings can fluctuate between tolerance and intolerance during their lifetimes, just as the U.S. national mood has ebbed and flowed between liberalism and conservatism for decades.[16] Working-class whites who joined Trump's movement were partly misled by his alarmism about a wrecked U.S. economy. In fact, the economic situation in various heavily white counties that changed sides had improved under Obama.[17]

While Trump was born into the business elite and ran a business empire embodying dog-eat-dog capitalism,[18] he cast himself as an anti-elitist populist eager to assist the underprivileged. However, we have seen that his program largely overlapped with the Republican Party's winner-take-all economics, including repealing "Obamacare," passing a tax plan primarily favoring the wealthy, and eviscerating financial and environmental regulations.

Even though the Democratic Party has also embraced aspects of winner-take-all economics, the G.O.P. categorically obstructed the Obama administration's moderate efforts to reduce wealth inequality and expand access to health care. Obama stressed that his rejected policy proposals "would make a huge difference with the white working class—and the black working class, and the Latino working class," and disputed the notion that Trumpism is explainable by how "both Republican and Democratic elites have neglected the white working class." Racial divisions have indeed been historically influential in persuading many whites to vote against their own economic interest. The 2016 election was no exception.

It is unclear how long the Republican Party can keep winning elections with a nearly all-white coalition. Trump's nativist, sexist, and incendiary rhetoric has alienated not only minorities but also millions of whites. Merely 38 percent of voters on election day had a favorable opinion of Trump. The same dismal proportion deemed him "qualified" for the presidency. Barely a third found him "honest and trustworthy." [19]

Nevertheless, legions of citizens were convinced that Hillary Clinton, a centrist with vast political experience, presented a graver threat to democracy. "The election of Hillary Clinton will lead to the destruction of our country," Trump warned. His supporters were persuaded that Clinton deserved to be imprisoned for mismanaging her email—a fitting picture in the age of mass incarceration and wild conspiracy-mongering. While numerous progressives felt lukewarm about or suspicious of Clinton, the reactions she stirred in conservative America were striking. Slogans on (unofficial) pins distributed at the Republican National Convention stated, "Life's a Bitch, Don't Vote for One" and "2 Fat Thighs, 2 Small Breasts . . . Left Wing," [20] recalling the exceptional influence of patriarchy in parts of the nation.

Much has been said about how Trump hurt the G.O.P.'s image, although he may have helped it in various ways, such as by making hardline establishment Republicans seem like centrists. Many experts previously considered the George W. Bush years the heyday of modern anti-intellectualism and reactionarism. Then came Sarah Palin, the Tea Party movement, and Donald J. Trump. Now Bush practically evokes a polished, well-read gentleman with a moderate ideology—notwithstanding his reintroduction of torture into Western civilization, vow to detain people forever without trial at Guantánamo, baseless invasion of Iraq, adamant embrace of the death penalty, promotion of abstinence-only sexual education, aspiration to outlaw abortion, attempt to pass a constitutional amendment banning gay marriage, and defense of winner-take-all economics.

It remains to be seen what Trump will actually do as president. He toned down his rhetoric after the election, suggesting that he may have been posturing. In any event, the demagogy Trump used to win the White House marked a defining historical moment in and of itself.

Trump's election and the growing influence of anti-immigrant European parties may signify that far-right populism will become normalized in the West. Trump's fiery and fact-free campaign rhetoric openly defied virtually every single norm of human decency. He was a celebrity with absolutely no government experience who touted his "common sense" and disdained education. For the approximately sixty-three million Americans who voted for Trump, these were either good reasons to elect him or nothing to worry about. While the Republican establishment recurrently resorted to disinformation to obstruct Obama's agenda, Trump intensified the weight of naked propaganda in U.S. politics. Alt-right news media like *Breitbart* are no longer on the fringe but a central part of Trump's coalition. Bestowing the status of president on Trump may also dignify him, making opponents more deferential and further normalizing his movement.

"Today, the United States; tomorrow, France. Bravo!" This was the reaction of Jean-Marie Le Pen—the founder of France's extreme-right National Front party—congratulating Trump on his victory. His daughter Marine Le Pen, who now heads the party, concurred: "Nothing is immutable. What has happened this night is not the end of the world, it's the end of a world." Florian Philippot, the party's vice president, struck an ominous tone: "Their world is collapsing. Ours is being built." Other European far-right leaders were jubilant.

The European far right is not a product of the same ideological nexus as the American far right. Christian fundamentalism is practically absent in modern Europe, anti-intellectual conspiracy-mongering has limited traction, and Europeans do not share a visceral suspicion of government programs like universal health care. We have seen that the European far right's ideology primarily stems from nativism and resentment of the establishment, including the European Union. Still, authoritarianism is a key dimension of the European far right's ideology. It may ultimately lead to a similar type of society as Trumpism but via a different path. In addition to receiving a greater proportion of the vote in recent decades, far-right parties have tilted certain mainstream European political parties rightward.

For the time being, however, political extremism is less mainstream in Europe than in America. The fact that the G.O.P., a mainstream conservative party, has aligned itself with fringe, far-right European parties is revealing. When it comes to their basic worldview, mainstream European conservatives are often closer to U.S. liberals than to U.S. conservatives. Because of its peculiar ideological evolution, conservative America has become an outlier in the West.

On the other hand, the over-the-top nature of Trumpism may be interpreted as the last throes of a peculiar ideology doomed by a demographic revolution. Yet predicting the future is a risky business. Illustratively, the ridiculed "Scopes Monkey Trial" of 1925 then seemed to be the nail in the coffin for creationists. Christian fundamentalism survived and grew into a powerful movement.[21] Likewise, when the Supreme Court abolished capital punishment in 1972, some thought that America was joining the rest of the West in abandoning executions.[22] States responded by enacting new death penalty statutes, which the court licensed in 1976.[23] Certain justices now appear disposed to hear another challenge to capital punishment's constitutionality.[24] American conservatives never moved on after *Roe v. Wade* made abortion a constitutional right in 1973. Trump stated that he would appoint justices who would reverse *Roe,* which would spark staunch resistance from Americans who support the right to abortion. This further suggests that Trump's election is perhaps best interpreted as part of the cycles of American exceptionalism.

The latest social developments can obscure longstanding dynamics. As this book went to press, the public debate focused on whether the 2016 presidential race was swayed by the spread of pro-Trump "fake news" on social media and allegations that Vladimir Putin's regime was involved in hacking the Democratic National Committee's computer network to help Trump. But the emergence of fake news should not eclipse the broader disinformation that started well before the 2016 election and that is partly rooted in America's subculture of anti-intellectualism. Attributing Trump's win mainly to Russian interference is also questionable. While these factors may indeed have contributed to the election's outcome, understanding Trump's rise requires us to look beyond the last few weeks of the 2016 campaign. The prior years, decades, and centuries shed light on the evolution of American democracy.

Various reforms could strengthen American democracy and improve the public's well-being. America could establish a genuine universal health care system with pricing regulations on medical treatment. Steps could be taken to undercut the influence of lobbyists in American government and overhaul the campaign finance system. The nation's colossal wealth inequality could be tackled in several ways, such as by reasonably raising taxes on the affluent and expanding the Earned Income Tax Credit. Unlike stereotypical welfare payments to the idle, the EITC provides underprivileged workers with supplementary income to help make ends meet. Sensible family planning could be promoted by discontinuing abstinence-only education and bolstering reproductive rights, including better access to contraception and abortion. Following the legalization of same-sex marriage, additional reforms could fully bar discrimination against LGBTQ people in the workplace and elsewhere. America could abolish the death penalty, revise the draconian sentencing laws that contributed to mass incarceration, abandon the "War on Drugs," tackle police brutality, and expand gun control. These reforms would improve the predicament of minorities, and specific measures could be taken to address institutional racism. When it comes to foreign policy, America could use its power more wisely by rethinking militarism and respecting international human rights, which would notably entail closing the Guantánamo detention camp and joining the International Criminal Court.

Several of these proposals seem obvious to experts and well-informed citizens. The intriguing question is why much of American society has fiercely resisted sensible laws and policies that other Western democracies have adopted. This book has aimed to provide answers by exploring the peculiar mindsets that lead so many Americans to oppose or only modestly support policies that would benefit them. Voting preferences in America are not all backwards, yet a sizable minority of Americans vote against their own interests.

A mix of national chauvinism, insularity, anti-intellectualism, and disinformation reinforces the status quo by leading myriad Americans to believe that the United States has nothing to learn from the rest of the world. However, there is nothing un-American about such reform proposals. Generations of Americans have advocated for them. Back in 1944, Franklin Roosevelt was already calling for a "Second Bill of Rights," encompassing health care, education, and a decent standard of living.

The Fox News pundit Bill O'Reilly contended that Obama's reforms, including a modest raise of the top income tax bracket from 35 to 39.6 percent, risked turning America into Sweden.[25] (Recall that the top income tax rate reached 90 percent under Eisenhower, which did not preclude high economic growth.) This led to a memorable episode of *The Daily Show* where an American comedian traveled to Stockholm to frantically warn incredulous Swedes that they were enslaved by universal health care, weeks of paid vacation, and "socialism." In reality, a study shows that Americans would much prefer the level of wealth equality in Sweden. A representative sample was asked to identify which of several pie charts had the ideal wealth distribution. Unbeknown to them, two depicted the wealth distributions in the United States and Sweden. A full 92 percent of Americans preferred the Swedish level.[26]

Improving wealth equality is not necessarily synonymous with resorting to Swedish tax levels. In *The Spirit Level,* Richard Wilkinson and Kate Pickett compare how Sweden and Japan achieved relatively high levels of income equality: "Sweden does it through redistributive taxes and benefits and a large welfare state. As a proportion of national income, public social expenditure in Japan is, in contrast to Sweden, among the lowest of the major developed countries. Japan gets its high degree of equality not so much from redistribution as from a greater equality of market incomes, of earnings *before* taxes and benefits." [27] Similarly, New Hampshire and Vermont are among the most equal American states, though Vermont has one of the highest tax burdens nationwide and New Hampshire one of the lowest. "The need for redistribution depends on how unequal incomes are before taxes and benefits," Wilkinson and Pickett note.[28]

Americans could learn from prosperous democracies that blend greater solidarity with a market economy, just as foreigners have historically followed examples set by American society. For instance, several countries looked to the U.S. Constitution and to FDR's Second Bill of Rights for inspiration when crafting their own constitutions.[29] In recent years, Europeans convinced that austerity measures are counterproductive have invoked FDR's New Deal policies. French progressives even created a reform initiative named "Roosevelt 2012." Simultaneously, Europeans have criticized the excesses of U.S. capitalism, demonstrating that foreigners perceive America as a model of both what to do and what not to do.

In the end, social democracy will not lead to utopian societies in America, Europe, or elsewhere. But "better the occasional faults of a government that lives in a spirit of charity than the consistent omissions of a government frozen in the ice of its own indifference," as Roosevelt emphasized.

AMERICAN DECLINE, A DOUBLE-EDGED SWORD

Decline may be the inevitable fate of any leading society. From the Roman Empire to the Mongol Empire and European colonial empires, countless dominant societies have faded over the course of history.[30] Perhaps it is America's turn to experience the cyclical rise and fall of civilizations.

Yet decline is not simply a matter of fate. Just as the ascent of civilizations is largely human-made, so is their downfall.[31] America's decline after little more than a century as a superpower seems far from inevitable at this stage. It remains the world's strongest economy. It is a leader in technology and multiple other fields. Its universities are widely recognized as the best in the world. It has great thinkers and innovators. In sum, there is much to admire about contemporary America.

American decline would be a negative development if it meant an inability to resolve the nation's problems. But if "decline" is taken to mean a reduction in U.S. power, it might not lead to worse living standards for Americans. A country does not have to be the world's top power for its citizens to lead satisfying lives. The people of Sweden, for example, enjoy higher living standards than Americans in various ways. Sweden is prosperous, yet it is neither economically dominant nor militarily powerful. The days of the Swedish Empire are long gone. By the same token, the average British or French person is not worse off today than their counterparts were at the peak of the British or the French Empire. Thanks to internal social progress, Britain and France have more just and equal societies now than when they were conquering colonies across the world. The same can be said of today's Germany, which found a way to thrive and remain influential without being belligerent.

It is therefore possible to imagine a scenario in which America is no longer a superpower but its citizens are better off. The decline of the United States may not have the disastrous consequences that many Americans fear. In fact, the country's current superpower status arguably contributes to its immobilism. So long as scores of Americans are persuaded that the United States is simply "the best," it will be difficult to envisage meaningful reforms to its political, legal, social, and economic systems. If pride comes before a fall, it is relevant that most Americans think they live in an inherently superior country chosen by God to lead the world.[32]

Those who oppose the idea of an American empire may take comfort in American decline. But the United States never had a genuine empire, and even its most reprehensible abuses of power, such as the Vietnam War and the 2003 invasion of Iraq, were generally less abusive than those of European colonial empires. The invasion of Iraq led to massive loss of life yet ultimately also to an Iraqi government—a government over which America had a measure of influence, but an Iraqi government nonetheless. Conversely, European colonial empires typically rejected the very notion of self-rule for those they conquered and often brutally repressed protest and independence movements.

If America has been wiser in its use of power than the European empires of yesteryear, this is partly because its rise as a superpower paralleled a global movement toward democracy and human rights—a trend that somewhat accelerated with the collapse of the authoritarian Soviet bloc. The United States has at times helped promote this trend, such as by pressuring dictatorships to transition toward democracy and playing a role in crafting international human rights treaties. It is thus important that the world's most influential country be a democracy, even though America has regularly sought to exempt itself from these treaties and certain aspects of its foreign policy are imperialistic.

The prospect of American decline should be approached warily, since the most serious contender to become the next global superpower is China, a totalitarian, one-party dictatorship. While China remains a largely rural and impoverished country, it is now the world's second economy and largest exporter.[33] It has the world's biggest population and a nuclear arsenal. Assuming that China does not evolve toward democracy, its rising clout may challenge democratic principles worldwide. The Chinese Communist Party engages in systematic censorship, rampant corruption, and state violence. The Nobel Peace Prize winner Liu Xiaobo is among the dissidents imprisoned for urging a nonviolent transition to democracy.

On the bright side, China's rapid development led to a reduction in poverty and better standards of living. But it has become a highly unequal country, as its newfound wealth is concentrated in the hands of the ruling class and the business elite. The Chinese system conciliates some of the least desirable aspects of communism and capitalism, yet certain voices laud its "efficiency." Its supporters affirm that the slow workings of democracy would stifle China's economic progress—as if economic development were incompatible with democracy. The Chinese Communist Party defiantly rejects calls for democracy and human rights, describing them as foreign concepts irreconcilable with Chinese values—as if communism came from China. Authoritarianism is obviously not ingrained in Chinese culture. Chinese philosophers such as Laozi and Zhuangzi already condemned tyrants more than two thousand years ago. Democracy has made progress in modern Asia, and there is no fundamental reason why it could not do so in China.

A democratic China could play a positive role on the international stage, but now the world has to contend with a Chinese government that sees no legitimacy in representative government or human rights. American power may prove to be the most viable bulwark against Chinese power as these countries keep competing for influence in coming decades. America's rise shows that democratic rule and economic development are not mutually exclusive.

China has thus far been remarkably unfazed by pressure from America and other democracies urging it to recognize basic human rights. The Chinese government denounces such lesson-giving as hypocrisy, and it is sometimes right. The only credible way to lead is by example, and the United States' harsh socioeconomic inequality and troubling human rights record undermine its calls for reforms abroad. The Chinese government makes a point of publishing reports emphasizing U.S. social injustices and human rights abuses.[34] Of course, differences of degree matter. China has a far worse human rights record than America. Still, America cannot convincingly call on China to discontinue its abuses when, for example, the CIA waterboarded alleged terrorists, slammed them into walls, chained them in uncomfortable positions for hours, stripped them of clothing, and forced them to stay awake for days.[35] The torture methods that America used to interrogate suspected terrorists were copied from a 1957 Air Force study of techniques that Chinese communists employed during the Korean War to elicit confessions from U.S. prisoners, including sleep deprivation, exposure, and prolonged stress positions. America then denounced these methods as "torture."[36] Moreover, the Bush administration's most prominent torture method, waterboarding, was a primary means of torture under the Spanish Inquisition.[37] Certain Americans protest that their nation's enemies resort to heavy-handed measures, leaving it no choice but to do the same. Yet America is a longstanding democracy that cannot be held to the same standard as dictators or terrorists. The expectations for America are high, as they should be for a superpower aspiring to lead the free world.

As Trump came into power, the evolution of democracy in America and the Western world took an uncharted path. Far-right European parties, Vladimir Putin, and other dictators hailed his election. Civil society and human rights defenders shuddered at the prospect of an authoritarian wave or the spread of illiberal democracy. People across the globe wonder what happened to the United States.[38]

America is no longer a commendable standard-bearer for democracy and human rights, although it once helped plant their seeds. A few generations ago, Tocqueville wrote admiringly: "In that land the great experiment was to be made, by civilized man, of the attempt to construct society upon a new basis; and it was there, for the first time, that theories hitherto unknown, or deemed impracticable, were to exhibit a spectacle for which the world had not been prepared by the history of the past."[39] America may eventually reclaim credibility as a global leader by building on its tremendous strengths, tapping into its enormous potential, and addressing the fundamental problems behind its decline. If it chooses that path, America could draw on its legacy of progress to fulfill the expectations of the great experiment in democracy in which it was a trailblazer. American exceptionalism is not set in stone.

ACKNOWLEDGMENTS

Innumerable people generously assisted me in this project, from loved ones to friends and scholars who reviewed the manuscript or shared insights, including colleagues at Stanford Law School. I express my gratitude to all, though special thanks go to Naomi Schneider and the University of California Press team, my literary agent Kate Johnson, my research assistant Nicole Bronnimann, Juliana Froggatt, Naomi Cahn, June Carbone, Susan Jacoby, Dorothy Roberts, Norman Spaulding, Rick Banks, John Donohue, David Sklansky, Bob Weisberg, Deborah Rhode, Michelle Mello, David Studdert, Nathaniel Persily, Beth Van Schaack, Allen Weiner, Jeanne Merino, Abbye Atkinson, Sarah Duranske, Thea Johnson, Justin Weinstein-Tull, Beth Colgan, Andrew Gilden, Morris Fiorina, Shanto Iyengar, Tanya Luhrmann, Amir Weiner, Nina Eliasoph, Bob O'Dell, Chandler Davidson, Bhargav Gopal, Mirte Postema, Keren Mock, Marie-Pierre Ulloa, Cóman Kenny, Francisco Moneta, Rick Greenberg, Catherine Paradeise, Jean-Claude Thoenig, Mireille Honeïn, the Stefani family, and my parents. Last but not least, I cannot forget Iaru and Annie for their exceptional kindness.

NOTES

Epigraph. Seymour Martin Lipset, *American Exceptionalism: A Double-Edged Sword* (Norton, 1997), 17.

INTRODUCTION

1. Institute for Criminal Policy Research, "World Prison Brief" (2016). As we will see in Chapter 7, the tiny archipelago of the Seychelles has technically surpassed America as the country with the highest incarceration rate.

2. Michelle Ye Hee Lee, "Fact Check: Does the United States Really Have 5 Percent of the World's Population and One Quarter of the World's Prisoners?," *Washington Post,* April 30, 2015.

3. Amnesty International, "Death Sentences and Executions in 2014" (2015), 64.

4. The prison-industrial complex encompasses correctional facilities and related services.

5. The court is officially named New York Appellate Division, First Department. It has jurisdiction over Manhattan and the Bronx.

6. Hector Merced is a composite character based on several of my clients. Certain case details have been modified to ensure privacy.

7. New York State's incarceration rate is 433 prisoners per 100,000 people, below the U.S. national average of 693. But New York State's incarceration rate is very high by international standards: approximately three times higher than Britain's, four times higher than France's, and eight times higher than Sweden's. See Institute for Criminal Policy Research, "World Prison Brief" (2016); Prison Policy Initiative, "States of Incarceration: The Global Context," accessed October 18, 2016, www .prisonpolicy.org/global/.

8. While the debate over mass incarceration has led to various reforms in parts of America, Chapter 7 describes how they have had a relatively limited scope.

9. Fyodor Dostoyevsky, *The House of the Dead,* trans. Constance Garnett, (1862), quoted in *The Yale Book of Quotations,* ed. Fred R. Shapiro (Yale University Press, 2006), 210.

10. Bryan Stevenson, "We Need to Talk about an Injustice," TED talk, March 2012.

11. For instance, see Seymour Martin Lipset, *American Exceptionalism: A Double-Edged Sword* (Norton, 1997), 18.

12. Alan Abramowitz, *The Polarized Public? Why American Government Is So Dysfunctional* (Pearson, 2013), 2.

13. While John McCain opposed the George W. Bush administration's use of torture, as we will see in Chapter 8, many other Republican leaders have supported torture, from Mitt Romney to Mitch McConnell, Marco Rubio, Ted Cruz, and Donald Trump.

14. Comparative research on mainstream conservative parties in various countries has found that "the U.S. Republican Party is an anomaly in denying anthropogenic climate change." Sondre Båtstrand, "More Than Markets: A Comparative Study of Nine Conservative Parties on Climate Change," *Politics and Policy* 43, no. 4 (2015): 538.

15. Ian Haney López, *Dog Whistle Politics: How Coded Racial Appeals Have Reinvented Racism and Wrecked the Middle Class* (Oxford University Press, 2015).

16. Lipset, *American Exceptionalism,* 19.

17. See generally Gallup, "Bush Ratings Show Historical Levels of Polarization," June 4, 2004; Gallup, "Obama Approval Ratings Still Historically Polarized," February 6, 2015.

18. Christopher Hare and Keith Poole, "The Polarization of Contemporary American Politics," *Polity* 46, no. 3 (2014): 428.

19. Isaac Asimov, "A Cult of Ignorance," *Newsweek,* January 21, 1980.

20. Despite the revelation that Iraq had no weapons of mass destruction or ties to Al-Qaeda, Americans proved "less sensitive about the reasons for going to war in Iraq than many experts expected." Thomas Ricks, *Fiasco: The American Military Adventure in Iraq* (Penguin, 2007), 108. In fact, we will see that many Americans still believe that invading Iraq was the right decision, regardless of how it contributed to the rise of ISIS.

21. See, for instance, Michael Cooper, "From Obama, the Tax Cut Nobody Heard of," *New York Times,* October 18, 2010.

22. Alexis de Tocqueville, *Democracy in America,* trans. Henry Reeve (Bantam, 2000), 4.

23. See generally Richard Hofstadter, *Anti-Intellectualism in American Life* (Vintage, 1966).

24. See, for example, Richard Wilkinson and Kate Pickett, *The Spirit Level: Why Greater Equality Makes Societies Stronger* (Bloomsbury, 2010), 155–56; James Whitman, *Harsh Justice: Criminal Punishment and the Widening Divide between America and Europe* (Oxford University Press, 2003), 200.

25. Gallup, "In U.S., 42% Believe Creationist View of Human Origins," June 1, 2014.

26. Pew, "Life in 2050," June 22, 2010.

27. See, for instance, Pew, "Many Americans Uneasy with Mix of Religion and Politics," August 24, 2006; Sarah Posner, "George W. Bush to Raise Money for Group That Converts Jews to Bring about Second Coming of Christ," *Mother Jones,* November 7, 2013; Ariel Levy, "Prodigal Son," *New Yorker,* June 28, 2010.

28. Pew, "One in 100: Behind Bars in America," February 2008.

29. David Garland, *The Culture of Control: Crime and Social Order in Contemporary Society* (University of Chicago Press, 2002), 99, 197.

30. An empirical study shows that the Supreme Court has grown friendlier to big business over time. Lee Epstein, William Landes, and Richard Posner, "How Business Fares at the Supreme Court," *Minnesota Law Review* 97 (2013): 1471–72.

31. Wilkinson and Pickett, *Spirit Level,* 148–50.

32. Scott Keyes, "As Alabama Cuts Benefits, Desperate Man 'Robs' Bank to Get Food, Shelter in Jail," *Think Progress,* July 11, 2013. Similar cases include those of Timothy Alsip in Oregon, Frank Morrocco in New York, and James Richard Verone in North Carolina. See Meredith Bennett-Smith, "Timothy Alsip, Oregon Homeless Man, Robs Bank for $1, Asks to Go to Jail to Access Healthcare," *Huffington Post,* August 28, 2013; Dan Herbeck, "Judge Refuses to Jail Ex-Convict on Quest for Health Coverage," *Buffalo News,* December 10, 2012; Tony Pierce, "$1 Bank Robbery Doesn't Pay Off for Man Who Said He Was Desperate for Healthcare," *Los Angeles Times,* June 21, 2011.

33. D.K., "Armed Police: Trigger Happy," *Democracy in America* (blog), *Economist,* August 15, 2014.

34. Small Arms Survey, "Estimating Civilian Owned Firearms" (2011).

35. Nearly a third of Americans think that "in the next few years an armed revolution might be necessary in order to protect our liberties." Fairleigh Dickinson University PublicMind Poll, "Beliefs about Sandy Hook Cover-up, Coming Revolution Underlie Divide on Gun Control," May 1, 2013.

36. United Nations Office on Drugs and Crime, "Global Study on Homicide" (2011), 93, 95.

37. Organisation for Economic Co-operation and Development, Better Life Index, "Safety," accessed October 17, 2016, www.oecdbetterlifeindex.org/topics /safety/"; Civitas, "Comparisons of Crime in OECD Countries" (2012); Peter Baldwin, *The Narcissism of Small Differences: How America and Europe Are Alike* (Oxford University Press, 2009), 78–87.

38. Lockyer v. Andrade, 538 U.S. 63 (2003). This precedent has largely barred other challenges to three-strikes laws.

39. Office of the United Nations High Commissioner for Human Rights, "US: 'Four Decades in Solitary Confinement Can Only Be Described as Torture,'" October 7, 2013.

40. International Human Rights Clinic at the University of Chicago Law School, American Civil Liberties Union, and Chicago Legal Advocacy for Incarcerated Mothers, "The Shackling of Incarcerated Pregnant Women: A Human Rights Violation Committed Regularly in the United States" (August 2013), 2–3.

41. Roper v. Simmons, 543 U.S. 551 (2005).

42. Human Rights Watch, "Against All Odds: Prison Conditions for Youth Offenders Serving Life without Parole Sentences in the United States," January 4, 2012. Iran is another country with virtually unparalleled draconian punishments for juveniles. Amnesty International, "Growing Up on Death Row: The Death Penalty and Juvenile Offenders in Iran," January 26, 2016.

43. Not only are draconian punishments and police shootings more common in the United States, but Americans are also more inclined to embrace military force than other Westerners. Jerome Karabel and Daniel Laurison, "An Exceptional Nation? American Political Values in Comparative Perspective" (Institute for Research on Labor and Employment Working Paper 136–12, University of California, Berkeley, 2012), 29–32.

44. Samuel Moyn, *The Last Utopia: Human Rights in History* (Belknap, 2010), 63.

45. Mugambi Jouet, "The Exceptional Absence of Human Rights as a Principle in American Law," *Pace Law Review* 34, no. 2 (2014): 704–8.

46. See, for example, Shanto Iyengar, James Curran, and Anker Brink Lund, "Media Systems, Public Knowledge and Democracy: A Comparative Study," *European Journal of Communication* 24, no. 1 (2009): 5–26.

47. U.S. State Department, "Valid Passports in Circulation (1989–Present)," https://travel.state.gov/content/passports/en/passports/statistics.html.

48. Bryan Bender and Sasha Issenberg, "Palin Not Well Traveled outside US," *Boston Globe,* September 3, 2008.

49. Non-Latino whites represent approximately 61.6 percent of the U.S. population. U.S. Census, "Quick Facts" (July 1, 2015, data), www.census.gov/quickfacts /table/PST045215/00.

50. Michael L. Millenson, "Why Obamacare Is Good for White People," *Health Care Blog,* October 30, 2012; Urban Institute and Robert Wood Johnson Foundation, "Characteristics of Those Affected by a Supreme Court Finding for the Plaintiff in King v. Burwell," January 2015. Chapters 5 and 6 cover other reasons why most Americans stand to gain from universal health care.

51. Stephen Mansfield, *The Faith of George W. Bush* (Tarcher, 2004), 108.

52. John Kingdon, *America the Unusual* (Worth, 1999), 55. See also 72.

1. ONE NATION, DIVISIBLE

1. Gallup, "Americans See U.S. as Exceptional," December 22, 2010. A later poll found fewer Americans convinced of U.S. superiority: Pew, "Most Americans Think the U.S. Is Great, but Fewer Think It's the Greatest," July 2, 2014. Given that the drop was strongest among Republicans, it might have been influenced by the G.O.P.'s recurrent claim that Barack Obama's policies have ruined America. The drop among Democrats might reflect preoccupation over the damaging gridlock in Washington and the rise of the Tea Party. In any event, a comparative international

study confirms that Americans are generally the Westerners proudest of their nationality. Jerome Karabel and Daniel Laurison, "An Exceptional Nation? American Political Values in Comparative Perspective" (Institute for Research on Labor and Employment Working Paper 136–12, University of California, Berkeley, 2012), 22–23, 32.

2. Public Religion Research Institute, "Most Americans Believe Protests Make the Country Better," June 23, 2015.

3. A chart tracking references to "American exceptionalism" in the U.S. media previously appeared in Jerome Karabel, "'American Exceptionalism' and the Battle for the Presidency," *Huffington Post,* December 22, 2011.

4. Jack Greene, *The Intellectual Construction of America: Exceptionalism and Identity from 1492 to 1800* (University of North Carolina Press, 1993), 6–7, 69.

5. John Adams, *A Dissertation on the Canon and Feudal Law* (1765), quoted in Robert Ferguson, *The American Enlightenment, 1750–1820* (Harvard University Press, 1997), 89.

6. Anders Stephanson, *Manifest Destiny: American Expansion and the Empire of Right* (Hill and Wang, 1995), especially xi, xii, 5–6 (quotes), 8, 49–51, 56, 60.

7. Alexis de Tocqueville, *Democracy in America,* trans. Henry Reeve (Bantam, 2000), 548.

8. Ted Morgan, *A Covert Life: Jay Lovestone: Communist, Anti-Communist, and Spymaster* (Random House, 1999), 41, 78, 91, 100–104. The linguist Ben Zimmer has underlined that it was Lovestone, not Stalin, who first used the expression "American exceptionalism." Zimmer, "Did Stalin Really Coin 'American Exceptionalism'?," *Slate,* September 27, 2013. Various other scholars have commented on the communist origins of the phrase. See, for instance, James W. Ceaser, "The Origins and Character of American Exceptionalism," *American Political Thought* 1 (2012): 6; Donald Pease, *The New American Exceptionalism* (University of Minnesota Press, 2009), 10; Mark Liberman, "The Third Life of American Exceptionalism," *Language Log,* February 23, 2012, http://languagelog.ldc.upenn.edu/nll/?p=3798; Karabel, "'American Exceptionalism.'" The Yale librarian Fred Shapiro identified a prior reference to "exceptionalism" in an 1861 London *Times* article on the U.S. Civil War, which evoked the chauvinistic definition that especially reemerged during the Obama presidency: "It is probable that the 'exceptionalism,' if one may use the word, on which the Americans rather pride themselves, will not prevail in the case of the struggle between North and South." "The Civil War in America," *Times* (London), August 20, 1861, quoted in Shapiro to American Dialect Society mailing list, September 29, 2013, http://listserv.linguistlist.org/pipermail/ads-l/2013-September/128665.html.

9. See Greene, *Intellectual Construction of America,* 4–5; Ceaser, "Origins and Character," 2; Seymour Martin Lipset, *American Exceptionalism: A Double-Edged Sword* (Norton, 1997), 18.

10. Besides the previously cited publications, a wide range of scholarship focuses on American exceptionalism. See, for instance, Peter H. Schuck and James Q. Wilson, eds., *Understanding America: The Anatomy of an Exceptional Nation* (Public

Affairs, 2008); Charles Lockhart, *The Roots of American Exceptionalism: Institutions, Culture and Policies* (Palgrave MacMillan, 2003); Michael Ignatieff, ed., *American Exceptionalism and Human Rights* (Princeton University Press, 2005).

11. Lipset, *American Exceptionalism,* 18.

12. Glenn Greenwald, "The Premises and Purposes of American Exceptionalism," *Guardian,* February 18, 2013.

13. See Sylvia Söderlind, "Introduction: The Shining of America," in *American Exceptionalisms: From Winthrop to Winfrey,* ed. Söderlind and James Taylor Carson (State University of New York Press, 2011), 1; Emily García, "'The Cause of America Is in Great Measure the Cause of Mankind': American Universalism and Exceptionalism in the Early Republic," in ibid., 52–53.

14. Donald Trump, *Time to Get Tough: Making America #1 Again* (Regnery, 2011), 155–56.

15. This finding is based on my review of the Republican platforms in the database of Gerhard Peters and John T. Woolley's American Presidency Project (www .presidency.ucsb.edu/) at the University of California, Santa Barbara. It should be noted that various platforms emphasized faith in American greatness even though they did not use the precise adjective "exceptional."

16. "American Exceptionalism," in "We Believe in America: Republican Platform 2012" (August 27, 2012), American Presidency Project, 39–50, www.presidency .ucsb.edu/papers_pdf/101961.pdf.

17. Preamble, "Republican Platform 2016" (July 18, 2016), American Presidency Project, i, www.presidency.ucsb.edu/papers_pdf/117718.pdf.

18. Steven Brill, *America's Bitter Pill: Money, Politics, Backroom Deals, and the Fight to Fix Our Broken Healthcare System* (Random House, 2015), 30–34, 93.

19. Harris Interactive, "'Wingnuts' and President Obama," March 23, 2010.

20. PolitiFact, "Mitt Romney Repeats Claim That Obama Went around the World Apologizing for the United States," September 22, 2011.

21. Andrew Sullivan, "The Big Lie," Daily Dish, *Atlantic,* November 9, 2010.

22. Harris Interactive, "'Wingnuts' and President Obama."

23. David Corn, "Donald Trump Says He Doesn't Believe in 'American Exceptionalism,'" *Mother Jones,* June 7, 2016.

24. Trump, *Time to Get Tough,* 155–56.

25. Hillary Clinton, speech at the American Legion National Convention, Cincinnati, August 31, 2016.

26. Ian Haney López, *Dog Whistle Politics: How Coded Racial Appeals Have Reinvented Racism and Wrecked the Middle Class* (Oxford University Press, 2015), 1, 4.

27. "Gerrymandering" refers to redrawing electoral districts for political gain. The term stems from the actions of Massachusetts Governor Elbridge Gerry, whose 1812 electoral map featured a district shaped like a salamander. His critics derisively called it a "gerry-mander." Carl Hulse, "Seeking to End Gerrymandering's Enduring Legacy," *New York Times,* January 25, 2016.

28. "On gerrymandering, much of the discussion tends to conflate the issue of increasingly 'safe seats' for one party or the other, which has occurred, with gerry-

mandering as the cause for the rise of these safe seats. Many empirical studies now conclude that the increasing geographic concentration of Democrats in urban areas, and their geographic isolation in college towns and certain other areas, is the major cause for the rise of these safe seats." Richard Pildes, "Romanticizing Democracy, Political Fragmentation, and the Decline of American Government," *Yale Law Journal* 124 (2014): 821 fn. 46. See also Nolan McCarty, Keith Poole, and Howard Rosenthal, *Polarized America: The Dance of Ideology and Unequal Riches* (MIT Press, 2016), 207 ("We are reluctant to see gerrymandering as a major source of the overall polarization of American politics."). Jill Lepore of Harvard aptly summarized the general consensus among political scientists: "First, polarization has taken place in both chambers at about the same time and rate and, since redistricting does not affect the Senate, it cannot wholly explain what's happened in the House. Second, much polarization in the House has taken place in districts that have not been redrawn by legislators. Third, much of the polarizing in gerrymandered districts preceded their redrawing. The best calculation is that redistricting accounts for no more than ten or twenty per cent of the polarization in the House. Gerrymandering is bad for all kinds of reasons, but polarization isn't one of them." Lepore, "Long Division," *New Yorker,* December 2, 2013, 77–78.

29. Christopher Hare and Keith Poole, "The Polarization of Contemporary American Politics," *Polity* 46, no. 3 (2014): 428.

30. Belgium and Canada, like the United States, are exceptional in this regard. See Katharine Young, "American Exceptionalism and Constitutional Shutdowns," *Boston University Law Review* 94 (2014): 991–92.

31. Pildes, "Romanticizing Democracy," 823.

32. Lisa Lerer, "Clinton Wins Popular Vote by Nearly 2.9 Million," *Associated Press,* December 23, 2016.

33. Elena Schneider, "Trump Explains Mussolini Quote," *Politico,* February 28, 2016.

34. "Father of Fascism Studies: Donald Trump Shows Alarming Willingness to Use Fascist Terms and Styles," *Democracy Now!,* March 15, 2016.

35. Dylan Matthews, "I Asked 5 Fascism Experts Whether Donald Trump Is a Fascist. Here Is What They Said," *Vox,* May 19, 2016; Peter Baker, "Rise of Donald Trump Tracks Growing Debate over Global Fascism," *New York Times,* May 28, 2016.

36. Alan Abramowitz, *The Polarized Public? Why American Government Is So Dysfunctional* (Pearson, 2013), 3.

37. Bill Adair and Angie Drobnic Holan, "PolitiFact's Lie of the Year: 'A Government Takeover of Health Care,'" December 16, 2010.

38. Brill, *America's Bitter Pill,* 30–34, 93.

39. Congressional Budget Office, "Insurance Coverage Provisions of the Affordable Care Act—March 2015 Baseline," March 2015, Table 2.

40. Andrew Romano and Daniel Stone, "The Necessary Man," *Newsweek,* September 19, 2010.

41. Jim Nunns, Len Burman, Jeff Rohaly, and Joe Rosenberg, "An Analysis of Donald Trump's Tax Plan," Tax Policy Center, December 22, 2015.

42. Abramowitz, *Polarized Public?*, 2.

43. McCarty, Poole, and Rosenthal, *Polarized America*, 12.

44. Jacob Hacker and Paul Pierson, "Confronting Asymmetric Polarization," in *Solutions to Polarization in America,* ed. Nathaniel Persily (Cambridge University Press, 2015), 59–70; Thomas E. Mann, foreword to *American Gridlock: The Sources, Character, and Impact of Political Polarization,* ed. James Thurber and Antoine Yoshinaka (Cambridge University Press, 2015), xxiv.

45. Nathaniel Persily, introduction to *Solutions to Polarization,* 6.

46. Morris Fiorina with Samuel Abrams and Jeremy Pope, *Culture War? The Myth of a Polarized America,* 3rd ed. (Longman, 2010), 55, 73, 76–77, 93, 206, 208. Fiorina's theory about the outsize role of political elites is bolstered by a study which found that "Democrats and Republicans now speak different languages to a far greater degree than ever before" because of increasingly partisan rhetoric framed by political consultants and campaign strategists. Matthew Gentzkow, Jesse Shapiro, and Matt Taddy, "Measuring Polarization in High-Dimensional Data: Method and Application to Congressional Speech" (National Bureau of Economic Research Working Paper No. 22423, July 2016), 23.

47. David Broockman and Christopher Skovron, "What Politicians Believe about Their Constituents: Asymmetric Misperceptions and Prospects for Constituency Control" (working paper, July 17, 2015), www.vanderbilt.edu/csdi/miller-stokes/08_MillerStokes_BroockmanSkovron.pdf.

48. Abramowitz, *Polarized Public?*, xii, 56–57; Hacker and Pierson, "Confronting Asymmetric Polarization," 63.

49. Abramowitz, *Polarized Public?*, 8, 16, 44–45, 54, 60, 105.

50. Ibid., 105; Pew, "Political Polarization in the American Public," June 12, 2014. By other estimates, "the highly politically active and knowledgeable citizens that scholars routinely indict for pulling politics to the extremes appear, if anything, less likely than their peers to support more extreme policies." David Broockman, "Approaches to Studying Policy Representation," *Legislative Studies Quarterly* 41, no. 1 (2016): 206.

51. Abramowitz, *Polarized Public?*, 2.

52. Ibid., xv, 60. Broockman, however, has questioned political scientists' findings regarding ideological consistency among conservative and liberals. Broockman, "Studying Policy Representation," 181–215.

53. Douglas Ahler and David Broockman, "Does Elite Polarization Imply Poor Representation? A New Perspective on the 'Disconnect' between Politicians and Voters" (working paper, March 14, 2016), https://people.stanford.edu/dbroock/sites/default/files/ahler_broockman_ideological_innocence.pdf.

54. Hare and Poole, "Polarization of Contemporary American Politics," 428.

55. Ibid.; Abramowitz, *Polarized Public?*, 2, 25–26, 42; Morris Fiorina, "If I Could Hold a Seminar for Political Journalists . . . ," *Forum* 10, vol. 4 (February 2013): 2–10.

56. Hare and Poole, "Polarization of Contemporary American Politics," 417. On realignment, see also Abramowitz, *Polarized Public?*, 45–61.

57. Pew, "Beyond Red vs. Blue: The Political Typology," May 4, 2011.

58. Pew, "Political Polarization in the American Public," June 12, 2014.

59. Shanto Iyengar and Sean Westwood, "Fear and Loathing across Party Lines: New Evidence on Group Polarization," *American Journal of Political Science* 59, no. 3 (2015): 691.

60. Giovanni Russonello, "Race Relations Are at Lowest Point in Obama Presidency, Poll Finds," *New York Times,* July 13, 2016.

61. Michael Norton and Samuel Sommers, "Whites See Racism as a Zero-Sum Game That They Are Now Losing," *Perspectives on Psychological Science* 6, no. 3 (May 2011): 215–18.

62. Scott Clement, "Republicans Embrace Trump's Ban on Muslims While Most Others Reject It," *Washington Post,* December 14, 2016.

63. Sam Roberts, "Projections Put Whites in Minority in U.S. by 2050," *New York Times,* December 17, 2009.

64. Guttmacher Institute, "In Just the Last Four Years, States Have Enacted 231 Abortion Restrictions," January 5, 2015.

65. Abramowitz, *Polarized Public?,* 65, 70–72.

66. Ibid., 65.

67. Fiorina, Abrams, and Pope, *Culture War,* 241.

68. According to Marc Hetherington, modern public opinion data on gay rights suggests that Americans are more polarized over this issue than Fiorina's interpretation of the data indicates. Proceeding by analogy, Hetherington showed that a narrow interpretation of statistical data could even support the conclusion that Northern and Southern whites were not truly polarized over race and civil rights in the 1960s. Hetherington, "Putting Polarization in Perspective," *British Journal of Political Science* 39, no. 2 (2009): 433–36.

69. Abramowitz, *Polarized Public?,* 10–11.

70. Sean F. Reardon and Kendra Bischoff, "The Continuing Increase in Income Segregation, 2007–2012" (Stanford Center for Education and Policy Analysis, 2016).

71. Raj Chetty, Nathaniel Hendren, and Lawrence Katz, "The Effects of Exposure to Better Neighborhoods on Children: New Evidence from the Moving to Opportunity Experiment," *American Economic Review* 106, no. 4 (2016): 855–902.

72. Bill Bishop, *The Big Sort: Why the Clustering of Like-Minded America Is Tearing Us Apart* (Mariner, 2009).

73. Chapter 2 describes how Fox News plays a more dominant role in conservative America than MSNBC does in liberal America. Fox News viewers also tend to be far less informed and more radical than their MSNBC counterparts.

74. Abramowitz, *Polarized Public?,* 86, 100.

75. McCarty, Poole, and Rosenthal, *Polarized America,* 9, 79.

76. That is a recurrent finding of the World Values Survey. See Karabel and Laurison, "Exceptional Nation?," 5–13; Lipset, *American Exceptionalism,* 71–76.

77. Abramowitz, *Polarized Public?,* 10–11.

78. "The Return of 'Drill, Baby, Drill,'" Editorial, *New York Times,* May 6, 2011.

79. Joseph Stiglitz, *Freefall: America, Free Markets, and the Sinking of the World Economy* (Norton, 2010), 219.

80. Again, this is a persistent finding of the World Values Survey. See Karabel and Laurison, "Exceptional Nation?," 16–21; Lipset, *American Exceptionalism,* 60–67.

81. Pew, "America's Changing Religious Landscape," May 12, 2015.

82. See generally Mugambi Jouet, "The Exceptional Absence of Human Rights as a Principle in American Law," *Pace Law Review* 34, no. 2 (2014): 101–42.

83. Atkins v. Virginia, 536 U.S. 304 (2002); Roper v. Simmons, 543 U.S. 551 (2005).

84. I present various nuances to this argument throughout the book, such as in Chapter 7, where I discuss how the death penalty was abolished in Europe despite public support.

85. Data suggest that, unlike in America, mainstream political parties in Western Europe have largely depolarized. See Philipp Rehm and Timothy Reilly, "United We Stand: Constituency Homogeneity and Comparative Party Polarization," *Electoral Studies* 29, no. 1 (2010): 40–53; Morris Fiorina, "Is the US Experience Exceptional?," Hoover Institution, October 26, 2016. Another study found that partisan animosity is worse in America than in Britain. Shanto Iyengar, Gaurav Sood, Yphtach Lelkes, "Affect, Not Ideology: A Social Identity Perspective on Polarization," *Public Opinion Quarterly* 76, no. 3 (2012): 405–31.

86. Peter Schwartzstein, "90 Percent of Europeans Would Vote for Obama," Reuters, October 31, 2012.

87. "Global Poll on the American Election," WIN/Gallup International, October 4, 2016.

88. Ethan Bronner, "For Many Abroad, an Ideal Renewed," *New York Times,* November 5, 2008.

89. T. R. Reid, *The Healing of America: A Global Quest for Better, Cheaper, and Fairer Health Care* (Penguin, 2010), 84–90.

90. Soonman Kwon, "Thirty Years of National Health Insurance in South Korea: Lessons for Achieving Universal Health Care Coverage," *Oxford Journal of Health Policy and Planning* 24, no. 1 (2009): 63–71.

91. Reid, *Healing of America,* 173.

92. Felicia Marie Knaul, Eduardo González-Pier, Octavio Gómez-Dantés, David García-Junco, Héctor Arreola-Ornelas, Mariana Barraza-Lloréns, Rosa Sandoval, et al., "The Quest for Universal Health Coverage: Achieving Social Protection for All in Mexico," *Lancet* 380, no. 9849 (October 6, 2012): 1259–79.

93. South African Constitution, Article 27(1)(a).

94. *Time* Magazine / ABT SRBI survey, October 9–10, 2011, http://swampland.time.com/full-results-of-oct-9–10–2011-time-poll/.

95. Jonathan Weisman, "Poll Finds Voters Deeply Torn," *Wall Street Journal,* November 8, 2011.

96. Data going back to the 1950s suggest that the public's mood swings to the left when conservatives are in power and to the right when liberals are. Larry Bartels,

Unequal Democracy: The Political Economy of the New Gilded Age (Princeton University Press, 2016), 289–90.

97. Thomas Piketty, *Capital in the Twenty-First Century,* trans. Arthur Goldhammer (Belknap, 2014), 321.

98. John Kingdon, *America the Unusual* (Worth, 1999), 10; Pildes, "Romanticizing Democracy," 808–17; Persily, introduction to *Solutions to Polarization,* 7.

99. Sarah Binder, "How We Count Senate Filibusters and Why It Matters," *Washington Post,* May 15, 2014; "Not Too Late to Curb the Filibuster," Editorial, *New York Times,* May 14, 2012; Steven S. Smith, "Partisan Polarization and the Senate Syndrome," in Persily, *Solutions to Polarization,* 219–21.

100. Andrew Moravcsik, "The Paradox of U.S. Human Rights Policy," in Ignatieff, *American Exceptionalism,* 184, 187.

101. Akhil Reed Amar, "Foreword: The Document and the Doctrine," *Harvard Law Review* 114 (2000): 61–62.

102. David R. Mayhew, "Supermajority Rule in the U.S. Senate," *Political Science and Politics* 36, no. 1 (2003): 31.

2. FROM THE AMERICAN ENLIGHTENMENT TO ANTI-INTELLECTUALISM

1. Trump was questioning aspects of Carson's controversial biography. Maggie Haberman, "Donald Trump Asks Iowans: 'How Stupid' Are They to Believe Ben Carson?," *New York Times,* November 13, 2015.

2. Angie Drobnic Holan, "All Politicians Lie. Some Lie More Than Others," *New York Times,* December 11, 2015.

3. Isaac Asimov, "A Cult of Ignorance," *Newsweek,* January 21, 1980.

4. As privacy requires, I have usually modified the names and identifying details of people I have interacted with.

5. Susan Jacoby, interview by Nick Gillespie, *After Words, Book TV,* C-SPAN2, May 1, 2008.

6. Peter Galbraith, *The End of Iraq: How American Incompetence Created a War without End* (Simon and Schuster, 2007), 83.

7. Alexis de Tocqueville, *Democracy in America,* trans. Henry Reeve (Bantam, 2000), 4.

8. Henry May, *The Enlightenment in America* (Oxford University Press, 1976), 314.

9. Peter Lindert and Jeffrey Williamson, "American Incomes before and after the Revolution," *Journal of Economic History* 73, no. 3 (2013): 725–65; Thomas Piketty, *Capital in the Twenty-First Century,* trans. Arthur Goldhammer (Belknap, 2014), 150–52.

10. May, *Enlightenment in America,* 29.

11. Leo Damrosch, *Tocqueville's Discovery of America* (Farrar, Straus and Giroux, 2010), 26.

12. On this point see also May, *Enlightenment in America,* 308–9.

13. Jacob Hacker and Paul Pierson, *Winner-Take-All Politics: How Washington Made the Rich Richer—and Turned Its Back on the Middle Class* (Simon and Schuster, 2010), 39.

14. Jack Greene, *The Intellectual Construction of America: Exceptionalism and Identity from 1492 to 1800* (University of North Carolina Press, 1993), 106–7, 132.

15. Susan Jacoby, *The Age of American Unreason* (Vintage, 2009), 37.

16. See generally Richard Hofstadter, *Anti-Intellectualism in American Life* (Vintage, 1966). See also Jacoby, *Age of American Unreason,* 37–38, 57; Michael Kazin, *The Populist Persuasion: An American History* (Basic, 1995), 12.

17. Tocqueville, *Democracy in America,* 58.

18. Ibid., 560.

19. Ibid., 58.

20. Hofstadter, *Anti-Intellectualism,* 154.

21. Robert Ferguson, *The American Enlightenment, 1750–1820* (Harvard University Press, 1997), 89, 109.

22. Marquis de Condorcet, "Influence of the American Revolution on the Opinions and Legislation of Europe" (1786), quoted in Greene, *Intellectual Construction of America,* 140.

23. Ibid., 131, 138–40; Denis Lacorne, *Religion in America,* trans. George Holoch (Columbia University Press, 2011), 2–12.

24. See, for example, Philippe Roger, *The American Enemy: The History of French Anti-Americanism,* trans. Sharon Bowman (University of Chicago Press, 2006).

25. Caroline Winterer, *American Enlightenments: Pursuing Happiness in the Age of Reason* (Yale University Press, 2016), 12.

26. As the historian Caroline Winterer has emphasized, the notion of a single "American Enlightenment" emerged in the twentieth century, although "American Enlightenments" may better describe this complex and multifaceted epoch. Ibid., 5–13.

27. Federalist Paper No. 49, available at www.congress.gov/resources/display /content/The+Federalist+Papers#TheFederalistPapers-49.

28. Ferguson, *American Enlightenment,* 86–87, 110.

29. Marist Poll, "7/1: Independence Day—Seventeen Seventy When?," July 1, 2011.

30. Annenberg Public Policy Center, "New Annenberg Survey Asks: 'How Well Do Americans Understand the Constitution?,'" September 16, 2011.

31. Andrew Romano, "How Dumb Are We?," *Newsweek,* May 20, 2011.

32. Jean-Marie Déguignet, *Mémoires d'un paysan bas-breton* (Pocket, 2001).

33. While anti-intellectualism has had less weight in France than in America, the French have long debated whether their high schools should prioritize practical instruction or the humanities. This enduring Gallic debate emerged in the nineteenth century. See Philippe Savoie, *La construction de l'enseignment secondaire (1802–1914): Aux origines d'un service public* (ENS Éditions, 2013), 138, 401–4.

34. Henry Louis Gates Jr., "Mister Jefferson and the Trials of Phillis Wheatley," Jefferson Lecture in the Humanities, National Endowment for the Humanities, Washington D.C., March 22, 2002.

35. Ta-Nehisi Coates, "Acting French," *Atlantic,* August 29, 2014.

36. Pew, "U.S. Religious Knowledge Survey," September 28, 2010.

37. Shanto Iyengar, James Curran, and Anker Brink Lund, "Media Systems, Public Knowledge and Democracy: A Comparative Study," *European Journal of Communication* (2009): 14.

38. Jacoby, interview on *Book TV.*

39. Claudia Goldin and Lawrence Katz, *The Race between Education and Technology* (Belknap, 2008), 12 (quote), 28, 154–55.

40. Ibid., 157, 197, 206.

41. Ibid., 4–5, 325 (quote).

42. Hofstadter, *Anti-Intellectualism,* 51.

43. Kazin, *Populist Persuasion,* 257–58.

44. Ioanna Kohler, "Gone for Good? Partis pour de bon? Les expatriés de l'enseignement supérieur français aux États-Unis," Institut Montaigne, November 2010, 22. See also Maïa de la Baume, "French Professors Find Life in U.S. Hard to Resist," *New York Times,* November 21, 2010.

45. Susan Dynarski, "New Data Gives Clearer Picture of Student Debt," *New York Times,* September 10, 2015.

46. Sam Stein, "McCain Backed Abolishing the Department of Education," *Huffington Post,* September 9, 2008.

47. Andrew Romano and Daniel Stone, "The Necessary Man," *Newsweek,* September 19, 2010.

48. Nina Eliasoph, *Avoiding Politics: How Americans Produce Apathy in Everyday Life* (Cambridge University Press, 1998).

49. John Adams, *A Dissertation on the Canon and Feudal Law* (1765), quoted in Ferguson, *American Enlightenment,* 89.

50. See, for example, Jacoby, *Age of American Unreason,* 250–51; Olivier Donnat, "Les pratiques culturelles des français à l'ère numérique: Eléments de synthèse 1997–2008," Culture Études, Ministère de la Culture et de la Communication, October 2009, 6; Pew, "A Snapshot of Reading in America in 2013," January 16, 2014.

51. David Riesman, "Preface to the 1961 Edition," in *The Lonely Crowd* (Yale University Press, 2001), lxiv.

52. Hofstadter, *Anti-Intellectualism,* 145–51, 155–57, 160 (first quote); May, *Enlightenment in America,* 312; Kazin, *Populist Persuasion,* 22 (second quote).

53. Hofstadter, *Anti-Intellectualism,* 192–96.

54. Ibid., 10 (quote), 226–27.

55. Elvin Lim, *The Anti-Intellectual Presidency: The Decline of Presidential Rhetoric from George Washington to George W. Bush* (Oxford University Press, 2008), 42.

56. Ibid., 43.

57. Hofstadter, *Anti-Intellectualism,* 227–29; Jacoby, *Age of American Unreason,* 283–84.

58. Jerome Karabel, "The Legacy of Legacies," *New York Times,* September 13, 2004; "Kerry Grades near Bush's While at Yale," *New York Times,* June 8, 2005.

59. Ron Suskind, *The Price of Loyalty: George W. Bush, the White House, and the Education of Paul O'Neill* (Simon and Schuster, 2004), 57–60, 88, 149, 153.

60. Tony Blair, *A Journey: My Political Life* (Knopf, 2010), 393.

61. John DiIulio to Ron Suskind, October 24, 2002, available at www.esquire .com/news-politics/a2880/dilulio/.

62. Larry Bartels, *Unequal Democracy: The Political Economy of the New Gilded Age* (Princeton, 2008), 163 (quote), 186.

63. "Iraq | Gallup Historical Trends," www.gallup.com/poll/1633/iraq.aspx.

64. Lim, *Anti-Intellectual Presidency,* 93 (quote), 96.

65. Even if Obama was born in Kenya, he would still be a "natural born citizen" eligible for the presidency because his mother was a U.S. citizen. Paul Clement and Neal Katyal, "On the Meaning of 'Natural Born Citizen,'" *Harvard Law Review Forum* 128 (2015): 161–64.

66. Harris Interactive, "'Wingnuts' and President Obama," March 23, 2010.

67. Barack Obama, "My Spiritual Journey," *Time,* October 16, 2006.

68. Josh Gerstein, "Should Obama Show His Faith?," *Politico,* October 19, 2010.

69. Lydia Polgreen, "A Question of Appearances: Obama Will Bypass Sikh Temple on Visit to India," *New York Times,* October 19, 2010.

70. Alex Theodoridis, "Scott Walker's View of Obama's Religion Makes Him a Moderate," *Washington Post,* February 25, 2015.

71. Public Policy Polling, "Trump Supporters Think Obama Is a Muslim Born in Another Country," September 1, 2015.

72. Ian Urbina, "Beyond Beltway, Health Care Debate Turns Hostile," *New York Times,* August 7, 2009.

73. Reed Abelson, "Census Numbers Show 50.7 Million Uninsured," *New York Times,* September 16, 2010.

74. Reed Abelson, "Ranks of Underinsured Are Rising, Study Finds," *New York Times,* June 10, 2008.

75. This was the conviction of Republican voters too. See Harvard School of Public Health and Harris Interactive, "Most Republicans Think the U.S. Health Care System Is the Best in the World. Democrats Disagree," March 20, 2008.

76. See, for example, Stanford Center on Poverty and Inequality, "State of the Union" (2016), 58–64; Commonwealth Fund, "U.S. Health Care from a Global Perspective" (2015); Organisation for Economic Co-operation and Development, "Why Is Health Spending in the United States So High?" (2011); T.R. Reid, *The Healing of America: A Global Quest for Better, Cheaper, and Fairer Health Care* (Penguin, 2010), 31–34.

77. Bill Adair and Angie Drobnic Holan, "PolitiFact's Lie of the Year: 'A Government Takeover of Health Care,'" December 16, 2010.

78. Steven Brill, *America's Bitter Pill: Money, Politics, Backroom Deals, and the Fight to Fix Our Broken Healthcare System* (Random House, 2015), 30–34, 93.

79. Adair and Holan, "PolitiFact's Lie of the Year."

80. Congressional Budget Office, "Insurance Coverage Provisions of the Affordable Care Act—March 2015 Baseline," March 2015.

81. Commonwealth Fund, "31 Million People Were Underinsured in 2014; Many Skipped Needed Health Care and Depleted Savings to Pay Medical Bills," May 20, 2015.

82. See generally Reid, *Healing of America,* 36–37; Mugambi Jouet, "The Exceptional Absence of Human Rights as a Principle in American Law," *Pace Law Review* 34 (2014): 714.

83. Glenn Kessler, "Fact-Check: Boehner's Claim That Obamacare Has Resulted in a 'Net Loss' of People with Health Insurance," *Washington Post,* March 17, 2014.

84. PolitiFact, "James Clyburn Says Republicans Sat on Sidelines for Passage of Social Security, Medicare, Medicaid," September 6, 2012.

85. Kaiser Family Foundation, "Health Tracking Poll," September 2013. Another poll similarly found that fewer than four in ten Americans realize that enrollees in new insurance plans can choose among different private health plans, whereas a quarter wrongly believe they are enrolled in a single government plan and another four in ten are unsure. Kaiser Family Foundation, "Health Tracking Poll," July 2014.

86. Kaiser Family Foundation, "Health Tracking Poll," September 2011.

87. Harris Interactive, "'Wingnuts' and President Obama."

88. Paul Farhi, "The E-mail Rumor Mill Is Run by Conservatives," *Washington Post,* November 18, 2011.

89. Pew, "Cable News Fact Sheet," April 29, 2015.

90. Public Policy Polling, "Americans Closely Divided on Brian Williams," February 26, 2015.

91. PolitiFact, "Jon Stewart Says Those Who Watch Fox News Are the 'Most Consistently Misinformed Media Viewers,'" June 20, 2011.

92. Lauren Feldman, Edward Maibach, Connie Roser-Renouf, and Anthony Leiserowitz, "Climate on Cable: The Nature and Impact of Global Warming Coverage on Fox News, CNN, and MSNBC," *International Journal of Press/Politics* 17, no. 1 (2012): 3. See also Bruce Bartlett, "How Fox News Changed American Media and Political Dynamics," June 3, 2015, https://papers.ssrn.com/sol3/papers.cfm?abstract_id=2604679; Fairleigh Dickinson University's PublicMind Poll, "Some News Leaves People Knowing Less," November 21, 2011; Kaiser Family Foundation, "Pop Quiz: Assessing Americans' Familiarity with the Health Care Law," February 2011; Program on International Policy Attitudes / Knowledge Networks Poll, "Misperceptions, the Media and the Iraq War," October 2, 2003.

93. Michael Grynbaum and John Herrman, "Breitbart, Reveling in Trump's Election, Gains a Voice in His White House," *New York Times,* November 13, 2016.

94. Shanto Iyengar, James Curran, Anker Brink Lund, Inka Salovaara-Moring, Kyu Hahn, and Sharon Coen, "Cross-National versus Individual-Level Differences

in Political Information: A Media Systems Perspective," *Journal of Elections, Public Opinion and Parties* 20, no. 3 (August 2010): 294–95.

95. Ibid., 294, 304 (quote).

96. Richard Hofstadter, *The Paranoid Style in American Politics, and Other Essays* (Vintage, 2008), 3, 65.

97. Michael Cooper, "From Obama, the Tax Cut Nobody Heard Of," *New York Times,* October 18, 2010.

98. Robert Hendin, "Poll Reveals Most Americans Don't Know They Got a Tax Cut," CBS News, February 12, 2010.

99. Tax Policy Center, "Historical Highest Marginal Income Tax Rates," www .taxpolicycenter.org/statistics/historical-highest-marginal-income-tax-rates.

100. Emmanuel Saez, "Striking It Richer: The Evolution of Top Incomes in the United States," UC Berkeley Economics Department, January 25, 2015.

101. As noted above, a study of conservative parties in nine countries found that "the U.S. Republican Party is an anomaly in denying anthropogenic climate change." Sondre Båtstrand, "More Than Markets: A Comparative Study of Nine Conservative Parties on Climate Change," *Politics and Policy,* 43, no. 4 (2015): 538. Still, a relative partisan divide exists in various countries. Pew, "The U.S. Isn't the Only Nation with Big Partisan Divides on Climate Change," November 6, 2015. However, both the extent and the intensity of the U.S. partisan divide over climate change are considerable, as illustrated by the conspiracy theories that Republican leaders promote. Pew, "Americans, Politics and Science Issues," July 1, 2015, 40–41; Pew, "Global Warming Seen as a Major Problem around the World," December 2, 2009; Institut français d'opinion publique, "Les français et le climato-scepticisme," November 15, 2010 (comparing poll data in France and the United States).

102. Andrew Moravcsik, "The Paradox of U.S. Human Rights Policy," in *American Exceptionalism and Human Rights,* ed. Michael Ignatieff (Princeton University Press, 2005), 187.

103. The filibuster is not a constitutional provision but a Senate rule.

104. Regarding the influence of America's situation on the negotiation process, see Coral Davenport, "Nations Approve Landmark Climate Accord in Paris," *New York Times,* December 12, 2015.

105. PolitiFact, "Jerry Brown Says 'Virtually No Republican' in Washington Accepts Climate Change Science," May 18, 2014.

106. Cordula Meyer, "'Science as the Enemy': The Traveling Salesmen of Climate Skepticism," *Der Spiegel,* October 8, 2010.

107. Bill Curry and Shawn McCarthy, "Canada Formally Abandons Kyoto Protocol on Climate Change," *Globe and Mail,* December 12, 2011.

108. Juliet Eilperin, "U.S. Plays Conflicted Role in Global Climate Debate," *Washington Post,* November 1, 2010.

109. "Republican Platform 2016" (July 18, 2016), American Presidency Project, 22, www.presidency.ucsb.edu/papers_pdf/117718.pdf.

110. "Into Ignorance," *Nature,* March 16, 2011.

111. Chris Mooney, "The Surprising Links between Faith and Evolution and Climate Denial," *Washington Post,* May 20, 2015.

112. PolitiFact, "Yes, Donald Trump Did Call Climate Change a Chinese Hoax," June 3, 2016.

113. Center for Responsive Politics, "Oil and Gas: Long-Term Contribution Trends," accessed October 29, 2016, www.opensecrets.org/industries/totals .php?cycle=2016&ind=E01.

114. Upton Sinclair, *I, Candidate for Governor: And How I Got Licked* (University of California Press, 1994), 109.

115. Coral Davenport and Marjorie Connelly, "Most Republicans Say They Back Climate Action, Poll Finds," *New York Times,* January 30, 2015.

116. Coral Davenport, "Supreme Court's Blow to Emissions Efforts May Imperil Paris Climate Accord," *New York Times,* February 10, 2016.

117. See the data on political polarization cited in Chapter 1.

118. Alan Abramowitz, *The Polarized Public? Why American Government Is So Dysfunctional* (Pearson, 2013), 2; Pew, "Beyond Red vs. Blue: The Political Typology," May 4, 2011.

119. Mike Lofgren, "Goodbye to All That: Reflections of a GOP Operative Who Left the Cult," *Truthout,* September 3, 2011.

120. John Nichols, "Why Dutch Far-Right Extremist Geert Wilders Has Come to Cleveland to Cheer On Donald Trump," *Nation,* July 20, 2016.

121. Jon Gabel, "Cancelled Non-group Plans: What We Know Now That We Did Not Know in October," *Health Affairs* blog, June 17, 2014.

122. Glenn Kessler, "Fact-Check: Obama's Pledge That 'No One Will Take Away' Your Health Plan," *Washington Post,* October 30, 2013.

123. Paul Krugman, "Varieties of Voodoo," *New York Times,* February 19, 2016.

124. Wendy Rahn and Eric Oliver, "Trump's Voters Aren't Authoritarians, New Research Says. So What Are They?," *Washington Post,* March 9, 2016; Holan, "All Politicians Lie."

125. Kyle Cheney, Isaac Arnsdorf, Daniel Lippman, Daniel Strauss, and Brent Griffiths, "Donald Trump's Week of Misrepresentations, Exaggerations and Half-Truths," *Politico,* September 25, 2016.

126. Brian Fung, "The British Are Frantically Googling What the E.U. Is, Hours after Voting to Leave It," *Washington Post,* June 24, 2016.

127. Émilie Trevert, "Les intellectuels entre haine et fascination," *Le Point,* October 20, 2008.

128. "Edgar Morin: 'Que connaissent Sarkozy et Guaino de mes thèses?,'" *Le Nouvel Observateur,* January 2, 2008.

129. The bystander made the first provocation, saying that shaking Sarkozy's hand would have "soiled" him.

130. Thomas Guénolé, "Les électeurs qui votent FN votent pétainiste," *Slate France,* June 8, 2014.

131. Abel Mestre, "34% des français 'adhèrent aux idées du Front national,'" *Le Monde,* February 12, 2014.

132. Abel Mestre, Caroline Monnot, and Isabelle Mandraud, "Le FN embarrassé par une nouvelle affaire russe," *Le Monde,* April 3, 2015.

133. Gerstein, "Should Obama Show His Faith?"

134. Harris Interactive, "'Wingnuts' and President Obama."

135. The FN won roughly 28 percent of the vote in the first round of the 2015 French regional elections. It may garner a higher proportion in the 2017 presidential elections. "Elections régionales: Ce qu'il faut retenir d'un premier tour dominé par le FN," *Le Monde,* December 6, 2015. See also Gregor Aisch, Adam Pearce, and Bryant Rousseau, "How Far Is Europe Swinging to the Right?," *New York Times,* July 5, 2016.

136. The FN certainly wants a more patriarchal society and has been blasted by feminist groups for years. Marion Maréchal Le Pen—a legislator and niece of Marine—especially wants to bar public funding for family planning and abortion. Still, social conservatism is not a huge part of the FN platform so far and Christian fundamentalists practically do not exist in France, as Chapters 3 and 4 explain.

137. Pew, "Beyond Red vs. Blue."

138. Nancy Murphy, "Addressing Social and Political Inequality at Home and Mobilizing Allies to Counter Global Threats Are Challenges for the Next President of the U.S., Stanford Expert Says," "Wide Angle: Election 2016," Stanford University, September 29, 2016.

139. See, for example, Philip Bump, "Donald Trump Took 5 Different Positions on Abortion in 3 Days," *Washington Post,* April 3, 2016.

140. George Orwell, *1984* (Signet, 1961), 214.

3. THE EXCEPTIONAL INFLUENCE OF CHRISTIAN FUNDAMENTALISM

1. Alexis de Tocqueville, *Democracy in America,* trans. Henry Reeve (Bantam, 2000), 352–53 (quote), 358.

2. Will Gervais, Azim Shariff, and Ara Norenzayan, "Do You Believe in Atheists? Distrust Is Central to Anti-atheist Prejudice," *Journal of Personality and Social Psychology* 101, no. 6 (2011): 1189–1206. See also, for instance, Husna Haq, "Ted Cruz: Atheists Shouldn't Be President. Why Are They So Vilified?," *Christian Science Monitor,* November 10, 2015.

3. This fascinating phenomenon has been the subject of anthropological research. See T. M. Luhrmann, *When God Talks Back: Understanding the American Evangelical Relationship with God* (Vintage, 2012), 72–100.

4. Pew, "America's Changing Religious Landscape," May 12, 2015, 4.

5. See, for example, Gallup, "In U.S., 42% Believe Creationist View of Human Origins," June 1, 2014; Pew, "Life in 2050," June 22, 2010, 15–16 (four in ten Americans expect Jesus to return by 2050). Additional evidence is provided throughout this chapter.

6. Pew, "Religious 'Nones' Are Not Only Growing, They're Becoming More Secular," November 11, 2015; Pew, "America's Changing Religious Landscape," 3–4, 10, 30. See also Pew, "'Nones' on the Rise," October 9, 2012, 9, 13, 22; Stephen Prothero, *Religious Literacy: What Every American Needs to Know about Religion—and Doesn't* (Harper, 2007), 31.

7. Nancy Gibbs, "Apocalypse Now," *Time,* June 23, 2002; Pew, "Many Americans Uneasy with Mix of Religion and Politics," August 24, 2006.

8. Pew, "U.S. Religious Knowledge Survey," September 28, 2010.

9. See also Pew, "Many Americans Don't Argue about Religion—or Even Talk about It," April 15, 2016.

10. This section draws on Henry May, *The Enlightenment in America* (Oxford University Press, 1976).

11. Ibid., 232–33, 326–27.

12. David Holmes, *The Faiths of the Founding Fathers* (Oxford University Press, 2006), 50–51.

13. May, *Enlightenment in America,* 133, 140–41, 149, 184–85, 197, 215, 231–33, 245, 259 (Vermont), 262–67.

14. Thomas Jefferson to William Short, August 4, 1820, in *Jefferson: Political Writings,* ed. Joyce Appleby and Terence Ball (Cambridge University Press, 1999), 402.

15. Robert Ferguson, *The American Enlightenment, 1750–1820* (Harvard University Press, 1997), 77.

16. Holmes, *Faiths of the Founding Fathers,* 85–86.

17. Thomas Jefferson to William Short, April 13, 1820, available at http://memory.loc.gov/cgi-bin/ampage?collId=mtj1&fileName=mtj1page051.db&recNum=1223.

18. Holmes, *Faiths of the Founding Fathers,* 87.

19. See, for instance, Gibbs, "Apocalypse Now"; Kenneth Woodward, "The Way the World Ends," *Newsweek,* November 1, 1999; PR Newswire, "Newsweek: Forty Percent of Americans Believe the World Will End as the Bible Predicts: A Battle between Jesus and the Antichrist at Armageddon," October 24, 1999; Pew, "Life in 2050," 15–16.

20. Thomas Jefferson to General Alexander Smith, January 17, 1825, in *The Writings of Thomas Jefferson,* vol. 7, ed. H. A. Washington (Riker Thorne, 1854), 394.

21. Thomas Jefferson, quoted in Frank Lambert, *Religion in American Politics: A Short History* (Princeton University Press, 2010), 39–40.

22. Benjamin Franklin, *Autobiography, and Other Writings* (Oxford University Press, 1999), 353.

23. Benjamin Franklin, quoted in May, *Enlightenment in America,* 129.

24. Holmes, *Faiths of the Founding Fathers,* 78.

25. John Adams to Thomas Jefferson, June 20, 1815, in *The Writings of Thomas Jefferson,* vol. 6, ed. H. A. Washington (Taylor and Maury, 1854), 473.

26. May, *Enlightenment in America,* 96–97. See also Holmes, *Faiths of the Founding Fathers,* 97–98, 136.

27. Ron Chernow, *Alexander Hamilton* (Penguin, 2004), 205, 659–60.

28. May, *Enlightenment in America,* 124, 173–75, 242, 285.

29. Thomas Paine, *The Age of Reason: Being an Investigation of True and Fabulous Theology* (G.E. Wilson, 1890), 74, 16.

30. Holmes, *Faiths of the Founding Fathers,* 59–71, 162.

31. May, *Enlightenment in America,* 232–33, 326–27.

32. Holmes, *Faiths of the Founding Fathers,* 141, 143, 150, 154.

33. May, *Enlightenment in America,* 232–33, 326–27. On the decline of deism, see also Holmes, *Faiths of the Founding Fathers,* 49.

34. Alexis de Tocqueville, *The Old Regime and the Revolution,* trans. Alan Kahan, vol. 1 (University of Chicago Press, 1998), 206.

35. This section draws on Richard Hofstadter, *Anti-Intellectualism in American Life* (Vintage, 1966), 55–116; May, *Enlightenment in America,* 42–44, 48, 54–55, 317–34; Prothero, *Religious Literacy,* 58–59, 109–17, 134–39; Nathan Hatch, *The Democratization of American Christianity* (Yale University Press, 1989); George Marsden, *Understanding Fundamentalism and Evangelicalism* (Eerdmans, 1990), 115; Mark Noll, *The Scandal of the Evangelical Mind* (Eerdmans, 1994), 59–64.

36. Dwight Moody, quoted in Hofstadter, *Anti-Intellectualism,* 108.

37. Susan Jacoby, *The Age of American Unreason* (Vintage, 2009), 45–46.

38. Hofstadter, *Anti-Intellectualism,* 55.

39. Charles Darwin, *Selected Letters on Evolution and Origins of Species,* ed. Francis Darwin (Courier, 1958), 249, 61; on his agnosticism, see 66.

40. Marsden, *Understanding Fundamentalism and Evangelicalism,* 59–61.

41. See Jaroslav Pelikan, *Whose Bible Is It?* (Penguin, 2006), 183–99.

42. Marsden, *Understanding Fundamentalism and Evangelicalism,* 15, 32.

43. Curtis Lee Laws, undated remarks at Chicago Moody Bible Institute, quoted in "Baptist Fundamentals," *Herald and Presbyter* 92, no. 29, July 19, 1922, 10.

44. Marsden, *Understanding Fundamentalism and Evangelicalism,* 3, 18, 30, 57; Pelikan, *Whose Bible Is It?,* 211.

45. Noll, *Scandal of the Evangelical Mind,* 114.

46. Harry Emerson Fosdick, "Shall the Fundamentalists Win?," *Christian Work* 102 (June 10, 1922): 716–22, available at http://historymatters.gmu.edu/d/5070/.

47. Harry Emerson Fosdick, *Evolution and Mr. Bryan* (American Institute of Sacred Literature, 1922), available at http://darrow.law.umn.edu/documents /Evolution_and_Mr_Bryan_Fosdick.pdf.

48. Fosdick, "Shall the Fundamentalists Win?"

49. Noll, *Scandal of the Evangelical Mind,* 101.

50. These matters are discussed at length in Ernest Sandeen, *The Roots of Fundamentalism: British and American Millenarianism, 1800–1930* (University of Chicago Press, 1970).

51. Marsden, *Understanding Fundamentalism and Evangelicalism,* 172.

52. Pew, "America's Changing Religious Landscape," 3–4, 10, 30. See also Pew, "'Nones' on the Rise," 13, 22; Prothero, *Religious Literacy,* 31.

53. "Religion | Gallup Historical Trends," www.gallup.com/poll/1690/religion.aspx. There is no definite consensus among scholars on how to define "evangelicalism." See Christian Smith, *Christian America? What Evangelicals Really Want* (University of California Press, 2002), 15–18; Conrad Hackett and Michael Lindsay, "Measuring Evangelicalism: Consequences of Different Operationalization Strategies," *Journal for the Scientific Study of Religion* 47, no. 3 (2008): 499–514.

54. Hackett and Lindsay, "Measuring Evangelicalism," 510.

55. Pew, "Spirit and Power: A 10-Country Survey of Pentecostals," October 2006, 94.

56. Pew, "America's Changing Religious Landscape," 12–13, 33–38.

57. The U.S. data source in Table 3 is from 2010 because more recent Gallup polls conflate "God" and "universal spirit." It is noteworthy that a 2014 poll showed that 7.1 percent of Americans identified as "atheists" or "agnostics," a figure similar to the 6 percent of nonbelievers in the 2010 Gallup poll. See Pew, "America's Changing Religious Landscape," 4.

58. For a study on Canada, see Timothy Avery, "One in Four Don't Believe in God, Poll Finds," *Toronto Star,* May 31, 2008. For more statistics, see Ipsos, "Supreme Being(s), the Afterlife and Evolution," April 25, 2011.

59. Pew, "Faith and the 2016 Campaign," January 27, 2016, 11.

60. Pew, "America's Changing Religious Landscape," 3–4.

61. Pew, "Religious 'Nones.'" See also Pew, "America's Changing Religious Landscape," 10 (emphasizing that "many people who are unaffiliated with a religion believe in God, pray at least occasionally and think of themselves as spiritual people"); Pew, "'Nones' on the Rise," 9; Prothero, *Religious Literacy,* 31.

62. Pew, "Millennials in Adulthood," March 7, 2014, 13.

63. Pew, "Religious 'Nones'"; Pew, "Religion among the Millennials," February 17, 2010, 1–2.

64. "Religion | Gallup Historical Trends."

65. "Europe's Irreligious," *Economist,* August 9, 2010. See also Michael Paulson, "Americans Claim to Attend Church More Than They Do," *New York Times,* May 17, 2014.

66. Peter Boyer, "The Covenant," *New Yorker,* September 6, 2010. Elaine Howard Ecklund's thought-provoking research indicates that, like Collins, a sizable segment of American scientists aim to blend modern scientific understanding with religious faith. Ecklund, *Science v. Religion: What Scientists Really Think* (Oxford University Press, 2012).

67. This finding has been constant over the years. See Jerome Karabel and Daniel Laurison, "An Exceptional Nation? American Political Values in Comparative Perspective" (Institute for Research on Labor and Employment Working Paper 136–12, University of California, Berkeley, 2012), 16–20; Pew, "Among Wealthy Nations U.S. Stands Alone in Its Embrace of Religion," December 19, 2002; Gallup, "Religiosity Highest in World's Poorest Nations," August 31, 2010; Pew, "The American–Western European Values Gap," November 17, 2011; Pew, "How Do Americans Stand Out from the Rest of the World?," March 12, 2015.

68. 107 Cong. Rec. H4527 (daily ed. July 11, 2002) (statement of Rep. Pence). Creationists know that their views can undermine their electoral chances, especially at the national level. In a 2009 TV interview, Pence unsurprisingly dodged questions about whether he accepted evolution, although he used creationist rhetoric: "We should teach all of the facts about all of these controversial areas." Pence, interview, *Hardball with Chris Matthews,* May 5, 2009.

69. Kitzmiller v. Dover Area School District, 400 F. Supp. 2d 707, 762 (M.D. Pa. 2005). On intelligent design, see also Michelle Goldberg, *Kingdom Coming: The Rise of Christian Nationalism* (Norton, 2007), 80–105.

70. Jon Miller, Eugenie Scott, and Shinji Okamoto, "Public Acceptance of Evolution," *Science* 313, no. 5788 (August 11, 2006): 765–66.

71. Gallup, "In U.S., 42% Believe Creationist View of Human Origins," June 1, 2014. Answers depend on the wording of the question. Another poll found that 31 percent of Americans think that humans have "existed in their present form since the beginning of time." Pew, "Religion and Science," October 22, 2015, 19. People appear likelier to interpret scripture literally when asked about specific stories. Six in ten Americans indicated that biblical accounts about God creating Earth in six days or Noah's Ark are true word for word. David Morris, "Poll: Jews Not to Blame for Jesus' Death," ABC News, February 15, 2004. Sixty-seven percent also indicated that the entire story behind Christmas—the virgin birth, the Star of Bethlehem, and the Wise Men from the East—is historically accurate. "The Christmas Miracle," *Newsweek,* December 5, 2004.

72. Harris Interactive, "Americans' Belief in God, Miracles and Heaven Declines," December 16, 2013.

73. Pew, "Public's Views on Human Evolution," December 30, 2013.

74. Data confirm that many religious Americans are not opposed to modern science. Elaine Howard Ecklund, David Johnson, Christopher Scheitle, "Individual Religiosity and Orientation towards Science: Reformulating Relationships," *Sociological Science* 2 (2015): 106–124.

75. Chris Barton, "Intelligent Design—Coming to a School near You," *New Zealand Herald,* August 27, 2005.

76. Stephen Moss, "Defying Darwin," *Guardian,* February 17, 2009; Sophia Deboick, "Creationist Claims in Northern Ireland," *Guardian,* June 19, 2010.

77. Parliamentary Assembly of the Council of Europe, Resolution 1580, "The Dangers of Creationism in Education," October 4, 2007.

78. The Discovery Institute, an arm of the religious right, called for replacing evolution with "a science consonant with Christian and theistic convictions." Discovery Institute, "The 'Wedge Document': 'So What?,'" 8, www.discovery.org /scripts/viewDB/filesDB-download.php?id=349.

79. Pew, "On Darwin's 200th Birthday, Americans Still Divided about Evolution," February 5, 2009.

80. Pew, "Religion and Science," 21. See also Virginia Commonwealth University Life Sciences Survey 2010, 10; Pew, "Americans Still Divided about Evolution."

81. Kurt Eichenwald, *500 Days: Secrets and Lies in the Terror Wars* (Simon and Schuster, 2012), 459–61.

82. Sarah Posner, "George W. Bush to Raise Money for Group That Converts Jews to Bring about Second Coming of Christ," *Mother Jones,* November 7, 2013.

83. Pew, "Many Americans Uneasy." Regarding belief in such prophecies, see Marsden, *Understanding Fundamentalism and Evangelicalism,* 77; Goldberg, *Kingdom Coming,* 72.

84. See, for instance, Ariel Levy, "Prodigal Son," *New Yorker,* June 28, 2010.

85. Religion was obviously not the main reason for invading Iraq, yet it can influence U.S. foreign policy, as we will see in Chapter 8.

86. Chapter 6 provides examples of such declarations when discussing evangelical politicians' views.

87. Nancy Gibbs, "Apocalypse Now," *Time,* June 23, 2002.

88. Pew, "Life in 2050."

89. Gibbs, "Apocalypse Now."

90. See, for example, David John Marley, "Ronald Reagan and the Splintering of the Christian Right," *Journal of Church and State* 48, no. 4 (2006): 851–68.

91. Selwyn Crawford, "In Disasters, Some See the Wrath of God," *Dallas Morning News,* September 30, 2005.

92. Public Religion Research Institute and American Academy of Religion, "Believers, Sympathizers, and Skeptics," November 22, 2014.

93. Noll, *Scandal of the Evangelical Mind,* 13–14 (Gulf War of 1991), 71 (American Revolution); Holmes, *Faiths of the Founding Fathers,* 153 (French Revolution and Napoléon); Sandeen, *Roots of Fundamentalism,* 233 (World War I).

94. Eichenwald, *500 Days,* 459–61.

95. Elaine Pagels, *Revelations: Visions, Prophecy, and Politics in the Book of Revelation* (Penguin, 2013), 1–35.

96. Bart Ehrman, *Jesus, Interrupted: Revealing the Hidden Contradictions of the Bible (and Why We Don't Know about Them)* (Harper, 2010), 13, 20, 183–89.

97. Ibid., 9–10, 29, 35–39.

98. Pew, "U.S. Religious Knowledge Survey."

99. Prothero, *Religious Literacy,* 1.

100. Luhrmann, *When God Talks Back,* 16–22.

101. Laurie Goodstein, "Gay and Transgender Catholics Urge Pope to Take a Stand," *New York Times,* July 28, 2015.

102. Carol Kurivilla, "Six Questions with a Black Mormon Feminist," *Huffington Post,* September 3, 2015.

103. Tocqueville, *Old Regime and the Revolution,* 206.

104. See generally Gervais, Shariff, and Norenzayan, "Do You Believe in Atheists?"

105. See, for example, Julian Baggini, "In God We Must," *Slate,* February 5, 2012.

106. Phil Zuckerman, *Society without God: What the Least Religious Nations Can Tell Us about Contentment* (New York University Press, 2010), 177–79.

107. Gallup, "Atheists, Muslims See Most Bias as Presidential Candidates," June 21, 2012. Another poll identifies atheism as the least desirable trait in a presidential candidate. Pew, "Faith and the 2016 Campaign," 3.

108. "Mr. Lieberman's Religious Words," Editorial, *New York Times*, August 31, 2000.

109. Zuckerman, *Society without God*.

110. Gallup, "U.S. Satisfaction with Religion Settling at Lower Levels," February 12, 2015.

111. See, for example, Hofstadter, *Anti-Intellectualism*, 238, 265; Prothero, *Religious Literacy*, 143.

112. Luhrmann, *When God Talks Back*, 299.

113. Laurence Iannaccone, "Why Strict Churches Are Strong," *American Journal of Sociology* 99, no. 5 (1994): 1180–211.

114. Hofstadter, *Anti-Intellectualism*, 55.

115. Tanya M. Luhrmann, interview by Terry Gross, *Fresh Air*, National Public Radio, April 9, 2012. See also Luhrmann, *When God Talks Back*, 72–100.

116. Jon Meacham, "The God Debate," *Newsweek*, April 9, 2007; Michelle Goldberg, "A Wolf in Sheep's Clothing," *Guardian*, December 18, 2008.

117. Denis Lacorne, *Religion in America*, trans. George Holoch (Columbia University Press, 2011), 27, 32, 147–49; Nathaniel Philbrick, *Mayflower: A Story of Courage, Community, and War* (Penguin, 2006), 177.

118. Lacorne, *Religion in America*, 2–8, 27.

119. Noah Feldman, *Divided by God: America's Church-State Problem—and What We Should Do about It* (Farrar, Straus and Giroux, 2005), 23.

120. See Ferguson, *American Enlightenment*, 73–74, 89.

121. Tocqueville, *Democracy in America*, 358.

122. See, for example, Jacoby, *Age of American Unreason*, 46; Zuckerman, *Society without God*, 111, 171–72.

123. This section partly draws on my *Public Books* article "Reading *Charlie Hebdo* across the Atlantic," May 5, 2015.

124. Céline Goffette and Jean-François Mignot, "Non, 'Charlie Hebdo' n'est pas obsédé par l'Islam," *Le Monde*, February 24, 2015.

125. CBS News Poll, "Mitt Romney's Race for the Nomination," February 13, 2007.

126. Clinton reported this event in a speech at Riverside Church, New York, August 29, 2004.

127. See, for example, these Media Matters in America articles: "CNN Still Fixated on Apocalypse Predictors," August 1, 2006; "CNN or CBN? Phillips Asks Apocalypse Authors: '[A]re We Living in the Last Days?,'" July 26, 2006; "In Middle East Conflict, Other Crises, Conservative Media Find Signs of Biblical Prophecy of Armageddon," July 25, 2006.

128. The episode is titled "The Midterms" and ran in the second season of *The West Wing*.

129. See, for example, Peter Steinfels, "Mormons Drop Rites Opposed by Women," *New York Times,* May 3, 1990.

130. Pew, "Mormons in America," January 12, 2012.

131. Richard Lyman Bushman, *Rough Stone Rolling: A Cultural Biography of Mormonism's Founder* (Vintage, 2007), 48–52, 289, 437–40.

132. Washington Post–ABC News poll, April 10, 2012.

133. Pew, "U.S. Religious Knowledge Survey."

134. Half of the public admits knowing "not very much" or "nothing" about Mormonism. "Polygamy" is one of the words that most often comes to people's minds when they are asked about Mormonism. Pew, "Americans Learned Little about the Mormon Faith, but Some Attitudes Have Softened," December 14, 2012.

135. Prothero, *Religious Literacy,* 142.

136. "In 1835, Smith bought some ancient Egyptian papyruses. One, he said, had been written by Abraham, the Jewish patriarch. He translated it and published it as the Book of Abraham. At the time, no one in America could read hieroglyphics, but when professional Egyptologists first saw facsimiles of Smith's papyrus, they recognized them as fragments from an ancient Egyptian Book of the Dead that bore no relation to his translation." "From Polygamy to Propriety," *Economist,* December 19, 2007.

137. Lawrence Wright, "The Apostate," *New Yorker,* February 14 and 21, 2011.

138. Ibid.

139. See Robert Wuthnow, *Inventing American Religion* (Oxford University Press, 2015).

140. Smith, *Christian America?,* 7, 48, 87–88, 122–23.

141. Pew, "Religious Groups' Views on Evolution," February 4, 2009; National Center for Science Education, "Statements from Religious Organizations on Evolution," http://ncse.com/media/voices/religion; Death Penalty Information Center, "Official Religious Statements on the Death Penalty," http://deathpenaltyinfo.org /religion-and-death-penalty#state.

142. Marc Hetherington and Jonathan Weiler, *Authoritarianism and Polarization in American Politics* (Cambridge University Press, 2009), 59–60.

143. However, "political party identification and race and ethnicity are stronger predictors of views about climate change beliefs than are religious identity or observance." Pew, "Religion and Science," 32. See also Chris Mooney, "The Surprising Links between Faith and Evolution and Climate Denial," *Washington Post,* May 20, 2015.

144. John Broder, "Climate Change Doubt Is a Tea Party Article of Faith," *New York Times,* October 20, 2010.

145. Daniel Schorr, "Reagan Recants: His Path from Armageddon to Détente," *Los Angeles Times,* January 3, 1988.

146. Edward Caudill, *Intelligently Designed: How Creationists Built the Campaign against Evolution* (University of Illinois Press, 2013), 118.

147. Marley, "Splintering of the Christian Right."

148. John F. Harris, "God Gave U.S. 'What We Deserve,' Falwell Says," *Washington Post,* September 14, 2001.

149. "Antichrist Is Alive, and a Male Jew, Falwell Contends," *New York Times,* January 16, 1999.

150. Marsden, *Understanding Fundamentalism and Evangelicalism,* 113.

151. Haynes Johnson, "Nuclear Arms in the Pulpit," *Boston Globe,* April 12, 1983.

152. "Election 2016: Exit Polls," *New York Times,* November 8, 2016.

153. Trump won 40 percent of the evangelical vote in the Republican primary, next to Cruz's 34 percent. NBC News, "Lacking a Clear Champion in 2016, White Evangelicals Voted for Trump," May 10, 2016. See also Maggie Haberman and Thomas Kaplan, "Evangelicals See Donald Trump as Man of Conviction, If Not Faith," *New York Times,* January 18, 2016. While data indicate that Trump supporters were somewhat less authoritarian than Cruz's, both groups shared far more authoritarian traits than Clinton or Sanders supporters. Wendy Rahn and Eric Oliver, "Trump's Voters Aren't Authoritarians, New Research Says. So What Are They?," *Washington Post,* March 9, 2016.

154. Hofstadter, *Anti-Intellectualism,* 55.

155. Morris Fiorina with Samuel Abrams and Jeremy Pope, *Culture War? The Myth of a Polarized America,* 3rd ed. (Longman, 2010), 169.

4. THE CULTURE WARS OF FAITH, SEX, AND GENDER

1. Gallup, "Americans Continue to Shift Left on Moral Issues," May 26, 2015; Pew, "Religious 'Nones' Are Not Only Growing, They're Becoming More Secular," November 11, 2015; Pew, "Religion among the Millennials," February 17, 2010, 1–2.

2. Pew, "U.S. Becoming Less Religious," November 3, 2015. See also Alan Abramowitz, *The Polarized Public? Why American Government Is So Dysfunctional* (Pearson, 2013), 68.

3. George Washington to Edward Newenham, June 22, 1792, available at http:// founders.archives.gov/documents/Washington/05–10–02–0324.

4. PolitiFact, "Jerry Brown Says 'Virtually No Republican' in Washington Accepts Climate Change Science," May 18, 2014.

5. "Political Party Platforms of Parties Receiving Electoral Votes, 1840–2016," American Presidency Project, University of California, Santa Barbara, www .presidency.ucsb.edu/platforms.php.

6. Guttmacher Institute, "In Just the Last Four Years, States Have Enacted 231 Abortion Restrictions," January 5, 2015.

7. Whole Woman's Health v. Hellerstedt, 136 S.Ct. 1001 (2016).

8. Timothy Williams, "The Surprise in the Hobby Lobby Comments," *New York Times,* July 3, 2014.

9. Stephen Kurczy, "Don't Ask, Don't Tell: How Do Other Countries Treat Gay Soldiers?," *Christian Science Monitor,* May 26, 2010.

10. Eric Bradner, "Pence in 1997: Working Mothers Stunt Emotional Growth of Children," CNN, July 19, 2016.

11. The Massachusetts State Senate voted unanimously to override Romney's veto, and its House did so by a 139–16 margin. Laura Bassett, "Mitt Romney Vetoed Contraception Bill for Rape Victims as Governor," *Huffington Post,* January 9, 2012.

12. James Davidson Hunter, "The Enduring Culture War," in Hunter and Alan Wolfe, *Is There a Culture War? A Dialogue on Values and American Public Life* (Brookings, 2006), 15.

13. Morris Fiorina, "Further Reflections on the Culture War Thesis," in Hunter and Wolfe, *Is There a Culture War?,* 84.

14. Abramowitz, *Polarized Public?,* 56–57, 82 (quote).

15. Marc Hetherington, "Putting Polarization in Perspective," *British Journal of Political Science* 39, no. 2 (2009): 433–36.

16. Pew, "Changing Attitudes on Gay Marriage," March 2014; Pew, "Roe v. Wade at 40: Most Oppose Overturning Abortion Decision," January 16, 2013; Pew, "Trends in Party Identification of Religious Groups," February 2, 2012.

17. Naomi Cahn and June Carbone, *Red Families v. Blue Families: Legal Polarization and the Creation of Culture* (Oxford University Press, 2010), 183.

18. Nicholas Kristof, "Tussling over Jesus," *New York Times,* January 26, 2011.

19. Catholic Church Internal Laws, "Substantive Norms," Article 5, www .vatican.va/resources/resources_norme_en.html.

20. Benedict gave these instructions when he was an influential cardinal, prior to becoming the pope. "Benedict's Answers to Big Questions," *Los Angeles Times,* April 20, 2005.

21. Pew, "What's a Sin? Catholics Don't Always Agree with Their Church," September 25, 2015.

22. Pew, "Most U.S. Catholics Rely Heavily on Their Own Conscience for Moral Guidance," April 19, 2016.

23. Carol Kuruvilla, "Meet the Evangelicals Who Cheered the SCOTUS Gay Marriage Ruling," *Huffington Post,* June 29, 2015.

24. Richard Cizik, interview by Terry Gross, *Fresh Air,* National Public Radio, July 28, 2010.

25. Richard Hofstadter, *The Paranoid Style in American Politics, and Other Essays* (Vintage, 2008), 21–23.

26. David Campbell, "A House Divided? What Social Science Has to Say about the Culture War," *William and Mary Bill of Rights Journal* 15 (2006): 59–74.

27. Ibid., 66–67; Noah Feldman, *Divided by God: America's Church-State Problem—and What We Should Do about It* (Farrar, Straus and Giroux, 2005), 196.

28. Like England, Scotland has a state-established church. Wales and Northern Ireland, the other main parts of the United Kingdom, do not.

29. Pew, "In Some European Countries, Church Membership Means Paying More Taxes," September 22, 2014. Regarding the limits of secularism in Europe, see also Peter Baldwin, *The Narcissism of* Small *Differences: How America and Europe Are Alike* (Oxford University Press, 2009), 170–71.

NOTES TO PAGES 116–119 · 303

30. Michelle Goldberg, *Kingdom Coming: The Rise of Christian Nationalism* (Norton, 2007), 25–27.

31. Feldman, *Divided by God,* 23.

32. John Adams, "Defense of the Constitutions of Government" (1787), quoted in Robert Ferguson, *The American Enlightenment, 1750–1820* (Harvard University Press, 1997), 42.

33. Stephen Prothero, *Religious Literacy: What Every American Needs to Know about Religion—and Doesn't* (Harper, 2007), 29.

34. Feldman, *Divided by God,* 33–38, 50–51, 81, 109; Mark Noll, *The Scandal of the Evangelical Mind* (Eerdmans, 1994), 64–65.

35. Feldman, *Divided by God,* 61–92.

36. George Marsden, *Understanding Fundamentalism and Evangelicalism* (Eerdmans, 1990), 10–11.

37. School District of Abington Township, Pennsylvania v. Schempp, 374 U.S. 203, 222 (1963). See also Feldman, *Divided by God,* 180–81; Engel v. Vitale, 370 U.S. 421 (1962).

38. See generally Bob Egelko, "'In God We Trust' Suit Rejected by Supreme Court," *San Francisco Chronicle,* March 8, 2011.

39. Town of Greece v. Galloway, 134 S.Ct. 1811 (2014).

40. Gallup, "Americans Indivisible on Pledge of Allegiance," May 4, 2004; Gallup, "Americans Approve of Public Displays of Religious Symbols," October 3, 2003.

41. Public Religion Research Institute, "Majority of Americans Still Support Contraception Coverage Mandate," June 2, 2014.

42. Pew, "South Carolina Valedictorian Reignites Debate on Prayer in School," June 13, 2013.

43. See, for example, Scalia's dissents in Lee v. Weisman, 505 U.S. 577 (1992) and McCreary County v. ACLU of Kentucky, 545 U.S. 844 (2005).

44. Antonin Scalia, "God's Justice and Ours," *First Things,* May 2002. In his comment about Americans, Scalia was quoting Justice William Douglas's opinion in Zorach v. Clauson, 343 U.S. 306 (1952).

45. Christian Smith, *Christian America? What Evangelicals Really Want* (University of California Press, 2002), 33–34, 102.

46. Goldberg, *Kingdom Coming,* 25–27.

47. Smith, *Christian America?,* 12, 42, 115.

48. Pew, "Many Americans Don't Argue about Religion—or Even Talk about It," April 15, 2016.

49. See, for example, Angelique Chrisafis, "'We Can No Longer Stay Silent': Fury Erupts over Sexism in French Politics," *Guardian,* May 13, 2016.

50. Goldberg, *Kingdom Coming,* 208–10.

51. See, for example, Julie Mianecki, "Obama Administration Calls on United Nations to Support Gay Rights," *Los Angeles Times,* March 23, 2011.

52. Sandra Day O'Connor, "The History of the Women's Suffrage Movement," *Vanderbilt Law Review* 49 (1996): 657–76.

53. Various American and foreign scientists contributed to the pill's discovery and development, but the New Jersey–born scientist Gregory Pincus is generally credited as its main inventor. Margaret Sanger, the American reproductive rights activist, notably spearheaded this breakthrough by urging Pincus to develop an effective contraceptive. See Jonathan Eig, *The Birth of the Pill: How Four Crusaders Reinvented Sex and Launched a Revolution* (Norton, 2015).

54. Ruth Bader Ginsburg, "Ratification of the Equal Rights Amendment: A Matter of Time," *Texas Law Review* 57 (1979): 938; Martha F. Davis, "The Equal Rights Amendment: Then and Now," *Columbia Journal of Gender and Law* 17 (2008): 425–28; Michael Kazin, *The Populist Persuasion: An American History* (Basic, 1995), 259.

55. Reva Siegel, "Constitutional Culture, Social Movement Conflict and Constitutional Change: The Case of the De Facto ERA," *California Law Review* 94 (2006): 1379.

56. Jeffrey Toobin, *The Nine: Inside the Secret World of the Supreme Court* (Anchor, 2008), 325–26, 348.

57. Smith, *Christian America?*, 182–86, 189.

58. Ibid., 182.

59. Goldberg, *Kingdom Coming,* 68.

60. Bart Ehrman, *Jesus, Interrupted: Revealing the Hidden Contradictions of the Bible (and Why We Don't Know about Them)* (Harper, 2010), 222, 280.

61. Cahn and Carbone, *Red Families v. Blue Families,* 1–2, 19–20.

62. Ibid., 78–84, citing Claudia Goldin and Laurence Katz, "The Power of the Pill: Oral Contraceptives and Women's Career and Marriage," *Journal of Political Economy* 110, no. 4 (2002): 730–70.

63. Thomas Diprete and Claudia Buchmann, *The Rise of Women: The Growing Gender Gap in Education and What It Means for American Schools* (Sage, 2013), 38, 183. On the relative economic progress of American women in recent decades, see also June Carbone and Naomi Cahn, *Marriage Markets: How Inequality Is Remaking the American Family* (Oxford University Press, 2014), 196.

64. Hunter, "Enduring Culture War," 15.

65. Goldberg, *Kingdom Coming,* 142, 208, 209.

66. Anna Peterson, "From Commonplace to Controversial: The Different Histories of Abortion in Europe and the United States," *Origins* 6, no. 2 (November 2012): http://origins.osu.edu/article/commonplace-controversial-different-histories-abortion-europe-and-united-states.

67. Charles Lockhart, *The Roots of American Exceptionalism: Institutions, Culture and Policies* (Palgrave MacMillan, 2003), 1.

68. Abramowitz, *Polarized Public?*, 68–69.

69. Pew, "Religion and Politics '08: John McCain," November 4, 2008.

70. See, for example, Cahn and Carbone, *Red Families v. Blue Families,* 92. These divergent views are also reflected in the parties' briefs in *Roe v. Wade.*

71. "Avortement: Ce qui a changé depuis le discours de Simone Veil," France 24, November 26, 2014.

72. Jean-Yves Le Naour and Catherine Valenti, *Histoire de l'Avortement: XIXe–XXe Siècle* (Seuil, 2003), 114–21, 192, 201–4, 262–70, 283; Lockhart, *Roots of American Exceptionalism,* 110–17.

73. Gaëlle Dupont, "Quarante ans après la loi Veil, l'IVG à nouveau débattue dans l'hémicycle," *Le Monde,* January 22, 2014.

74. Guttmacher Institute, "231 Abortion Restrictions."

75. Ashifa Kassam, "Spain Abandons Plan to Introduce Tough New Abortion Laws," *Guardian,* September 23, 2014.

76. Abramowitz, *Polarized Public?,* 76–77; Gallup, "Abortion Is Threshold Issue for One in Six U.S. Voters," October 4, 2012.

77. "In Portugal, Abortion Legal but Many Doctors Refuse to Perform Them," WBEZ 91.5, July 18, 2012, www.wbez.org/shows/worldview/in-portugal-abortion-legal-but-many-doctors-refuse-to-perform-them/5a63e08f-7ea0-4a9b-a9a5-4eac4ad570cf.

78. Center for Reproductive Rights, "The World's Abortion Laws: Fact Sheet," June 2013.

79. Guttmacher Institute, "State Policies in Brief: An Overview of Abortion Laws," June 1, 2014.

80. See, for example, Lockhart, *Roots of American Exceptionalism,* 105–17; Federico Fabbrini, "The European Court of Human Rights, the EU Charter of Fundamental Rights and the Right to Abortion: *Roe v. Wade* on the Other Side of the Atlantic?," *Columbia Journal of European Law* 18 (2011): 1–53.

81. Guttmacher Institute, "State Policies in Brief."

82. "Abortion | Gallup Historical Trends," www.gallup.com/poll/1576/abortion.aspx#3.

83. Morris Fiorina with Samuel Abrams and Jeremy Pope, *Culture War? The Myth of a Polarized America,* 3rd ed. (Longman, 2010), 81–84.

84. "Abortion | Gallup Historical Trends."

85. For a discussion of this change since the early twentieth century, see Justin Garcia, Chris Reiber, Sean Massey, and Ann Merriwether, "Sexual Hookup Culture: A Review," *Review of General Psychology* 16, no. 2 (2012): 161–76.

86. See generally Nancy Jo Sales, *American Girls: Social Media and the Secret Lives of Teenagers* (Knopf, 2016); Peggy Orenstein, *Girls and Sex: Navigating the Complicated New Landscape* (Harper, 2016).

87. Amy Schalet, *Not under My Roof: Parents, Teens, and the Culture of Sex* (University of Chicago Press, 2011), 173, 178.

88. See ibid., 197.

89. Jacob Gersen and Jeannie Suk, "The Sex Bureaucracy," *California Law Review* 104 (2016): 912.

90. Ibid., 913.

91. See, for instance, Kate Carey, Sarah Durney, Robyn Shepardson, Michael Carey, "Incapacitated and Forcible Rape of College Women: Prevalence across the First Year," *Journal of Adolescent Health* 56, no. 6 (June 2015): 678–80.

92. Marsden, *Understanding Fundamentalism and Evangelicalism,* 55–56.

93. Gallup, "Americans Continue to Shift Left."

94. Center for Reproductive Rights, "European Standards on Subsidizing Contraceptives" (2009).

95. Organisation for Economic Co-operation and Development, "Marriage and Divorce Rates," July 7, 2015.

96. Gallup, "Fewer Young Americans Say I Do—to Any Relationship," June 8, 2015.

97. An exception was the case of Dominique Strauss-Kahn, who was accused of rape in New York while director of the International Monetary Fund. Strauss-Kahn, who had been considered likely to win the 2012 French presidential election, fell into disfavor and chose not to run.

98. Andy Barr, "Haley Will 'Resign' If Affairs Proved," *Politico,* June 4, 2010.

99. Cahn and Carbone, *Red Families v. Blue Families,* 28, 39, 118.

100. Ibid., 8, 13.

101. Ibid., 8, 21–24, 45, 104, 111–12.

102. Schalet, *Not under My Roof,* 3 (quotes), 4, 9–10.

103. Ibid., 7 (quote), 20.

104. Sarah Kliff, "The Future of Abstinence," *Newsweek,* October 27, 2009.

105. Goldberg, *Kingdom Coming,* 108, 120–22, 126, 135, 139–40, 145, 147.

106. Kliff, "Future of Abstinence."

107. Government Accountability Office, "Abstinence Education: Efforts to Assess the Accuracy and Effectiveness of Federally Funded Programs" (2006), 5, 14–19, 20.

108. Goldberg, *Kingdom Coming,* 135–36.

109. Cahn and Carbone, *Red Families v. Blue Families,* 176.

110. Ibid., 4, 42–43, 175.

111. Rob Stein, "Health Bill Restores $250 Million in Abstinence-Education Funds," *Washington Post,* March 27, 2010.

112. Cahn and Carbone, *Red Families v. Blue Families,* 87.

113. Andrew Koppelman, "Why Discrimination against Lesbians and Gay Men Is Sex Discrimination," *New York University Law Review* 69 (2004): 237–38.

114. Pew, "Changing Attitudes on Gay Marriage."

115. Biblical quotations in this book come from the New Revised Standard Version.

116. Cahn and Carbone, *Red Families v. Blue Families,* 128.

117. Koppelman, "Discrimination against Lesbians and Gay Men," 249.

118. Dudgeon v. United Kingdom, 45 Eur. Ct. H.R. (1981).

119. See Scalia's dissent in *Lawrence;* Martha Minow, "The Controversial Status of International and Comparative Law in the United States," *Harvard International Law Journal Online* 52 (2010): 1–25.

120. Gallup, "Public Shifts to More Conservative Stance on Gay Rights," July 30, 2003.

121. "Gay and Lesbian Rights | Gallup Historical Trends," www.gallup.com /poll/1651/gay-lesbian-rights.aspx.

122. Pew, "Changing Attitudes on Gay Marriage."

123. Kurczy, "Don't Ask, Don't Tell."

124. Ibid.

125. Gallup, "In U.S., Broad, Steady Support for Openly Gay Service Members," May 10, 2010.

126. Ed O'Keefe and Craig Whitlock, "'Don't Ask, Don't Tell' Report: Little Risk to Allowing Gays to Serve Openly," *Washington Post,* November 30, 2010.

127. Dana Milbank, "John McCain at His Fieriest before 'Don't Ask, Don't Tell' Vote," *Washington Post,* December 18, 2010.

128. Anthony Faiola, "British Conservatives Lead Charge for Gay Marriage," *Washington Post,* March 30, 2012.

129. Pew, "The American–Western European Values Gap," November 17, 2011.

130. Patrick Healy, "Hopefuls Differ as They Reject Gay Marriage," *New York Times,* November 1, 2008.

131. Civil Forum on the Presidency, Saddleback Church, Lake Forest, CA, August 16, 2008.

132. George W. Bush, interviewed by Cynthia McFadden, *Nightline,* Australian Broadcasting Corporation, December 8, 2008.

133. Pew, "Faith and the 2016 Campaign," January 27, 2016, 11.

134. Kevin Kruse, *One Nation under God: How Corporate America Invented Christian America* (Basic, 2015), xii–xiii, 72–75, 81–84, 124, 242.

135. David Domke and Kevin Coe, *The God Strategy: How Religion Became a Political Weapon in America* (Oxford University Press, 2010), 4–6, 39–45 (Clinton quote on 44).

136. Ibid., 14–17.

137. Ibid., 33–34, 61–64, 89–97.

138. John Kerry, speech at Pepperdine University, September 18, 2006, quoted in ibid., 142.

139. Maggie Haberman and Thomas Kaplan, "Evangelicals See Donald Trump as Man of Conviction, If Not Faith," *New York Times,* January 18, 2016.

140. "Prime Minister Julia Gillard Speaks to Jon Faine," Australian Broadcasting Corporation, June 29, 2010.

141. Pew, "Faith on the Hill," January 5, 2015.

142. Fiorina, Abrams, and Pope, *Culture War?,* 241.

5. BETWEEN DEMOCRACY AND PLUTOCRACY

1. America has the worst score of any Western nation on the Gini index, a statistical measure of income inequality. "Gini Index," *The World Factbook,* Central Intelligence Agency; Lane Kenworthy and Timothy Smeeding, "Growing Inequalities and Their Impacts in the United States: Country Report for the United States" (Gini Growing Inequalities' Impacts Project, January 2013).

2. Thomas Piketty, *Capital in the Twenty-First Century*, trans. Arthur Gold-hammer (Belknap, 2014), 297, 291, 320; Jacob Hacker and Paul Pierson, *Winner-Take-All Politics: How Washington Made the Rich Richer—and Turned Its Back on the Middle Class* (Simon and Schuster, 2010), 22–25, 36; Robert Reich, *Aftershock: The Next Economy and America's Future* (Knopf, 2010), 19; "Changes in U.S. Family Finances from 2010 to 2013: Evidence from the Survey of Consumer Finances," *Federal Reserve Bulletin* 100, no. 4 (September 2014): 1–41.

3. Paul Krugman, *The Conscience of a Liberal* (Norton, 2009), 18.

4. Robert Healy, "From Reagan's Past, Grist for the Carter Mill," *Boston Globe,* September 10, 1980.

5. Piketty, *Capital,* 321.

6. See the empirical evidence discussed in Chapter 1.

7. Tax Policy Center, "An Analysis of Donald Trump's Tax Plan," December 22, 2015; Nicholas Confessore, "9 Times Donald Trump Complained about Taxes," *New York Times,* October 2, 2016 (quote). Given that Trump repeatedly made contradictory statements throughout his campaign, one could not state with certainty what his economic policies as president would be when this book went to press. See, for example, Peter Eavis, "Donald Trump's Plan to Raise Taxes on Rich: Just Kidding," *New York Times,* May 11, 2016; Binyamin Appelbaum, "Conflicting Policy from Trump: To Keep, and Remove, Tax Cut," *New York Times,* September 16, 2016.

8. Piketty, *Capital,* 152.

9. Krugman, *Conscience of a Liberal,* 32.

10. See Lochner v. New York, 198 U.S. 45 (1905); Hammer v. Dagenhart, 247 U.S. 251 (1918).

11. Oliver Wendell Holmes, dissenting opinion in *Lochner,* 198 U.S. 45.

12. Krugman, *Conscience of a Liberal,* 35.

13. Cass Sunstein, *The Second Bill of Rights: FDR's Unfinished Revolution and Why We Need It More Than Ever* (Basic, 2004), 41.

14. Piketty, *Capital,* 506–7.

15. Sunstein, *Second Bill of Rights,* 94–95.

16. Seymour Martin Lipset and Gary Marks, *It Didn't Happen Here: Why Socialism Failed in the United States* (Norton, 2001), 73–75.

17. Alan Brinkley, "With Justices for All," *New York Times,* March 25, 2010.

18. These were Justices Hugo Black, William Douglas, Robert Jackson, Felix Frankfurter, Frank Murphy, Stanley Reed, and Wiley Rutledge. FDR also promoted Harlan Fiske Stone to chief justice.

19. Dwight Eisenhower to Edgar Eisenhower, November 8, 1954, quoted in Hacker and Pierson, *Winner-Take-All Politics,* 189.

20. Ibid., 96–97; Steven Brill, *America's Bitter Pill: Money, Politics, Backroom Deals, and the Fight to Fix Our Broken Healthcare System* (Random House, 2015), 32.

21. Piketty, *Capital,* 97, 506–7.

22. Emmanuel Saez, "Striking It Richer: The Evolution of Top Incomes in the United States," UC Berkeley Economics Department, January 25, 2015, 5 fn. 7.

23. Brill, *America's Bitter Pill,* 21–23.

24. PolitiFact, "Dean Claims Social Security and Medicare Were Passed without Republican Support," August 28, 2009.

25. Healy, "From Reagan's Past."

26. Krugman, *Conscience of a Liberal,* 111.

27. Larry Bartels, *Unequal Democracy: The Political Economy of the New Gilded Age,* 1st ed. (Princeton, 2008), 226, 234, 240.

28. See generally Alan Abramowitz, *The Polarized Public? Why American Government Is So Dysfunctional* (Pearson, 2013), 25–26.

29. Brill, *America's Bitter Pill,* 30–34, 93.

30. Piketty, *Capital,* 297, 291, 320; Hacker and Pierson, *Winner-Take-All Politics,* 22–25, 36; Reich, *Aftershock,* 19; Federal Reserve Bulletin, "Changes in U.S. Family Finance from 2010 to 2013" (2014); PolitiFact, "Warren: The Average Family in the Bottom 90 Percent Made More Money 30 Years Ago," January 13, 2015.

31. Edward Wolff, "Household Wealth Trends in the United States, 1962–2013" (National Bureau of Economic Research Working Paper, 2014), 49.

32. Hacker and Pierson, *Winner-Take-All Politics,* 46.

33. PolitiFact, "Bernie Sanders Says Walmart Heirs Own More Wealth Than Bottom 40 Percent of Americans," July 31, 2012.

34. Reich, *Aftershock,* 61; Hacker and Pierson, *Winner-Take-All Politics,* 22.

35. Hacker and Pierson, *Winner-Take-All Politics,* 34–37; Piketty, *Capital,* 314, 321. This does not mean that factors like technological skills play no role in wage inequality among workers. But such technological advances also occurred in Western nations where inequality is less acute than in America. Claudia Goldin and Lawrence Katz, *The Race between Education and Technology* (Belknap, 2008), 291–92, 329.

36. Economic Policy Institute, "Top CEOs Make 300 Times More Than Typical Workers," June 21, 2015.

37. Hacker and Pierson, *Winner-Take-All Politics,* 61.

38. Eric Dash, "Fiorina Exiting Hewlett-Packard with More Than $42 Million," *New York Times,* February 12, 2005.

39. Piketty, *Capital,* 330–35, 508–9.

40. That is the conclusion of a comprehensive statistical study of 1,779 policy issues. See Martin Gilens and Benjamin Paige, "Testing Theories of American Politics: Elites, Interest Groups, and Average Citizens," *Perspectives on Politics* 12, no. 3 (2014): 564–81.

41. Stanford Center on Poverty and Inequality, "State of the Union" (2016), 15–23.

42. America ranks last among Western nations on the Gini inequality index. See n. 1, above.

43. Bartels, *Unequal Democracy,* 296.

44. David Auerbach and Arthur Kellermann, "A Decade of Health Care Cost Growth Has Wiped Out Real Income Gains for an Average US Family," *Health Affairs* 30, no. 9 (2011): 1630–36.

45. Piketty, *Capital,* 321–24.

46. These findings were based on 2002 and 2004 data. See Larry Bartels, *Unequal Democracy: The Political Economy of the New Gilded Age,* 2nd ed. (Russell Sage, 2016), 126–27.

47. Saez, "Striking It Richer." This statistic excludes government transfers, such as Social Security and nontaxable benefits.

48. See Sarah Binder, "How We Count Senate Filibusters and Why It Matters," *Washington Post,* May 15, 2014; "Not Too Late to Curb the Filibuster," *New York Times,* May 14, 2012; Steven S. Smith, "Partisan Polarization and the Senate Syndrome," in *Solutions to Polarization in America,* ed. Nathaniel Persily (Cambridge University Press, 2015), 219–21.

49. Aaron Blake, "Will the Fiscal Cliff Break Grover Norquist's Hold on Republicans?," *Washington Post,* November 26, 2012.

50. "The Return of 'Drill, Baby, Drill,'" *New York Times,* May 6, 2011.

51. Joseph Stiglitz, *Freefall: America, Free Markets, and the Sinking of the World Economy* (Norton, 2010), 219.

52. Jill Lepore, "Tea and Sympathy," *New Yorker,* May 3, 2010.

53. Jane Mayer, *Dark Money: The Hidden Story of the Billionaires behind the Rise of the Radical Right* (Doubleday, 2016), 58–59, 76, 147.

54. Alison Fitzgerald and Justin Blum, "Republicans Voting against Stimulus Then Asked Obama for Money," *Bloomberg,* February 22, 2010.

55. Jerry Markon and David Fallis, "Paul Ryan Has Record of Pushing for and Earmarking Federal Funds for His District," *Washington Post,* August 17, 2012.

56. Melinda Henneberger, "Michele Bachmann's New Book Matches Her Political Message," *Washington Post,* November 23, 2011.

57. Bartels, *Unequal Democracy,* 1st ed., 131.

58. Rosalind Helderman, "Trump Agrees to $25 Million Settlement in Trump University Fraud Cases," *Washington Post,* November 18, 2016.

59. Robert Yoon, "$153 Million in Bill and Hillary Clinton Speaking Fees, Documented," CNN, February 6, 2016.

60. Philip Rucker and Rosalind Helderman, "At Time of Austerity, 8 Universities Spent Top Dollar on Hillary Rodham Clinton Speeches," *Washington Post,* July 2, 2014.

61. Rosalind Helderman and Michelle Ye Hee Lee, "Inside Bill Clinton's Nearly $18 Million Job as 'Honorary Chancellor' of a For-Profit College," *Washington Post,* September 5, 2016; "Hillary's For-Profit Education," *Wall Street Journal,* September 14, 2015.

62. Peter Whoriskey, "Growing Wealth Widens Distance between Lawmakers and Constituents," *Washington Post,* December 26, 2011.

63. Center for Responsive Politics, "Millionaires' Club: For First Time, Most Lawmakers Are Worth $1 Million–Plus," January 9, 2014.

64. William M. Welch, "Tauzin Switches Sides from Drug Industry Overseer to Lobbyist," *USA Today,* December 16, 2004.

65. Brill, *America's Bitter Pill,* 232.

66. In a 2010 case called *SpeechNOW.org v. Federal Election Commission,* 599 F.3d 686, the D.C. Circuit Court interpreted *Citizens United v. FEC,* 558 U.S. 310 (2010), as allowing unlimited "independent expenditures" by individual persons. The Supreme Court declined to review that decision, effectively endorsing it. The FEC then issued an advisory opinion on July 22, 2010, interpreting *Citizens United* and *SpeechNOW* as allowing unlimited individual contributions to Super PACs. See Cynthia Bauerly and Eric Hallstrom, "Square Pegs: The Challenge for Existing Federal Campaign Finance Disclosure Laws in the Age of the Super PAC," *NYU Journal of Legislation and Public Policy* 15 (2012): 329–62.

67. See the amicus briefs filed by Mitch McConnell, the Senate Republican leader, in *Citizens United* and *McCutcheon v. FEC,* 134 S.Ct. 1434 (2014), and the amicus brief of the Republican National Committee in *United States v. Danielczyk,* 683 F.3d 611 (2012), before the Fourth Circuit Court of Appeals.

68. Source: Center for Responsive Politics.

69. Source: ProPublica.

70. Mayer, *Dark Money,* 314.

71. *Citizens United,* 558 U.S. at 314.

72. Nathaniel Persily and Kelli Lammie, "Perceptions of Corruption and Campaign Finance: When Public Opinion Determines Constitutional Law" (University of Pennsylvania Law School Research Paper, 2004).

73. *McCutcheon,* 134 S.Ct. at 1441.

74. Mugambi Jouet, "Is the Supreme Court Disconnected from the Real World?," *Hill,* April 22, 2014.

75. *McCutcheon,* 134 S.Ct. at 1450.

76. "Which Presidential Candidates Are Winning the Money Race," *New York Times,* June 22, 2016.

77. Carrie Levine, Michael Beckel, and Dave Levinthal, "Donald Trump Dismantles Hillary Clinton's Big Money Machine," *Time,* November 9, 2016.

78. Gilens and Paige, "Testing Theories of American Politics," 576. Another study found that *Citizens United* helped Republican candidates win several state elections. See Tilman Klumpp, Hugo Mialon, and Michael Williams, "The Business of American Democracy: *Citizens United,* Independent Spending, and Elections," *Journal of Law and Economics* 59, no. 1 (2016): 1–43.

79. Manuel Funke, Moritz Schularick, and Christoph Trebesch, "The Political Aftermath of Financial Crises: Going to Extremes," *Vox,* Centre for Economic Policy Research, November 21, 2015.

80. Piketty, *Capital,* 297.

81. Nicholas Kristof, "A Banker Speaks, with Regret," *New York Times,* November 30, 2011.

82. Stiglitz, *Freefall,* 113. See also this blog post by the French economist Anne Lavigne: "Pourquoi le subprime ne peut exister en France," *Mutatis mutandis,* August 18, 2007.

83. Stiglitz, *Freefall,* 1–3, 13, 88, 113.

84. Ibid., 7–9.

85. Ibid., 162–63.

86. Paul Krugman, "Disaster and Denial," *New York Times,* December 14, 2009.

87. Stiglitz, *Freefall,* 10–11.

88. ProPublica, "Bailout Tracker," February 16, 2016.

89. Binyamin Appelbaum and David Herszenhorn, "Financial Overhaul Signals Shift on Deregulation," *New York Times,* July 15, 2010.

90. William Cohan, "'Too Big to Fail' Banks Thriving a Few Years after Financial Crisis," *New York Times,* January 22, 2016; Emily Glazer and Peter Rudegeair, "J. P. Morgan Posts Record Earnings, but Can Good Times Last?," *Wall Street Journal,* January 14, 2016.

91. They included Leon Cooperman and Stephen Schwarzman. See Chrystia Freeland, "'First Do No Harm' Prescription Issued for Wall Street," *Financial Times,* April 28, 2009.

92. This section partly draws on Mugambi Jouet, "The Exceptional Absence of Human Rights as a Principle in American Law," *Pace Law Review* 34, (2014): 711–15.

93. Reed Abelson, "Census Numbers Show 50.7 Million Uninsured," *New York Times,* September 16, 2010; Abelson, "Ranks of Underinsured Are Rising, Study Finds," *New York Times,* June 10, 2008.

94. Congressional Budget Office, "Insurance Coverage Provisions of the Affordable Care Act—March 2015 Baseline," March 2015.

95. Robert Pear, "On Health Exchanges, Premiums May Be Low, but Other Costs Can Be High," *New York Times,* December 9, 2013.

96. Commonwealth Fund, "31 Million People Were Underinsured in 2014," May 20, 2015.

97. Kimberly Barlow, "Romoff Is UPMC's Top Wage Earner," *University of Pittsburg Times,* May 29, 2014.

98. Ezra Klein, "Why an MRI Costs $1,080 in America and $280 in France," *Washington Post,* March 15, 2013. See also Brill, *America's Bitter Pill,* 4–5, 232–36.

99. Steven Brill, "Bitter Pill: Why Medical Bills Are Killing Us," *Time,* February 20, 2013.

100. T. R. Reid, *The Healing of America: A Global Quest for Better, Cheaper, and Fairer Health Care* (Penguin, 2010), 36–37. See also PolitiFact, "Feinstein Says U.S. Is Only Nation to Rely Heavily on For-Profit Insurers for Basic Health Care," March 11, 2010.

101. David Himmelstein, Deborah Thorne, Elizabeth Warren, and Steffie Woolhandler, "Medical Bankruptcy in the United States, 2007: Results of a National Study," *American Journal of Medicine* 122, no. 8 (2009): 741–46.

102. PolitiFact, "Former U.S. Rep. Patrick Kennedy Says Most Bankruptcies in U.S. Are Due to Health Care Costs," July 29, 2012.

103. Robert Seifert and Mark Rukavina, "Bankruptcy Is the Tip of a Medical-Debt Iceberg," *Health Affairs* 25, no. 2 (2006): w89–w92.

104. Reid, *Healing of America,* 31.

105. Klein, "Why an MRI Costs $1,080."

106. Brill, *America's Bitter Pill,* 235–36.

107. Elisabeth Rosenthal, "Price for a New Hip? Many Hospitals Are Stumped," *New York Times,* February 11, 2013.

108. Center for Responsive Politics, "Health Lobbying," accessed November 6, 2016, www.opensecrets.org/industries/lobbying.php?cycle=2016&ind=H.

109. Brill, "Bitter Pill."

110. Bruce Bartlett, "What Your Taxes Do (and Don't) Buy for You," *New York Times,* June 7, 2011.

111. Ellen Nolte and Martin McKee, "Variations in Amenable Mortality—Trends in 16 High-Income Nations," *Health Policy* 103, no. 1 (November 2011): 47–52.

112. Reid, *Healing of America,* 3, 32. See also Commonwealth Fund, "U.S. Health Care from a Global Perspective" (2015).

113. Stanford Center on Poverty and Inequality, "State of the Union," 58–64.

114. Harris Interactive, "Most Republicans Think the U.S. Health Care System Is the Best in the World; Democrats Disagree," March 20, 2008.

115. Eric Roper, "Bachmann: Criticize Health Care Plan and Forget about Being Treated," *Star Tribune,* February 2, 2010.

116. Ian Urbina and Katherine Seelye, "Senator Goes Face to Face with Dissent," *New York Times,* August 11, 2009.

117. Reid, *Healing of America,* 51, 232; Diane Archer, "Medicare Is More Efficient Than Private Insurance," *Health Affairs* blog, September 20, 2011; Paul Krugman, "Medicare Saves Money," *New York Times,* June 12, 2011.

118. See, for example, Kenneth Thorpe, "An Analysis of Senator Sanders Single Payer Plan," January 27, 2016. Other experts disagree that Sanders's plan would be far costlier than presented. See, e.g., David Himmelstein and Steffie Woolhandler, "On Kenneth Thorpe's Analysis of Senator Sanders' Single-Payer Reform Plan," *Huffington Post,* January 29, 2016.

119. Timothy Jost, "The Affordable Care Act: What's There to Like about It?," *Engage* 13, no. 3 (October 2012): 13.

120. Andrew Wilper, Steffie Woolhandler, Karen Lasser, Danny McCormick, David Bor, and David Himmelstein, "Health Insurance and Mortality in US Adults," *American Journal of Public Health* 99, no. 12 (2009): 2289–95.

121. Institute of Medicine, "America's Uninsured Crisis" (2009).

122. Reid, *Healing of America,* 231, 242.

123. Ibid., 231.

124. Ibid., 230.

125. Abby Goodnough, "Distaste for Health Care Law Reflects Spending on Ads," *New York Times,* June 20, 2012. While a significant minority of nonwealthy Americans stand against their own interest by opposing health care reform, affluent voters are far likelier to oppose it. Andrew Gelman, "Economic Divisions and Political Polarization in Red and Blue America," *Pathways* (2011): 4.

126. Healy, "From Reagan's Past."

127. Abelson, "50.7 Million Uninsured;" Abelson, "Ranks of Underinsured Are Rising."

128. Henneberger, "Michele Bachmann."

129. Randy Krehbiel, "Coburn Sour on Economy," *Tulsa World,* August 18, 2011.

130. Piketty, *Capital,* 567.

131. See generally Sylvain Cypel, "Why French Workers Are So Mad," *New York Times,* June 8, 2016.

132. Willem Adema, Pauline Fron, and Maxime Ladaique, "Is the European Welfare State Really More Expensive?: Indicators on Social Spending, 1980–2012; and a Manual to the OECD Social Expenditure Database (SOCX)" (OECD Social, Employment and Migration Working Papers, no. 124, 2011), 21.

133. Piketty, *Capital,* 174, 510 (quote).

134. Thomas Piketty, "2007–2015: Une si longue récession," *Le Monde* blog, January 8, 2016. See also Peter Goodman, "Europe's Economy, after 8-Year Detour, Is Fitfully Back on Track," *New York Times,* April 29, 2016.

135. World Bank, "GDP Per Capita" (2015).

136. Rebecca Ray and John Schmitt, "No-Vacation Nation," Center for Economic and Policy Research (2007); Sarah Jane Glynn and Jane Farrell, "The United States Needs to Guarantee Paid Maternity Leave," Center for American Progress, March 8, 2013.

137. See, for example, Seymour Martin Lipset, *American Exceptionalism: A Double-Edged Sword* (Norton, 1997), 32.

138. Karl Marx and Friedrich Engels, *The Communist Manifesto,* trans. Samuel Moore (Penguin, 2002), 235.

139. Lipset, *American Exceptionalism,* 35.

140. The rest of this section partly draws on my *Truthout* article "Paul Ryan's Misconceived Rugged Individualism," October 13, 2012.

141. Abramowitz, *Polarized Public?,* 112–13.

142. Spencer Magloff, "Tea Party Protester Sorry for Mocking Man with Parkinson's," CBS News, March 25, 2010.

143. David Weiner, "Wheelchair-Bound Woman Shouted Down at New Jersey Health Care Town Hall," *Huffington Post,* September 2, 2009; Rachel Weiner, "Tea Party Patriots Attack Family Who Lost Daughter and Grandchild," *Huffington Post,* November 23, 2009.

144. See Sunstein, *Second Bill of Rights,* 90.

145. U.N. Office on Drugs and Crime, "Percentage of Homicides by Firearm, Number of Homicides by Firearm and Homicide by Firearm Rate per 100,000 Population," accessed October 16, 2016, www.unodc.org/documents/data-and-analysis/statistics/Homicide/Homicides_by_firearms.xls.

146. Robin Abcarian, "Paul Ryan Says His Abortion Stance Is Unchanged, Matches Romney's," *Los Angeles Times,* October 10, 2012.

6. MILLIONS STANDING AGAINST THEIR OWN ECONOMIC INTEREST

1. Baruch Spinoza, *Theological-Political Treatise,* trans. Michael Silverthorne and Jonathan Israel (Cambridge University Press, 2007), 6.

2. Tax Policy Center, "An Analysis of Donald Trump's Tax Plan," December 22, 2015.

3. David Fahrenthold, "Trump Boasts about His Philanthropy. But His Giving Falls Short of His Words," *Washington Post,* October 29, 2016; Alexandra Berzon, "Donald Trump's Business Plan Left a Trail of Unpaid Bills," *Wall Street Journal,* June 9, 2016; Steve Reilly, "Hundreds Allege Donald Trump Doesn't Pay His Bills," *USA Today,* June 9, 2016; Rosalind Helderman, "Trump Agrees to $25 Million Settlement in Trump University Fraud Cases," *Washington Post,* November 18, 2016; David Fahrenthold, "Trump Foundation Admits to Violating Ban on 'Self-Dealing,' New Filing to IRS Shows," *Washington Post,* November 22, 2015; PolitiFact, "Fact-Checking the *Funny or Die* Video about Trump-Brand Products Made Overseas," July 25, 2016.

4. John Kingdon, *America the Unusual* (Worth, 1999), 55, 72 (quote). See also Jerome Karabel and Daniel Laurison, "An Exceptional Nation? American Political Values in Comparative Perspective" (Institute for Research on Labor and Employment Working Paper 136–12, University of California, Berkeley, 2012), 13.

5. Seymour Martin Lipset, *American Exceptionalism: A Double-Edged Sword* (Norton, 1997), 38–39.

6. Larry Bartels, *Unequal Democracy: The Political Economy of the New Gilded Age,* 1st ed. (Princeton University Press, 2008), 64–97; Nolan McCarty, Keith Poole, and Howard Rosenthal, *Polarized America: The Dance of Ideology and Unequal Riches* (MIT Press, 2016), 75; Andrew Gelman, *Red State, Blue State, Rich State, Poor State: Why Americans Vote the Way They Do* (Princeton University Press, 2010), 10–17.

7. "Election 2016: Exit Polls," *New York Times,* November 8, 2016. As this book went to press shortly after the election, data breaking down the exit polls by both income and race were not yet available. However, prior data suggest that Trump supporters earn relatively high household incomes despite being less educated and likelier to work in blue collar occupations than the average citizen. Overall, the Trump coalition appears economically diverse. See Jonathan Rothwell and Pablo Diego-Rossell, "Explaining Nationalist Political Views: The Case of Donald Trump" (working paper, November 2, 2016), https://papers.ssrn.com/sol3/papers.cfm?abstract_id=2822059; Nate Silver, "The Mythology of Trump's 'Working Class' Support," *FiveThirtyEight,* May 3, 2016.

8. Bartels, *Unequal Democracy,* 72–73. These statistics are limited to votes for either the Democratic or the Republican presidential candidate, leaving aside third parties and blank ballots.

9. "Exit Poll," in "Presidential Election Results," "Decision 2012," NBC News, http://elections.msnbc.msn.com/ns/politics/2012/all/president/.

10. Gelman, *Red State, Blue State,* 9.

11. John Huber and Piero Stanig, "Voting Polarization on Redistribution across Democracies" (paper prepared for the Annual Meetings of the American Political Science Association, Philadelphia, PA, 2006).

12. For example, see Lipset, *American Exceptionalism,* 72–75; Bartels, *Unequal Democracy,* 162–63.

13. Pew, "The U.S.'s High Income Gap Is Met with Relatively Low Public Concern," December 6, 2013.

14. Larry Bartels, *Unequal Democracy: The Political Economy of the New Gilded Age,* 2nd ed. (Princeton University Press, 2016), 109.

15. Stanford Graduate School of Business and Rock Center for Corporate Governance, "Americans and CEO Pay: 2016 Public Perception Survey on CEO Compensation," 4.

16. Sorapop Kiatpongsan and Michael Norton, "How Much (More) Should CEOs Make? A Universal Desire for More Equal Pay," *Perspectives on Political Science* 9, no. 6 (2014): 587–93.

17. Bartels, *Unequal Democracy,* 1st ed., 153.

18. Ibid., 163, 179, 186.

19. Gelman, *Red State, Blue State,* 62; PolitiFact, "'Red State Socialism' Graphic Says GOP-Leaning States Get Lion's Share of Federal Dollars," January 26, 2012.

20. Gelman, *Red State, Blue State,* 22.

21. Dana Milbank, "A Tea Party of Populist Posers," *Washington Post,* October 20, 2010.

22. Naturally, Trumpism was not limited to the South. See generally Neil Irwin and Josh Katz, "The Geography of Trumpism," *New York Times,* March 12, 2016. A prior study further indicates that poor people typically vote Democrat but poor states vote Republican. Gelman, *Red State, Blue State,* 22.

23. Ralph Vartabedian, Richard Serrano, and Ken Bensinger, "Despite Working-Class Image, Ryan Comes from Family of Wealth," *Los Angeles Times,* August 25, 2012.

24. Jill Lepore, "Tea and Sympathy," *New Yorker,* May 3, 2010.

25. Stephanie Mencimer, "The Supreme Court Is about to Hear the Case That Could Destroy Obamacare," *Mother Jones,* February 9, 2015.

26. Bartels, *Unequal Democracy,* 2nd ed., 289, 312–15, 341, 353. Compelling data demonstrate that politicians are barely receptive to ordinary citizens' concerns, unlike those of the wealthy. Martin Gilens and Benjamin Paige, "Testing Theories of American Politics: Elites, Interest Groups, and Average Citizens," *Perspectives on Politics* 12, no. 3 (2014): 564–81.

27. The "Tea Party movement" as such seemed to decline toward the end of Obama's presidency, although its concerns remained omnipresent among the Republican base and were reinvigorated by Trump's movement.

28. George Orwell, *1984* (Signet, 1961), 207.

29. Bartels, *Unequal Democracy,* 1st ed., 3–4, 66, 72–73, 89–90; Morris Fiorina with Samuel Abrams and Jeremy Pope, *Culture War? The Myth of a Polarized America,* 3rd ed. (Longman, 2010), 241.

30. Gelman, *Red State, Blue State,* 91, 172.

31. Bartels, *Unequal Democracy,* 1st ed., 3–4, 66, 72–73, 89–90.

32. In 2008, for instance, "whites with family incomes below $50,000 who attended religious services more than once a week voted for John McCain over Barack Obama by better than a two-to-one margin." Alan Abramowitz, *The Polarized Public? Why American Government Is So Dysfunctional* (Pearson, 2013), 65.

33. This section partly draws on my *Truthout* article "Religious and Free-Market Fundamentalism Have More in Common Than Their Fans in the Tea Party," July 21, 2012.

34. See Meredith Shiner, "G.O.P. Begins Rollback of Wall Street Reform," *Politico,* March 16, 2011.

35. Illustratively, we saw in Chapter 3 that Michele Bachmann has claimed that scores of Nobel Prize–winning scientists are creationists.

36. Tom Cohen, "Tea Party: Bring on a Government Shutdown," CNN, April 6, 2011.

37. Naomi Cahn and June Carbone, *Red Families v. Blue Families: Legal Polarization and the Creation of Culture* (Oxford University Press, 2010), 8, 13.

38. Abramowitz, *Polarized Public?,* 16–17, 78–82, 114.

39. David Campbell and Robert Putnam, "Crashing the Tea Party," *New York Times,* August 16, 2011.

40. Abramowitz, *Polarized Public?,* 114.

41. Ibid., 80.

42. Julian Borger, "Cultural Conservatives Tighten Grip in Congress," *Guardian,* November 5, 2004.

43. Michelle Goldberg, *Kingdom Coming: The Rise of Christian Nationalism* (Norton, 2007), 3.

44. "Jim DeMint, Chris Christie Skipping CPAC 2011," *Huffington Post,* January 24, 2011.

45. Maggie Haberman, "Michele Bachmann Steals the Show in Iowa," *Politico,* March 26, 2011.

46. Mark Duel, "'Gays Are Part of Satan and Their Life Is Bondage': Bachmann's Thoughts on Homosexuality," *Daily Mail* (UK), July 13, 2011.

47. Brian Ross, Rhonda Schwartz, Matthew Mosk, and Megan Chuchmach, "Michele Bachmann Clinic: Where You Can Pray Away the Gay?," ABC News, July 11, 2011.

48. Michele Bachmann, speech at the Living Word Christian Center, Brooklyn Park, Minnesota, October 14, 2006.

49. Pew, "Beyond Red vs. Blue: The Political Typology," May 4, 2011. See also Abramowitz, *Polarized Public?,* 16–17, 78–82.

50. Guttmacher Institute, "Unintended Pregnancies Cost Federal and State Governments $21 Billion in 2010," March 2, 2015.

51. Joseph Stiglitz, *Freefall: America, Free Markets, and the Sinking of the World Economy* (Norton, 2010), 219.

52. Goldberg, *Kingdom Coming,* 46, 169.

53. Diana Butler Bass, "God in Wisconsin," *Huffington Post,* May 25, 2011.

54. See, for example, Sam Brownback, "What I Think of Evolution," *New York Times,* May 31, 2007.

55. 107 Cong. Rec. H4527 (daily ed. July 11, 2002) (statement of Rep. Pence).

56. Stephen Braun, "Palin Canny on Religion and Politics," *Los Angeles Times,* September 28, 2008.

57. Media Matters for America, "Beck, Carlson Noted That Apocalyptic August 22 Predictions Were Wrong," August 23, 2006.

58. Tara Golshan, "10 Things We Learned about Trump Adviser Steve Bannon from This Recently Surfaced Speech," *Vox,* November 17, 2016.

59. Dinesh D'Souza, *The Enemy at Home: The Cultural Left and Its Responsibility for 9/11* (Broadway, 2008).

60. Robin Abcarian, "Paul Ryan Says His Abortion Stance Is Unchanged, Matches Romney's," *Los Angeles Times,* October 10, 2012.

61. Abramowitz, *Polarized Public?,* 16–17, 78–82. See also Pew, "Beyond Red vs. Blue."

62. Pew, "Palin V.P. Nomination Puts Pentecostalism in the Spotlight," September 12, 2008.

63. Kevin Kruse, *One Nation under God: How Corporate America Invented Christian America* (Basic, 2015), 37–39.

64. Ayelish McGarvey, "Carter's Crusade," *American Prospect,* April 5, 2004.

65. Richard Hofstadter, *Social Darwinism in American Thought* (Beacon, 1992), 200.

66. Andrew Koppelman, "The Nonproblem of Fundamentalism," *William and Mary Bill of Rights Journal* 18 (2010): 917. See also Michael Kazin, *The Populist Persuasion: An American History* (Basic, 1995), 42–45.

67. This section features excerpts of my article "The Polarization of the American Dream," published by *Collier's* in October 2012.

68. Stanford Center on Poverty and Inequality, "State of the Union" (2016), 52; Economic Mobility Project, "Does America Promote Mobility as Well as Other Nations?," November 2011; Economic Mobility Project, "Is the American Dream Alive and Well?," May 25, 2007.

69. Economic Mobility Project, "Economic Mobility of the States," April 2012.

70. Matt Kibbe, *Real Time with Bill Maher,* HBO, July 29, 2011.

71. Jack Greene, *The Intellectual Construction of America: Exceptionalism and Identity from 1492 to 1800* (University of North Carolina Press, 1993), 69.

72. Ibid., 102 (quote), 104. See also Thomas Piketty, *Capital in the Twenty-First Century,* trans. Arthur Goldhammer (Belknap, 2014), 150–51.

73. Greene, *Intellectual Construction of America,* 107.

74. Piketty, *Capital,* 152; Peter Lindert and Jeffrey Williamson, "American Incomes before and after the Revolution," *Journal of Economic History* 73, no. 3 (2013): 725–65.

75. Piketty, *Capital,* 150–52.

76. Jared Diamond, *Guns, Germs, and Steel: The Fates of Human Societies* (Norton, 1997), 77–78.

77. Cass Sunstein, *The Second Bill of Rights: FDR's Unfinished Revolution and Why We Need It More Than Ever* (Basic, 2004), 198–99.

78. Barack Obama, speech in Osawatomie, Kansas, December 6, 2011.

79. Bartels, *Unequal Democracy,* 2nd ed., 338.

80. Nicholas Confessore, "9 Times Donald Trump Complained about Taxes," *New York Times,* October 2, 2016.

81. Bartels, *Unequal Democracy,* 1st ed., 153.

82. Pew, "Most See Inequality Growing, but Partisans Differ over Solutions," January 23, 2014.

83. Ibid.

84. For example, see David Shipler, *The Working Poor: Invisible in America* (Vintage, 2005).

85. See generally Piketty, *Capital,* 297, 291, 320.

86. Economic Mobility Project, "Economic Mobility and the American Dream: Examining Income Differences," March 2012.

87. Barbara Ehrenreich, *Nickel and Dimed: On (Not) Getting By in America* (Holt, 2008), 108, 118 (quote), 178, 180, 184–85, 208.

88. Shipler, *Working Poor,* x.

89. As discussed in this chapter's first section, research by Gelman, Bartels, and other political scientists demonstrates that the rich are likelier than the poor to oppose the welfare state.

90. Pew, "Most See Inequality Growing."

91. Lipset, *American Exceptionalism,* 108–9.

92. Gelman, *Red State, Blue State,* 102; Bartels, *Unequal Democracy,* 1st ed., 95; Huber and Stanig, "Voting Polarization."

93. Kazin, *Populist Persuasion,* 36–41, 59–61, 147.

94. Paul Krugman, *The Conscience of a Liberal* (Norton, 2009), 92–93, 106, 178.

95. Ian Haney López, *Dog Whistle Politics: How Coded Racial Appeals Have Reinvented Racism and Wrecked the Middle Class* (Oxford University Press, 2015), 58.

96. Ibid., 1.

97. Ibid., 4.

98. Rick Perlstein, "Lee Atwater's Infamous 1981 Interview on the Southern Strategy," *Nation,* November 13, 2012.

99. Paul Krugman, "Love for Labor Lost," *New York Times,* September 1, 2013; U.S. Office of Family Assistance, "Characteristics and Financial Circumstances of TANF Recipients, Fiscal Year 2015" (2016). The programs typically identified as "welfare" are Temporary Aid to Needy Families and its predecessor, Aid to Families with Dependent Children. Other anti-poverty programs exist, such as Medicaid and the Supplemental Nutrition Assistance Program, which dispenses food stamps.

100. Harris Interactive, "'Wingnuts' and President Obama," March 23, 2010.

101. Michael Norton and Samuel Sommers, "Whites See Racism as a Zero-Sum Game That They Are Now Losing," *Perspectives on Psychological Science* 6, no. 3 (May 2011): 215–18.

102. López, *Dog Whistle Politics,* 55–56, 108–11.

103. "Racial Attitudes," in "Polling the Tea Party," *New York Times,* April 10, 2010.

104. David E. Campbell and Robert Putnam, "Crashing the Tea Party," *New York Times,* August 16, 2011.

105. William Emmons and Bryan Noeth, "Why Didn't Higher Education Protect Hispanic and Black Wealth?," Federal Reserve Bank of St. Louis, *In the Balance* 12 (2015).

106. See Devah Pager, Bruce Western, and Bart Bonikowski, "Discrimination in a Low-Wage Labor Market: A Field Experiment," *American Sociological Review* 74, no. 5 (2009): 777–99.

107. Families are considered "low income" if they have an income below 200 percent of the poverty level. See Margaret Simms, Karina Fortuny, and Everett Henderson, "Racial and Ethnic Disparities among Low-Income Families," Urban Institute, August 2009. Whites, Latinos, and blacks respectively constitute 61, 17, and 13 percent of the U.S. population. U.S. Census, "Quick Facts" (2015 data), www.census.gov/quickfacts/table/PST045215/00.

108. Suzanne Mettler, "Our Hidden Government Benefits," *New York Times,* September 19, 2011. See also Mettler, "Reconstituting the Submerged State: The Challenges of Social Policy Reform in the Obama Era," *Perspectives on Politics* 8, no. 3 (September 2010): 803–24.

109. Sunstein, *Second Bill of Rights,* 135.

110. Ira Katznelson, *When Affirmative Action Was White* (Norton, 2005), 22–23, 140.

111. Alberto Alesina, Edward Glaeser, and Bruce Sacerdote, "Why Doesn't the US Have a European-Style Welfare State?," *Harvard Institute of Economic Research* 1933 (2001): 49–51.

112. Needless to say, the horrors of the Holocaust epitomize the capacity of Europeans to scapegoat and persecute minorities. That being noted, in 1933 Jews represented barely 1.7 percent of Europe's population, which was much less diverse than America's. See United States Holocaust Memorial Museum, *Holocaust Encyclopedia,* s.v. "Jewish Population of Europe in 1933: Population Data by Country." Although anti-Semitism was part of anti-socialist and anti-communist rhetoric in Europe, Jews were not widely perceived as the main recipients of national health insurance or the welfare state.

113. See generally Andrew Higgins, "Right Wing's Surge in Europe Has Establishment Rattled," *New York Times,* November 8, 2013.

114. See, for instance, Michael Millenson, "Why Obamacare Is Good for White People," *Health Care Blog,* October 30, 2012. *King v. Burwell,* 135 S.Ct. 2480, a major 2015 Supreme Court decision, rejected an attempt to eviscerate Obama's health care reform. More than 60 percent of the people who would otherwise have become uninsured were white. See Urban Institute and Robert Wood Johnson Foundation, "Characteristics of Those Affected by a Supreme Court Finding for the Plaintiff in *King v. Burwell,*" January 2015.

115. Richard Hofstadter, *The Paranoid Style in American Politics, and Other Essays* (Vintage, 2008), 51.

116. This is especially true for legislative elections. See International Institute for Democracy and Electoral Assistance, Voter Turnout Database, www.idea.int/themes/voter-turnout.

117. Turnout is generally lower for nonpresidential elections in both America and France.

118. Data suggest that voter turnout is higher in swing states. Carl Bialik, "Voter Turnout Fell, Especially in States That Clinton Won," *FiveThirtyEight,* November 11, 2016; Susan Page, "Voter Turnout Higher in Swing States Than Elsewhere," *USA Today,* December 23, 2012. But turnout also tends to be high in various nonswing states. James Gimpel, Karen Kaufmann, and Shanna Pearson-Merkowitz, "Battleground States versus Blackout States: The Behavioral Implications of Modern Presidential Campaigns," *Journal of Politics* 69, no. 3 (2007): 795. Moreover, another study concluded that voters in swing states do not have significantly higher turnout. Alan Gerber, Gregory Huber, David Doherty, and Conor Dowling, "Are Voting Norms Conditional? How Electoral Context and Peer Behavior Shape the Social Returns to Voting" (2016), http://huber.research.yale.edu/materials/56_paper.pdf.

7. MASS INCARCERATION, EXECUTIONS, AND GUN VIOLENCE

1. Recall that our definition of the West does not include Latin American nations, some of which have much higher murder rates.

2. Alexis de Tocqueville, *Democracy in America,* trans. Henry Reeve (Bantam, 2000), 694.

3. Lawrence Friedman, *American Law in the Twentieth Century* (Yale University Press, 2002), 92–95.

4. Alexis de Tocqueville and Gustave de Beaumont, *On the Penitentiary System in the United States and Its Application in France,* trans. Francis Lieber (Carey, Lea and Blanchard, 1833). "We have signaled . . . the advantages of the penitentiary system in the United States," Tocqueville and Beaumont emphasized (106).

5. Michelle Ye Hee Lee, "Fact Check: Does the United States Really Have 5 Percent of the World's Population and One Quarter of the World's Prisoners?," *Washington Post,* April 30, 2015.

6. Prison Policy Initiative, "States of Incarceration: The Global Context 2016," www.prisonpolicy.org/global/2016.html.

7. Institute for Criminal Policy Research, "World Prison Brief" (2016).

8. Freedom House, "Freedom in the World 2015."

9. Institute for Criminal Policy Research, "World Prison Brief." See also Lisa Mahapatra, "Why Are So Many People in US Prisons?," *International Business Times,* March 19, 2014.

10. James Whitman, *Harsh Justice: Criminal Punishment and the Widening Divide between America and Europe* (Oxford University Press, 2003), 71–72.

11. U.S. Bureau of Justice Statistics, "Prisoners in 2014," September 2015, 16.

12. Whitman, *Harsh Justice,* 63, 71–72, 83.

13. John Pfaff, "The Micro and Macro Causes of Prison Growth," *Georgia State University Law Review* 28 (2012): 1241.

14. See Civitas, "Comparisons of Crime in OECD Countries" (2012); Peter Baldwin, *The Narcissism of Small Differences: How America and Europe Are Alike* (Oxford University Press, 2009), 78–87.

15. William Stuntz, *The Collapse of American Criminal Justice* (Belknap, 2011), 2–3, 34.

16. Ibid., 224–25.

17. Ibid., 223–24, 235.

18. Stuntz, *Collapse of American Criminal Justice,* 242.

19. Susan Jacoby, *The Age of American Unreason* (Vintage, 2009), 137, 149–53.

20. Christian Henrichson and Ruth Delaney, "The Price of Prisons: What Incarceration Costs Taxpayers," Vera Institute of Justice, January 2012, 2.

21. David Garland, *The Culture of Control: Crime and Social Order in Contemporary Society* (University of Chicago Press, 2002), 90.

22. As John Pfaff noted, "Canada's crime rates have risen and fallen roughly in sync with those in the United States, yet its incarceration rate barely budged from 100 per 100,000 between 1981 and 2001. An increase in crime thus does not inexorably lead to an increase in prisoners." Pfaff, "Causes of Prison Growth," 1246.

23. Garland, *Culture of Control,* 20, 58, 62.

24. Ibid., 143.

25. See, for instance, Eva Nilsen, "Decency, Dignity, and Desert: Restoring Ideals of Humane Punishment to Constitutional Discourse," *UC Davis Law Review* 41 (2007): 111–75.

26. Rummel v. Estelle, 445 U.S. 263 (1980).

27. Lockyer v. Andrade, 538 U.S. 63 (2003). As Justice O'Connor's majority opinion stated, in California "petty theft with a prior conviction" was "punishable either as a misdemeanor or as a felony" at the prosecutor's discretion. In *Lockyer* "the prosecutor decided to charge the two counts of theft as felonies rather than misdemeanors" (67). That underscored the drive to inflict the harshest possible sentence. Leandro Andrade, the petty offender, thus received a sentence of fifty years to life, meaning that he must serve fifty years in prison before being eligible for parole. Because he was thirty-seven when sentenced, he was likely condemned to die in prison.

28. Harmelin v. Michigan, 501 U.S. 957 (1991).

29. See generally Shanto Iyengar, James Curran, Anker Brink Lund, Inka Salovaara-Moring, Kyu Hahn, and Sharon Coen, "Cross-National versus Individual-Level Differences in Political Information: A Media Systems Perspective," *Journal of Elections, Public Opinion and Parties* 20, no. 3 (August 2010): 294.

30. Katherine Beckett and Theodore Sasson, *The Politics of Injustice: Crime and Punishment in America* (Pine Forge, 2000), 77–87; Opportunity Agenda, "An Overview of Public Opinion and Discourse on Criminal Justice Issues" (hereafter "Opportunity Agenda Report"), August 2014, 18.

31. Marc Fisher, "Democratic Party Platform: An Uneven Progression over the Years," *Washington Post,* September 4, 2012.

32. Marshall Frady, "Death in Arkansas," *New Yorker,* February 22, 1993.

33. Bill Clinton, quoted in Michelle Alexander, *The New Jim Crow: Mass Incarceration in the Age of Colorblindness* (New Press, 2012), 56.

34. See Paul Duggan, "'Too Easy for Him': For Witnesses in Oklahoma City, a Long Day Brought Little Relief," *Washington Post,* June 12, 2001.

35. Michelle Alexander, "Why Hillary Clinton Doesn't Deserve the Black Vote," *Nation,* February 10, 2016.

36. DiIulio was among the criminologists who filed an amicus brief in *Miller v. Alabama,* 132 S.Ct. 2455 (2012), a challenge to life sentences for juveniles. See also Elizabeth Becker, "As Ex-Theorist on Young 'Superpredators,' Bush Aide Has Regrets," *New York Times,* February 9, 2001.

37. Carol Steiker, "Capital Punishment and American Exceptionalism," in *American Exceptionalism and Human Rights,* ed. Michael Ignatieff (Princeton University Press, 2005), 77. Only a tiny number of countries have judicial elections. In particular, certain Swiss cantons elect judges, and appointed judges on Japan's Supreme Court face retention elections that tend to be a formality. These elections are vastly different in practice than those in America, which exist on a far larger scale and in a far more politicized environment. Jed Handelsman Shugerman, "The Twist of Long Terms: Judicial Elections, Role Fidelity, and American Tort Law," *Georgetown Law Journal* 98 (2010): 1351 fn. 3; Adam Liptak, "Rendering Justice, with One Eye on Re-election," *New York Times,* May 25, 2008. Other examples similarly differ from American judges campaigning on their willingness to impose death sentences or draconian prison terms. In France, for instance, lower court commercial and labor judges are elected professionals who usually lack legal training. They have no jurisdiction over criminal cases. Amalia D. Kessler, *"Marginalization and Myth: The Corporatist Roots of France's Forgotten Elective Judiciary,"* American Journal of Comparative Law 58 (2010): 681–83.

38. Whitman, *Harsh Justice,* 71.

39. See Carol Steiker, "Capital Punishment," 71–72; Carol Steiker and Jordan Steiker, "No More Tinkering: The American Law Institute and the Death Penalty Provisions of the Model Penal Code," *Texas Law Review* 89, no. 2 (2010): 390–96.

40. See Richard Wilkinson and Kate Pickett, *The Spirit Level: Why Greater Equality Makes Societies Stronger* (Bloomsbury, 2010), 155–56; Whitman, *Harsh Justice,* 200.

41. Chris Suellentrop, "The Right Has a Jailhouse Conversion," *New York Times,* December 24, 2006.

42. Vera Institute of Justice, "Confronting Confinement," June 2006.

43. Institute for Criminal Policy Research, "World Prison Brief" (2014 data).

44. Keith Humphreys, "There's Been a Big Decline in the Black Incarceration Rate, and Nobody's Paying Attention," *Washington Post,* February 10, 2016.

45. Sentencing Project, "Fewer Prisoners, Less Crime: A Tale of Three States," July 23, 2014.

46. Brown v. Plata, 563 U.S. 493, 511 (2011).

47. Rob Kuznia, "An Unprecedented Experiment in Mass Forgiveness," *Washington Post,* February 8, 2016.

48. FBI Uniform Crime Reports (2014). See also Christopher Ingraham, "Every Minute, Someone Gets Arrested for Marijuana Possession in the U.S.," *Washington Post,* September 28, 2015.

49. James Forman Jr., "Racial Critiques of Mass Incarceration: Beyond the New Jim Crow," *NYU Law Review* 87, no. 1 (2012): 24–25; U.S. Bureau of Justice Statistics, "Prisoners in 2014," 16.

50. Laurence Steinberg, "The Influence of Neuroscience on US Supreme Court Decisions about Adolescents' Criminal Culpability," *Nature Reviews Neuroscience* 14 (2013): 513–18.

51. See, for example, George Will, "More Prisoners, Less Crime," *Washington Post,* June 22, 2008.

52. See PolitiFact, "Fact-Checking Bill Clinton's Philly Defense of His Controversial Crime Bill," April 8, 2016.

53. See John Pfaff, "Bill Clinton Is Wrong about His Crime Bill. So Are the Protesters He Lectured," *New York Times,* April 12, 27.

54. See generally Brennan Center for Justice, "What Caused the Crime Decline?" (2015).

55. Stuntz, *Collapse of American Criminal Justice,* 26. See also Shaila Dewan, "The Real Murder Mystery? It's the Low Crime Rate," *New York Times,* August 2, 2009.

56. OECD Better Life Index, "Safety," accessed October 17, 2016, www.oecdbetterlifeindex.org/topics/safety/. The U.S. homicide rate is approximately 5.2 per 100,000 people, compared to 1.5 for Canada, 0.8 for Italy, 0.4 for Austria, and 0.2 for the United Kingdom, for example.

57. "ACLU Nationwide Poll on Criminal Justice Reform," July 15, 2015.

58. Pew, "Voters Want Big Changes in Federal Sentencing, Prison System," February 12, 2016. Another poll had similar findings: Reason-Rupe, "Poll: 77% of Americans Favor Eliminating Mandatory Minimum Prison Sentences for Nonviolent Offenders; 73% Favor Restoring Voting Rights," October 21, 2014.

59. "Republican Platform 2016" (July 18, 2016), American Presidency Project, 39–40, www.presidency.ucsb.edu/papers_pdf/117718.pdf.

60. "2016 Democratic Party Platform" (July 21, 2016), American Presidency Project, 14–16, www.presidency.ucsb.edu/ws/index.php?pid=117717.

61. David Alan Sklansky, "The Changing Political Landscape for Elected Prosecutors," *Ohio State Journal of Criminal Law* 14, no. 2 (Spring 2017).

62. Opportunity Agenda Report, 31.

63. Ibid., 20.

64. Gallup, "More Americans Say Crime Is Rising in US," October 22, 2015.

65. Opportunity Agenda Report, 3 (summarizing the findings of various studies). Another study found that only half of whites believe the justice system is discriminatory. See Christopher Ingraham, "In a Post-Ferguson World, Americans Increasingly Doubt the Notion of Colorblind Justice," *Washington Post,* September 23, 2014.

66. David Graham, "Systemic Racism or Isolated Abuses? Americans Disagree," *Atlantic,* May 7, 2015; Giovanni Russonello, "Race Relations Are at Lowest Point in Obama Presidency, Poll Finds," *New York Times,* July 13, 2016.

67. PolitiFact, "Trump's Pants on Fire Tweet That Blacks Killed 81% of White Homicide Victims," November 23, 2015.

68. Sentencing Project, "Race and Punishment: Racial Perceptions of Crime and Support for Punitive Policies" (2014).

69. U.S. Bureau of Justice Statistics, "Prisoners in 2014"; U.S. Census, "Quick Facts" (2015 data) www.census.gov/quickfacts/table/PST045215/00.

70. See, for example, Alexander, *New Jim Crow,* 117–18; PolitiFact, "Hillary Clinton Says Blacks More Likely to Be Arrested, Get Longer Sentences," February 26, 2016; Sonja Starr and M. Marit Rehavi, "Mandatory Sentencing and Racial Disparity, Assessing the Role of Prosecutors and the Effects of *Booker,*" *Yale Law Journal* 123 (2013): 2–80. Latinos may be undercounted among prisoners partly because states did not define them as a separate group for years. Forman, "Racial Critiques of Mass Incarceration," 59–61.

71. Alexander, *New Jim Crow,* 99–100, 126–27.

72. Ibid., 126–27; Stuntz, *Collapse of American Criminal Justice,* 4.

73. Alexander, *New Jim Crow,* 72–78.

74. Forman, "Racial Critiques of Mass Incarceration," 47–48.

75. Rebecca Hetey and Jennifer Eberhardt, "Racial Disparities in Incarceration Increase Acceptance of Punitive Policies," *Psychological Science* 25, no. 10 (2014): 1949–54.

76. Jennifer Eberhardt, Paul Davies, Valerie Purdie-Vaughns, and Sheri Lynn Johnson, "Looking Deathworthy: Perceived Stereotypicality of Black Defendants Predicts Capital-Sentencing Outcomes," *Psychological* Science 17, no. 5 (2006): 383–86.

77. See, for example, Steiker and Steiker, "No More Tinkering," 396–402.

78. Franklin Zimring, *The Contradictions of American Capital Punishment* (Oxford University Press, 2004), 88–89.

79. This paragraph draws on my *Slate* article "The Human Toll of Antonin Scalia's Time on the Court," February 17, 2016.

80. Oral arguments, McCleskey v. Kemp, 481 U.S. 279, October 15, 1986 [emphasis mine].

81. State v. Santiago, 318 Conn. 1, 14 (2015).

82. My Stanford colleague John Donohue notably provided key empirical evidence in these proceedings. See "An Empirical Evaluation of the Connecticut Death Penalty System since 1973: Are There Unlawful Racial, Gender, and Geographic Disparities?," *Journal of Empirical Legal Studies* 11, no. 4 (2014): 637–96.

83. Thomas Miles and Adam Cox, "Does Immigration Enforcement Reduce Crime? Evidence from 'Secure Communities,'" *Journal of Law and Economics* 57 (2014): 951.

84. Bianca Bersani, "An Examination of First and Second Generation Immigrant Offending Trajectories," *Justice Quarterly* 31, no. 2 (2014): 315–43. See also Pew, "Crime Rises among Second-Generation Immigrants as They Assimilate," October 15, 2013.

85. Whitman, *Harsh Justice,* 46.

86. See ibid., 79; Adam Liptak, "U.S. Prison Population Dwarfs That of Other Nations," *New York Times,* April 23, 2008.

87. Alexander, *New Jim Crow,* 158–59.

88. Sentencing Project, "Trends in U.S. Corrections," December 2015.

89. The United Kingdom is an exception in this area, as it has defied European Court of Human Rights decisions on prisoners' voting rights.

90. Whitman, *Harsh Justice,* 198.

91. Forman, "Racial Critiques of Mass Incarceration," 36–45.

92. Elizabeth Hinton, Julilly Kohler-Hausmann, and Vesla Weaver, "Did Blacks Really Endorse the 1994 Crime Bill?," *New York Times,* April 13, 2016.

93. See Kate Stith and Steve Koh, "The Politics of Sentencing Reform: The Legislative History of the Federal Sentencing Guidelines," *Wake Forest Law Review* 28 (1993): 233–90.

94. Forman, "Racial Critiques of Mass Incarceration," 58–59.

95. U.S. Bureau of Justice Statistics, "Prisoners in 2014"; Death Penalty Information Center, "Execution Database," accessed August 22, 2016, www.deathpenaltyinfo .org/views-executions.

96. Hetey and Eberhardt, "Racial Disparities in Incarceration."

97. Forman, "Racial Critiques of Mass Incarceration," 64.

98. Pew, "One in 100: Behind Bars in America," February 28, 2008.

99. Garland, *Culture of Control,* 99, 197. See also Lee Epstein, William Landes, and Richard Posner, "How Business Fares at the Supreme Court," *Minnesota Law Review* 97 (2013): 1471–72.

100. Will, "More Prisoners, Less Crime."

101. Regarding the interrelated evolution of capitalism and penitentiary systems since the nineteenth century, see Bernard Harcourt, *The Illusion of Free Markets: Punishment and the Myth of the Natural Order* (Harvard University Press, 2011).

102. Mugambi Jouet, "In Prison Debate, Race Overshadows Poverty," *Salon,* March 1, 2013.

103. Wilkinson and Pickett, *Spirit Level,* 148–50.

104. Ibid., 155.

105. Alberto Alesina, Edward Glaeser, and Bruce Sacerdote, "Why Doesn't the US Have a European-Style Welfare State?" (Harvard Institute of Economic Research Paper No. 1933, 2001), 56. Loïc Wacquant further discusses the relationship between harsh attitudes toward both poverty and crime in *Prisons of Poverty* (University of Minnesota Press, 2009).

106. Wilkinson and Pickett, *Spirit Level,* 246.

107. Hamilton Project, "Ten Economic Facts about Crime and Incarceration in the United States," Brookings Institution, May 1, 2014, 13.

108. Suzanne Kirchhoff, "Economic Impacts of Prison Growth," Congressional Research Service, April 13, 2010.

109. See, for example, Maples v. Thomas, 132 S.Ct. 912 (2012) (noting that lawyers in capital cases are "undercompensated"); David Ovalle, "New Fee Rules Rile South Florida Defense Lawyers," *Miami Herald,* June 23, 2012; Joseph Slobodzian, "Philadelphia Courts Increase Pay for Capital Defense," *Philadelphia Inquirer,* February 29, 2012.

110. Sandra Day O'Connor, speech to the Minnesota Women Lawyers Association, July 2, 2001.

111. Ruth Bader Ginsburg, speech at the University of the District of Columbia, April 9, 2001.

112. See Pew, "Religious Groups' Views on Evolution," February 4, 2009; National Center for Science Education, "Statements from Religious Organizations on Evolution," http://ncse.com/media/voices/religion; Death Penalty Information Center, "Official Religious Statements on the Death Penalty," http://deathpenaltyinfo .org/religion-and-death-penalty#state.

113. Assemblies of God, "Capital Punishment," accessed May 5, 2016, www.ag .org/top/Beliefs/contempissues_08_capital_punish.cfm.

114. "Death Penalty | Gallup Historical Trends," www.gallup.com/poll/1606 /death-penalty.aspx.

115. Stephen Prothero, *Religious Literacy: What Every American Needs to Know about Religion—and Doesn't* (Harper, 2007), 38.

116. See, for instance, Bart Ehrman, *Jesus, Interrupted: Revealing the Hidden Contradictions of the Bible (and Why We Don't Know about Them)* (Harper, 2010).

117. Roper v. Simmons, 543 U.S. 551 (2005); Atkins v. Virginia, 536 U.S. 304 (2002).

118. Antonin Scalia, "God's Justice and Ours," *First Things,* May 2002.

119. Douglas Martin, "W. J. Stuntz, Who Stimulated Legal Minds, Dies at 52," *New York Times,* March 20, 2011.

120. Empirical evidence does not suggest that faith-based rehabilitation programs are more effective than secular ones. Alexander Volokh, "Do Faith-Based Prisons Work?," *Alabama Law Review* 63 (2011): 43–95.

121. Roper, 543 U.S. 551 (2005).

122. "The few countries in which juveniles were previously reported to be serving life sentences without parole have either changed their laws or explained that juvenile offenders can apply for parole." Brief of *Amici Curiae* Amnesty International et al., 3–4, in *Miller,* 132 S.Ct. 2455 (2012).

123. Sentencing Project, "Juvenile Life without Parole: An Overview," July 1, 2016.

124. Oral arguments in *Jackson v. Hobbs,* companion case to *Miller,* 132 S.Ct. 2455 (2012), March 20, 2012.

125. Graham v. Florida, 560 U.S. 48 (2010).

126. Miller, 132 S.Ct. 2455 (2012).

127. Mugambi Jouet, "The Exceptional Absence of Human Rights as a Principle in American Law," *Pace Law Review* 34, no. 2 (2014): 705–8.

128. Noémie Buffault, "Prisons: La France, championne des fouilles au corps abusives," *Rue89,* September 7, 2011.

129. Whitman, *Harsh Justice,* 76.

130. Institute for Criminal Policy Research, "World Prison Brief."

131. Office of the United Nations High Commissioner for Human Rights, "US: 'Four Decades in Solitary Confinement Can Only Be Described as Torture'—UN

Rights Expert," October 7, 2013; Amnesty International, "The Edge of Endurance: Prison Conditions in California's Security Housing Units" (2012).

132. International Human Rights Clinic at the University of Chicago Law School, American Civil Liberties Union, and Chicago Legal Advocacy for Incarcerated Mothers, "The Shackling of Incarcerated Pregnant Women: A Human Rights Violation Committed Regularly in the United States" (August 2013).

133. See Leslie Meltzer Henry, "The Jurisprudence of Dignity," *University of Pennsylvania Law Review* 160, no. 1 (2011): 169–233.

134. For a broader analysis, see Jouet, "Exceptional Absence of Human Rights."

135. Samuel Moyn, *The Last Utopia: Human Rights in History* (Belknap, 2010), 63.

136. Gallup found 61 percent support in 2015: "Death Penalty | Gallup Historical Trends," www.gallup.com/poll/1606/death-penalty.aspx. However, Pew found that support had dropped to 49 percent in 2016 from 56 percent in 2015: "Support for Death Penalty Lowest in More Than Four Decades," September 29, 2016.

137. Zimring, *Contradictions of American Capital Punishment,* 10–11, 23.

138. BBC, "Support for Death Penalty Drops Below 50% for the First Time," March 26, 2015.

139. Jean-Baptiste de Montvalon et Gérard Courtois, "Une France moins pessimiste où les idées du FN s'enracinent," *Le Monde,* May 6, 2015.

140. Swedish Wire, "Sweden Enjoys 100 Years without Executions," November 23, 2010.

141. Alexander Bickel coined "the counter-majoritarian difficulty" to refer to the question of whether courts can legitimately overturn legislation supported by a democratic majority: *The Least Dangerous Branch: The Supreme Court at the Bar of Politics* (Bobbs-Merrill, 1962), 16.

142. This language stems from *Trop v. Dulles,* 356 U.S. 86 (1958), 101, an influential precedent. We will see in the next chapter that in the twenty-first century the justices have showed growing interest in international human rights standards.

143. Amnesty International, "Death Sentences and Executions in 2013" (2014).

144. Gregg v. Georgia, 428 U.S. 153 (1976); Furman v. Georgia, 408 U.S. 238 (1972). If *Gregg* had gone the other way, it might have permanently abolished capital punishment and ended the debate about American exceptionalism in this area. See Carol Steiker, "Capital Punishment," 86.

145. Amnesty International, "List of Abolitionist and Retentionist Countries."

146. Death Penalty Information Center, "The 2% Death Penalty: How a Minority of Counties Produce Most Death Cases at Enormous Costs to All" (2013).

147. National Research Council of the National Academies, "Deterrence and the Death Penalty" (2012).

148. Death Penalty Information Center, "States without the Death Penalty Have Had Consistently Lower Murder Rates," www.deathpenaltyinfo.org/deterrence-states-without-death-penalty-have-had-consistently-lower-murder-rates.

149. See generally Steiker and Steiker, "No More Tinkering," 419–20.

150. Judge Arthur Alarcón and Paula Mitchell, "Executing the Will of the Voters?: A Roadmap to Mend or End the California Legislature's Multi-billion-Dollar Death Penalty Debacle," *Loyola of Los Angeles Law Review* 44 (2011): S41–S224. See also Carol Williams, "Death Penalty Costs California $184 Million a Year, Study Says," *Los Angeles Times,* June 20, 2011.

151. Death Penalty Information Center, "Innocence and the Death Penalty," as of October 16, 2016, www.deathpenaltyinfo.org/innocence-and-death-penalty.

152. See generally Innocence Project, "Causes," www.innocenceproject .org/#causes.

153. O'Connor, speech to the Minnesota Women Lawyers Association, July 2, 2001, quoted in Zimring, *Contradictions of American Capital Punishment,* 164.

154. "Death Penalty | Gallup Historical Trends," 2015 data.

155. Death Penalty Information Center, "Execution Database."

156. Culture is not set in stone. American attitudes toward executions have changed over time and will probably continue to evolve. See David Garland, "Capital Punishment and American Culture," *Punishment and Society* 7 (2005): 365–66.

157. Glossip v. Gross, 135 S.Ct. 2726 (2015).

158. U.S. Bureau of Justice Statistics, "Capital Punishment, 2013—Statistical Tables," December 19, 2014, 14.

159. See, for example, Daniel Wood, "Death Row: Does Personal Reform Count?," *Christian Science Monitor,* November 29, 2005.

160. Denis Diderot, "Letter on the Blind for the Use of Those Who See" (1749), in *Diderot's Early Philosophical Works,* trans. and ed. Margaret Jourdain (Open Court, 1916), 81.

161. Zimring, *Contradictions of American Capital Punishment,* 51.

162. Austin Sarat, *When the State Kills: Capital Punishment and the American Condition* (Princeton University Press, 2002), Chapter 3, "Killing Me Softly."

163. David Garland, *Peculiar Institution: America's Death Penalty in the Age of Abolition* (Belknap, 2010), 11–12.

164. Zimring, *Contradictions of American Capital Punishment,* 11.

165. Swedish Wire, "Sweden Enjoys 100 Years without Executions."

166. Zimring, *Contradictions of American Capital Punishment,* 59–62.

167. For example, see Kathleen Garcia, "Death Penalty Hurts—Not Helps—Families of Murder Victims," *Nashua Telegraph,* March 28, 2010.

168. Zimring, *Contradictions of American Capital Punishment,* 1, 48.

169. Murder Victims' Families for Reconciliation, "Voices," accessed October 16, 2016, www.mvfr.org/mvfr_voices.

170. Zimring, *Contradictions of American Capital Punishment,* 56, 62.

171. According to the FBI Uniform Crime Reports, 13,741 murders and non-negligent manslaughters occurred in 2013.

172. See generally Steiker and Steiker, "No More Tinkering."

173. Furman, 408 U.S. 238, 309 (1972).

174. Zimring, *Contradictions of American Capital Punishment,* 56.

175. A journalist then interviewed me. See Associated Press, "Georgia Man Executed for 1983 Rape and Murder of 2-Year-Old Niece," *Access North Georgia,* July 19, 2004.

176. The "poisonous cocktail" metaphor invites consideration of the multiple factors that scholars have suggested explain the exceptional harshness of American law, some of which are beyond this book's scope.

177. Zachary Elkins, "Rewrite the Second Amendment," *New York Times,* April 4, 2013; Elkins and Tom Ginsburg, "U.S. Gun Rights Truly Are American Exceptionalism," *Bloomberg View,* March 7, 2013. The constitutions of Haiti and Iran also mention guns, although Elkins and Ginsburg found their provisions too ambiguous to include in the tally for the Comparative Constitutions Project. People in various other nations have relatively broad access to firearms, but it is not a constitutional right for them. See PolitiFact, "Marco Rubio Says Second Amendment Is Unique in Speech to NRA," April 29, 2014.

178. Canada and Ireland are exceptions, as their people are "only" six times less likely to be killed by firearms than Americans. U.N. Office on Drugs and Crime, "Percentage of Homicides by Firearm, Number of Homicides by Firearm and Homicide by Firearm Rate per 100,000 Population" (2008–10 data), accessed October 16, 2016, www.unodc.org/documents/data-and-analysis/statistics/Homicide/Homicides_by_firearms.xls. See also PolitiFact, "'Americans Are 20 Times as Likely to Die from Gun Violence as Citizens of Other Civilized Countries,' Says Author Lisa Bloom," January 17, 2014.

179. U.N. Office on Drugs and Crime, "Percentage of Homicides by Firearm" (2010 data).

180. William Krouse, "Gun Control Legislation," Congressional Research Service, November 14, 2012, 8–10.

181. "Guns | Gallup Historical Trends," www.gallup.com/poll/1645/guns.aspx.

182. See David Chen, "Bloomberg Says Out-of-State Gun Show Dealers Often Violate Law," *New York Times,* October 7, 2009.

183. PolitiFact, "Frank Lautenberg Claims a Loophole Allows Individuals Convicted of Domestic Violence to Purchase Guns," May 3, 2012.

184. Melody Gutierrez, "Gov. Jerry Brown Signs 6 Gun-Control Bills, Vetoes 5," *San Francisco Chronicle,* July 1, 2016.

185. Laura Vozzella, "McDonnell Signs Bill Lifting One-Handgun-per-Month Limit," *Washington Post,* February 28, 2012.

186. Ian Urbina, "Fearing Obama Agenda, States Push to Loosen Gun Laws," *New York Times,* February 23, 2010.

187. The shooter's gun purchase should technically have been barred because of his mental illness, but Virginia failed to adequately comply with federal guidelines. Michael Luo, "Cho's Mental Illness Should Have Blocked Gun Sale," *New York Times,* April 20, 2007.

188. Nick Carbone, "Colorado Theater Shooter Carried 4 Guns, All Obtained Legally," *Time,* July 21, 2012.

189. Tim Steller, "Gun Used in Shooting Spree Bought at Tucson Store," *Arizona Daily Star,* January 9, 2011.

190. Michael Luo, "Felons Finding It Easy to Regain Gun Rights," *New York Times,* November 13, 2011; Luo, "Some with Histories of Mental Illness Petition to Get Their Gun Rights Back," *New York Times,* July 2, 2011.

191. Small Arms Survey, "Estimating Civilian Owned Firearms" (2011).

192. For instance, see "Packing Guns in the Daycare Center," *New York Times,* November 30, 2015. Research indicates that such laws worsen gun violence. See John Donohue III, Abhay Aneja, and Alexandria Zhang, "The Impact of Right to Carry Laws and the NRC Report: The Latest Lessons for the Empirical Evaluation of Law and Policy" (Stanford Law and Economics Online Working Paper No. 461, September 4, 2014).

193. Gallup, "Despite Criticism, NRA Still Enjoys Majority Support in U.S.," October 22, 2015.

194. Nicholas Confessore, Michael Cooper, and Michael Luo, "Silent since Shootings, N.R.A. Could Face Challenge to Political Power," *New York Times,* December 17, 2012.

195. See Glenn Reynolds and Brannon Denning, "*Heller*'s Future in the Lower Courts," *Northwestern University Law Review* 102 (2008): 2035–44.

196. Adam Liptak, "A Liberal Case for Gun Rights Sways Judiciary," *New York Times,* May 6, 2007; Jill Lepore, "Battleground America," *New Yorker,* April 23, 2012.

197. District of Columbia v. Heller, 554 U.S. 570 (2008). *Heller* concerned Washington D.C., but the court extended the ruling to the states in *McDonald v. Chicago,* 561 U.S. 742 (2010).

198. Gallup, "Americans Want Stricter Gun Laws, Still Oppose Bans," December 27, 2012.

199. Chris Cillizza and Scott Clement, "President Obama Has the Public on His Side on Gun Proposals," *Washington Post,* January 17, 2013.

200. Fairleigh Dickinson University PublicMind Poll, "Beliefs about Sandy Hook Cover-Up, Coming Revolution Underlie Divide on Gun Control," May 1, 2013.

201. Jerome Karabel and Daniel Laurison, "An Exceptional Nation? American Political Values in Comparative Perspective" (Institute for Research on Labor and Employment Working Paper 136–12, University of California, Berkeley, 2012), 29–32.

202. I am referring here not simply to U.S. law but also to the disinclination to prosecute and punish police officers who unjustifiably kill suspects.

203. Jamiles Lartey, "US Police Kill More in Days Than Other Countries Do in Years," *Guardian,* June 9, 2015.

204. Republican presidential primary debate, Simi Valley, CA, September 7, 2011.

205. Ryan Lizza, "The Duel," *New Yorker,* February 1, 2016.

206. Leo Damrosch, *Tocqueville's Discovery of America* (Farrar, Straus and Giroux, 2010), 169.

207. Gallup, "Americans Want Stricter Gun Laws."

1. Peter Galbraith, *The End of Iraq: How American Incompetence Created a War without End* (Simon and Schuster, 2007), 83.

2. Kurt Eichenwald, *500 Days: Secrets and Lies in the Terror Wars* (Simon and Schuster, 2012), 459–61.

3. Program on International Policy Attitudes (PIPA), "Misperceptions, the Media and the Iraq War," October 2, 2003, 6; Rick Shenkman, *Just How Stupid Are We? Facing the Truth about the American Voter* (Basic, 2009), 6.

4. Joby Warrick, *Black Flags: The Rise of ISIS* (Doubleday, 2015), 76–80,104–5; Jane Cramer and A. Trevor Thrall, introduction to *Why Did the United States Invade Iraq?*, ed. Cramer and Thrall (Routledge, 2012), 1; John Duffield, "Oil and the Decision to Invade Iraq," in ibid., 154.

5. Jane Cramer and Edward Duggan, "In Pursuit of Primacy," in Cramer and Thrall, *Why Did the United States Invade Iraq?*, 206–7.

6. Besides skepticism of the Bush administration's intelligence, geopolitical interests partly shaped the French government's opposition to the war. Evidence suggests that France contemplated joining the invasion if it had seemed in its advantage. John Vinocur, "A Different Take on France's Role in Iraq," *New York Times,* March 20, 2007.

7. Tony Blair's controversial decision to join the Bush administration's invasion of Iraq is a notable exception to this trend.

8. Andrew Gelman, *Red State, Blue State, Rich State, Poor State: Why Americans Vote the Way They Do* (Princeton University Press, 2010), 114–15; Gallup, "Fewer in U.S. View Iraq, Afghanistan Wars as Mistakes," June 12, 2015.

9. CNN-ORC Poll, March 4, 2016, available at http://i2.cdn.turner.com/cnn /2016/images/03/04/rel4d.-.threats.draft.guantanamo.pdf.

10. Associated Press–NORC Center for Public Affairs Research, "Balancing Act: The Public's Take on Civil Liberties and Security," September 2013.

11. Andrew Moravcsik, "The Paradox of U.S. Human Rights Policy," in *American Exceptionalism and Human Rights,* ed. Michael Ignatieff (Princeton University Press, 2005), 187.

12. Available at www.youtube.com/watch?v=cPu9RhMIQdg.

13. Available at www.youtube.com/watch?v=Pwe-pA6TaZk&nohtml5.

14. Gallup, "Americans See U.S. as Exceptional," December 22, 2010. A later poll found a decline in the share of Americans convinced of U.S. superiority, though this may be due to other factors, as Chapter 1 notes. See Pew, "Most Americans Think the U.S. Is Great, but Fewer Think It's the Greatest," July 2, 2014.

15. Scott Shane, "The Opiate of Exceptionalism," *New York Times,* October 19, 2012.

16. Alexis de Tocqueville to his mother, May, 14, 1831, quoted in Leo Damrosch, *Tocqueville's Discovery of America* (Farrar, Straus and Giroux, 2010), 23.

17. Alexis de Tocqueville, *Democracy in America,* trans. Henry Reeve (Bantam, 2000), 457.

18. Pew, "The American–Western European Values Gap," November 17, 2011.

19. Public Religion Research Institute, "Most Americans Believe Protests Make the Country Better," June 23, 2015.

20. Alan Abramowitz, *The Polarized Public? Why American Government Is So Dysfunctional* (Pearson, 2013), 10–11.

21. Robert Ferguson, *The American Enlightenment, 1750–1820* (Harvard University Press, 1997), 79.

22. "Letter of Thomas Jefferson to John Banister, Junior" (October 15, 1785), in A.J. Morrison, *The Beginnings of Public Education in Virginia, 1776–1860: Study of Secondary Schools in Relation to the State Literary Fund* (D. Bottom, superintendent of public printing, 1917), 20.

23. John Archdale, *A New Description of That Fertile and Pleasant Province of Carolina* (1707), quoted in Jack Greene, *The Intellectual Construction of America: Exceptionalism and Identity from 1492 to 1800* (University of North Carolina Press, 1993), 76. See also Anders Stephanson, *Manifest Destiny: American Expansion and the Empire of Right* (Hill and Wang, 1995), 11.

24. "Bras d'honneur: Longuet assure avoir voulu s'opposer au 'procès de la colonisation' en Algérie," *Le Monde,* November 1, 2012.

25. Pew, "U.S. Religious Knowledge Survey," September 2010.

26. Bryan Bender and Sasha Issenberg, "Palin Not Well Traveled outside US," *Boston Globe,* September 3, 2008.

27. Passport Canada / Passeport Canada, "International Comparison of Passport-Issuing Authorities" (2012). See also U.S. Department of State, "Valid Passports in Circulation (1989–Present)," report in "Passport Statistics," https://travel.state.gov/content/passports/en/passports/statistics.html.

28. Natalie Avon, "Why More Americans Don't Travel Abroad," CNN, February 4, 2011.

29. Shenkman, *Just How Stupid Are We?,* 22.

30. Andrew Romano, "How Ignorant Are Americans?," *Newsweek,* March 20, 2011.

31. Shenkman, *Just How Stupid Are We?,* 21.

32. Jacob Hacker and Paul Pierson, *Winner-Take-All Politics: How Washington Made the Rich Richer—and Turned Its Back on the Middle Class* (Simon and Schuster, 2010), 109.

33. See generally Shanto Iyengar, James Curran, Anker Brink Lund, Inka Salovaara-Moring, Kyu Hahn, and Sharon Coen, "Cross-National versus Individual-Level Differences in Political Information: A Media Systems Perspective," *Journal of Elections, Public Opinion and Parties* 20, no. 3 (2010): 299–300.

34. Charles Lockhart, *The Roots of American Exceptionalism: Institutions, Culture and Policies* (Palgrave MacMillan, 2003), ix.

35. John Kingdon, *America the Unusual* (Worth, 1999), ix.

36. Jerome Karabel and Daniel Laurison, "An Exceptional Nation? American Political Values in Comparative Perspective" (Institute for Research on Labor and Employment Working Paper 136-12, University of California, Berkeley, 2012), 22–23, 30.

37. Gallup, "Americans See U.S. as Exceptional."

38. Harris Interactive, "Most Republicans Think the U.S. Health Care System Is the Best in the World, Democrats Disagree," March 20, 2008.

39. Roper v. Simmons, 543 U.S. 551 (2005); Atkins v. Virginia, 536 U.S. 304 (2002).

40. Anne-Marie Slaughter, "A Brave New Judicial World," in Ignatieff, *American Exceptionalism and Human Rights,* 277–303.

41. "A Respect for World Opinion," *New York Times,* August 2, 2010.

42. Joseph Ellis, "Immaculate Misconception and the Supreme Court," *Washington Post,* May 7, 2010.

43. Gelman, *Red State, Blue State,* 114–15.

44. Marc Hetherington and Johnathan Weiler, *Authoritarianism and Polarization in American Politics* (Cambridge University Press, 2009), 27–28.

45. Gallup, "Fewer in U.S. View Iraq, Afghanistan Wars as Mistakes."

46. Robert Pape and James Feldman, *Cutting the Fuse: The Explosion of Global Suicide Terrorism and How to Stop It* (University of Chicago Press, 2010), 2.

47. Ibid.

48. Rukmini Callimachi and Jim Yardley, "From Amateur to Ruthless Jihadist in France," *New York Times,* January 17, 2015.

49. Maxime Vaudano, "La France était dans le viseur de l'État islamique bien avant les frappes en Syrie," *Le Monde,* November 19, 2015.

50. Madjid Zerrouky, "La France n'est pas l'un des premiers fournisseurs de djihadistes," *Le Monde,* June 12, 2015.

51. Andrew Preston, *Sword of the Spirit, Shield of Faith: Religion in American War and Diplomacy* (Anchor, 2012), 603–4.

52. Media Matters, "Beck Hosted Rosenberg to Discuss Briefing of White House," October 19, 2006.

53. Bob Woodward, *Plan of Attack* (Simon and Schuster, 2004), 379.

54. Eichenwald, *500 Days,* 459–61.

55. Warrick, *Black Flags,* 93.

56. Julian Baggini, "In God We Must," *Slate,* February 5, 2012.

57. "Company Offers to Stop Putting Biblical References on Military Scopes," CNN, January 21, 2010.

58. George H. W. Bush, *All the Best: My Life in Letters and Other Writings* (Simon and Schuster, 2014), 501. See also David Holmes, *The Faiths of the Founding Fathers* (Oxford University Press, 2006), 177.

59. Richard Cooper, "General Casts War in Religious Terms," *Los Angeles Times,* October 16, 2003.

60. Nicholas Schmidle, "Getting bin Laden," *New Yorker,* August 8, 2011.

61. Pape and Feldman, *Cutting the Fuse,* 10–11, 20–26.

62. Thomas Ricks, *Fiasco: The American Military Adventure in Iraq* (Penguin, 2007), 238–39, 264–67, 270–97.

63. Fred Kaplan, *The Insurgents: David Petraeus and the Plot to Change the American Way of War* (Simon and Schuster, 2013).

64. Malcolm Byrne, ed., "CIA Confirms Role in 1953 Iran Coup," National Security Archive, George Washington University, August 19, 2013.

65. Colin Powell, *My American Journey* (Ballantine, 2003), 338.

66. Testimony of Tony Blair before the Iraq Inquiry commission, January 29, 2010.

67. See generally Cramer and Thrall, *Why Did the United States Invade Iraq?*, 1; Ricks, *Fiasco,* 90–94; "In 2003, U.S. Experts Doubted Key Iraq War Claim," Reuters, December 11, 2014.

68. A 2006 scholarly survey of 227 experts on U.S. foreign policy and international relations is instructive. The vast majority concluded that the Bush administration did not truly believe its own rhetoric about Iraq being a genuine WMD or terrorism threat. Cramer and Thrall, *Why Did the United States Invade Iraq?*, 3–7, 24.

69. Ron Suskind, *The Price of Loyalty: George W. Bush, the White House, and the Education of Paul O'Neill* (Simon and Schuster, 2004), 70–86, 96, 187–88, 258. Regarding geopolitical interests, see also Duffield, "Oil and the Decision to Invade Iraq," 144–66.

70. Colin Powell, *It Worked for Me: In Life and Leadership* (Harper, 2014), 217–18; George Tenet, *At the Center of the Storm: My Years at the CIA* (HarperLuxe, 2007), 464.

71. Joel Roberts, "Plan for Iraq Began on 9/11," CBS News, September 4, 2002.

72. Ricks, *Fiasco,* 40, 66–67.

73. Stephen Kotkin, *Armageddon Averted: The Soviet Collapse, 1970–2000* (Oxford University Press, 2008), 183–88, 244 n. 3.

74. PIPA, "Misperceptions, the Media and the Iraq War," 6; Shenkman, *Just How Stupid Are We?*, 6.

75. Karabel and Laurison, "Exceptional Nation?," 22–23, 29–32.

76. U.S. Department of Defense, Operation Iraqi Freedom fatalities, November 25, 2016, available at www.defense.gov/casualty.pdf; Amy Hagopian, Abraham Flaxman, Tim Takaro, Sahar Esa Al Shatari, Julie Rajaratnam, Stan Becker, Alison Levin-Rector, et al., "Mortality in Iraq Associated with the 2003–2011 War and Occupation: Findings from a National Cluster Sample Survey by the University Collaborative Iraq Mortality Study," *PLOS Medicine,* October 15, 2013.

77. John Tirman, *The Deaths of Others: The Fate of Civilians in America's Wars* (Oxford University Press, 2012), 3, 167–68.

78. Arthur Schlesinger Jr., "History and National Stupidity," *New York Review of Books,* April 27, 2006.

79. Duffield, "Oil and the Decision to Invade Iraq," 154; Warrick, *Black Flags,* 76–80, 104–5.

80. Pape and Feldman, *Cutting the Fuse,* 22–23.

81. Justifications were stronger for invading Afghanistan than Iraq, as the Taliban regime had sheltered Al-Qaeda. But America was not fighting for its "freedom" in Afghanistan either.

82. "Iraq War Illegal, Says Annan," BBC, September 16, 2004. See also Asli Bâli, "Justice under Occupation: Rule of Law and the Ethics of Nation-Building in Iraq,"

Yale Journal of International Law 30 (2005): 433: "This war was widely considered illegal under both international law and the rules of the prevailing international peace and security system established (largely by the United States) in the post–World War II era."

83. See generally Bâli, "Justice under Occupation," 433; Moravcsik, "U.S. Human Rights Policy," 184.

84. Naturally, that does not mean that no human rights violations exist in these countries.

85. Harold Hongju Koh, "America's Jekyll-and-Hyde Exceptionalism," in Ignatieff, *American Exceptionalism and Human Rights,* 118.

86. Moravcsik, "U.S. Human Rights Policy," 184.

87. Ibid., 178–79, 192; John Gerard Ruggie, "American Exceptionalism, Exemptionalism, and Global Governance," in Ignatieff, *American Exceptionalism and Human Rights,* 323.

88. Robert Marquand, "Dutch Still Wincing at Bush-Era 'Invasion of The Hague Act,'" *Christian Science Monitor,* February 13, 2009.

89. Moravcsik, "U.S. Human Rights Policy," 187.

90. France is another exception among Western democracies in this area. See International Court of Justice, "Declarations Recognizing the Jurisdiction of the Court as Compulsory," www.icj-cij.org/jurisdiction/index.php?p1=5&p2=1&p3=3.

91. This vote was on May 20, 2009.

92. Connic Bruck, "Why Obama Has Failed to Close Guantánamo," *New Yorker,* August 1, 2016.

93. "Presidential Candidates Compete over Their Embrace of Torture," *Economist,* February 13, 2016; Emmarie Huetteman, "Senate Panel's Republicans Dismiss Torture Report as 'Partisan,'" *New York Times,* December 9, 2014; "On Torture, Romney's Wrong," *Los Angeles Times,* October 3, 2012.

94. Associated Press–NORC Center for Public Affairs Research, "Balancing Act."

95. Matt Sledge, "Obama, Romney Both Promise an Increase in Military Spending," *Huffington Post,* October 23, 2012.

96. PolitiFact, "Ron Paul Says U.S. Has Military Personnel in 130 Nations and 900 Overseas Bases," September 14, 2011.

97. Gallup, "Americans Less Likely to See U.S. as No. 1 Militarily," February 15, 2016.

98. Dwight Eisenhower, farewell address, January 17, 1961.

99. Peter Finn and Anne Kornblut, "Obama Creates Indefinite Detention System for Prisoners at Guantanamo Bay," *Washington Post,* March 8, 2011.

100. Glenn Greenwald, "Obama Wins the Right to Detain People with No Habeas Review," *Salon,* May 21, 2010.

101. Barack Obama, interviewed on *Charlie Rose,* PBS, June 16, 2013.

102. Andrew Bacevich, "Non-believer," *New Republic,* July 7, 2010.

103. Milton Bearden, "Afghanistan, Graveyard of Empires," *Foreign Affairs,* November–December 2001.

104. Matthew Rosenberg and Michael Shear, "In Reversal, Obama Says U.S. Troops Will Stay in Afghanistan to 2017," *New York Times,* October 16, 2015. See

also Rosenberg, "Taliban Run into Trouble on Battlefield, but Money Flows Just the Same," *New York Times,* June 13, 2014; Azam Ahmed, "Taliban Making Military Gains in Afghanistan," *New York Times,* July 26, 2014; Rod Norland, "Study Finds Sharp Rise in Attacks by Taliban," *New York Times,* April 19, 2013.

105. Akmal Dawi, "Despite Massive Taliban Death Toll No Drop in Insurgency," VOA News, March 6, 2014; Aamir Latif, "Taliban Finds Fertile Recruiting Ground in Pakistan's Tribal Refugee Camps," *U.S. News and World Report,* February 9, 2009.

106. For instance, see Dylan Welch, "Women, Girls Increasingly Victims in Afghan War, U.N. Says," Reuters, February 19, 2013; Alissa Rubin, "Record Number of Afghan Civilians Died in 2011, Mostly in Insurgent Attacks, U.N. Says," *New York Times,* February 4, 2012.

107. Jami Forbes and Brian Dudley, "Increase in Taliban Efforts to Recruit from Afghan Government and Security Forces," Combating Terrorism Center at West Point, November 2013.

108. International Human Rights and Conflict Resolution Clinic (Stanford Law School) and Global Justice Clinic (NYU School of Law), "Living under Drones: Death, Injury, and Trauma to Civilians from US Drone Practices in Pakistan," September 2012, 10–12.

109. Tirman's *Deaths of Others* discusses this issue at length.

110. International Human Rights and Conflict Resolution Clinic and Global Justice Clinic, "Living under Drones," vi–vii.

111. Human Rights Watch, "'Between a Drone and Al-Qaeda': The Civilian Cost of US Targeted Killings in Yemen" (2013). See also Amnesty International, "Will I Be Next? US Drone Strikes in Pakistan" (2013).

112. International Human Rights and Conflict Resolution Clinic and Global Justice Clinic, "Living under Drones," vii-viii, 131–37; Human Rights Watch, "'Between a Drone and Al-Qaeda,'" 24–27.

113. Anne Barnard and Neil MacFarquar, "Paris and Mali Attacks Expose Lethal Qaeda-ISIS Rivalry," *New York Times,* November 20, 2015.

114. Ryan Lizza, "The Duel," *New Yorker,* February 1, 2016.

115. Finn and Kornblut, "Prisoners at Guantanamo Bay"; Greenwald, "No Habeas Review," *Salon,* May 21, 2010; "Obama to Appeal Detainee Ruling," *New York Times,* April 10, 2009; Charlie Savage, "Obama Upholds Detainee Policy in Afghanistan," *New York Times,* February 21, 2009.

116. Documented on *The Daily Show,* June 15, 2010.

CONCLUSION

1. In particular, recall the discussion of *Lawrence v. Texas* and "Don't ask, don't tell" in Chapter 4.

2. See the data discussed in Chapter 3, including Gallup, "In U.S., 42% Believe Creationist View of Human Origins," June 1, 2014; Pew, "Life in 2050," June 22, 2010.

3. See generally Robert Pape and James Feldman, *Cutting the Fuse: The Explosion of Global Suicide Terrorism and How to Stop It* (University of Chicago Press, 2010).

4. Alexis de Tocqueville, *Journey to America,* trans. George Lawrence (Doubleday, 1971), 271–72, quoted in Leo Damrosch, *Tocqueville's Discovery of America* (Farrar, Straus and Giroux, 2010), 140.

5. The vast majority of hate crimes appear to have been perpetrated by Trump supporters, although Trump supporters also faced abuse. See generally Southern Poverty Law Center, "More Than 400 Incidents of Hateful Harassment and Intimidation Since the Election," November 15, 2016; Eric Lichtblau, "U.S. Hate Crimes Surge 6%, Fueled by Attacks on Muslims," *New York Times,* November 14, 2016.

6. PolitiFact, "Pro-Clinton Super PAC Ad Says Trump 'Mocked' Disabled Reporter; Evidence Supports Claim," June 13, 2016.

7. The campaign's anti-bullying message was strategically announced by Melania Trump, to "soften her husband's coarse image" with a view toward "swaying undecided voters and women who have been wary of the Republican nominee." Alan Rappeport, "Melania Trump, Solo in Pennsylvania, Tries to Smooth Husband's Rough Edges," *New York Times,* November 3, 2016.

8. Source: U.S. Census.

9. United States Census Bureau, "2010 Census Shows Nation's Hispanic Population Grew Four Times Faster Than Total U.S. Population," May 26, 2011.

10. United States Census Bureau, "2010 Census Shows Asians Are Fastest-Growing Race Group," March 21, 2012.

11. Christopher Ingraham, "Chris Rock Is Right: White Americans Are a Lot Less Racist Than They Used to Be," *Washington Post,* December 1, 2014.

12. United States Census Bureau, "2010 Census Shows Interracial and Interethnic Married Couples Grew by 28 Percent over Decade," April 25, 2012.

13. "The Success of the Voter Fraud Myth," *New York Times,* September 19, 2016.

14. Justin Levitt, "A Comprehensive Investigation of Voter Impersonation Finds 31 Credible Incidents Out of One Billion Ballots Cast," *Washington Post,* August 6, 2014. See also John Ahlquist, Kenneth Mayer, and Simon Jackman, "Alien Abduction and Voter Impersonation in the 2012 U.S. General Election: Evidence from a Survey List Experiment," *Election Law Journal* 13, no. 4 (2014): 460–75.

15. Lee Drutman, "How Race and Identity Became the Central Dividing Line in American Politics," *Vox,* August 30, 2016.

16. Larry Bartels, *Unequal Democracy: The Political Economy of the New Gilded Age,* 2nd ed. (Russell Sage, 2016), 289–90.

17. Jeff Guo, "Yes, Working Class Whites Really Did Make Trump Win. No, It Wasn't Simply Economic Anxiety," *Washington Post,* November 11, 2016.

18. See, for example, David Fahrenthold, "Trump Boasts about His Philanthropy. But His Giving Falls Short of His Words," *Washington Post,* October 29, 2016; Alexandra Berzon, "Donald Trump's Business Plan Left a Trail of Unpaid Bills," *Wall Street Journal,* June 9, 2016; Steve Reilly, "Hundreds Allege Donald

Trump Doesn't Pay His Bills," *USA Today,* June 9, 2016; Rosalind Helderman, "Trump Agrees to $25 Million Settlement in Trump University Fraud Cases," *Washington Post,* November 18, 2016; David Fahrenthold, "Trump Foundation Admits to Violating Ban on 'Self-Dealing,' New Filing to IRS Shows," *Washington Post,* November 22, 2015.

19. Chris Cillizza, "The 13 Most Amazing Findings in the 2016 Exit Poll," *Washington Post,* November 10, 2016.

20. Emma Kate-Symons, "Misogynist Anti-Hillary Paraphernalia and Calls for Jail Time Feature Heavily at RNC," *New York Times,* July 19, 2016.

21. George Marsden, *Understanding Fundamentalism and Evangelicalism* (Eerdmans, 1990), 59–60.

22. Furman v. Georgia, 408 U.S. 238 (1972).

23. Gregg v. Georgia, 428 U.S. 153 (1976).

24. See the dissent of Justices Breyer and Ginsburg in *Glossip v. Gross,* 135 S.Ct. 2726 (2015), discussed in Chapter 7.

25. Bill O'Reilly, "Is America Sliding towards Socialism?," Fox News, February 20, 2009.

26. Michael Norton and Dan Ariely, "Building a Better America—One Wealth Quintile at a Time," *Perspectives on Psychological Science* 6, no. 1 (2011): 9–12. Wealth inequality has increased in Sweden in recent decades, as in other European nations. Thomas Piketty, *Capital in the Twenty-First Century,* trans. Arthur Goldhammer (Belknap, 2014), 344.

27. Richard Wilkinson and Kate Pickett, *The Spirit Level: Why Greater Equality Makes Societies Stronger* (Bloomsbury, 2010), 183–84.

28. Ibid., 246.

29. Cass Sunstein, *The Second Bill of Rights: FDR's Unfinished Revolution and Why We Need It More Than Ever* (Basic, 2004), 3.

30. Mugambi Jouet, "Does American Exceptionalism Foster American Decline?," *Truthout,* February 5, 2013.

31. Naturally, environmental and other factors partially or fully beyond human control can contribute to the rise and fall of civilizations. See Jared Diamond, *Collapse: How Societies Choose to Fail or Succeed* (Penguin, 2011).

32. Gallup, "Americans See U.S. as Exceptional," December 22, 2010; Public Religion Research Institute, "Most Americans Believe Protests Make the Country Better," June 23, 2015.

33. "Country Comparison: Exports," in Central Intelligence Agency, *The World Factbook* (2016).

34. See, for example, the following article in Xinhua, a media agency run by the Chinese government: "China Hits Back with Report on U.S. Human Rights Record," April 21, 2014.

35. Scott Shane, "U.S. Practiced Torture after 9/11, Nonpartisan Review Concludes," *New York Times,* April 16, 2013.

36. Scott Shane, "China Inspired Interrogations at Guantánamo," *New York Times,* July 2, 2008.

37. Cullen Murphy, *God's Jury: The Inquisition and the Making of the Modern World* (Houghton Mifflin, 2012), 92–94.

38. See generally Griff Witte and Simon Denyer, "After Trump's Victory, the World Is Left to Wonder: What Happened to America?," *Washington Post,* November 9, 2016; Jean-Philippe Rémy, "Cette Afrique qui vote Trump en secret," *Le Monde,* November 10, 2016; WIN/Gallup International, "Global Poll on the American Election," October 4, 2016.

39. Alexis de Tocqueville, *Democracy in America,* trans. Henry Reeve (Bantam, 2000), 27.

INDEX

Page numbers in italic refer to illustrations.

23–27, 263; polarization of American
society and, 6–7, 21, 27; possible end of,

American exceptionalism *(continued)*
263–67; religion and, 8, 35–37, 80, 92,
113; roots of, 6, 22–23, 281n8

American Revolution, 48, 58, 96

Anglican Church (Church of England,
Episcopal Church), 102, 110, 119, 135, 215

Annan, Kofi, 239, *240*, 251

anti-intellectualism, 7, 14, 40, 42, 73, 263;
Christian fundamentalism and, 9, 81,
86, 173, 215; conspiracy theories and,
63–73, 78–79; criminal justice and, 195,
203; disinformation and, 63; economic
interests and, 169, 170; in European
politics, 76; extremism and, 78;
historical roots of, 46–59; influence in
the South, 8, 44–45; Iraq war and, 233;
poor quality of public education and,
52; in U.S. politics generally, 45–46,
59–63. *See also* conspiracy theories,
disinformation, and propaganda

anti-Semitism, 33, 77

Archdale, John, 237

Asia, 13, 39, 191, 235, 272

Asian-Americans, 186, 264

Assemblies of God, 215–16

atheism, 64, 84, 92; in America
(population percentage), 90, 297n57;
church–state separation and, 122;
Soviet Union and, 140, 248;
Tocqueville on, 98; unacceptability in
American politicians, 99, 300n107

Atwater, Lee, 187–88

Australia, 6, 17, 95, 142; belief in God
(population percentage), 90; Christian
fundamentalism absent in, 81, 88, 100;
conservatives in, 165; death penalty
abolished in, 220; health care spending,
160; homicide by firearms in, *229*; incarceration rate, *4*, *202*; liberal American
worldview and, 27; modernist worldview
in, 114; political parties in, 164

"Axis of Evil," 244, 246

Bachman, Rep. Michele, 94, 112, 125, 151,
160; on "Obamacare," 188; on social
and fiscal conservatism, 174–75

Bachus, Spencer, 156

Bannon, Stephen, 69, 177

Baptists, 102

Bartels, Larry, 62, 170, 173, 320n89

Beck, Glenn, 68, 177, 188

Benedict XVI, Pope, 93, 118, 303n20

Benghazi plot, 7

Berlusconi, Silvio, 77, 249

Bible, 82, 85, 88, 100, 142; Book of
Revelation, 83, 95, 96; death penalty
and interpretation of, 215–16;
economics and, 178; King James Bible,
121; "Manifest Destiny" and, 22;
scholarly research on, 86; sex and
gender roles in, 125; sexual morality in,
135; Ten Commandments, 115, 120, 123

Bible, belief in literal veracity of, 7, 21, 36,
89, 97, 298n71; absence in Europe, 81,
99; age of the earth, 115; Christians in
disagreement with, 80, 87; creationism
and, 101; ideological purity and, 173;
polls and intensity of belief, 109; Bill
Clinton and, 105; Tea Party activists
and, 174

Bible Belt, 17, 32, 80, 113, 132, 195

Biden, Joe, 119, 229, 245

"big government," 34, 143, 147, 151, 176;
blamed for 2008 financial crisis, 156;
economic interests of voters and, 172;
Tea Party opposition to, 174, 189; white
Southerners' distrust of, 191

Bin Laden, Usama, 245, 248, 259

"birtherism." *See* conspiracy theories,
disinformation, and propaganda

Bismarck, Otto von, 165

Black Lives Matter, 33, 205

Blair, Tony, 61, 247, 249, 333n7

Boehner, John, 20, 30, 49, 50, 54; accuracy
of statements by, 75; "Obamacare"
attacked by, 68; Obama conspiracy
theories and, 65; "small business" of,
171

Bolton, John, 253

"both-sides-ism," 30, 31

BP oil spill (Gulf of Mexico, 2010), 34, 150

Brady v. Maryland (1963), 197

Brat, David, 30, 176

Breitbart News website, 69, 177, 266

Christian fundamentalism, 5, 8, 14, 36, 42, 80–82; abortion and, 127; absent in Europe, 81, 88, 266; American view of religious liberty and, 104–105; anti-intellectualism and, 9, 81, 86, 173, 215; apocalyptic biblical prophecies and, 88, 94–96, 245, 262; climate change and, 111, 115, 174, 215; creationism and, 86–88, 92–94, 114, 262; criminal justice and, 195; "culture wars" and, 40; division with moderate faith, 88–92; evolution from Enlightenment to Christian fundamentalism, 82–88; as exception in Western world, 8, 35–37, 80, 92, 113; extremism and, 78; impact on American society, 8–9, 81–82, 109–12; indoctrination to, 100–102; Iraq war and, 81, 94–96, 111, 232, 233, 244–45, 299n85; market funda-mentalism and, 178–79; origin of "fundamentalism" term, 86; paro-chialism and, 241; political impact of, 9; religious illiteracy of, 96–97; rise of evangelicalism, 84–86; secular public education resented by, 53; split of American Protestantism, 86–88; Trump campaign and, 9, 112, 262, 302n153. *See also* evangelical Christians; religion

Christianity, 37, 80, 82–84, 99, 120; born-again, 89, 112, 138, 177; capitalism and, 176; Great Awakenings, 85; liberal-moderate, 36, 88. *See also* Catholics; Protestants

Christie, Chris, 29, 184

Citizens United v. Federal Election Commission (2010), 10, 153, 166, 312n78

civil rights, 147, 188, 191, 198, 220, 285n68; Democratic Party and, 32, 147; gay rights compared to, 117

Civil War, 6, 16, 188, 281n8

climate change, 7, 21, 36, 37, 44, 45, 72, 73, 75, 111, 278n14; alleged myth and hoax of, 31, 43, 71–73, 111, 115, 174, 215, 262; Christian fundamentalism and, 9, 111, 115, 174; Fox News viewers and, 69; Kyoto Protocol and, 72, 239, *240*

Clinton, Bill, 39, 72, 77, 104–5, 132, 189; criminal justice and, 3, 200, 205; "Don't ask, don't tell" policy and, 136–37; death penalty and, 200; international law and, 254; strategic political use of religion, 140, *141*

Clinton, Hillary, 3, 28, 33, 77, 99, 302n153; accuracy of statements by, 75; "American exceptionalism" invoked by, 26; criminal justice and, 3, 204, 205; death penalty and, 201; European views of, 38; health care reform of, 39; income level of supporters, 169; Iraq invasion supported by, 232; Obama conspiracy theories and, 65; popular vote in 2016 election won by, 41; Protestantism of, 119; strategic political use of religion, 142; traditional gender roles and, 131–32; vote of minorities and, 264; wealth inequality and, 143, 144, 152

Coburn, Sen. Tom, 162, 178, 188, 230

Coe, Kevin, 140

Cold War, 94, 111, 120, 140, 248

Collins, Francis, 92

colonialism, European, 236, 237–38, 249, 258, 270

communism, 8, 22, 51, 146, 164–65; "American exceptionalism" phrase, origins of, 22–23, 281n8; Chinese Communist Party, 272; dissidents and protest against, 248; individual rights under, 167; U.S. Communist Party, 22, 23

Condorcet, Marquis de, 48

Congress, U.S., 27, 142, 147, 161, 171, 257; financial regulation and, 157; partisan polarization of, 7, 144; wealth inequality and, 152. *See also* House of Representatives; Senate

conservatism, American, 5, 17, 42, 68, 264; climate change and, ix, 31, 71; crea-tionism embraced by, 94; democracy and, 164–67; growing radicalism of, 6; market fundamentalism and, 151, 175; mood swings of public opinion and, 286n96; as outlier in Western world, 6, 34–39, 267; sexual prudishness of,

129–130; ultratraditionalist worldview and, 80, 114. *See also* traditionalist worldview

conspiracy theories, disinformation, and propaganda, ix, 7, 8, 31, 43, 44, 51, 63–73, 75–76, 79, 141, 144, 159–60, 168–69, 188, 207, 241, 244, 261, 263–64, 267; anti-immigrant, 76, 210; climate change and, 31, 43, 71–73, 111, 115, 174, 215, 262; creationism and, 94; democracy and, 63, 73–76; economic interests of voters and, 171; Iraq invasion and, 7, 250–51; by leftists, 31, 68; normalization of, 7, 79, 266; of Republican Party, 75–76, 266; Obama's "forged" birth certificate, ix, 5, 20, 26, 29, 43, 45, 64–66, 78, 188, 261; Obama as secret Muslim, 5, 20, 26, 64–66, 78, 141, 172, 261; "socialized medicine" and, 6, 7, 15, 66–67, 75, 109, 146, 161–62, 174, 241; "tyranny" of Obama administration, 68–71. *See also* anti-intellectualism

Constitution, U.S., 40, 49, 124, 144, 255, 269; church–state separation and, 120; death penalty and, 221; Eighth Amendment, 11, 199, 209, 218, 221; First Amendment, 120, 121, 122, 123, 139; influence on constitutions of other nations, 48, 241–42, 269; institutional gridlock and, 40–41, 71–72, 145, 192–93; Nineteenth Amendment, 124; originalism doctrine and, 242; ratification of treaties and, 40, 71–72, 233, 251–55; religious liberty and, 103, 108; Second Amendment, 227, 228–29, 230

contraception, 8–9, 36, 80, 131, 177; birth-control pill, 124; Catholic Church teachings about, 118; Christian fundamentalist hostility to, 110; family model in blue states and, 125–26; insurance coverage for, 115–16; "morning-after pill," 116–17; public funding for, 126, 131, 133–34; public health insurance and, 37–38

Copenhagen Accord, 72, 255

creationism, 37, 53, 92–94, 101, 298n68; age of the earth and, 115; Scopes "Monkey Trial" and, 86, 179, 267; teaching of, 92–93, 123, 176. *See also* evolution, theory of

Crèvecœur, J. Hector St. John de, 47, 48

criminal justice, 7, 12, 44, 112; degeneration of, 195–207; human rights and, 218–21, 222, 224–25, 262; lynchings, 195, 208; as microcosm of American exceptionalism, 3–4, 9–11, 194–95, 207, 262; prison-industrial complex, 2, 167, 277n4; in red and blue states, 37, 195; "War on Drugs" and, 1, 208. *See also* death penalty; mass incarceration

Cruz, Ted, 20, 24, 28, 278n13; on the American Dream, 183; on divine origin of constitutional rights, 176; evangelical Christianity of, 112, 116, 302n153; Iowa caucus (2016) and, 43; "Obamacare" attacked by, 70; Obama conspiracy theories and, 65; strategic political use of religion, 142; torture supported by, 256; war plans of, 260

Cuba, *4*, 77, 196

"culture wars," 8, 33, 113–14, 123–24; feminism and, 124–27; gay rights and, 134–38; of the Obama years, 114–17; sexual morality and, 129–34; strategic political use of religion and, 138–142; voters' economic concerns and, 173; war over abortion, 127–29

Czechia, 90

Darwin, Charles, 86, 92

"death panels," 7, 45, 66

death penalty, 1, 10, 23, 110, 129, 178–79, 214, 221–27; abolition of, 38, 195, 206, 211, 267, 268; Christian faith and, 15; Democratic Party leaders and, 37; human rights and, 219; opposition to, 226–27; popular support for, 220–21, 221–26, 329n136; racism and, 208–9

Declaration of Independence, 48, 49, 120–21

de Gaulle, Charles, 236

Déguignet, Jean-Marie, 50–51

DeLay, Tom, 112, 175–76

DeMint, Jim, 174

democracy, 79, 86, 110, 271; anti-intellectualism and, 48, 49, 50; anti-intellectual populism as loss for, 73–76; conservative conception of, 164–67; economic failures of, 162–64; emergence from the Enlightenment, 7–8, 82; in Europe, 103; illiberal, 273; populism and, 60; religion and, 123; restricted 19th-century notions of, 46; voter turnout and, 193; without human rights, 207. *See also* social democracy

Democracy in America (Tocqueville), 6

Democratic Party, 2, 16, 19, 187, 280n1; American Dream and, 182–83; anti-intellectual politicians in, 63; chauvinism and, 241; *Citizens United* decision opposed by, 153; conservative Democrats, 32; criminal justice and, 200, 203, 211; "culture wars" and, 114, 115; economic agenda of, 143, 265; foreign policy and, 233–34; gay marriage and, 136; international law/institutions and, 252, 255; Iraq invasion and, 242; leftward shift of, 5; New Deal coalition, 32, 147; "Obamacare" and, 75, 160; partisan polarization and, 27–34, 284n46; race and class of supporters, 170, 173, 178; racial segregation and, 147; regional divide and, 114; religion and, 80, 91; Senate majority under Obama, 73–74; strategic political use of religion, 139, 140; winner-take-all economics and, 265

Denmark, 38, 99, 161; belief in God (population percentage), 90; GDP (gross domestic product) of, 163; homicide by firearms in, *229*; social mobility in, 180

Diderot, Denis, 84n, 225

DiIulio, John, 61–62, 201, 324n36

disinformation. *See* conspiracy theories, disinformation, and propaganda

Disraeli, Benjamin, 165

Dodd-Frank Act, 157

"dog whistles," 5, 26, 187, 189

Domke, David, 140

"Don't ask, don't tell" policy, 136–37, 178

Dostoyevsky, Fyodor, 3

Douglass, Frederick, 51, 211

D'Souza, Dinesh, 177

Dukakis, Michael, 200

Dylan, Bob, 58, 98

education, 9, 33, 52–54, 81, 100; church–state separation and, 121; creationism in public schools, 93–94; evangelical revivalist view of, 85; populist attitude toward, 43; quality of American universities, 12, 15, 240; skepticism of, 7, 8, 47–48, 63, 79

egalitarianism, 6, 8, 46–47, 53, 172

Ehrenreich, Barbara, 185

Ehrman, Bart, 96, 216

Eisenhower, Dwight, 40, 60, 70, 77, 146, 257; on religious freedom, 107; strategic political use of religion, 140, *141*

Electoral College, 28, 41, 192, 193

Engels, Friedrich, 164

Enlightenment, 8, 43, 48, 59–60, 98, 110, 167; American Enlightenment, 49, 57, 261, 288n26; anti-Christian attitudes during, 104; in France, 84, 225; religion and U.S. Founding Fathers, 82–84

Environmental Protection Agency, 72, 146

environmental regulation, 36, 37, 71–73, 164, 263, 265

Episcopal Church. *See* Anglican Church

Equal Rights Amendment (ERA), 124–25

Europe: American Revolution and, 48; anti-intellectualism in, 50–51; belief in God (population percentage), 90; Christian fundamentalism absent in, 88, 266; colonial empires of, 49, 270; conservatives in, 16, 164, 267; crime compared to United States, 11, 195, 196; death penalty abolished in, 220; demagogy and extremism in, 76–78; Eastern, 6n; elementary education in, 52–53; emigration to America from, 33, 181; European Union, 38, 76, 78, 266; evolution of democracy in, 8; far-right movements in, 38, 76–78, 191, 266–67, 273; feudalism in, 46, 181; health care system in, 34, 191; immigration into, 13; liberal American worldview and, 27, 80, 267; "old Europe" epithet during Iraq

Francis, Pope, 93
Frank, Thomas, 173
Franklin, Benjamin, 49, 58, 83
Freedom Caucus, 30
French Revolution, 48, 96
Freudianism, 86
Front National (FN) (French political party), 77, 191, 266, 294nn135–136. *See also* Le Pen, Jean-Marie; Le Pen, Marine

Garland, David, 199
Gates, Henry Louis, 51
Gault, In re (1967), 198
gay marriage (same-sex marriage), 40, 56, 95, 113; reform beyond legalization, 268; Supreme Court ruling in favor of, 114, 115, 116
gay rights, 7, 80, 104, 117, 123–24; broader implications of, 134–38; Christian fundamentalist hostility to, 102; "culture wars" and, 117, 124, 173; partisan polarization and, 33, 285n68; religious divide and, 118; Tea Party opposition to, 174. *See also* homosexuality; LGBTQ people/issues
Gelman, Andrew, 171, 320n89
Germany, 38, 128, 161, 270; belief in God (population percentage), 90; East and West Germany, 248; GDP (gross domestic product) of, 163; health care spending, 158, *160*; homicide by firearms in, *229*; incarceration rate, *4*, *202*; Iraq war opposed by, 233, 249; military budget of, *257*; race and criminal justice in, 210; social mobility in, 180
gerrymandering, 27, 282nn27–28
GI Bill, 190
Gideon v. Wainwright (1963), 198
Giffords, Rep. Gabrielle, 228
Gillard, Julia, 132, 142
Gingrich, Newt, 24, 30, 68, 189
Ginsburg, Justice Ruth Bader, 214, 218, 224
Giuliani, Rudolph, 24, 29
Glass-Steagall Act (1933), 155
globalism, 12, 234–35

global warming. *See* climate change
God Strategy, The (Domke and Coe), 140
Gorbachev, Mikhail, 248
Gore, Al, 38, 41
government shutdown (2013), 27–28
Graham, Billy, 178, 245
Great Awakenings, 85
Great Depression, 25, 40, 145, 155
Great Gatsby, The (Fitzgerald), 21
Great Recession, 7, 174
Greene, Jack, 181
Greenspan, Alan, 155–56
Guantánamo camp, 11, 12, 25, 219–220, 257, 265; human rights and closing of, 268; liberal–conservative divide and, 233; Obama's failure to close, 255, 256, 260; opposition to, 36
Gulf War (1991), 96, 247
guns: countries with constitutional right to bear arms, 227, 331n177; culture of violence in America and, 230–31; homicide by firearms, 227, *229*; lax gun control, 10–11, 20, 166, 194, 228, 231; mass/school shootings, 176, 228; Second Amendment and, 227, 228–29, 230

Haley, Nikki, 132
Hall, Ralph, 72, 115
Hamilton, Alexander, 83–84, 230
Hannity, Sean, 24
Harding, Matt, 234
Harris, Sam, 105
Hatch, Sen. Orrin, 160
hate crimes, 188, 263, 339n5
health care, 6, 12, 20, 31, 129, 143, 262; American Dream and, 183; expanded access to, 265; health care reform, 7, 13, 34, 35, 69, 268; history of efforts toward universal health insurance, 146; Medicaid, 320n99; medical costs and, 168; as pillar of democracy, 165; in prison, 10; public's ignorance about, 67, 291n85; single-payer system, 34; Supreme Court and, 172; universal health care in Western world and international community, 6, 36, 39, 42, 164; wealth inequality and absence of,

157–162. *See also* Affordable Care Act; Medicare; "socialized medicine"

Henry, Patrick, 84

Heritage Foundation, 25, 67, 174, 180

Hetherington, Marc, 117, 285n68

Hindus, 89, 97, 103, 122

Hispanics. *See* Latinos

Hitler, Adolf, 77, 157, 233, 249

Hobby Lobby (2014) Supreme Court decision, 116

Hofer, Norbert, 77

Hofstadter, Richard, 47, 48, 53, 70; on "conspiratorial fantasy," 72; on religious ultratraditionalists, 101, 112

Hollande, François, 77, 132, 243

Holmes, Justice Oliver Wendell, 144

Holocaust, 13n, 77, 128, 239

homophobia, 123, 135

homosexuality, 8–9, 33, 80, 175; Catholic Church teachings about, 118; Christian fundamentalist hostility to, 101, 110; patriarchy and, 134; tolerance of, 36, 177. *See also* gay rights

House of Representatives, 30, 120, 152, 155, 156. *See also* Congress, U.S.

Houston, Charles Hamilton, 147

Hubbard, L. Ron, 108

Huckabee, Mike, 64–65, 68, 112, 125, 177

human rights, 5, 7, 11–12, 21, 110, 201–202, 233; in China, 272; death penalty and, 220, 222, 224; democracy and, 218–221; European Court of Human Rights, 13, 136, 210, 219; Inter-American Court of Human Rights, 255; international treaties, 40; United Nations and, 252; Universal Declaration of Human Rights, 220; U.S. prison system and, 11, 194

Hungary, 78, 261n

Hunter, James Davidson, 117

Hussein, Saddam, 247, 248; lumped together with Al-Qaeda, 62, 232, 233, 242, 251; secular dictatorship of, 62

ignorance, 7, 43, 44, 51, 52, 79, 81, 97, 239–241. *See also* anti-intellectualism

immigration, 5, 78, 87; as divisive issue in Western world, 38; emigration to

Europe from former colonies, 191; European attitudes toward, 13, 51, 77–78, 191, 210, 266; nativist riots against Catholic immigrants, 103, 121; xenophobia and perceived threat of, 3, 33, 43, 207, 209–10

incarceration rate, U.S., 1, 8, 204, 277n1; increase to world-record levels, 39–40; in international comparison, 4, 10, 196, 277n7, 323n22; juvenile incarceration rate, *202. See also* mass incarceration

India, 64, 97, *257*

individualism, 6, 165, 166, 167, 194, 263

Inhofe, Sen. James, 72, 111, 115

"intelligent design," 92–93, 93, 176. *See also* creationism

International Criminal Court (ICC), 253–55, 268

international law, 12, 36, 252–53

internet. *See* mass media

Iran, 1, 124, 196, 221, 252; in "Axis of Evil," 246; incarceration rate, *4*; nuclear deal with, 65

Iraq, invasion of (2003), 12, 25, 34, 57, 139, 238, 278n20; alleged alliance between Al-Qaeda and Saddam Hussein, 62, 232, 233, 242, 251; apocalyptic biblical prophecies and, 94–96, 111, 232, 244, 299n85; Bush's ignorance and, 45, 232–33; Christian fundamentalism and, 81, 94–96, 111, 232, 233, 244–45, 299n85; civilian deaths in, 247, 250; consequences of war in, 45, 62, 232, 233, 262, 270; false intelligence and, 7, 62, 232, 233, 247–48, 333n6; Fox News viewers and, 69; insurgency and counterinsurgency in, 245–46; Middle East destabilized by, 45, 232, 262; opposition to, 36, 233, 242, 258; references to World War II and, 249; rise of ISIS and, 232, 242, 250, 262; terrorists radicalized by, 243, 259; Vietnam War comparison, 40, 250–51; weapons of mass destruction and, 62, 232, 278n20

Ireland, 42, 128; belief in God (population percentage), 90, 91; homicide by firearms in, *229*; incarceration rate, 196

ISIS (Islamic State in Iraq and Syria), 45, 62, 243, 260, 278n20; Iraq war and, 232, 242, 250, 262; Obama conspiracy theories and, 65

Islam, 92, 97; caricatures of Muhammad in *Charlie Hebdo*, 104; fundamentalist, 245; Koran, 97, 101, 238; as object of intolerance in the West, 88. *See also* Muslims

Islamism, 5, 26, 45, 246

Israel, 94, 95

Italy: belief in God (population percentage), 90, 91; female suffrage in, 124; health care spending, *160*; incarceration rate, *4*, 196; labor unions in, 147

Jackson, Andrew, 60

Jacoby, Susan, 47, 52

Japan, 39, 61, 249, 269, 324n37; health care spending, *160*; incarceration rate, *4*; military budget of, *257*

Jay, John, 84

Jefferson, Thomas, 49, 58, 60, 84; American nationalism and, 236–37; views of religion, 82–83, 121

Jehovah's Witnesses, 89, 101

Jesus Christ, 9, 80, 81, 82, 83, 85, 87, 88, 91, 94–95, 96–97, 98, 106, 107, 111, 112, 138, 141, 178, 216

Jesus Movement (Jesus People), 97–98

Jews, 87, 89, 99, 103, 217; Christian apocalypticism and, 94–95; church–state separation and, 122; in Europe, 191

Jim Crow segregation, 124, 147, 211

Jindal, Bobby, 177

John Paul II, Pope, 248

Johnson, Lyndon B., *141*, 146, 147, 148

Kagan, Justice Elena, 241

Katrina, Hurricane, 7, 95

Katz, Lawrence, 53

Kennedy, John F. (JFK), 60–61, 77, 119, *141*, 176

Kennedy, Justice Anthony, 127, 153

Kenya, 14, 17, 20, 64, 65, 250

Kerry, John, 38, 141

King, Martin Luther, Jr., 58, 191, 211, 226

Kingdon, John, 16, 169, 240

King v. Burwell (2015), 65, 172, 321n114

Koch brothers, 151, 171

Korea, North, 1, 221, 252

Korea, South, 39, *160*

Korean War, 250, 272

Krugman, Paul, 156

Ku Klux Klan, 189

Kyoto Protocol, 72, 239, *240*, 255

labor unions, 147, 178, 186

Lafayette, Marquis de, 48

laissez-faire economics, 6, 145, 155, 173–74

LaPierre, Wayne, 228

Latin America, 39, 322n1

Latinos, 186, 189–190, 265; criminal justice system and, 194, 200, 207, 208, 326n70; increasing population of, 264

Lawrence v. Texas (2003), 136

League of Nations, 251–52

Le Pen, Jean-Marie, 77, 266

Le Pen, Marine, 77, 266, 294n136

Le Pen, Marion Maréchal, 294n136

LGBTQ people/issues, 5, 40, 95, 134, 262, 268; Catholic Church and, 98; legal victories under Obama, 114. *See also* gay rights

liberalism, American, 6, 17, 68, 74, 264, 267; dominant worldview of Western nations and, 34–38; evolution accepted by, 94; modernist worldview of, 80; mood swings of public opinion and, 286n96; sexual openness of, 129–130. *See also* modernist worldview

Lieberman, Joe, 99

Lim, Elvin, 62, 63

Limbaugh, Rush, 70, 117, 188

Lipset, Seymour Martin, 6–7, 23, 165, 169, 186

Lockhart, Charles, 240

López, Ian Haney, 187

Lovestone, Jay, 22–23, 281n8

Luhrmann, Tanya, 97, 100, 101–102

Luther, Martin, 52, 81, 97, 105

Lutheran Church, 110, 215

Madison, James, 49, 83, 121

Maher, Bill, 105

New Deal, 32, 41, 108, 148, 184, 192, 269; conservative acceptance of, 146; denounced as "fascism," 143, 147; Glass-Steagall Act (1933) and, 155; race and class in relation to, 190; Supreme Court and, 145

New Jim Crow, The (Alexander), 208

New York, 1–3, 162, 194, 204, 277n5, 277n7

New Zealand, 6, 17, 95; American fundamentalist proselytizing in, 93; Christian fundamentalism absent in, 81, 88, 100; conservatives in, 165; death penalty abolished in, 220; female suffrage in, 124; health care spending, *160*; incarceration rate, *4*; liberal American worldview and, 27; modernist worldview in, 114; political parties in, 164

1984 (Orwell), 79, 172

Nixon, Richard, 25, 60, 62, 146; environmental regulation and, 73; health insurance supported by, 67; strategic political use of religion, 140, *141*; Supreme Court and, 198

Norquist, Grover, 150

North/Northern states, 6, 41, 88, 180

Norway, 38, 163, 180, 196

Obama, Barack, 12–13, 14, 77, 131, 133, 280n1; accuracy of statements by, 75; "American exceptionalism" invoked by, 26, 235; anti-intellectual critics of, 48, 54; "apology tour" of, 25; Bush counterterrorism policies continued by, 255–56, 258, 260; climate change and, 71, 73, 234; conspiracy theories about forged birth certificate and Islamism of, ix, 5, 20, 26, 29, 43, 45, 64–66, 78, 141, 172, 188, 261; "culture wars" under, 114–17; death penalty and, 200–201; division of American society under, 20–21, 27; economic program of, 188; electoral victories of, 27–28, 63, 264; European views of, 38; as first black president, 12, 26, 39, 66, 188–89, 192, 261; foreign policy of, 233–34, 243, 245; gay marriage issue and, 138; as global citizen, 238; health care reform of, 13, 30, 34, 35, 148,

157, 161, 241, 321n114; international community and, 39; partisan redefinition of "American exceptionalism" and, 4–5, 7, 20, 23–27; as presidential candidate, 168, 317n32; race relations under, 33; religious beliefs of, 105; Republican obstructionism and, 40, 41, 71–72, 73–74, 150, 169, 188, 189, 265–66; as "socialist," 41, 164, 175, 176; strategic political use of religion, 139, 141; Supreme Court and, 28, 241; surveillance state and, 258; "tyranny" of Obama administration, 67–71, 75; use of torture discontinued by, 40, 256; vote of minorities and, 264; Wall Street economy and, 156–57; "War on Terror" and, 254; wealth inequality and, 149–150

"Obamacare." *See* Affordable Care Act

Obergefell v. Hodges (2015), 134, 136

Occupy Wall Street, 172

O'Connor, Justice Sandra Day, 127, 199, 223, 323n27

O'Neill, Paul, 61, 247

Orbán, Viktor, 77, 261n

O'Reilly, Bill, 269

Orwell, George, 79, 166, 172

Paine, Thomas, 47, 49, 84

Pakistan, 245

Palin, Sarah, 12, 29, 45, 238, 265; anti-intellectualism of, 59, 63, 86; Christian fundamentalism of, 86, 105, 112, 177; conspiracy theories and, 64; on "death panels," 66; far-right economic views of, 177; feminism invoked by, 126; Obama criticized/mocked by, 48, 188

Pape, Robert, 242–43

Paris Agreement (2015), 71–72, 73

patriarchy, 98, 110, 123, 124–27, 129, 130, 134, 261–62, 265

patriotism, 235–38. *See also* nationalism

Paul, Sen. Rand, 184

Paxton, Robert, 29

Pence, Mike, 92, 116, 176, 298n68

Perry, Rick, 16, 25, 45, 73, 177; Christian fundamentalism of, 112; as death penalty supporter, 230

Pétain, Marshal Philippe, 77

Petraeus, Gen. David, 137, 246
Piketty, Thomas, 163
Pilgrims, 102
Planned Parenthood, 7, 116, 175
Pledge of Allegiance, 19, 80, 120, 122
plutocracy, 151–54
Poland, 42, 90, 91, 128
polarization, partisan, 5–6, 27, 79, 144, 286n85; American Dream and, 182–85; anti-intellectual populism and, 74; in international comparison, 34–38; liberals and conservatives in different worlds, 27–34; religion and, 88, 118–19
police shootings, 10, 33, 206–207, 230, 280n43
populism, 6, 8, 50; anti-intellectualism and, 74; Jacksonian, 60; Trump as far-right populist, 29, 31
pornography, 112
Portugal, 42, 49, 90, 128
Powell, Colin, 247–48
presidential election (2016), ix–x, 3, 5, 28, 30–31, 43, 46, 67, 263–67; criminal justice and, 3, 207; Clinton and, 132, 142, 154, 205, 261, 265; Democratic Party platform, 206; polarization of American society and, 144; race and class of voters, 168, 169, 316n7; racial divisions and, 265; religion and, ix, 9, 112, 116, 142; Republican National Convention, 74, 207; Republican Party platform, 72, 115, 206; Republican primary candidates, 43, 46, 126; Sanders campaign, 30–31, 142, 160–61, 164, 172; Trump and, xi–x, 28–29, 43, 127, 144, 154, 168–69, 230, 263
presidential elections, 170, 173; of 1952, 60; of 1980, 140; of 1988, 200; of 2008, 168, 317n32; of 2012, 116, 150, 151
Princeton Theological Seminary, 88
PRISM program, 258
progress, 8, 11, 13, 42; American expansion and, 21; historical cycles and, 40, 264
Progressive movement, 144
propaganda. *See* conspiracy theories, disinformation, and propaganda

Protestants, 119, 131; mainline, 89, 110, 118, 217; Protestant Reformation, 52, 81, 85, 97, 105; split of American Protestantism, 86–88, 98, 118
Prothero, Stephen, 97
Puritans, 102
Putin, Vladimir, 29, 74, 77, 244, 267, 273

Quakers, 98, 102, 215

race, 6, 186–192; criminal justice system and, 206–207; economic solidarity hindered by race divisions, 9; mass incarceration and, 207–12; partisan polarization and, 32; police shootings and, 10
racism, 12, 28, 33, 51, 98, 253; dog whistle politics and, 23–27, 187; in Europe, 13, 51, 191, 210, 266; institutional and systemic, 3, 12–13, 191–92, 207–12
Reagan, Ronald, 23, 54, 70, 94, 125, 169; on the American Revolution, 237; apocalyptic biblical prophecies and, 111; "big government" opposed by, 147, 165; on capital punishment, 225; Christian fundamentalism and, 112, 140, 175; Cold War and, 248; on national health insurance, 162; strategic political use of religion, 140–41, *141*
Reconstruction period, 7, 27
Rehnquist, Chief Justice William, 124–25, 136, 198
religion, 6, 8, 44; death penalty and, 214–17; deism, 82, 83, 84, 99; education as obstacle to faith, 49; historical evolution in America, 82–88; moral society and, 98–100; movement of new faiths into mainstream, 106–108; national chauvinism and, 19, 241; partisan polarization and, 32, 33; Pledge of Allegiance and, 19; politicians' strategic use of, 138–142; religious affiliations in America, 89; secular government in relation to, 102–104; sociopolitical role in the

religion *(continued)*
    United States, 34–35; U.S. Founding
    Fathers and, 82–84. *See also* Christian
    fundamentalism; separation of church
    and state
reproductive rights, 21, 80, 123–24, 127–34
Republican Party (G.O.P.), 2, 19, 278n13,
    280n1; American Dream and, 182–85;
    "American exceptionalism" and, 4–5, 7,
    20, 23–27, 39; anti-intellectualism in,
    43, 45–46, 49–50, 54, 59–76, 78–79; as
    the "anti-science party," 115; chauvinism
    and, 241; Christian fundamentalism
    and, 80, 111, 112, 114–16, 178, 302n153;
    Citizens United decision supported by,
    153, 312n78; climate change and, 5,
    71–73, 115, 278n14, 292n101; criminal
    justice and, 203, 204; "culture wars"
    and, 114–15; establishment of, 29–30, 31,
    74, 75; extremism and rightward shift
    of, 5–6, 28–34, 78–79, 69–70, 127, 144,
    147, 267; foreign policy and, 233–34;
    gerrymandering and, 27; international
    law/institutions and, 252, 255; Iraq
    invasion and, 242; liberal Republicans,
    32, 74; nationalism and, 238; New Deal
    and, 143, 146; "Obamacare" denounced
    by, 31, 42, 66–68, 144, 159–60, 162, 169,
    171, 264; Obama conspiracy theories
    and party leadership, 65; obstruc-
    tionism of, 40, 41, 71–72, 73–74, 150,
    169, 188, 189, 265–66; partisan
    polarization and, 27–34, 284n46; race
    and class of supporters, 170, 316n7; rate
    of support for gay marriage, 136;
    regional divide and, 114; "Southern
    Strategy" of, 187–88; strategic political
    use of religion, 139; taxation policy of,
    150; Tea Party influence on, 172, 317n27;
    wealth inequality and, 143, 152
Rice University, 15, 44, 54–56, 91
Roberts, Chief Justice John, 125, 134, 153,
    154, 198
Robertson, Pat, 95, 109
Roe v. Wade (1973), 42, 127, 267
Romney, Mitt, 20, 25, 28, 31, 278n13;
    abortion politics and, 116–17, 303n11;
    American exceptionalism invoked by,

24, 235, 236; European views of, 38; on
    government dependence, 184; health
    insurance supported by, 67, 161;
    Mormon faith of, 107, 108; on Obama
    and welfare reform, 189; Obama
    conspiracy theories and, 65; religious
    beliefs of, 105; "small business" of, 171;
    torture supported by, 256; on war
    against the Taliban, 260; wealth
    inequality and, 151–52
Roosevelt, Eleanor, 11, 220
Roosevelt, Franklin Delano (FDR), 32, 77,
    140, *141*, 166, 270; New Deal and, 143,
    269; "Second Bill of Rights"
    proposition of, 145, 148, 268, 269;
    Supreme Court and, 145, 309n18
Roosevelt, Theodore, 60, 77
Rubio, Marco, 20, 24, 112, 134, 278n13; on
    "big government," 156; on earth's age,
    115; on religion and government, 176;
    torture supported by, 256
Rumsfeld, Donald, 248
Russia, *4*, 6n, 252, 256, *257*
Rwanda, genocide in, 225
Ryan, Paul, 28, 151, 162, 167, 171, 177–78;
    on class and social mobility, 180; "A
    Roadmap for America's Future," 184

Sanders, Bernie, 30–31, 142, 172, 302n153;
    accuracy of statements by, 75; as
    "democratic socialist," 164; health care
    proposals of, 160–61, 314n118; wealth
    inequality and, 144
Sanger, Margaret, 58
Santorum, Rick, 24, 54, 65, 116;
    Catholicism of, 119; Christian
    fundamentalism of, 112; on class in
    America, 180; global warming rejected
    by, 111; "Obamacare" attacked by, 66;
    on teaching of creationism, 176
Sarkozy, Nicolas, 76–77, 164, 185, 293n129
Saudi Arabia, 1, 221, 246, 252, *257*
Scalia, Justice Antonin, 28, 90, 119, 136,
    209, 216–17, 304n44
Scandinavia, 196; penal practices in, 213,
    221. *See also* Denmark; Norway;
    Sweden
Scheffer, David, 254

Schlafly, Phyllis, 124

science, 7, 9, 14, 21, 262; American religion and, 80, 81, 100; anti-intellectual politicians and, 60; blended with religious faith, 92, 297n66; Christian fundamentalist hostility to, 87; climate change and, 71, 72–73; practicality and, 47

Scientology, Church of, 108–9

Scopes "Monkey Trial" (1925), 86, 179, 267

Senate, 40, 41, 120, 192, 256; science committee, 115; treaty ratification procedure and, 72, 254–55. *See also* Congress, U.S.

separation of church and state, 9, 81, 93, 103, 119–122; conflicts over secularism, 120–22; JFK's speech on, 176; liberal modernist support for, 80; traditionalist desire for more religion in government, 122–23

separation of powers, 40, 192

September 11, 2001 (9/11) attacks, 52, 95, 112, 177, 234, 239; orchestrated from Afghanistan, 258, 336n81; "War on Terror" and, 260

sex, 7, 9, 177; "culture wars" and, 8–9; moralizing attitudes toward, 129–134; premarital, 101, 110, 113, 129, 131, 174; sexual revolution, 14, 129, 198

sexism, 28, 123, 126–27, 130, 265

sexual education, abstinence-only, 36, 80, 102, 114, 129, 133, 266; opposed by religious Americans, 122–23; poor women and, 123

Shapiro, Fred, 281n8

Sikhs, 103

"Silent Majority," 198

slavery, 22, 41, 46, 48, 182, 211, 237

Smith, Adam, 47

Smith, Joseph, 105, 106, 107, 301n136

Snowden, Edward, 23, 258

social Darwinism, 179

social democracy, 164, 165, 210, 269–70

socialism, 164–65

"socialized medicine," 6, 7, 15, 30, 75, 146; Christian fundamentalism and, 109; conspiracy theories about, 66–67; political divide and, 241. *See also* Affordable Care Act; health care

social media, 59, 69, 79

Social Security, 31, 144, 146, 190

South Africa, *4*, 39

Southern Baptist Convention, 105, 110, 215

South/Southern states, 6, 15, 16, 29, 31, 32, 41, 171, 180, 230–31; African-American evangelicals in, 178; anti-intellectualism in, 8, 44–45; attitudes toward education, 44, 47; Christian fundamentalism in, 88, 91; electoral college system and, 41; harsh justice and capital punishment in, 1, 37, 195, 196, 208, 209, 222, 225–26; lag of education in, 53; lynchings in, 208; partisan polarization in, 31; racism, segregation, and slavery in, 32, 41 37, 147, 187, 189, 208, 209, 252; Republican Party support in, 32, 147, 187; social mobility in, 180; Trump supporters in, 171

Soviet Union (USSR), 68, 111, 159, 164, 239; collapse of, 248, 271; propaganda in, 51

Spain, 42, 49, 128, 249; belief in God (population percentage), 90; Franco regime, 51; health care spending, *160*; homicide by firearms in, *229*

Spinoza, Baruch, 84n, 168

Stalin, Joseph, 22, 68, 239, 281n8

"Star-Spangled Banner, The" (U.S. national anthem), 19, 34–35, 194

"states' rights," 26, 187, 188

stem-cell research, 102

Stephanson, Anders, 21–22

Stevenson, Adlai, 60

Stevenson, Bryan, 3–4

Stiglitz, Joseph, 35, 151, 156, 175

Stuntz, William, 217

Super PACs (political action committees), 153, 154

Supreme Court, 11, 28, 41, 90, 124, 144; Catholic justices of, 119; church–state separation and, 93, 120, 122; criminal justice and, 197–98, 199, 204, 221; death penalty cases and, 37, 214, 218, 267; gay marriage and, 114, 115, 116; gun control and, 229; human rights and, 220, 221, 329n142; Roosevelt's New Deal and, 145, 309n18

Supreme Court cases: *Brady v. Maryland*
(1963), 197; *Brown v. Board of Education*
(1954), 147, 198; *Citizens United v.
Federal Election Commission* (2010), 10,
143, 153; *Gideon v. Wainwright* (1963),
198; *Hobby Lobby* (2014), 116; *King v.
Burwell* (2015), 65, 172, 321n114;
Lawrence v. Texas (2003), 136; *Mapp v.
Ohio* (1961), 197; *McCleskey v. Kemp*
(1987), 209; *Miranda v. Arizona* (1966),
197; *Obergefell v. Hodges* (2015), 134, 136;
In re Gault (1967), 198; *Roe v. Wade*
(1973), 42, 127, 267
Sweden, 38, 99, 161, 270; belief in God
(population percentage), 90; GDP
(gross domestic product) of, 163; health
care spending, *160*; incarceration rate, *4*,
196, *202*, 277n7; social mobility in, 180;
support for death penalty in, 221, 225;
wealth distribution in, 269, 340n26
swing states, 34, 193, 322n118
Switzerland, 163, 324n37
Syria, 243, 252

Taiwan, 39
Taliban, 52, 239, *240*, 258–59, 260, 336n81
talk radio, 69. *See also* mass media
Tauzin, Rep. Billy, 152–53
taxation, 35, 70, *71*, 143, 144; "Bush tax
cuts," 62, 170; Earned Income Tax
Credit (EITC), 268; health care and,
161; proposal to abolish federal income
tax, 174; tax cuts for the wealthy, 36,
151, 168, 264–65; tax rates of the
wealthy, 70, *71*, 146, 269
Tea Party, 16, 25, 30, 74, 265, 280n1;
American Dream and, 180; anti-
intellectualism and, 63; "big government" denounced by, 25, 171, 174;
financial crisis of 2008 and, 154; health
care reform opposed by, 165–66; ignorance about taxes, 70; influence on the
Republican Party (G.O.P.), 172,
317n27; minimal government position
of, 151, 171; moneyed interests and, 171;
Obama conspiracy theories and, 45, 63,
64; perceived as extreme/far right, 36;
racial politics and, 189

television (TV), 58–59, 63, 69, 105. *See also*
mass media
Tenet, George, 247–48
terrorism, 34, 40, 65, 243, 259. *See also*
"War on Terror"
Texas, 15–16, 45, 54, 80, 91, 193; Bush
(George W.) as governor of, 16, 45, 138;
capital punishment in, 222, 224;
conception of morality in, 113; sexual
mores in, 131; state laws on abortion,
115; three-strikes law, 199
Thomas, Justice Clarence, 119, 136
Tocqueville, Alexis de, 6, 8, 17, 22, 263,
273; on American justice, 195, 322n4;
on anti-intellectualism in America, 47;
on culture of violence in America,
230–31; on national chauvinism, 235;
praise for the United States, 22, 48,
263, 273; on religion in America, 80,
84, 98, 103; on value of equality in
America, 46–47
torture, 5, 12, 31, 38; Bush administration's
use of, 11, 34, 272, 278n13; U.S.
methods copied from Chinese
communists, 272; U.S. methods
mirroring Spanish Inquisition, 272
"tough on crime" movement, 2, 3, 8, 202,
203, 205
traditionalist worldview, 9, 112, 113–14, 117,
126, 135–36. *See also* "culture wars";
conservatism, American
Truman, Harry, 77, 140, *141*, 146
Trump, Donald, 3, 20, 28, 40, 178, 234,
238; abortion politics and, 116; accuracy
of statements by, 75, 76; advisors and
associates of, 69, 177; American Dream
and, 182; "American exceptionalism"
and, 24, 26; anti-establishment image
of, ix, 30, 31; anti-intellectualism of, 59,
262; bigoted presidential campaign of,
3, 33, 65, 188, 207, 261, 263–65; business
empire of, 152, 168–69, 264; Christian
fundamentalism and, ix, 9, 112, 262,
302n153; on climate change as "hoax,"
73; contradictory statements of, 26, 79,
144, 309n7; conspiracy theories and
disinformation of, ix, 7, 29, 31, 43, 65,
73, 75–76, 79, 144, 168–69, 188, 207,

261, 263–64; corruption and fraud of, 152, 168–69, 264; criminal justice and, 3, 207; criticized by Republican establishment, 29; on deportation of Mexicans, 209–10; division of American society under, 20–21; election of 2016 and, 28–29; evangelical Christian support for, 9, 82, 112, 142; executive power at disposal of, 260; ignorance of policy-making, 50, 266; machismo and misogyny of, 126–27; "Make America Great Again" slogan, 26, 263; Muslim immigrants vilified by, ix, 7, 33, 66; "Obamacare" attacked by, 67, 70, 158, 169; perceived as extreme/far right, 36; popular vote lost by, 192; as populist, 29, 31, 42, 144, 168–69, 183, 230, 263–67; post-election rhetoric of, 266; Putin and, 74, 267, 273; race and class of supporters, 168, 169, 316n7; racial politics and, 3, 188–89, 207; as reality TV star, 58, 263; Russian support for, 38, 74, 267, 273; torture supported by, 5, 230, 256, 278n13; unfavorable popular opinions of, 265; vow to assassinate terrorists, 259–260; wealth inequality and, 152, 168–69, 183
Trump, Melania, 339n7
two-party system, 32

Ukraine, 74
unilateralism, 39, 251–55
United Nations (U.N.), 17–18, 36, 72, 124, 219, 239; Human Rights Commission, 11; international criminal tribunals, 253–55; League of Nations' failure and, 252; women's rights and, 125, 253
United States: absence of universal health care in, 6, 10, 35, 66–67, 157–62, 268; belief in God (population percentage), 90; capital punishment retained by, 221–27; class-based society in, 186; continental expansion of, 21–22; contradictions of, 13–14, 44, 52–59, 66, 124, 129–130, 261–62; decline of, 39–42, 270–73; Enlightenment and founding of, 49; as first modern democracy, 7–8, 46–49, 167, 181;

health care spending, *160*; homicide by firearms in, 227, *229*; human rights and, 11–12, 218–21; insularity of, 234–35, 238–242; intellectual life in, 57–58; labor unions in, 147; military budget of, 23, 256, *257*; polarization in, 5–6, 27–39; religiosity in, 34–35; religious affiliations in, 89, 297n57; as "shining city upon a hill," 5, 23; United Nations and, 252

Valls, Manuel, 77
Vanderbilt, Cornelius, 182
Veil, Simone, 128
Vietnam War, 40, 52, 97, 191, 242, 250, 271
Voltaire, 83, 84n, 176
voter turnout, 192–93, 322n117

Walker, Scott, 24, 65, 112, 176
Wall Street, 34, 154–57, 166, 178
warfare, 21, 129, 233, 245, 251, 258; America's wars since World War II, 250; Christian fundamentalism and, 81, 94–96, 111, 232, 233, 244–45, 299n85; European reservations about, 249
"War on Crime," 11
"War on Drugs," 1, 208
"War on Terror," 7, 11, 16, 233, 234, 244; Christian fundamentalism and, 81, 94–96, 111, 232, 233, 244–45, 299n85; as endless struggle, 259; Iraq invasion and, 61, 251; use of torture in, 31. *See also* terrorism
Warren, Chief Justice Earl, 197, 198
Warren, Rick, 101, 102
Washington, George, 84, 114
wealth inequality, 9–10, 31, 39, 44, *71*, 149, 170–72, 186, 262; acuteness in the United States, 143, 172, 308n1; American Dream and, 180, 183; anti-intellectualism and, 170, 172; decline of public education and, 53; democracy and, 162–64; market fundamentalism and, 150–164, 173–75; mass incarceration and, 213–14; social contract and, 144–150; technological skills and, 148, 310n35; Wall street economy and, 154–57

welfare state, 164, 169, 184, 320n89; in Europe, 35, 180, 191; middle class and, 190; "welfare" as racially charged word, 188

Western world (the West), 6, 27, 117, 210, 241; attitudes toward immigration, 17; Christian fundamentalism mostly absent in, 81, 173; criminal justice in, 3, 196; defined, 6n, 322n1; demagogy and extremism in, 78; economic agenda of political parties in, 164; far-right populism in, 266; liberal American worldview and, 6, 34–38; modernist worldview as norm in, 114; public TV broadcasting in, 69; wealth inequality in, *71*

What's the Matter with Kansas? (Frank), 173

Whitman, James, 210

Wilders, Geert, 74, 77

Will, George F., 213

Wilson, Woodrow, 251

Winthrop, John, 23

women, 5, 46; abortion war and, 127–29; American women and gender equality, 261–62; feminism and, 124–27. *See also* "culture wars"; feminism; patriarchy

working class, 5, 62, 148, 168, 169, 186, 192, 316n7

World War I, 96, 234, 251

World War II, 61, 70, 96, 108, 146, 234; American citizens' ignorance about, 239; genocide during, 13n, 225; human rights standards after, 220; League of Nations' failure and, 252; role in debate over 2003 Iraq invasion, 249–50; surge of immigration to Europe following, 186

xenophobia. *See* immigration

Yellen, Janet, 157

Yemen, 221, 255, 259

Yugoslavia, genocide in, 225, 253–54

Zimring, Frank, 225

Zuckerman, Phil, 99

EUROPE'S CONSTITUTIONAL MOSAIC

This book emerged from an extended seminar series held in Edinburgh Law School which sought to explore the complex constitutional arrangements of the European legal space as an inter-connected mosaic. There has been much recent debate concerning the constitutional future of Europe, focusing almost exclusively upon the EU in the context of the (failed) Constitutional Treaty of 2003–5 and the subsequent Treaty of Lisbon. The premise of the book is that this focus, while indispensable, offers only a partial vision of the complex constitutional terrain of contemporary Europe. In addition it is essential to explore other threads of normative authority within and across states, embracing internal challenges to state-level constitutional regimes; the growing jurisprudential assertiveness of the Council of Europe regime through the ECHR and various democracy-building measures; as well as Europe's ever thicker relations, both with its border regions and with broader international institutions, especially those of the United Nations. Together these developments create increasingly dense networks of constitutional authority within the European space. This fluid and multi-dimensional dynamic is difficult to classify, and indeed may seem in many ways impenetrable, but that makes the explanatory challenge all the more important and pressing. Without this fuller picture it becomes impossible to understand the legal context of Europe today or the prospects of ongoing changes. The book brings together a range of experts in law, legal theory and political science from across Europe in order to address these complex issues and to supply illustrative case-studies in the topical areas of the constitutionalisation of European labour law and European criminal law.

Europe's Constitutional Mosaic

Edited by

Neil Walkcr

Jo Shaw

and

Stephen Tierney

·HART·
PUBLISHING

OXFORD AND PORTLAND, OREGON
2011

Published in the United Kingdom by Hart Publishing Ltd
16C Worcester Place, Oxford, OX1 2JW
Telephone: +44 (0)1865 517530
Fax: +44 (0)1865 510710
E-mail: mail@hartpub.co.uk
Website: http://www.hartpub.co.uk

Published in North America (US and Canada) by
Hart Publishing
c/o International Specialized Book Services
920 NE 58th Avenue, Suite 300
Portland, OR 97213–3786
USA
Tel: +1 503 287 3093 or toll-free: (1) 800 944 6190
Fax: +1 503 280 8832
E-mail: orders@isbs.com
Website: http://www.isbs.com

British Library Cataloguing in Publication Data

Data Available

ISBN: 978-1-84113-979-1

Typeset by Columns Design XML Ltd, Reading
Printed and bound in Great Britain by
TJ International Ltd, Padstow, Cornwall

Acknowledgements

The present volume emerged from a series of five seminars held at Edinburgh Law School during the academic year 2008–9. The main funding for the seminar series came from a small grant from the British Academy, and we are extremely grateful for their support. We are also very grateful to Gavin Anderson, Daniel Augenstein, Christina Boswell, Ailsa Henderson, Chris Himsworth, Claudio Michelon, Drew Scott and Elaine Webster for moderating discussion or supplying comments to the main papers at the various seminars. The seminars were well-attended, provoked much debate and challenged our main speakers to revise or rethink their draft papers for publication. Sincere thanks are due to our contributors for taking this task so seriously, and also to Ruth Dukes, Cormac MacAmhlaigh and Kimmo Nuotio for providing excellent contributions to the final volume outside the context of the original seminar series. On the editorial side, we very much appreciate the work of Stephen Thomson and Conrado Hübner Mendes in helping prepare the manuscript for publication. Finally, we would like to thank Conrado (again) and all the administrative staff of the Law School's Research Office, especially its head Alison Stirling, for their sterling efforts in organising the seminar series.

The editors
Old College, Edinburgh
March 2011.

Contents

1

Introduction
A Constitutional Mosaic? Exploring the New Frontiers of Europe's Constitutionalism

NEIL WALKER AND STEPHEN TIERNEY

I.   SETTING THE SCENE

A.   Question of Europe

THE CONSTITUTIONAL TRAJECTORY of Europe scarcely constitutes a novel field of enquiry. In recent years we have seen a wealth of scholarly analysis addressing the European constitutional present and speculating about its future. That there has been so much attention upon constitutionalism on a continental scale is unsurprising. We inhabit an age of 'post-national' constitution-building and constitution-branding. Over the past European decade the new post-national phase has reached an unprecedented pitch of intensity, triggered by the establishment of the Convention on the Future of Europe by the European Council at Laeken in December 2001. That initiative led to the publication of a Draft Treaty establishing a Constitution for Europe in 2003, its adoption in modified form by the subsequent Intergovernmental Conference, and its eventual and terminal defeat in referendums in Holland and France in 2005. In turn, the gap left by the failure of the 'big-C'[1] project was quickly filled by a more familiar 'small-c' instrument. A Reform Treaty, which retained the vast majority of the content of the aborted Constitutional Treaty but evacuated all the more obvious signs and conceits of constitutional ambition, was signed at Lisbon on 13 December 2007, finally entering into force on 1 December 2009.

---

[1]   See eg N Walker, 'Big "C" or small "c"? (2006) 12 *European Law Journal* 75–81.

Yet just as the Laeken Declaration did not signal the beginning of the new European constitutionalism, the conclusion of the new Lisbon project has surely not marked its end. In part, this is because the constitutional current of the European Union runs deeper than the events of the last decade. The social and political forces that made the contemplation of a Constitutional Treaty for the EU possible – and its deep disputation inevitable – have not simply disappeared. The increasing legal and political authority of the European Union and its developing forms of cultural identity mean that constitutionalism – traditionally such a close companion to similar developments at the state level – remains a key, if controversial, discourse and practice for those seeking to explain, justify and frame the progress of the new supranational polity and the challenges it poses to the state system.

But there is a broader reason why European constitutionalism extends beyond the events of the last decade. For it is the particular legal and institutional structure of the EU rather than Europe more generally that has been the dominant concern in recent work; so much so, indeed, that the former is often offered as a synonym for the latter. This elision is no mere linguistic shortcut, but carries a suggestion of some significance. It speaks to a tendency to address the EU's constitutional machinations as a free-standing and encompassing normative project for the continent, and so to treat the implications of the changes enacted or envisaged for the institutions of the Union and its Member States as if the EU occupies and controls all the available transnational legal space.

The premise of this book is that a focus on the EU as the key agent of non-state constitutional activity in Europe, while important, offers an incomplete picture of the complex constitutional configuration – or 'mosaic' – of contemporary Europe. Our purpose is to complement existing analysis with a work addressing this broader constitutional context. The volume, while paying due regard to the continuing impor- tance of the EU's familiar constitutional relations with its Member States, explores other threads of legally-coded publicly sourced authority that (together with various new or strengthened threads of transnational *private* authority)[2] apply within and across states, and which both act upon and are acted upon by the states and the EU alike. These other normative

---

[2] There is also a burgeoning literature on the growth of forms of privately sourced 'constitutional' authority; that is to say, forms of authority which make no direct claim to represent the public but which are nevertheless involved in the pursuit of the kinds of collective goods, and/or are subject to the kinds of 'public interest' constraints, normally associated with publicly established constitutional bodies. The analysis of these trends lies beyond the scope of the present volume. For a notable example under the label of 'societal constitutionalism', see G Teubner, 'Fragmented Foundations: Societal Constitutionalism Beyond the Nation State' in P Dobner and M Loughlin (eds), *The Twilight of Constitutional-ism?* (Oxford, Oxford University Press, 2010) 327–44.

threads of public authority have been by no means neglected in the legal literature to date. But they have tended to be addressed somewhat discretely, in a manner that pays little regard to their contribution to the wider *constitutional* landscape of Europe.

What are these other normative threads? They include, quite centrally, the developing institutional apparatus of Europe's other major post-war integrationist initiative, the Council of Europe. Confronted with a new frontier of opportunity after the end of the Cold War and the demise of Soviet Europe, the Council of Europe continues today to augment its constitutional personality through its ever more pervasive involvement in the life of Europe's new and existing states – both those within or seeking to join the EU and those situated at or beyond its margins – and through its increased role in the formation of binding legal obligations, including treaty-making with states outside Europe. A key specialism of the Council of Europe, and an area of constitutional inquiry in its own right, is, of course, human rights. Under the aegis of the Council, the European Court of Human Rights (ECtHR) responds to an ever broader and deeper set of challenges, the outcome of which is an expanding and increasingly dense body of case law that not only challenges the rights supremacy of its signatory states but also promises more overlap, and the possibility of future tension, in its relationship with the EU, and in particular its Court of Justice.

Constitutionally ambitious normative claims at the internal, sub-state territorial level in Europe's many and architecturally various federal and multinational polities are also deserving of our attention in posing an increasing challenge to the unitary self-assurance of states and the supra-state polity-building assumptions of the EU. Finally, and at the opposite extreme, the new transnational normative threads tend more and more to overlap the outer boundaries of Europe. Europe in its various institutional guises has increasingly 'thick' legal relations with other international institutions, perhaps most prominently today with the United Nations Security Council but also with key global sectoral regimes such as the World Trade Organization (WTO), as well as with the 'constitutional' features of 'international law' generically conceived.

Together, these various relations create increasingly dense networks of legal authority within and beyond the continent. 'Europe' is revealed as a more complex, fluid, multi-dimensional category – and also a more recondite one – than in most received understandings of the contours of public authority, and one that merits close investigation. But if this tells us something about 'where' our volume is located, what of the two other key concepts in our title, namely 'constitutional' and 'mosaic' itself?

B.   The Constitutional Dimension

The unsettling of old taken-for-granted certainties about the role of a previously dominant state-centred constitutionalism within the European and, indeed, global scheme in recent years has been both energising and destabilising for constitutional analysis. On the one hand, never before has discussion of law and politics so frequently, so explicitly and so self-consciously occurred within a constitutional register. On the other hand, never before has there been a less settled view as to the proper locus and centre of gravity of the constitutional idea, or indeed as to whether the constitutional idea retains *any* significant locus and role in the new transnational circumstances.[3] Constitutional ideas, in other words, are today more widespread than they have previously been, and more ambitious in their jurisdictional claims, but, equally, the nature and extent of their jurisdiction is more keenly contested than before.

How, then, should we handle the deeply disputed quality of the very concept with which we seek to depict the new complexity of legal relations in Europe? And this is joined by a second and more fundamental question: how can we justify the choice of such a disputed concept at the core of our analytical framework in the first place? The short answer to the first question is that we adopt a permissive approach. As we shall see, our various contributors do bring somewhat different understandings and expectations of constitutionalism to the table, or at least vary in their emphases. Given the contested character of what they are dealing with, this is no more than was to be expected, and could only have been avoided by the kind of question-begging conceptual dictat that would have defined certain possibilities out of their consideration in advance. Nevertheless, our embrace of diversity might seem to purchase inclusiveness at the price of coherence. For how can we talk meaningfully about – still less systematically investigate – a social and political phenomenon for which we lack agreed terms of reference?

On deeper reflection, however, the unresolved and underspecified quality of constitutionalism appears both manageable and, indeed, healthily inevitable. On the one hand, there is in fact sufficient overlapping consensus about what is going on in European 'constitutional' terms for the danger of incoherence, and of an attendant analytical confusion or vacuity, to be averted. On the other hand, what remains at issue is implicit in the very idea of constitutionalism, and speaks to a sense of uncertainty,

---

[3] Recent volumes exploring both sides of this coin include Dobner and Loughlin (eds), n 2 above; JL Dunoff and JP Trachtman (eds), *Ruling the World? Constitutionalism, International Law and Global Governance* (Cambridge, Cambridge University Press, 2009); J Klabbers, A Peters and G Ulfstein, *The Constitutionalization of International Law* (Oxford, Oxford University Press, 2009).

divergence and open possibility that tells us something important about the very character of the modern political age. An exploration of these points allows us to address the second question of the basic justification of a constitution-centred approach.

We should begin that exploration by acknowledging that constitutionalism and the idea of constitutional government typically refer to factors located at different levels of analysis, and that the nature and degree of controversy differ depending on the kinds of factors and the level of analysis with which we are concerned. In the first place, there is little controversy over constitutionalism conceived of as an arsenal of *normative resources*. Whether we are talking about normative forms (eg a legal order with its own system of internal hierarchy and independence of external authority, or the different formal methods of achieving a constitutional settlement), or normative structures (eg Parliaments, executives, Ombudsmen, Supreme Courts), or normative doctrines (fundamental rights, separation of powers, proportionality, subsidiarity), there is scant disagreement about what counts in historical and conventional terms as constitutional or not, or about how, where and when these normative materials now manifest themselves on the European transnational scene. Granted, the ways in which constitutional norms – form, structure and substance – are put together differs radically between different state settings, between the state and the post-state setting, and indeed between different post-state settings. But if we are interested not in the shape of the whole but in the disaggregated normative parts, then there is little doubt or controversy that contemporary Europe has witnessed the dissemination – some would say fragmentation – of constitutional ideas well beyond their state domicile, and even beyond their EU 'second home'.

In the second place, constitutionalism tends to be associated not only with its normative resource pool but also with *an underlying complex of public power*. Here there is already more scope for controversy. For some, constitutionalism in its fullest sense is parasitic upon an underlying complex of public power modelled upon or in some way analogous to that of the state, while for others the state-centredness of constitutionalism is merely a contingency of modern history. Yet the kind of disagreement to which this gives rise, though sometimes styled as all or nothing – as categorical[4] – can be (and often is) more productively understood as a matter of degree. While there may be significant disagreement about just how much public power non-state polities possess, and just how much underlying legitimacy, we are bound to acknowledge that the spread of

---

[4] See eg D Grimm, 'The Achievement of Constitutionalism and its Prospects in a Changed World' in Dobner and Loughlin (eds), above n 2, 3–22.

constitutional norms beyond the state has *in some measure* been accompanied – underpinned, indeed – by a corresponding shift in the architecture of
public power. No one can deny that, whether we are talking about the
expanding social, economic and security mandate of the EU, or the
ECtHR's maturing concern with continental standards of human rights
protection and public order, or the UN Security Council's enhanced powers
of intervention in the collective affairs of state and non-state polities and in
the individual affairs of their citizens, or the increasing political and
cultural autonomy of the federal or quasi-federal parts of Europe's
multinational states, what we are observing is a significant dispersal of the
very idea of public power and its corresponding authority structures away
from its state stronghold.

We would contend that these areas of overlapping consensus over the
spread of constitutionally familiar normative resources and the shift in the
underlying political architecture provide enough by way of shared terms of
reference for the significance of what remains unavoidably at issue in the
transnational constitutional debate to become a matter of common
acknowledgement and engagement rather than one of mutual incompre-
hension. In that common acknowledgement of and engagement with
divergent possibilities, moreover, we are alerted to one of the defining
features of the modern age.

Constitutionalism, understood in a third and broadest sense as the very
organising frame of the political realm, is by its very nature Janus-faced. It
is simultaneously concerned with achieved structures of power and the
normative resources these draw upon, and with ways of ideally conceiving
of and projecting the organisation of authority. It is, therefore, both
profane institutional reality and *symbolic aspiration*. And in its double
perspective, constitutionalism puts on vivid display its modernist credentials as a constructivist idea. The constitutional framing of the political
speaks to our sense of collective capacity to make over the world in our
own terms, rather than (as in the pre-modern imaginary) to seek and
manage the world's conformity with a pre-given order of things.[5] And such
a constructivist ambition involves a striving that is invariably marked both
by a record of existing accomplishment and by a supplement of unrealised
and unresolved potential.

Accordingly, the contestation that lies at the heart of European constitutionalism is not just about the taking of a state-fertilised idea away from its
roots, and over whether and to what extent this is feasible and desirable.
For, in a more basic methodological sense, contestation and the plasticity
of social and political possibilities are built into the very DNA of modern

---

[5]   See eg N Walker, 'Constitutionalism and the Incompleteness of Democracy' (2010) 39
Rechtsfilosofie en Rechtstheorie 206–33.

constitutionalism. When we argue, as our contributors do, over the proper and projected balance of constitutional authority between the states and the EU, or between the EU and the Council of Europe, or between the local and the regional, or between the regional and the global, we are not arguing *against* the grain of constitutionalism. Rather, we are operating *within* the modern tradition of the contentious construction of our collective futures, albeit no longer in a universe dominated by nation states, as in the high modern age, but in the politically multiform context of today. To retain a constitutional mode of analysis, therefore, is not some blindly anachronistic imposition of the old upon the new. Rather, it is a way of trying to understand the nature and limits of the adaptive relevance of our most prominent and resilient inherited categories of modern legal and political thought to the significantly altered circumstances of twenty-first century transnational Europe.

C. The Matrix Metaphor

What, finally, of the matrix metaphor itself? How useful is it as a means of depicting and exploring Europe's contemporary constitutional circumstances? We offer some preliminary points by way of general justification of the mosaic metaphor before addressing its particular utility to the case in hand.

We should begin with a declaration of modesty. New labels will only ever take us so far in making sense of the shifting European and global constitutional order. They can be no more than orienting devices, encouraging new directions and fresh insight. There are already in circulation countless terms that have sought to convey the novelty of Europe's changing constitutional order. Reflecting the weight of prior analysis, most of these have been concerned primarily with the EU and with its newly staked place in the previously state-centric order of constitutional relations. Some such terms have stressed the idea of novelty itself, referring to supranational Europe's *sui generic* character,[6] or its status as an 'unidentified political object'.[7] In more assertive formulations, this unidentified object may approximate to a compound democracy,[8] a transnational

---

[6] See eg DN MacCormick, *Who's Afraid of the European Constitution?* (London, Socictas, 2005).

[7] As described by Jacques Delors in 1985. For discussion, see H Drake, *Jacques Delores: Perspectives on a European Leader* (London, Routledge, 2000) 5.

[8] See S Fabbrini, *Compound Democracies: Why the United States and Europe are Becoming Similar* (Oxford, Oxford University Press, 2009).

consociation,[9] a commonwealth,[10] a post-Hobbesian non-state,[11] a *Bund*,[12] a *federation d'états-nations*,[13] or a form of 'multi-level constitutionalism'[14] – to name but a few of the candidate neologisms. None of these terms should be taken too seriously. Their status is not analytical but expressive. They do not speak to mutually exclusive scientific paradigms of explanation (even if they are sometimes treated as if they do), but are merely so many loose evocations of an imprecisely understood and unfinished transformation. The 'mosaic' idea joins these terms – albeit now with a somewhat broader and less EU-centred frame of reference – less as a conceptual rival than as an additional stimulant in a cumulative exercise of thick description.[15]

It is clear that, understood in these unassuming terms, the mosaic idea does have something to offer us. The primary meaning of mosaic is of a picture or decoration made of differently coloured pieces of inlaid stone, glass or similar substance. Often, however, as it is in our own case, the mosaic terminology is used in an active metaphorical sense to depict anything resembling such a picture or decoration in the diversity of its composition.

There are two additional and related features of the mosaic idea, at least as understood in its more developed forms, which enhance its suggestiveness in the present context. First, as in the notion of an aerial mosaic or a photo-mosaic, the mosaic idea has gradually been extended in a *representational* direction. Here its primary value is no longer aesthetic, and no longer confined to the familiar and somewhat limiting image of a multi-chrome structure made out of monochrome pieces.[16] Rather, it is descriptive, providing a picture or a map of some underlying 'real world' (whether

---

[9] See eg R Dehousse, 'European Institutional Architecture After Amsterdam: Parliamentary System or Regulatory Structure?' (1998) 35 *Common Market Law Review* 595.

[10] See eg DN MacCormick, *Questioning Sovereignty: Law, State and Nation in the European Commonwealth* (Oxford, Oxford University Press, 1999).

[11] See P Schmitter, 'If the Nation-State Were to Wither away in Europe, What Might Replace It?' in S Gustavsson and L Lewin (eds), *The Future of the Nation State* (London, Taylor and Francis, 1996).

[12] See M Avbelj, *Theory of the European Bund* (PhD thesis, European University Institute, 2009).

[13] See O Beaud, *Théorie de la Fédération* (Paris, Presses Universitaires de France, 2007).

[14] See I Pernice, 'Multilevel Constitutionalism and the Treaty of Amsterdam: European Constitution-Making Revisited?' (1999) 36 *Common Market Law Review* 703–50; 'Multilevel Constitutionalism in the European Union' (2002) 27 *European Law Review* 511–29.

[15] 'Mosaic' terminology has been used previously in the European context, but to describe the composition of the diverse field of EU *theory* rather than the pattern of European institutions or constitutional forms; see T Diez and A Wiener, 'Introducing the Mosaic of Integration Theory' in A Wiener and T Diez (eds), *European Integration Theory* (Oxford, Oxford University Press, 2004).

[16] The limitations of the most familiar version of the mosaic image have been characterised by Rogers Brubaker in this way in the somewhat different (but not entirely unrelated) context of a critique of Will Kymlicka's 'groupist' approach to the structure of national or

'natural world' or, as in the present case 'socio-political world') structure in all its multiform and fluid complexity. Secondly, as our cover image indicates and as Sionaidh Douglas-Scott demonstrates to striking effect in her chapter (chapter five), sometimes the mosaic is deployed purely as a *visual* or pictorial metaphor with no textual intermediation. That is to say, the metaphor consists of the image itself, in its independent signifying power, and in the implication that what it depicts cannot be adequately conveyed in words. Or, translated into the immediate context, the visual quality of the matrix metaphor speaks quite literally to its representational ambition, and in so doing dramatises the fact that we struggle to find in our existing vocabulary the terms necessary to capture something possessing such an emergent and unprecedented character.

Let us now look in more depth at the impression the mosaic metaphor conveys about the changing European constitutional scene. Here we proceed in two stages. First, the mosaic metaphor assists us in developing a series of general contrasts between the state-centred and so-called 'Westphalian' European constitutional configuration of the high modern period and the emerging post-national configuration. In turn, this allows us to indicate a set of constitutional challenges that are distinctive to the new 'mosaic' phase.

Regarding the contrast with a state-centred configuration, the idea of a constitutional mosaic suggests an emergent pattern exhibiting four distinguishing features. It is a pattern based on the *plurality* rather than the *singularity* of the constitutional field; the *diversity* rather than the *uniformity* of its parts; the *heterarchical* rather than the *hierarchical* quality of the relations between these parts; and the *fluidity* rather than the *fixity* of the internal and external boundaries.

The most basic property of the constitutional mosaic is its plural or composite quality. Whereas the state-based constitutional order is a discrete and self-contained whole, and knows only 'international' as opposed to constitutional relations with other discrete and self-contained state-based constitutional orders, the European constitutional mosaic is a thing of many interdependent parts. The states, the EU, the Council of Europe and the various other transnational or international constitutional instruments and orders that thread across and beyond the European continent, each has only partial constitutional jurisdiction. In addition, all

ethnic communities and the relationship between them; see R Brubaker, 'Myths and Misconceptions in the Study of Nationalism' in J Hall (ed), *The State of the Nation: Ernest Gellner and the Theory of Nationalism* (Cambridge, Cambridge University Press, 2008) 272–306; see also H De Schutter, 'Towards a Hybrid Theory of Multinational Justice' in S Tierney (ed), *Accommodating Cultural Diversity* (Aldershot, Ashgate, 2007) 35–58.

are closely mutually engaged, with adjacent and interlocking competence over matters as diverse as trade, migration, the environment, criminal law, social law and human rights.

Diversity rather than the uniformity of the parts is the second outstanding feature of the constitutional mosaic. The polity 'pieces' are no longer based upon the same basic state template. Rather, they are highly variable in form. On the state-like end of the spectrum, we have the still capacious if no longer monopolistic state authorities, the sub-state nations with sovereign aspirations, and the ever more prominent supranational remit of the EU, which has seen five Treaty-based extensions of jurisdiction and a trebling of its membership in 20 years. At the other end of the spectrum we have the Council of Europe, whose remit has remained much narrower, but which has considerably deepened in impact and widened in territorial scope, as well as various global institutions of even more restricted remit and still broader territorial scope.

The new mosaic, at least if viewed from the disinterested 'outside' – as in the idea of the aerial or photo-mosaic – also exhibits a very flat structure. Whereas constitutional authority within the state is hierarchically structured and closely concentrated at the top, the distribution of authority between the states and the various other new post-state polities forms a heterarchical pattern across these widely dispersed sites. There is no agreed meta-authority standing above these various polities, but merely so many site-specific claims to authority whose recognition and endorsement at other constitutional sites is not automatic, but may be refused, recast, qualified or otherwise disputed.

Finally, the mosaic metaphor, certainly if understood in its more advanced representational and visual modalities, emphasises the crowded and unsettled nature of the internal and external frontiers of the emerging European constitutional map. Whereas boundary shifts and disputes at the margins of constitutional orders are the exception under the more clearly and stably demarcated state-based system, once constitutional sites boast complexly overlapping jurisdictions but lack an authoritative place of common monitoring and authoritative point of common resolution between these jurisdictions, such movements and disputes multiply in number and amplify in significance.

Considered together, these mosaic features of plurality, diversity, heterarchy and fluidity raise a number of new issues and pose a number of new challenges to constitutional forms of governance in the European domain. These issues and challenges may be grouped under the heads of *authority*, *legitimacy*, *identity* and *contestability*. In substance, if not necessarily under these labels, these are the topics with which our various authors engage in their individual chapters, and so they should not detain us long at this preliminary stage. Let us, however, say a few introductory words about each.

The centrality of the question of authority has already been broached. Within the mosaic structure final authority is dispersed and disputed across the European domain. Indeed, much of the recent and burgeoning literature on constitutional pluralism, to which the articles in the present volume constitute a notable addition, is concerned with how this should be negotiated.[17] Does constitutional heterarchy provide an opportunity for a better balance between different forms of authority, and for a more rational, civilised or egalitarian way of resolving differences? Or does it represent a descent into confusion, uncertainty, unpredictability and parochialism? And, at an even deeper level, what are the implications of the fact that the very heterarchical pattern of authority is itself undesigned and unplanned, a mere 'disorder of orders'?[18] What, in other words, follows in terms of the legibility and steerability of the entire complex from the fact that the mosaic, unlike the discrete state constitutional miniatures that preceded it, is a product of many (collective) artists, none of whom had artistic control over the whole, and all of whom would offer a different perspective on the overall tableau and would offer different projections as to its preferred future development?

The challenge of legitimacy has to do with the ways in which the different sites of authority can be justified both in their own internal claims and in their claims against each other. We begin from the premise that, while pre-modern constitutional government was often suspicious of democracy and its intimations of untrammelled popular authority, democracy has certainly become the main and default basis of legitimacy within the modern world of constitutional government. If that is so, then Europe's constitutional mosaic poses two forms of challenge to that default constitutional legitimacy. In the first place – and this has been a constant theme of relations between states and both their sub-state 'national' interlocutors and the supranational EU – where we find various and overlapping pre-democratic claims of 'peoplehood' and demos-constituting authority, democracy itself cannot adjudicate on the legitimacy of the different claims. Secondly, many of the new claims to constitutional authority lack *any* direct democratic legitimacy, still less contending claims. Instead, they seek legitimacy on grounds that may be quite distinct from democracy, or which may qualify rather than complement democracy. Whether we are dealing with claims to individual political or economic rights under the ECHR or the new EU Charter of Rights, or the claims to the virtues of expertise and of freedom from political passions and pressures by the bureaucratic decision-makers of the EU Commission or the WTO, or the

---

[17] See eg M Avbelj and J Komarek, 'Four Visions of Constitutional Pluralism' EUI Working Papers 2008/21, at: papers.ssrn.com/sol3/papers.cfm?abstract_id=1334219.

[18] N Walker, 'Beyond Boundary Disputes and Basic Grids: Mapping the Global Disorder of Normative Orders' (2008) 6 *International Journal of Constitutional Law* 373–96.

supposedly all-trumping claims of 'security' on the part of the UN Security Council, or the indirectly democracy-respecting work of democracy promotion, anti-discrimination and minority protection of various EU and Council of Europe bodies working in the wider Europe, constitutional legitimacy in the mosaic world rests less, or less obviously, on democratic foundations than it does in a state-centred world. To what extent this is inevitable, and to what extent justifiable, remain pressing questions.

The question of identity is often given less attention in the post-national constitutional literature, but is an equally vital and urgent one. As Michel Rosenfeld has recently reminded us,[19] the very idea of modern constitutional identity – or subjectivity – reflects a commitment, in the name of liberty and equality, to inaugurate politically significant forms of collective being different from and irreducible to (although, paradoxically, invariably also drawing upon) other forms of pre- or extra-constitutional identity, whether these are based on nationality, religion, ethnicity, gender or other affiliation. Constitutional identity in the modern age, then, was about replacing a cross-cutting diversity of specific roles and status attributes with an inclusive singularity. What happens, then, when constitutional identity *itself* becomes multiple and cross-cutting? What happens – as is increasingly occurring throughout Europe and in the environs of its external frontiers in particular – when constitutional claims to 'citizenship' and its rights and responsibilities are made or received simultaneously and in a complex pattern of mutual support and competition at sub-state, state, supranational, functionally transnational and global levels? Positively, this can lead away from a reductive uniformity to bespoke forms of political identity. Negatively, it can contribute to the fracturing of the constitutional self, and to new forms of disorientation before and detachment from the body politic.

Finally, we should say something about the increasingly intense contestation at the boundaries of the new mosaic. Clearly, boundary questions can arise in any institutional context, in the work of legislatures testing the limits of their jurisdiction, concerning the *vires* of high executive action, or in the intrusive detail of administrative implementation or operational delivery. Yet it is also an undeniable feature of the constitutional politics of the mosaic that such boundary questions are often, in their highest profile instances, conducted in judicial settings. We should not be surprised, then, that much of the discussion in the chapters that follow is taken up with jurisdictional disputes within or around the borders of the mosaic involving Europe's highest courts. Whether it is the *Bundesverfassungsgericht* (German Constitutional Court), concerned with the latest Treaty chapter

---

[19] M Rosenfeld, *The Identity of the Constitutional Subject: Selfhood, Citizenship, Culture and Community* (New York, Routledge, 2010).

of the extension of EU authority,[20] or the European Court of Justice (ECJ) looking inwards and engaging with nationally sensitive questions of the definition of citizenship[21] or the regulation of labour markets,[22] or the EU looking outwards and engaging with the globally sensitive question of anti-terrorist security,[23] or the ECtHR debating its extra-territorial jurisdiction over supposedly universal human rights[24] or the ECtHR negotiating the terms and extent of its monitoring role over the EU as its transnational neighbour,[25] judicial forms of constitutional disputation in the mosaic age tend more and more to raise fundamental and highly-charged questions of demarcation. As Miguel Maduro has said, judges working at the margins and in the crevices of the mosaic must increasingly engage in 'meta-teleological reasoning',[26] looking not just to the wider telos and justification of the relevant rules at issue but also to the wider telos and justification of the very legal order responsible for these rules, and now even to how this wider telos is informed by the host legal order's relationship with adjacent legal orders. There are two vital challenges here – one substantive and the other structural. Substantively, how can and how do judges think 'beyond' the normative structure exhibited by their own legal order – their own piece of the mosaic? Structurally, how should we respond to the fact that the proliferation of boundary issues tends to lead to a new level and quality of judicialisation of high political issues? Is the propensity to empower the judges unavoidable, and is it a development to be welcomed or criticised?

II. OUTLINE OF CHAPTERS

The volume emerges from a seminar series convened by the three editors at the Edinburgh School of Law over the course of the academic year 2008–09. The seminars sought to explore our key research theme of the complex constitutional arrangements of the European legal space, considered as an inter-connected mosaic. Five seminars were held, engaging in turn with the current relationship between the EU and its Member States,

---

[20] BVerfG, 2 BvE 2/08, judgment of 30 June 2009.
[21] Case C-135/08 *Rottmann v Freistaat Bayern*, ECJ, judgment of 2 March 2010.
[22] Case C-341/05 *Laval un Partneri Ltd v Svenska Byggnadsarbetareförbundet* [2007] ECR I-11767; Case C-438/05 *International Transport Workers' Union v Viking* [2007] ECR I-10779.
[23] Joined Cases C-402/05 P and C-415/05 P *Kadi and Al Barakaat International Foundation v Council and Commission* [2008] ECR I-6351.
[24] *Bankovic v Belgium and others* (2001) 11 BHRC 435.
[25] *Bosphorous Hava Yollari Turizm v Ireland* (2006) 42 EHRR 1.
[26] See eg Miguel Maduro, 'Interpreting European Law: Judicial Adjudication in a Context of Constitutional Pluralism' (2007) 1(2) *European Journal of Legal Studies* 1.

the developing profile of the European Convention on Human Rights, the wider Europe of the Council of Europe and EU Enlargement, the role of European regions and nations below the state, and the relationship between Europe and global legal forms and structures. In each seminar two speakers delivered main papers, and these were followed by short discussion papers offered by other contributors, then broader debate within the seminar plenary. Each of these seminars forms the basis for one part of the book. From these seminars we also gained a sense that our understanding of the general structural momentum behind the development of the new European legal space and of the extent of national resistance to the establishment of the mosaic structure would be augmented by studies looking at the formation of particular areas of law. So we commissioned papers which allowed us to add a final part of case-studies of two areas of law – criminal law and labour law – whose strong statist pedigree has long provided a powerful counter-current to transnational European developments.

The contributors to the volume are all acknowledged experts from the fields of public law and legal theory or, in two cases where an 'outside' voice was deemed most pertinent, from political science (Sasse and Requejo). In addition, many of the commentators came from law's neighbour disciplines, so underlining the interdisciplinary flavour of the whole.

In Part One on the European Union, the two contributions by Cormac Mac Amhlaigh and Julio Baquero Cruz seek in their different ways to go beyond received ways of understanding the constitutional quality of Europe's main supranational presence. Mac Amhlaigh examines the future through the lens of the early modern past. He sets out to demonstrate that each of the three main trends within EU constitutionalist discourse – legalist, neo-republican and processual – tends to understate the sovereigntist deep structure of the EU's claim to constitutional authority. Only if we think of the EU as a proto-sovereign order, he argues, can we hold the mosaic in place, so to speak, and make proper sense of the degree and quality of constitutional contestation in the European domain. Cruz's focus is more squarely on the relationship between the EU and its Member States, and, in particular, on the three main candidate understandings of that relationship – state-centred, integrationist and pluralist. He sees each of these positions as telling us only part of the story, and as tending to become locked into a self-corroborating pattern to the exclusion of the other narratives. He proposes instead, as a means of blending the explanatory and normative insights of the first three perspectives, an exceptional and non-system-threatening capacity for Member States to express their disagreement with the Union based upon a theory of 'institutional disobedience'.

In Part Two, Andrew Williams begins by questioning the conventional wisdom that the ECHR is the jewel in the crown of international systems of human rights protection. He claims that the ECHR is instead a conceptual and practical failure, not least because it does not sufficiently articulate the universality and indivisibility of rights protection, or adequately memorialise the conditions of inhumanity which prompted the Convention in the first place. He proposes to move beyond the mosaic of diverse institutional forms of human rights protection in Europe, and to vest the key human rights jurisdiction not in the ECHR but in the politically more powerful and legally more expansive EU. Sionaidh Douglas-Scott takes a rather different view. She concludes that the ECHR, precisely because of the singularity of its remit, should in fact be *the* human rights constitution for Europe, with its Court building on its recent practice of 'pilot' judgments to provide a more selective and directive role than at present. Furthermore, aided and abetted by the post-Lisbon accession of the EU to the ECHR, the ECtHR should exercise as firm and vigilant an authority over the EU as it does over the European states. Unlike Williams, moreover, Douglas-Scott does not view the divided institutional hierarchy of the mosaic structure as being necessarily an impediment to rights protection, provided that in each system human rights stands at the pinnacle of a shared hierarchy of *values*.

In Part Three, Jo Shaw initiates discussion of Europe's wider frontiers by addressing head-on the constitutional identity question posed above, in the context of the shifting, multi-layered and mutually uncoordinated citizenship regimes of the new former Yugoslavian states of South Eastern Europe. Citizenship of these seven states, she argues, is influenced by a complex range of internal, regional, EU, pan-European and wider international normative sources, as well as by the conflicted contemporary constitutional history of the post-Communist dissolution of the multinational and multi-ethnic Yugoslavia. Amongst the most important of these influences, she stresses, are changes both *within* the EU – and in particular the increasing political substance invested in the idea of supranational citizenship – and changes *to* the EU in the form of a further expansion of membership that will gradually embrace all the states of the region. Gwen Sasse also dwells on the constitutional politics of the wider Europe – including questions of ECHR compliance and issues of statelessness, multiple citizenship and the protection of national minorities – in the context of a general study of the value of the apparently institutionally weak Council of Europe as a norm entrepreneur. Given the 'soft' means at its disposal, the Council of Europe will always be more effective as a norm producer and developer than as a norm enforcer. As Sasse's study shows, the Council of Europe's resourcefulness in overcoming its weaknesses and playing to its strengths is greater than is often appreciated, not least through its institutional flexibility and capacity for innovation, its resilience and ability to play the long game, and its appreciation of inter-institutional synergies across the constitutional mosaic.

In Part Four Hans Lindahl cuts to the heart of the debate over sub-state constitutional recognition by asking to what extent the normative idea of reciprocity between groups – which he argues is essential to the very integrity and singularity of a constitutional settlement – can succeed in reconciling political plurality and legal unity in the face of strong group claims to cultural distinctness. Drawing upon the famous example of the Quebec secession adjudication, Lindahl criticises a number of diversity-friendly positions for failing to appreciate the full implications of the internal relationship between constitutional singularity and reciprocity, and so contemplating within constitutional singularity expressions of distinctiveness that are incompatible with reciprocity, and, it follows, with constitutional singularity itself. In conclusion, drawing on the example of the introduction of a national secession mechanism in the EU in the Lisbon Treaty, Lindahl posits, against the pluralism-threatening logic of strict constitutional reciprocity, the intriguing notion of 'para-constitutionality'. This involves contemplation within the constitutional vehicle itself of a partial suspension of the constitutional regimentation of reciprocity so as to allow the detailed negotiation and plotting of an *asymmetrically* conceived secession – one that follows from the wishes of the seceding party alone. Ferran Requejo starts from a different philosophical place than Lindahl, from the premise of the deep political imperative rather than the constitutional limitation of the recognition of the distinctiveness and autonomy of sub-state groups. He criticises the conceptual straitjacket imposed by conventional understandings of liberal democracy, and, following a survey of the viability of different forms of institutional design for diversity, concludes that only plurinational federal models and so-called partnership models can do full justice to the need to accommodate difference within constitutional singularity in the states of Europe today.

Anne Peters commences Part Five with a wide-ranging overview of the ways in which international organisations within and beyond Europe's regional theatre may display their constitutional credentials. The point of her focus on international organisations and their sectoral constitutions is to highlight the dispersed nature of the global constitutional order or mosaic. Global constitutionalism, in her view, is multi-level and nested rather than hierarchical and monolithic. To the modest extent that it is possible, the commonality of constitutional identity of the different international organisations, European and otherwise, depends upon their separate adherence not only to key modes and mechanisms of constitutional authority but also to shared constitutional values, including those associated with parliamentary democracy. For his part, Jan Klabbers takes a more ambitious view of what would be required for a genuinely global constitutionalism. He notes the strong case that could be made for some kind of cohesive infrastructure of institutions as well as of values and also, crucially, for a set of agreed secondary rules regulating the relationship between different sites of primary rules, including European and global sites. He goes on to argue, however, that the tension between this kind of universal code and the autonomous and necessarily particularising claims and commitments of those postulating a specifically European constitutional order is extremely difficult, if not impossible, to reconcile. Rather than common rules, he asserts, the best we can hope for in inter-site relations is an appeal to extra-legal, or at least legally irreducible virtues such as honesty, humility and seeing the bigger picture. Only thus, he concludes, might it become appropriate to talk of a global constitutional mosaic.

In Part Six, Kimmo Nuotio introduces the subject of European criminal law as a key barometer of transnational constitutional possibilities. He makes the point that criminal and constitutional law each has highly particularising tendencies as expressions of national culture, while the immediacy of new collective action problems and externalities at the European level mean that there is also a strong drive towards the generation of transnational criminal and constitutional law norms both in the Council of Europe and, more prominently today, in the EU. As well as being similar in how they connect the national to the transnational, criminal law and constitutional law are also mutually constitutive. Criminal law and the various common commitments it articulates (or does not) can relay constitutionally significant messages about the development (or not) of new forms of solidarity at the supranational level. Reciprocally, the supranational management of the continuing differences between national criminal justice regimes requires constitutional rules of coordination, as in the robust constitutionalisation of mutual recognition and mutual assistance dimensions of criminal justice in recent supranational treaties. National criminal law differences, he concludes, can therefore provide an impediment to the development of European constitutional rules, but they also act as a catalyst for new forms of European constitutional law.

In the final chapter, Ruth Dukes examines the role of another mainstay of European national law, namely labour law, in the making of a European constitutional settlement. Whereas the infiltration of criminal law into the European transnational constitutional mosaic has been gradual and 'bottom-up', in the case of labour law the relevant dynamic has been 'top-down'. The constitution of the EU single market – the economic constitution – was unbalanced from the outset, and the history of transnational labour initiatives, from the development of the social dialogue to the incorporation of justiciable social rights into the EU Charter of Rights and the increasingly social rights-friendly jurisprudence of the ECtHR, can be seen as so many attempts to correct that original sin. Nevertheless, Dukes concludes, the combination of the resilience of the deep formative bias of the EU and the strong residual sovereigntist desire of the states to retain jurisdiction over the main areas of labour law means that labour law continues to maintain only a fragile and derivative presence in the transnational constitution.

These last two case studies offer a valuable corrective to an overly institutional approach to the development of the constitutional field, and to the danger that such an approach treats the deepening of the transnational as inevitable and inexorable. They remind us that Europe's constitutional prospects depend not just upon contemporary innovations in structural engineering but also upon long material and cultural histories. And in so doing, they warn that underneath the normative modelling, the institutional decline of the state and rise of the transnational is not necessarily matched – or at least not evenly so across policy areas and jurisdictions – at the societal level. Perhaps, then, a final value of the mosaic metaphor lies in its simple reminder that constitutional construction is ultimately a matter of the design and manipulation of surface forms, and in the caution that the framing and transformative power of these surfaces depends upon an ever precarious capacity to capture and harness unruly underlying forces.

Part One

The European Union

2

The European Union's Constitutional Mosaic: Big 'C' or Small 'c', Is that the Question?

CORMAC MAC AMHLAIGH*

I. INTRODUCTION

THE EUROPEAN UNION is, in many ways, the *locus classicus* of contemporary post-state constitutionalism. Its quasi-federal nature, along with recent attempts to draft a self-styled 'constitutional treaty' for the supranational polity, has put it at the vanguard of constitutional theorising beyond the state. As such, any metaphorical mosaic of European constitutionalism must have the European Union close to, if not right at, its centre.

A mosaic is made up of individual fragments which, taken together, make up an image or representation. As such it is more than the sum of its parts and requires some distance and perspective in order to be truly appreciated. However, this contribution will focus on one, or a small number of 'tiles' of Europe's broader constitutional mosaic, that of European constitutional discourse. More specifically, it will interrogate the various notions of constitutionalism that have been applied in the EU context, and the related issue of what, precisely, it means for the EU to be constitutional.

As the chapter will demonstrate, EU constitutional discourse is, in itself, a 'mosaic within a mosaic', revealing a variegated picture of EU constitutionalism as a complex array of interpretations of the constitutional concept. This focus on EU constitutional discourse as opposed to the reception of the EU's constitutional claims in its Member States[1] or the broader European mosaic of interlocking normative orders, reveals that there are some gaps in the EU constitutional picture, due in the main to EU

---

* The University of Edinburgh.
[1] See Baquero Cruz's contribution to the current volume (ch 3).

constitutional discourse's alienated relationship with the concept of sovereignty. The chapter argues that sovereignty provides (to push the mosaic metaphor to stretching point) the 'grout' for EU constitutionalism's own mosaic; perhaps not the brightest or most beautiful aspect of the picture but absolutely essential to the existence of the constitutional mosaic itself.

II.   CONSTITUTIONALISM AND THE EUROPEAN UNION

Constitutionalism has been the *leitmotif* of European Union legal studies for almost a generation.[2] It has become an article of faith amongst European lawyers[3] that the EU is a constitutional entity, notwithstanding its genesis in a set of international treaties set up by sovereign states. As is well known, in a series of seminal judgments on the nature of the treaty system which established the then European Economic Community (EEC),[4] the EU's judicial arm, the European Court of Justice (ECJ), set the foundations for the EU as a constitutional polity in a similar manner to the US Supreme Court's elevation of the United States Constitution in its famous *Marbury v Madison* decision.[5] To summarise what is considerably well-trodden ground,[6] in a series of cases, the ECJ found that the EU legal order, unusually for an international treaty system, contained the following characteristics: that individuals can rely directly on EU primary and

---

[2] Some of the pioneering work in this regard includes Eric Stein, 'Lawyers, Judges and the Making of a Transnational Constitution' (1981) 75 *American Journal of International Law* 1; Federico Mancini, 'The Making of a Constitution for Europe' (1989) 26 *Common Market Law Review* 595; Joseph HH Weiler, 'The Transformation of Europe' (1991) 100 *Yale Law Journal* 2403.

[3] Whereas lawyers have been at the vanguard of EU constitutional discourse, political theorists have been taking an increasing interest in constitutionalism as part of a more general 'normative turn' in EU integration. For an overview, see Richard Bellamy and Dario Castiglione, 'Legitimizing the Euro-"polity" and its "Regime": The Normative Turn in EU Studies' (2003) 2(7) *European Journal of Political Theory* 7.

[4] Since the entry into force of the Lisbon Treaty in December 2009 all of the bits and pieces of the organisation (EC etc) have now all been assimilated into one EU. In the light of this significant simplification exercise, 'EU' will be used throughout this chapter as a generic identifier for both today's EU and the other entities which preceded it, including the European Economic Community, European Community, Community law etc.

[5] *Marbury v Madison* 5 US (1 Cranch) 137 (1803). Daniel Halberstam, 'Constitutionalism and Pluralism in Marbury v. Madison' in Miguel Maduro and Loic Azoulai (eds), *The Past and Future of EU Law: Revisiting the Classics on the 50th Anniversary of the Rome Treaty* (Oxford, Hart Publishing, 2010).

[6] Perhaps the most detailed statement of the development is still Weiler's 'The Transformation of Europe', above n 2.

secondary law in national courts without the requirement of prior implementing measures by national authorities;[7] that EU law overrides any
provision of national law in cases of conflict;[8] that the ECJ enjoys exclusive
competence to decide questions on the validity and application of EU law;[9]
and that the EU entails a principle of implied powers whereby it may
assume certain powers in order for it to achieve the objectives stipulated in
the Treaties.[10]

In this way, the system of European integration established by the Treaty
of Rome had, by judicial fiat, metamorphosed into something new, *sui
generis*, which resembled more closely the constitutional structure of a
federal system than that of a classic treaty system under international law
such as the United Nations or North Atlantic Treaty Organization. Upon
this fertile ground, EU constitutional discourse has taken root and flour-
ished in EU legal studies.[11] The constitutional idea has also made forays
into EU and national politics,[12] a development reaching its zenith with the
Constitutional Treaty in 2005. As is well-known, this was rejected in
referendums in France and The Netherlands, but a rehashed and semi-
digested form of the original dish was served up in the Lisbon Treaty which
finally came into force, after a few wobbles, on 1 December 2009.

The EU's reform agenda of the past decade, both successes and failures,
has been the subject of much comment and debate both in academic circles
and further afield,[13] and it is not my intention to contribute to that

---

[7] Known as the 'direct effect' of EU Law first established by the court in Case 26/62,
Van Gend en Loos v Nederlandse Administratie der Belastingen [1963] ECR 1, 13.

[8] Hitherto known as the supremacy, but now the primacy of EU law: Case 6/64, *Costa v
Ente Nazionale Energie Elettrica (ENEL)* [1964] ECR 585. This has now been formally
recognised in Declaration 17 attached to the Lisbon Treaty.

[9] Case 314/85, *Firma Foto-Frost v Hauptzollamt Lübeck-Ost* [1987] ECR 4199.

[10] See, for example, Case 22/70, *European Commission v European Council* [1971] ECR
263.

[11] EU Constitutional literature is now legion. Some recent examples include Neil Walker,
'Reframing EU Constitutionalism' in Jeffrey Dunoff and Joel Trachtman (eds), *Ruling the
World? Constitutionalism, International Law and Global Governance* (Cambridge, Cam-
bridge University Press, 2009); Miguel Maduro, 'The Importance of Being Called a Constitu-
tion: Constitutional Authority and the Authority of Constitutionalism' (2005) 3 *International
Journal of Constitutional Law* 373; Joseph HH Weiler and Marlene Wind, *European
Constitutionalism Beyond the State* (Cambridge, Cambridge University Press, 2003).

[12] See for example, the proposals for a European constitution by Alterio Spinelli as far
back as the 1950s: Andrew Glencross, 'Altiero Spinelli and the Idea of the US Constitution as
a Model for Europe: The Promises and Pitfalls of an Analogy' (2009) 47(2) *Journal of
Common Market Studies* 287.

[13] See (2005) 2/3 *International Journal of Constitutional Law* (Special Issue) 163–515;
Andrew Moravcsik, 'What Can we Learn from the collapse of the European Constitutional
Project?' (2006) 47:2 *Politische Vierteljahresschrift* 219; Neil Walker, 'A Constitutional
Reckoning' (2006) 13(2) *Constellations* 140 and 'Not the European Constitution' (2008)
15(1) *Maastricht Journal of European and Comparative Law* 135–41.

particular debate here.[14] Rather, as already noted, in this contribution, I will focus on one particular tile of Europe's constitutional mosaic; specifically the ways in which the constitutional idea itself has been theorised in this robustly constitutional but non-state entity.

In order to do so, the chapter will first provide a glance at the conceptual landscape of EU constitutional discourse, tracing the divergent threads of the constitutional concept employed therein. It then critiques these conceptions of constitutionalism as failing to explicitly recognise the essential signifier of the constitutional idea: sovereignty. It goes on to illustrate problems with the forms constitutionalism adopted, arguing that a sovereignty-inspired conception of EU constitutionalism provides a better and more coherent rendering of the EU constitutional picture. It finds that the ECJ's early 'constitutionalising' judgments as well as its recent *Kadi* decision, are sufficient evidence of the EU's sovereignty claims, and so support this sovereigntist reading of EU constitutionalism.

III.   EXCAVATING THE EU'S CONSTITUTIONAL MOSAIC

EU constitutional discourse is acquiring a venerable pedigree, due in no small part to the broad acceptance of the ECJ's seminal judgments on the nature of the EU's treaty system.[15] A fundamental aspect of the success of the Court's constitutionalisation was the willingness of national actors, particularly national courts, to 'play the constitutional game' with the ECJ and act as joint protagonists in the construction of the European constitutional façade.[16] Moreover, the ECJ's subsequent christening of the treaties as the polity's 'constitutional charter'[17] added a formal veneer to the already substantial and broadly accepted constitutional character of the EU legal system by national legal actors. As such, constitutionalism has remained an important 'academic artifact'[18] of European integration notwithstanding the fact that it has undergone various challenges and a 'reformation'[19] in its first half-century.[20]

---

[14] See Cormac Mac Amhlaigh, 'Revolt by Referendum? In search of a European Constitutional Narrative' (2009) 15(4) *European Law Journal* 552.

[15] For a sceptical position on this question, see Baquero Cruz's contribution to the current volume (ch 3).

[16] See generally, Miguel Maduro, *We the Court* (Oxford, Hart Publishing, 1998).

[17] Case 294/83, *Parti Ecologiste 'Les Verts' v European Parliament* [1986] ECR 1339. See also the recent *Kadi* decision (discussed below, n 124).

[18] Joseph HH Weiler, *The Constitution of Europe* (Cambridge, Cambridge University Press, 1999) 223.

[19] *ibid*, ch 6.

[20] Perhaps the biggest challenge to EU constitutionalism in recent years has been the assertion of national constitutional supremacy in the face of EU law by national constitutional

Notwithstanding the indisputable pedigree of EU constitutionalism as a distinct field of inquiry, its precise dimensions and nature are not easily tied down. This is in large part due to divergent approaches to theorising EU constitutionalism in the discourse. The major fault-lines which shape the increasingly complex field of EU constitutional discourse relate to the concept of constitutionalism adopted, the question of how or why the EU can be constitutional, as well as the question of how constitutionalism can make a contribution to the EU's well-publicised legitimacy problems, perhaps most clearly demonstrated by the failure of the Constitutional Treaty itself. Thus, navigating the terrain of EU constitutional discourse in the era of the 'post-constitutional'[21] Lisbon Treaty is complex.

In this contribution, this complexity is managed by identifying trends in EU constitutional discourse organised according to the conception or form of constitutionalism adopted. In this regard, three distinct trends in EU constitutional discourse are identified; legalist, neo-republican and processual.

The first of these trends of EU constitutional discourse, the legalist trend, remains the most faithful – some might argue parochial – to the legal origins of EU constitutionalism, based on a characterisation of the law of the treaties as having effects similar to domestic constitutional law.[22] As such, it emphasises the importance of a hierarchical system of positive law as the essence of constitutionalism, where the constitution itself is the 'fundamental law'[23] of the system. Thus, the significance of the ECJ's constitutionalisation of the treaties was the elevation of what was essentially a species of international law to the status of the 'law of the land',[24] with the treaties playing a role analogous to national constitutions in domestic legal systems.

---

courts, notably the German constitutional court in its decision regarding the constitutionality of German ratification of the Maastricht and Lisbon Treaties. See *Brunner v European Union Treaty*, [1994] CMLR 57; *Lisbon Case*, BVerfG, 2BvE 2/08 from 30 June 2009, available at: www.bverfg.de/entscheidungen/es20090630_2bve000208.html.

[21] Alexander Somek, 'Postconstitutional Treaty' (2007) 8:12 *German Law Journal* 1121.

[22] See generally, Neil MacCormick, 'Beyond the Sovereign State' (1993) 56 *Modern Law Review* 1, 'The Maastricht-Urteil: Sovereignty Now' (1995) 1 *European Law Journal* 259, and *Questioning Sovereignty* (Oxford, Oxford University Press, 1999) (hereinafter 'QS'); Catherine Richmond, 'Preserving the Identity Crisis: Autonomy, System and Sovereignty in European Law' (1997) 16(4) *Law and Philosophy* 337; Frank Dowrick, 'A Model of the European Communities' Legal System' (1983) 3 *Yearbook of European Law* 169; ML Jones, 'The Legal Nature of the European Community: A Jurisprudential Model Using Hart's Model of Law and Legal System' (1984) 17 *Cornell International Law Journal* 1; Ines Weyland, 'The Application of Kelsen's Theory of the Legal System to European Community Law – The Supremacy Puzzle Resolved' (2002) 21 *Law and Philosophy* 1.

[23] Neil Walker, 'Fundamental Law' in *Stair Memorial Encyclopedia of the Laws of Scotland* (Re-issue 4) (Scotland, Butterworths Law, 2001) *Constitutional Law*, 29–82.

[24] Weiler, 'The Transformation of Europe', above n 2.

Conceptually, this purely legalistic form of EU constitutional discourse entails a legal positivist theory of law and constitutionalism, where legal ontology is predicated on a single source of legal *validity*, the constitution, which sits at the apex of a hierarchically ordered system of norms.[25] As the fundamental law of a system, the constitution cannot, itself, depend on a higher norm for its own validity if it is meaningfully to constitute the fundamental law. This presents a puzzle for legal theory given that the normative system is incapable of accounting for its own validity. Legal theory has attempted to solve this puzzle by postulating the authority of the constitution on a basic norm *presupposed* in relation to it[26] as a kind of ideal of reason, or by basing the validity of the constitution on a 'social fact' of obedience pursuant to a 'rule of recognition'.[27]

Applying legalist approaches of constitutionalism to the EU then, it can be argued that the ECJ, in developing the constitutional doctrines of EU law, presupposed a basic norm in relation to the Treaty system, thereby equating it with a domestic constitutional order in legal terms.[28] Alternatively, the ECJ's seminal judgments can be said to have prompted a change in the national 'rule of recognition'[29] as to the validity of laws prevailing on the territories of Member States.[30]

This legalist constitutionalism has been given its clearest expression in the EU context in the work of the late Neil MacCormick.[31] As part of his more general theory of post-sovereignty, MacCormick argued that the concept of sovereignty entails both a legal and political dimension. The legal dimension relates to the constitutive rules of the legal system where '[s]overeign power is that which is enjoyed ... by the holder of a constitutional power to make law, so long as the constitution places no restrictions on the exercise of that power'.[32] In this regard, legal sovereignty is a proxy for legalist constitutionalism. Political sovereignty on the other hand, is political power unrestrained by higher political power, which relates to the 'interpersonal power over the conditions of life in a human community or society'.[33] In arguing in favour of the primacy of legal sovereignty, MacCormick rejects a hegemonic political sovereignty,

---

[25] Paradigmatically expressed in Hans Kelsen's account of a legal system. See Hans Kelsen, *General Theory of Law and State* (Cambridge MA, Harvard University Press, 1946).

[26] *ibid*, ch 10.

[27] HLA Hart, *The Concept of Law*, 2nd edn (Oxford, Clarendon Press, 1994).

[28] Richmond, 'Preserving the Identity Crisis' and Weyland, 'The Application of Kelsen's Theory', above n 22.

[29] Hart, *The Concept of Law*, above n 27, 94.

[30] In the UK context, see Paul Craig, 'Sovereignty of the United Kingdom Parliament after Factortame' (1991) 11 *Yearbook of European Law* 221; William Wade, 'Sovereignty – Revolution or Evolution?' (1996) 112 *Law Quarterly Review* 568.

[31] MacCormick, 'Beyond the Sovereign State' and 'The Maastricht Urteil', above n 22.

[32] *QS*, above n 22, 127.

[33] *QS*, 127.

finding it is not relevant to entities with standing constitutional traditions.[34] In such a situation, described as a *rechtstaat* or 'law state', MacCormick argues that law and legal sovereignty can exist independently of an overarching political sovereignty.[35] As such, conceptually speaking, a hierarchical (constitutional) legal system can be decoupled from the concept of sovereignty and can be replicated at non-state, and importantly non-sovereign, sites such as the EU.[36] On this account, then, there is no incoherence in claiming that the EU enjoys a hierarchical constitutional legal order but is not, at the same time, a sovereign entity.

The second significant trend in EU constitutionalism adopts a concept of constitutionalism as a 'set of legal and political instruments limiting power'.[37] This reflects a republican conception of the nature and function of constitutions as 'checks and balances' on the exercise of public power through the rule of law, the separation of powers, federalism and fundamental rights protection.[38] This in turn is predicated on ideals of republican liberty, which is ensured through the fragmentation of political power.[39] The transportation of these republican-inspired ideals to the EU level provides for a form of federal neo-republican constitutionalism with a *communautaire* twist.[40] Whereas with classic republican constitutional

---

[34] *QS*, 128.

[35] *QS*, 128–9.

[36] *QS*, 129, 131.

[37] Maduro, 'The Importance of Being Called a Constitution', above n 11, 333.

[38] This conception of constitutionalism is a particular feature of much German scholarship on EU Constitutionalism. See, for example, Dieter Grimm, 'Does Europe Need a Constitution?' (1995) 1(3) *European Law Journal* 282 and 'Integration by Constitution' (2005) 3(2–3) *International Journal of Constitutional Law* 193; Ingolf Pernice, 'Multilevel constitutionalism in the European Union' (2002) 27 *European Law Review* 511 and 'The Treaty of Lisbon: Multilevel Constitutionalism in Action' (2009) 2/09 Walter Hallestein Institut Working Paper, 15 *Columbia Journal of European Law* 349; Armin von Bogdandy, 'The European Union as a Supranational Federation: A conceptual attempt in the light of the Amsterdam Treaty' (2000) 6 *Columbia Journal of European Law* 27. There is also more than a hint of republican ideals informing Maduro's writings on EU constitutionalism. See 'The Importance of Being Called a Constitution', above n 11, and 'Europe and the constitution: what if this is as good as it gets?' in Weiler and Wind (eds), *European Constitutionalism Beyond the State*, above n 11; Maduro, 'Contrapunctual Law: Europe's Constitutional Pluralism in Action' in Neil Walker (ed), *Sovereignty in Transition* (Oxford, Hart Publishing, 2003).

[39] In this regard, classic republican theory endorses a strong separation of powers doctrine. For a paradigmatic statement see Baron de Montesquieu (Charles de Secondat), *The Spirit of the Laws* [1748], Anne Cohler, Basia Miller and Harold Stone (eds) (Cambridge, Cambridge University Press, 1989), especially Book II: 'On the law that form political liberty in its relation with the constitution'. This theme has been taken up in political theory in recent years through the writings of Philip Pettit and Richard Bellamy who adopt a republican conception of political liberty in terms of independence from arbitrary power or nondomination. See Philip Pettit, *Republicanism: A Theory of Freedom and Government* (Oxford, Oxford University Press, 1999), particularly ch 2; Richard Bellamy, *Political Constitutionalism: A Republican Defence of the Constitutionality of Democracy* (Cambridge, Cambridge University Press, 2007).

[40] Pernice, 'Multilevel Constitutionalism', above n 38.

theory, the constitution is an expression of the constituent power where 'the people as a whole adopted the Constitution',[41] which in turn provides the mechanism through which government is restrained, the primary checks on power in EU constitutionalism are overwhelmingly *functional*, where the exercise of power is limited to the achievement of the specific aims or objectives stipulated in the Treaties, such as the establishment of the internal market. In this regard, EU neo-republican constitutionalism protects the prerogative of the Member States against the unauthorised exercise of what is deemed to be delegated sovereign power by the EU's institutions. In the EU context, this neo-republican constitutionalism thus prioritises the constitutional principles of subsidiarity, the principle of the conferral of powers as well as a strong doctrine of ultra vires.[42] Moreover, whereas institutional design is an important element of this neo-republican EU constitutional discourse,[43] law is the primary mechanism of control which patrols the exercise of power by EU institutions as enforced by the courts, primarily the ECJ.[44] The development of a strong fundamental rights jurisprudence from the ECJ,[45] which was crowned by the EU's own bill of rights,[46] is an extra safeguard against abuse of power by the EU institutions, and enhances EU constitutionalism's neo-republican credentials. As such, this trend in EU constitutional discourse implies a unique form of federal republican constitutionalism; where sovereign states, rather than citizens, play a leading role and the concept of 'public' in the *res publica* is elusive.

A third, more recent trend in EU constitutional discourse, is one which conceptualises the idea of constitutionalism in terms of a *process*.[47] Thus,

---

[41]   Stephen Griffin, 'Constituent Power and Constitutional Change in American Constitutionalism' in Martin Loughlin and Neil Walker (eds), *The Paradox of Constitutionalism* (Oxford, Oxford University Press 2007) 49.

[42]   See above n 38.

[43]   Maduro, 'The Importance of Being Called a Constitution', above n 11.

[44]   There is an affinity between the role of law in neo-republican EU constitutional discourses and approaches in political science to European integration such as Giandomenico Majone's conceptualisation of the EU as a 'regulatory state' or Moravcsik's recent work on the democratic deficit in the EU, in the sense that they all posit a strong role for law in keeping the EU's institutions in check and therefore see law as the primary source of legitimacy in the EU. See Giandomenico Majone, *The Dilemmas of European Integration* (Oxford, Oxford University Press, 2005); Andrew Moravcsik, 'In Defence of the 'Democratic Deficit': Reassessing Legitimacy in the European Union' (2002) 40(4) *Journal of Common Market Studies* 603.

[45]   See, for example, Case 11/70, *Internationale Handelsgesellschaft mbH v Einfuhr- und Vorratsstelle für Getreide und Futtermittel* [1970] ECR 1125; Case 4/73, *Nold v European Commission* [1974] ECR 491; Case C-112/00, *Schmidberger v Austria* [2003] ECR I-5659; Case C-36/02, *Omega Spielhallen- und Automatenaufstellungs-GmbH v Oberbürgermeisterin der Bundesstadt Bonn* [2004] ECR I-9609.

[46]   Charter of Fundamental Rights of the European Union, [2007] OJ C303, 14 December 2007.

[47]   The notion is eloquently presented by Bankowski and Christodoulidis, who use the metaphor of the journey to capture the processual conception of constitutionalism. Zenon

rather than defining constitutionalism in terms of static legal hierarchies or formal structures of restraint, this processual approach views constitutionalism as a forum for contestation regarding the values of the political community, where reasonable disagreement is articulated and debated. James Tully's critical and practical constitutionalism is exemplarily of the approach to constitutionalism upon which this third trend in EU constitutional discourse relies.[48] Central to Tully's 'agonistic'[49] conception of constitutionalism, is the acceptance of disagreement 'all the way down',[50] where contestation is central to the constitutional concept itself; something to be celebrated rather than a pathology to be remedied.[51] Thus, reasonable disagreement is both inevitable and profound both within and over the rules of constitutional law.[52] No rule, procedure or agreement is sheltered or protected from contestation or enjoys a higher status or protection contrary to conventional 'entrenched' constitutionalism.[53] Moreover, not only is the subject-matter of contestation unlimited, but also the process of contestation itself is perpetual. As Tully remarks, '[n]o sooner is a constitutional principle, rule or law laid down as the basis of democratic institutions then it is itself open in principle to democratic challenge, deliberation and amendment'.[54] The cornerstone of such dialogic contestatory constitutionalism is *audi alteram partem*,[55] or 'hear the other side', and this is virtually the only certainty which processual constitutionalism offers, given that everything else, up to and including the framework within which the process takes place, is up for contestation.

Bankowski and Emilios Christodoulidis, 'The European Union as an Essentially Contested Project' in Zenon Bankowski and Andrew Scott (eds), *The European Union and its Order* (Oxford, Blackwell, 1999). Examples of the processual approach in EU constitutional discourse include Joshua Cohen and Charles Sabel, 'Directly-Deliberative Polyarchy' (1997) 3 *European Law Journal* 313; Jo Shaw, 'Postnational Constitutionalism in the European Union' (1999) 6:4 *Journal of European Public Policy* 579 and 'Process, Responsibility and Inclusion in EU Constitutionalism' (2003) 9(1) *European Law Journal* 45; Emilios Christodoulidis, 'Constitutional Irresolution: Law and the Framing of Civil Society' (2003) 9(4) *European Law Journal* 401; Michael Wilkinson, 'Civil Society and the Re-imagination of European Constitutionalism' (2003) 9:4 *European Law Journal* 451.

[48] James Tully, 'The Unfreedom of the Moderns in Comparison to Their Ideals of Constitutional Democracy' (2002) 65 *Modern Law Review* 204 (hereinafter 'UM') and *Public Philosophy in a New Key*, 2 vols, (Cambridge, Cambridge University Press, 2009). Although for critique of Tully's approach from within processual constitutional thinking, see Christodoulidis, 'Constitutional Irresolution', above n 47.

[49] Tully, 'UM', above n 48, 208.
[50] UM, 218.
[51] UM, 218.
[52] UM, 218.
[53] UM, 207.
[54] UM, 208.
[55] UM, 218.

Applying this approach to the EU[56] represents a break from teleological accounts of European integration towards political and economic union.[57] It also therefore represents a departure from legalistic approaches to EU constitutionalism, with their path-dependent linear logic of integration,[58] preferring a conceptualisation of the EU in terms of an 'essentially contested concept'.[59]

Moreover, the processual constitutional approach also represents a departure from the certainties which inform the neo-republican approach. For the neo-republican approach, EU constitutionalism represents a clear division of labour between the EU institutions and that of its Member States which, as noted, remain the 'masters of the treaties'. This implies that there are clearly identifiable and objective criteria against which the EU's activities can be evaluated, and in particular, criticised, the *sotto voce* implication being that the sovereign nation-state remains the only truly legitimate political actor. As such, the role of the EU's constitution is to keep the EU's institutions in check by solidifying in law the limitations of the legitimate exercise of the EU's powers. For processual constitutionalism, the picture is not so simple. Constitutionalism as process does not allow for such a clear-cut distinction between competences which allow for a definitive carving up of EU and Member State powers. The legitimacy or otherwise of both EU and Member State competences and their exercise are imminently contestable. Thus, the legitimatory monism which informs neo-republican approaches – essentially legitimacy through legality – is but one aspect of a richer tapestry of EU constitutionalism. Different constituencies will perceive the legitimacy of the exercise of EU and Member State powers differently, and this pluralism must necessarily be factored into the EU constitutional design.

In sum, with respect to some of the fundamental questions which are central to the concerns of EU constitutionalism such as the *finalite* of integration and the appropriate levels of government within the EU constitutional space, disagreement in the EU runs deep and is manifested in a variety of ways, including (admittedly decreasing) national vetoes and treaty 'opt outs';[60] not to speak of the broader dissent among national electorates regarding the nature and role of integration more generally, as was manifested in the failed attempts to draft a self-styled constitutional

[56]   It should be noted that Tully has, himself, commented upon the EU; see Tully, *Public Philosophy*, above n 48.

[57]   See Ernst Haas, *The Uniting of Europe* (London, Stevens & Sons, 1958).

[58]   Jo Shaw, 'European Union Legal Studies in Crisis? Towards a New Dynamic' (1996) 16 *Oxford Journal of Legal Studies* 231.

[59]   Bankowski and Christodoulidis, 'The European Union as an Essentially Contested Project', above n 47.

[60]   Perhaps the most salient in recent times being Poland and the UK's opting out of parts of EU's charter of fundamental rights.

treaty for the polity. Thus, according to this processual trend, an epistemic approach to constitutionalism based on diversity and contestation as opposed to unity, consensus or legally-demarcated competences is both practically and normatively more desirable than modern enlightenment constitutional forms, in a context where 'the very social basis of the polity remains highly contested and very fluid'.[61]

IV.   BIG 'C' OR SMALL 'C': IS THAT THE QUESTION?

What is clear from this mapping exercise of the terrain, is that EU constitutional discourse is varied and complex; a 'mosaic within a mosaic'. However what also emerges is that EU constitutional discourse is part of a more general trend which attempts to forge a new trajectory in the career of the concept from its more familiar state setting. It can be argued that the conception of constitutionalism employed in the EU constitutional discourses represents a *parsing* of the state-based constitutional concept into its constituent parts; fundamental law, checks and balances, constituent power, democratic deliberation etc, and a subsequent *fusion* of the various bits and pieces of the constitutional puzzle for the purposes of their application to a new post-state site. In this way, EU constitutional discourse is engaged in constitutional experimentalism, involving innovations in the (state-based) constitutional idea to suit the particular – and peculiar – circumstances of a post-state supranational polity. Thus, notwithstanding its strong genetic resemblance to state constitutionalism, the concept of constitutionalism employed in EU constitutional discourse, be it legalist, neo-republican or processual, represents, to a certain extent, a *reinterpretation* of its post-Westphalian state variety. This new venture of the constitutional idea trades under a variety of different brand names including 'low intensity constitutionalism',[62] constitutionalism 'with a small c'[63] or 'constitutionalism lite';[64] the EU itself a constitutional body without a soul,[65] a constitutional site yes, but of a different, more anemic form than that of its statist cousin. EU constitutionalism has been spun from the same cloth as national constitutionalism but with a new (more frugal) design more suitable to the conditions and requirements of the supranational polity.

---

[61] Jo Shaw, 'Postnational Constitutionalism', above n 47, 586–7.
[62] Maduro, 'The Importance of Being Called a Constitution', above n 11, 334.
[63] Neil Walker, 'Big "C" or small "c"' (2006) 12:1 *European Law Journal* 12.
[64] Jan Klabbers, 'Constitutionalism Lite' (2004) 1:31 *International Organizations Law Review* 31.
[65] Maduro, 'As Good as it Gets', above n 38, 77.

Perhaps the most salient aspect of this reinterpretation of the constitutional idea in the EU context is its almost complete elision of the concept of sovereignty, primarily due to the fact that the EU is not considered a state and therefore does not enjoy sovereignty. Rather, in the process of parsing and fusing which has been the hallmark of EU constitutionalism, the concept of sovereignty has not made the cut. As such, EU constitutional discourse eschews any suggestions that the *fact* of (small 'c') EU constitutionalism equates with the existence of, or even trajectory towards, a sovereign Europe. Rather, the various trends of EU constitutional discourse entail a conception of constitutionalism which attempts to do without the concept of sovereignty either as a 'social fact' of power or as a normative discourse of the foundation of authority such as constituent power.[66]

As such, the legal positivist tradition which informs legalist approaches to EU constitutionalism whether couched in terms of a *Grundnorm*, rule of recognition or *rechtstaat* has little to say about the concept of sovereignty more generally.[67] Indeed, for MacCormick, who inherits this positivist legacy, twenty-first century Europe is a decidedly sovereignty-free zone. In decoupling hierarchical constitutional law in terms of institutional normative order from a political concept of sovereignty through the notion of the *Rechtstaat*, MacCormick established that the EU could enjoy a constitutional legal order without necessarily being sovereign. Extrapolating from this, MacCormick continues that, not only is the EU not sovereign, but its Member States do not enjoy sovereignty either, due to the fact that they are bound by EU law.[68] Given this state of affairs, MacCormick argues that Europe has moved 'beyond the sovereign state'.[69] In doing so, certain aspects of the state idea have evolved and enjoy continued relevance, such as constitutionalism and law, but others, like sovereignty, are, at least in Europe, becoming increasingly redundant.

An ambivalence with respect to the concept of sovereignty also surrounds neo-republican approaches to EU constitutionalism. Along with the idea of checks and balances, another central tenet of republican theory is the idea of popular sovereignty, where sovereignty resides with a people as opposed to stemming from royal or divine sources.[70] However, in respect

---

[66] Which in normative constitutional discourse is equated with popular sovereignty and constituent power. See Andreas Kalyvas, 'Popular Sovereignty, Democracy, and the Constituent Power' (2005) 12:2 *Constellations* 223.

[67] Carl Schmitt famously critiqued Hans Kelsen's pure theory by claiming that he 'solved the problem of the concept of sovereignty by negating it'. Carl Schmitt, *Political Theology* (Chicago IL, Chicago University Press, 2005) 21.

[68] *QS*, above n 22, 132.

[69] The one slight qualification to this is that MacCormick acknowledges that sovereignty is still relevant externally; that is both the EU and its Member States enjoy a 'compendious legal external sovereignty' to the rest of the world: *QS*, 133.

[70] This is, perhaps, most clearly illustrated in Rousseau's conception of sovereignty as the exercise of the *volunte generale*. Jean-Jacques Rousseau, *The Social Contract* [1762] (Oxford,

of neo-republican EU constitutional discourse, in the absence of the orthodox repository of republican sovereignty, a sovereign European people, the only viable surrogate is that of the sovereign states which created the polity in the first place. Thus, the EU's Member States remain 'masters of the treaties' who have 'pooled' or 'limited' their sovereignty but ultimately retain the final say in matters European.[71] On this view, whereas European *law* can be considered constitutional, its politics remains resolutely international through intergovernmental bargaining reflecting the 'dual character of supranationalism'.[72] Not only does this 'dual character' create problems for the coherence of the idea of EU constitutional *authority* and its implicit hierarchical ordering, but it presupposes a republican discourse without a public.

Processual forms of EU constitutionalism share a common starting point in repudiating sovereignty and attempting to prise open the rigid categories and identities imposed by this modernist concept.[73] In this regard, the processual accounts of constitutionalism serve to highlight and overcome the inadequacies of state-based constitutionalism, and particularly the concept of sovereignty.[74] It is precisely the limitations offered by the concept of sovereignty which have prompted the turn towards more processual, deliberative models of constitutionalism and democratic experimentalism.[75] With its emphasis on 'partisanship, dissent, disagreement, contestation and adversarial reasoning',[76] processual constitutionalism leaves little room for the putative unity and homogeneity imposed

Oxford University Press, 1994) Book II, ch 2. See also John McCormick, 'People and Elites in Republican Constitutions, Traditional and Modern' in Loughlin and Walker (eds), *The Paradox of Constitutionalism*, above n 41.

[71] See Maduro, 'The Importance of Being Called a Constitution', above n 11.

[72] Maduro, 'The Importance of Being Called a Constitution', above n 11, 335. See also for the original account Joseph HH Weiler, 'The Community System: the Dual Character of Supranationality' (1981) 1 *Yearbook of European Law* 267 and 'The Transformation of Europe', above n 2.

[73] For a clear, if somewhat extreme, illustration of this idea, see Michael Hardt and Antonio Negri, *Empire* (Cambridge MA, Harvard University Press, 2000), *Preface*.

[74] Richard Bellamy and Dario Castiglione, 'Building the Union: The Nature of Sovereignty in the Political Architecture of Europe' (1997) 16(4) *Law and Philosophy* 421.

[75] Indeed, in some more radical forms of EU processual constitutionalism such as Cohen and Sabel's 'directly deliberative polyarchy', sovereignty is even accused of causing a broader failure of politics in the twentieth century. Their response to this failure is to fracture centralised political power and with it, leave behind the concept of sovereignty. See Cohen and Sabel, 'Directly-Deliberative Polyarchy', above n 47, 314.

[76] Tully, 'UM', 219.

through state-based conceptions of popular sovereignty. Processual constitutionalism, therefore, relies on the 'diffusion'[77] of sovereignty where the
notion is either repudiated or is ubiquitous such that 'nowhere is it
particularly important'.[78]

In many ways, the absence of an overt discussion of sovereignty in EU
constitutional discourse is not particularly surprising. The very objective of
parsing the concept of constitutionalism into small and big 'c's was to
enable the use of parts of the constitutional idea without the big 'C'
baggage of sovereignty. In particular, one of the apparent main stumbling
blocks of EU constitutionalism is the absence of a Europe-wide *pouvoir
constituant* which would 'consciously will a European political
existence'.[79] This deficiency permeates much political theorising at the EU
level and is genetically linked to the 'no-demos' debate.[80] Thus, parsing the
idea of constitutionalism into a 'small c' form permits the use of the
constitutional idea in respect of the EU without foundering on its lack of
thick political community or sovereign people. Small 'c' constitutionalism,
then, is constitutionalism without a constituent power, a people, and
therefore sovereignty.

This reinterpretation of the idea of constitutionalism to suit the circumstances of the EU, is redolent of the various shades and degrees of familiar
state-based concepts which have populated non-state sites that make up
the broader tapestry of global legal transnationalism of which the EU is but
one, particularly salient, example. However, profound problems of 'translation'[81] affect this wider development, perhaps the most serious of which
is ensuring that the state-based concept adopted retains its epistemological
purchase as a 'way of world-making' beyond its domicile. In order to
ensure this, the relevant 'signifier'[82] of the state-based concept must be
retained. It is submitted that, with respect to the notion of constitutionalism, this signifier is the concept of sovereignty. This claim can be supported
by examining the evolution of the concept of modern constitutionalism at
the state level. For this a brief excursus into the evolution of the state is
warranted.

---

[77] Hans Lindahl, 'Sovereignty and Representation in the EU' in Walker (ed), *Sovereignty in Transition*, above n 38, 92.

[78] Neil Walker, 'Late Sovereignty in the European Union' in Walker (ed), *Sovereignty in Transition*, above n 38, 15.

[79] Paraphrasing Schmitt, see *Constitutional Theory* (Duke NC, Duke University Press, 2008) 127. On the question of constituent power and EU constitutionalism see Walker, 'Post-Constituent Constitutionalism? The Case of the European Union' in Loughlin and Walker (eds), *The Paradox of Constitutionalism*, above n 41.

[80] For a general overview, see Weiler, *The Constitution of Europe*, above n 18, ch 8.

[81] Neil Walker, 'Postnational Constitutionalism and the Problem of Translation' in Weiler and Wind (eds), *European Constitutionalism Beyond the State*, above n 11.

[82] Walker, 'Postnational Constitutionalism and the Problem of Translation' in Weiler and Wind (eds), *European Constitutionalism Beyond the State*, above n 11.

A. Constitutionalism and the State

The idea of constitutionalism has enjoyed a long and illustrious career featuring both in the politics of the ancient world as well as appearing at the vanguard of political theories of transnationalism and globalisation.[83] However, in its modern form, constitutionalism is inextricably linked to the co-evolution of the state and the concept of sovereignty as a form of political and legal organisation.[84]

The state emerged out of the governing arrangements of the medieval period, incorporating feudal bonds and the overarching authority of the Roman church.[85] Central to its development was the emergence of an idea of sovereignty which entailed the centralisation of power in one locus as opposed to the prevailing fragmented power arrangements.[86] This was achieved, to a large extent, through the adoption of law – latterly positive law – as a form of rule which, given its universal application and simplifying tendencies, provided both an intelligible and efficient means of transmitting the power of the sovereign to an ever broader constituency.[87] Law's general and universal application made it a useful tool in the dissemination of political power, given that it could traverse the various extant societal divisions; regional, sectoral and patrimonial. This, in turn, enhanced efficiency by obviating the need for 'particularized modes of conflict resolution'.[88]

As Thornhill notes, this rise in the use of legal forms in sites which evolved into states was indispensible to the rise of the *political power* of the sovereign and the development of an autonomous political realm central to the concept of sovereignty, but distinct from, and superior to, morality, economy and perhaps most fundamentally, ecclesiastical authority.[89] This increase in the use of legal forms of rule in turn provoked

---

[83] See generally, Charles McIlwain, *Constitutionalism: Ancient and Modern* (Indianapolis IN, Liberty, 1975); Bardo Fassbender, *The United Nations Charter as the constitution of the international community* (Leiden, Martinus Nijhoff, 2009); Jeffrey Dunoff, 'The politics of international constitutions: the curious case of the WTO' in Jeffrey Dunnof and Joel Trachtman (eds), *Ruling the World? Constitutionalism, International law, and Global Governance* (Cambridge, Cambridge University Press, 2009); Gunther Teubner, 'Societal Constitutionalism: Alternatives to State-Centered Constitutional Theory?' in Christian Joerges, Inger-Johanne Sand and Gunther Teubner (eds), *Transnational Governance and Constitutionalism* (Oxford, Hart Publishing, 2004).

[84] Chris Thornhill, 'Towards a historical sociology of constitutional legitimacy' (2008) 37 *Theory and Society* 161.

[85] See generally Michael Oakeshott, *On Human Conduct* (Oxford, Clarendon, 1975) ch 3; David Held, *Democracy and the Global Order* (Cambridge, Polity, 1995) Pt II; and Martin van Creveld, *The Rise and Decline of the State* (Cambridge, Cambridge University Press, 1999).

[86] See particularly Oakeshott, *ibid.*

[87] Thornhill, 'Towards a historical sociology', above n 84, 172.

[88] Thornhill, 'Towards a historical sociology', above n 84, 171.

[89] Martin Loughlin, *The Idea of Public Law* (Oxford, Oxford University Press, 2003).

the extrapolation of legally informed theoretical principles which attempted to validate the origins and actions of political institutions[90] and coincided with the rise of theories of political legitimacy which predicated the legitimacy of sovereignty and the autonomy of the political on natural law or the social contract.[91] This development reached its zenith during the Enlightenment where this twofold development of functional autonomy and philosophical justification was fused in a concept of constitutionalism made up of a *pouvoir constituant* and *pouvoir constitué*.[92]

What is clear from this evolution is that the modern constitutional idea emerged *as a facet of the concept of sovereignty*. The concept of constitutionalism under conditions of political modernity, therefore, is incorrigibly anchored in the concept of sovereignty, which is, in turn, an expression of the autonomy of the political realm.[93] The modern concept of constitutionalism then, has a specific teleology, that of serving the ends of the maintenance of sovereignty and the preservation of autonomy of the political by tracing 'the boundaries between the political system and other areas of social practice, and in so doing ... preserv[ing] its autonomy and legitimacy as concentrated around a set of evidently limited political issues'.[94]

If, at root, constitutionalism is an expression of sovereignty, then a constitutional discourse which ignores the concept of sovereignty is problematic. As such, constitutionalism relates to a specific form of power – *sovereign* power – which in turn implies an autonomous realm of legitimate authority that makes claims to hierarchy and obedience. Therefore constitutional discourse necessarily presupposes claims to *ultimate authority* and *hierarchy*. To dismiss this essential aspect of constitutionalism, it is submitted, is to dismiss the essence of the constitutional idea itself, making a 'sovereignty-less' constitutionalism oxymoronic. The oxymoronic nature of a constitutionalism without sovereignty creates problems for the characterisation of the EU as a constitutional polity in EU constitutional discourse. These manifest themselves in each of the trends in EU constitutional discourse outlined above which, on close analysis, betray deficiencies or incoherencies in their characterisation of the EU as a constitutional polity.

---

[90] For an early account of this development see Walter Ullman, 'The Development of the Medieval Idea of Sovereignty' (1949) 64 *English Historical Review* 1.

[91] Thornhill, 'Towards a historical sociology', above n 84, 173.

[92] Thornhill, 'Towards a historical sociology', above n 84, 173. See also Griffin, 'Constituent Power and Constitutional Change' and Lucien Jaume 'Constituent Power in France: The Revolution and its Consequences' in Loughlin and Walker (eds), *The Paradox of Constitutionalism* (Oxford, Oxford University Press, 2007).

[93] Loughlin, *The Idea of Public Law*, above n 89.

[94] Thornhill, 'Towards a historical sociology', above n 84, 175.

First, with regard to the legalistic forms of EU constitutionalism, sovereignty provides the key ingredient which distinguishes the EU from other forms of legal organisation as a genuinely constitutional polity. In removing the constitutional idea from the conceptual context of sovereignty, legalistic accounts of EU constitutionalism run the risk of definitional inflation such that defining the EU in constitutional terms proves to be of limited heuristic value. Even if we bracket MacCormick's not uncontroversial post-sovereignty thesis, which arguably, like Kelsen, dismisses the essential political element of sovereignty,[95] there is a question as to the 'added value' of describing the EU as constitutional in terms of *Rechtstaat*. If the requirements of constitutionalism relate to a basic idea of an institutional normative order, what is it that differentiates the EU *qua* constitutional entity from other forms of post-state (and indeed sub-state) legal forms? Such a minimalist concept of constitutionalism runs a real risk of succumbing to the charges of 'golf club governance' levelled at the attempt to draft a constitutional-style document for the EU.[96] The constitutional epithet simply becomes yet another label for the supranational structure, yet another proxy for the empty idea of the *sui generis* polity. It is the sovereignty claims at the EU level which make the EU constitutional and distinguish this particular legal system from other forms of inter-state cooperation.

This problem of definitional inflation is also present in neo-republican accounts of EU constitutionalism, where the use of law as a restraint on political and administrative power is evidenced at many diverse sites at both the post-state and sub-state level. This account of constitutionalism, moreover, has an affinity with the Global Administrative law movement which, somewhat paradoxically, attempts to distance itself from the post-state constitutional discourse as a much more modest way of capturing the increasing transnationalisation of constitutional values and legal forms.[97] However, to this inflationary problem can be added a basic question of logical consistency. If constitutionalism as a form of restraining power is adopted in the absence of sovereign power, as the neo-republican view seems to espouse, the question arises as to *what form of power is being restrained?* As noted above, constitutionalism emerged as a facet of sovereignty and, as such, in its legitimating function, it was aimed at restraining *sovereign* power. If EU constitutionalism does not relate to sovereign power, or if sovereign power is absent at the EU level, then the

---

[95] For a critique in this vein see Loughlin, *The Idea of Public Law*, above n 89, 88–93.

[96] This refers to UK Foreign Minister Jack Straw's claim, during the drafting of the Constitutional Treaty, that even golf clubs have constitutions. See *The Economist*, 12 October 2002.

[97] See Benedict Kingsbury et al, 'The Emergence of Global Administrative Law' (2005) 68 *Law and Contemporary Problems* 15, and Benedict Kingsbury, 'The Concept of "Law" in Global Administrative Law' (2009) 20:1 *European Journal of International Law* 23–57.

restraining function of constitutionalism, which is at the forefront of neo-republican accounts, becomes logically incoherent. If the EU is not sovereign, then what need is there for *constitutional* law to restrain it?

Finally, with respect to the processual trend of EU constitutionalism, disagreement, which is axiomatic in processual constitutionalism, requires an *a priori agreement* regarding with whom, and over what, to disagree. Sovereignty provides the vital *frame* within which deliberation can take place. Without such agreement, the disagreement central to processual constitutionalism can never get off the ground. The concept of sovereignty, with its claims to ultimate authority and hierarchy over individuals and its *conscious designation of certain issues as political*, allows actors to identify themselves as participants in the deliberative process, as well as providing a 'particular' over which to deliberate. Without such a non-negotiable, non-contestable agreement providing a fulcrum around which disagreement can gravitate, contestation becomes chaotic unmediated 'noise'.

Therefore EU constitutionalism needs the concept of sovereignty in order to ensure the conceptual coherence of the idea of EU constitutionalism as well as to ensure that constitutionalism retains its practical utility as a way of producing a relevant political way of knowing and understanding the EU. Thus, for the EU to be characterised as a constitutional polity, it must simultaneously be a sovereign polity.

V.   LOCATING SOVEREIGNTY IN THE EU

As noted above, justifications of sovereignty in modern constitutionalism have revolved around the notion of *pouvoir constituant*, the power to constitute legitimate order.[98] From the perspective of modern accounts of constitutional origins, the search for sovereignty in the EU constitutional order is prima facie inauspicious. The EU's constitutional order is not the product of a revolutionary overthrow of an *ancien regime*. Indeed, it was arguably not conceived of in constitutional terms at all when the original treaties were signed by the founding six Member States in the 1950s.

However, the discourse of a constituent power in modern constitutionalism, as noted, is part of the *justificatory narrative* of sovereign power and therefore sovereignty precedes constitutionalism. This, then, begs the question of what *sovereignty* constitutes. Sovereignty, can be defined as a normative claim to a particular type of authority: *ultimate* authority over a

---

[98]   See Kalyvas, 'Popular Sovereignty', above n 66.

particular territory and people.[99] As a form of normative claim, or 'speech act', then, sovereignty does not relate to a simple 'fact' of power, nor can it be equated with an ethnic, cultural or historic community.[100] Rather, sovereignty relates to an unambiguous assertion of ultimate authority which is 'plausible'[101] in the sense that it is heeded to a significant degree by those over whom the claim is made, reflecting the 'relational' nature of the concept.[102] Moreover, as Werner and de Wilde note, as a claimed status to ultimate authority, sovereignty is always at stake – permanently contestable,[103] and so sovereignty claims are therefore necessarily *iterative*. As a result of the precarious nature of sovereign status, assertions of sovereignty are likely to be more pronounced where that status is threatened or weak;[104] empty sovereign vessels make the most noise.

Moreover, as noted above, given that the justificatory discourse of sovereignty and its derivations such as constitutionalism, are concerned with the validity or justification of political power which is exogenous to the justificatory discourse itself, sovereignty claims are always *self-validating*. The very emergence of the concept of sovereignty itself as explaining the centralisation of power in the state required a justification independent of existing justificatory forms such as feudalism or Christendom to seal its autonomy. Thus, sovereign claims always appear self-referential and self-norming when viewed from an external point of view. In this way, initial sovereign claims, paradigmatically declarations of independence, always constitute a transgression of established order.[105] Revolutions are never legal.[106]

Therefore, to dismiss the possibility of an EU sovereignty claim due to the fact that it cannot be said to entail a credible constituent power is, it is submitted, to put the cart before the horse. Sovereign claims to authority

[99] See generally Wouter Werner and Jaap de Wilde, 'The Endurance of Sovereignty' (2001) 7(3) *European Journal of International Relations* 283 and Walker, 'Late Sovereignty in the European Union' in Walker (ed), *Sovereignty in Transition*, above n. 38.

[100] Werner and de Wilde, 'The Endurance of Sovereignty', above n 99. Hobbes, notably in this regard, was clear in predicating his theory of sovereignty on a 'commonwealth by design [civitas institutiva]': Thomas Hobbes, *On the Citizen*, Richard Tuck and Michael Silverthorne (eds) (Cambridge, Cambridge University Press, 1998 [1641]) 102.

[101] Walker, 'Late Sovereignty in the European Union' in Walker (ed), *Sovereignty in Transition*, above n. 38, 17.

[102] Werner and de Wilde, 'The Endurance of Sovereignty', above n 99, and Loughlin, *The Idea of Public Law*, above n 89.

[103] Werner and de Wilde, *ibid*, 287.

[104] *ibid*, 286.

[105] For example, the US declaration of independence, a paradigmatic sovereignty claim, was, from the point of view of the *ancien regime* UK constitutional order, a breach of the established order. On this point see Hans Lindahl, 'Acquiring a Community: The *Acquis* and the Institution of European Legal Order' (2003) 9(4) *European Law Journal* 433, 434.

[106] Hannah Arendt, *On Revolution* (London, Penguin, 1990). See also Jacques de Ville, 'Sovereignty without sovereignty: Derrida's *Declarations of Independence*' (2008) 19 *Law and Critique* 87.

and hierarchy *necessarily precede the justification and validation of these claims* through justificatory discourses such as that of a constituent power.[107] To insist upon an ontological constituent power to justify sovereign claims in *any* constitutional context is to reify the concept of sovereignty and willfully to ignore the necessarily unjustifiable origins of *any* sovereignty claim.[108] Therefore, rather than a putatively credible constituent power, the necessary a priori of a constitutional discourse is an unambiguous and plausible claim to ultimate authority made within an institutional context to which such justificatory discourses can attach. This, it is argued, is present in the ECJ's interpretation of the EU's legal and political system.

A. We the Court

The early judgments of the ECJ, as noted, were the original catalyst for the evolution of EU constitutional discourse. However, they can also be interpreted in terms of sovereignty claims on behalf of the EU.[109] For example, in establishing the doctrine of direct effect in *Van Gend en Loos*, the ECJ found that[110]

> the [then EEC] Treaty is more than an agreement which merely creates mutual obligations between the contracting states ... [t]he Community constitutes a new legal order of international law for the benefit of which states have limited their sovereign rights, albeit within limited fields, and the subjects of which comprise not only their Member States but also their nationals.

Thus, the Court was claiming a particular status for the EU's legal system which was not evident from a literal reading of the Treaties. In this way, the ECJ's interpretation constituted a *transgression* of established order through legal interpretation.[111] It is this transgressive interpretation which supports the contention that the decision constitutes a sovereignty claim. As noted above, sovereignty claims are always unauthorised from the point of view of the *status quo*, an act of 'seizing the initiative'.[112]

The decision constitutes a transgression of established order because the Court had no prior authority to interpret the Treaty system in this way.

---

[107] Which is the basis of the 'no demos' thesis in EU constitutional discourse. See Joseph HH Weiler, 'Does Europe Need a Constitution? Demos, Telos and the German Maastricht Decision' (1995) 1(3) *European Law Journal* 219.

[108] Something which Hobbes himself, acknowledged, finding that 'there is scarce a Commonwealth in the world, whose beginnings can in conscience be justified': Thomas Hobbes, *Leviathan*, Richard Tuck (ed) (Cambridge, 1996 [1651]) 486.

[109] See Lindahl, 'Sovereignty and Representation in the EU', above n 77.

[110] *Van Gend en Loos*, [1963] ECR 1, 12.

[111] Lindahl, 'Acquiring a Community', above n 105, 434.

[112] Lindahl, 'Acquiring a Community', above n 105, 440.

Under a conventional – one could say *ancien regime* – reading, the Treaties were international agreements signed by sovereign states, and binding under international law only, and only had domestic effect in accordance with national constitutional requirements. However, the Court deliberately rejected this conventional reading by finding that the Treaty system constituted a 'a new legal order of international law',[113] basing its finding on less than convincing evidence.[114] However, it is precisely the paucity of evidence for such a reading of the Treaties as a new legal order which makes this interpretation a transgression. Were the Treaty structure to unambiguously assert the novelty of the treaty system vis-à-vis international law, then the ECJ's claims would have appeared very conventional.[115]

This initial transgression of established order by the ECJ was quickly followed by a strong claim to the *autonomy* of the EU legal system, validated in self-referential language in the *Costa v ENEL* decision. In this decision in particular, a clear sovereignty claim is discernable presupposing the existence of an autonomous European political realm. In answering a preliminary reference from an Italian court with respect to the role of EU law in national legal systems, the Court found that[116]

> by contrast with ordinary international treaties, the EEC Treaty has created its own legal system which, on the entry into force of the Treaty, became an integral part of the legal systems of the Member States and which their courts are bound to apply.

In this passage, the Court supplemented its transgressive reading of the Treaties with an unambiguous assertion of the sovereign authority of the legal order. In doing so, the Court went on to articulate the logical corollary of autonomy as a sovereignty claim by emphasising the *hierarchical* nature of the EU's legal system, where[117]

> the transfer by the States from their domestic legal system to the Community legal system of the rights and obligations arising under the Treaty carries with it a permanent limitation of their sovereignty rights, against which a subsequent

---

[113] *Van Gend en Loos*, [1963] ECR 1, 12.

[114] Gráinne de Búrca, 'Sovereignty and the Supremacy Doctrine of the European Court of Justice' in Neil Walker (ed), *Sovereignty in Transition*, above n 38.

[115] There are those who argue that the ECJ's assertions of the constitutional doctrines of the Treaty system were highly conventional – a perfectly reasonable interpretation of the text of the Treaty and its structural implications, and so anything *but* transgressive. See, for example, J Baquero Cruz, 'The Changing Constitutional Role of the European Court of Justice' (2006) 34 *International Journal of Legal Information* 223–45. However, while one could quibble with the transgressive nature of the establishment of direct effect in isolation, it is argued that it is but one factor in a broader picture of the Court's activity which *cumulatively* constitute a sovereignty claim (see further below).

[116] *Costa v ENEL*, [1964] ECR 585, 593.

[117] *ibid*, 594.

unilateral act incompatible with the concept of Community cannot prevail. Consequently, Community law is to be applied regardless of any domestic law, whenever questions relating to the interpretation of the Treaty arise.

Thus, the Court held that the EU entailed a sovereign legal order through its authority and autonomy. Moreover, this sovereignty claim serves to demarcate an autonomous political realm of the EU. The autonomy of the political realm relates to the notion that the political domain has distinct 'purposes, concerns or interests that set it apart from the divisive activities of sectarian social actors and the aims that motivate them'.[118] Therefore, the assertion of an EU political domain implies that the EU has its own purposes, concerns and interests distinct from those of its Member States. As much was intimated by the Court in this decision where it found that the then EEC is not concerned with the politics of its Member States or their relations *inter se*, but with its own particular concerns and interests expressed in the 'terms and spirit of the Treaty'[119] with its own clear objectives whose attainment cannot be jeopardised by the politics of its Member States.[120]

Moreover, as noted, the transgression implicit in initial sovereignty claims necessarily entails a self-validating justification of the assertion of that sovereignty. This self-validation is clearly illustrated by the ECJ's reasoning in support of the autonomy of the legal system:[121]

> [T]he law stemming from the Treaty, an *independent* source of law, could not, because of its special and original nature, be overridden by domestic legal provisions, however framed, without being deprived of its character as Community law, and without the legal basis of the Community being called into question.

The Court reasons that EU law is independent and original and as such, cannot be overridden by provisions of national law, because if it were susceptible to national law override, then it would not be independent and original;[122] the Court effectively ends up back where it started. As noted, every sovereign claim entails such circular logic (witness the 'self evident truths' of the US declaration of independence) and where the sovereign claim is made in a legal register such as in the EU context, the tautology is particularly pronounced given the strong justificatory nature of law as a normative discourse. Thus, the fact that the Court was effectively 'pulling

---

[118] Joshua Flaherty, 'The Autonomy of the Political' (Unpublished PhD Thesis, Massachusetts Institute of Technology, 2003) 7.
[119] *Costa v ENEL*, [1964] ECR 585, 593.
[120] *ibid*, 594.
[121] *ibid*, 594.
[122] Lindahl, 'Sovereignty and Representation in the EU', above n 77, and de Burca, '*Sovereignty and the Supremacy Doctrine*', above n 114, 115.

itself up by its own bootstraps',[123] simply serves to reinforce its nature as a necessarily self-validating sovereignty claim.

Thus, these early decisions can be interpreted as sovereignty claims in respect of the EU where the ECJ claimed the ultimate authority of the EU legal system over national systems through a transgressive reading of the treaties supported by explicitly self-validating normative claims. Moreover, in this regard, the ECJ was staking a claim to the sovereignty of the EU and the autonomy of a European political realm, such that the concerns and interests of the EU were independent of those of its constituent Member States.

As noted above, as a claimed status, sovereignty is precarious and must be defended through reiterations of the sovereignty claim. Moreover, such iterations tend to be more forceful when sovereign status is threatened or at risk. This applies as much to the ECJ's assertion of the sovereignty of the EU as to any other sovereignty claim. There are many ECJ decisions which constitute an iteration of the EU's sovereignty claims. However, the Court's *Kadi* decision, one of the most important in recent years, is a particularly clear example of the iterative nature of the EU's sovereignty claims.[124]

B. '*Kadi* Justice' or Sovereignty Claim?

This important decision involved a challenge to the validity of an EU Regulation in the context of 'smart sanctions' adopted by the United Nations Security Council aimed at individuals who were suspected of belonging to Al-Qaida.[125] The effect of the resolution was effectively to freeze the assets of any individual or organisation which appeared on the suspect list. The EU adopted a number of measures to implement resolutions, particularly Regulation No 467/2001, which listed Kadi in its annex as a person suspected of supporting terrorism and whose assets in EU Member States were duly frozen. Mr Kadi brought an action against his listing pursuant to the Regulation, challenging its validity on the grounds of inter alia breaches of fundamental rights, which, he claimed, were protected under the EU's legal order. In particular, he argued that his listing pursuant to a secret procedure resulting in the sequestering of personal assets violated his rights to property and to due process. Both the ECJ and

---

[123] Bruno de Witte, 'Direct Effect, Supremacy and the Nature of the Legal Order' in Paul Craig and de Burca (eds), *The Evolution of EU Law* (Oxford, Oxford University Press, 1999) 199.

[124] Joined Cases C-402/05 P and C-415/05 P, *Kadi and Al-Barakaat International Foundation*, judgment of 3 September 2008, [2008] ECR I-6351 (hereinafter *Kadi*).

[125] For a detailed overview see Hinoja Martinez, 'The Legislative Role of the Security Council in its fight against Terrorism: Legal, Political and Practical Limits' (2008) 57 *International and Comparative Law Quarterly* 333.

its Advocate-General found that the EU Regulation which implemented the UN resolutions violated basic due process rights as well as the right to property which were protected under the EU's legal system,[126] and the Regulation was duly invalidated.[127]

The decision has prompted much commentary ranging from the lawfulness of the basis of the EU Regulation,[128] to the potential problems for the uniformity of international law provoked by the judgment[129] and the redefinition of the relationship between international law and EU law.[130] However, as noted, the judgment also constitutes a robust iteration of the EU's sovereignty claim.

In its reasoning, the Court at several junctures in a long and complex judgment stressed the autonomy of the legal system as it had done almost 50 years previously. However, in this decision, the ECJ extrapolated from this claim finding that[131]

> the review by the Court of the validity of any Community measure in the light of fundamental rights must be considered to be the *expression*, in a community based on the rule of law, of a constitutional guarantee stemming from the EC Treaty *as an autonomous legal system which is not to be prejudiced by an international agreement*. The question of the Court's jurisdiction arises in the context of the *internal and autonomous order of the community* within whose ambit the contested regulation falls and in which the Court has jurisdiction to review the validity of Community measures in the light of fundamental rights (my emphasis).

Moreover the context within which this case was decided, one of 'competing claims to authority',[132] is paradigmatic of when sovereignty claims are most likely to be asserted. Legally speaking, the case presented a conflict between the obligations of the EU's Member States under the EU Treaty system and their obligations under the UN Charter (of which they are all signatories) including Security Council resolutions under Article 25 of the UN Charter. According to Article 103 of the Charter, the obligations of Member States must *prevail over any other international obligations* assumed by the states, therefore including the obligations assumed by EU

---

[126]   *Kadi*, [2008] ECR I-6351, paras 348, 352 and 370.

[127]   *Kadi*, [2008] ECR I-6351, para 372.

[128]   Takis Tridimas and Jose Gutierrez-Fons, 'EU Law, International Law, and Economic Sanctions against Terrorism: The Judiciary in Distress?' (2009) 32 *Fordham International Law Journal* 660.

[129]   G de Burca, 'The EU, the European Court of Justice and the International Legal Order after Kadi' (2009) 51 *Harvard International Law Journal* 1–49.

[130]   de Burca, *ibid*, and Samantha Besson, 'European Legal Pluralism after *Kadi*' (2009) 5(2) *European Constitutional Law Review* 237.

[131]   *Kadi*, [2008] ECR I-6351, paras 316–17.

[132]   Werner and de Wilde, 'The Endurance of Sovereignty', above n 99, 286. In this regard, they highlight how Hobbes, Bodin and Schmitt developed their own theories of sovereignty against a backdrop of political instability.

membership. Article 307 (now Article 351 TFEU) of the EC Treaty, moreover, provided that obligations assumed under the EC Treaty will not be affected by international obligations undertaken *prior* to EU membership, which clearly includes the UN Charter and measures taken thereunder, including Security Council resolutions. Interpreting this provision on the prior assumption of international obligations by the EU's Member States, the ECJ found that this would lead to the primacy of the Charter in matters of secondary Community law *only*.[133] It would not, the Court found, permit 'any challenge to the principles that *form part of the very foundations of the Community legal order*' (my emphasis),[134] and therefore could not authorise any derogation from the 'principles of liberty, democracy and respect for human rights and fundamental freedoms'[135] protected by the EU. Thus, the Court was reasserting the autonomy of the community legal order and its own jurisdiction to review the impugned measures as an expression of the sovereignty of the system as a whole. Moreover, this independence was asserted not, or not only, internally as against national legal orders – which was the case in *Costa* – but rather *externally*, as against the international legal order, and the UN Charter in particular when this system potentially challenged the autonomy of the EU's system by claiming primacy over the EU system as was argued in the case. In this regard the Court was making a clear sovereign claim in the sense of asserting the independence from international law of the EU's legal order. Thus, the EU no longer constitutes a 'new order of international law' but is an autonomous, sovereign order, which is *emphatically not* subject to the international legal order which applies in the EU only in accordance with and on the terms of, EU law. In asserting this independence from international law, the Court was asserting the robustly *dualist* nature of the EU legal order vis-à-vis the reception of international law, a classic sovereign prerogative exercised by states in the international system.[136] Thus, the EU was asserting the autonomy of the EU political realm in the teeth of the 'international law of international laws' that is the UN Charter with its clear requirement of primacy under Article 103.[137]

---

[133]   *Kadi*, [2008] ECR I-6351, para 307.

[134]   *Kadi*, [2008] ECR I-6351, para 304.

[135]   *Kadi*, [2008] ECR I-6351, para 303.

[136]   See Ian Brownlie, *Principles of Public International Law* (Oxford, Oxford University Press, 2008) ch 2. In the context of the UK, a classically dualist state, see *R v Secretary of State for the Home Department, ex parte Brind* [1991] 1 AC 696 (HL).

[137]   Contrast the ECJ's approach with the approach of the UK's House of Lords in its Al Jedda judgment, *R (Al Jedda) v Secretary of State for Defense* [2007] UKHL 58, [2008] 1 AC 332. Here the House of Lords found that the UK's obligations assumed under the UN Charter took precedence over national fundamental rights protections contained in the Human Rights Act and the UK's obligations under the European Convention of Human Rights. EU law was not engaged in this case.

Finally, as well as asserting its autonomy externally, the ECJ in this decision was asserting its sovereignty internally by simultaneously justifying this autonomy through the language of fundamental rights protection. As described above, constitutionalism is a facet of sovereignty and has served to maintain and preserve the autonomy of the political realm. Constitutional rights, in particular, have in played a particularly important role in this function. As Thornhill notes,[138]

> constitutional rights are ... the forms in which states have produced generalized and normatively acceptable descriptions of their activities and foundations: they are also the normative prerequisites of state legitimacy ... By guaranteeing constitutional rights, a state acts to articulate and to reinforce the conditions of its necessary functional autonomy and to provide a theoretical explanation of its legitimacy in terms likely to command respect from and integrate those to whom rights are applied.

The ECJ's development of a fundamental rights jurisprudence has been well documented.[139] However, to reiterate, it is significant that fundamental or constitutional rights were also at stake in the *Kadi* decision in the sense that as well as asserting its autonomy as against international law, the Court was simultaneously legitimating its sovereignty claim internally in the language of fundamental rights.

In sum, in order to discover an unambiguous sovereignty claim in the EU context which can support EU constitutional discourse, one need look no further than the catalyst for the constitutional discourse itself; the ECJ's important early decisions. Moreover, these claims have permeated the ECJ's case law over the years, reflecting the iterative nature of sovereignty claims. The *Kadi* case in particular, provides a recent and robust iteration of these sovereignty claims. This, in turn, presupposes the autonomy of an EU political realm with its own concerns and interests over and above the politics of its Member States.

VI.   CONCLUSION

This contribution has sought to argue that the EU constitutional discourse is a complex and variegated element within Europe's broader constitutional mosaic, which has remained incomplete due to the absence of the concept of sovereignty. Sovereignty, it was argued, essentially keeps the mosaic in place. It vitiates the charge of definitional inflation which can be

---

[138] Thornill, 'Towards a Historical Sociology', above n 84, 176.
[139] See above n 45. For an overview, see Craig and de Burca, *EU Law*, 4th edn (Oxford, Oxford University Press, 2008) ch 11.

levelled, in particular, at legalist forms of EU constitutional discourse, as not all rule-based entities such as golf clubs can be described as constitutional; it is only those which make sovereignty claims and to which an autonomous political realm can be attributed which warrant the epithet constitutional. Moreover, the EU's sovereignty claims provide ballast to the checks and balances of the neo-republican accounts of EU constitutionalism. Checks and balances only make sense when *sovereign* power is at stake as it, in the final analysis, constitutes the threat to *political* liberty. Finally, sovereignty provides the frame for processual constitutional discourse. It is in this regard that the self-authorising logic of sovereignty is most pronounced, given that the sovereignty claim itself cannot be part of the deliberative process. However, it also highlights the role of sovereignty in facilitating disagreement, even radical disagreement, which has practical normative effects.

To include the concept of sovereignty in EU constitutionalism, it was argued, diminishes these risks and helps to firmly root the EU as a constitutional polity. Without sovereignty, EU constitutionalism can only be a partial theory of the EU which is vulnerable to charges of conceptual incoherence and definitional inflation. The EU's sovereignty claims indicate precisely what is unique about the EU as a constitutional polity.

Thus, the EU is a constitutional polity precisely because it makes claims to sovereignty both over its Member States and externally, against the international community as a whole, as was demonstrated in the ECJ's *Kadi* decision. That the EU's sovereignty claims occur in the context of court judgments as opposed to declarations of independence – the sovereignty register of choice in modernity – does not undermine their status as unambiguous claims to sovereignty and the autonomy of an EU political realm. Rather, the sovereignty claims of the ECJ clarify the nature of the EU as a form of legal and political activity, ensuring that the picture presented is one which is both familiar and intelligible to those over whom it claims to govern.

The EU's sovereignty has always been precarious and it has had to constantly nurture this relationship to preserve and maintain its autonomous political realm, a task which is becoming increasingly difficult. EU sovereignty is of a much more attenuated nature than the sovereignty of its Member States and the legitimacy problems in terms of lack of identification, affiliation and understanding from its citizens – attributes central to the *relational* concept of sovereignty – that were so painfully exposed during the ratification crises of the Constitutional and Lisbon treaties, are major problems which the constitutional polity faces. The solution to stabilising the EU's sovereignty claims is beyond the scope of this contribution. However, a remedy is impossible without a proper diagnosis, which requires an adequate representation of the EU. In constructing this representation, whereas constitutionalism provides the 'tiles' of this particular mosaic, sovereignty provides its overall shape.

3

An Area Of Darkness: Three Conceptions of the Relationship Between European Union Law and State Constitutional Law

JULIO BAQUERO CRUZ*

And even now, though time has widened, though space has contracted and I have travelled lucidly over that area which was to me the area of darkness, something of darkness remains, in those attitudes, those ways of thinking and seeing, which are no longer mine.

VS Naipaul

I. INTRODUCTION

A N AREA OF *Darkness* is the title of a remarkable book by VS Naipaul. The writer, or rather his fictional counterpart (or else an ideal mind that strives to stand between and above both, on the proper grounds of literary art), born in Trinidad to Indian parents who were also born there, educated at Oxford on a fellowship, travels to India for the first time. It is the land of his ancestors, but he knows little about it. Only his readings on India,[1] some family traditions and a number of memories maintain the link with it. When he is there, at first sight he seems an Indian to the Indians, but he knows he is an outsider, and they can feel

* Member of the Legal Service of the European Commission. Visiting Professor at Sciences Po (Paris). All opinions expressed in this chapter are purely personal and are not necessarily shared by the institution for which I work. This paper was presented at the School of Law at The University of Edinburgh on 10 October 2008 and at a seminar at the Centro de Estudios Políticos y Constitucionales in Madrid on 14 October 2008. Thanks are due to the participants at both venues for their comments and criticism.
[1] But he might have 'been reading the wrong books', as someone tells him at the beginning of his journey (VS Naipaul, *An Area of Darkness* (London, Picador, 2002) 21).

it too. There is something odd about him, something unfamiliar in his way of speaking, in his attitudes. Too British, perhaps; one of those emigrants that come back for a holiday, they might think. But he gets along, with his dubious status as an insider and also as an outsider, a sort of double agent in India, which will always remain for him what the title announces: an area of darkness. Of darkness surrounding him with so many new things, uncanny things as well and a mix of attraction and repulsion, of familiarity and strangeness, to that India he is starting to discover. Of darkness, also and mainly, within him, for his experiences are discovering whole new dimensions of his own personality; new reactions, a new self which slowly emerges through the book, revealing its character precisely in the space left blank by the fracture of that self – the fracture between the insider and the outsider – revealing a character, moreover, which is tainted by a deep sense of loss and a deep pessimism, both about India and about himself.

This book and the situation of its desolate narrator provide a rich and very productive metaphor for the position of the European Community lawyer and of European Community law itself (or European Union lawyer and European Union law, if you will, now that the 'Community' has become legal history) when they travel to the sometimes uncanny territories of the laws of the Member States and find themselves transfigured, almost unrecognisable, a very different thing indeed. That experience is also an experience of dislocation, of loss, and it might lead to pessimism about the status, value and identity of European Union law. But it could also lead to an attempt to establish a more solid mechanism to mediate between the original self of Community law and the distorted self it sees when it looks into the mirror of State law, that area of darkness in which things slowly emerge, but only the other way around.[2] And it is, in any event, a curious and unavoidable experience.

From one point of view, it is clear that for more than half a century the law of European integration has been radically altering the European legal landscape, and it will probably continue to alter it. This transformation is the juridical counterpart of spectacular changes in the political landscape since the 1950s. But the new reality can be seen in many different lights and from many different angles. There is no consensus on a common perspective, but several competing and often contradictory conceptions. In particular, the relationship between the law of European integration and the constitutional laws of the Member States has traditionally been problematic, at least around the edges (where, paradoxically, the 'core' becomes essential) and will probably remain so for a long time. And that

---

[2] For a similar point of view about the distortion of Union law when seen from the perspective of international law, see Joseph HH Weiler, *The Constitution of Europe* (Cambridge, Cambridge University Press, 1999) 290, quoting *Alice in Wonderland*: 'that's just the same ... only things go the other way'.

means that the transformative potential of the supranational law of the European Union sometimes encounters resistance from actors that are crucial for its proper application.

Here as elsewhere, interpretation is not only passive but also constitutive and reflexive. It does much more than just perceiving its object. It creates and changes what it interprets, and at the same time it immediately changes or reinforces the identity of the interpreting subject vis-à-vis the interpreted object. Even the seemingly descriptive proposition with which I began the previous paragraph is loaded with normative assumptions. Many will disagree with the adverb 'radically' or with the adjective 'spectacular'. Some may argue that the alteration has been limited at most, even that there has not been any essential alteration and only limited changes. Our interpretations thus tend to produce several versions of the European Union and its law, and also different views of national constitutional law and of the relationship between the two.

This flexibility, at its base a flexibility about the very meaning of being a Member State of the European Union or a European citizen, is an indispensable political and legal condition for the existence of the Union – in particular of our enlarged Union. It opens up a space of compromise, a meeting place of sorts, which can only exist surrounded by a grey zone in which endless processes of definition and redefinition of boundaries and relationships take place at all levels between norms and practice. Such flexibility is both a strength and a weakness of the European Union. It might be something difficult to sustain in the long run, but at present it seems to be a constitutive characteristic of the Union.

The advantages and disadvantages of such openness and flexibility are clear in the relationships between European Union law and the constitutional laws of the Member States. These relationships find their most important institutional locus (although not the only one) in the interaction between the European Court of Justice and national constitutional courts or courts exercising constitutional functions. There we find a curious mixture of competition and cooperation, understood in various ways. The mixture might be inevitable, for there are no clear and generally accepted institutional hierarchical links between these courts.[3] A degree of competition might even be beneficial, at least as long as it does not degenerate into outright rivalry. Cooperation, on the other hand, is also subject to interpretation; and what the European Court of Justice understands as

---

[3] The procedural connection through preliminary references (Article 267 TFEU) presents a hierarchical element in the obligation to refer imposed on national courts of last resort. Breaches of this obligation, however, are rarely effectively sanctioned – which means that the contours of the obligation become blurred. On these issues, see my article: 'De la cuestión prejudicial a la casación europea: Reflexiones sobre la eficacia y la uniformidad del Derecho de la Unión' (2005) *Revista Española de Derecho Europeo* 35.

dialogue and cooperation might not exactly coincide with the 'relation of cooperation' proposed by the German Constitutional Court. Beyond competition and cooperation, however, there are two other forms of relationship that might be as important as or even more important than the first two: deference, which can be implicit or explicit. And deference may sometimes become indifference, that is, a situation in which institutions pursue their objectives in an isolated way, without taking into account the behaviour or even the presence of other institutions, discounting the fact that they are part of a wider normative and institutional framework of increasing interconnection. Competition, cooperation, deference and indifference: sometimes one prevails, sometimes another, but in general these four attitudes are always present in the background of the relationship between national constitutional courts and the European Court of Justice.

To continue thinking about this question, I set out to examine the three predominant narratives of the relationship between Union law and state constitutional law, which roughly correspond to the main visions of the Union as a political entity and to the main theories of integration. I should like to address first the state-centred conceptions. Then I turn to the law of integration. Thirdly, I focus on legal pluralism, an attempt to supersede the first two perspectives. To conclude I address the more difficult themes of institutional disobedience and the area of darkness that remains between these perspectives.

II.   STATE-CENTRED CONCEPTIONS

There are several state-centred conceptions out there, but they all share a common trait: the dogmatic preference for the state and its people as the predominant political community, and for constitutional law as the predominant structuring law of that community. European Union law is seen and actually allowed to exist only as part of that framework, in the terms and within the limits established by national law. The European Union is not and cannot be an autonomous entity. It has not yet severed the umbilical cords that link it to the constitutional laws of the various Member States, the true 'masters of the Treaty'. Its law is just a more effective kind of international law, but not fundamentally different from it.

As a result of that predominant point of view, state-based constitutionalism, an essentially rational product of the modern mind, usually remains pre-modern when it looks beyond its boundaries – when its purely national perspective defines an identity by opposing itself to other identities. Beyond the state, state-centred constitutionalism becomes suffused with political theology, with axiomatic notions such as state, people, identity, sovereignty

and constituent power, which constitute the unproven dogmatic foundations of the whole constitutional building and also, sometimes, the
generally unconscious basis of a form of legal nationalism. Unconscious
indeed and barely visible: it is so deeply engrained in the legal cultures of
the Member States that it usually passes unnoticed, at least among jurists.
This conception is the natural consequence of the mythical theories of
national constitutional origins, which establish a permanent framework,
sometimes held to be 'eternal', over and above future generations –
something that reminds one of Burke's curious contract between the living
and the dead.

From that point, when constitutionalism looks beyond the borders of the
nation-state, there is indeed only a tiny step to move onto the romantic or
counter-revolutionary rhetoric of a Joseph de Maistre or an Edmund
Burke.[4] According to these thinkers, it would be impossible, a revolutionary folly, to try to write constitutions out of the blue. Constitutions would
just reflect national character and tradition. They are mainly composed of
unwritten rules, which might be codified but can never be changed. They
are just effects, not causes. In the same way, many traditional constitutional jurists argued that the 'utopian' exercise of drafting a 'Constitution
for Europe' produced a monster instead of a 'real' constitution. And even
that monster has failed to see the light. For them, the whole idea was
misguided from the start.

The most radical state-centred conception is a sort of *constitutional
solipsism* aimed at avoiding tackling the issue. This position considers
European Union law as something intrinsically *foreign* and different. It
always moves, as it were, on another plane. It can never be part of the
same picture. It is extra-constitutional or a-constitutional. As a result, the
two cannot meet or collide. Issues of Union law are thus characterised as
issues of *mere* statutory law, to be resolved by ordinary courts, taking into
account ordinary law. Constitutional courts could not possibly bother with
them.[5] This position is the result of seeing state constitutional law as a
constant function, unaffected by Union law and its evolution. The latter
might change, of course, but by its very nature it cannot invade the

---

[4] See *Considérations sur la France* (1797) and *Essai sur le principe générateur des
constitutions politiques et des autres institutions humaines* (1814) in Joseph-Marie de
Maistre, *Œuvres*, Pierre Glaudes (ed) (Paris, Laffont, 2007) 177, 333; Edmund Burke,
Reflections on the Revolution in France (London, Penguin, 1969).

[5] That was, for a long time, the position of the Spanish Constitutional Court, which
variously considered 'infraconstitutional' or 'extraconstitutional' the possible conflicts
between Community law and internal law (see, for example, judgments 64/1991 and
45/1996).

privileged sphere of state constitutional law. From this perspective, European Union law is forever condemned to remain a different kind of law, and state constitutional law will forever maintain its core functions and attributes.

There are more sophisticated and realistic versions of the state-centred approach, of course, designed to preserve a space for state constitutional law against a European Union law that is sometimes perceived as 'an incoming tide that cannot be held back',[6] and even as 'a tidal wave bringing down our sea walls and flowing inland over our fields and houses – to the dismay of all'.[7] Such a defence of 'our fields and houses' usually takes the form of a general acceptance of the supremacy of European Union law, with a number of reservations and the possibility of a last resort intervention by a constitutional court if in an exceptional case there is a need to preserve the core values and principles of the state constitutional order. This is the case in which the Schmittian decision on the exception stands as the small shrine in which sovereignty is preserved, in general – but not always – without actual consequences for integration. Those reservations are sometimes coupled with an attitude of 'benign' neglect with regard to European Union law.

The judgment of the German Constitutional Court on the Treaty of Lisbon[8] – a sophisticated and rather convoluted restatement of the Maastricht-Urteil with some additional teeth and dubious practical consequences for the decision-making process of the European Union – is the most recent example of this approach. The courageous reader of this piece of legal writing will certainly notice that in the world it represents everything is seen through the peculiar lens of German constitutional law, which becomes the beginning and the end of an axiomatic and ultimately, in spite of all its turns, rather simple circular reasoning. The European Union and its law are reinterpreted and sometimes distorted through that curious lens. The state and its constituent power are presented as untouchable mythical figures. Their withering away would require an unthinkable dramatic act. There is no effort on the part of the German court to see itself as a participant, in the same way as German political institutions, in a larger institutional and legal community that transforms itself gradually

---

[6] Lord Denning MR in *HP Bulmer Ltd v J Bollinger SA (No 2)* [1974] Ch 401, 418–19 (CA).

[7] Lord Denning, *Introduction to the European Court of Justice: Judges or Policy Makers?* (London, Bruges Group, 1990) 7–8. Both quotations by Lord Denning are mentioned in the introduction to Catherine Barnard and Okeoghene Odudu (eds), *The Outer Limits of EU Law* (Oxford, Hart Publishing, 2009) 1.

[8] BVerfG, 2 BvE 2/08, 30 June 2009. See Daniel Thym, 'In the Name of Sovereign Statehood: A Critical Introduction to the *Lisbon* Judgment of the German Constitutional Court' (2009) 46 *Common Market Law Review* 1795. See also Katrin Auel and Julio Baquero Cruz, *Karsruhe's Europe* (Paris, Notre Europe, 2010).

without any need for dramatic events. There is no hesitation on its part about what course to take and no consideration at all of the negative consequences that its behaviour could have on all the other actors and systems concerned, not to speak of its effects on the common enterprise of integration. Its normative horizon really starts and ends with German constitutional law. The so-called 'eternity clause', the ultimate basis of the case law of the German Constitutional Court on European integration, is clearly suffused with political theology, and points to an unreconstructed legal eschatology in which the historically grounded mistrust of democratic politics leads to a blind trust of the politics of law, carried out by that very German Constitutional Court, with very negative potential consequences for the European project – and perhaps also for Germany.[9]

Radical and less radical, sophisticated and less sophisticated, all state-centred conceptions present a common impediment: their incapacity and sometimes outright unwillingness to 'think European', to embrace integration, to adopt an internal point of view with regard to the European Union and its law, and to work towards the consolidation of a common European legal culture. They tend to see the European Union and its law from a purely external perspective, as the mere sum of the Member States, as a political and legal complement to them. The nation-state is thus taken as the *natural* political community which strives to maintain itself for an indefinite and ideally eternal time – sometimes, and only in a number of areas, with the help of integration – and to achieve a just and stable social, economic and political order within its borders. Only the democracy of the nation-state is natural and truly democratic: that of the Union lacks the necessary preconditions of democracy, and can only and will always be an artificial and imperfect *ersatz*. In the same way, legal things beyond the state also lack that natural basis: they are artificial constructs to be regarded with diffidence and to be narrowly construed. As a result, only the constitution of the nation-state is a true constitution and can reign supreme. In the last analysis and as a matter of principle, European Union law must always be subordinate to it, even if that subordination only becomes visible in the unlikely but crucial exceptional case.

From the point of view of state-centred conceptions, the European Union, its institutions and its law appear transfigured, interpreted as very soft and essentially provisional commitments. They would represent a 'balance of powers', as argued by Paul Kirchhof, former judge of the

---

[9] The German court has later softened its approach in its more deferential and pragmatic judgment of 6 July 2010 (2 BvR 2661/06) (limiting the scope of its ultra vires review of Union law to acts which are manifestly in breach of the limits of the powers of the Union and which lead to a structurally significant shift in the division of powers between the Union and the Member States).

German Constitutional Court and the mastermind of the Maastricht-Urteil.[10] The irony is that the system of the 'balance of powers' brings to memory the tragic experience of European history. It dates back to the Westphalian system of sovereign states, based indeed on a balance between powers, none of which could be hegemonic, and on recurrent European wars, which functioned as a regulatory mechanism of sorts. That was indeed the foundation of the 'European system' until 1945.

As Ortega y Gasset predicted, post-war political and legal arrangements, including European integration, were designed to overcome the balance of powers through formal institutions and binding law. The objective: to prevent hegemonic dreams and wars at the heart of Europe. The only thing these legal and institutional arrangements have to do with the 'balance of powers' is that they were precisely meant to overcome it.[11]

History, however, has its mysterious ways. It could be that Kirchhof's reinterpretation and rewriting of the story of integration is the legal counterpart of Alan Milward's thesis on the reinforcement of the nation-state through European integration: domestic social and economic choice alone would explain the choice for integration; legal integration would then be an avatar of national social and economic interests. State-centred constitutionalism may indeed have a close relationship with the intergovernmental theories of political integration, such as those developed by Milward or Moravcsik, which also explain integration from the exclusive point of view of states' power and preferences.[12]

It may be interesting to transpose Alan Milward's thesis to the relationships between national constitutional law and European Union law. Consider the constitutional law of France, Germany or Italy in 1945. It was torn to pieces, ineffective, worth nothing as the basic law of a political community. But from that moment it was reconstructed as part of the European rescue of the nation-state. The law of integration, together with the Council of Europe, the European Convention on Human Rights and other institutions and norms, could be seen in retrospect as so many parts of a post-war plan to reinvent and reinforce state constitutional law, framing it into wider institutional and normative structures. This plan would be part of the project, based on economic and social objectives, to reconstruct and reinforce the nation-state. The law of integration would, in other words, provide the Member States with a certainty, seriousness and irreversibility concerning their mutual commitments that could not be had in the context an

---

[10] Paul Kirchhof, 'The Balance of Powers between National and European Institutions' (1999) 5 *European Law Journal* 225.

[11] On Ortega's ideas about the European system and its future, see my article: 'Europa invertebrada: una conversación con Ortega' (2006) *Revista de Occidente* 129.

[12] See Alan S Milward, *The European Rescue of the Nation-State*, 2nd edn (London, Routledge, 2000); Andrew Moravcsik, *The Choice For Europe: Social Purpose And State Power From Messina To Maastricht* (Ithaca NY, Cornell University Press, 1998).

international public law agreement that reflected mere interdependence and just a 'balance of powers'. 'Law' would thus be one of the main factors that could explain the states' choice for European integration.

This would mean that the reinforcement of state constitutional law constitutes the main objective and at the same time the ultimate limit of the law of integration, at least from one perspective. When state constitutional law has been reconstructed, we might have reached the upper limit of European Union law. It could even be that after national constitutional law has successfully reinvented and stabilised itself, in part with the help of supranational law, the law of integration could start a process of decay and fragmentation, or at least would start experiencing new difficulties in its evolution (or stop evolving altogether, reaching a measure of stability) and probably also a legitimacy crisis.

Milward's views can be criticised. We may wonder, to begin with, whether institutionalisation and legal integration were just avatars of economic and social policy choices. As I have argued, it could be that the choice for the law and the institutions of integration was not only a collateral effect of first-order economic and social objectives. Binding the Member States in a system of common law and institutions was probably a first-order aim in its own right, regardless of substantive policy choices. The structural elements of the Treaties of Paris and Rome were at least as important as the substantive policies that were introduced in them. They were an open and empty form that had its own value and could be put to various substantive uses.

III.   THE LAW OF INTEGRATION OR CONSTITUTIONALISM BEYOND THE STATE

The law of integration, in contrast, strives hard to 'think European' and to lay down the foundations of a European legal culture that can travel across borders and become truly common ground as a technique, as a language, and as a carrier of shared values and principles.[13]

In contrast to state-centred constitutionalism, the law of integration has no origins, no mythical foundations. It only has unprivileged beginnings. It is a programme for the future. There is, to be sure, a certain measure of mythical content in the foundational period, in the rhetoric of the 'founding fathers', in the leading cases of the 1960s on direct effect and supremacy, in the attempt to enact a 'Treaty establishing a Constitution for

---

[13]   See Pierre Pescatore, *Le droit de l'intégration* (Leiden, Sijthoff, 1972); Mauro Cappelletti, Monica Seccombe and Joseph HH Weiler, *Integration through Law: Europe and the American Federal Experience* (5 vols) (Berlin and New York, Walter de Gruyter, 1985–88).

Europe', and also in the drafting of a Charter of Fundamental Rights,[14] but so far these are for the most part unsuccessful attempts at creating a political mythology. Moreover, they are harmless attempts in that they do not have the undemocratic drawbacks of some state constitutional law. Indeed, the rules for the revision of many constitutions typically require stronger majorities than the rules that were followed for their adoption, and sometimes the revision of certain provisions is simply impossible, as in the case of the 'eternity' clause of the German Basic Law. These are clear examples of the imposition of the will of one generation over the will of future generations, and they present problems from the point of view of democratic theory. In contrast, the rules followed for the adoption of the Treaty are identical to the rules established for its revision and for the accession of new Member States. In addition, Member States can withdraw from the Union (a possibility now confirmed in Article 50 of the Treaty on European Union as revised by the Treaty of Lisbon). It is in this fundamental sense that I argue that the Treaty has no origin, but only unprivileged beginnings that can always be put into question and revised with the same majorities that were needed to adopt it.

According to the logic of the law of integration, the progressive reception of European Union law in national legal cultures would lead to the establishment of an ordered relationship along the lines devised by Union law itself, in an automatic process that can be seen as the legal counterpart of the 'spillover' of neo-functional theories. The acceptance of its supremacy would be part of the European path of civilisation. As Pescatore argued, the principles of direct effect and supremacy are founded on important normative and practical considerations. They would be indispensable for the law of integration. Thus, according to him, it is difficult to see how national courts could oppose the clear logic of these principles in the long run,[15] a clear logic that resembles very much the main characteristics of law as set out in Kelsen's *Pure Theory of Law*[16]: a 'pure' law without a context.

Perhaps because that 'purity' was better adapted to its ends, the law of integration discounted the resilience of a different logic based on state-centred constitutionalism. It thought that that logic was going to recede and accept that inclusion in a larger, more comprehensive, political community would require the acceptance of its law and an enlargement of the horizons, both in terms of law and in terms of justice, of national legal cultures. European Union law and its institutions would have to be in charge of policing the borders between the European Union legal system and national legal orders, for that function could not possibly be decentralised without endangering

---

[14]   See my article: 'What's Left of the Charter? Reflections on Law and Political Mythology' (2008) 15 *Maastricht Journal of European and Comparative Law* 65.

[15]   Pescatore, *Le droit de l'intégration*, above n 13, 89.

[16]   Hans Kelsen, *Reine Rechtslehre* (Vienna, Österreichische Staatsdruckerei, 1992).

integration. Those institutions should be trusted to do that, since they are as democratic as they can be in a system of integration, and not fundamentally undemocratic or less democratic than the institutions of the Member States – with which they are in close contact through the interface between systems and that of the Council. At the ideal end of the process of legal integration, there would be a harmonious coming together to form a new composite legal system, based on common principles and on a large consensus about the way in which legal orders should interact with each other, especially in case of conflict.

The demise of the Treaty establishing a Constitution for Europe gives us a chance to rediscover the basic constitutional qualities of the law of integration and of integration through law with their main elements: majority voting, institutionalisation, legislation, the rule of law, primacy, direct effect, state liability, etc. In many ways, the law of integration was, and in part remains, a technocratic utopia, but unlike state constitutionalism it is one that is not static and closed. It has no blueprint. It is a flexible and in many ways undefined utopia.

It is this essential and novel aspect of the law of integration that is discounted when European Union law is presented as the minimum common denominator of 'constitutional traditions'. The Charter, presented as a mere codification of common constitutional traditions, not changing anything in the legal landscape, is a case in point. The main idea behind this reduction is a quest for acceptability. If the law of integration is only that, then there would be no reason for state constitutional lawyers to fear it: they would see it as something familiar, as *almost the same thing*. 'Tradition', in particular, is used here as a codeword for continuity, something that is carried on from state law to European Union law, something that, in the minds of European jurists, represents the security and certainty of moving in chartered territory, 'our own fields and houses', as Lord Denning put it. This explains the important role of that rhetoric in the case law of the European Court of Justice.

But European Union law is more, probably much more, than a mere codification of 'common constitutional traditions'. In fact, the main elements of the law of integration do not belong to any 'common constitutional tradition', for those traditions were confined to the inner borders of nation-states. And in five decades the law of integration has produced a 'tradition' of its own. From this perspective, we readily understand the emphasis given by the pioneers of the law of integration to the *specificity* of Community law vis-à-vis both international law and national law. Pescatore and others[17] insisted on the fact that Community

---

[17] See, for example, L-J Constantinesco, 'La spécificité du Droit communautaire' (1966) 1 *Revue trimestrielle du droit européen* 15.

law was a new system of law, not classifiable under previous categories of law. A new law, a new legal system, was also the message of the European Court of Justice in its seminal cases on direct effect and supremacy. The rhetoric of *constitutionalisation*, as neo-functional as the law of integration – and its continuation in a way – abandoned the quest for *specificity* and embraced a search for *recognition* as an established branch of the law that in the meantime had recovered the prestige it had lost with the Second World War.

The law of integration is thus a modern enterprise through and through, and one that is deeply imbued with the usual trust the modern man puts in reason and rationality. In many ways, it is a project that takes to a continental plane the modern project of constitutionalism, which was originally circumscribed to the nation-state. Thus, it was clear that sooner or later it would end up adopting the vocabulary of constitutionalism and clashing with the basic tenets of state-based constitutionalism.

The ambitious project of the law of integration has obviously encountered a number of difficulties, and some of them may well have become endemic. The law of integration has always had a problematic and ambivalent mode of being. Torn between the domestic, the federal and the international, it has always seemed much more effective than most international law and yet somewhat less effective than most domestic and federal law. Even today, its authority does not seem to be as solidly established as that of other more traditional legal systems. It can never be taken for granted. It is always changing, never stable, sometimes improving, sometimes decaying, inevitably linked to the ups and downs of political integration. European Union law itself and its doctrinal elaboration may be well developed in theory and in the case law, but social reality and the behaviour of legal actors in the Member States do not always correspond to it. The more European Union law develops in words and structure, the more the social and legal reality of some Member States seems to resist that development, and the wider becomes the gap between the ideal order of things expressed in Union law and things as they are and tend stubbornly to remain. That resistance may sometimes be rebellious but most of the time it is due to ignorance and habit. And even though the law of European integration may be seen as a success in terms of acceptance and effectiveness, especially when compared to the law of other international and regional organisations, European Union law still presents many shortcomings in its actual application: it is an imperfect system of law.[18]

---

[18] This and the following three paragraphs are based on my 'Francovich and Imperfect Law', in Miguel Poiares Maduro and Loïc Azoulai (eds), *The Past and Future of EU Law: The Classics of EU Law Revisited on the 50th Anniversary of the Rome Treaty* (Oxford, Hart, 2010) 418–22.

These difficulties have to do with legal culture rather than with legal principles and techniques. As I have already argued, national legal cultures are deeply engrained. Like the state, they become habits and tend to be perceived as something natural – the conspicuous 'law of the land'. Thus, most national legal actors still live in a self-contained word in which external objects, including European Union law, are seen with suspicion if they are seen at all. Quite often Union law is not applied when and as it should be. This problem may be graver in peripheral countries, in countries that still have a short experience as Member States of the European Union, or in countries with judicial systems that do not perform well in general, also with regard to state law. To a variety of extents, however, it is present in all of them, even in the founding Member States that have well-functioning judicial and administrative institutions, and it does not take much to find cases in which Union law is blatantly ignored or misinterpreted. Hence if one reads a handbook on European Union law or just the *European Court Reports* one will not have a realistic view of it, but a highly idealised view of the legal system that is only part of the story. Like Naipaul's traveller, we will have been 'reading the wrong books'. To have the complete picture one needs to examine carefully its practical reception in the legal orders of the Member States. And there the picture usually becomes a bit blurred and sometimes somewhat bleak.

Even if these difficulties might be shared by all legal systems, one cannot deny that the mode of being of European Union law is more problematic than that of the laws of more conventional political communities. The difference is essential, for the 'existence' of Union law depends on its continuing acceptance by the legal systems of the Member States, the very 'existence' of which as closed and self-contained systems is being constantly put into question by Union law itself. This tension is characteristic of federal systems in their initial, critical or final phases. In the European Union, however, that tension seems to be consubstantial to the usual state of the system, and no durable equilibrium seems to be available. From a legal and also from a political point of view, the European Union seems to be condemned to be a crisis system, always as if about to begin or seeming to approach its end, never attaining a lasting balance.

The problematic mode of being of European Union law is clear in many examples. The *Francovich* line of case law is one of them.[19] *Francovich*'s declaration that state liability is inherent in the system of the Treaty, and the gradual development of the legal contours of that liability, actually seem to transmit the opposite message: that the system has resources to

---

[19] Cases C-6/90 and C-9/90 *Francovich and Bonifaci v Italy* [1991] ECR I-5357; Cases C-46/93 and C-48/93 *Brasserie du Pêcheur v Bundesrepublik Deutschland and R v Secretary of State for Transport ex parte Factortame and others* [1996] I-1029; Case C-224/01 *Köbler* [2003] ECR I-10239.

cope with non-compliance; that Union law is 'normal' and effective law. Yet *Francovich*, more than any other judgment, speaks to us about the uncertainty of European Union law, about the imperfect and unfinished character of the rule of law in the European Union. In looking for a final sanction, for closure, for 'normality', *Francovich* exposes the fragility and openness of the system.

Consider also *the Directive*: the preferred source of secondary law, with its ambiguous status and its uncertain scope and effects, becoming almost invisible once 'transubstantiated' into state law. Or *the Council*, that hybrid institution, permeating almost the whole political process with its power, theoretically open to democratic deliberation and qualified majority voting yet practically trapped, most of the time, in diplomatic bargaining and consensus decision-making. Or *preliminary references*, too many to be properly dealt with yet only the tip of the iceberg of those that should be raised if the third paragraph of Article 267 TFEU, as interpreted in *CILFIT*,[20] were strictly respected.

Confronted with these difficulties, European Union law has developed a number of strategies of 'internalisation' and 'incorporation', which render it flexible and plural from within and more palatable to the constitutional orders of the Member States.[21] Such strategies can only work, however, to the extent that the guardians of those constitutional orders are willing to engage in a productive dialogue with the institutions of integration. Before unilateral and direct threats to supremacy, however, Union law has only been able to repeat the predictable and ineffectual response: *supremacy!* Like most legal systems, European Union law does not have the legal instruments needed to cope with extreme cases of disagreement, other than ignoring them. But by ignoring them it runs the risk of drifting further apart from reality, of becoming a voice in the wilderness.

These examples reveal the ambiguity of design and the political tensions of the European Union and its law. They show that the law of integration has not overcome the resistance of national legal cultures; that for the time being its ambitious programme is in part condemned to remain utopian.

IV.   LEGAL OR CONSTITUTIONAL PLURALISM

Following a third way of sorts, some have tried to bridge the gap between state-centred conceptions and the law of integration through dynamic and

---

[20]   Case 283/81, *CILFIT v Ministero della Sanità* [1982] ECR 3415.
[21]   On these strategies, see Loïc Azoulai, 'The Future Constitutional Role of the European Court of Justice' in Julio Baquero Cruz and Carlos Closa Montero (eds), *European Integration from Rome to Berlin, 1957–2007: History, Law and Politics* (Brussels, Peter Lang, 2009) 229.

bi-directional models.[22] They are the legal counterparts of third generation political theories of integration such as multi-level governance.[23] They have a clearly post-modern flavour in their rejection of hierarchy and their insistence on complexity, openness, discourse and the like. They take into account the shifts and evolutions through time of the systems of law at play, seeing them as reciprocally engaged in an open-ended process of informal dialogue. They have come to be known as legal or constitutional pluralism.

There are several pluralisms out there, more or less radical in the consequences they extract from their approach, but they are all characterised by a number of common traits.

First, the pluralists would like to stand beyond the European point of view and also beyond any particular national perspective. They would like to see things from far away, as if with a telescope, and try to adopt a neutral stance.

Secondly, this point of departure leads them to the recognition of the normative claims of both sides and to the search for a compromise.

Thirdly, such a compromise is sought on the basis of what is common, and on the recognition of what is different. This may explain the usual emphasis of pluralists on the existence of 'common constitutional traditions' to be discovered through deliberation. Hence also the need to protect what is not common, the specific traits of national constitutional identities; for plurality is perceived as a value in itself, often quite independently from the merits of its underlying substance in concrete situations.

Finally, this leads them to prefer to leave forever open the issue of supremacy, an openness that becomes embedded in the compromise. Thus, the supremacy of European Union law would generally be recognised by national constitutional orders, but unilateral exceptions would exist, through judicial or political means, whenever they are justified by the need to preserve a particular constitutional identity and hence the pluralism of the system as a whole.

Like the other two accounts, pluralism is not without problems, especially when presented as a normative ideal and not just as a description of the imperfect relationship between European Union law and state constitutional law.[24] As a description of the current state of affairs, it may be

---

[22] See Neil Walker, 'The Idea of Constitutional Pluralism' (2002) 65 *Modern Law Review* 317; Miguel P Maduro, 'Contrapunctual Law: Europe's Constitutional Pluralism in Action' in Neil Walker (ed), *Sovereignty in Transition* (Oxford, Hart, 2003) 501; Mattias Kumm, 'The Jurisprudence of Constitutional Conflict: Constitutional Supremacy in Europe before and after the Constitutional Treaty' (2005) 11 *European Law Journal* 262.

[23] See, for example, Liesbet Hooghe and Gary Marks, *Multi-level Governance and European Integration* (Lanham, Rowman and Littlefield, 2001).

[24] For a more detailed critique, see my article: 'The Legacy of the Maastricht-Urteil and the Pluralist Movement' (2008) 14 *European Law Journal* 389, 412, 418.

correct, at least in some Member States. But then constitutional pluralism could just be seen as a second best solution for a slow transitional period towards legal orthodoxy – something like Wittgenstein's famous ladder, to be thrown away once one has climbed up on it and gained the height needed to see the world correctly.[25] Then, in other words, it would not be the sort of dialectic *Aufhebung* that some believe it to be, but a more modest and pragmatic attempt to bridge the seemingly intractable gap that lies between state-centred conceptions and the law of integration. As a normative ideal, like a ladder where some would like to stay and an *Aufhebung* of sorts, however, pluralism might be somewhat uncomfortable and less appealing when its possible consequences are considered.

First, the neutrality it purports to adopt is difficult if not impossible in the world of law. Confronted with actual conflicts that call for a solution, neutrality and undecidability are unsustainable. With their contempt for hierarchy, the pluralists actually seem to favour practical solutions that are closer to the exceptional reservations of sovereignty favoured by state-based constitutional theories than they are to the position of the law of integration. As a result, it would not be a genuine middle ground but a more sophisticated version of state-centred theories. In addition, we have not seen any convincing proposal of how a non-hierarchical legal order would work in practice whilst remaining a legal *order*. For if we want it to remain an order, a system of law needs at least a measure of normative hierarchy that necessarily implies a degree of institutional hierarchy. In most cases, the questioning of the supreme character of European Union law only leads to the replacement, in a number of exceptional cases, of one hierarchy by another.

Secondly, the compromise legal pluralism tries to achieve may be positive in political terms but it would sometimes sacrifice the position of individuals, who would not know in advance which institution will ultimately adjudicate on their rights and obligations and on the basis of which rules. This is problematic, for the position of individuals should be at the centre of our reflection. This deserves emphasis, since in its quest for institutional compromises pluralism tends to marginalise the position of individuals, which the legal systems involved and their institutions are supposed to serve, and to sacrifice important dimensions of the rule of law.

Thirdly, the tension between the search for common constitutional traditions and the need to preserve constitutional diversity may fatally undermine deliberation, if the emphasis on specificity, difference and identity – all of them easily *constructible* and open to political manipulation – leads to irreconcilable positions.

---

[25] Ludwig Wittgenstein (trans David Pears and Brian McGuinness), *Tractatus Logico-Philosophicus*, 2nd edn (London, Routledge, 2001), proposition 6.54.

Finally, pluralists tend to consider that the absence of a final decision on the issue of supremacy is an essential part of the structure of European Union law, even its very foundation, ignoring the fact that such explicit 'pluralistic' episodes are relatively rare in the actual practice of law in Europe.

V. INSTITUTIONAL DISOBEDIENCE

It is that rarity referred to above that made me think that the phenomenon sometimes described as legal or constitutional pluralism could not be seen as the normal state of affairs and even less as the very foundation of the relationship between European Union law and state constitutional law. My intuition was always the opposite: that if we want the institutional and legal machinery to work at all, its normal state should be supremacy and loyal cooperation through the preliminary rulings procedure; that express disagreement should remain exceptional, an extraordinary escape valve from the system, not part of its essence.

At present, however, the European Union system cannot cope with or make sense of express disagreement. It has no space for it. For some time I just thought that there was no solution to this problem, that the two first positions were incommensurable, that neither of them was fully accurate, that pluralism was vague, confusing and unworkable as a bridge between the European and the national positions, for none of them is open to discussing its fundamental assumptions and that would impair a genuine dialogue.[26] Hence it seemed to me that we were just stuck with what was not really a substantive problem but a problem related to the incompatible points of view adopted by different actors in the discourse around supremacy; a problem of legal culture, therefore, that could only be resolved by the slow evolution of the various legal cultures involved.

Only later on, and quite coincidentally, did I start to think about the issue from the angle of institutional disobedience. Elsewhere I have indeed proposed to conceive of the attitude of national constitutional courts or courts that carry out constitutional review in terms of institutional disobedience, which would be a special case of civil disobedience carried out by institutions.[27] Following the classical theory of civil disobedience, institutional disobedience can be defined as 'a public, non-violent, conscientious yet political act contrary to law usually done with the aim of

---

[26] See David Bohm, *On Dialogue* (London and New York, Routledge, 2004) 8–9.
[27] See my article: 'Legal Pluralism and Institutional Disobedience in the European Union' in Jan Komárek and Matej Avbelj (eds), *Constitutional Pluralism in the European Union and Beyond* (Oxford, Hart Publishing, forthcoming, 2011).

bringing about a change in the law or policies of government'.[28] The theory of civil disobedience tends to legitimise some extreme forms of political action and at the same time imposes a number of conditions on it. Some are explicitly mentioned in the definition. Others can be deduced from it. Thus, unlike rebellion or revolution, civil disobedience 'expresses disobedience to law within the limits of fidelity to law'.[29] It is meant to correct a particular injustice within an otherwise generally just and accepted system of law. Secondly, disobedient actors must be ready to accept the consequences of their action. Thirdly, their action must be based on fundamental principles and they must carry out a balance of costs and benefits before taking that course.[30] Finally, all the channels of change of the system must have been tried in vain beforehand. In such a way, civil disobedience is clearly limited to some extreme cases, as a last resort in the framework of otherwise generally just and well-functioning constitutional democracies, where recourse to it might be needed to reopen an urgent debate on some fundamental issue.

The theory of civil disobedience can be transposed to the institutional arena, although institutions may be subject to even stronger constraints before having recourse to it. But in extreme cases and as a last resort, especially in the context of divided-power systems characterised by double and sometimes conflicting loyalties, institutions might decide to act contrary to the law of one of the systems in order to prompt legal change. Institutional disobedience can thus be seen as a possible but risky political voice that should remain exceptional and mostly silent. Used sparingly, properly and intelligently, it can be a stabilising device, a sort of escape valve in complex systems when they are confronted with difficult situations in which the usual channels of change are blocked or of no avail. Used negligently, however, it can damage the very foundations of the polity. The particular configuration of institutional disobedience in divided-power or federal systems, with their problems of double loyalty, is of especial interest to the concrete situations that may arise in the European Union.

This is, it seems to me, what national constitutional courts or courts exercising constitutional review are trying to do when they voice actual or potential reservations to the absolute supremacy of European Union law. The same would apply to comparable action on the part of the political institutions of the Member States, and also to popular protest through the *institutional* mechanism of referenda. These institutions seem to be saying: if there is a higher principle in danger we may want to reserve ourselves the

---

[28]   John Rawls, *A Theory of Justice*, reproduced in Hugo A Bedau (ed), *Civil Disobedience in Focus* (London and New York, Routledge, 1991) 104. For the definition, Rawls relies on Hugo A Bedau, 'On Civil Disobedience' (1961) 58 *Journal of Philosophy* 653.

[29]   *ibid*, 106.

[30]   *ibid*, 10.

possibility of disobeying Union law. Should the case arise, we will not be doing it because we want to overturn the European Union or to abandon it. We actually see the European Union as a generally just system. We would be doing it as a plea for reconsideration in a particular case. It would indeed be a public, non-violent and conscientious breach of the common law with the aim of bringing about a legal or a political change. The higher moral rules justifying such a departure could be found in the quintessence of the common constitutional traditions. The state would be ready to accept the consequences of its breach within the sphere of Union law (for example, liability, an infringement action, a judgment against the state, a fine, etc). And the European Union legal order and its institutions could be convinced by the plea for reconsideration – changing the law – or could take the argument into account and reject it with good reasons. Thus, the idea of institutional disobedience could complement and improve the traditional approach of the law of integration to the relationship between Union law and state constitutional law. It could provide a way to think about, frame and cope with exceptional cases of disagreement.

As in the other contexts, in the European Union such conduct can never be seen as the normal state of the law, of politics and of the interaction between the two. It is indeed highly anomalous and risky. It is also a highly ambiguous course of action, one that stands in uncomfortable proximity to exit and disloyalty, at the very limits of acceptable political and legal discourse. But sometimes, in very extreme cases, it might be a useful way to foster debate, to lead to positive changes and to unveil certain deficits.

The normative framework of civil and institutional disobedience imposes a number of limits on the occasions in which to use it and the way to do so. An institution of a Member State that considers following that course of action should not do it lightly.

First, a higher principle should be in grave, actual and imminent danger. This principle should essentially be common to the systems concerned. If it is a principle peculiar to the legal order of the Member State concerned, the disobedient institution should give convincing reasons explaining why it deserves the respect of all.

Secondly, the institution has to see whether the available legal and/or political procedures (for example, preliminary references – including a preliminary reference asking the European Court of Justice to reconsider its position[31] – and political negotiations) to express dissent and to prompt change have been used and with what result. In other words, institutional

---

[31] A preliminary ruling does not have to be the end of the judicial dialogue in the framework of Article 267 TFEU. The leading authorities are Case 14/86 *Pretore di Salò* [1987] ECR 2545, and Case 69/85 *Wünsche* [1986] ECR 947. A new submission cannot be used as an appeal against a preliminary ruling, but it can ask for a clarification or even reconsideration in the light of new facts or arguments.

disobedience has to be a last resort and not a first and only resort, as is sometimes the case in the Union. For example, in the European Arrest Warrant case,[32] the German Constitutional Court annulled the German provisions transposing the framework decision without referring a question to the European Court of Justice, as suggested by the German government. The annulment was, supposedly, limited to issues falling within the margin of appreciation of German legislature when transposing the framework decision, but such a finding was only possible after a complex and dubious interpretation of the framework decision itself, an issue that should have been referred to the European Court. In other situations, such as the prior constitutional review of a treaty amendment, in which a preliminary reference is not possible because the new treaty is not yet part of European Union law, national institutions should behave with special prudence. In such cases, it might be preferable national courts to reserve constitutional review for concrete cases arising once the new treaty is in force, and limit themselves to flagrant abstract problems and violations which are quite unlikely to exist. This was done by the Spanish Constitutional Court with regard to fundamental rights protection in its declaration on the Treaty establishing a Constitution for Europe.[33] In contrast, in its judgment on the Treaty of Lisbon,[34] the German Constitutional Court took the opposite route, putting forward very concrete interpretive provisos and conditions for the constitutionality of that Treaty, instead of reserving its judgement for concrete cases in which it would have the opportunity to request the guidance of the European Court of Justice. I wonder what would happen to the European Union if every court exercising constitutional review in the Member States engaged in such a procrustean exercise before a Treaty amendment came into force.

Thirdly, the institution concerned has to weigh the pros and cons of the route of institutional disobedience in the particular case, and be ready to accept all the political and legal consequences of its disobedience for itself, for the Member State, for the other Member States and for the European Union as a whole. We would also have to consider certain limits based on political and legal prudence. Since the institutions involved consider the system to which they belong to be 'nearly just', maintain their general loyalty to it and do not intend to overthrow it but only to adjust it in one particular aspect which they deem unjust, they should avoid endangering or destroying it. Now, the European Union is a fragile system in which there are only minorities, all of which can be disobedient at some point for one reason or another. Indeed, each Member State is a minority and all the

---

[32] BVerfGE, 2 BvR 2236/04, 18 July 2005.
[33] Declaration 1/2004 of 13 December 2004 (in *Boletín Oficial del Estado*, 4 January 2005, No 3, Supplement, 5).
[34] See n 8 above.

peoples in the Member States are in a minority position within the Union. In such a system, the parties concerned may well have to approach the possibility of institutional disobedience with even greater prudence.

Finally, if it is done, it has to be done publicly and explicitly, and not by paying lip-service to European Union law. The cases of sheer silent ignorance of Union law would never qualify as institutional disobedience. Indeed, non-cooperation in the Union is more common than is thought, not because of open opposition to a system that is considered to be unjust in whole or in part, but because of the mere ignorance and inertia of national legal actors. This form of passive resistance may be more damaging than institutional disobedience. It is, in any case, not a legitimate form of institutional resistance, but mere disloyal behaviour in a system of integration.

Some may think that these ideas are not too far away from some of the softer versions of constitutional pluralism, such as those of Kumm and Ferreres Comella. They consider that, in spite of a 'strong interpretative presumption' in favour of the supremacy of European Union law, national courts may still have 'legitimate reasons for setting aside Union law when it collides with *specific* national constitutional rules that form an essential part of a member state's constitutional identity'. According to them, this possibility could be grounded on Article 4 of the Treaty on European Union, which commits the European Union to respecting the 'national identities' of the Member States, 'inherent in their fundamental structures, political and constitutional'. This provision is thus seen 'as authorizing national courts to set aside Union law on certain limited grounds'.[35] Insofar as my own position is no more than a refinement of the traditional stance of the law of integration and theirs is a soft version of the pluralist conception – itself an attempt to bridge the gap between state-centred perspectives and the law of integration – it is only natural that similarities exist. However, essential differences remain.

First, their insistence on particularistic and interpretable notions ('specific', 'identity') is fundamentally different from my concern for the functioning of the common system and for the need to explain to all actors concerned why a specific national constitutional feature would deserve the respect of all. These are important requirements of any form of legitimate institutional disobedience. These requirements would lead, it seems to me, to a much more restrained and exceptional practice of disobedience on the part of national institutions than their proposal.

---

[35] Mattias Kumm and Victor Ferreres Comella, 'The Primacy Clause of the constitutional Treaty and the Future of Constitutional Conflict in the European Union' (2005) 3 *International Journal of Constitutional Law* 473, 483, 491–92.

Secondly, I am not convinced by their interpretation of Article 4 of the Treaty on European Union. As I have argued elsewhere,[36] it may be more reasonable to think that this provision confirms the decision of the Member States to entrust the European Court of Justice with the competence to resolve all constitutional conflicts that arise in the judicial arena, that is, a provision that 'internalises' such conflicts to avoid the disruptive shadow of unilateral constitutional review by national courts. From the point of view of the common system, such exceptional review can only be grounded at the margins of the legal order, beyond the law, and that is why the theory of institutional disobedience, which is a theory about the limits of the legal order, may be relevant to our discussion.

VI. CONCLUSION

The notion of institutional disobedience might be a good description of what is going on when national institutions, including courts exercising constitutional review, resist in one way or another, actually or potentially, the supremacy of European Union law.[37] I also think it could be a fairly good prescriptive guide for what should and should not be done in such difficult and rare circumstances. Finally, from the perspective of the emergence and consolidation of a shared European legal culture, the notion of institutional disobedience could become a useful tool to think about and discuss these problems, not only from the particular point of view of the law of integration, but also from the other two perspectives outlined above, which may not be as incommensurable as they sometimes seem.

It could, indeed, but I do not think that it will. The three conceptions of the relationship between Union law and state constitutional law described above and the boundaries they trace seem to be rigidly defined and there is little ground for development. It is curious to see how these issues seem to be connected to the fortunes and misfortunes of European integration, as if the political mood of integration conditioned the evolution of Union law. In a way, the decision of the German Constitutional Court on the Treaty of Lisbon can be seen as a collateral effect of the political crisis the European Union has been experiencing since the rejection of the Treaty establishing a

[36] See my article 'The Legacy of the Maastricht-Urteil', above n 24, 417–18.
[37] It is also very similar to what the European Court of Justice itself did when it resisted the supremacy of international public law in the *Kadi* case, in view of the lack of protection of fundamental rights within the system of the United Nations (Case C-402/05 P *Kadi and Al Barakaat v Council and Commission* [2008] ECR I-6351). On *Kadi*, see my article: 'La réception de l'arrêt Kadi de la Cour de justice des Communautés européennes' in Edouard Dubout et Sébastien Touzé (eds), *Les droits fondamentaux: charnières entre ordres et systèmes juridiques* (Paris, Pedone, 2010) 117–44.

Constitution for Europe. Without the crisis, the decision might have been very different. In this field, the law sometimes seems to be a mere reflection of political developments.

Which means, probably, that the theoretical debate on the nature of European Union law and on its relationship with state constitutional law is not only exhausted, for the positions are well defined and perhaps even over-theorised, but also useless, because it is in practice – a practice dominated by a politics of law – that these issues are discussed. And it is there, in practice, where they are under-theorised, approached from dogmatic positions, and rendered barren by a rigid conception of the state and its constitutional law.

Without a defined identity, in hard times, the European jurist seems to be condemned to a nomadic existence, wandering endlessly in an area of darkness, never sure of the solidity of the ground beneath his feet.

Part Two

The European Convention on Human Rights

4

Burying, Not Praising the European Convention On Human Rights: A Provocation

ANDREW WILLIAMS*

I. INTRODUCTION

T
HE THEME OF Europe's constitutional mosaic is extraordinarily apt for the study of human rights across this continent. It entreats us to think about the overall picture and patterns of the European constitutional landscape and the means by which human rights have been entertained, formed, abused and enforced on multiple levels. With the European Union providing one backdrop, the Council of Europe another, with national constitutions all reflecting and challenging a notion of a transcontinental human rights vision, we are certainly experiencing an increasingly complicated pattern of legal expression and practice. It is this 'mosaic' (for want of a better word) that I have been attempting to chart over a number of years, although undoubtedly my focus has been primarily on the EU. Taken together I would like to think that this corpus of work is a form of constitutional mosaic project in itself, but I recognise that this volume of essays is a better reflection of the scope of the theme.

The purpose of this chapter, nonetheless, is to focus on one aspect of the European *human rights* mosaic. Although it is dangerous to think of treating any one element of the picture in isolation, there is justification for looking to the regime established by the European Convention on Human Rights (ECHR) and the Council of Europe as worthy of special analysis. Why? Because it not only represents a vital product of an important European human rights institution in its own right, but it also provides inspiration and perhaps irritation to all human rights initiatives throughout the continent. It is a backdrop for all things related to human rights, in

* School of Law, University of Warwick.

practice, in doctrine, in adjudication and in politics. Either it acts as a justification for developing human rights jurisprudence at national and regional level or it is there as a normative background against which the correctness of decisions or policies of European governments can be assessed.

This is not to say, however, that the subject should be treated as some kind of hagiography. The prevailing view maybe that the ECHR and its Court (ECtHR) is a shining achievement for human rights, 'the crown jewel of the world's most advanced international system for protecting civil and political liberties'.[1] And the jurisprudence that has developed over the decades may be presented as strong evidence for the success of law's ability to fulfill human rights. But accompanying this story is a firmly held belief that the system is a 'victim of its own success'.[2] For all the good judgments delivered, the system suffers from structural problems that hinder good adjudication. Problems of case selection, delays in review, the under-enforcement of decisions, to name but three, all provoke considerable concern. Such critique has become so prevalent that it too has become part of the orthodox view. The basic system is seen as sound, as generally successful, but certain structural constraints prevent it from being what it might be. Hence, when looking to improve the condition of human rights *through* the system, attention is focused upon structural and practical reform rather than re-evaluating its principled foundations.

But what if we questioned the basic premise of this orthodoxy? What if we suggested that instead of a system grounded on success it was grounded on failure? And instead of being a victim of success, it perpetrated its own failings? Surely, then, the search for 'solutions' (through procedural changes) will always be in vain? Indeed, by looking at addressing *some* symptoms of *some* perceived problems, the sense of success and failure running in parallel would most likely be perpetuated rather than 'solved'.

The purpose of this chapter is to consider an alternative perspective. It is deliberately provocative. It starts by making a heretical statement: we should seek to bury the ECHR and the ECtHR as encompassing a human rights regime, not praise it. Contemplating reform or even expansion would therefore be redundant. Of course, this is intended to echo Mark Antony's ironic speech. And in doing so, the prospect of inferring the opposite of what is said is also apparent. For perhaps when we look carefully enough we can reaffirm faith in the regime rather than condemn it. But I do not want to assume that to be the case. The point of the provocation is to get to the core of what the regime is about. And we need

---

[1]   Laurence Helfer, 'Redesigning the ECHR: Embeddedness as a Deep Structural Principle of the European Human Rights Regime' (2008) 19 *European Journal of International Law* 125–59.

[2]   *ibid.*

to keep an open mind about that if we are not to slip into an unquestioning self-satisfaction. That means we have to challenge the orthodoxy of success and failure to see if it can withstand critique.

II.   FIVE PROPOSITIONS

The approach I intend to take is to put forward a series of propositions. Each one will provoke resistance but that is the averred intention. After that I want briefly to look at some of the consequences if the argument presented is accepted. The propositions are:

> First, that the ECHR and the ECtHR have failed human rights conceptually and practically.
> Secondly, that the number of 'good' decisions made over the years does not necessarily remedy or even justify this dual failure.
> Thirdly, that recent decisions have exposed the failure I describe in the first proposition.
> Fourthly, that systemic problems perpetuate the failure but their resolution cannot solve the underlying failure.
> Fifthly, that remedying the failure(s) requires a fundamental re-conceptualisation of the central purpose of human rights in line with a more plausible account of their appeal *and* an institutional and constitutional settlement at the European level.

I will have something to say about all propositions, although the last will receive less attention overall. The claim I make there I need to reserve to a longer work, currently in progress, although I will try to sketch some of the key arguments I will develop elsewhere.

A. First Proposition

The ECHR and the ECtHR have failed human rights conceptually and practically. On the face of it, this proposition might seem difficult to justify. It goes against the grain of the eulogies supporting these institutions of European civilisation after the Second World War. And there is a *reason* for the orthodox position I have already outlined. This has rested on the understanding that both the normative text of the Convention and the institutional development of the Court have been necessary and desirable inventions for Europe. Once consistently articulated claims along these lines have become institutionalised, backed up by evidence of changes in national law following landmark decisions, the tendency has been to assume that the achievements are many and good. The narrative of success has become self-sustaining even in the absence of a deeper review of the whole picture.

But we cannot rely on the weight of narrative opinion as the foundation for evaluation if we are to question the system more fully. We must also consider the evidence for counterpoint views. In this respect there has been considerable critique offered by, among others, Steven Greer and Marie-Bénédicte Dembour.[3] During the course of the former's assessment of the history of the ECHR and the ECtHR's jurisprudence, Greer identifies several systemic problems that have arisen over the past half century. These are most pressing issues but still speak to the orthodox critique that is founded on the belief that the Convention and its Court are indubitably valuable institutions that merely require reform in order to make them 'work'. Changes in procedures and institutional structures are deemed to be capable of solving any manifest problems and will presumably ensure the successful continuing development of the Convention. Without doubt these are very pertinent critiques and practical suggestions. Indeed, I will appreciate them in a little more detail later. However, at this preliminary stage of my argument we need to look beneath the practical aspects and question some of the underlining assumptions of this orthodoxy.

In the first instance, I want to challenge the reliance upon the canonical Convention text as a satisfactory way in which human rights can ever be represented and fulfilled. One of Orhan Pamuk's characters in *The Black Book*, obsessed with the maintenance of the perfect archive, has the revelation that 'even the greatest and most authoritative texts in the world, were about dreams, not real life, dreams conjured up by words'.[4] This disjuncture between the moment of the text, its genesis and the reality of its later application to concrete situations is obviously not a concern restricted to the ECHR. It applies to all texts that are produced in the name of human rights (or otherwise). But it does seem to be particularly apposite for the Convention and its moment in history.

What, then, lay behind the dream of the Convention? Surely it had to have been the trauma of the Second World War and the totalitarian era that preceded it. Surely it was a reaction to the terrifying systemic and systematic violence of governments that operated without moral constraint and without regard for the suffering they inflicted. Surely also it was the product of and reaction to the specific horrors of the Holocaust. It would be ridiculous to suggest that all these matters did not provide the moral

---

[3]   S Greer, *The European Convention on Human Rights: Achievements, Problems, and Prospects* (Cambridge, Cambridge University Press, 2006) and M-B Dembour, *Who Believes in Human Rights? Reflections on the European Convention* (Cambridge, Cambridge University Press, 2006).

[4]   O Pamuk, *The Black Book* (London, Faber & Faber, 2006) 82.

impetus for constructing the Convention, or indeed that the authors of the text did not have in mind the images of genocide, war and atrocity when conceiving norms that would apply regardless of location.[5] Such terrible events, and a determination that some safeguard against them happening again be instituted, rather than the construction of an ideal model of society, must have been uppermost in the minds of those creators of the text. And yet, if this were so, where in the Convention was the statement of outrage regarding institutionalised killing and industrial genocide? Where was the attempt to acknowledge the atrocious potential of racism and supremacism? Where was the articulation of responsibility for actions perpetrated *outside* national territorial borders? These matters may have appeared in the rhetoric of the Assembly of the Council of Europe that debated the Convention as it was drafted. Memoirs and writings of the key players at this time may have recorded the moral genesis of the human rights and freedoms that were discussed. But the text itself was and remains a neutered document when considered in the light of its probable dream. As a reaction to and recognition of the inhumanity that can overwhelm any nation, as a means for recording the outrage of a right-minded continent, and as a conduit for setting the standards for all to observe *in the light of the potential for brutality and atrocity* that disrespect for the objects of human rights can produce, the Convention was a singular failure.

This might seem a very thin critique in terms of the conceptualisation of human rights, particularly when set against the subsequent application of the Convention. But it is a framing issue that should not be dismissed too easily. For, when it comes to providing guidance to those authorised to interpret the Convention's rights and freedoms, the conceptual purpose of its text surely has an important role to play. It may be a 'living instrument' but not to the disregard of its original purpose. So, faced with questions of extra-territoriality, for instance, the genetic inspiration for its standards should presumably make an adjudicator think more than twice before adopting a strict interpretation of jurisdiction. The absence of a contextual statement, which must include the violence casually meted out by regimes not only within but outside its borders, has, however, meant that the ECtHR has perhaps not received the reminder that should be ever-present. In this sense, the Convention has failed any conception of human rights

---

[5] Pierre-Henri Teitgen, one of the authors of the original draft for the Convention, reminded the Assembly of the Council of Europe, when presenting the motion recommending the adoption of a convention on human rights, of his experiences with the Gestapo and his family's losses in Dachau, Mauthausen and Buchenwald. See Council of Europe, *Collected Edition of the Travaux Préparatoires of the European Convention on Human Rights* vol 1 (Preparatory Commission of the Council of Europe, Committee of Ministers, Consultative Assembly) (Martinus Nijhoff, 1975) 48–50.

that includes memorial goals. The value of memory in addressing past atrocity was ignored when it came to the finally agreed text.

This was not the only conceptual failure. A fundamental contradiction was also built into the Convention. It emerged from an opposition constructed between the necessary 'universal' nature of human rights adopted *and* their particular purpose and interpretation within a specific locality: Europe. On the one hand, the Convention was drafted in the light of the Universal Declaration of Human Rights of 1948 (UDHR). It stated explicitly that it was aimed 'at securing the universal and effective recognition' of those rights in that declaration.[6] Since then it has become part of the system's self-affirming rhetoric that the 'Convention represented the first step towards the collective enforcement of certain of the rights set out in the Universal Declaration'.[7]

On the other hand, it was conceived in a period of intense dreaming of political realignment and reconstruction. The Convention represented part of a powerful parochial (or relativist) political statement of intent: to provide greater unity between European states through a new order for Europe. The 'maintenance and further realisation' of rights was 'one of the methods by which' the aim of 'greater unity between' Members of the Council of Europe was written into the Convention. In this respect, the rights enshrined were to give the people *of* Europe a set of core standards that would forever cast a light on their national governments' practices and that would provide some degree of assurance of protection against extreme visions of social management. But in conceptualising these standards an extremely narrow beam was constructed, one that did not embrace the universal quality attributed to human rights as a concept. Brian Simpson's extraordinary tome, *Human Rights and the End of Empire*, provides the greatest insight into the history of this endeavour.[8] Highlighting the vacillating and ultimate antipathy of the British Government towards creating a meaningful institution of European union, Simpson unveils the parochial interests that helped determine the conceptual and practical architecture of the Convention, the Court of Human Rights and the Council of Europe within which this all was set. And the story is not a particularly edifying one. The political intervention by the British and other authors of the Convention in the interests of then current concerns (mostly with the loss of colonial power and world influence; with the desperate need for economic regeneration; and with the fear of the

---

[6] See the Preamble to the European Convention on Human Rights, Rome, 4 November 1950 (213 UNTS 221).

[7] See, eg, European Court of Human Rights Annual Report 2008, 9 (Registry of ECtHR, Strasbourg 2009).

[8] AWB Simpson, *Human Rights and the End of Empire: Britain and the Genesis of the European Convention* (Oxford, Oxford University Press, 2001).

communist threat externally from the USSR and internally from home-grown European far-left movements) had an enormous impact on the conceptual skeleton of the Convention. In essence, it ensured that the rights were limited, only partially reflected the scope of the UDHR, paid little or no heed to the past, made no attempt to mention – let alone address – the potential of systemic violence re-emerging, restricted their application on the basis of legal technicality, and gave no succour to rights which might suggest support for a centralised economic system.

All of this was and is quite understandable. An appreciation of the context of the times, and indeed the forces of *realpolitik*, is vital to understanding why the Convention was designed in its original form. But even so, there is redolent within the text and what we know of the negotiations which gave it form, a sense of a conceptual approach that was highly constrained towards human rights. The political environment was, if anything, antithetical to the creation of a legal instrument that would advance 'human' as opposed to some other form of rights. There were no statements of an underlying principle of human dignity (or anything remotely akin to such a universalising ideal) as there were in the UDHR. There were few, if any, references to notions of universality which might have been interpreted as endorsing a notion of international comradeship. In particular, the legalistic restriction on jurisdiction of Article 1 of the Convention was pursued with the direct intention of excluding colonial territories. The inclusion of Article 15 and the ability of states to derogate from the application of rights in times of war reinforced a sense of contingency, and this was further emphasised by various limitations and qualifications on many of the particular rights. And of course there were few references to rights that attached to communities rather than individuals, casting doubt on ideas about the indivisibility of human rights or their collective value.

Some of this could be put down to the intention to construct an instrument that was legally binding, something the UDHR was certainly not. But in making this commitment through a very restricted vision of human rights that were *capable of being binding* a political statement was made. It intimated that only a limited number of 'rights' could be contemplated as falling within that restricted category. But what did this make of those other rights that were to be excluded? And what comment did it make on the validity of the UDHR? In effect, the choice of a particular set of rights deemed enforceable, ostensibly in part fulfillment of the UDHR (which in turn by definition attempted to identify a universal list of human rights) was a political and arguably pragmatic decision that challenged its own stated purpose. For it called into question at a fundamental level the ability to *realise* the corpus of human rights now purportedly to be defended internationally. And if it was not possible to defend the whole range of agreed rights in a democratic and still relatively affluent Europe, how could that broader catalogue be promoted as being of universal application?[9]

Of course, many will deny that such concern with a general conception has any validity. They will also deny the coherence of a universal notion of human rights. The positions adopted by commentators from Joseph Raz to Michael Ignatieff (and by the authors of the Convention) deny the plausibility of such an interpretation. For them, and many others, human rights have meaning *because of the text*, not in spite of it. They exist because the text states they exist and States Parties have accepted their applicability in their individual legal systems. Consequently, the Convention cannot be said to have failed human rights conceptually. The only issue of conceptual relevance rests in the moment of judicial interpretation. This would be an empirical matter to be determined through the classic method of analysis of Court judgments. We only ask then: do they accord with the text?; do they act in good faith when compared with the terms of the document that provides the authority for judgment?

But such a reading seems odd. The Convention was deliberately framed with reference to the UDHR. This was the authoritative instrument from which it took its cue. It was acknowledged as contributing to the realisation of the dream of a universal declaration on human rights. It was supposed to take a general moral statement applicable throughout the world and find a means by which it could be promoted effectively in a specific region. That being so, the Convention's particularist approach conceptually contradicted the purpose and content of the UDHR. Within the Convention's own terms the contradiction can only undermine *any* conception of human rights. It will forever stand as a challenge to its own generation.

For these key reasons of memorialisation and clarity regarding universalism, the Convention failed human rights conceptually. This is not to say that there is *a* concept of human rights to which one *has* to adhere. Rather, the text failed to make any sensible choice between a number of possibilities, some of which appear in its wording and some of which can be inferred from the context of its creation. If only at the level of needing *some* conception of human rights in a document purportedly designed to give them substance, the Convention failed.

But the general conceptual failure, I suggest, has been accompanied by more specific failures of ideal. There are two further areas of concern: first, the limitations that have been adopted for particular rights and the application of the Convention in general; and secondly, the systemic

---

[9] Affluent in comparison to the colonial world lying beyond Europe.

weaknesses that have constantly restricted the Convention's ability to respond to human rights challenges. I will look at these only very briefly to sketch the argument I am making.

First, then, the limitations or qualifications that were negotiated for the majority of rights in the Convention sit uneasily in comparison with their supposed counterparts in the UDHR. Admittedly, the international Bill of Rights that followed the UDHR in 1966 incorporated some limited qualifications to certain rights, but at the time of its creation the Convention deliberately set about *restricting* the possible impact of those rights. One example will suffice. Let us compare Article 8 of the ECHR, which related to respect for family life, and Article 12 of the UDHR. The latter provides that

> [n]o one shall be subjected to arbitrary interference with his privacy, family, home or correspondence, nor to attacks upon his honour and reputation. Everyone has the rights to the protection of the law against such interference or attacks.

The Convention article, on the other hand, states that:

> 1. Everyone has the right to respect for his private and family life, his home and his correspondence.

> 2. There shall be no interference by a public authority with the exercise of this right except such as is in accordance with the law and is necessary in a democratic society in the interests of national security, public safety or the economic well-being of the country, for the prevention of disorder or crime, for the protection of health or morals, or for the protection of the rights and freedoms of others.

The extensive qualifications introduced have given life not to human rights but to the 'margin of appreciation' principle that recognises and favours an acknowledgment, in essence, of the importance of the parochial 'public interest'. In terms of human rights this is again a direct contradiction. For the notion of the 'public interest' that can be attached to the 'human' element of 'human rights' must be unlimited in its conception of 'the public'. That is an inherent quality of the language of universality applied to human rights. It is what distinguishes them from those 'rights' otherwise constructed without any sense of humanity necessarily informing their content, let alone their application. Although the debate about the nature of human rights is by no means resolved, it remains a plausible contention, as James Griffin for one has recently put it, that a human right is 'a right that we have simply in virtue of being human'.[10] The humanity that is implied in human rights requires a way to be found for their realisation, *not* a surrender to the practical barriers put in their way by legal

[10] J Griffin, *On Human Rights* (Oxford, Oxford University Press, 2008) 2.

jurisdiction and political partiality. That, it could be said, is part of the promise of 'human rights', their transcendence of the political at least at the level of their conceptual recognition. As David Luban argues, 'human rights are the demands of all of humanity on all of humanity'.[11]

In the context of the immediate aftermath of the Second World War and the suffering inflicted by governments unconcerned with appeals of humanity, it seems reasonable to me that the notion of human rights was intended to evoke a greater awareness of human bond beyond mutual citizenship. Borders were to be transcended, which, of course, suggests that any understanding of public interest should have been conceived in this light. The Convention contravened this position.

This is not to say the approach of the Convention is or was unreasonable per se. There is undoubtedly much to be said for the need for each state to be able to manage its laws and its social and political choices in its own way. The protection of a plurality of ethical responses to dilemmas of conflicts between individual and collective interests may well be considered a notable virtue. So long as the essence of the right concerned is not undermined, governments should have the ability to make decisions that interfere with individual rights for the benefit of the wider community. Similarly, there are many theorists who argue that any universal idea of human rights existing independently of a system that constructs their parameters and contents is an empty dream. The Benthamite attribution of 'nonsense' to human rights as an ungrounded ideal remains a strong critique. It is reflected in the argument that the 'rights' aspect of the notion requires a system that not only identifies those who hold those rights but also those to whom those rights are addressed (the 'obliged', we might call them) *and* the extent to which the holders can expect the obliged to respond to their claims. The 'nonsense' of human rights is then said to occur when the logic of 'all humanity owing an obligation to all humanity' is applied to political systems. How can they in reality respond to such an overarching idea without diluting its impact to the point of impossibility? Far better, it is argued, to rely on existing state law to provide definition and certainty in realising designated human rights at the very point where they are needed: at particular state institutions exercising power over people's lives. Such 'rights realism' remains a strong argument for allowing the 'text' to rest not too heavily on human rights concepts but rather on its own terms.

But can this approach really accord with a notion of 'human' as opposed to other types of rights? If we attribute any universalist characteristics to

---

[11] D Luban, 'Just War and Human Rights' (1980) 9:2 *Philosophy and Public Affairs* 160–81, 174.

human rights, then clearly such potential restrictions can excuse consider-able infringements on the liberty of people. It also reflects a dimension that arises through the adjudication process. If there is to be a concept of human 'rights', the margin of appreciation inspired by the qualifications on some rights might tip the balance too far towards 'interests' rather than rights.[12]

This potential structural failing of human rights as a concept is mirrored and extended through the introduction of Article 15 and the powers of states to derogate from most rights under the Convention.[13] Simpson again tells the story of how this provision was produced in an 'amateurish fashion' and immediately became a concern for certain states with regard to colonies.[14] The uncertainty attached to how the Convention rights should apply to territories outside the immediate jurisdiction of State Parties may have been of acute concern in the late 1950s when direct colonialism was nearing its end, but it remains a significant problem in practice. The history of Turkish involvement beyond its borders and recent practices of the United Kingdom in Iraq and Afghanistan as well as Russia in Chechnya, have been beset by an inherent failure in the Convention to come to grips with its terms of application. But the irony lies precisely in the fact that this failure was most obvious when it was drafted. The colonial question was very much alive at the time, and, as noted, it has only been fairly recently that similar problems have been revived in disparate and perhaps unpredictable ways. Nonetheless, the initial failure to address the scope of application and the scope of derogation in an effective way has left a legacy that continues to have considerable implica-tions for human rights. It further undermines the universality of the concept and gives impetus to the idea that we are not dealing with human rights at all, but rather some other form of rights. In the case of the Convention we might term these 'European rights' perhaps. These would be related to but not synonymous with human rights.

The second area of concern arises from systemic weaknesses in the whole structure of the Convention. Steven Greer identifies the most significant of these as 'case overload', the inability to enforce judgments of the Court, the ineffective means adopted to improve the application of the Convention, and the jurisprudential confusion involved in adopting an

[12] I do not mean here interests in the sense of the 'interest' rather than 'will' theory of rights. The interest theory of rights suggests rights as a vehicle for the recognition and enforcement of people's interests, very broadly conceived. In the present instance I have instead in mind a more narrowly conceived set of political 'interests', focusing on the institutions of power within a society.
[13] The notable exceptions are Article 2 (right to life) other than as a result of 'lawful acts of war', Article 3 (right not to be tortured etc), Article 4 (the prohibition of slavery), and Article 7 (no crime without law).
[14] Simpson, *Human Rights*, above n 8, 875 et seq.

'individual justice' model rather than a 'constitutional justice' model.[15] In essence, the last issue again takes us back to the conceptual failing. It speaks of a confusion of purpose that applies to international human rights as global phenomena. Should international rights instruments act as a means for interfering in the affairs of states *and* providing a direct channel for individuals to seek redress? Or should those courts, tribunals or commissions constructed by these instruments provide general guidance on errors, flaws and abusive practices that can inform future procedures adopted by states parties both specifically and collectively? The Convention as developed through the jurisprudence of the Court has failed to make this choice. And as a result the sense of human rights promoted by the regime has become confused. When weighed with the 'crises' (as Greer calls them) of case overload and ignored decisions, the impact of this conceptual uncertainty serves to undermine both human rights as transcendental in character or as having particular application to the lives of all.

In sum, therefore, we have a system that has failed to address significant questions about human rights and their composition and character. Greer's critique that there has been an inadequate determination of the appropriate model of justice adopted (the individual or the constitutional) is part of this problem. But so too is the failure to adopt a conception of justice constructed with a plausible notion of human rights in mind.

B.   Second Proposition

My second proposition follows from the understanding that the Convention system is conceptually flawed from the perspective of a plausible understanding of human rights. The political constraints placed on the meaning of human rights through the Convention text, which were the result of perceived national interests and the preservation of national sovereignty (themselves both antithetical, I would suggest, to the underlying appeal of the human rights discourse in contemporary international law), has meant that we cannot look to the practice of the ECtHR in order to provide an effective counterbalance. In other words, it would be expecting too much to rely on the jurisprudence of any court to remedy what is a theoretically defective constituting text. Indeed, any court which attempted to remedy a constitutional flaw through its judgments could be admonished for its lack of respect for the internationally negotiated text *and* have its judgments questioned on the basis of an unjustified activism that might even contradict the authorising instrument. That would put in jeopardy the whole mantle of legitimacy placed on the Convention.

---

[15]   See Greer, *The European Convention on Human Rights*, above n 3.

For this reason, the number of 'good' decisions made over the years is unlikely to remedy or even justify the failure of the Convention as I have described. That is not to say that the judgments handed down over the years possess scant value. Undoubtedly we can point to a whole welter of decisions which have helped further particular human rights, giving them greater definition, wider application and directive clarity. We might not be able to claim that individuals who brought the cases to Court have benefited (mainly due to the delays in reaching judgment, that have undermined the usefulness of decisions for people alleging abuse). Additionally, we might not be able to suggest that States Parties have uniformly honoured their obligations to make necessary changes to their practices or laws to reflect the 'good' judgments. The systemic failings already mentioned demonstrate that any confidence that good decisions will lead to positive action has to be muted. But even so, there are many instances where there has been a positive development of Convention rights benefiting societies and individuals alike in the medium and longer term. At least that is the argument. The difficulty, however, is demonstrating whether this impact is of any great overall consequence. Have the good decisions merely reinforced the failings by emphasising the restricted application of human rights in the European sphere? Have they given greater weight to civil and political rights at the expense of other rights, particularly collective ones, which remain outside the Convention's remit? Have they entrenched the sense that indivisibility as a reliable, even useful, notion of human rights is practically impossible except through the lens of a tight reading of civil and political rights, or at best as a result of discriminatory practices?[16]

Ultimately we lack a clear cost-benefit analysis that would help answer these questions. Maybe that is because it is emotively difficult to talk about human rights in such technical terms. Given their pedigree – the dreams that are often referred to as providing their appeal – constructing a balance sheet along these lines can be difficult to accept. Richard Rorty has pointed to this 'sentimental' quality to human rights in their modern mythology.[17] Even if we would like to address rights in a more technical fashion, thus providing them with some sense of substantive achievement, the allure of human rights does not rely on calculations. They generate emotional responses, gut-reactions, that have more to do with people's sense of justice than they do with respecting legal articulation of those rights. But some

---

[16] Eg, Ken Roth provides an indication of the restricted significance of economic and social rights in advocating that they provide grounds for legal action only in limited circumstances. In so doing he eschews the justiciability of many rights other than where there is evidence of discrimination. See K Roth, 'Defending Economic, Social and Cultural Rights' (2004) 26 *Human Rights Quarterly* 63–73.

[17] R Rorty, 'Human Rights, Rationality, and Sentimentality' in S Shute and S Hurley (eds), *On Human Rights: The Oxford Amnesty Lectures 1993* (Oxford, Oxford University Press, 1993) 111–34.

method of evaluation still needs to be conducted, something which remains largely haphazard in the analysis of the Convention system and its jurisprudence. But even with the limited information available it is clear that the respect for the ECtHR's rulings is certainly suspect.

We can see this most clearly in the ability of State Parties to ignore the infrequent but vital occasions when the Court attempts to intervene to *prevent* human rights violations. The bulk of its work, it should be remembered, relates to pronouncing on violations that have already occurred. That is inevitable for any tribunal. But the emergency intervention is an important testing ground for determining the ability of a system of law to respond to human rights claims in the raw, so to speak. In this regard, the ECtHR has the power to impose interim measures against a State Party under Rule 39 of its Court Rules. This states that the

> Chamber or, where appropriate, its President may, at the request of a party or of any other person concerned, or of its own motion, indicate to the parties any interim measure which it considers should be adopted in the interests of the parties or of the proper conduct of the proceedings before it.

Rule 44A, added in 2004, requires that

> [t]he parties have a duty to cooperate fully in the conduct of the proceedings and, in particular, to take such action within their power as the Court considers necessary for the proper administration of justice.

Clearly, such interim measures can only follow if there is an urgent matter to address. And the Court will only issue such measures if there is clear evidence provided by the applicant of an imminent violation. It would be plausible to maintain that any requirement of interim measure provides *the* most acute moment for the testing of the Convention's efficacy to protect human rights. And yet despite this, both Italy and the United Kingdom have recently taken decisions to return non-citizens to other jurisdictions even though there is a real risk of their suffering torture as a result, and even though the Court requested the relevant governments to delay such forced return until the Court could consider the matter.[18] Quite apart from the moral demands of the particular cases, such blatant disrespect of the institution of the Convention is hard to understand except within the terms of an instrument that is fundamentally incapable of intervention for human rights in an effective manner. No matter how 'good' the decisions reached, which is of course a subjective matter for many, the invocation of political exigencies allows governments to follow whatever path seems appropriate. Here as elsewhere, the margin of appreciation, which was introduced by

---

[18] See Report by Thomas Hammarberg, Commissioner for Human Rights of the Council of Europe, following his visit to Italy on 13–15 January 2009, Part IV, Strasbourg, 16 April 2009 and the case of *Al Sadoon v UK* (Application no 61498/08), decision on admissibility by the European Court of Human Rights (Fourth Section), sitting on 30 June 2009.

the Court as a conceptual clarification of the Convention's application (and indeed a judicial acknowledgement that the conceptual design of the text was flawed or at best incomplete), reinforces the undercurrent of contingency in human rights terms within the whole system.

Of course, such a proposition can and will be countered by those who believe in the general impact attributed to the Convention on the improvement in human rights in Europe over the last 50 years. And the evidence of change can be presented in a positive fashion. It would indeed be churlish to suggest that the Convention and the decisions produced by the ECtHR have had no positive influence on the development of human rights cultures in Europe. But how much of this is really a product of Court judgments? Where is the solid evidence that decisions have not only altered laws and changed practices but also have had permanent and widespread effect? Perhaps such evidence is unnecessary. Perhaps it is even unwelcome. For to encourage faith in a system so that it prevails over time the last thing one really needs is hard evidence that can be challenged and subjected to critique. Far better to have a 'sense' of achievement, backed up by reiterated messages from the institutions related to the system and their commentators that change has and is being effected for the better. In this case, whatever approach we take to this research question, 'good decisions' are pretty much irrelevant. They neither prove nor disprove contentions of success or achievement.

C. Third Proposition

It might seem a little ironic, given the above, that my next proposition should make more of 'bad' decisions than I say is possible for 'good decisions'. But in truth the arguments involved are different. 'Bad' decisions can expose the conceptual failure that I maintain underscores the Convention. They can provide an insight not only into the quality of the judges who have the task of interpreting the 'text' but also the parameters of judgement which the text demands. Indeed, it is when judges of great virtue act in *spite* of the text that we can discern an underlying flaw in its composition. Similarly, when they fail to look beyond the constraints of that text we can also discover failings inhabiting it. Of course, this requires a theoretical approach to the Convention that does not accept the 'law as text' and 'law as practice' dichotomy. Each reflects the value of the other.

Yet there is clearly something rather nebulous about using such terms as 'good' and 'bad' judgments. These designations are themselves likely to be the product of judgement. And that is in turn likely to be a subjective matter unless we can identify a plausible basis for making pronouncements one way or another. This returns us to the conceptual underpinning of human rights integral to the first proposition. Without becoming embroiled in discussion about the meaning or foundations of human rights, I will only refer to one quality which I believe can be plausibly assumed: that for a human rights text to be considered just that – a human rights text – it has to be applied *humanely*.

I want to use one case, *N v United Kingdom*, to illustrate my claim; one that I appreciate will require considerably more support through the examination of other cases that I cannot undertake here.[19] Nonetheless, the case of *N* seems to me of great significance in my propositional scheme.

The facts of the case are quickly drawn. N was a Ugandan citizen who had sought asylum in the United Kingdom. She was an HIV sufferer and began to receive anti-retroviral drugs whilst her claim for asylum was still being considered. The Secretary of State then refused her application. N appealed on the grounds that it was clear that if she were returned to Uganda her access to treatment would be severely affected and her life expectancy would be dramatically reduced. This would be a violation of Article 3 of the ECHR. Her appeals through the UK system failed. When the case was referred to the ECtHR, a similar conclusion was reached. The Court determined that only in 'exceptional circumstances' would the expulsion of a failed asylum seeker fall foul of Article 3. The Convention was expressed as being aimed at protecting civil and political rights. Its purpose was inferred as attempting to manage a balance between communal interests on the one hand and the individual's on the other. It did not offer any significant possibility for equalising 'care' (be it health or any other type of care one might imagine) among State Parties and was not designed to address economic and social rights. Consequently, it could not be used to protect those from non-State Parties and in effect be used as a means of addressing global inequalities in health care. This was the central premise of the judgment. It recognised the unpalatable possibility of a contrary finding opening the 'floodgates' to people from outside any State Party to receive free health care. That would be placing 'too great a burden on the contracting states' it was held.

The dissenting judgment of Judges Tulkens, Bonello and Spielmann highlighted the way in which this decision reflects the underlying failure of human rights apparent in the Convention and its system. Two particular arguments are relevant for my purposes.

First, they alluded to the unsatisfactory statement by the majority of the Court that the ECHR was essentially an instrument of civil and political rights, that could not, and indeed should not, be deployed to provide relief or even guidance on wider notions of human rights. Although the dissenters were able to point to previous decisions that there is in theory

---

[19]   *N v United Kingdom* (Application no 26565/05), Grand Chamber, Strasbourg, 27 May 2008.

'no water-tight division' between the two sets of rights, the fact remains that the Convention was conceived in narrow terms.[20] The indivisibility of human rights was from the outset denied by the Convention.

Secondly, the dissenters also objected to the application of a logic of derogation in this case. They recognised that although some balancing exercise had been prevalent early in the life of the Convention system, whereby the 'communal interest' was weighed against the position of the individual, such an approach could not be applied to Article 3. This provision has often been lauded as the 'absolute' right within the Convention, suggesting that it holds a position that denies the legitimacy, from a human rights perspective, of any balance of interests in its application. If someone is found to suffer inhumane treatment at the hands of a State Party then there can be no social interest that would forgive it. This interpretation, the dissenters suggested, was sacrosanct. It had been forged through the case law concerned with returning migrants to their country of origin where they faced a real prospect of torture or ill-treatment.[21] But of course, the Convention does not really offer this protection. It was not designed to do so. The majority of the Court was correct in its interpretation *because of the instrument's very failure that I outlined in the first proposition.* The Convention, in its partial adoption of the human rights idea, denied those same human rights. Providing a politically parochial determination of a balance of interests within its language and structure ensured that human rights were always to be contingent and *subject to* the rights of states.

It is in this sense that the decision in *N* was 'bad' – not from a Convention point of view but rather from a human rights perspective. The same could be said for two other fairly recent cases, *Behrami/Saramati* and *Leyla Şahin v Turkey*.[22] Although I do not have space to examine these judgments they are both correct in their findings in terms of the Convention and both indicative of the central failures I suggest exist.

D.   Fourth Proposition

All of which brings me to my fourth and reasonably short proposition. It is short because it is really a restatement of an element of the first proposition. I have already referred to the systemic problems identified by Steven Greer in his leading work on the ECHR regime. And this fourth proposition merely contends that such problems are further evidence of the

---

[20] The dissenters relied on the case of *Airey v Ireland* (1979) 2 EHRR 305, para 26.

[21] *Chahal v United Kingdom* [1996] ECHR 54, 15 November 1996.

[22] *Joined Cases Behrami v France* and *Saramati v France, Germany and Norway* (2007) 45 EHRR SE10; and *Leyla Şahin v Turkey* (Application no 44774/98), Strasbourg, 10 November 2005, [2005] ECHR 819.

failures of the Convention. The problems of case overload, delay, failure of implementation of judgments, failure to tackle persistent offenders and failure to give priority to rights, all further reinforce my central claim. They are indicative of a system that demonstrates its inability to overcome its underlying conceptual failings. But remedying these problems through an increasing number of additional protocols is a fruitless exercise. If they are even in part the product of a central conceptual failure then however much we might tinker with the details of procedure, however much the rules of the Court and the structures of its operation might be developed, we will never escape that condition. All they can hope to do is diminish some of the injustices made more apparent through the operation of the system itself. So, for instance, speeding up the resolution of cases may well address the wholly egregious sight of the human rights violated struggling to access and obtain some possible just conclusion to their plight (which, because of the requirement that domestic remedies be exhausted before the Convention system can be accessed, is always anyway going to be protracted) but it will not assist in cases such as N. All we may get is less drawn-out processes. But this will not mean that the decisions the Court delivers will be or can be any better as a result or that they may somehow remedy the underlying problem of the Convention.

E.   Fifth Proposition

Despite this argument we should not bury the Convention system just yet. No doubt we can point to many benefits it has supposed to have delivered. But perhaps in order to make it flourish we must extract and memorialise more of its generative ideals and indeed its subsequent popular, if not intellectual, appeal. This will require, I argue, the adoption of a more plausible basic conception of the *purpose* of human rights. This purpose can, in the words of Thomas Pogge, be identified as to 'work for an institutional order and public culture that ensure that all members of society have secure access to the objects of their human rights'.[23] The objects in this case must transcend borders and speak to a public interest that is based on a notion of human rights that focuses on human suffering rather than property.[24] For good or ill, it also means the society being

---

[23] T Pogge, *World Poverty and Human Rights: Cosmopolitan Responsibilities and Reform* (Cambridge, Polity, 2002) 65.

[24] Such re-conceptualisation remains a work-in-progress but can be witnessed from such recent works as A Williams, 'Human Rights and Law: Between Sufferance and Insufferability' (2007) 122 *Law Quarterly Review* 132–57; I Wall, 'On Pain and the Sense of Human Rights' (2008) 29 *Australian Feminist Law Journal* 53; K Woods, 'Suffering, Sympathy, and (Environmental) Security: Reassessing Rorty's Contribution to Human Rights Theory' (2009) 15:1 *Res Publica* 53–66.

addressed in our case is European. Whatever the objections may be to this designation the fact is that so long as the Convention holds itself out as a regional enterprise (which remains an interim measure in the absence of a global regime of human rights that is effective) we cannot hope to find a solution to the problems and failings of the Convention without considering how it can interact and combine with the institutional presence and operation of that other significant institution, the European Union. The continuing attempt to maintain jurisdictional boundaries, which are supposed to ring-fence judicial authorities amongst other things, is not tenable in the long run. A dream of a 'zone of human rights in Europe' with inter-locking but ultimately independent legal human rights regimes will merely perpetuate the unsatisfactory development of competing systems that fail to do justice to human rights both in theory and practice.[25]

This is where the image of a constitutional mosaic might encourage the perpetuation of an unsatisfactory condition of human rights in Europe. Dividing up responsibility and jurisdiction may well allow the failings of the Convention to go unaddressed. Alternatively, I suggest that in order to maintain the Convention's legitimacy and its ability to act as a means for attaining 'justice', which are key to its continuing acceptance and therefore survival, the Convention system has to look beyond mere structural matters of undertaking judgement. It also requires a reading of 'human rights law' that is more blatant in its determination to reflect enduring and universal values. The very nature of the current Convention will not allow that to happen. Its concentration on particular rights, namely the civil and political, with limited and tangential incorporation of the broader spectrum that has been developed during its lifetime, *and* its separation from the political field that human rights inhabit at the parochial level, means it does not have the necessary tools to operate effectively *for* human rights as reconceived. It is a partial instrument with partial application. Similarly, the inability of the Court to make up its mind whether its role is to dispense 'individual' or 'constitutional' justice, as Greer mentions, hardly inspires confidence that the judicial element of the system can compensate for such defects.

But what does this mean for the future of the Convention? By way of conclusion, my fifth proposition is perhaps more provocative than those that precede it. For, I maintain that remedying the conceptual and practical failings of the system would require a fundamental re-conceptualisation of the central purpose (or values) of human rights in line with a more plausible account of their appeal. This would in turn mean extending the

---

[25] My evaluation of the unsatisfactory human rights regime constructed in the EU need not be repeated here but can be found in A Williams, *EU Human Rights Policies: A Study in Irony* (Oxford, Oxford University Press, 2004). Further examination of this subject can be found in A Williams, *The Ethos of Europe* (Cambridge, Cambridge University Press, 2010).

substantive reach of the ECHR and the Court to such a degree that both must cease to exist in their current or projected recognisable form. Any perpetuation of the distinction between civil/political rights and those related to economic, social and cultural matters as well as collective interests (and I include here issues related to resources, the environment, minorities and migration) would be unacceptable. Ideally what is required is the reconstruction of institutions designed to give effect to the re-conceptualised purpose. From a practical perspective the most plausible way of achieving this lies with that more rounded and perhaps grounded institution, the European Union.

This proposition is bound to infuriate those who see all that the EU does as antithetical to the achievement of human rights, or indeed those who see the Convention system as a counterpoint to the EU. But the EU offers the opportunity for developing the centrality of humanity in the idea of human rights that the concept requires. Its Charter of Fundamental Rights is a more complete instrument than the ECHR in terms of contemporary notions of the scope and objects of human rights whilst embracing the history and form of the Convention text. It has also been produced through a much more transparent and participatory process than the Convention, and has the benefit of building on the former and making it more relevant to the current era of globalised economies with interdependent systems afflicted by inter-related dangers.

This does not mean the Charter has been perfected. It remains also a partial instrument from a human rights perspective. It also lacks the legal machinery needed to give it effect. And this is where the Convention *system* will not be buried. For there is much to be said for the development of the European Court of Human Rights, unleashed from its restricted Convention roots, which can fully embrace the constitutional model of justice for human rights with which it has so far only felt able to flirt. In this it has the pedigree that the European Court of Justice, with all its flaws of philosophy when it comes to justice (as I claim elsewhere), does not.[26] Similarly, the human rights mechanisms and systems of the Council of Europe offer considerably more satisfying value than those possessed by the EU organs, and in particular the repressed Fundamental Rights Agency.[27]

If this merger does not happen and the EU survives in its current form, then the Convention will continue to be undermined by comparison to the EU's spread of policy, if not law. The Convention system will also be starved of the political and economic clout of the EU. And the possibilities offered by the EU for human rights (whether or not they are fully realised)

---

[26] A Williams, 'Taking Values Seriously: Towards a Philosophy of EU Law' (2009) 29:3 *Oxford Journal of Legal Studies* 549–77.

[27] By this I allude to the highly restricted mandate adopted for the EU FRA.

mean that any competition between the two systems will result in the undermining of the continuing appeal of the Convention regime. If the EU does not survive it is conceivable that the Convention will be reinvigorated as the only means by which human rights can be advanced continentally. But even then, it will be exposed as so limited in its authority (merely by comparison with the EU's previous potential for human rights practice and legal exposition) that it will suffer by retrospective comparison.

This leaves a considerable amount of work to be done. At the very least it requires us to look beyond the currently offered solution (which is aimed at legitimating the EU more than it is the Convention system) of accession by the EU to the ECHR. We will need to revisit what is meant by human rights; what role they are supposed to play in the economic and social life of individual states; what structures of judgement are necessary to give effect to them; and how systems of scrutiny and intervention can be developed that make human rights more central to European politics. Of course, this will also entail the constant need to reflect on the nature of sovereignty and European law. The lack of a philosophy of the latter is an enduring problem of both the Convention and the EU systems. But perhaps the aura of the Convention and its ability to survive despite consistently challenging some political interests (albeit ineffectively) will remain its most important attribute. In that sense, it would remain alive, much as the *Magna Carta* remains alive for England: an historically vital text lessening in relevance as the years pass, but one from which has emerged a more effective, coherent and relevant human rights regime.

5

Europe's Constitutional Mosaic: Human Rights in the European Legal Space – Utopia, Dystopia, Monotopia or Polytopia?

SIONAIDH DOUGLAS-SCOTT*

I.   INTRODUCTION

AVID CERNY'S *ENTROPA* (a name which perhaps should have signalled that all was not as it seemed) was an enormous mosaic installed in the European Council Justis Lipsius building in Brussels in January 2009. It was commissioned by the European Union to be a positive representation of a unified Europe, and originated with the Czech EU Council Presidency's attempt to present the EU from the perspectives of 27 artists from the individual EU Member States. Before the work was unveiled, the Czech Deputy Prime Minister, Alexandr Vondra, stated that *Entropa* epitomised the motto for the Czech presidency in Europe, 'A Europe Without Borders' – a celebration of European diversity and national cultural identities, continuing to comment that '[s]culpture, and art more generally, can speak where words fail'.[1] Alas, this work of art spoke in a way both undesired and unpredicted by its sponsors.

Once unveiled it proved shocking – for example, revealing Bulgaria as a series of crude, hole-in the-floor toilets, and The Netherlands as drowning under floods, with only a few minarets surfacing from the water. The United Kingdom, known for its Euro-scepticism and relative isolation from the Continent, is 'included' as a missing piece (an empty space) at the top-left of the work.

Although initially *Entropa* may look like a project to decorate official space, on a closer look it appears not as a playful analysis of national

* Professor of European and Human Rights Law, University of Oxford.
[1] *NY Herald Tribune*, January 2009.

Fig 1: Entropa, by David Cerny

stereotypes but rather as a mad display of national traumas and complexes. Individual states in this mosaic are 'constructed' by artists who turned out to be non-existent. Despite Cerny's claim that he had not wished to insult anybody, just to highlight the difficulty of communication, the work appeared to be a massive hoax, a mockery, instead of an artistic representation of the diversity and solidarity of the European Union. Due to this controversy, the sculpture was removed from the Council building and reinstalled in the Centre of Contemporary Art in Prague in June 2009, in the presence of guests including the former Czech President, Václav Havel.

Is *Entropa* a gross allegory of contemporary Europe? It is to be hoped that this is not the situation we have in Europe, an *Entropa* of human rights, a diverse, risible space devoid of any coherent, laudable European values? Yet the varying regimes and processes which exist regarding human rights protection across the European continent are so diverse, complicated and often confusing in their application that it sometimes feels as if the European mosaic has mutated into Entropy.

This chapter seeks to analyse and interrogate this situation, to highlight its problem spots and fault-lines and to suggest mechanisms whereby the worst outcomes may be avoided. In order to do this, I proceed by way of three different analyses. First, what does it mean to have a 'European' human rights regime? This enquiry questions whether, in presenting such a regime as 'European', we thereby render incoherent and dilute in value different human rights protections which are too diverse to be grouped together in this way. Secondly, this chapter asks whether the increasing use of the term 'constitutional' in this context is justified? And if so, what added value does it lend to human rights protection in Europe? Thirdly, if we acknowledge a European 'mosaic' in this context, as a means of capturing this diverse and complex state of affairs, what then emerges from such a reading – from acknowledgment of juxtaposition, contrast, overlap – an overall picture capable of coherence, or a situation verging towards chaos and Entropy?

II.   EUROPE

What is the 'Europe' of human rights and what impact does 'Europe' have on human rights protection?

A.   Legal Geography

Geography is important. There are at the very least two separate human rights geographies of Europe. One concerns an organisation of 27 Member States, and the other, one of 47. Whatever the overlap of aims, specific rights and cultures, this difference in geography is significant.

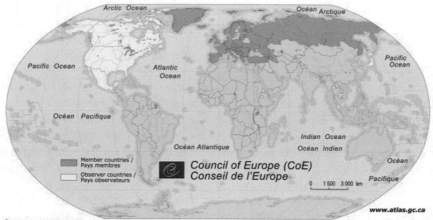

Fig 2: Council of Europe membership

Figure 2 shows a map of the Member States of the Council of Europe. As one can see, its territory stretches over a huge swathe of the Earth – we even find it creeping up on the extreme left of the map, due to the vast expanse of Russia.

One may contrast this membership with the territory of the EU, as illustrated by *Figure 3* below. In fact, *Figure 3* is not a map of the EU as such, being slightly too wide for that, and including some of Turkey and some Central European territory which is not part of the EU – but it clearly covers far less territory than the previous map. What is interesting about this map is that it is a 'mosaic' – compiled from many shots taken from satellite images in space. So it sits nicely with the theme of this collection, but it also captures the fact that we are more and more being 'watched' in a surveillance society in which the EU is playing its part – one in which security state Europe threatens our human rights. Indeed, increasing surveillance (both by the state and by private parties) and infringement of privacy increasingly raise human rights issues, so this map is itself a 'symptom' of our contemporary European human rights situation, as well as also being a map, helping us to chart the geography of EU human rights.

Differences in geography are significant. In the case of the European Convention on Human Rights (ECHR), geography can affect compliance. The ECHR includes Member States such as Russia and Turkey, which raise specific problems (regardless of the separate question of whether we see Russia and Turkey as sufficiently 'European'). Russia raises serious compliance problems for the ECHR, in turn raising rule of law concerns. It has been dissatisfied with judgments against it from the European Court of Human Rights – for example, several judgments finding Chechens to have

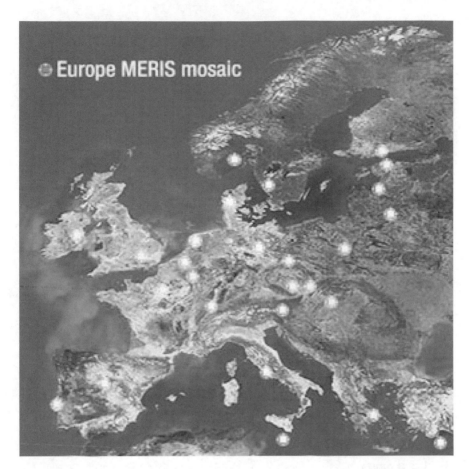

Fig. 3

been ill-treated or tortured;[2] also with the *Ilascu*[3] judgment in which Russia was found to have breached Article 3 of the ECHR in Transnistria. There have been significant problems with Russian compliance – see for example the *Burdov*[4] judgment, which concerned compensation for those suffering nuclear radiation from Chernobyl. There have been other forms of lack of co-operation. For a long time Russia refused to ratify the 14th Protocol to the ECHR, thus hindering the improvement of the institutional enforcement mechanisms of the ECHR – officially because it claimed not to favour the move to one-judge admissibility panels, but in reality,

---

[2] There are many European Court of Human Rights judgments on cases from Chechnya – for example, *Baysayeva v Russia* (Application No 74237/01), judgment of 5 April 2007, *Akhmadova and Sadulayeva v Russia* (Application No 40464/02), judgment of 10 May 2007.
[3] *Ilascu v Moldova and Russia* (2005) 40 EHRR 46.
[4] *Burdov v Russia (No 2)* (2009) 49 EHRR 2.

probably due to an unwillingness to cooperate. Less legally, former ECHR President Luzius Wildhaber claimed[5] to have been poisoned on a trip to Russia, perhaps in retaliation to some unfavourable judgments against Russia. Indeed, the former Communist states with the poorest human rights records are often former constituents of the USSR – including of course Russia itself – which have 'at best a very ambivalent sense of European identity'.[6]

The membership of Turkey raises some similar problems. For a long time not considered sufficiently 'European' to be a member of the EU, Turkey has not suffered a similar fate in relation to the ECHR. But its treatment of the Kurds has, like Russia's relations with the Chechens, created a lot of work for the ECtHR, including fact-finding missions to eastern Turkey, so casting the Strasbourg Court into the role of a Court of First Instance.

It is no accident that a vast proportion of applications to the ECtHR comes from these states. If we add to this fact the existence of other conflicts such as that in Georgia, regarding which the first applications are now being received at the European Court of Human Rights, it can be seen that there exists within the Council of Europe a geography which aids and abets in the construction of a human rights profile. These changes are also, however, in turn capable of changing the nature of the European Court's role, perhaps actually making it more constitutional – a state of affairs which will be discussed later in this chapter.

For the present, however, it is sufficient to note that for the Council of Europe, what exists is a matter of a post-Western,[7] or even maybe a post-European,[8] as well as a possibly post-national, human rights profile.

B.   Legal Space

So it is the case that the Council of Europe (COE) and the EU do not share the same geographical legal space of human rights. What exists is more likely to take the shape of two concentric circles, with a very large area of common ground in the first circle. Although comity has largely character-ised the relationship between the two European courts, there is some jealousy over this shared territory of the EU and COE, evidence of a fear

---

[5]   See eg 'I was poisoned by Russians, human rights judge says', *The Guardian*, 31 January 2007.

[6]   Steven Greer, *The European Convention on Human Rights* (New York, Cambridge University Press, 2006) 126.

[7]   See Gerard Delanty, 'Peripheries and borders in a post-western Europe', *Eurozine*, 20 December 2007.

[8]   See William Outhwaite, *European Society* (Cambridge, Polity Press, 2008).

that the EU might seek to usurp or marginalise[9] the COE's role in the human rights field – a fear expressed by Pierre Drzemczewski,[10] a fear whose realisation may have been rendered more likely by the now binding nature of the EU Charter of Fundamental Rights, since the Lisbon Treaty came into force. The Juncker report specifically addressed this relationship. In this report, Prime Minister Jean-Claude Juncker proposed that a working rule be established, according to which

> the decisions, reports, conclusions, recommendations and opinions of [the Council of Europe] monitoring bodies: 1. will be systematically taken as the first Europe-wide reference source for human rights; 2. will be expressly cited as a reference in documents which they produce.[11]

This means taking something which today is simply a practice, and turning it into a rule for EU'.[12]

So there exists a certain amount of tension and competition over this European human rights legal space – in fact, what is even described in a recent *Justice* report as 'an unsightly scrap'.[13]

We find geography intruding again to an extent in the issue of jurisdiction. The European Court of Human Rights has referred to the ECHR operating within the 'legal space of the contracting parties'.[14] But what is within this legal space? Not Belgrade in the former Yugoslavia, according to the Strasbourg Court in *Bankovic*, which stated that the ECHR was 'not designed to be applied throughout the world, even in respect of the conduct of contracting parties'.[15] Yet elsewhere, the European Court has stated that it should 'avoid a vacuum in human rights protection'.[16] What exactly does this mean? How do we know if territory will be brought within the ECHR jurisdiction?[17] And then why not Iraq? Afghanistan? If not already?

---

[9] Elsewhere the fear that the EU is becoming an 'Empire' has been expressed, partly due to an aggressive application of its rules to its neighbours, evidencing imperial politics – see Jan Zielonka, *Europa as Empire* (Oxford, Oxford University Press, 2007).

[10] Eg Pierre Drzemczewski, 'The Council of Europe's Position with Respect to the EU Charter of Fundamental Rights' (2001) 22 *Human Rights Law Journal* 31.

[11] Jean-Claude Juncker, Council of Europe / European Union: 'A Sole Ambition for the European Continent', Report to the Heads of State and Government of the Member States of the Council of Europe (11 April 2006). See also Memorandum of Understanding Between the Council of Europe and the European Union, adopted at the 117th Session of the Committee of Ministers, CM(2007)74 (10 May 2007).

[12] *ibid*. Accession of the EU to the ECHR (ongoing at the time of writing) also raises the issue of whether the ECHR should be seen as hierarchically superior.

[13] *Justice*, 'Human Rights and the Future of the European Union' (April 2008) *Justice Futures Series* p 5.

[14] *Bankovic and others v Belgium and others* (Application No 52207/99) (2001) 11 BHRC 435.

[15] *ibid*.

[16] *Cyprus v Turkey* (2002) 35 EHRR 30.

[17] See on this R *(Al-Jedda) v Secretary of State for Defence* [2008] 1 AC 332 (HL), and R *(Al-Skeini and Others) v Secretary of State for Defence* [2007] UKHL 26. Also *Al Saadoon and Mufdhir UK* (Application No 61498/08) in which territory occupied by UK troops in Iraq was held to fall within the jurisdiction of the ECHR.

C. Different Geography, Different History

All of this large 'European' space does not have a shared history, nor a single route to modernity and post-modernity. A landmass stretching from Cape Finisterre to Vladivostok is simply too large for this. Enlargement brought a change in Europe as a geopolitical entity. If we consider the post-Second World War Europe, and in particular the EEC, which colonised the word 'Europe' for quite some time, we see a region born out of reconciliation between France and Germany and then dedicated to economic prosperity. However, this earlier understanding can no longer dominate our conception of Europe – and other strands of meaning, each with its own history, enter the scene. Scuzs[18] divided Europe into three distinct regions: western/Carolingian; central European; and Eastern, which is closely linked with Russia and with no clear Eastern frontier. If Europe has previously looked to classical civilisation and Renaissance art to find its heritage and values, then it should now also look to Byzantium, Andrei Rublev and the Ottoman Empire.

There are also the 'darker' recent histories that shape this diversity of human rights Europe.[19] If the EEC was born out of an attempt to avoid the conflict of the Second World War, we have to add to that more recent pasts which involve conflict in Chechnya, Georgia, Eastern Turkey, foul prison conditions in Russia, as well as concerns arising over lustration[20] in eastern and central Europe. Russia presents a huge challenge, with an autocratic past and no tradition of democracy, and whose former President Putin has stated that he wanted a 'quick fix of dictatorship through law'.[21]

'Europe' now attempts to surmount these challenges. Although they arise from countries which are now members of the European Union (Lithuania, Poland, Czech republic[22]), the lustration cases have, so far at least, come knocking at the doors of the Strasbourg rather than the

[18] J Scüzs, 'Three Historical Regions of Europe' in John Keane (ed), *Civil Society and the State* (London, Verso, 1988).

[19] See eg Christian Joerges and Navraj Singh Ghaleigh (eds), *Darker Legacies of Law in Europe: The Shadow of National Socialism and Fascism Over Europe and Its Legal Traditions* (Oxford and Portland OR, Hart Publishing, 2003).

[20] Lustration (from the Latin lustration – 'purification by sacrifice') is used to denote 'purification' of state organisations from their 'sins' under the Communist regime and it is mainly used in the context of public life of post-Communist Central and Eastern Europe. It is a measure barring officials and collaborators of a former regime from positions of public influence. Various states adopted laws relating to lustration in Central and Eastern Europe, some of which were significantly stricter than others, and all of which were adopted in the early to mid-1990s.

[21] Quoted in Jeffrey Kahn, 'Russian Compliance with Articles Five & Six of the European Convention of Human Rights as a Barometer of Legal Reform & Human Rights in Russia' (2002) 35 *University of Michigan Journal of Law Reform* 641.

[22] See, for example, *Matyjek v Poland* (Application No 38184/03), judgment of 24 April 2007.

Luxembourg court, raising conflicts between a public working through and seeking exposure of a Communist past, and the individual's desire for privacy and fair trial. Purification, however vigorous, does not necessarily conquer the past. The Communist past also provides the impetus for a recent innovation of the European Court of Human Rights in the shape of the 'pilot judgment', first really explicated in the case of *Broniowski* concerning the right to property beyond the Bug river, and later maintained in *Hutton Czapska*.[23] The situation of the Roma, in Central Europe, displaced after the fall of Communism, causes concern.[24] The *Vajnai*[25] case, concerning the banning of the red star in Hungary, held by the Strasbourg Court to infringe the freedom of expression on the grounds that Hungary is now a stable democracy able to cope with divisive signs of its past, might be seen as an example of a more successful working through. This extension to the East has also greatly increased the number of applications to the European Court of Human Rights, threatening its very ability to function.

Out of this very diverse geography and history, is it possible to distil any particular values to underpin our notion of Europe? Human rights might seem to be one of the best candidates, but *which* human rights? If the COE feels threatened by an emerging EU in this field, and if the European Court of Human Rights finds itself dealing with some very different types of human rights issues beyond the remit of EU jurisdiction, does this also mean that human rights in Europe is simply too diverse for any underlying unifying values of the European space? It should be noted that, due to the fact that the focus of this chapter lies with transnational protection, this section has not even attempted discussion of national human rights regimes, which add a third dimension to human rights protection across the continent.[26] If there exists a lack of unifying values and approaches, does it really matter? Does it affect protection of human rights in this area? These questions will be carried over into the next two sections and some attempted resolution offered in the conclusions.

---

[23] *Broniowski v Poland* (2006) 43 EHRR 1; *Hutten-Czapska v Poland* (2006) 45 EHRR 4.

[24] Roma cases, *Nachova v Bulgaria* (2005) 39 EHRR 793.

[25] *Vajnai v Hungary* (Application No 33629/06), judgment of 8 July 2008). Interestingly also a parallel action was also brought in the ECJ, which was found to be inadmissible.

[26] The *Omega* case (Case C-36/02 *Omega Spielhallen v Oberbürgermeisterin der Bundesstadt Bonn* [2004] ECR I-9606) revealed a concept of dignity singular to one Member State. The *Grogan* case (Case C-158/91 *Society for the Protection of Unborn Children Ireland Ltd (SPUC) v Grogan* [1991] ECR I-4685) regarding the Irish abortion ban (a situation which would now be extended to Malta and Poland) also reveals the problems which can result from one Member State's taking a particular and isolated view of human rights.

III.   'CONSTITUTIONAL'

Does Europe have a 'constitutional' mosaic in the human rights field, and if so, does this aid and abet human rights protection? A first thought is that, if the concept of 'Europe' is problematic, then the term 'constitutional' is just as much so. It might also seem that enlargement of both institutions – COE and EU – increasing their diversity, should make them look even less like a state, but does that make them less able to be 'constitutional'? Or might this situation even be compared to a return to a 'neo medieval' situation?[27]

Much has been written about the 'constitutional' nature of the EU. Yet, however much academics have fixated on the topic, a 'constitutional' EU has been a notion that proved unpopular with the European public in the debacle over the failed Constitutional Treaty. Even if aspects of contemporary EU law may possess de facto 'constitutional' features, it appears that the European public does not think of them as such. Nevertheless, human rights may be able to fulfill a 'constitutional' role across Europe. National human rights may play an important role in domestic constitutions. But the most obvious medium for a transnational role for human rights would seem to be the ECHR rather than the EU, and this section therefore focuses on the ECHR.

Quite a lot has been written about the 'constitutional' ECHR recently, although this subject is not yet the growth industry that characterises the 'constitutional' nature of the EU. A contemporary preoccupation among human rights jurists and lawyers is that of how the European Court of Human Rights in many ways now acts as a constitutional court for Europe. As we find this idea coming from members of the Court itself (for example, former Presidents Luzius Wildhaber and Rolf Ryssdael, and the Court's former Registrar Paul Mahoney[28] – and surely not for self-aggrandising purposes) as well as from prominent academics such as Steven Greer,[29] we should take it seriously.

---

[27]   For use of this term, see Zielonka, *Europe as Empire*, above n 9; also Marlene Wind, 'The European Union as a polycentric polity: returning to a neomedieval Europe' in Marlene Wind and Joseph HH Weiler (eds), *European Constitutionalism Beyond the State* (Cambridge, Cambridge University Press, 2003).

[28]   Luzius Wildhaber, 'A Constitutional Future for the European Court of Human Rights?' (2002) 23 *Human Rights Law Journal* 161; Rolv Ryssdal, 'On the road to a European constitutional Court' in (1991) *Recueil des cours de l'Académie de droit européen* 3; Mahoney, 'New Challenges for the European Court of Human Rights Resulting from the Expanding Caseload and Membership' (2002) 21 *Pennsylvania State International Law Review* 101, 105.

[29]   Greer, *The European Convention on Human Rights*, above n 6, 126.

A. What Does it Mean for the ECHR to be 'Constitutional'?

But what would it mean for the ECHR and European Court of Human Rights to be more 'constitutional' in any case? The ECHR provides a basic Charter of Rights for its Member States.[30] So much is clear – but does this mean it has a 'constitutional' function? It would take a very large and long enquiry to expound on what a constitution is, and what it does, and whether it can be applied to transnational entities, and whether if it could, it would take on a different meaning. Jacques Delors described the EU as an 'unidentified political object' and perhaps that is the best way of describing the ECHR and its institutions. However, one has to work with some conceptual framework so, in good company,[31] I will work very loosely with Raz's writings on the nature of a constitution, which are general enough to capture examples other than the paradigm nation state, and give a basis on which to work, but precise enough to be helpful in this context.

Raz argues that a constitution, at least in its richer sense, is (i) constitutive of the legal and political structure, (ii) stable, (iii) written, (iv) superior to other laws, (v) justiciable, (vi) entrenched and (vii) expresses a common ideology.[32] The ECHR fits with some but not all of these characteristics. The main problem seems to lie with Raz's first 'constitutional characteristic' – the notion that constitutions are constitutive of political and legal structure, given that the ECHR[33] does no real constituting of the executive or legislature. It does not aspire to do the many and varied things that national constitutions do, nor does it contain the range of powers that characterise national constitutions. On the other hand, the task that it performs, namely to set limits on how states may treat peoples, has come, at least in the twentieth century, to be seen as one of the basic elements of a constitution – Bradley and Ewing describe this area of constitutional law as 'one branch of human learning and experience that helps make life in today's world less brutish than it might otherwise be'.[34]

The ECHR may also fail to conform with Raz's stipulated fourth characteristic of constitutions, namely their posited superior nature as law. Although the ECHR is in any case, as an international treaty, binding on

---

[30] Per Beddard, *Human Rights and Europe*, 3rd edn (Cambridge, Cambridge University Press, 1993) 5.

[31] See Wojciech Sadurski, 'Partnering with Strasbourg: Constitutionalization of the European Court of Human Rights, the Accession of Central and East European States to the Council of Europe, and the Idea of Pilot Judgments' (2009) 9(3) *Human Rights Law Review* 397–53.

[32] Joseph Raz, 'On the Authority and Interpretation of Constitutions: Some Preliminaries' (2001) 2 *Anuario de Derechos Humanos, Nueva Epoca*

[33] Although its parent organisation, the Council of Europe, does so in a very weak sense.

[34] Anthony Bradley and Keith Ewing, *Constitutional and Administrative Law*, 14th edn (Harlow, Pearson, 2007) 417.

states, as we shall discuss, its status as superior to other laws is complex. But the ECHR does comply with all of what Raz characterises as the key features of a constitution. Sadurski, for example, characterises it as 'largely if not fully constitutional'.[35]

One view of the ECHR's 'constitutional' nature sees it as part of the developing narrative of the ECHR more generally. The ECHR was originally set up as a defence of liberal democracy against totalitarianism – as a 'collective insurance policy' for its members. As the Cold War developed, it played its part in the ideological battle between West and East, which included human rights law. With the coming down of the Iron Curtain, this role was lost, given that the ECHR's primary role could no longer be that of defending liberal democracy against Communism. For a while it was even suggested that it suffered from an identity crisis.[36] However, according to this account, it was then that a new 'constitutional' future provided a tentative answer, a new role for the ECHR in a new century – an example of the evolution of the ECHR, another illustration of its ability to operate as a 'living instrument'.[37] This account locates the ECHR firmly at the centre of contemporary politics and European history as well as suggesting it may offer a guiding role in the transformation of Europe.

Another approach is to suggest that a constitutional role might also provide a solution to the overloading of the Court, requiring some sort of streamlining of applications, so that the system becomes less geared to individual and more to constitutional justice. Again, underlying this is the notion that the Court may offer guidance and steering, that it may have a broader role in the development of values.

However, it is the case that, until quite recently, the Court has been relatively constitutionally conservative. In the early 1990s, Conor Gearty described the case law of the Court as pertaining to a 'due process' methodology without any great substantive philosophy, with a reluctance to give judgments at a high level of generality.[38] Yet it can be said that its style became more general and supranational in the 1990s, and in 1991 Ryssdal described the ECHR as an 'embryo of a European Constitution'.[39] Also, the Court has been growing in confidence in handling the ECHR as 'an instrument of European public order' – a term increasingly used in the

---

[35]   Sadurski, 'Partnering with Strasbourg', above n 31.
[36]   Stéphanie Hennette-Vauchez, 'Divided in Diversity: National Legal Scholarship(s) and the European Convention of Human Rights' EUI-RSCAS Research Paper 2008/39.
[37]   Per *Tyrer v United Kingdom* (1978) 2 EHRR 1.
[38]   Conor Gearty, 'The European Court of Human Rights and the Protection of Civil. Liberties: an Overview' (1993) 52 *Cambridge Law Journal* 89–127.
[39]   Ryssdal, 'On the road', above n 28.

1990s – for example in *Loizidou* and again in *Bosphorus*.[40] For example, the previous President of the Court, Luzius Wildhaber, maintained that the Court should increasingly concentrate on judgments of principle which 'build up the European "public order"' and which place the Court in its true 'constitutional role'[41].

The European Court of Human Rights also works on the basis of a set of principles which could be identified as 'constitutional'. Stephen Greer has usefully categorised the following as 'primary' constitutional principles: teleogical interpretation, the 'rights' principle (effective protection of Convention rights), the democracy principle, principles of legality, fairness and the rule of law, balancing and priority to rights; and as 'secondary' constitutional principles he designates: autonomous interpretation, dynamic interpretation positive obligations, subsidiarity, proportionality, absolute necessity, non-discrimination and margin of appreciation.[42] We might quibble with the naming of some of these as 'principles' rather than interpretive tools and also their categorisation as of secondary or primary importance, but these are undoubtedly concepts which the Court uses in its reasoning, and some of them, at least, have a 'constitutional' look to them.

B.   Pilot Judgments

Those who wish to stress the ECHR's constitutional nature point to the 'pilot judgments' which it has been giving with increasing frequency since the *Broniowski* case.[43] This is a new, very important and possibly 'constitutional' departure. In the traditional view, the Strasbourg Court is seen as providing justice in the *individual* case, specific to the facts of that case, and as giving declaratory judgments, leaving it to the national authorities to implement the judgments in the ways they see fit, providing they comply with them. However, given the huge flow of applications, many of them from Central and Eastern European states,[44] often relating

---

[40]   *Loizidou v Turkey* (1995) 20 EHRR 99; *Bosphorus Hava Yollari Turizm v Ireland* (2006) 42 EHRR 1.

[41]   Wildhaber, 'A Constitutional Future', above n 28, 163. See also Garlicki in *Ocalan v Turkey* (2005) 41 EHRR 985 and the Court itself in *Mamatkulov and Askarov v Turkey* (2005) 41 EHRR 494.

[42]   Greer, *The European Convention on Human Rights*, above n 6, 195.

[43]   *Broniowski v Poland* (2006) 43 EHRR 1 concerned Poland's failure to implement compensatory measures in respect of persons repatriated from the 'territories beyond the Bug River' in the aftermath of the Second World War who had had to abandon their property. According to the Polish Government, the anticipated total number of people entitled to such measures was nearly 80,000.

[44]   But see *Sejdovic v Italy* (2004) 42 EHRR 360 regarding systemic problems with Article 6 in Italy. Also *Greens and MT v UK* (Applications 60041/08, 60054/08) judgment of 23 November 2010 in which the European Court delivered a pilot judgment against the UK regarding its failure to remedy the situation regarding the inability of prisoners to vote in

to systemic flaws in those country's legal systems (usually arising out of their past history, for example land claims under Communism) which provoke continuously repetitious breaches of human rights, the Court instigated the pilot judgment which sets out in general terms what the state must do to remedy breaches, often involving changes to legislation. In these cases, the Court goes beyond the facts of individual litigation and acts more like a constitutional court, enabling it to shape domestic law in more general terms.[45] It also means that the Court has responded to *general legislative* measures rather than *individual* state acts which breach the Convention, ie declaring national legislation incompatible with the Convention.[46] However, it should be noted that the Court has been attacked for its pilot judgments. Judge Zagrebelsky, writing in a partly dissenting opinion in *Hutten-Czapska v Poland*, suggested that, by indicating the need for a state to amend its own legislation to solve a general problem affecting individuals other than the applicant, the Court usurped the role of the Committee of Ministers and entered the realm of politics.

C.   Lack of Coherence/Unconstitutional Features

However, other factors in the ECHR's make-up and development militate against a constitutional nature. Perhaps the most obvious is the 'margin of appreciation',[47] described by Lester as producing for the ECHR a 'pernicious variable geometry'.[48] This doctrine has also been criticised for providing a case law which is 'highly casuistic',[49] and also criticised by members of the Court itself.[50] The need to interpret the ECHR as a 'living instrument', already mentioned, can also lead to unpredictable results, depending on when the Court will feel able to find a common European approach from which to draw. Its reasoning in looking to international trends, is rarely very transparent.[51]

---

elections. The issue of prisoners' voting rights has caused great animosity in some quarters in the UK, illustrating the resistance to the ECtHR taking on a more forceful role.

[45] See also Council of Europe Committee of Ministers resolution inviting the Court to identify in judgments systematic problems, adopted 12 May 2004 (Res(2004)3). Since March 2011, the Pilot Judgment procedure has been codified in Rule 61 of the European Court's rules.

[46] See Garlicki, 'Cooperation of courts: The role of supranational jurisdictions in Europe' (2008) 6 *International Journal of Constitutional Law* 37; also earlier cases which might be some evidence of the general approach, ie *Marckx v Belgium* (1979) 2 EHRR 330.

[47] *Handyside v United Kingdom* (1979–80) 1 EHRR 737.

[48] Lord Lester of Herne Hill, 'Universality Versus Subsidiarity: A Reply' (1998) 1 *European Human Rights Law Review* 73, 75.

[49] Janneke Gerards, 'Judicial Deliberations in the European Court of Human Rights' in Nick Huls, Maurice Adams and Jacco Bomhoff (eds), *The Legitimacy of Highest Courts' Rulings – Judicial Deliberations and Beyond* (The Hague, TMC Asser Press, 2009) 407–36.

[50] Eg Judge de Meyer in *Z v Finland* (1997) 25 EHRR 371.

[51] See *Goodwin v United Kingdom* (2002) 35 EHRR 18; *Selmouni v France* (2000) 29 EHRR 403.

Secondly, although the Court has also chosen to give autonomous meanings to Convention concepts, such as 'civil servant', rather than looking to find a common meaning from Member States,[52] it lacks other features which might emphasise an autonomous, constitutional, nature – such as the supremacy and direct effect possessed by EU law. Although as an international treaty it binds states at international law level, its status in national law is unclear and differs from state to state. In some countries it has constitutional status – such as in Austria – but by no means all. In quite a few it has only the same status as an ordinary statute (Germany and Italy). In a recent survey, 21 out of 32 constitutional courts surveyed declared themselves not bound by Strasbourg pronouncements.[53]

In the well-known *Görgülü* case[54] of 2004, the German Constitutional Court declared that whilst domestic courts were bound to give European Court of Human Rights judgments full effect, those judgments had limited *res judicata* effect and were not binding *erga omnes*. The German Constitutional Court stated that German courts should not violate prior ranking (ie constitutional) law. This undermines the growing *erga omnes* effect which European Court judgments have, at least as far as their interpretive value is concerned. Contrast this to the position in EU law, under the preliminary reference system, in which national courts must apply European Court of Justice rulings, and also the situation in which a Court of Last Instance may have to review a judgment, final in national law, on the basis of a subsequent ECJ ruling.[55]

There is also the fact that the European Court of Human Rights has over the past 10 years or so been presented with cases of the most severe rights violations – for example, prison conditions in Russia (*Kalashnikov*[56]) and mistreatment of Chechens by Russia, as well as cases of torture in Turkey, for example as in *Aksoy*.[57] Many of these cases have focused on specific individual victims rather than on underlying trends of official human rights abuses, so lessening any more general or 'constitutional' effect. In some of these cases the Court has had to make its own investigations, relieving the appellant from the requirement of exhausting domestic remedies, thus acting like a Court of First Instance and again lessening 'constitutional' impact. This contrasts with most of the Court's activities pre-1992, which

---

[52] *Pellegrin v France* (2001) 31 EHRR 26.
[53] Nico Krisch, 'The Open Architecture of European Human Rights Law' (2008) 71 *Modern Law Review* 183.
[54] *Görgülü*, BVerfGE, 2 BvR 1481/04, judgment of 14 October 2004. See also *R v Horncastle* [2009] UKSC 14 in which the UK Supreme Court refused to follow the decision of the ECtHRs in *Al Khawaja v UK* (2009) 49 EHRR 1.
[55] Case C-453/00 *Kühne & Heitz NV v Productschap vor Pluimvee en Eieren* [2004] ECR I-837.
[56] *Kalashnikov v Russia* (2003) 36 EHRR 34.
[57] *Aksoy v Turkey* (1997) 23 EHRR 553.

on the whole did not deal with very serious rights violations and which have been described as 'fine tuning'.[58] However, for some, including Wildhaber, this intervention, to deal with terrible rights abuses, aids rather than detracts from the Court's status as a constitutional court.[59]

Further, the ECHR was designed, and still operates, so as to provide for *individual* justice, although, given its huge overloading, individual justice is unlikely in most of the applications it receives, 95 per cent of which are ruled inadmissible. Indeed, the Interlaken Declaration of February 2010, issued by the 'High Level Conference on the Future of the European Court of Human Rights' resolved to preserve the Court's twofold functions of constitutionalism and adjudication. The Court's methodology has been criticised as inadequate and unstructured overall. Greer is one of a host of critics of the Court, complaining that it is insufficiently rigorous in its judgments, often just deciding cases on the individual facts, bedevilled by the margin of appreciation and unstructured 'balancing' attempts.[60]

Overall, we could say that the Court has no conclusive purposive theory of its own legal order, unlike the ECJ – it lacks the 'certaine idee de L'Europe' (of course this may be no bad thing!). Furthermore, we should not assume that constitutionalism at a transnational level need look the same as at a national level. Wildhaber has described the Court as a 'quasi constitutional court sui generis' – perhaps the best way to describe it.

D. Impact of Constitutionalism

The most important question, however, is what the impact of constitution-alisation of the ECHR *could be* for human rights protection in Europe. Constitutionalisation is often thought as a positive force – resulting in unity and harmony, and establishing the rule of law by taming politics. Is it, will it, be positive, or will it lessen human rights protection?

An immediate worry in the Strasbourg context has been that, in a rush for 'constitutional' justice, individual justice will be lost, with individual cases sacrificed to a greater constitutional accommodation. Yet this may be a false dichotomy. Given its present backlog and huge rate of applications (about 40,000 per year, around 98 per cent of which fail) individual justice in Strasbourg is, in any case, unattainable for most.

Greer suggests that the most important role for the ECHR is to provide national institutions, particularly national courts, with a clear indication of the constitutional limits provided by Convention rights on the exercise of

---

[58] Sadurski, 'Partnering with Strasbourg', above n 31, 401.
[59] Wildhaber, 'The European Court of Human Rights – Reflexions on my 15 years in Strasbourg', speech in Sydney, Australia on 21 August 2008.
[60] Greer, *The European Convention on Human Rights*, above n 6, 323.

national public power. This involves generating a case law embodying shared European values, identifying structural problems and scrutinising plausible allegations of serious rights abuse even where not systemic in nature.[61] Wildhaber writes that the aim of granting individual relief is secondary to the 'primary aim of raising the standard of human rights protection'.[62] Therefore the Court should not be a small claims tribunal for Europe. It should instead project an 'abstract' constitutional identity, which leaves considerable scope to national authorities to fashion a range of equally Convention-compliant national norms and in providing a constitution for a partial polity, ie one with executive and judicial but no legislative functions.

A constitutional solution for the Court also helps resolve the problem of how to target most effectively the Court's very scarce resources – by focusing on the most serious violations in Europe and by ensuring that those cases which actually reach the Court are fully reasoned judgements capable of projecting the maximum impact. A greater constitutional identity for the Court may also help compensate for the fact that the Council of Europe's intergovernmental nature and the process of execution of judgments by the Committee of Ministers (ie political and diplomatic, rather than by court control) are unlikely to produce significant improvements in Convention compliance.

Therefore, cases should be primarily selected for adjudication by the Court more because of their *constitutional significance* for Europe as a whole and less because of implications for applicants. This means that cases from states with a high violation rate but low rates of compliance, such as Russia, should feature more prominently (as indeed they do) in the Court's docket than cases from high compliance/low violation states. This requires a change in criteria of admissibility for the ECHR, to involve a test based on the seriousness of the violation, which would bring the ECHR's admissibility process more in line with the German Constitutional Court and US Supreme Court. It would also require a broadening of the 'victim' test in order to bring more systemic violations to the Court's attention. Although some of the reforms of Protocol 14 to the ECHR, now in force, aid in improving ECHR mechanisms, as do the institutionalisation of pilot judgments, more is needed to create a greater constitutional profile for the ECtHR.

Lastly, the Court's method of adjudication should become more constitutionally rigorous. The failure of the Court to develop a coherent constitutional model for interpreting the Convention, and constant use of

---

[61]   Greer, *The European Convention on Human Rights*, above n 6.
[62]   Wildhaber, 'The European Court of Human Rights – Reflexions on my 15 years in Strasbourg', speech in Sydney, Australia on 21 August 2008.

the margin of appreciation has sometimes lent its judgments an unsatisfactory character, lacking in depth and authority.

If the Strasbourg Court were able successfully to adapt in the above ways, promoting a more 'constitutional' ECHR and Court, it is suggested that this would undoubtedly ameliorate human rights protection in Europe overall, fitting the Strasbourg mechanism in a more positive way into the overall European mosaic.

IV.   CONSTITUTIONAL MOSAIC

However, it is not enough to consider the ECHR in isolation. It is one, albeit important, part of Europe's constitutional mosaic. The way in which these pieces fit together is important for human rights protection. What are the other elements which go toward the patterned mosaic of human rights Europe?

A.   'Musing' about Mosaics

I want first to consider the concept of 'mosaic', the theme of this collection. The origins of this term are uncertain. It is believed by some to derive from the Greek term *mousaikòn*, meaning work worthy of the Muses. The connection between the Muses and mosaic artwork is rather uncertain, but it may be that early mosaics were often dedicated to the Muses so that the form and the inspiration for this artform became inextricably associated. Alternatively, it may be the case that ancient temples dedicated to the Muses (*mouseion* in Greek, source of our modern 'museum') were often decorated with mosaic murals. In any case, the term mosaic has come to mean the art of creating images with small pieces of coloured glass, stone or other material.

Mosaics have developed over time, developing in ever more complicated patterns and for different uses. Mathematically-modelled mosaics exist, drawing on the work of Roland Penrose and Escher, as well as the satellite images of our planet. There is also Mosaic Europe – an interactive map – a game where you name all the countries, within a time limit, and there are winners and losers, and of course *Entropy*.

What kind of a mosaic is this then – Europe's constitutional mosaic? There are different inter-relationships and patterns. The relationship between the ECHR and its signatory states is not the same as that between the EU – which is not yet a member of the ECHR – and the ECHR. Overall, the varying combinations suggest a very great complexity – closer to Escher than the original tessellations of the ancient world. In order to examine this complex subject it helps to highlight several areas for a greater focus.

B.   The Relationship between the ECHR and its Member States

This is varied. As already mentioned, the ECHR has a different status in different states. In some, such as Austria and The Netherlands, it has constitutional rank. In some, such as Germany, it has the status of ordinary law, and in others its status lies somewhere in between. Its status also depends on whether that country operates a monist or dualist approach to international law and whether (in the past) they have incorporated the ECHR.

Also, due to the margin of appreciation, the Convention may have a different impact in different states. Freedom of expression may be overridden in some countries under certain circumstances – eg *Otto Preminger*; *Muller v Switzerland*,[63] but not others. Different countries have ratified different Protocols and there exists a great variety of reservations among the Member States. Many have, however, not ratified Protocol 12 on discrimination (the UK has not done so) raising an issue as to whether the ECHR might have reached a saturation point with rights.

National courts have also responded differently to European Court of Human Rights judgments. Studies of constitutional courts in Central and Eastern European states such as Hungary and Poland show that although these courts cite the European Court, they usually give very little analysis of its case law. So these courts appear to be upholding ECHR standards but without much reference to the ECHR itself.[64] The case of *Görgülü* has already been mentioned, in which the German Constitutional Court stated that German courts could disregard Strasbourg in so far as its judgments were incompatible with the central elements of domestic law. Krisch suggests that the *Görgülü* example should be seen as the norm of the relationship between the ECHR and its Member States, but not, however, as a particularly fractious, troubling one.[65] For Krisch, a study of the supposedly compliant ECHR states reveals pluralism below the surface, but he believes that the system works through accommodation rather than friction. However, there are reasons to believe that this is not what has been termed a 'monotopia' – namely, an area of zero friction.[66]

Therefore, it seems that different standards might operate between different countries within the ECHR, given the recent large influx of new Member States. Some of these new members face considerable problems with rights compliance – in particular Russia, eg with regard to its prison conditions. Over 10 years ago, Mark Janis[67] worried that the participation

---

[63]   *Otto Preminger Institute v Austria* (1994) 19 EHRR 34; *Muller v Switzerland* (1991) 13 EHRR 212.
[64]   Sadurski, 'Partnering with Strasbourg', above n 31.
[65]   Krisch, 'The Open Architecture of European Human Rights Law', above n 53.
[66]   This term is used in Ole B Jensen and Tim Richardson, *Making European Space* (London, Routledge, 2004).
[67]   Mark Janis, 'Russia and the Legality of Strasbourg Law' (1997) 1 *European Journal of International Law* 93.

of Russia would increase the possibility of the ECHR being disobeyed and flouted. He feared that Russia would not be able to internalise the laws of the ECHR. Herbert Hart[68] suggested that the minimum conditions for legal validity and the existence of a legal system were not orders backed by threats, but the existence of generally obeyed rules and of secondary rules of change, adjudication and recognition accepted by officials. Cases like *Ilascu* and *Burdov*, in which Russia has failed to accept judgments of the European Court quite openly, indicate the lack of an 'internal point of view'. Russia has denounced the perceived 'politicisation' of the Court, which has repeatedly ruled against Russia for human rights abuses. Furthermore, unlike Turkey, there is no lure of EU membership to hold out to Russia, which does not want to join the EU. The Parliamentary Assembly of the Council of Europe sought to suspend Russia's membership over its conduct in Chechnya, but the Committee of Ministers declined to go along with this. So matters of compliance have returned to the European Court. This has placed the Court in a very invidious position, namely, a choice between giving a ruling which it fears will not be complied with, or to apply lesser standards to Russia, and hence to develop a two-tier standard of justice within the ECHR.

The relationship between the ECHR and its Member States reveals a variegated, incoherent and possibly diseased mosaic pattern and standard of justice. And mosaic disease in fact exists[69] – it is a well-known plant disease. Indeed it is a virus, which means it is a living organism. The shape it takes may be seen in *Figure 4* below. Varying standards of justice, compliance rates and national reception of the ECHR give rise to concern – this is the first of my suggested 'flashpoints'.

Fig 4: Turnip mosaic virus symptoms on the internal leaves of cabbage[70]

---

[68]   Herbert LA Hart, *The Concept of Law* (Oxford, Clarendon Press, 1994).

[69]   See eg Samuel J Martin, *The Biochemistry of Viruses* (Cambridge, Cambridge University Press, 1978).

[70]   Photo courtesy of TA Zitter, Cornell University, Ithaca, NY; available at: vegetablemdonline.ppath.cornell.edu/PhotoPages/CropHosts/Cabbage.htm.

C.   Relationship between the EU and the ECHR – overlapping jurisdictions

The second 'flashpoint' concerns the jurisdictional overlap between the EU and the ECHR. Why are there two supranational organisations in Europe dealing with human rights? Is this excessive? Does it improve or overcomplicate human rights protection in Europe? Early European integration pioneers saw the Council of Europe as a bitter disappointment and lost opportunity – Monnet for example referred to it as 'entirely valueless' – and they therefore chose to go down their own separate route, initially with no Bill of Rights.[71] The story of human rights protection in the EU is well known and will be swiftly stated. Originally lacking a Bill of Rights, the ECJ introduced an unwritten bill of rights into EC law, by way of recognition as general principles of law of those fundamental rights as are to be found in national constitutions and international human rights treaties. Such treaties include the ECHR.[72] Then came the Charter of Fundamental Rights (CFR), proclaimed by the EU's institutions in 2000,[73] to which the ECJ has been referring since 2006,[74] and binding since the entry into force of the Lisbon Treaty in December 2009. To have two treaties and two international organisations dealing with the rights in the ECHR causes complexity and some problems, which will not necessarily be resolved by the proposed accession of the EU to the ECHR, as provided by the Lisbon Treaty amendments.

(i)   The Charter of Fundamental Rights

This may be illustrated by a closer look at the CFR. An obvious point is that the CFR is also much wider in scope than the ECHR, which is largely civil and political in focus. Moreover, even those ECHR rights which are contained in the CFR are not expressed in identical terms. For example, Article 6 of the CFR – the right to liberty and security – is expressed in one clause, whereas in Article 5 of the ECHR it is expressed in five. Yet Article 52(3) of the CFR states that CFR rights are to be interpreted in the same way as the ECHR. The ECHR also contains different restriction clauses for each right, whereas the CFR contains a general limitation clause. Furthermore, the ECHR binds its Member States in all their activities whereas Article 51 of the CFR binds Member States only when they are implementing EC law. The opt-outs obtained by the UK and Poland in the

---

[71]   AW Brian Simpson, *Human Rights and the End of Empire* (Oxford, Oxford University Press, 2004) 224.
[72]   Case 36/75 *Rutili v Ministre de l'intérieur* [1975] ECR 1219.
[73]   Which at last becomes legally binding under the Treaty of Lisbon.
[74]   Case C-540/03 *European Parliament v Council of the European Union* [2006] ECR I-5769, para 25.

negotiations to the Lisbon treaty could also create problems.[75] The United Kingdom and Poland may then opt out of provisions of the CFR (at least where interpreted as going beyond existing UK law) but not out of the ECHR. So,[76] Poland would not be bound if the ECJ declared homosexual marriages lawful under the CFR, but might become so if the European Court of Human Rights so decided. Yet the ECJ has stated in its case law that it will apply the ECHR as interpreted by the European Court of Human Rights as spelling out constitutional principles common to all Member States. So what would happen in a case like this? As the ECJ seems now to be referring to the CFR more and more, this problem will increase.

The point is also one of conceptual diversity – to what extent are the two organisations even dealing with the same rights?[77] This point is illustrated in differing conceptions of discrimination between EU and ECHR – illustrated in the discrimination cases brought by the Roma.[78]

(ii)   The Nature of the ECJ's Human Rights Jurisdiction

The ECJ could have a very broad human rights jurisdiction. If we leave aside Article 51 of the CFR, then the ECJ has interpreted its human rights jurisdiction quite expansively on some occasions. *Carpenter*[79] is an obvious example. Although a tentative connection with the Internal Market may often be found, as in *Carpenter*, it often seems as if a fundamental rights claim in itself lies at the centre of the case. In *Chen*, and *Lindqvist*,[80] EC secondary legislation was raised to bring the case easily within the ECJ's competence. The ECJ could in fact go further with this jurisdiction,

---

[75]   For example, Article 2 of Protocol 7 to the Lisbon Treaty reads: 'To the extent that a provision of the Charter refers to national laws and practices, it shall only apply to Poland or the United Kingdom to the extent that the rights or principles that it contains are recognised in the law or practices of Poland or of the United Kingdom'.

[76]   This situation is specifically cited as problematic by Luzius Wildhaber, Speech in Australia 2008, 'The European Court of Human Rights – Reflexions on my 15 years in Strasbourg'.

[77]   Sacha Prechal and Bert van Roermund, *The Coherence of EU Law: The Search for Unity in Divergent Concepts* (Oxford, Oxford University Press, 2008).

[78]   See also Samantha Besson, 'Gender Discrimination under EU and ECHR Law: Never Shall the Twain Meet?' (2008) 8 *Human Rights Law Review* 647.

[79]   Case C-60/00 *Mary Carpenter v Home Secretary* [2002] ECR I-6279, in which the ECJ held that EC law applied (namely Art 49 EC) due to the applicant's husband being involved with procurement of advertising in other Member States – seen as most commentators as a tentative connection with a fundamental rights issue and immigration law at the kernel of the case.

[80]   Case C-200/02 *Zhu and Chen v Home Secretary* [2004] ECR I-9925; Case C-101/01 *Criminal proceedings against Bodil Lindqvist* [2003] ECR I-12971; Case C-380/05 *Centro Europa 7* [2008] ECR I-349.

giving itself an ever broader foundation[81] to decide human rights cases, but so far has not very often done so – perhaps for reasons of accommodation with the ECHR? But it may choose to do so in the future. In *Kadi*, the ECJ stressed a strong commitment to fundamental rights.[82] The ECJ is growing in magnitude as a human rights court and the European Court of Human Rights might even be content for the ECJ to take certain cases off its hands and lessen its burden of cases. It also has a broader range of rights to deal with.

(iii)   The European Court of Human Rights and the European Union

The COE's fear of marginalisation has already been discussed.[83] This fear was also illustrated in the discussions leading up to the setting up of the EU's Fundamental Rights Agency (FRA). The FRA has not been charged with ensuring compliance with human rights, but rather acting as a pole of expertise and human rights advice. It has no power to issue regulations, examine individual complaints, or act under Article 7 of the Treaty on European Union (TEU). This rather modest role is explained by the position taken by the COE, which feared that the FRA would duplicate the work of monitoring bodies of the COE.[84] That such a scrap should take place reveals Europe at its worst: jealousies undermining human rights protection.

The EU is not at present a signatory of the ECHR and therefore cannot be a defendant in Strasbourg. However, as early as 1958, the European Commission of Human Rights, in *X and X v Germany*,[85] held that, if an international obligation were to prevent a Member State of the ECHR from performing that state's ECHR obligations, then that state could be nonetheless responsible under the ECHR. However, in *M & Co v Germany*,[86] decided in 1990 (in which the applicant was claiming breach of the right to a fair trial under Article 6 of the ECHR in the course of the execution of an ECJ judgment in a competition case), whilst stating that

---

[81] For example Case C-299/95 *Kremzow v Austria* [1997] ECR I-2629; Case C 328/04 *Vajnai* [2005] ECR I 8577. Also see Opinion of AG Sharpston in Case C-34/09 *Ruiz Zambrano*, nyr for suggestions on the scope of application of EU fundamental rights law.

[82] Joined cases C-402/05P and C-415/05P *Kadi and Al Barakaat* [2008] ECR I-6351.

[83] See eg PACE, Memorandum of Understanding Between the Council of Europe and the European Union, Recommendation No 1743 (2006).

[84] See also Juncker Report, above n 83.

[85] *Mr and Mrs X v Federal Republic of Germany* Application No 235/56 (Commission Decision 10 June 1958).

[86] *M & Co v Germany* (1990) 64 DR 138.

Member States are responsible for all acts and omissions of their domestic organs allegedly violating the Convention regardless of whether the act or omission in question is a consequence of domestic law or ... of the necessity to comply with international obligations,

the European Commission of Human Rights held that a transfer of powers to an international organisation by a Member State would not be incompatible with that state's obligations under the ECHR, provided that, within the international organisation, fundamental rights would receive 'equivalent protection'. This judgment of the European Commission seemed to have been influenced by the similar doctrine developed by the German Bundesverfassungsgericht (German Constitutional Court) in its *Solange II* case.[87] The European Commission found that the EC legal system did provide equivalent protection and deemed the action inadmissible. The *M & Co* finding was, however, criticised by former President Ryssdal of the European Court of Human Rights.[88]

The same standard of 'equivalence' was applied by the European Court of Human Rights in *Bosphorus*.[89] The *Bosphorus* case leaves one feeling uneasy, principally because in its focus on 'equivalence' it sets a lower level of scrutiny than the scrutiny given by the Court to Member State domestic institutions. The Court also stated in *Bosphorus* that equivalence need not mean identical human rights protection. The presumption of equivalent protection by the EU is rebuttable, but only in the case of 'manifest deficiency' by the EU. As the concurring judgments[90] stressed, 'manifestly deficient' is a high threshold to set, suggesting that the Strasbourg court does not want to become involved unless outrageous breaches of human rights are at issue – an approach which is deferential to Luxembourg. It is also the case that no Luxembourg judgment has yet been overturned by Strasbourg.[91]

What is worrying is that in *Bosphorus*, the Court did not closely scrutinise the ECJ's proportionality review, but transformed the issue into one of cooperation in general. In the words of Judge Ress, international cooperation cannot be the basis for limits on the role of the Court.[92] This is particularly troubling at a time when applicants are increasingly turning

---

[87] *Re Wuensche Handelsgesellschaft*, BVerfG [1987] 3 CMLR 225–65, decision of 22 October 1986.

[88] Ryssdal, 'On the road to a European constitutional Court', above n 28.

[89] *Bosphorus Hava Yollari Turizm v Ireland* (2006) 42 EHRR 1.

[90] *Bosphorus*, Joint Concurring Opinion of Judges Rozakis, Tulkens, Traja, Botoucharova, Zagrebelsky and Garlicki, 42 EHRR 4.

[91] But see *Matthews v United Kingdom* [2002] ECHR 592 in which the Court appeared to be indirectly reviewing the legality of primary EC legislation (notably the European Community Act 1976) which applied in the UK.

[92] See *Bosphorus*, above n 89, concurring opinion of Judge Ress.

to Strasbourg with complaints against the EU. Indeed, it is unlikely that the Bosphorus 'presumption of equivalence' will survive accession of the EU to the ECHR.

What might then be examples of 'manifest deficiency'? Certain EU-adopted laws under the Area of Freedom, Security and Justice (AFSJ)?[93] What if a decision of the ECJ were at issue? Indeed, the ramifications of such a finding would be immense and could threaten the supremacy of EC law, problematising the ECJ's relationship with national courts. What if the measure at issue were one taken by the European Commission with no implementing measure by the Member States, ie a *Senator Lines*[94] type case? What would the European Court of Human Rights do then? What must be avoided is a 'Bermuda triangle'[95] or Black Hole of human rights in which in pursuit of a plethora of institutional possibilities, a victim is left with no forum in which to challenge a rights violation.

The relationship between the EU and the ECHR has never really been clarified. The ECJ has never claimed to be bound by the European Court of Human Rights. Indeed, the first reference made by the ECJ to actual Strasbourg jurisprudence was only in 1996 in *P v S*, (when it referred to *Rees v UK*,[96] a rather puzzling choice) a striking delay given that the ECJ had been citing the ECHR itself for over 20 years.

The ECJ also states that the ECHR is not binding, but rather a 'source of inspiration'. What this means is not clear. Whenever a court treats a legal source as a persuasive authority rather than a precedent this can reduce certainty, broadening the legal arguments which can acceptably be taken into consideration. But the controversial nature of persuasive authority can be seen in the arguments in the US Supreme Court over whether it is permissible to cite and draw upon foreign precedents.[97] Will accession of the EU to the ECHR clarify this relationship between the two courts and

---

[93] For an example of EU legislation which might seem to violate ECHR standards, see EU-PNR (Passenger Name Record): Proposal for a Council Framework Decision on the use of Passenger Name Record (PNR) for law enforcement purposes (17 April 2009, EU doc no 5618/1/09, pdf), which requires retention of all passenger name records of all flights into and out of the EU.

[94] *Senator Lines GmbH v The 15 Member States of the European Union* (Application No 56672/00), judgment of 10 March 2004.

[95] Garlicki, 'Cooperation of courts', above n 46.

[96] Case C-13/94 *P v Cornwall County Council* [1996] ECR I-2143; *Rees v UK* (1986) 9 EHRR 56 – a puzzling choice in that the Court rejected Rees's claim, that the UK's refusal to amend her birth certificate following gender reassignment surgery, breached Art 8 of ECHR – hardly a human rights victory.

[97] Specific examples of judicial parochialism, such as that of US Supreme Court Justice Scalia in the juvenile death penalty case of *Roper v Simmons* – 'More fundamentally, however, the basic premise of the Court's argument – that American law should conform to the laws of the rest of the world' – ought to be rejected out of hand', per Justice Scalia, *Roper v Simmons* 543 US 551 (2005) 125 S Ct 1183, 1226.

result in the hierarchical superiority of the ECtHR? In fact, both Article 6(2) TEU and Protocol No 8 to the Lisbon Treaty set very strict limits to ensure that accession shall not affect the competences of the EU and that it make provision to preserve the specific characteristics of EU law. This illustrates a fear of encroachment by the ECtHR on the autonomy of EU law.

However, a more usual fear when it comes to the relationship between the ECHR and the EU is the development of diverging standards between the two transnational courts, due to their concurrent human rights jurisdiction. Yet the ECHR has been recognised by the ECJ as an integral part of EC law for nearly 40 years and there has not been a single case in which the ECJ has *gone against* Strasbourg's interpretation of the ECHR. The usually cited cases of conflict do not actually provide good examples – note that in *Roquette* the ECJ took trouble to reverse its earlier decision in *Hoechst*.[98] The relationship between the Courts has been generally friendly. In *Moustaquim*, the European Court of Human Rights referred to the EU as a 'special legal order'.[99] Callewaert has recently referred to the 'Unionisation' of the ECHR and the 'Conventionalisation' of the EU.[100]

We should also note that there are key differences between these Courts. The European Court of Human Rights was set up as a freestanding human rights court in 1959 to protect individuals against human rights abuses by Member States of the ECHR. The ECJ was established with a much broader jurisdiction as the Court of Justice of the European Communities. However, Luxembourg is aware that fundamental rights may not always have the same application in the EU context, at least where companies are asserting them. In such a case the ECHR case law may not be straightforwardly applied. In the 2006 case of *SGL Carbon*[101] Advocate-General Geelhoed suggested that '[i]t is not possible simply to transpose the findings of the European Court of Human Rights without more to legal persons or undertakings', also noting that case law from other jurisdictions, such as that under the US Fifth Amendment right against self-incrimination, could not be invoked by companies. The different contexts of these two courts – with Strasbourg acting as freestanding human rights court, and Luxembourg possessing a much wider jurisdiction, comprising a

---

[98]   Case C-88/99 *Roquette Frères SA v Direction des Services Fiscaux du Pas-de-Calais* [2000] ECR I-10465, para 23, 29.

[99]   *Moustaquim v Belgium* (1991) 13 EHRR 802.

[100]   Johan Callewaert, '"Unionisation" and "Conventionalisation" of Fundamental Rights in Europe' in Jan Wouters, André Nollkaemper and Erika De Wet (eds), *The Europeanisation of Public International Law: The status of Public International Law in the EU and its member states* (The Hague, TMC Asser Press, 2008).

[101]   Case C-301/04, *European Commission v SGL Carbon* [2006] ECR I-5915.

very large number of (sometimes competing) policies – should not be overlooked as a factor constraining and sometimes shaping human rights interpretations.

(iv) The EU's Area of Freedom Security and Justice

This raises important challenges for human rights. It did not exist just over a decade ago, but over the last 10 years the EU has adopted a plethora of measures, including the European Arrest Warrant, and a Europe-wide definition of terrorism. All of this activity belies claims made in the context of constitutional debate over the EU, by those such as Moravscik or Haltern, that EU legitimacy is not so important because it is not a state and its powers are mainly economic.[102] The AFSJ deals with matters that are crucial, namely, the relation between individual and the state or authorities. It is crucial that if the AFSJ is to be developed it is achieved in the spirit of a 'constitutional moment', as a space of hope, rather than what Pocock has called a 'Machiavellian moment'[103] (ie an attempt to remain stable by any means in the face of a stream of irrational events).

Development of this area has taken the EU into areas of law previously not within its competence but which are crucial when it comes to human rights protection – arrest warrants, privacy, surveillance, taking of evidence etc. Does the fact that each Member State of the EU is a member of the ECHR provide adequate protection for human rights, given the scope of the AFSJ? The ASFJ is premised on mutual trust[104] as illustrated by the European Arrest Warrant. If Member States take this mutual trust seriously then they must act, eg under the Arrest Warrant, without a case-by-case verification of fundamental rights, which risks compromising those rights, and specifically the ECHR.[105] In *Pellegrini*[106] the European Court of Human Rights declared that there is a duty on courts to satisfy themselves that an applicant has had a fair trial under another legal system. However, under EU law, especially in the context of the Arrest Warrant, the precise extent of Member State ability to refuse to cooperate is debatable and perhaps not justified on the basis of national constitutional rights unless the fundamental right is one recognised by the EU. But for a right to be recognised among general principles of EU law it is not necessary that all

---

[102] See eg Andrew Moravscik, 'In defence of democratic deficit: reassessing legitimacy in the EU' (2002) 40(4) *Journal of Common Market Studies* 603; Ulrich Haltern, 'Pathos and Patina: the failure and promise of constitutionalism in the European imagination' (2003) 9 *European Law Journal* 14.

[103] John GA Pocock, *The Machiavellian Moment: Florentine Political Thought and the Atlantic Republican Tradition*, revised edn (Princeton NJ, Princeton University Press, 2003).

[104] As made clear in the EU's Tampere programme in the late 1990s.

[105] See eg *Sejdovic v Italy* (2006) 42 EHRR 360.

[106] *Pellegrini v Italy* (2002) 35 EHRR 44.

Member States give it the same scope, as illustrated by the *Omega* case, in which the ECJ stated that the circumstances in which the right to dignity may be protected may vary among states of the EU.

There therefore exists a risk of fragmentation in the AFSJ as a result of the absence of a common understanding of the requirements of fundamental rights between the Member States of the EU. This could be avoided if the EU legislated to establish common standards between EU Member States above the minimum in the ECHR, or set up monitoring mechanisms. Development in the field of personal data illustrates this – at long last, Council Framework Decision 2008/977/JHA of 27 November 2008 on the protection of personal data processed in the framework of police and judicial cooperation in criminal matters has been adopted – very necessary, given the proliferation of data exchanges under the principle of availability.[107] But it can be very difficult to ensure agreement between Member States in matters of harmonisation, as attempts to secure agreement in the field of procedural rights have shown.[108] Also, if the EU acts to harmonise rights in this area, it may be seen as usurping either the COE or national legislatures.[109] This is unfortunate. A risk of clashes with the COE should not be seen as a way for the EU to avoid action.

In conclusion, there are several unanswerable questions regarding the relationship between the European Court of Human Rights and the EU which cause concern. The problems discussed above are also not ameliorated by the prospect of EU accession to the ECHR, now provided for by Art 6(2) of the Lisbon Treaty. Expansion of the EU's competence over the ASFJ causes concern, as well as increasing the capacity of the EU to violate rights as a polity, as do its Member States.

Overall, I suggest that this examination of Europe's constitutional mosaic in the human rights field may be seen as provoking certain 'flashpoints' of concern, which may be summarised in the following way:

1.   The nature of the relationship between the ECHR and its Member States – how to deal with the worst violations without fear of double standards?

[107] The principle of availability is the idea that information needed to fight crime should be able to cross borders of the EU without obstacles. The principle of availability is also one of the key items in the 2005 Hague Programme and the EU has been working hard to put it in action since then.

[108] In Spring 2004, the Commission proposed that minimum safeguards for criminal proceedings be agreed by Member States by way of a framework decision on procedural rights. This measure had still not been adopted at time of writing.

[109] It is significant in this regard that, at the Justice and Home Affairs Council meeting of 4–5 December 2006, it was concluded that 'the main outstanding issues of the proposal relate to the question whether to adopt a Framework Decision or a non-binding instrument, and the risk of developing conflicting jurisdictions with the European Court of Human Rights'. 147 Press Release 15801/06 (Presse 341), 2768th Meeting of the JHA Council of the European Union (4–5 December 2006) 12.

2. The prospect of competition between the EU and COE over territory, which damages rights protection – eg the Fundamental Rights Agency remit was lessened as result.
3. The question of adequacy of the ECJ as a human rights court – is it capable of taking a broader, more general human rights role, especially given the EU's expanding competence over areas which threaten the liberty of the individual?
4. The unsatisfactory *Solange* paradigm, namely:
    (i)   its reflection in the European Court of Human Rights' *Bosphorus* case law – namely that there is lesser scrutiny when an international organisation's conduct is at issue *so long as* protection is deemed 'equivalent';
    (ii) also the current fact that the ECJ is not exercising its human rights jurisdiction to its full possibilities, eg it does not always take as broad a view of the scope of its jurisdiction as in the *Carpenter* case, *so long as* not needed;
    (iii) to the above we should add a further element – that Member States of the EU are not exercising their human rights jurisdiction (to review EU acts for rights violations, as originally threatened by the German Constitutional Court in *Solange I*) to the full *so long* as they do not perceive the need.

The situation just described in this Section patently results in much structural complexity. Mireille Delmas-Marty, writing about European law generally, has described a situation in which 'incomplete pyramids surrounded by strange loops are mocking the old hierarchies'.[110] The complex human rights jurisdiction of the ECJ and the Court of Human Rights, as well as their Member States, provides a striking illustration of a European legal space of overlapping jurisdictions and segmented authority. Luzius Wildhaber, former president of the Court of Human Rights, recently described the relationship between the ECJ, the Strasbourg Court and national courts as a '*deétriplement fonctionnel*'. The fluidities and crossings of this legal world bring to mind the innovations of recent science – of non-Euclidian geometry, Borromean knots and Moebius bands – summoning a situation of great complexity, or perhaps a new or neo- medievalism?[111] The relationship between these different jurisdictions is symbiotic, incremental and unpredictable – for example, the first European court to refer to the EU Charter of Fundamental Rights was the Court of Human Rights (in *Goodwin*), not the ECJ, which took six years of the CFR's existence to refer to it.

---

[110] Mireille Delmas-Marty, *Towards a truly common law: Europe as a laboratory for legal pluralism* (Cambridge, Cambridge University Press, 2002).
[111] See Jan Zielonka, *Europe as Empire*, above n 9.

European legal space is therefore not clearly defined. Sousa Santos[112] uses the expression 'living on the frontier' to capture a more general sense in which individuals never completely belong to one space or another. Many legal terms and systems have a blurry quality. Their areas of application are not delineated by hard and fast borders but rather spill over into neighbouring areas. This is certainly the case in European human rights law, which in the twenty-first century does not provide an example of the kind of formal legal rationality described by Max Weber, who invoked 'the unitary characteristics of a legal system of a well-ordered State'.[113] The current European human rights *acquis*, however, leaves room for possibilities behind the alternative binary poles of certainty and chaos – anticipating the conceptualisation of fuzzy logic – not the constricting 'Either/Or' of a formal mechanistic jurisprudence, but the 'Both/And' of a less clockwork-like world. What we seem to have in the European legal space is 'Both/And'.[114]

However, it must be questioned whether these intricate spatial morphologies actually improve European human rights protection. For all the various possibilities, in such a complex jurisdictional space attaining a (sometimes negative) result may take years. The case of *Poirrez*,[115] in which the applicant was ultimately successful[116] in the Court of Human Rights after suits in the French courts and the EU courts, took 13 years. The *Bosphorus* litigation took 11 years in all, with no final favourable result for the applicant. Yet the very origins of the doctrine of precedent itself lie in the instrumental value of efficiency and economy of judicial effort – the same point should not be argued too often.[117] With such growing complexity it has even been suggested that there may be a need for a 'private international law of human rights'.[118]

Again, this situation can be usefully captured by an image. Another mosaic serves as a possible illustration. This one is of the Carina Nebula, a distant galaxy, notably full of Black Holes.

---

[112] Boaventura de Sousa Santos, *Towards a New Legal Common Sense* (Cambridge, Cambridge University Press, 2002).

[113] Max Weber, *On Law in Economy and Society* (Cambridge MA, Harvard University Press, 1954).

[114] See Gillian Rose, *The Broken Middle* (Oxford, Blackwell, 1992).

[115] *Koua Poirrez v France* (2005) 40 EHRR 2.

[116] Poirrez was originally denied disability allowance on the basis of his Algerian nationality, despite his adoption by a French citizen. The Court found a breach of Art 14 and Protocol 1, Art 1 ECHR.

[117] Neil MacCormick and Zenon Bankowski, 'Rationales for Precedent' in Neil MacCormick and Robert Summers (eds), *Interpreting Precedents* (Aldershot, Ashgate, 1992).

[118] Rick Lawson, 'The contribution of the agency to the implementation in the EU of international and European human rights instruments' in Philip Alston and Olivier de Schutter (eds), *Monitoring Fundamental Rights in the European Union* (Oxford, Hart Publishing, 2005) 229–51.

Fig 5: The Carina Nebula

The extraordinary image of the Carina Nebula in *Figure 5* was released by the European arm of the Hubble science community to celebrate 6,209 days in space. The Carina Nebula is a vast complex of gas, dust, stars, forces and energy situated 7,500 light years from Earth. Interestingly, as noted, this image too is a mosaic – made up of 50 frames from the Advanced Camera for Surveys on board Hubble. It portrays a region many hundreds of light years across, with huge quantities of solar material – stars of all sizes, masses, temperatures and brightnesses forming as well as dying, and gas and dust blown and whirling into all manners of shapes. There are Black Holes, dark matter and all sorts of imponderable, perplexing shapes. This is a beautiful but disturbing image. With its hugeness, its mysteries and multiplications, it might be compared to the European human rights space delineated above. But surely, no more than *Entropa*, is this a desirable prototype for Europe. What prospects exist then for improvement?

V.   A BETTER MOSAIC?

Legal pluralism (namely a situation in which two or more legal systems co-exist within the same geographical space) is a concept many scholars turn to as a natural approach in these complex circumstances.[119] However, this European constitutional pluralism is not the classic legal pluralism of

---

[119]   See eg Neil Walker, 'The Idea of Constitutional Pluralism' (2002) 65(3) *Modern Law Review* 317; Nicholas Barber, 'Legal Pluralism and the European Union' (2006) 12 *European Law Journal* 306; Neil MacCormick, *Questioning Sovereignty: Law, State and Nation in the European Commonwealth* (Oxford, Oxford University Press, 1999).

legal anthropology and colonial law,[120] nor even that of socio-legal theory, in which, although several legal systems are competing over the same juridical territory, only one of them (usually state law) claims for itself the position of ultimate legal authority.[121] In classical legal pluralism, what is required is that the dominant legal system becomes more responsive to the claims of other systems.[122] Instead, within Europe what exist are overlapping jurisdictions in which there are competing claims for ultimate legal authority, even if not over interpretation of the ECHR itself.

We might note that there are so many human rights claims in Europe that one court could not possibly hear them all. Strasbourg is currently overwhelmed. The quality of judicial decisions could improve as a result of this plurality of courts – as each is able to learn from the other. There is unlikely to be an all-out conflict between the ECJ and the European Court of Human Rights, as both stand to lose too much from such a conflict – Luxembourg would not wish to see its decisions overturned by Strasbourg and Strasbourg would not wish to become marginalised by Luxembourg. It is also perhaps apposite that given the multi-dimensional 'post-modern'[123] nature of the European space there should be no final arbiter of human rights, and more than one candidate for a European 'constitutional court'. This situation illustrates a Rawlsian 'overlapping consensus',[124] applied not just within one polity, but across a wider Council of Europe of 47 states, in a situation of what Taylor has called 'deep diversity' and differing goals.[125] Such a situation, again, might be fitting in a Europe in which there is no common constitutional language in any case; in which in some countries' constitutional courts with strong judicial review of legislation exists, and in others, such as the UK, there is an ongoing debate over the very notion of the constitutional order – ie as to whether a 'common law' constitution exists.[126] In such circumstances, a variety of human rights jurisdictions in Europe can reinforce rather than compete with each other, hopefully producing an eventual favourable ruling, as in *Poirrez*. No

---

[120] For examples of this see eg Leopold J Pospisil, *Anthropology of Law – A Comparative Theory* (New York, Harper & Row Publishers, 1971); Sally Falk Moore, 'Law and Social Change: The Semi-Autonomous Social Field as an Appropriate Subject of Study' (1972–73) 7 *Law and Society Review* 720.

[121] Matej Avbelj, 'The EU and the Many Faces of Legal Pluralism: Toward a Coherent or Uniform EU Legal Order?' (2006) 2 *Croatian Yearbook of European Law and Policy* 377.

[122] *ibid.*

[123] eg Jacques Derrida, *The Other Heading: Reflections on Today's Europe* (Bloomington IN, Indiana University Press, 1992).

[124] John Rawls, 'The idea of an overlapping consensus' (1987) 7(1) *Oxford Journal of Legal Studies* 1.

[125] Charles Taylor, *Multiculturalism and the Politics of Recognition* (Princeton NJ, Princeton University Press, 1994).

[126] See eg Adam Tomkins, *Our Republican Constitution* (Oxford, Hart Publishing, 2005); and Jeffrey Goldsworthy, *The Sovereignty of Parliament* (Oxford, Oxford University Press, 1999) for examples of differing interpretations of the British Constitution.

jurisdiction can avoid applying human rights. In this way, Europe may be expressed as possessing a *ius commune* of human rights. This more positive vision presents an argument for maintaining the current jurisdictionally complex status quo. It also provides another example of what Weiler has termed 'normative supranationalism'[127] – whereby, when the political processes stall, the courts can proceed with integration.

The pressing question is however still this: can there be order rather than chaos in this situation? How to avoid a nightmare of oversupply of competing rules? The general response of pluralists (but not all of them[128]) seems to be that of *heterarchy*, namely the recognition of equally credible claims to ultimate legal authority within respective legal spaces – what amounts to a 'non-order of orders'.[129] The most radical heterarchical approach is Walker's epistemological pluralism, in which legal systems are recognised as separate legal spaces, each with different foundations, systems and methods of knowledge, and in cases of conflict there exists no independent viewpoint, or final authority, by which disputes may be settled.[130] Other heterarchical pluralisms take a less extreme perspective and attempt to find some solution to the reconciliation of apparently irreconcilable claims. Some of these in fact seem to revert to monism in this attempt, eg Kumm,[131] would allow national constitutional courts the final say in resolving disputes. Maduro, on the other hand, aims for 'best fit' between national and supranational principles, and thus harmony, by contrapunctual relationships between competing legal orders – to be achieved by greater inclusion of participants, ie courts, politicians and individuals in EU legal discourse.[132] Weiler suggests the principle of constitutional tolerance, mutual respect and recognition – Europe's 'Sonderweg'.[133] Joerges, within the context of the EU, suggests conflict of laws as a strategy for conflict avoidance.[134]

---

[127] Joseph HH Weiler, 'The Community System: The Dual Character of Supranationalism' (1981) 1 *Year Book of European Law* 268.

[128] For example, *hierarchical* pluralists do not take this approach. For a discussion of adherents to this viewpoint, see Avbelj, *The EU and the Many Faces of Legal Pluralism*. See also Neil MacCormick, 'Juridical Pluralism and the Risk of Constitutional Conflict' in MacCormick, *Questioning Sovereignty*.

[129] Walker, 'The Idea of Constitutional Pluralism', above n 119.

[130] *ibid*.

[131] Mattias Kumm, 'The Jurisprudence of Constitutional Conflict: Constitutional Supremacy in Europe before and after the Constitutional Treaty' (2005) 11(3) *European Law Journal* 299.

[132] Miguel Poiares Maduro, 'Contrapunctual Law: Europe's Constitutional Pluralism in Action' in Neil Walker (ed), *Sovereignty in Transition* (Oxford, Hart Publishing, 2003).

[133] Joseph HH Weiler, 'In defence of the status quo: Europe's constitutional Sonderweg' in Joseph HH Weiler and Marlene Wind, *European constitutionalism beyond the state* (Cambridge, Cambridge University Press, 2003).

[134] Christian Joerges, 'European Law as Conflict of Laws' in Christian Joerges and Jürgen Neyers, 'Deliberative Supranationalism Revisited', EUI Working Paper Law No 2006/20.

What most, but not all, of these approaches have in common is a looking *outside* of law for resolution. Whether through politics[135] or through deference, accommodation and comity. Often this recognition is perceived as describing what is actually going on – ie the European Court of Human Rights' recognition of the EU as offering 'equivalent protection', or the German Constitutional Court's *Solange* jurisprudence which provide examples of judicial comity. Such accommodation seems to arise spontaneously through the actions of those involved. However, it also reflects a desire to avoid legal fetishism, as well as recognition that there is only so much that law can do, faced with an oversupply of competing rules in sensitive situations. Perhaps there is also a recognition that this unsettled hierarchy in Europe is not truly a threat to the rule of law as was state defiance of federal rule in the nineteenth century United States.[136]

This is all very well. Comity and resignation have their place. But is this the best that can be done – a resigned sigh and the feeling that, in this pluralistic space, we leave it to politics, judicial comity, accommodation? Does this resignation result in the best quality of protection for human rights in Europe? This seems to neglect two important factors. First, it ignores law's *normative* role – its capacity to provide substantive solutions – what Habermas calls the dual nature of law, taking account of its viability as a normative solution to hotly contested issues (as well as its facticity, its factual content).[137] Must we give up on this role for law just because we are apparently dealing with something overly complex because more than one legal system is at issue? Secondly, it ignores the fact that in the case of human rights in particular 'muddling though' should not be the best we can do.

Some situations do unavoidably seem to have to be left to politics: the relationship between the European Court of Human Rights and the Council of Europe on the one hand, and Russia on the other, probably cannot be left to law alone, particularly as it seems that Janis's point is a pertinent one – that Russia or at least many of its officials have not internalised the ECHR.[138]

But there are other areas in which there might be improvements. Hierarchy might be preferable to the heterarchy of modern legal pluralism, but a hierarchy far from the traditional monism of legal positivism. How would things change if we put *human rights* at the top of a hierarchical, monist perspective? If we took human rights as our internal point of view? It has been claimed that, within each of these pluralist systems, participants

[135] See Krisch, 'The Open Architecture of European Human Rights Law', above n 53.
[136] See Archibald Cox, *The Court and the Constitution* (Boston MA, Houghton Mifflin, 1987).
[137] Jürgen Habermas, *Between Facts and Norms* (Cambridge, MA, MIT Press, 1996).
[138] Janis, 'Russia and the Legality of Strasbourg Law', above n 67.

view their own system internally.[139] Yet the human rights victim does not necessarily take a Hartian internal point of view towards their own system. Instead, they may feel more attached to Strasbourg and the shadow constitution of the ECHR.

It has been suggested that human rights might become a foundation for the EU legal order.[140] Direct effect and supremacy were the original foundations created by the ECJ for a Community that had the Common Market as its vision. However, with the Common Market now largely achieved, fundamental rights could take its place as the foundation, especially at a time when hopes for a more 'constitutional' Europe seem to have been abandoned. The ECJ is therefore finding its feet as a human rights court and, as a keystone of the EU constitutional order, human rights could take their place in a way that they already do in Germany or South Africa – whose whole legal orders are informed by human rights. EU law also presents potential advantages to litigants over actions in Strasbourg. Although direct access to the ECJ is quite limited under Article 263 of the TFEU, the applicant need not exhaust all domestic remedies, as is required to get a hearing in Strasbourg, but may get a ruling from Luxembourg by way of a (indirect) preliminary reference from a domestic court. Domestic courts also have the power to set aside national measures which conflict with EC human rights law – which provides a much faster remedy than a Strasbourg law suit and subsequent enforcement by the Committee of Ministers. The EU has a much bigger budget than Strasbourg and a bigger staff.[141] Cases such as *Pupino* show that the ECJ is willing to use its human rights jurisdiction and apply Strasbourg case law to Member States directly. Thus, even those Member States in which the status of precedents from the European Court of Human Rights is still unclear may be forced to apply it, giving the Convention added strength through EU law. Furthermore, as EU competence increases, so does its human rights competence, with a possible corresponding decline in Strasbourg jurisdiction which is restricted to Member States' domestic law – an ever dwindling field. The ECJ could also decide to focus on the Charter, which provides a greater spectrum of rights than the ECHR, thus possibly displacing the ECHR within the EU as a source of rights.

In fact the ECJ could become the main curial forum for human rights protection within the EU. This would free up the Court of Human Rights

---

[139] Krisch, 'The Open Architecture of European Human Rights Law', above n 53. For a possibly different view, see Barber, 'Legal Pluralism and the European Union', above n 119.

[140] Eg Armin von Bogdandy, 'The European Union as a Human Rights Organization? Human Rights and the Core of the European Union' (2000) 37 *Common Market Law Review* 1307. Andrew Williams, *The Ethos of Europe* (Cambridge, Cambridge University Press, 2010).

[141] The European Court of Justice has over 800 full time staff, the European Court of Human Rights 458. See eg See Andrew Drzemczewski, 'The Internal Organisation of the European Court of Human Rights' (2000) 7 *European Human Rights Law Review* 233.

to spend more time on the high violation/low compliance cases which have a truly serious impact. If the Court of Human Rights were to give more 'constitutional' and rigorously reasoned judgments this would give national courts and the ECJ a stronger foundation to follow where necessary. But this would not mean that the Court of Human Rights would ignore the EU and the Member States within its territory. What it could mean, however, is that the EU rather than its Member States became the main focus of litigation in Strasbourg. This would be best achieved in tandem with accession of the EU to the ECHR – something provided for in the Lisbon Treaty[142] (although, as already remarked, problematic, given Russia's refusal to ratify Protocol 14). As the EU has increased in competence, so has its capability both to violate and protect human rights. With regard to the ECHR, the EU should be treated as a polity rather than just the sum of its members who are within Strasbourg jurisdiction. This might seem awkward – it might seem to violate relations of comity between the two. On the other hand, it should keep the EU on its toes as far as human rights is concerned. This would also underline that the ECHR *is* Europe's Constitution at a time when the EU's own constitutional efforts have stalled.

Perhaps we could look instead to this last mosaic – still polytopic, overlapping, but with a clearer order of its own, as a paradigm for this projected solution.

This mathematical mosaic obviously provides a greater vision of order than the Carina Nebula. It is highly complex, hugely multiple, overlapping and yet still clear in structure, indeed all of its components share the same structure. There are no Black Holes. We might posit for this shared structure the idea of human rights – an overall priority, as seen by the clarity of this form, reproduced again and again, and salient as the central, dominant image. As a pictorial metaphor for European human rights protection this dodecahedral tessellation has its attractions. Yet of course, it is merely a projection, one way of looking at things, as also is the mosaic of the Carina Nebula. As such it is an aspiration, not a representation of reality.

VI.   CONCLUSIONS

If we were to organise a set of priorities for the European constitutional mosaic, which truly took seriously the imperative of internalising and

---

[142] Art 6 TEU, as amended by the Treaty of Lisbon, states that the EU shall accede to the ECHR.

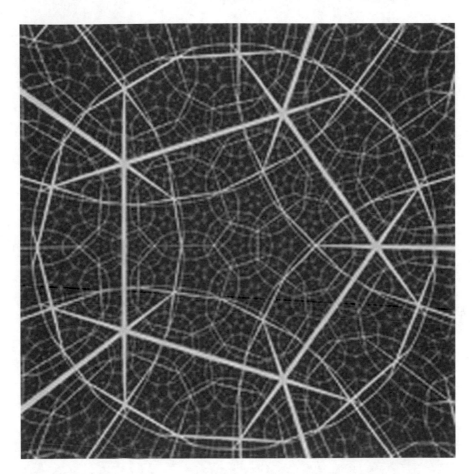

Fig 6: A perspective projection of a dodecahedral tessellation in H3.
Four dodecahedra meet at each edge, and eight meet at each vertex, just like a cubic
tessellation in E3

prioritising human rights, then instead of the ordering of Europe's 'flashpoints' above, the ordering might look like this.

1. It would stress the importance of the ECHR as a Constitution for
   Europe, something that all Europeans can internalise, although
   acknowledging that some might do so more than others. (In Germany,
   loyalty and constitutional patriotism, may lie primarily with the Basic
   Law and the rights it provides, and if the Basic Law provides superior
   protection to the ECHR, then this is acceptable, but human rights are
   still the priority in both systems.) Yet, in many jurisdictions, the ECHR
   provides the only viable rights protection. What is certainly necessary
   is for the European Court of Human Rights to adopt a more

'constitutional' role, giving more guidance for domestic courts, leaving more time for the Court to deal with major violations.

2. There is a need for revision of the relationship of the Court of Human Rights with the EU. In this case, there should be less comity. The EU has the potential to be as serious a rights violator as its Member States, as its increased competences in the field of the AFSJ illustrate. The relationship between the Court of Human Rights and EU should reflect this – which the position after *Bosphorus* does not currently do. Accession of the EU to the ECHR should ameliorate this.

3. However, the ECJ could itself take a bigger role in human rights. It has potentially a very broad jurisdiction (including rights which are not in the ECHR). It is also the case that more 'constitutional' judgments from the Court of Human Rights would give the ECJ more to go on. This could also aid the EU in its efforts to internalise rights more.

4. In this way, the 'Bermuda triangle' or Black Hole of rights protection, feared by those such as Judge Garlicki, could be more effectively avoided.

Such a re-ordering results in both hierarchy (ie human rights as pinnacle) and heterarchy (no one court is in overall control) and whilst we should remember Conor Gearty's warning, that, in the context of human rights, 'There is no certainty of a happy ending',[143] this would provide a way forward for Europe's constitutional mosaic.

---

[143] Conor Gearty, *Can human rights survive* (Cambridge, Cambridge University Press, 2006).

Part Three

The Wider Europe

6

The Constitutional Mosaic Across the Boundaries of the European Union: Citizenship Regimes in the New States of South Eastern Europe

JO SHAW*

I. INTRODUCTION

I N ANY CONSTITUTIONAL settlement, citizenship claims a central place. This observation is as valid for that dimension of citizenship – often termed nationality under international law – which constitutes and formalises the link between a particular individual and a particular state, as it is for the other dimension which is concerned with the institutions, rights and practices through which a person attains and exercises full membership of a community. Citizenship continues to determine, above all, who belongs within a given constitutional settlement and thus who has the right to determine – and to share in – its future. It concerns, in Hannah Arendt's famous phrase, the 'right to have rights', the most basic of rights.[1] It is central, therefore, to state-building and to polity-building more generally.

* Salvesen Chair of European Institutions, University of Edinburgh. This chapter draws on work ongoing in the context of the European Research Council-funded CITSEE project: *The Europeanisation of Citizenship in the Successor States of the Former Yugoslavia* (ERC Advanced Grant 230239); I am very grateful to members of the project team (Igor Štiks, Jelena Dzankic, Gezim Krasniqi, Eldar Sarajlic and Ljubica Spaskovska for discussion and input; I would also acknowledge the input of Felicita Medved). See www.law.ed.ac.uk/citsee for more details of CITSEE, including material such as Country Profiles, which have been used in the preparation of this chapter. CITSEE works closely with the EUCITAC/EUDO-Citizenship Observatory Project funded by EC Commission DG JLS (eudo-citizenship.eu), based on a project funded by the British Academy (www.law.ed.ac.uk/citmodes). The financial support of all of these funding bodies is acknowledged with thanks.

[1] H Arendt, *Origins of Totalitarianism*, new edn (New York, Harcourt Brace Jovanovich, 1973) 293.

Even so, citizenship is rarely *just* national. For example, international law has taken a position on what constitutes 'nationality' for the purposes of what should be recognised by states, namely a 'genuine link' between the citizen and the state.[2] In addition, states frequently sign up voluntarily to a range of international legal instruments which impose conditions and restrictions (eg in the name of human rights) upon the answers to the question which is ostensibly one for states alone, namely the definition of 'who is a citizen?'. Sometimes the imposition of international norms results from actions of the international community rather than from the voluntary choices of states. One example would be where it is for the purpose of humanitarian intervention or in order to foster security and stability within a region. Even within states, there may be variation in relation to citizenship rights and practices between different sub-national units, especially in federal or quasi-federal states, and – even more frequently – substantial contestation between sub-national units and the federal 'centre' around, for example, the question of who should vote in sub-national elections.[3]

In the light of such challenges to national 'hegemony' over the concept and practices of citizenship, the central task of this chapter is to illuminate the network of normative sources that shape the legal status of citizenship in Europe today. For these purposes it looks not only at the paradigm case of multi-level citizenship in Europe today, namely citizenship of the Union under the EU Treaties, but it also uses the case study of the citizenship regimes of the new states of South Eastern Europe (ie those states now existing on the territory of the former Yugoslavia[4]). This is a region which has been profoundly affected not only by the operation of EU law, as each of the states prepares (or has prepared, in the case of Slovenia) for the challenges of accession to the EU, but also by multiple sources of 'beyond-the-state' law. The former Yugoslavia represents a classic scenario of fragmentation, disintegration and partial reintegration under the shadow of international and European (Union) law, with the result that we can see clearly – as the metaphor underpinning this collection would have

---

[2]   *Liechtenstein v Guatemala (Nottebohm)* [1955] ICJ Rep 4.

[3]   J Shaw, 'Political Rights and Multilevel Citizenship in Europe' in E Guild, K Groenendijk and S Carrera (eds), *Illiberal Liberal States: Immigration, Citizenship and Integration in the EU* (Farnham, Ashgate, 2009) 29–49.

[4]   'Yugoslavia' has taken a number of different legal forms: the (first) interwar Yugoslavia (originally the Kingdom of Serbs, Croats and Slovenes until 1929) until the Axis powers invaded in 1941; the (second) post-war Yugoslavia which was the Democratic Federal Yugoslavia until late 1945, Federal People's Republic of Yugoslavia until 1963 and the Socialist Federal Republic of Yugoslavia (SFRY) thereafter until dissolution in 1991–92; and finally the (third) Yugoslavia or Federal Republic of Yugoslavia (FRY) comprising the two non-secessionist republics remaining after dissolution. This state was established in 1992 and existed until 2003, when it was replaced by the State Union of Serbia and Montenegro, which existed until Montenegro declared independence in 2006.

it – the mosaic-like character of the broader constitutional framework which is evolving for these seven states.[5] There are also areas of profound tension *between* the states in relation to questions of citizenship, where it is possible to see spillover from one (national) legal order to another. Somewhat surprisingly, however, in such a scenario of intense state-building where questions of sovereignty have often been debated and contested, little attention has thus far been paid to the issues raised by the complex and overlapping citizenship regimes of these states.[6] This chapter aims to begin the process of filling this gap, at least from a legal point of view, building in particular on the earlier work of Štiks, who observed in 2006 how these states had – almost without exception – used citizenship as a tool of 'ethnic engineering' in the context of the process of state-building.[7]

This chapter shares the basic pluralistic assumptions of this collection as a whole that national constitutional frameworks are nested within broader transnational and supranational structures in which multiple sources of normative authority often compete for centrality, or come into conflict with each other. Institutional means to adjudicate conflict are needed from time to time, as well as day-to-day mechanisms for avoiding conflict and friction between the systems. The relationship is, moreover, iterative and two way, with much of the structure of the supranational constitution of the EU itself – and indeed of the wider legal framework provided by the Council of Europe and other international organisations and legal regimes – being underpinned by national constitutional sources as well as national

[5] In the order in which they became independent and recognised by the international community: Slovenia, Croatia, Macedonia, Bosnia, Serbia, Montenegro and Kosovo. When dealing with Kosovo, the EU still routinely refers to Kosovo 'under UN Resolution 1244', as it has not been recognised by all Member States of the EU, nor is it yet a member of the United Nations. However, it has a separate legal and constitutional system, incorporating its own citizenship regime, and for these purposes it is treated unconditionally as a 'state'.

[6] The limited work includes M Dika, A Helton and J Omejec (eds), 'The Citizenship Status of Citizens of the Former SFR Yugoslavia After its Dissolution' (1998) 3(1–2) *Croatian Critical Law Review* 1 (now rather outdated) and S Imeri (ed), *Rule of Law in the Countries of the Former SFR Yugoslavia and Albania: Between Theory and practice* (Gostivar, Association for Democratic Initiatives, 2006). There are also some single country case studies: F Medved, 'From civic to ethnic community? The evolution of Slovenian citizenship' and F Ragazzi and I Štiks, 'Croatian citizenship: from ethnic engineering to inclusiveness' in R Bauböck, B Perchinig and W Sievers (eds), *Citizenship Policies in the New Europe*, 2nd edn (Amsterdam, Amsterdam University Press, 2009) 305, 339.

[7] I Štiks, 'Nationality and Citizenship in the Former Yugoslavia: From Disintegration to European Integration' (2006) 6 *Southeast European and Black Sea Studies* 483; other work by Štiks includes: I Štiks, 'A Laboratory of Citizenship: Nations and Citizenship in the Former Yugoslavia and its Successor States', (PhD Dissertation, Northwestern University (June 2009)/Sciences Po, Paris (March 2009)); I Štiks, 'A Laboratory of Citizenship: Shifting Conceptions of Citizenship in Yugoslavia and its Successor States', CITSEE Working Paper 2010/2 (www.law.ed.ac.uk/citsee).

mechanisms for implementation. The various sources are, on that argument, as much mutually reinforcing as they are in competition with each other. The legitimacy of the whole does not depend upon one source or another, but upon the composite constitutional structure providing the fundamental human goods that we demand in order to sustain the good life. However, this chapter is primarily descriptive and interpretative in its approach, and approaches the question of the constitutional mosaic as a useful metaphor for illuminating cases of plural normative authority, rather than as an invitation to engage in further theory-building.

As the case study of citizenship regimes in the former Yugoslavia will show, this region remains unstable in citizenship (and indeed many other constitutional) terms. It is often argued that the costs of non-integration of the new states now to be found on the territory of the former Yugoslavia within all aspects of Europe's constitutional mosaic are greater than those of integration, not least because of the wider effects of these instabilities. However, integration within the EU does not necessarily and automatically imply a simplification of the sources of constitutional authority or the resolution of the fragmented pattern of the mosaic into a discernible picture with settled constitutional structures in a unified framework. On the contrary, whilst the former Yugoslavia offers a fascinating laboratory within which to study the interaction of multiple sources of constitutional authority as these operate upon the case of citizenship, it is not necessarily so different in its fundamental character to other cases within the European Union, such as the United Kingdom, Spain and Belgium, where state constitutional authority is contested from below. The difference in the former Yugoslavia is that in some contexts sovereignty remains contested by other neighbouring states as well as from below, not least because of the single constitutional root of all the citizenship regimes in that of the former Socialist Federal Republic of Yugoslavia (SFRY), which itself had a multi-level system with both federal and republican-level citizenship. Furthermore, many of the actions undertaken by external authorities have been and continue to be contested by domestic political actors.[8] Whilst there may be multiple sources of normative authority enveloping the region and its new states, the levels of compliance at the national and local level are often in practice very low, and friction both with international legal regimes and also as between the neighbouring states is high. Legal change, therefore, will rarely be sufficient on its own.

In this chapter, the term 'citizenship regime' is given a specific meaning. It denotes certain key legal statuses which are central to the exercise of civil rights, political membership and – in many cases – full socio-economic

---

[8] See T Freyburg and S Richter, 'National identity matters: the limited impact of EU Political conditionality in the Western Balkans' (2010) 17 *Journal of European Public Policy* 263.

membership in a particular territory. Specifically, this includes 'nationality' in the sense of the internally and externally recognised link between the citizen and the state,[9] and thus the body of law which sustains this link, such as rules and processes governing acquisition and loss, as well as key themes such as toleration or rejection of dual or multiple nationality, the treatment of de jure and de facto statelessness, and the rules which govern effective access to a given citizenship status, such as requirements of civic registration. The latter are often important issues in regions which have seen violent conflict, war and forced population movements, especially in the case of socially, politically and legally marginal groups such as the Roma, who are the most vulnerable to the long-term exclusionary effects of forced population movements. However, other groups of internally displaced persons also find it difficult to resolve their citizenship status after conflicts.

Where applicable, the concept of citizenship regime must also include the status and rights attaching to citizenship of the European Union (and the connection between EU citizenship and national citizenship), as well as the effects of EU law, such as rules on visa liberalisation or facilitated entry mechanisms (eg for students or those seeking family reunification), although – as we shall see – Union citizenship is different in character to national citizenship. It also includes certain statuses of internal 'quasi-citizenship' for non-national residents where these extend to electoral rights and related political rights which are normally restricted to national citizens alone, and of external 'quasi-citizenship' for non-nationals residing outside the territory of the state, who receive special benefits as former nationals (or their descendants) or ethnic kin groups related to the protector state. Beyond the formal rules, citizenship regimes also include the official and unofficial 'ideologies' which sustain the rules themselves, in given political contexts (ie within and across the boundaries of polities).

More generally, a citizenship regime could be said to encompass certain key individual and collective rights protected by national and international human rights law, such as minority rights and non-discrimination rights, which profoundly impact upon the exercise of full civic membership within a society and a polity, in particular the right to non-discrimination on grounds of race or ethnic origin, gender and religious affiliation. This is the case even where the exercise of these rights is not strictly limited by reference to citizenship status or where the source of the norm being invoked for protection is not to be found in the national constitution or legislation, but in international law. However, the latter points fall largely outside the scope of this chapter.

---

[9] This is, of course, a technical use of the term 'nationality', which is quite different to the way that 'nationality' is often used in Slavic languages (eg *nactionalnost* or *narodnost* in Croatian) to denote an ethnic conception of 'national' identity.

The discussion starts with a presentation of the significance and character of citizenship of the European Union. Membership of the EU and thus the achievement for their citizens of the status of citizens of the Union is a central foreign policy goal of all of the South Eastern European states whose citizenship regimes will be under discussion in the latter part of the chapter. It is also a stated goal of the EU and its Member States, albeit one with a rather long-time horizon in some cases. It is thus logical to present at the outset the curious multi-level character of the EU's own citizenship regime before moving to a closer examination of those of the seven new states of South Eastern Europe and the dense networks of norms stemming from sources beyond the state which impact upon these regimes.

II.   THE PLACE OF (UNION) CITIZENSHIP IN EUROPE'S
CONSTITUTIONAL MOSAIC

A.   The Relationship between Union Citizenship and National Citizenship

Although scholarly opinion is divided as to the precise significance of national citizenship in an increasingly globalised world,[10] the EU's complex scenario of multi-level citizenship has paradoxically contributed to strengthening the significance of holding the citizenship of one of the Member States, when compared to holding the citizenship of a third country (or indeed of a candidate state). It has not, in that sense, contributed to the erosion of national citizenship as an institution, despite the activist nature of much of the European Court of Justice's (ECJ) recent case law in this area. The Court's case law has thus far had little to say directly about (national) citizenship; indirectly, however, it has strengthened the alternative reference point of residence rather than national belonging, at least for those EU citizens who are resident in other Member States, by extending residence-based access to certain benefits and educational entitlements[11] and by imposing restrictions on the exercise of national competences vis-à-vis mobile EU citizens in some surprising areas,

[10] For a somewhat partial review of the debates see R Hansen, 'The poverty of postnationalism: citizenship, immigration, and the new Europe' (2009) 38 *Theory and Society* 1; see also C Joppke, 'The vulnerability of non-citizens' (2009) 39 *Perspectives on Europe* 18; C Joppke, 'Transformation of Citizenship: Status, Rights, Identity' (2007) 11 *Citizenship Studies* 37.
[11] Case C-85/96 *Martínez Sala v Freistadt Bayern* [1998] ECR I-2691; Case C-184/99 *Grzelczyk v Centre public d'aide sociale d'Ottignies-Louvain-La-Neuve* [2001] ECR I-6193.

such as the national rules which regulate surnames.[12] It has also permitted the portability outside the national jurisdiction of some benefits and entitlements, in order not to penalise EU citizens for exercising free movement rights.[13] Even so, Member States still remain substantially unconstrained so far as concerns the regulation of acquisition and loss of national citizenship.

Thus in the EU, the root of citizenship lies at the national level. 'Citizenship of the Union', introduced by the Treaty of Maastricht in 1993, is limited in its personal scope by reference to the national citizenship laws of the Member States. EU citizens are the nationals of the Member States, according to Article 9 of the Treaty on European Union (TEU),[14] and Union citizenship is intended to have a secondary function in comparison to national citizenship:

> Every national of a Member State shall be a citizen of the Union. Citizenship of the Union shall be additional to national citizenship and shall not replace it.

The same point is repeated in Article 20 of the TEU.

The ECJ is now beginning to take up the task of elaborating further upon the significance of the connection between national citizenship and Union citizenship, and thus upon the effects of national regulation of access to and loss of national citizenship, in ways that might in the future prove significant for the states of the former Yugoslavia. In *Micheletti*,[15] even before the introduction of Union citizenship, the Court confirmed that while Member States remain competent alone to define the scope of their citizenship laws in order to determine who are their citizens, they must act with due regard to EU law. Thus when the host state is faced with a person who has the nationality of a Member State and also the nationality of a third state, it is obliged to recognise that part of a person's dual (or multiple) nationality which gives them access to free movement and non-discrimination rights. Post-Maastricht this means that Member States must recognise the Union citizenship of nationals of other Member States also holding the nationality of a third state, or – as in the case of *Chen* – benefiting from broad *ius soli* rules governing acquisition by birth.[16]

---

[12] Case C-148/02 *Garcia Avello v Belgian State* [2003] ECR I-11613; Case C-353/08 *Grunkin and Paul v Grunkin-Paul and Standesamt Stadt Niebüll* [2008] ECR I-7639.
[13] Eg Case C-11/06 *Morgan v Bezirksregierung Köln* [2007] ECR I-9161; Case C-224/98 *D'Hoop v Office National de l'Emploi* [2002] ECR I-6191.
[14] References are to the Treaty on European Union (TEU) and the Treaty on the Functioning of the European Union (TFEU) with their post-Lisbon formulation and numbering unless otherwise indicated.
[15] Case C-369/90 *Micheletti v Delegacion del Gobierno en Cantabria* [1992] ECR I-4239.
[16] Case C-200/02 *Zhu and Chen v Secretary of State for the Home Department* [2004] ECR I-9925.

The Court confirmed the autonomy of the Member States in *Kaur*,[17] holding that in order to determine who was a national of the United Kingdom for the purposes of determining the scope of the Treaty *ratione personae*, it was essential to refer to the 1972 and 1982 declarations made by the UK and appended to the treaties, stating which persons it regarded as its citizens for the purposes of the application of EU law (even though declarations are not normally regarded as having the same value as the EU Treaties themselves).

In the 2010 case of *Rottmann*,[18] despite a rather cautious opinion from Advocate General Maduro, the ECJ has adopted a formula for articulating the relationship between national citizenship, EU citizenship and the requirements of EU law which Member States might in the future find quite intrusive in an arena which they have hitherto guarded as largely one for the unfettered exercise of national sovereignty – ie the choice of who should be their citizens. The case concerned the issue of a decision by Germany to withdraw naturalisation from the applicant Rottmann, where the decision granting naturalisation had been obtained by fraud. That is, the applicant had failed to disclose that he was subject to criminal proceedings in Austria. On naturalisation in Germany, Rottmann had, by operation of law, lost his Austrian citizenship. As he would not automatically re-acquire Austrian citizenship in event of loss of German citizenship obtained by fraud, he would be stateless. He would also, at least temporarily, lose his EU citizenship and all the rights such as free movement rights associated with it.

The Court noted the well-established principle that while it is for each Member State to lay down the conditions for the acquisition and loss of nationality, they must nonetheless do so 'having due regard to Community law'[19] in 'situations covered by European Union law'.[20] The essence of Advocate-General Maduro's Opinion was that the loss of citizenship here was not related to the exercise of free movement rights in such a way as to render it subject to scrutiny under EU law. He contrasted Rottmann's situation with one where a person is deprived of the citizenship acquired after an exercise of free movement because of political or trade union activities, and drew attention also to the scenario where Member States would be concerned about mass naturalisations of third country nationals in circumstances that could amount to a breach of the duty of sincere cooperation under Article 4 of the TEU. The Court, in contrast, made a

[17]   Case C-192/99 *R v Secretary of State for the Home Department, ex parte Kaur* [2001] ECR I-1237.
[18]   Case C-135/08 *Rottmann v Freistaat Bayern*, judgment of 2 March 2010; Opinion of Advocate-General Maduro of 30 September 2009.
[19]   *Rottmann*, para 39.
[20]   *ibid*, para 41.

very strong and broad statement about the 'reach' of Union citizenship and consequently the capacity of Member States to withdraw national citizenship where that results in the loss of Union citizenship:

> It is clear that the situation of a citizen of the Union who, like the applicant in the main proceedings, is faced with a decision withdrawing his naturalisation, adopted by the authorities of one Member State, and placing him, after he has lost the nationality of another Member State that he originally possessed, in a position capable of causing him to lose the status conferred by Article 17 EC [ie Union citizenship] and the rights attaching thereto falls, *by reason of its nature and its consequences*, within the ambit of European Union law (emphasis added).[21]

In *Rottmann* the connection which the Court draws between EU law and national law is the simple fact that by losing national citizenship a person will also lose EU citizenship rights. This seems to be a step beyond the approach in *Micheletti* where the Court formulated the issue thus:

> [I]t is not permissible for the legislation of a Member State to restrict the effects of the grant of the nationality of another Member State by imposing an additional condition for recognition of that nationality *with a view to the exercise* of the fundamental freedoms provided for in the Treaty.[22]

This matches more closely the approach taken by Advocate General Maduro, but it is arguable that the Court's most recent approach represents a logical continuation of other aspects of its citizenship case law where it has gradually attenuated the link between citizenship and free movement.[23] The *Rottmann* formulation is justified by reference to the oft-repeated statement that 'citizenship of the Union is intended to be the fundamental status of nationals of the Member States',[24] but significantly the Court omitted the second part of the original quotation which went on to refer to the equal treatment principle and the transnational element of Union citizenship.[25] This seems to elevate Union citizenship *within* the Member States to a higher level. Later on, the Court emphasised once again 'the importance which primary law attaches to the status of citizen

---

[21] *ibid*, para 42.

[22] *Micheletti*, above n 15, para 10.

[23] Case C-148/02 *Garcia Avello v Belgian State* [2003] ECR I-11613; see also Case C-353/08 *Grunkin and Paul v Grunkin-Paul and Standesamt Stadt Niebüll* [2008] ECR I-7639.

[24] *Rottmann*, above n 18, para 43.This quotation was originally to be found in Case C-184/99 *Grzelczyk v Centre public d'aide sociale d'Ottignies-Louvain-La-Neuve* [2001] ECR I-6193, para 31. Note the small (but significant?) change in wording from 'destined' to 'intended'.

[25] The original quotation in *Grzelczyk* went on to state that Union citizenship enables 'those who find themselves in the same situation to enjoy the same treatment in law irrespective of their nationality, subject to such exceptions as are expressly provided for'.

of the Union'.[26] Accordingly, having decided that EU law applies in principle in a situation such as this, the Court concluded that it is for the national court to determine whether the national laws, regulations and measures taken are proportionate in all the circumstances, having regard to the implication of the loss of Union citizenship for the person affected. It did not give any further guidance to the national court on this matter or attempt to decide the issue itself, as it had done in other cases.

The longer term implications of *Rottmann* are yet to be discerned, and whilst the case does not change the fundamental character of Union citizenship, which remains derivative from the status of national citizenship for each individual who holds it, it does seem to change some aspects of the legal connection between the two statuses, and to open up an avenue which could be exploited to challenge a variety of aspects of national citizenship laws. Such challenges could come from aggrieved individuals, or indeed *Rottmann* could be used by the European Commission in the context of accession conditionality in order to pressurise candidate states to alter certain problematic aspects of their citizenship laws. This point will be discussed in more detail in Section IV(B) below. One implication in terms of cases brought before both the national courts and the ECJ could be that since national decisions which result in a person losing their Union citizenship (or perhaps also, not gaining EU citizenship) are now subject to judicial review in this manner, they must – by definition – be reasoned, in order to allow a Court to scrutinise the basis on which they are taken. This will have an impact upon what are often discretionary powers relating to naturalisation residing with national executives.

B.   The Character of Union Citizenship

As a legal status, citizenship of the Union gathers together a set of rights largely associated with the exercise of free movement rights, including political rights giving a Union citizen the rights to stand and vote under the same conditions as nationals when resident in a Member State other than the one of which she is a national, in both local elections and European Parliamentary elections. Under the reforms introduced by the Treaty of Lisbon, the language of citizenship is linked increasingly to the language of democracy and representation, in order to insist, for example, that the European Parliament is the Parliament of Union citizens.[27] Thus in future we may see the concept of citizenship in the EU context filled out to a

---

[26]   *Rottmann*, above n 18, para 56.

[27]   J Shaw, 'The constitutional development of citizenship in the EU context: with or without the Treaty of Lisbon' in I Pernice and E Tanchev (eds), *Ceci n'est pas une Constitution – Constitutionalisation without a Constitution?* (Baden-Baden, Nomos, 2009) 104.

greater extent and made more meaningful for 'static' citizens. However, so far as concerns the current legally enforceable rights, it is essentially in relation to the mobile European citizen that the specific impact of EU law can be felt, and has indeed been felt in a series of cases which have gradually eroded various aspects of the welfare and immigration 'sovereignty' of the Member States.[28] According to the ECJ,

> Union citizenship is destined to be the fundamental status of nationals of the Member States, enabling those who find themselves in the same situation to enjoy the same treatment in law irrespective of their nationality, subject to such exceptions as are expressly provided for.[29]

It has repeated this point in numerous judgments since 2001. Clearly, at the present time, this statement must be read in the light of the limited scope of Union citizenship, which is constrained by reference to the limited competences of the Union itself as determined by the founding Treaties; but so far as concerns mobility *within* the EU and across the borders of the Member States for Union citizens it is increasingly the reference point of residence that matters most, rather than national citizenship.[30] In that sense, Union citizenship could be called a species of *transnational* citizenship.[31]

Meanwhile, for those who find themselves at or beyond the margins of the territory of the Union, national citizenship as a status remains decisive because it gives access to the full benefits of Union citizenship. For the 'new' Member State citizens, the situation is precarious. Much has been made of the limited free movement rights granted to citizens of the Member States which joined the Union in 2004 and 2007. Most Member States have applied transitional periods in order to restrict labour market access for Union citizens, whose status has widely been characterised as that of second-class citizens.[32] Thus national citizenship matters here, as it does for third country nationals. In that sense, Union citizenship is definitely neither a form of *postnational* membership itself,[33] nor a

---

[28] See *Martinez Sala* and other cases cited in n 11 above in relation to welfare sovereignty; as regards immigration sovereignty, see Case C-413/99 *Baumbast and R v Secretary of State for the Home Department* [2002] ECR I-7091; C-127/08 *Metock and others v Minister for Justice, Equality and Law Reform* [2008] ECR I-6241.

[29] *Grzelczyk*, above n 11, para 31.

[30] G Davies, '"Any Place I Hang My Hat?" or: Residence is the New Nationality' (2005) 11 *European Law Journal* 43.

[31] J Fox, 'Unpacking "Transnational Citizenship"' (2005) 8 *Annual Review of Political Science* 171.

[32] N Rollason, 'Citizenship and the Expanding European Union: The Rights of New EU Nationals' in A Baldaccini, E Guild and H Toner (eds), *Whose Freedom, Security and Justice?: EU Immigration and Asylum Law and Policy* (Oxford, Hart Publishing, 2007).

[33] This term is particularly associated with the work of Yasemin Soysal: Y Soysal, *Limits of Citizenship. Migrants and Postnational Membership in Europe* (Chicago and London, University of Chicago Press, 1994).

mechanism which in and of itself will lead to the withering away of the significance of national citizenship – even – as *Rottmann* shows, for citizens of the 'old' Member States.

In states which are (still) outside the external borders of the EU, individuals can become Union citizens in two ways: either by gaining the nationality of an existing Member State (with all the attendant difficulties associated with naturalisation, such as contending with possible requirements of renunciation or release,[34] passing citizenship/language tests, and demonstrating possible 'virtue' requirements); or because the state of which they are a national itself becomes a Member State. It is important to note that many of the states at or just beyond the boundaries of the present EU (including all of those in the former Yugoslavia) are new, or renewed states, with citizenship regimes and rules on acquisition and loss of national citizenship which have been devised or substantially amended during the 20 years or so which have elapsed since the fall of the Berlin Wall, the collapse of the Soviet Union and the end of the Cold War.[35] Some of these are (sometimes fragile and weak) states with unstable and changing citizenship regimes (often overlapping in important ways with the regimes of other neighbouring states which may have originated in a single state of origin), and in some cases they are states where there are contested sovereignty claims on the part of different national groups or continuing protectorate statuses pursuant to situations of war and violent conflict. In the region studied here, Kosovo and Bosnia-Herzegovina are two cases in point.

In the post-1989 'transition' states, there are frequently groups of national minorities, whose status has been formed by a combination of historical population flows combined with boundary changes that have occurred throughout the twentieth century and into the twenty-first. 'Immigration' in its twentieth and twenty-first century guises has not constituted these groups of minorities, but rather other historical forces, generally outwith the agency of individuals, who find their formal status as citizens changing without them changing their location. In such circumstances, concepts such as citizenship and nationality have quite different meanings, even though it may be overly simplistic to talk of an East-West divide in the context of citizenship.[36]

---

[34] For a reflection on the implications of this in an intra-EU context see D Kochenov, 'A Glance at Member State Nationality – EU Citizenship Interaction' (forthcoming 2010), draft version available at www.unc.edu/euce/eusa2009/papers/kochenov_05E.pdf.

[35] On the character of citizenship politics in new states, see O Shevel, 'The Politics of Citizenship Policy in New States' (2009) 41 *Comparative Politics* 273.

[36] See A Liebich and R Bauböck (eds), 'Is there (still) an East-West divide in the conception of citizenship in Europe?', RSCAS Working Paper 2010/19, eudo-citizenship.eu/docs/RSCAS_2010_19.pdf.

Reflections upon more general questions about citizenship and enlargement were the subject of an earlier paper, which called for the specifics of national constitutional, legal and political conditions to be given close attention in the context of assessing the process of national accommodation of new (post-2004) Member States with the requirements of EU law.[37] This chapter meanwhile adopts a different angle of approach to some of the same material, as it seeks to figure out in more detail the place of citizenship in Europe's constitutional mosaic by taking into account not only the national constitutional specifics, but also the multiple sources of normative authority from beyond the state, which contribute to determining the patterns of the mosaic. Specifically, it does so by looking at one highly contested region rather than at the question of enlargement more generally. This is the territory of the former Yugoslavia, which dissolved from 1991 onwards, partly as a result of the end of the Cold War and changes in the priorities of the United States and other great powers, but also because of the rise of nationalist and ethnic politics and the dominance of political elites who used nationalist politics for their own ends, with the disastrous end result, in several cases, of war and crimes against humanity such as ethnic cleansing. These in turn caused widespread population displacement and statelessness, which in some cases have persisted until the present day.

III.   SITUATING THE EVOLVING CITIZENSHIP REGIMES IN THE NEW STATES
OF SOUTH EASTERN EUROPE

The case of the seven states which are now to be found on the territory of the former SFRY shows clearly the effects of transition, disintegration and partial re-integration processes in relation to the evolution and operation of citizenship regimes in new states. We can term these seven states, for the purposes of this chapter, either the new states of South Eastern Europe, or the new Balkan states.[38] Due to lack of space, this chapter cannot provide

---

[37] J Shaw, 'Citizenship and Enlargement: The Outer Limits of EU Political Citizenship' in C Barnard and O Odudu (eds), *The Outer Limits of EU Law* (Oxford, Hart Publishing, 2009).

[38] All of these terms could be contested. Strictly speaking, Slovenia has never been viewed as a 'Balkan' state, but obviously its inclusion in Yugoslavia from its inception as the Kingdom of the Serbs, Croats and Slovenes in 1918 until Slovenia's declaration of independence in 1991 continues to tie its citizenship regime to those of the other states of the region which were, like Slovenia, republics in the former Yugoslavia (Croatia, Bosnia-Herzegovina, Serbia, Montenegro and Macedonia), as well as to that of Kosovo, which was never a republic, but was an automous province within the Republic of Serbia with republic-like competences and representation within Federal institutions, after the last 1974 SFRY Constitution was adopted. It should also be pointed out that the term 'successor states' of the

even an outline description of the regimes of all seven states;[39] rather, it proceeds by picking out the dimensions which help to illustrate the complexity of the constitutional mosaic and its specific character as regards the regulation of membership questions.

The choice of this case study is justified by the fact that the region which the European Commission now terms the Western Balkans[40] is an enclave within the EU, and is an arena of enduring political and constitutional instability encompassing some 'weak states',[41] which is uniquely proximate to the EU itself. For much of the 1990s, the dissolution of Yugoslavia represented one of the most difficult foreign policy challenges for the EU and its Member States – a challenge which, in the view of many, both the EU and its leading Member States, failed rather comprehensively.[42] Even now, while officially all of the states are at least potential EU Member States, it is hard to discern precisely whether this region is an arena of EU enlargement policy or foreign policy.[43]

One of the seven post-Yugoslav states, Slovenia, has been a member of the EU since 2004 and thus its citizens are EU citizens. It is also within the Schengen zone, requiring it to apply the same visa rules and border controls as the other Schengen members (subject to local border traffic agreements), including towards states that were originally part of the same country. And – as an indicator of the degree of its integration within the

former Yugoslavia is a problematic term, since it is clear that only former SFRY republics can strictly be successor states. In 1992, there were five successor states: Slovenia, Bosnia-Herzegovina, Croatia, Macedonia and the FRY (or – as it became after 2003 – the State Union of Serbia and Montenegro). In 2006, Montenegro seceded, but formally Serbia was declared the successor of their Union. Kosovo seceded unilaterally from Serbia in 2008 but, as it was never a republic, it cannot in that narrow sense be a 'successor state'; the Badinter Commission of 1991 specifically restricted recognition processes to entities which had been SFRY republics, on the basis of the continued subsistence of republican boundaries. Finally, some of the states, such as Serbia or Croatia, might baulk at being termed 'new'.

[39] For more details, see Štiks, 'Laboratory of Citizenship: Shifting Conceptions', above n 7. See also the material and especially the country reports provided via the Country Profile section of the CITSEE project website: www.law.ed.ac.uk/citsee/countryprofiles/. One prominent issue which this chapter does not address is the question of 'entity' citizenship, adding a multi-level element to citizenship in Bosnia: see E Sarajlic, 'The Bosnian Triangle: Ethnicity, Politics and Citizenship', CITSEE Working Paper 2010/06, 15–16.

[40] Once again this term excludes Slovenia, although it was a Republic of the former SFRY and it also includes Albania, which, due to ethnic ties with neighbouring Kosovo and the ethnic Albanian minorities in Macedonia and Montenegro, is definitely part of the post-Yugoslav future although it was not part of Yugoslavia itself.

[41] See generally D Kostovicova and V Bojicic-Dzelilovic (eds), *Persistent State Weakness in the Global Age* (Aldershot, Ashgate, 2009); D Jano, 'How Legacies of the Past and Weakness of the State Brought Violent Dissolution and Disorder to the Western Balkan States' (July 2009) 14 *Journal of Peace, Conflict and Development*, available at: www.peacestudiesjournal.org.uk, and papers.ssrn.com/sol3/papers.cfm?abstract_id=1438662.

[42] L Silber and A Little, *The Death of Yugoslavia*, rev edn (London, Penguin Books / BBC Books, 1996).

[43] G Noutcheva, 'Fake, partial and imposed compliance: the limits of the EU's normative power in the Western Balkans' (2009) 16 *Journal of European Public Policy* 1065, 1066.

EU – it has adopted the Euro as its currency.[44] Three out of the other six states share land borders with two or more Member States if one includes Slovenia in this tally (Croatia, Serbia and the Former Yugoslav Republic of Macedonia[45]). Two of the three which do not have land borders with EU Member States are located just across the Adriatic from Italy (Bosnia-Herzegovina[46] and Montenegro). Only landlocked Kosovo has neither sea nor land borders with EU Member States. Conversely, five Member States (Hungary, Romania, Bulgaria, Greece and Italy), not including Slovenia, have land or sea borders with the states in the region, and additionally Austria, Italy and Hungary have land borders with Slovenia.

All the Western Balkan states have been offered a 'European' perspective by the EU and its Member States, with Croatia nearing the end of its protracted negotiations for an accession treaty, and likely to be a Member State by 2011 or 2012, despite ongoing bilateral difficulties with Slovenia and some questions over its compliance with the requirements imposed by the International Criminal Tribunal for the Former Yugoslavia established in the Hague. Its citizens have generally benefited, throughout the period since the dissolution of Yugoslavia and Croatia's declaration of independence in 1991, from visa-free travel in the EU Member States, although the United Kingdom imposed visa requirements for six years until 2006. Macedonia is recognised as a candidate state, although it has not begun negotiations for accession and the EU has been postponing making a decision on this question, not least because of the dispute over its name with Greece. However, its citizens have benefited from visa liberalisation and greater freedom of movement for the purposes of business and leisure travel to the Schengen area since 19 December 2009,[47] along with the citizens of Montenegro and Serbia. Both of these states have applied for membership of the EU, but are not recognised as candidate states. Serbia did so most recently, on 22 December 2009, having taken its inclusion in visa liberalisation along with the unblocking of an interim trade agreement – which is part of the Stabilisation and Association Agreement process – as the green light from the EU institutions and Member States to submit an application. At the beginning of 2010, Montenegro was awaiting a decision of Council of Ministers as to whether to seek an Opinion from the Commission on its application.

[44] It is interesting to note that both Kosovo and Montenegro have unilaterally adopted the Euro as their currency.

[45] Hereinafter referred to as 'Macedonia'.

[46] Hereinafter referred to as 'Bosnia'.

[47] Council Regulation 1244/2009, amending Regulation (EC) No 539/2001, listing the third countries whose nationals must be in possession of visas when crossing the external borders and those whose nationals are exempt from that requirement, [2009] OJ L336/1, based on a Commission proposal of 15 July 2009: CON(2009) 366. The UK seems likely to remove the visa requirement one year later than the Schengen zone states.

Meanwhile the citizens of Bosnia and Kosovo (along with those of Albania, which has – like Montenegro and Serbia – submitted an EU membership application but has not been recognised as a candidate state) were not given visa liberalisation in the first phase, but Bosnia and Albania, at least, although not Kosovo, were deemed to have fulfilled the relevant conditions imposed in relation to the Schengen area by the end of 2010.[48] For Kosovo, the prospect of visa liberalisation and the reduction in its significant level of physical isolation seems a more distant prospect, not least because it has not been recognised as a state by five of the 27 Member States[49] and thus does not have formal contractual relations with the EU in the absence of a consensus of the Member States necessary under the Common Foreign and Security Policy. This is so even though it hosts the largest EU civilian mission aimed at bringing stability and promoting the rule of law internally: EULEX. It has also not been recognised by its neighbours Serbia and Bosnia, or by significant international players such as Russia and China, which can veto its membership of the United Nations.

The region thus offers an example of a complex tapestry of legal relationships with the EU and its Member States, not just in the area of passport control and visas but also in other matters which lie outwith the scope of this chapter, such as trade relations and other conditions of economic transition and integration with the EU which form part of a route map to accession. But in truth little illustrates the point better than what happened to the different groups of persons who – before 1991 – would all have enjoyed comprehensive visa-free travel throughout Europe and many other parts of the world on the basis of what was, in the heyday of Tito's Yugoslavia, the valuable red passport.[50] Whilst some are now EU citizens, others have since faced substantial physical isolation as citizens of new states. We shall return in due course to the issue of visa liberalisation.

Whilst the EU has been and remains an important 'player' in the Western Balkans, there are numerous other international and regional organisations which have been engaged in this region in the process of trying directly or indirectly to sow the seeds which would lead to enhanced recognition and implementation of key norms associated with liberal and democratic constitutionalism under the rule of law. These include norms stemming from international and European human rights treaties, as well as more inchoate norms of good governance, democracy and neighbourly

---

[48] Council of the European Union, Visa liberalisation for Albania and Bosnia and Herzegovina, 8 November 2010, http://www.consilium.europa.eu/uedocs/cms_data/docs/pressdata/en/jha/117555.pdf

[49] Cyprus, Greece, Romania, Slovakia and Spain have not recognised Kosovo.

[50] See www.followstamps.com/other/dok-yupassport1.JPG. Images of the new passports can be found on the CITSEE website.

relations. The 'interplay' between these institutions, if not necessarily the norms that they have been seeking to bring into play, has not always been comfortable.[51] A non-exhaustive list of such organisations must include: NATO; the Council of Europe (especially the Venice Commission but also other relevant treaty frameworks adopted under its aegis such as the European Convention on Nationality and the Framework Convention on the Protection of National Minorities, and the latter's institutional enforcement mechanisms); the Organization for Security and Cooperation in Europe (OSCE); the Stability Pact for South Eastern Europe and its successor, the Regional Cooperation Council; the UN Security Council; the United Nations High Commissioner for Refugees (UNHCR); the United Nations Development Programme (UNDP) and other UN agencies; not to mention numerous special-purpose instruments and institutions of the international community and of the EU and its Member States, specifically designed to bring conflict to an end and to deal with post-conflict situations in the protectorate or quasi-protectorate states of Bosnia and Kosovo or to deal with war crimes and crimes against humanity (eg the International Criminal Tribunal for the Former Yugoslavia). The region and its states have been the subject of numerous international plans, some of which have been given the legal force of treaties or UN Security Council Resolutions, but by no means all. All these plans nonetheless have been the means through which norms have been identified for more or less explicit transplantation into the internal legal sphere, or into trans-border relations between states. Many of these have impacted directly or indirectly upon citizenship questions, even though the states are ostensibly largely free under international and European law to set their own norms in this domain, as we have seen. It is important to note that in this chapter our concern is not with the broader ideational dimensions of norm transfer that often accompany the discussion of the EU as a foreign policy actor in the Western Balkans or elsewhere,[52] but specifically with the impact of legal norms. It is an exercise in understanding the operation of law in its wider political and societal context.

Section IV outlines out the main mechanisms which structure the interface between the international or European normative orders and the state-level legal orders by identifying the main sources and forms of 'norm' which are being 'exported' via those mechanisms into the state-level legal and constitutional orders. Of course, the use of the term 'export' here conveys the sense that the process is exclusively uni-directional. That is not by any means the full story, as we shall see evidence of how *national* rules

---

[51] See U Caruso, 'Interplay between the Council of Europe, OSCE, EU and NATO' (2007) Report compiled for the MIRICO FP6 project available at: www.eurac.edu/NR/rdonlyres/ 4EA381B7–95DD–4750–A2D4–528E463863C3/0/ReportoninterplayWEB.pdf.

[52] Noutcheva, 'Fake, partial and imposed compliance', above n 43.

on citizenship acquisition and loss have transnational effects upon neighbouring states, and also of cases where EU-level policies, for example visa liberalisation, have been influenced by the scope and nature of national citizenship. The typological outline in Section IV is limited to brief statements about the various forms of intervention or interposition of international norms, with examples of how this impacts upon citizenship laws, institutions and practices. It is not comprehensive in nature. Indeed, an institutionally-focused survey of the significance of each of the international organisations cited above, along with their respective 'legal' systems, for the seven new states under discussion here, using a broad framework of disintegration and reintegration, would be too vast an enterprise for a single chapter. Whilst the main focus is upon 'vertical' relationships between state-level legal orders and those in the international or regional sphere, some attention is also paid to the horizontal challenges stemming from the way in which the citizenship regimes of the new states substantially overlap and impact upon each other. Woven into the discussion is a focus on two key dimensions of citizenship: first, the conditions under which citizenship is defined and thus the main mechanisms which allow individuals to become citizens (and conversely which restrict access to citizenship), and secondly the implications of this for mobility both within the region and – crucially – to and across the Member States of the EU.

Descriptively, what emerges from this survey of mechanisms is some evidence of a greater degree of openness towards the outside in relation to issues of citizenship definition – even in cases where such openness has not been directly mandated as a result of international action – but also many examples of as yet unresolved tensions and frictions stemming from the fact that each of the seven citizenship regimes has sprung, directly or indirectly, from the same source (the SFRY regime). This has the result that many of the regimes are effectively overlapping rather than exclusive in character. All of this suggests that a multi-perspectival approach to assessing these citizenship regimes alongside each other will be a complex endeavour, requiring a detailed study going well beyond the rather elliptical survey of rules and practices given here.

IV.   THE CONSTITUTIONAL MOSAIC IN PRACTICE: INSTRUMENTS AND NORMS

Without claiming to provide a comprehensive overview, this section identifies six principal mechanisms whereby instruments and norms of a constitutional character having their source outwith the state gain an impact upon domestic law, and specifically upon the national citizenship regimes of the new states of South Eastern Europe. Five of these categories are directly concerned with the impact of international norms, and they are closely intertwined. For example, compliance with international human rights norms represents a key element of conditionality for the purposes of preparation for accession to the EU under the Copenhagen Criteria. The precise distinction between direct intervention and direct supervision by international organisations may often be hard to discern, although the former is associated more with military interventions and their direct consequences, and the latter with civilian missions; equally the distinction between formal and more informal interventions by the EU, other organisations and indeed by third states is rather fine. Furthermore, external actors do not engage only with governmental organisations within the region, but also with organisations within civil society, both those which are of local origin and also those which are international organisations, such as the Open Society Institute or Helsinki Committee, with a local base. The sixth category focuses on overlaps between the systems, and how these impact upon the respective domestic systems.

A.   Adoption of and Compliance with International Norms

With the exception of Kosovo, all the new states – as they emerged – have become members of the United Nations and the Council of Europe. This has implied – under the aegis of the latter organisation – signing and ratifying key treaties such as the European Convention on Human Rights (ECHR) and permitting the right of individual petition to the judicial institutions of Strasbourg.

ECHR norms have a limited impact upon citizenship rules and regulations as such. The European Court of Human Rights (ECtHR) has consistently held that 'no right to acquire or retain a particular nationality is as such included among the rights and freedoms guaranteed by the Convention or its Protocols'.[53] The ECHR does, however, impact upon the exercise of rights consequent upon citizenship, especially political rights. This point is well illustrated by a case brought against Moldova,[54] in which the applicants challenged Moldovan rules banning dual nationals from holding public posts, including posts as Members of Parliament. The citizenship rules themselves remain unaffected. This would mean that Moldova would be at liberty, like other states, to correct the human rights violation by abolishing dual nationality. Whether or not to allow dual

---

[53] See, for example, a case concerning a former Yugoslav Republic: *Makuc and others v Slovenia* (Application No 26828/06), partial decision on admissibility of 31 May 2007, [2007] ECHR 523, para 160.

[54] *Tănase and Chirtoacă v Moldova* (Application No 7/08), judgment of 18 November 2008.

nationality is a free choice of states; having chosen to allow it, Moldova is under an obligation to treat all citizens equally. A set of related questions emerged in *Sejdić and Finci*,[55] concerning an application brought against Bosnia by members of the Roma and Jewish communities. They successfully argued that they had experienced discrimination on grounds of race and ethnic origin because of the effects of the Bosnian post-Dayton constitution, which limits certain political rights, such as the right to stand for the collective Bosnian Presidency, to self-declared members of the three 'constituent peoples' of Bosnia (the Bosniacs, Croats and Serbs). Again, all citizens must be treated equally, and *Sejdić and Finci* represents an important first case on the application of the freestanding non-discrimination principle in Article 1 of Protocol 12 to the ECHR.

One of the most infamous citizenship 'incidents' to result from the dissolution of Yugoslavia has been brought before the ECtHR (the Court), and awaits a final judgment.[56] The *Makuc* case concerns the fate of citizens of former Yugoslav republics other than Slovenia who were resident in Slovenia on the date of independence, and who – for whatever reason – either could not or would not apply for Slovenian citizenship under the conditions prescribed by section 40 of the 1991 Slovenian Citizenship Act. There were three requirements which they needed to meet: they must have acquired permanent resident status in Slovenia by 23 December 1990, be actually residing in Slovenia and have applied for citizenship within six months after the Citizenship Act entered into force (ie 28 February 1992). Those who did not apply, or who did apply and whose applications were rejected, were – on the orders of the Ministry of Interior – erased from all registers from that date and effectively rendered non-persons. Having repeated, as noted above, its well-known mantra concerning the limited effects of the ECHR in relation to the 'right' to a nationality, the Court none the less noted that an arbitrary denial of citizenship – such as that alleged by the applicants who were all erased – could raise issues under Article 8 of the Convention because of the possible impact upon the private life of the applicant.[57] In this case, because the actual 'erasure' took place before Slovenia acceded to the Convention in 1994, the Court declared that part of the application inadmissible from a temporal perspective. However, it did decide to adjourn for further examination and argument issues related to the denial of a retrospective right of permanent residence for those of the Erased who did eventually succeed in establishing the legality of their residence in Slovenia and to the continued denial of an effective remedy (notwithstanding two Slovenian Constitutional Court

---

[55]   *Sejdić and Finci v Bosnia and Herzegovina* (Application Nos 27996/06 and 34836/06), judgment of the Grand Chamber, 22 December 2009.
[56]   See *Makuc*, above n 53.
[57]   See *Makuc*, above n 53, para 160.

judgments condemning the actions of the Government[58]). It remains to be seen what position the Court will take on these matters. Medved[59] interprets the case of the Erased as part of a more general drift in Slovenia away from a civic conception of citizenship, visible in the initial determination of the citizenry and influenced by international 'best practice', towards a more ethnic-nation approach. This latter has more in common with the approaches taken by most of the other new states of South Eastern Europe. Moreover, in 2010, it seemed that the region was heading towards a related incidence of erasure, almost 20 years after the initial dissolution of Yugoslavia. Human rights advocates in Montenegro have highlighted the profound difficulties which members of the Roma community are having in obtaining citizenship papers in Montenegro, after the dissolution of the State Union with Serbia, and consequent upon the adoption of the new Montenegrin citizenship law and also the law on foreigners, mandated by the European Commission as part of the 'tidying up' process leading towards visa liberalisation and accession candidature.[60] Existing papers, such as those obtained during the period of the Federal Republic of Yugoslavia, or under the State Union, are being rendered nugatory in the newly independent Republic.[61]

By comparison with the ECHR, acceptance of other conventions specifically concerned with questions of nationality and citizenship is patchier. Bosnia and Croatia have signed but not ratified the core European norms on nationality, the 1997 European Convention on Nationality.[62] Only Macedonia and Montenegro have actually ratified the Convention, and for Macedonia the decision to do so in 2003 was a central element in its 'civic' and 'non-ethnic' redefinition of its constitution and its citizenship law in the aftermath of the Ohrid Framework Agreement of 2001, which brought to an end an armed rebellion by Macedonia's substantial Albanian community which threatened the very survival of the state.[63] Only Montenegro has signed and ratified the more recent 2006 Council of Europe Convention on the avoidance of statelessness in relation to State

---

[58] For more details see V Jalušič and J Dedić, '(The) Erasure – Mass Human Rights Violation and Denial of Responsibility: The Case of Independent Slovenia' (2008) 9 *Human Rights Review* 9; also Medved, 'From civic to ethnic community', above n 6.

[59] Medved, 'From civic to ethnic community', above n 6.

[60] For details on Montenegrin citizenship law, see J Dzankic, 'Transformations of Citizenship in Montenegro: a context-generated evolution of citizenship policies', CITSEE Working Paper 2010/03.

[61] Interview with Aleksandar Sasa Zekovic, Podgorica, 29 March 2010.

[62] European Convention on Nationality, Strasbourg 6 November 1997, entry into force 1 March 2000, ETS No 166.

[63] See generally L Spaskovska, 'Macedonia's Nationals, Minorities and Refugees in the Post-Communist Labyrinths of Citizenship', CITSEE Working Paper 2010/05. The issue of the Ohrid Agreement is discussed in the text to n 92 below.

succession.[64] On the other hand, reflecting concerns on the status of minorities which express themselves in particular in the context of EU conditionality (see Section B below), all of the states except Kosovo have signed and ratified the 1995 Framework Convention on the Protection of National Minorities,[65] a convention which it is safe to say was specifically drafted with post-1989 Central and Eastern Europe in mind. Like the ECHR, this is not a text which directly addresses itself to issues of citizenship (or statelessness), but it obviously has some effects.[66]

Thus far, in its condition of internationally supervised independence, Kosovo has not been able to join any key international organisations concerned with human rights and fundamental freedoms, including the United Nations and the Council of Europe. As it requires a two-thirds majority of members of the Council of Europe for accession, and it has been recognised by more than two-thirds of the Council of Europe's 47 member countries, accession to the latter became a prospect in 2010. In terms of fundamental rights norms, however, the scenario in relation to Kosovo is more a case of Section C discussed below, as Kosovo's explicit adhesion to international human rights standards was written into the Ahtisaari Plan or 'Comprehensive proposal for the Kosovo Status Settlement' of 2007, which in turn largely determined the contours of Kosovo's post-independence Constitution as the basis for a multi-ethnic state based on civic rather than ethnic principles.[67] However, the United Nations Interim Administration in Kosovo (UNMIK) adopted a number of technical agreements relating to key Conventions, especially the Framework Convention on National Minorities.[68] This enables the enforcement bodies which supervise these international instruments to scrutinise Kosovo's performance under key headings. However, it does not engage Kosovo's full international responsibility under these Conventions.

---

[64] Council of Europe Convention on the avoidance of statelessness in relation to State succession, Strasbourg 19 May 2006, entry into force 1 May 2009, ETS No 200.

[65] Framework Convention on the Protection of National Minorities, Strasbourg 1 February 1995, entry into force 1 February 1998, ETS No 157.

[66] See, for example, the comments on access to citizenship for minorities in the Committee of Ministers' recommendation of 14 January 2009 following the first cycle of reports, opinions, comments and recommendations after Montenegro's 2006 accession to the Convention: www.coe.int/t/dghl/monitoring/minorities/3_FCNMdocs/Table_en.asp#Montenegro.

[67] For details of the Ahtisaari Plan see the website of the United Nations Special Envoy for Kosovo: www.unosek.org/unosek/en/statusproposal.html. See further below at n 84.

[68] See Agreement between the United Nations Interim Administration Mission in Kosovo (UNMIK) and the Council of Europe on technical arrangements related to the Framework Convention for the Protection of National Minorities, 4 June 2006.

B. Conditionality in Relation to Prospects of Accession to the EU

It would be wrong to view conditionality too simplistically, as either coercive or voluntary in character. It can be both simultaneously. Conditionality engages a complex set of pressures and motivations on the part of the actors on both sides of the bargain.

The status of the seven states in relation to the EU has already been set out above and need not be repeated here. Potential accession to the EU implies not just direct pre-accession compliance with the rules of EU law (as well as all the necessary economic and political adjustments), but also other forms of legal and political compliance at earlier stages of looser integration, as the potential candidate state is guided along a Commission-devised 'roadmap' towards integration, eg through the Stabilisation and Association Process. One of the aims of such 'roadmaps', such as those in relation to visa liberalisation, is to render the process ostensibly more technical and less political, although one of the by-products of such an approach is that it reveals the inconsistency of EU policies. Western Balkan states have been required to issue biometric passports to achieve visa liberalisation, and only those citizens of the three states which achieved Schengen visa liberalisation in December 2009 who actually possess biometric passports can benefit from the new regime. Croatia has been extremely slow to start issuing biometric passports, yet its citizens have visa-free travel and – in relation to the Schengen states – have always benefited from this status.

As we have seen in Section II(A), the relationship between EU law and national citizenship laws and policies is a rather difficult one, especially since the judgment of the ECJ in the *Rottmann* case.[69] It would be incorrect to state that these national rules fall strictly outwith the scope of EU law. Even so, hitherto, Member States have thought themselves relatively unconstrained in their implementation of policies on acquisition and loss of citizenship, subject to compliance with obligations otherwise arising under EU law such as the duty to recognise dual citizenship, established in *Micheletti*.[70] However, for candidate states, broader human rights compliance is supposed to be a heavier burden, where a substantial impact on, for example, problematic citizenship policies might expect to be seen. Furthermore, there is an as yet undiscovered potential for the Commission in the *Rottmann* case, which it may choose to use proactively in relation to candidatures. Hitherto, there has been a signal failure to apply conditionality consistently, as evidenced by the failure of the EU institutions to use Slovenia's pre-accession process to force progress in relation to a situation (the erasure) which has not only been characterised

---

[69] See n 18 above and the accompanying discussion.
[70] See n 15 above.

as a serious human rights violation by organisations such as Amnesty International[71] and the Justice Initiative of the Open Society Institute,[72] but which has also drawn negative comment, because of its effects in relation to statelessness, from actors such as the Council of Europe Commissioner for Human Rights. But the rather hidden fate of the Erased failed to make a substantial dent in the overall success rate of Slovenia, which has been widely seen in international spheres as the only success story of the dissolution of Yugoslavia and a deserving member of the '2004 team' – ie the first post-1989 enlargement of the EU towards Central and Eastern Europe.[73] On the other hand, Bosnia will undoubtedly be expected to implement constitutional reforms to correct the human rights violation identified in the *Sejdić and Finci* judgment[74] on the political rights of non-members of its 'constituent peoples' before it can expect to make further progress towards accession. It will be interesting to see how Montenegro's putative 'erasure' scenario is treated in the future.

Visa liberalisation policies also have effects upon the citizenship policies of the former Yugoslav states. Since the liberalisation policy still excludes two of the six states which remain outside the EU (Bosnia and Kosovo), it will clearly affect the motivations of citizens of those states to seek other passports – especially since Bosnia and Kosovo are two of the states which are relatively tolerant, in different ways, of dual and indeed multiple nationality.[75] For example, it is estimated that there are more than 500,000 Croatian passport-holders resident in Bosnia – a relic of the willingness of the Croatian authorities to give passports to non-resident citizens whose acquisition of Croatian citizenship after independence was specifically facilitated in earlier versions of its citizenship law.[76] This policy sees Bosnian Croats as full members of the Croatian nation and is consistent with a general Croatian policy of using ethnic preferences in order to determine the limits of its citizenship laws. Likewise, Bosnian Serbs will be able to acquire Serbian passports, either by establishing 'residence' in Serbia or by taking advantage of a citizenship law that has become more open towards granting passports to non-resident co-ethnics since Serbia

---

[71] See, most recently, Amnesty International Briefing, Slovenia: Submission to the UN Universal Periodic Review: Seventh session of the UPR Working Group of the Human Rights Council, February 2010, AI Index EUR 68/004/2009, 8 September 2009.

[72] See U Boljka, 'The Unfinished Business of the Fifth Enlargement Countries. Country Report: Slovenia' (Sofia, Open Society Institute, European Policies Initiative, 2009) 16–17.

[73] A similar failure in relation to the situation of the Russian minorities and stateless persons in Estonia and Latvia before 2004 can also be observed; see Shaw, *Citizenship and Enlargement*, above n 37, 70–83.

[74] See above n 55.

[75] Sarajlic, *The Bosnian Triangle*, above n 39, 19–21; G Krasniqi, 'The challenge of building an independent citizenship regime in a partially recognised state: the case of Kosovo', CITSEE Working Paper 2010/04, 17–18.

[76] See Ragazzi and Štiks, *Croatian citizenship*, above n 6.

constitutionally redefined itself as 'the state of the Serbian people and of all citizens living in Serbia'.[77] It seems that only the third 'constituent people', Bosnia's Muslim citizens or 'Bosniacs', will be likely to continue to require visas in the future in order to access the Schengen area, especially those who suffered both the consequences of war and of post-war reconstruction and were unable to obtain the passports of Western states as did many Bosnian refugees who left the country. This reinforces, unfortunately, a perception that the EU does not recognise – in its dealings with Bosnia – the fact that it was this group who suffered the most during the 1992–95 wars in Bosnia.

In the context of Kosovo and Serbia, the EU has adopted a set of measures differentiating between different 'classes' of citizenship, which seems difficult to justify in view of fundamental principles of non-discrimination. Paragraph 4 of the preamble to Regulation 1244/2009[78] states:

> For persons residing in Kosovo as defined by the United Nations Security Council Resolution 1244 of 10 June 1999 (referred to as Kosovo (UNSCR 1244)) and persons whose citizenship certificate has been issued for the territory of Kosovo (UNSCR 1244), a specific Coordination Directorate in Belgrade will be in charge of collecting their passport applications and the issuance of passports. However, in view of security concerns regarding in particular the potential for illegal migration, the holders of Serbian passports issued by that specific Coordination Directorate should be excluded from the visa-free regime for Serbia.

The casual reference to 'illegal migration' as the justification for drawing this distinction has the effect of continuing the stigmatisation of that part of the Balkans, for visa liberalisation only affects short-term travel and not long-term residence or work regimes. Those determined to travel illegally to the EU and to work there will continue to do so, regardless of the existence of the visa regime. The statement also has implications for both Serbians and Kosovans, and indicates that EU policies can themselves be affected by domestic contingencies such as the capacity to distinguish between different categories of Serbian documents. As Serbia does not recognise the independence of Kosovo, and on the contrary sees that territory as still being subject to its sovereign jurisdiction, citizens of Kosovo are – simultaneously – citizens of Serbia.[79] Indeed, for pragmatic reasons, many Kosovans have hitherto retained Serbian documents, and this measure appears to be a step intended to reduce the benefits for them of so doing. Equally, of course, this measure has the effect of removing

---

[77] See Štiks, 'Laboratory of Citizenship: Nations and Citizenship', above n 7, 208–10.
[78] See above n 47. See also Article 1(2) of the Regulation.
[79] See Krasniqi, 'The challenge of building an independent citizenship regime', above n 75.

ethnic Serbian Kosovans – some of whom have also taken up Kosovan documents as well as Serbian ones, also for pragmatic reasons – from the ambit of the visa liberalisation regime. To that extent, Serbia appears to have agreed to a regime which may benefit the majority of its population, but which discriminates between different groups of citizens, both on the basis of residence and on the basis of ethnicity, and it will be interesting to see whether it is challenged internally. Of course, either group can seek to establish a 'residence' in Serbia, spurious or otherwise, and seek to obtain documents through that means. Indeed, as is often commented, those who seek ways around the law, or who are prepared to act illegally, are rarely those who are inconvenienced or stigmatised by visa regimes.[80] On the contrary, it is 'ordinary' citizens who bear the brunt.

Equally, one of the factors pointing in favour of early implementation of visa liberalisation for Macedonia is the fact that such a policy would relieve some of the pressure which has arisen because of the willingness of Bulgaria to give passports to Macedonians – whom some in Bulgaria see in any event as belonging to the Bulgarian nation – on the basis of rather spurious residence qualifications in Bulgaria, because they have studied at an university in Bulgaria, or on the basis of special measures benefiting non-resident citizens.[81] Again, this may be evidence of domestic policies spilling over into the EU arena. However, since Bulgaria is already a Member State – albeit one subject to transitional restrictions on freedom of movement for labour purposes – and Macedonia has not even begun its accession negotiations, the likelihood is that this route will continue to be seen as an attractive one for some Macedonians in order to acquire a passport more highly valued within the EU context.

C.   Direct Intervention by International Organisations

In the context of violent conflict in the region, there have been numerous occasions when international organisations have intervened directly, both to prevent conflict and also for humanitarian reasons, including to provide aid and to protect the interests of refugees and internally displaced persons (IDPs). NATO and the UN and its various agencies have been most directly engaged in these processes, along with the Council of Europe and the EU itself. With regard to refugees and IDPs, questions of access to citizenship, in particular via civic registration processes, have often been raised with

[80] E Neumayer, 'Unequal Access to Foreign Spaces: How States use Visa Restrictions to Regulate Mobility in a Globalized World' (2006) 31(1) *Transactions of the Institute of British Geographers* 72.

[81] See D Smilov and E Jileva, *Report on Bulgaria*, EUDO-Citizenship Observatory, available at: eudo-citizenship.eu/docs/CountryReports/EUDO-2009-Bulgaria-linked.pdf, p 17; Spaskovska, *Macedonia's Nationals*, above n 63, 23.

the successor states by international organisations, and they continue to be raised in the context of EU accession conditionality, especially with regard to groups such as the Roma.[82] However, in terms of direct impact upon citizenship questions, it is the role of the United Nations Interim Administration Mission in Kosovo (UNMIK), and also of the UN Special Envoy in Kosovo, Martti Ahtisaari, which require more detailed discussion.[83]

During the period of international administration (1999–2008), up to the date of Kosovo's unilateral declaration of independence, UNMIK decided to create a separate civil registry for Kosovo residents to deal with the fact that persons born after 1999 were undoubtedly stateless as they had no opportunity to be entered into the registers of the Federal Republic of Yugoslavia (FRY),[84] which continued to claim sovereignty over the territory even after the UN Security Council adopted Resolution 1244 obliging the FRY military and police forces and administration to withdraw completely from the territory. Indeed, most civil registers were destroyed or confiscated after 1999 by the FRY administration, as a result of which even those born before 1999 had difficulties in presenting official papers especially as many were lost or destroyed during the conflicts at the end of the 1990s. Consequently, UNMIK began to issue ID cards and also travel documents for those who could prove that they were 'habitual residents' of Kosovo. Krasniqi has obtained figures showing that UNMIK issued around 1,600,000 ID cards and 600,000 travel documents between 2000 and 2008, effectively beginning the process of reconstituting the citizenry of what became – in 2008 – the Republic of Kosovo.[85]

The transition to supervised independence for Kosovo came under the conditions of compliance with externally imposed principles of statehood. However, in practice, the UN Security Council was unable to endorse the plan for independence developed under the leadership of the UN Special Envoy, Martti Ahtisaari, leading in February 2008 to an unilateral declaration of independence and the adoption of the documents and symbols of statehood based on the democratic, secular and multi-ethnic principles which Kosovo signed up to in the context of the Ahtisaari plan. This affects also the terms of citizenship under the Kosovan Constitution and Law on Citizenship adopted shortly after independence. This law enables not only habitual residents during the UNMIK period but also pre-war

---

[82] For an example, see the Commission 2009 Progress Report on Macedonia, SEC(2009) 1335, 21, which refers to 3,000 to 5,000 Roma, ethnic Albanians and ethnic Turks still lacking personal documents.

[83] See generally Krasniqi, 'The challenge of building an independent citizenship regime', above n 75.

[84] This refers to the 'rump' state comprising Serbia and Montenegro and in existence until 2003 when it was replaced by the State Union of Serbia and Montenegro.

[85] Krasniqi, 'The challenge of building an independent citizenship regime', above n 75, 7–11.

residents of Kosovo and their descendants to acquire Kosovan citizenship – and is even-handed as to whether these persons are of Albanian or Serbian ethnicity. It is, as Krasniqi argues, an open and inclusive solution to the task of defining a citizenry, which is close to the so-called 'new state' solution identified by Rogers Brubaker when discussing the post-Soviet successor states.[86] This is because – unlike the other six states – Kosovo was not a republic of the former Yugoslavia and thus there was no republican-level citizenship upon which the initial determination of the citizenry could be based. As a law drafted and adopted by the Kosovan Parliament under a fast-track procedure supervised by the officials of the International Civilian Office (ICO), the Kosovan Law on Citizenship owes less than some of the other laws drawn up during that phase of develop- ment to examples drawn from other post-Yugoslav states such as Slovenia, as was often the practice of the ICO officials.[87] Whether – given the relatively mono-ethnic character of Kosovo, which has an Albanian majority group amounting to 90 per cent of the population – it is possible in practice to give effect to a civic conception of citizenship remains to be seen.

D.   Direct Supervision by International Organisations

Whilst it might be appropriate to describe the period of UNMIK adminis- tration of Kosovo as a direct *intervention* by an international organisation, it would be best to describe the current situation as an incidence of direct *supervision*. This involves the final stages of the UNMIK phase, taking the form of the ICO and the EU Special Representative for Kosovo (EUSR) (whose functions are expected to be wound down over a period of time), combined with an anticipated long-term presence for the largest EU civilian mission ever established (EULEX: the EU Rule of Law Mission). In that context, continued impacts upon citizenship and related matters can be seen as Kosovo finishes the task of reconstituting its citizenry through measures relating to civic and electoral registers, as well as the detailed implementation through administrative instructions of the Citizenship Law. Here, direct evidence of the importation of best practices can be seen, for example, in the procedures established to deal with requests for citizenship through the Citizenship Office and the Appeal Committee of

---

[86] *ibid*, 2; see R Brubaker, 'Citizenship Struggles in Soviet Successor States' (1992) 26 *International Migration Review* 269. See also more recently Shevel, above n 35.
[87] Interview in ICO office October 2009.

Citizenship, which has tight deadlines for making its decisions and which will – for the foreseeable future – be subject to scrutiny in its work by EULEX.[88]

In Bosnia, a similar quasi-protectorate scenario is in place, with the Office of the High Representative retaining substantial powers since the Dayton Agreements, similar to those of the ICO, EUSR and EULEX in Kosovo. The High Representative imposed the citizenship legislation in Bosnia after Dayton, two years before it was enacted by the state parliament.[89] In practice, also, the peculiarities of Bosnia's post-Dayton constitutional settlement have given considerable veto powers to the representatives of the two sub-state 'entities', and progress has thus been blocked in relation to important aspects of the constitution which is widely recognised as not being in conformity with international human rights norms. It is interesting to speculate whether – in the citizenship-related field of electoral rights – the case of *Sejdić and Finci* brought before the ECtHR[90] might achieve outcomes which the High Representative in Bosnia cannot.[91] For it is anticipated that the Bosnian Constitution will have to be amended to make it possible for persons not self-declaring as members of the three 'constituent peoples' of Bosnia to be elected to the collective Presidency and the House of the Peoples.

E. Other Forms of International Pressure

Throughout the region, more traditional forms of international pressure can be discerned, exercised both by other international organisations with a presence in the region which do not have the powers of the ICO/EUSR or EULEX in Kosovo or the High Representative in Bosnia, or by neighbouring states with particular interests to promote and by states with particular regional interests or responsibilities such as the United States, Russia and many Member States of the EU. In all of these cases, states and international organisations make use of the normal channels of diplomatic influence and pressure, many of which are not visible in public. Such pressures will cover, of course, not only citizenship issues but also other norms of good governance such as democracy, transparency and good administration. It is thus harder to state, for example, the extent to which Bulgaria experiences pressure from its EU partners not to grant citizenship to Macedonians, or whether some attempts have been made to persuade

---

[88] On procedures, see in particular Krasniqi, 'The challenge of building an independent citizenship regime', above n 75, 19–20.
[89] See Sarajlic, 'The Bosnian Triangle', above n 39, 11.
[90] See above at n 55.
[91] See Sarajlic, 'The Bosnian Triangle', above n 39, 23–24, 25–26.

Slovenia finally and fully to regularise the situation of the Erased.[92] It is certainly clear that at a certain point in the late 1990s and early 2000s Croatia did come under pressure – as part of an international policy to force it to allow the return of Serb refugees – to permit Croatian Serbs to access, if they so wished, Croatian citizenship. Croatia never pursued the Slovenian option of 'erasing' the residents who were citizens of other former Yugoslav republics, but the military successes of the Croatian army in the Krajina, Slavonia and elsewhere in 1995 led to large numbers of refugees amongst the Serb community who subsequently found it hard to return to Croatia from what was then the FRY, and to reassert the citizenship which they retained at least in theory.

Macedonia, however, does provide one very good example of a 'citizenship effect' of external pressure which it would be appropriate to include under this fifth rather ad hoc category. This concerns the Ohrid Framework Agreement, which was negotiated under the guidance of mediators from the US and the EU, as well as with more informal and private advice from the French politician and jurist Robert Badinter. Badinter is well known for having headed the Arbitration Commission of the Peace Conference on the former Yugoslavia appointed by the Council of Ministers in 1991 to attempt to devise some reliable criteria for determining when – and which – states seceding from Yugoslavia should receive international recognition by the EU and its Member States. The agreement was signed by both the international mediators and the representatives of the various ethnic Macedonian and Albanian parties, and it successfully brought to an end an armed rebellion by Albanian radicals which was threatening the stability of the state. The agreement itself recognised the importance of Macedonia being a multi-ethnic state governed on the basis of republican secular principles, and it led to the introduction of a form of consociationalism through constitutional amendments giving vetoes to both communities in the process, at all levels of government. Macedonia was constitutionally re-designated as a 'civic and democratic state', replacing the previous definition of Macedonia as primarily the state of the Macedonian people, 'as well as citizens living within its borders who are part' of the minorities. This exclusionary definition had been supported by a Citizenship Law of 1992, which established a lengthy 15-year continuous residence period, which effectively excluded many Albanian and Roma minority residents from citizenship of the new republic. This was reduced

---

[92] In March 2010, the Slovenian Parliament again amended its law to bring a final closure on the issue of the Erased, enabling a further tranche of those erased to recover their permanent resident status; see Balkan Insight, 'Slovenia Parliament amends law on erased', www.balkaninsight.com/en/main/news/26402/, 9 March 2010. However, the opposition parties have attempted to call a further referendum on this question, reckoning on the existence of a continuing tension between resolving the situation of the Erased and perceptions of national identity in what remains a new state.

in a new law of 2004 to an eight-year residence period.[93] Moreover, in its most recent amendment of 2008, it is possible to see further external influence upon Macedonian citizenship laws. Responding to international pressure that consistently highlighted the continued problems with refugees and IDPs, the amendment established that refugees could apply for Macedonian citizenship if they had been legally resident in Macedonia for six years prior to the application. It was also specifically aimed at settling the position of refugees from Kosovo, as it abolished the requirement that a person seeking naturalisation must have been released from their previous citizenship (in this case Serbian citizenship) and also removed the requirement that such persons must not have been subject to criminal prosecution in their country of citizenship.[94] In practice, many Kosovan Albanians had been subject to criminal prosecutions in Serbia.

F. Overlapping Citizenship Regimes Between Neighbouring States

As we have noted at several points in this chapter, one of the features of the citizenship regimes under consideration is that they all stem from a single historical root, namely the citizenship regime of the former Yugoslavia, with its dual system of republican/federal citizenship. This factor, along with cross-republic mobility, transnational family ties and more historical links which developed over centuries in the Balkans, explains why there are often points of overlap and friction between the citizenship regimes of these states, of an extent and an intensity which goes beyond other neighbouring pairs or sets of states (eg Belgium/France; Benelux states; Nordic states).

These factors account, for example, for the importance and high prevalence of dual nationality as between pairs of states (eg Croatia/Bosnia; Croatia/Serbia; Serbia/Bosnia; Serbia/Kosovo; Macedonia/Bulgaria, etc) as well as with those third countries permitting dual nationality that have been the most common destinations for emigrant Yugoslavs and citizens of post-Yugoslav states. In that context, the position in Montenegro – which acquired its independence in 2006 – is of considerable interest. Montenegro discourages dual citizenship, most particularly because of the relationship with Serbia (up to 30 per cent of the Montenegrin population identify themselves as Serbian and thus dual citizenship could have a profound impact upon voting arithmetic).[95] Dual citizenship is only

---

[93] See Spaskovska, 'Macedonia's Nationals', above n 63, 12.
[94] See *ibid*, 14.
[95] See Dzankic, 'Transformations of Citizenship in Montenegro', above n 60, especially 1–2, 16–17.

permitted in the context of reciprocity, once agreements have been concluded with other states; so far, an agreement has only been concluded with Macedonia. Montenegro's policy choice, which is significant for the purposes of state-building and community cohesion, therefore impacts upon the citizenship regimes of the *other* neighbouring states, because it seeks exclusivity for Montenegrin citizenship in a manner which the other regimes, with the exception of Bosnia which also has a reciprocity clause, do not.

The overlapping character of the citizenship regimes of the seven states also accounts for the sensitivities which attached in particular to the initial definition of the citizenry in each of the states at the point of independence/secession/state redefinition. As we saw in the case of the Erased in Slovenia, this was seen to pose a particular challenge in relation to the question of 'who are the citizens?', as no single state could be in any substantial respect isolated or insulated from the others. Indeed, as Oxana Shevel argues, 'the politics of national identity (defined as contestation between citizenship policymaking elites over the question of the nation's boundaries) is a particularly important source of citizenship policies in new states'.[96] But difficulties arose more generally because there had been a number of changes to the definitions of citizenship at both the federal and the republican levels whilst socialist Yugoslavia existed, and there were subtle differences between each of the states. Many citizens were not aware of the significance of republican citizenship and the registers of citizens were often incomplete or incorrect. As a result, there were many cases in the immediate aftermath of independence of persons finding themselves involuntarily stateless because it turned out they were not registered where they expected to be, or their registration did not have the effect of giving them the citizenship of the state where they might have resided for many years, or even were born. The impact of these rules also caused profound difficulties in relation to access to property, since – as Verdery has shown – during the post-socialist transition citizenship and property rights intersected in important ways during phases of privatisation as well as periods of conflict, violence and forced population mobility.[97] In the EU – ie where European norms of non-discrimination on grounds of nationality apply – it is, of course, unlawful to link property ownership to nationality in that way.

[96]   Shevel, 'The Politics of Citizenship Policy', above n 35, 274.
[97]   K Verdery, 'Transnationalism, Nationalism, Citizenship and Property: Eastern Europe since 1989' (1998) 25 *American Ethnologist* 291.

V. CONCLUSIONS

This chapter has covered a wide range of issues, having started with an analysis of the place of Union citizenship in the EU context, before shifting focus to look at the impact of the mosaic of constitutional and constitutional-like norms which impinge upon the citizenship regimes of a complex region – the former Yugoslavia – which remains unstable and in transition even 20 years or more after the fall of the Berlin Wall.[98] Moreover, it is a region that has not, for the most part, conformed to the patterns of post-socialist transition, which are visible in the states of Central and Eastern Europe which acceded to the EU in 2004 and 2007. Despite the lack of attention that citizenship has generally received in the context of the dissolution of Yugoslavia, it is not surprising that questions of membership definition have been of acute relevance in the context of a painful transition from a single multinational and multi-ethnic state, composed of republics most of which were themselves (increasingly) multi-ethnic in character, into seven often ethnically defined states. This is all the more so because there were increasingly large numbers of transnational families in Yugoslavia as a result of labour migration after the Second World War and the impact of the policies of the Yugoslav National Army. Such families, along with ethnic groups that have suffered specific policies of ethnic cleansing in a number of different contexts (eg Serbs in Croatia; Croats and Bosniacs in Bosnia), have often been internally or indeed externally displaced throughout the 1990s and into the 2000s.

The intention in this chapter was not, of course, to make the argument that the relations between Union citizenship and the citizenship of the Member States are completely straightforward, as cases such as *Micheletti*, *Kaur* and especially *Rottmann* have clearly shown, or to try to argue that integration in the EU or the role of EU citizenship represents some sort of panacea for the citizenship troubles of the new states of South Eastern Europe. The paradoxical effects of the EU on borders are, as is well known, as much to redefine them as they are to remove them altogether.[99] However, it is worth noting that even where EU citizenship is at its most challenging for the national citizenships of the Member States, it is still a less fraught scenario than that which faces the citizenship regimes of the new states of South Eastern Europe, engaging with multiple sources of normative authority making connections to the EU and its Member States, to each other and to other third countries. Even so, it should not be

---

[98] See I Štiks, '"The Berlin Wall Crumbled Down upon Our Heads!": 1989 and Violence in the Former Socialist Multinational Federations', (2010) 24 *Global Society* 91.

[99] N Walker, 'Beyond Boundary Disputes and Basic Grids: Mapping the Global Disorder of Normative Orders' (2008) 6 *International Journal of Constitutional Law* 375; T Diez, 'The Paradoxes of Europe's Borders' (2006) 4 *Comparative European Politics* 235.

thought that external pressures, whether vertical or horizontal in character, are the only forces in the shaping of the national citizenship laws of the seven states now established in the territory of the former Yugoslavia. Endogenous factors, such as the ethnic mix of the states or internal historical and institutional factors and questions of national identity, also play a role.

By the same token it should not be concluded that the international dimension of the constitutional mosaic, so far as it affects citizenship, somehow automatically undermines the legitimacy of the existing constitutional settlements. It would be wrong to suggest that these seven states will only reach a state of stability once they kick (almost all) the international norms out and start, as mature national systems, to deal with their own problems through predominantly national solutions. On the contrary, the experience of the EU in relation to citizenship surely suggests otherwise, as we saw in Section II, which charted the complex and still evolving relationship between EU citizenship and national citizenship for the Member States. For with stability and mature constitutional systems, along with greater economic prosperity, will – most likely – come also EU membership for these states and thus the complexities of a multi-level citizenship settlement that this involves, albeit with only limited constraints directly upon the capacity of states to determine the contours of their own citizenry. But if the EU continues to develop along its present (political) lines, as the Treaty of Lisbon has shown, a greater political substance is likely to be invested in EU citizenship, with consequential effects upon national *political* citizenship, if not the rules on acquisition and loss.

In that context, the patterns of the constitutional mosaic will change for the new states of South Eastern Europe, as a result of changes *within* the EU of an institutional and a legal character, as well as changes *to* the EU (ie the expansion of membership). Some of the arrangements discussed in this chapter will wither away, but others – such as the ECHR – may remain and develop, as civil and political rights become increasingly intertwined in the case law of the European Court of Justice. However, even when the last of the seven states in the region becomes a member, the heritage of its complex and often tortured history is likely to be evident in the continued intertwining of state-building and citizenship as presented here.

7

The Council of Europe as a Norm Entrepreneur: The Political Strengths of a Weak International Institution

GWENDOLYN SASSE*

I. INTRODUCTION

IN EUROPE'S DENSE institutional environment the Council of Europe acts as a reservoir of norms. Its Convention for the Protection of Human Rights and Fundamental Freedoms (1950) is a normative cornerstone which has gained visibility and legal assertiveness over time, in particular through the European Court of Human Rights (ECtHR). The Council of Europe develops and formalises norms linked to human rights, democracy and the rule of law, puts in place monitoring and enforcement mechanisms, and offers advice on constitutional and legal issues. The 'soft' nature of its remit and the difficulties attached to enforcing its norms underpin the image of the Council of Europe as a relatively weak institution. *The Economist*'s verdict on the Council of Europe's Parliamentary Assembly sums up a widely shared view about the Council of Europe in general: 'This body's members are moonlighting – in wordy, worthy and well-deserved obscurity – from their main jobs as national lawmakers in the 47 Member States. It is the sort of place that makes even the European Parliament look important'.[1]

This statement illustrates a number of facts and perceptions. The Council of Europe is clearly less visible than the EU, NATO or the UN. It often gets confused with the EU and its component parts, and its own institutional make-up and decision-making procedures are less talked

* University of Oxford.
[1] 'Laying down the law, or just laying down?', *The Economist*, 25 September 2008. See: edwardlucas.blogspot.com/2008/09/europe-view-no-100-council-of-europe.html.

about than the EU institutions. The Parliamentary Assembly of the Council of Europe (PACE), staffed by Member State parliamentarians for whom this job is an add-on (in contrast to the European Parliament), is a consultative body. Its often highly critical reports and non-binding resolutions tend to get wider media coverage than the actual decision-making body of the Council of Europe – the Committee of Ministers – which is made up of the Member States' foreign ministers and their permanent representatives based in Strasbourg. This imbalance in public visibility and the lack of follow-up of numerous PACE resolutions have created an image of PACE as a talking-shop whilst distracting from its role in the preparation of the Council of Europe's binding legal instruments, most notably its foundational Convention for the Protection of Human Rights. The quote from *The Economist* combines a verdict on the Council of Europe's lack of importance with an equally widely shared perception of the institution and the norms it tries to uphold as being 'worthy'. It is this tension between 'weak' and 'worthy' that this chapter seeks to explore.

The creation of the Council of Europe as an institution centred on a set of broad ideas, and its remit to translate these ideas into more specific legal instruments (over 200 to date) form part of the construction, routinisation and empowerment of norms. There is hardly a year in the Council of Europe's existence without a new treaty or protocol being opened for signature. A higher degree of institutionalisation increases the visibility, continuity and outreach of norms, and thereby their potential strength. However, the identification of a norm entrepreneur – in this case the Council of Europe – says little yet about the nature of its entrepreneurship and the lifecycle of the norms it promotes. What is missing from the analysis of the Council of Europe as a norm entrepreneur is an understanding of how norms come onto the Council of Europe's agenda in the first place, and how they are moulded and turned into legally-binding instruments that are then regularly reviewed, adjusted and extended. Some norms cascade and others do not, or do so only with a significant time-lag or have unintended consequences. Some Council of Europe treaties lie dormant for several years before a minimum number of Member States ratify them and thereby allow them to enter into force. There are often long temporal lags in the multi-stage ratification process of the Member States, and, depending on the issue at stake, there are countries that delay or categorically oppose even the first stage of the domestic ratification process. Checkel has pointed to the existence of a mismatch between institutionalised regional and domestic norms. He links this mismatch to increased levels of normative contestation in domestic politics, which make social learning less likely.[2] The Council of

---

[2] Jeffrey Checkel, 'Why Comply? Social Learning and European Identity Change' (2001) 55 *International Organization* 553–88.

Europe is actively involved in creating this mismatch. This raises several questions: Why would Member States agree to the codification of norms that they have no intention of ratifying? Why would they risk becoming entangled in an international normative and legal discourse that their respective governments are trying to avoid 'at home'?[3] It would be much easier to not cooperate or subvert the norm production inside the Council of Europe. Yet Member States tend not to block this process. This is part of what former Council of Europe Secretary-General Terry Davis has referred to as 'the best kept secret in Europe'.[4]

This chapter starts from a simple premise: even among the institutions with a remit for norm production some are more prolific and generate 'stickier' norms than others. Why? This chapter will address four plausible explanations for the sustained norm production and credibility of the Council of Europe: its institutional structure and ways of operating; its normative remit and institutional innovations; the coherence of its normative framework; and its interaction with other institutions with overlapping remits. These factors will be discussed through a number of 'hard' cases of norm production. While there is clear variation in the national compliance with Council of Europe norms – both between 'ratifiers' and 'non-ratifiers' of a particular treaty and within the group of 'ratifiers' – the focus on norm production is harder to substantiate in terms of variation in the outcome. There are plenty of ideas that are raised in PACE, for example, that are never codified as binding Council of Europe norms. The working of this filtering mechanism needs to be unpacked in more detail in further research, as does the related question of how certain norms appear on the Council of Europe agenda in the first place. This chapter will limit itself to analysing the underlying paradox: each Council of Europe treaty – including the Convention on Human Rights, which limited the range of rights included in the UN Declaration – is a compromise negotiated by Member State representatives. Even the compromise formula is often in direct juxtaposition to some national domestic preferences.

---

[3] Based on archival evidence, Anne Deighton has demonstrated that Member States were caught between the utility (in terms of Europe's image) and the potentially subversive nature (in relation to their own domestic or imperial practices) of the human rights focus enshrined in the foundational documents of the Council of Europe. See Anne Deighton, *Writing Europe into the World*, Paper given at the European Studies Centre at St Antony's College, University of Oxford, 4 February 2010.

[4] Terry Davis, 'The Council of Europe – the best kept secret in Europe', Lecture at the De Montfort University, Leicester, 13 January 2010.

II.   THE COUNCIL OF EUROPE'S CAPACITY AS A NORM ENTREPRENEUR

Regime theorists have suggested that international norms emerge when a hegemonic actor, defined in terms of economic or military power, pushes them, but this argument struggles to explain the adoption of human rights norms.[5] Alternative explanations of the emergence of norms have concentrated on strongly held beliefs and 'moral proselytysing' on the part of individuals,[6] or the interactions between non-governmental actors and norm entrepreneurs within governments or international organisations. Advocacy networks have been singled out as a necessary (though not sufficient) condition for bringing normative concerns to the attention of decision-makers through persuasion (as they lack direct access to state resources) and paving the way for an international norm to be formulated and adopted.[7] This line of argument stops short of unpacking the dynamics in the process of norm production once an issue has emerged on the agenda.

Finnemore and Sikkink have mapped the life-cycle of a norm as a linear process that moves from the emergence of a norm to norm acceptance via a tipping point at which a critical mass of relevant actors are willing to institutionalise the norm through a process of norm implementation.[8] The distinction between norm acceptance and norm implementation is fuzzy. Sunstein had used the evocative term of a 'norm cascade' to capture the momentum behind norm acceptance gathering speed.[9] More recently, Saurugger has pointed out that the process of norm creation and implementation does not have to be a linear one. She traces the translation of the norm of 'participatory democracy' into a constitutional norm at the EU level (through the Constitutional Treaty and the Lisbon Treaty), a process that reflects the ongoing struggle of different actors for power and legitimacy behind the institutionalisation of a norm which remains contested and is only partially implemented.[10] The legal and political consolidation of the EU has gone hand in hand with an increase in the

    [5]   John Ikenberry and Charles Kupchan, 'Socialization and Hegemonic Power' (1990) 44 *International Organization* 283–315; Stephen Krasner, 'Sovereignty, Regimes, and Human Rights' in Volker Rittberger (ed), *Regime Theory and International Relations* (Oxford, Clarendon Press, 1995).
    [6]   Ethan Nadelmann, 'Global Prohibition Regimes: The Evolution of Norms in International Society' (1990) 44 *International Organization* 479–526.
    [7]   Kathryn Sikkink, 'Transnational Politics, International Relations Theory, and Human Rights' (1998) 31 *Political Science and Politics* 516.
    [8]   Martha Finnemore and Kathryn Sikkink, 'International Norm Dynamics and Political Change' (1998) 52 *International Organization* 887–917.
    [9]   Cass Sunstein, 'Social Norms and Social Roles' in Cass Sunstein (ed), *Free Markets and Social Justice* (New York, Oxford University Press, 1997) 32–69.
    [10]   Sabine Saurugger, 'The Social Construction of the Participatory Turn: The Emergence of a Norm in the European Union' (2010) 49 *European Journal of Political Research* 471–95.

contestation of this process. The discursive framing of the integration process as 'constitutionalisation' nurtured strong opposition and led to the rejection of the Constitutional Treaty in two national referenda and its subsequent reframing as the Lisbon Treaty.[11] Despite its deepening and widening norm production the Council of Europe has escaped a similar veto point.

A. Institutional Structure and Modus Operandi

The Council of Europe's institutional structure combines elements that could both facilitate and hinder norm production. The Statute (1949) defines the aim of the Council of Europe as 'achieving greater unity between its members' through 'discussion of questions of common concern and by agreements and common action'.[12] Article 15a states that the Committee of Ministers

> shall consider the action required to further the aim of the Council of Europe, including the conclusion of conventions and agreements.

From the very beginning norm production – defined as a momentum for the progressive development of the foundational norms in the form of treaties – was inscribed in the definition of the Council of Europe. Thus, norm production has been the explicit cornerstone of the Council of Europe's activity. This is not a guarantee for the successful codification of norms, but it provides an intra-institutional explanation for the Council of Europe's norm activism: without it the Council of Europe would lose its raison d'être. Similarly, the Council of Europe's Member States share a baseline agreement on wanting to maintain the institution itself and therefore have to permit at least a degree of norm production. It creates a positive image both for internal and external consumption. The Council of Europe re-invents itself continuously by adjusting its remit to respond to topical challenges (eg democratisation in Eastern Europe, democratic citizenship, social cohesion) with an explicit link to its original mission.[13] It thus actively anchors and reinforces its legitimacy as an institution in a changing political environment.

The Council of Europe's remit – unlike that of the Organization for Security and Co-operation in Europe (OSCE) – is not framed in security terms (Article 1 of the Statute explicitly excludes national defence issues),

---

[11] *ibid*, 485–88.

[12] Statute of the Council of Europe, London, 5 May 1949 (as amended) CETS No 001, Art 1.

[13] See, for example, the speeches at the Council of Europe's Warsaw Summit 2005, as cited in Aline Royer, *The Council of Europe* (Strasbourg, Council of Europe, 2010) 19.

and the United States is an observer rather than a full member (unlike in the case of the OSCE). The Council of Europe is not seen as threatening a country's national interests. It is effectively a single-issue institution hinged on the principle of human rights. This principle, tied to the concepts of democracy and the rule of law, has been gradually extended into a wide range of different policy fields. The process of norm production itself is facilitated by the Council of Europe's relatively simple institutional structure. The decision-making body, the Committee of Ministers, is made up of the Member States' foreign ministers and, on a day-to-day basis, of their permanent representatives based in Strasbourg. A secretariat coordinates Council of Europe meetings and activities, and PACE (including the elected post of Commissioner for Human Rights, created in 1999), the Congress of Local and Regional Authorities of Europe and, since 2005, the Conference of International NGOs (bringing together over 400 NGOs) act as consultative bodies on the development and enforcement of norms. The streamlined structure, in particular the focus on one decision-making body, limits intra-institutional competition, while incorporating different national and sub-national constituencies into the discussion and preparation of the treaties and their enforcement mechanisms. The consultative bodies represent national and sub-national deputies from the Member States, but through an intensive reporting system these bodies represent a link to other national and transnational constituencies, including advocacy networks. The extensive use of external rapporteurs on thematic or country-specific issues regularly channels expert knowledge and a degree of field experience into the institution. Both are particularly needed on new topics or issues that are politically tricky to raise in a domestic arena.

One of the best examples of agenda-setting on the part of PACE is its influence on the idea and content of the Convention on Human Rights. PACE had urged the Committee of Ministers in 1949 to adopt a convention that would ensure the 'effective enjoyment by all persons ... of the rights and fundamental freedoms referred to in the UN Declaration of Human Rights', and the PACE Legal Affairs Committee was instructed to draft the text.[14] In 1951 an amendment of the Council's Statute gave PACE the right to set its own agenda, but PACE failed subsequently to become a constituent assembly. PACE is involved in different types of agenda-setting – within PACE and vis-à-vis the Committee of Ministers and the Member States. In an institution primarily focused on norm production and enforcement, the Committee of Ministers cannot but engage with recommendations and proposals generated by PACE as well as its input into the drafts of treaties. The norm-centred remit of the Council of Europe

[14]   *ibid*, 20.

guarantees PACE that it will be heard, though many of its proposals do not make it to the next stage of legal codification.

Only a small number of issues require a unanimous vote in the Committee of Ministers. These include the suspension of membership, recommendations to Member State governments or an amendment to the Statute articles defining the remit of the Council of Europe, the voting procedure or the institutional structure, including the status of PACE. The Committee of Ministers has the capacity to extend the unanimous vote to any issue 'on account of its importance',[15] for example issues of institutional reform. Rules of procedure and financial and administrative regulations can be changed by a simple majority of the Committee members. Resolutions related to new members or associate members require a two-thirds majority of all those entitled to sit on the Committee. All other resolutions, including the budget, treaties and amendments, require a two-thirds majority of the representatives casting a vote and a majority of those entitled to vote (each Member State has one vote). The same majorities are required to authorise the publication of any explanatory report.[16] Given that each Member State can choose whether or not to ratify a treaty, these thresholds for putting a treaty in place (and any future amendments) are set relatively low. This means that at least some Member States have to maintain the institution's momentum through treaty ratification and opening themselves up to monitoring.

With a slender zero-growth annual budget of €205 million, the Council of Europe operates under significant financial constraints.[17] One third of its budget is tied to the ECtHR. As the share for the ECtHR has increased, other areas of Council activity have contracted, thereby lowering the visibility of the Council of Europe's range of activities while reinforcing the ECtHR as its core pillar. Despite the Council of Europe putting its members on an equal footing in its voting procedures, France, Germany, Italy, Russia and the United Kingdom contribute more financially than they would have to and thereby increase their informal influence.[18] However, these Member States are too heterogeneous in their political systems and in their definition of national interests – including their approach to the legal codification of human rights, minority rights or dual citizenship – to push or prevent certain norms as a bloc. Their influence is best understood as a certain scope for agenda-setting or, in extreme cases, a veto on a decision that requires unanimity (see Russia's veto on ECtHR reform discussed below).

---

[15] Statute of the Council of Europe, CETS No 001 Art 20.
[16] *ibid*, Art 20.
[17] Royer, *The Council of Europe*, above n 13, 19.
[18] Even the Council of Europe's in-house publication admits as much; see Royer, *The Council of Europe*, above n 13, 9.

The Council of Europe changes with the norms it develops. Each treaty opens up the space for a sub-set of Member States to endorse the extension of norms into a new or revised issue area. A complex layering of Member State commitments is the result. Depending on the issue at stake, there is a degree of peer pressure on Member States as the number of ratifications goes up. The volume and detail of the monitoring that forms part of each treaty enforcement mechanism creates new points of contact between the Committee of Ministers (and its thematic working groups and treaty-specific advisory committees) and the Member State governments, between PACE and a wider range of Member State actors, and between PACE and the Committee of Ministers. Within the Council of Europe (and among aspiring Member States) the legitimacy of the foundational norms is beyond debate. Member States diverge in their views on the continuous (re-)interpretation of norms and extension into new policy fields of institutional reforms, but the fact that each new treaty draws its inspiration and legitimacy from specific thematic precursors as well as the overall body of Council of Europe norms limits the scope for any Member State actor to take an opposing view from the outset, in contrast to the bread-and-butter issues of many EU negotiations.

The Council of Europe, with its norm-based definition of democracy, is procedurally even further removed from democratic accountability than the EU with its directly elected European Parliament and the representation of the whole range of national ministries in the Council of Ministers.[19] Norm entrepreneurship, in particular mechanisms of naming and shaming, may benefit from this insulation (the annual meetings of the foreign ministers and the weekly meetings of their deputies take place behind closed doors and the minutes are confidential). The fact that only the foreign ministers – rather than a wider representation of the Member States' cabinets as in the EU's case – are represented in the Committee of Ministers, and that there is only one scheduled high-level meeting a year, with the permanent representatives based in Strasbourg meeting on a regular basis, reduces internal politicisation and increases the likelihood of an agreement being brokered while limiting a minister's fear of political fall-out 'at home'. The overall low public visibility of the Council of Europe further lifts the pressure on government representatives vis-á-vis their electorate and the media. However, in order for the consensus to be sustained that certain norms are not up for democratic contestation, the legitimacy of the Council of Europe's foundational norms and the Member States' commitment to these norms need to be continuously re-asserted.

---

[19]   The procedural democratic deficit is counterbalanced by the right to individual petition under the Convention on Human Rights. Originally this was optional; today it is obligatory for all Member States.

The Council of Europe's membership structure is bound to shape its role as a norm entrepreneur. The effect of the rapid enlargement from 13 relatively similar Member States in 1989 to the 47 Member States of today is a contradictory one. The Council of Europe's flexible institutional structure facilitated its engagement with some Central and Eastern European countries both prior to and after 1989. The push from Eastern Europe and the former Soviet Union for legitimation through membership provided the Council of Europe with a new political role and a momentum for institutional innovation. The Council of Europe put in place an admission process that allows for (soft) post-accession conditionality. By now the reference to 'like-minded countries in Europe' in the preamble to the Statute of the Council of Europe has been stretched to include a highly heterogeneous group of regimes, ranging from old Western European democracies and consolidating democracies in Central and Eastern Europe integrated (or integrating) into the EU and NATO, to post-conflict countries with unstable political systems and (semi-) authoritarian regimes with unresolved 'stateness' issues. In 2008 the Council of Europe was confronted with the first war between two of its Member States (Russia and Georgia). The post-1989 enlargement of the Council of Europe has had a clear effect on the content of norm production, with norms such as the protection of national minorities and statelessness being codified in new conventions.

It is too early, however, to determine clear effects of the enlargements beyond the EU Member States on the Council of Europe's legitimacy as an institution. Over time it may become harder to maintain the institution's credibility as an anchor of human rights and democracy if countries like Armenia and Azerbaijan, accepted in 2001, continue to make little or no attempt at democratisation, if Bosnia and Herzegovina, accepted in 2002, fails to stabilise, and if the conflicts in Chechnya and Georgia remain unaffected by Council of Europe membership obligations. The disparate interests, legacies and normative frameworks of the Council of Europe members could lead to deadlocks and stalling in norm production, a process which would erode the institution's credibility.

B. Normative Remit and Institutional Innovation

The Council of Europe has a dual function: the development and enforcement of norms. As the latter clearly depends on a whole range of factors, many of which are outside the control of the Council of Europe, activism in norm production and the design of enforcement mechanisms are the primary means of securing institutional survival and credibility in Europe's crowded legal and political space. As long as there is some evidence of enforcement and an active attempt to prevent the gap between norm production and enforcement from becoming too wide, the Council of Europe acts within fairly realistically framed expectations and long-time horizons. The process of managing the gap between norm production and enforcement is complex, as norm production and enforcement are being pursued simultaneously at different levels in the institution and its Member States. Its institutional structure, as discussed above, insulates the Council of Europe from direct public or democratic scrutiny. Its low visibility and a widespread perception of institutional weakness limit the immediate damage potentially costly decisions, such as the accession of Armenia and Azerbaijan, could otherwise have. The way in which the Council of Europe compensates for its apparent weaknesses is by linking norm production, in particular the widening normative remit, to institutional adaptation.

The Council of Europe's remit is focused but open-ended. The foundational norms of the Council of Europe form a package that is hard for any democratic or democratising state – or a regime keen to present itself as democratising – to question. Human rights are potentially the most 'subversive' norm from a state's perspective.[20] The decision to make the Convention on Human Rights, including the right to individual petition, obligatory for all Member States follows through on the original idea. The possibility of the EU acceding to the Convention under the Lisbon Treaty could be the next step in this process of institutional adaptation. Over time the Council of Europe has extended the principle of human rights into spheres closely connected with state sovereignty, such as migrant rights and the protection of national minorities. The principle of democracy, originally nebulously framed as 'genuine democracy' in the preamble to the Statute of the Council of Europe, has been spelled out by potentially more intrusive norms, such as multiple citizenship and inclusion in diverse societies. Whilst the adoption of these more specific norms is optional for Member States, the emphasis since the end of the Cold War has switched to encouraging countries to move towards democracy by admitting a range of hybrid and non-democratic states as members in the hope of changing their political systems and normative reference points from within the institution.

(i)   Eastern Enlargement

The end of the Cold War raised the profile and visibility of PACE and the Council of Europe, but only because the Council of Europe actively used and shaped the political space opening up in front of it. Not only did its normative focus find a natural new home in Eastern Europe; it had cultivated some relations with Eastern Europe before 1989. When the

---

[20]   Sikkink, 'Transnational Politics', above n 7, 516–23.

Council of Europe was established, several Central and Eastern European countries had been observers, though the Cold War then interrupted these links. In the 1980s the Council of Europe had reached out to the early transition countries, in particular Poland. PACE made the first step towards enlarging the Council of Europe: from 1989 Central and East European countries were given 'guest status'. This rapid engagement provides an example of agenda-setting on the part of PACE. It did not only raise the issue of engaging with Eastern Europe within the Council of Europe and beyond, it also opened up an institutional path for this engagement.

The Council of Europe swiftly expanded on the notion of 'guest status', partly following up on the earlier actions of PACE and partly in response to the push from Central and Eastern European countries that saw institutional membership as an anchor for their new regimes and the first step towards integration into Western institutions. The Council of Europe's admission criteria, as spelled out in the Statute, are vague. Article 4 states that European states

> deemed to be able and willing to fulfil the provisions of Article 3 may be invited to become a member of the Council of Europe by the Committee of Ministers.

Article 3, in turn, stipulates that every member has to

> accept the principles of the rule of law and of the enjoyment by all persons within its jurisdiction of human rights and fundamental freedoms, and collaborate sincerely and effectively in the realisation of the aim of the Council.

The Council of Europe put in place a more detailed procedure for accession at its Summit of Heads of State and Government in Vienna on 9 October 1993.

In a dense period of institutional activity in Europe, the Council of Europe followed the European Council in Copenhagen which had laid down the 'Copenhagen criteria' for EU accession in June 1993. Similar to the Copenhagen criteria, the Council of Europe added democracy, the rule of law and human rights, free elections, respect for international law and acceptance of the jurisdiction of the European Court of Human Rights as explicit membership criteria.[21] The Committee of Ministers remained the decision-making body regarding accession, but PACE took on a more prominent role in the admission process through the monitoring and assessment of the credentials of potential Member States.[22] The membership criteria and the accession procedure were elaborated, but in practice

---

[21] The Vienna Declaration of the Council of Europe, 9 October 1993. See:https://wcd.coe.int/wcd/ViewDoc.jsp?id=621771&Site=COE.

[22] PACE asks legal experts, including from the ECtHR, to draw up an opinion on the country in question, and a number of PACE members visit the country as rapporteurs.

the process remained flexible. The Council of Europe was the institution most open to the push from Eastern Europe, including an early move beyond the EU candidate countries.

In contrast to the EU, the Council of Europe interpreted membership conditionality as a post-accession instrument. This policy is logically linked to the reluctance of the Council of Europe to contemplate a Member State's expulsion – a possibility under Article 8 of the Statute in cases of non-compliance with the principles in Article 3 – and to a preference for attempting to change Member States from within.[23] Since 1994 new members commit themselves to ratifying the Convention on Human Rights within a year of joining (including the protocols, especially Protocol 6 on the abolition of the death penalty). In addition, they have to sign the Convention on the Prevention of Torture and the Social Charter and ratify them without delay. A somewhat flexible list of other treaties is usually added, including the Convention on Extradition, the European Charter on Local Self-Government and the Framework Convention for the Protection of National Minorities (FCNM).[24] The Council of Europe can further insist on institutional and legal changes, for example a reform of the Member State's civil code. The flexible institutional formula for accession was stretched to an extreme with the admission of Armenia and Azerbaijan in 2001, with PACE asserting and the Committee of Ministers accepting that both countries were 'moving towards a democratic, pluralist society'.[25]

The enlargement of the Council of Europe preceded the EU's own elaboration of its accession procedure, but the sequence in the admission process followed a different path. It started with Hungary (1990), Poland and Czechoslovakia (1991), but then mixed what were to become early and late EU accession countries – Bulgaria (1992), Estonia, Lithuania and Slovenia (1993) – and already in 1995 went beyond the EU's accession agenda when admitting Latvia, the Former Republic of Yugoslavia, Moldova and Ukraine. By doing so, it also paved the way for the EU's engagement with non-accession countries through the EU's European Neighbourhood Policy (ENP).

The institutional innovation of admitting new members with outstanding commitments required the introduction of a new monitoring mechanism. In the case of the Council of Europe this has meant the monitoring of Member States – rather than candidate states only, as in the case of the EU. While the EU has been reluctant to extend internal Member

---

[23]   Pamela A Jordan, 'Does Membership Have Its Privileges?: Entrance into the Council of Europe and Compliance with Human Rights Norms' (2003) 25 *Human Rights Quarterly* 3, 660–88.

[24]   Royer, *The Council of Europe*, above n 13, 40.

[25]   PACE Opinions No 221 (Armenia's application for membership of the Council of Europe) and No 222 (Azerbaijan's application for membership of the Council of Europe) (2000).

State monitoring, as the lengthy discussions about the EU Agency for Fundamental Rights have shown, the Council of Europe built on its existing institutional practice of monitoring Member States under the Convention on Human Rights (including monitoring the implementation of ECtHR rulings) and monitoring the signatories of the various treaties. The Committee of Ministers set up its own monitoring system of Member States in 1994 – in the form of thematic monitoring (for example, on the freedom of expression and information, the functioning of democratic institutions, local democracy and action against intolerance and racism) and individual country monitoring.[26] It applies to all Member States. The decision to proceed with thematic monitoring lies with the Committee of Ministers, but PACE, the Secretary-General or a Member State can recommend it (as in 2000 and 2003 when PACE and the Secretary-General asked for the monitoring of human rights in Chechnya). Originally with the new East European members in mind, PACE initiated its monitoring of new Member States in 1993; in 1995 the principle of monitoring was widened to include all Member States. This was followed up with a special monitoring commission in 1997 to ensure the 'honouring of obligations and commitments by member states'.[27] As of the beginning of 2010, 11 East European and post-Soviet states are still being monitored. Turkey has been the only long-term Council of Europe member to be subjected to country-specific PACE monitoring (concluded in 2004).[28]

The Council of Europe's third institutional pillar, the consultative Congress of Local and Regional Authorities, provides a further example of the widening of the normative remit through institutional innovation in reaction to political changes. It started as a loose conference and became a permanent body in 1962. The European Convention on Local Self-Government, which it had helped to shape, has been in force since 1988. It stipulates political, financial and administrative autonomy for local authorities and, in turn, became a prominent point of reference for Central and East European transition states. The 1993 Vienna summit of the Council of Europe upgraded the Congress to the status of third pillar of Council of Europe: the aim to promote local democracy in Central and Eastern Europe propelled a request for better representation of local and regional authorities. The Congress submits proposals on local and regional democracy to PACE and the Committee of Ministers – again the mandate is framed in proactive terms. Since 1996 the Congress has had its own monitoring procedure for observing the functioning of local and regional democracy in the Member States. In May 2008 the Congress adopted the

[26] Declaration on Compliance with Commitments Accepted by the Member States of the Council of Europe, adopted by the Committee of Ministers on 10 November 1994.
[27] Parliamentary Assembly of the Council of Europe, Resolution 1107 (1997).
[28] Royer, *The Council of Europe*, above n 13, 41.

draft European Charter of Regional Democracy, a yet more controversial norm across the Member States whose regional governance arrangements vary widely.

Almost a decade after its first involvement in Central and Eastern Europe, the Council of Europe decided at its Warsaw summit in 2005 to discuss its relations with the EU more systematically. By this point eight Central and East European countries had joined the EU; two more were to follow in 2007; and the Western Balkan countries had been given a membership perspective, though the time-line was still uncertain. After the first two eastern enlargements (plus Malta and Cyprus) EU Member States now make up the majority of members of the Council of Europe (25 of 46 members in 2004, 27 of 47 members since 2007). This considerable overlap in membership links the Council of Europe and the EU, but it could also eclipse the distinctive role of the Council of Europe. At the Warsaw summit the Council of Europe asked Jean-Claude Juncker for a report on Council of Europe-EU relations. His suggestions included the EU's accession to the Convention on Human Rights (now possible under the Lisbon Treaty), a joint legal and judicial system, EU recognition of the Council of Europe as the expert authority on human rights in Europe, the EU's adoption of the Statute of the Council of Europe by 2010, greater involvement of the public and the appointment of higher-profile Secretaries-General to enhance the institution's visibility and political weight.[29] The proposals have only been partially been implemented, but, in particular, the recognition of the Council of Europe as the pre-eminent normative authority has been strengthened.

In 1990 the European Commission for Democracy through Law (Venice Commission) was set up as a partial agreement under the Council of Europe. The idea was to create a forum for independent experts to discuss constitutional and international law issues. It has concentrated on four areas: constitutional assistance, elections and referenda, co-operation with constitutional courts and a series of transnational studies. Since 2002 it has been an 'enlarged agreement' that allows states that are not members of the Council of Europe to join. Initially, the Venice Commission was primarily used by states wanting to join the Council of Europe and the EU to help bring their legal systems in line with Council of Europe standards. Gradually, the Venice Commission has become a more general point of reference for advice on constitution- and law-making. The consultation process is voluntary and non-binding. Since 2002 the European Court of Human Rights (ECtHR) has referred to the opinions of the Venice

---

[29]   Royer, *The Council of Europe*, above n 13, 19.

Commission (so far in 45 cases), thereby creating an additional feedback effect into national systems regardless of a Council of Europe member's implementation of an opinion.[30]

(ii)   ECtHR Reform and Institutional Innovation

Russia's relationship with the Council of Europe has been an uneasy one. In 1995 PACE had suspended Russia's membership application due to the first Chechen war, but in 1996 Russia became a Council of Europe member. In 2000–01 PACE suspended Russia's voting rights in response to the human rights violations in the second Chechen war. This step followed a number of critical PACE resolutions asking the Committee of Ministers to suspend Russia's Council of Europe membership. Russia's furious rhetoric in response to these steps indicates that a hybrid or authoritarian regime is not immune to shaming by the Council of Europe and values its membership. In the aftermath of the Russian-Georgian war, PACE has repeatedly called on Russia to revoke its recognition of Abkhazia and South-Ossetia, but the fact that the conflict involves two Council of Europe Member States has limited the moral leverage of the institution.

Against this backdrop, the issue of reforming the ECtHR and Russia's veto over institutional reform have been one of the biggest internal challenges for the Council of Europe. As the Court is intrinsically tied to the legitimacy of the Council of Europe as a whole and presents the most tangible measure of the Council of Europe's effectiveness, the need for institutional reform to secure the right to individual petition has become ever more pressing in view of a backlog of cases (estimated to grow from over 100,000 cases today to about 300,000 cases within five years) and the fact that many cases take about six years to be decided. Given that Russia accounts for the largest share (about one-third) of pending cases, Russia's interest in streamlining the court's procedures had to be limited from the outset. As reforms of the court system go to the heart of the Council of Europe's institutional structure, they are approached as decisions that require unanimity among the Member States.

The ECtHR reform, embodied in a Protocol to the Convention on Human Rights (1998), abolished the Commission's vetting of incoming applications, created a single full-time Court of Human Rights, abolished the Committee of Minister's jurisdiction to decide on the merit of the cases not going to the Court, guaranteed automatic individual petition without a

---

[30] Council of Europe Directorate of Communication, *Peace through Democracy and Democracy through Law – 20 Years since the Establishment of the Venice Commission of the Council of Europe*, Press release 376 (2010).

state declaration and reduced the number of judges deciding the admissibility of a case.[31] The next reform in 2004 (Protocol 14) proved more controversial and was blocked by Russia for over three years. According to Protocol 14 one ECtHR judge (out of the 47 national judges) can decide the admissibility of a case, 'repetitive' cases can be grouped together; cases can be thrown out on the basis of posing 'no significant disadvantage', a panel of three judges (instead of seven) can rule in routine cases, and Member States can be brought in front of the Court by the Committee of Ministers if they refuse to enforce a judgment.[32] In 2006 Russia had signed Protocol 14, but the Russian State Duma had subsequently voted against its ratification. The then Deputy Foreign Minister, Grigorii Kazarin, tried to persuade parliamentarians by emphasising that Russia's refusal to ratify the Protocol would prevent it from coming into force and damage Russia's international reputation. President Vladimir Putin, by contrast, warned of the politicisation of the Court and signalled his support for the refusal to ratify.[33] The Duma committee vetting the Protocol listed so-called human rights concerns as its reasons to caution against ratification, namely the extension of the term of judges and the possibility to dismiss cases more easily.

Over time Russia's veto and delaying tactics became more costly for the Council of Europe in both operational and reputational terms, and ultimately led to a significant institutional innovation.[34] There were discussions to drop the reform of procedural changes via time-consuming protocols requiring unanimity and instead to enable procedural changes under a Statute which would allow the Committee of Ministers – still by unanimity – to issue resolutions without amending the Convention each time. In the end, the format of the reform procedure remained in place. At the Madrid Council of Foreign Ministers in May 2009 the Council of Europe paved the way for a two-tier system allowing for a fast-track procedure to be applied immediately to those ratifying a revised version of Protocol 14, thereby removing the veto power of any one Member State. The Committee of Ministers had prepared a draft protocol ahead of the Madrid Council, based on the proposal put forward by the ECtHR

[31]   Protocol No 11 to the Convention for the Protection of Human Rights and Fundamental Freedoms, restructuring the control machinery established thereby, 11 May 1994; entered into force on 1 November 1998 (CETS No 155); see: conventions.coe.int/Treaty/EN/Treaties/html/155.htm.

[32]   Protocol No 14 to the Convention for the Protection of Human Rights and Fundamental Freedoms, restructuring the control machinery established thereby, 13 May 2004, entered into force 12 May 2009, CETS No 194; see: conventions.coe.int/Treaty/EN/Treaties/Html/194.htm.

[33]   'Russia prompts crisis of European human rights justice', *BBC News*, 9 December 2009; see: news.bbc.co.uk/2/hi/8402806.stm.

[34]   A Mowbray, 'Crisis Measures of Institutional Reform for the European Court of Human Rights' (2009) 9 *Human Rights Law Review* 647–56.

President Jean-Paul Costa[35] and a draft by PACE,[36] alongside an alternative option based on individual state declarations allowing the Court to use its new mechanisms when dealing with cases from the state in question. Following the first option, Protocol 14-Bis, adopted in May 2009 by the Committee of Ministers and immediately opened for signature, created a procedural way out of the institutional deadlock and set a precedent for similar future scenarios. The innovation of a sub-protocol open to all but with binding effect on only those Member States who ratify it paved the way for a partial and differentiated approach to core institutional reforms.

Russia was represented inside the Council of Europe throughout the discussions of Protocols 14 and 14-Bis. By December 2009 nine Member States had ratified Protocol 14-Bis. As an emergency measure – deliberately framed as provisional – it entered into force immediately after the first three ratifications. Eight further members had signed it by this stage. PACE rapporteurs criticised Russia for its general conduct vis-à-vis individual claimants and NGOs, and requested a special report on Russia's refusal to ratify Protocol 14. This demonstrates that fundamental institutional reform issues can become a public matter in contrast to the Council of Europe's business as usual. The Secretary-General of the Council of Europe, Thorburn Jagland, held talks with Russian President Dimitrii Medvedev in late December 2009, and Medvedev himself eventually adopted a positive stance on the Protocol, tying it to a domestic political agenda when several draft laws on legal reform were under preparation. He called for an end to 'legal nihilism' in Russia and for court reform that would enable Russian citizens to seek redress in Russian courts rather than in Strasbourg. Russian Justice Minister Aleksandr Konovalov made a similar public statement calling for Russian courts to take the ECtHR case law into account.[37] On 15 January 2010 the Duma overwhelmingly voted in favour of the ratification of Protocol 14. Mikhail Margelov, the head of the International Affairs Committee of Russia's upper chamber, the Federation Council, tried to use the momentum by calling for the overdue

---

[35] *ibid*, 648.

[36] Committee of Ministers, *Letter from the Chairman of the Ministers' Deputies to the President of the Assembly*, 21 April 2009, Doc No 11864; see: assembly.coe.int/Mainf.asp?link=/Documents/WorkingDocs/Doc09/EDOC11864.htm.

[37] Anton Burkov, 'Ratification of Protocol 14 to the Convention on Human Rights', *EU-Russia Centre*, 26 February 2010; see: www.eu-russiacentre.org/our-publications/column/ratification-protocol-14-convention-human-rights-forced-measure-decision-reform-european-court-human-rights.html. In the first issue of its 2010 bulletin the Supreme Court of the Russian Federation published a judgment of the Presidium of the Supreme Court of the Russian Federation which refers to a violation of the Convention on Human Rights as an admissible ground for reopening of a criminal case (*ibid*).

abolition of the death penalty. Russia's Constitutional Court had prolonged the moratorium on capital punishment in late 2009 and declared
that the process towards the abolition of the death penalty was 'irreversible'.[38]

The fear that Protocol 14-Bis would lift any remaining pressure on
Russia proved wrong.[39] In January 2010 PACE revived its discussion about
suspending Russia's membership in connection with the recognition of
Abkhazia and South Ossetia. In response, the Russian delegation threatened to leave the Council of Europe. This timing should have hardened
Russia's position on ECtHR reform further. The fact that the opposite
happened underlines that, on balance, Russia remains interested in being a
full member of the club. Even if the calculation that the acceptance of the
ECtHR reform would soften the Council of Europe's stance on Abkhazia
and South Ossetia played into Russia's decision to ratify Protocol 14, the
potential fall-out of a higher number of ECtHR judgments against the
Russian government, showing up the shortcomings of the Russian court
system, had to be the more important consideration. With all Council of
Europe members having ratified Protocol 14, Protocol 14-Bis has been
superseded.

The cases of Eastern enlargement, and Russia's veto over ECtHR reform
demonstrate the willingness and ability of the Council of Europe and its
Member States actively to adjust the normative remit through institutional
innovations in view of external and internal political challenges. Russia's
veto over reforming the ECtHR has been the hardest institutional challenge
for the Council of Europe so far.

C.   Normative Coherence

The Council of Europe's institutional structure and the remit adjustments
through institutional innovation underpin a cumulative process of norm
production that raises the issue of normative coherence, both internally
and vis-à-vis other international actors. At least some degree of external
and internal coherence will be necessary in order for an international
institution with an explicit remit of norm production to gain and retain
credibility. The Council of Europe's codified norms are rooted in international law, most notably the UN Declaration of Human Rights, but the
ongoing development of the foundational norms could easily lead to
inconsistencies or overall incoherence. For despite being rooted in international law, over time the Council of Europe has confronted many issues

---

[38]   'Russia ratifies human rights agreement', *Financial Times*, 15 January 2010.
[39]   Antoine Buyse, 'Protocol 14 Bis – The Interim Solution', *ECtHR Blog*, 4 May 2009;
see: echrblog.blogspot.com/2009/05/protocol-14-bis-interim-solution.html.

that international law has avoided (eg on national minorities). Internally, path dependence has characterised the Council of Europe's norm production, but this process has not always been a linear one. On some norms, most notably the death penalty and dual nationality, the Council of Europe has fully or partially reversed its position.

Through interviews with Council of Europe officials and national negotiators Checkel established a discursive 'taken-for-grantedness' of the status of Council of Europe treaties and the norms they codify, including a lack of opposition to the controversial norm of minority rights.[40] This acceptance of the existence of Council of Europe norms underpins at least a shared perception of internal norm coherence. The Council of Europe's internal coherence is built around the Convention on Human Rights. All subsequent treaties have expanded on this normative basis. Council of Europe treaties either explicitly reframe an earlier treaty or implicitly build on the overall body of Council of Europe law and adapt the basic principles to new policy areas. The Council of Europe continuously invokes and reinforces its founding principles through its norm production and the celebration of symbolic occasions.[41]

Another way of ensuring norm coherence is the creation of explicit or implicit cross-linkages between Council of Europe treaties, thereby linking different policy fields. In order to keep each treaty open to Member State ratification, they tend to refer back only to the Convention on Human Rights. However, there are implicit references and thematic links between the treaties. The 'European Convention on the Participation of Foreigners in Local Public Life' of 1992 (in force since 1997), for example, builds on ideas in the European Charter on Local Democracy of 1985 (in force since 1988), and links up with the Convention on the Status of Migrant Workers of 1977 (in force since 1983) and the references to 'effective participation' in the FCNM of 1995 (in force since 1998).

(i) Abolition of the Death Penalty

The abolition of the death penalty has been one of the most prominent Council of Europe norms, in particular with regard to the new Member States in Eastern Europe and the former Soviet Union. The death penalty was allowed and used as part of the Nuremburg trials. Thus, the Council of Europe and even the Convention on Human Rights accepted it, and the norm remained in place for the next 30 years. In the 1970s the issue rose

---

[40] Checkel, 'Why Comply? Social Learning and European Identity Change', above n 2, 482.

[41] See, for example, the speech by PACE President Lluis Maria de Puig on the occasion of the 60th anniversary of the Council of Europe on 27 April 2009, cited in Royer, *The Council of Europe*, above n 13, 3.

on the Council of Europe's agenda when the Scandinavian countries abolished the death penalty (Sweden and Finland in 1972 – the latter joined the Council of Europe only in 1989; and Denmark in 1978) and three further abolitionist countries (Portugal, Spain and Liechtenstein)[42] joined the Council of Europe. The issue got its first airing in PACE only with difficulty.[43] Once the issue had been opened up for debate, primarily by EC Member States inside the Council of Europe interested in changing the norm in line with their domestic preferences, the momentum for norm change started to build. In 1980 PACE called for the abolition of the death penalty 'for crimes committed in times of peace'. The decision by France in 1981 (reinforced by the Netherlands in 1982) to abolish the death penalty for all crimes added weight to the abolitionist position. The Council of Europe's Protocol 6 to the Convention on Human Rights (opened for signature in 1983) introduced a first significant change by redefining the parameters for the application of the norm by ruling out the use of the death penalty in peacetime. In a second step, the abolition of the death penalty was made compulsory for future Member States. This step was talked about from 1989 and formalised in 1996.[44] Since 1997 no Council of Europe member has used the death penalty. All new Member States were obliged to introduce a moratorium immediately and ratify Protocol 6 within a year of joining (Russia is the only member that has not ratified Protocol 6 although it has – with the exception of cases in Chechnya – upheld its 1996 moratorium).[45] Finally, Protocol 13 to the Convention on Human Rights of 2002 abolished the death penalty also for crimes committed during war (ratified by all members apart from Azerbaijan and Russia). This protocol came after the 50th anniversary of the European Convention on Human Rights in November 2000. For the Council of Europe such occasions are routinely used to rhetorically reinforce the institution's rationale and anchor a new stage in the process of norm development.

The normative discourse about the death penalty has progressed along a path from the legally and politically tolerated use of the death penalty after the Second World War to the insistence on its complete abolition in all

[42] Portugal joined the Council of Europe and abolished the death penalty for all crimes in 1976; Spain joined in 1977, was among the first five countries ratifying Protocol 6 to the Convention on Human Rights, and abolished the death penalty for ordinary crimes in 1978 and for all crimes in 1995; Liechtenstein became a member of the Council of Europe in 1978 and abolished the death penalty for all crimes in 1987.

[43] Royer, *The Council of Europe*, above n 13, 28.

[44] Council of Europe, Parliamentary Assembly Resolution 1097, 28 June 2006. By 1990 only 6 of 12 EC states had already abolished the death penalty; by 2001 9 of by then 15 EU Member States had abolished it for all crimes, and 25 out of the then 43 Council of Europe members still had it on their statute books.

[45] Belarus – not a Council of Europe member – is the only remaining European country still using capital punishment.

Council of Europe Member States and attempts to export this norm internationally. Gradually, the legal, political and geographical remit of the norm of abolition have been stretched. The Council of Europe has begun to go beyond its members by calling on countries with an observer status, most notably the United States and Japan, to follow the example of the Member States in their non-application and abolition of the death penalty. In its resolutions and recommendation to that effect PACE has interpreted the Council of Europe observer status – defined by the Committee of Ministers' Statutory Resolution 93(26) – as implying compliance with the Council of Europe's basic norms, including the abolition of the death penalty.[46] In an attempt to make the norm truly international, the Council of Europe reacted to the hanging of Saddam Hussein in 2006 by calling for the worldwide abolition of the death penalty.[47] It was also involved in the preparation of the 2007 and 2008 UN Assembly Resolutions on a global moratorium on the death penalty.

The Council of Europe developed the norm of the abolition of the death penalty within the framework of its Convention on Human Rights (and the UN's Declaration of Human Rights). It supplied the anchor for a norm reversal in European political and legal discourse. In turn, it also provided a reference point for the EU, which became more outspoken on the issue – rhetorically after the Maastricht Treaty and substantively after the Amsterdam Treaty, which envisaged a stronger foreign policy role for the EU. In particular, in its relations with third countries the EU's growing emphasis on norms and values, including the abolition of the death penalty, reflects this ideational shift.[48]

(ii) Multiple Nationality

Citizenship marks another area of active Council of Europe involvement and normative change over time. The Convention on the Reduction of Dual Nationality and on Military Obligations in Cases of Multiple Nationality (1963) promoted the elimination of dual citizenship, seen as a dual privilege in terms of rights clashing with principles of equality and democracy.[49] In its preamble the Convention states that

---

[46] Council of Europe Parliamentary Assembly, Recommendation 1522 (2001), Resolutions 1253 (2001), 1349 (2003) (Abolition of the death penalty in Council pf Europe Observer states) and 1560 Promotion by Council of Europe member states of an international moratorium on the death penalty (2007).

[47] Royer, *The Council of Europe*, above n 13, 30.

[48] Ian Manners, 'Normative Power Europe: A Contradiction in Terms?' (2002) 40 *Journal of Common Market Studies* 245–52.

[49] Mark Miller, 'Dual Citizenship: A European Norm?' (1989) 23 *International Migration Review* 948.

cases of multiple nationality are liable to cause difficulties and … joint action to reduce as far as possible the number of cases of multiple nationality … corresponds to the aims of the Council of Europe.[50]

In Chapter 1, which no signatory can include in its reservations, Article 1 clearly states that nationals of full age who have acquired 'of their own free will' another nationality, 'shall not be authorised to retain their former nationality'. Chapter 2, also excluded from reservations, recognises the fact that instances of multiple nationality exist, and explicitly allows Member States to go beyond the Convention in their attempts to limit these instances (Chapter 2, Article 4). Few Member States ratified it.

The detailed explanatory report accompanying the 1997 European Convention on Nationality acknowledges that the issues surrounding nationality have grown in scope and complexity and are 'not sufficiently considered' in the 1963 Convention.[51] The extent of labour migration in Europe, the need to facilitate the integration of long-term residents, the growing number of marriages between spouses of different nationalities, the freedom of movement within the EU, the need to avoid statelessness and provide guidance for the new nationality laws in Central and Eastern Europe as well as the principles of gender equality (with regard to spouses acquiring nationality or passing on their nationality to their children) and non-discrimination are singled out as necessitating the Council of Europe's re-think and its ambition 'to consolidate in a single text the new ideas' on nationality.[52] This process occurred in several stages over two decades: two Committee of Minister resolutions in 1977, the 1977 Protocol to the Convention, PACE recommendations in the 1980s, the 1993 Protocol (allowing multiple nationality in three cases: second-generation migrants, spouses of mixed marriages, and children of mixed marriages), a feasibility study on 'modern solutions to issues relating to nationality suitable for all European States' and a multi-year process of drafting and consulting on a new convention, in which the Committee of Experts on Nationality played an important role. Whilst the explanatory report clearly states that the underlying assumption of the 1963 Convention was that multiple nationality was undesirable, it retains a link by emphasising the fact that the earlier Convention already acknowledged the existence of multiple

[50] Convention on the Reduction of Dual Nationality and on Military Obligations in Cases of Multiple Nationality, Strasbourg, 6 May 1963, entered into force 28 March 1968 (ETS No 43). See: conventions.coe.int/Treaty/Commun/QueVoulezVous.asp?NT=043&CM=8&DF=02/07/2010&CL=ENG.

[51] Explanatory Report, European Convention on Nationality, Strasbourg, 6 June 1997 (ETS No 166), Introduction, available at http://conventions.coe.int/treaty/EN/treaties/html/166.htm.

[52] A domestic Member State issue – a French parliamentarian's concern about the legal limbo of a person in his constituency – provided one of the concrete moments behind the reconsideration of the 1963 Convention. See Miller, 'Dual Citizenship', above n 49, 949.

nationality. This provides the basis for building normative coherence, expanding on the notion of 'automatically' acquired citizenships. Moreover, it is framed to go beyond the link between multiple nationality and military obligations, and to deal comprehensively with all aspects of nationality, including principles, acquisition (for example stipulating a maximum period of 10 years of residence before the application for naturalisation), retention, loss, recovery, procedural rights, nationality in the context of state succession (to avoid statelessness), social and economic rights for habitually resident non-nationals (with the exception of employment in the public service jobs concerned with the exercise of sovereign powers), and cooperation between states.

The tension between the 1963 and 1997 Conventions is strongest in Article 7 (1997) on the loss of nationality. The Explanatory Report admits as much: signatories are said now to have a choice rather than an obligation to provide for the deprivation of nationality in cases of voluntary acquisition.[53] Furthermore, the will of the individual is recognised as 'a relevant factor in the permanence of the legal bond with the State'.[54] The 1997 Convention on Nationality is nevertheless meant to be complementary to the 1963 Convention. The Explanatory Report emphasises that a state can sign either or both conventions. The 1997 Convention is defined as being 'neutral' on the issue of desirability of multiple nationality; Article 15 reflects the variation in Member State law and practice. Signatories to Chapter I of the 1963 Convention, however, are restricted to allowing multiple nationality only in a limited number of cases. The Explanatory Report spells out that despite the complementarity of the Conventions their effect might be different: Member States whose internal law allows multiple nationality are unlikely to bind themselves by the 1963 Convention when they could adopt the 1997 Convention.[55]

Nationality issues, as defined by the Council of Europe, map a path of norm re-definition from the prevention of dual citizenship to a gradual widening of the Council of Europe remit and a simultaneous shift towards a greater emphasis on nationality as a right, which includes a recognition of multiple nationality as a reality that needs to be accommodated rather than abolished.[56]

(iii)   Prevention of Statelessness

Over time several norms subsumed under 'nationality' have gained greater visibility in the Council of Europe's norm entrepreneurship. Among these is

---

[53] Explanatory Report accompanying 1997 Convention, Art 7(1)(a).
[54] *Ibid*, Art 8.
[55] *Ibid*, Art 26.
[56] *Ibid*, Chapter II, Art 4(a).

the prevention of statelessness. According to Article 15 of the UN Declaration of Human Rights everyone has a right to a nationality. The UN Convention on the Reduction of Statelessness of 1954 was adopted in 1961 and entered into force in 1975. By 2007 only 34 UN Member States had ratified the Convention, among them 14 Council of Europe Member States, primarily from Eastern Europe and the former Soviet Union, where the experience of imperial and federal collapse had increased the scope for statelessness. The Council of Europe's 1997 Convention on Nationality, which includes the prevention of statelessness (Article 18), builds on codified UN norms and UNHCR activism as well as numerous bilateral activities, in particular in cases of state succession. The Council of Europe proceeded to single out this norm and codify it in a separate Convention on the Avoidance and Reduction of Statelessness. It was opened for signature in 2006 and entered into force in 2009 after three Member States (Norway, Moldova, Hungary) had ratified it (the only other Member State ratifying since 2009 has been Montenegro).[57]

In the preparation of this Convention non-binding instruments were taken into account, such as draft articles by the UN International Law Commission and the Declaration of the Venice Commission on the Consequences of State Succession for Nationality, the Recommendation of the Committee of Ministers on the Avoidance and Reduction of Statelessness and the practical experience of Member States.[58] The new Council of Europe Convention gives the issue of statelessness greater visibility. However, it reflects the minimum compromise that allowed its adoption in the first place, thereby pointing to the sensitive nature of the issue and continuing disagreement among the Member States. Given that Member States know they will not face immediate pressure to ratify the resulting Convention, such disagreement in itself is an acknowledgement of the more long-term relevance of Council of Europe norms. The only instance of statelessness the compromise Convention addresses is that linked to the circumstances of state succession – the norm that had already been enshrined in principle in the 1997 Convention on Nationality. States are not obliged to grant a person nationality based on their most effective link or expressed will, but the Convention sets out a number of minimum standards aimed at preventing statelessness. After intensive discussion the decision was made to stick to the formulation of the Convention on Nationality.[59]

---

[57] Council of Europe Convention on the Avoidance of Statelessness in relation to State Succession, Strasbourg, 19 May 2006, (CETS No 200).

[58] Committee of Ministers, Recommendation No R (99) 18 (adopted 15 September 1999); see also Roland Schärer, 'The Council of Europe and the Reduction of Statelessness' (2006) 25 *Refugee Survey Quarterly* 33–39.

[59] *ibid*, 34–37.

The most important provision in the Convention deals with the responsibilities of the predecessor state and the successor state, clarifying that at least one successor state has to be responsible for those with habitual residence on the territory at the moment of state succession or those who were habitually resident in a third state but had an 'appropriate' connection with the successor state. The definition of 'habitual residence' does not require formal qualification (and states are asked in the case of potential statelessness to lower their requirements of proof), and birth in the territory or republic-level citizenship in a federal state that disintegrates are covered. If the predecessor state still exists, it should not withdraw nationality (Article 6) – this is considered a primary responsibility even if an individual was habitually resident somewhere else. Nationality can only be withdrawn if an individual acquires a different citizenship, but a state cannot use this argument as a reason before an individual has taken up another citizenship (Article 7). There is no option for an individual habitually resident in one successor state to choose the nationality of another successor state. Article 9 creates a secondary obligation for states faced with state succession to facilitate the acquisition of nationality in favour of persons lawfully and habitually residing in the territory who have become stateless as a result of state succession. This clause is similar to, though more specific than that in the 1997 Convention on Nationality. The 2006 Convention affirms the principle of avoiding second-generation statelessness and asks for automatic citizenship at birth, thereby going beyond the 1997 Convention on Nationality. It further reinforces clauses from the 1997 Convention, such as the timely processing of applications and the need for international cooperation on the issue. Article 15 spells out the non-retroactivity of the Convention, a clear example of the way the Council of Europe proceeds in the presence of opposition. The new Convention does not cancel out the 1997 Convention but rather acts as a protocol that updates the content of the Convention.[60]

The norm of the prevention of statelessness is rooted in early UN (and League of Nations) principles, gaining in importance over time – partly as a result of the widening of the Council of Europe's perspective on nationality and partly in reaction to the political realities in Eastern Europe – and was singled out as a norm in its own right through a new treaty. However, the norm has remained contested and for the time being the Council of Europe approach is to define a minimum standard in particular circumstances (ie state succession).

The three norms discussed here – the abolition of the death penalty, multiple nationality and the avoidance of statelessness – illustrate different pathways in the evolution of Council of Europe norms. In the three cases

[60] *ibid.*

norm coherence had to be crafted to anchor, respectively, a complete norm reversal, a partial redefinition and widening of the norm, and the introduction of a new separate norm.

D.   Interactions with other International Institutions

For a norm-centred institution like the Council of Europe recognition by others as a norm entrepreneur is particularly important. Internal and external norm coherence are a basis for this recognition, but this coherence is more likely to be noticed and 'recognised' through some form of action on the part of the Council of Europe itself. One way of ensuring this recognition is through fostering linkages with other international actors. From the very beginning the Council of Europe has supplied a link between different international institutions. These linkages underpin institutional rivalries,[61] but they also form part of the Council of Europe's easily underestimated strength. Europe has emerged as the region with the highest density of international institutions with partly overlapping membership structures and remits that locate normative or constitutional authority beyond the state. Within this 'series of reinforcing frames' the Council of Europe stands out due to its 'normative ambition and increasing trumping (over domestic norms)'.[62]

Today the Council of Europe acts in a complex environment of institutions and norms that it has helped to create. It originally translated parts of the UN rights agenda in a European context still overshadowed by the experience of war, and provided an institutional precursor to the component parts of what has become the EU. It also contributed actively to the revamping of the OSCE in the 1990s, in particular the creation of the OSCE Parliamentary Assembly,[63] and developed its norm on minority protection in a dialogue with the OSCE (see below). The Council of Europe feeds off norms developed elsewhere or re-connects with the codified norms of another actor whose original normative inspiration may

[61] In its own publications the Council of Europe refers to the EU and its institutional precursors as 'competitors'; see Royer, *The Council of Europe*, above n 13, 6.

[62] Neil Walker, 'Taking Constitutionalism Beyond the State' (2008) 56 *Political Studies* 525, 535.

[63] Thomas Buchsbaum, 'The CSCE and International Organisations: Expanding Cooperation with the Council of Europe' in Michael Lucas (ed), *The CSCE in the 1990s: Constructing European Security and Cooperation* (Baden-Baden, Nomos, 1993) 137. See also Declaration of the CSCE Parliamentary Assembly, 5 July 1992; PACE Recommendation 1184 (1992) on the work of the CSCE on the eve of the Third Summit (Helsinki, 9–11 July 1992), adopted on 6 May 1992; PACE Recommendation 993 (1993) on the general policy of the Council of Europe, adopted on 3 February 1993.

have come from the Council of Europe. This mechanism affects the content of norm production as well as the Council of Europe's image and position vis-à-vis other international actors.

Both the Council of Europe and the EU (and its institutional precursors) were born out of the same intention: to overcome the divisions in Europe and safeguard future stability. Despite this shared starting-point, the two institutions were built on different premises – 'twins separated at birth'.[64] The mission of the EC/EU was to pursue political stability and cooperation through economic integration, while the Council of Europe pursued the same goal through the promotion of democracy, human rights and the rule of law, based on an expanding set of codified rights-based norms. Over time, the EU has adopted a more value-oriented approach. This has given the Council of Europe (and the OSCE) a more visible role during Eastern enlargement and prepared the ground for the transfer of norms, albeit primarily in one direction, from the Council of Europe to the EU. One prominent way to promote human rights-related norms has been their inclusion in the admission criteria of international institutions.

(i)   Protection of National Minorities

The pathway of the norm of minority protection illustrates both the gradual extension of the Council of Europe's normative remit into new areas and the interaction between international institutions. Compared to the UN, which has been hesitant to codify a norm based on the concept of 'national minority',[65] the Convention on Human Rights included a reference to 'association with a national minority' under Article 15 on non-discrimination, thereby providing the basis for the future elaboration of a norm centred on national minorities. Several PACE recommendations in the 1990s – in particular Recommendation 1201 (1993) on an additional protocol on national minorities to the Convention on Human Rights – the CSCE Paris Charter (1990), which tied 'peace, justice, stability and democracy' to the protection and promotion of the ethnic, cultural, linguistic and religious identity of national minorities, the EU's Badinter Arbitration Commission linking state recognition to the treatment of minorities, and the EU's inclusion of the 'respect for and the protection of minorities' in its Copenhagen criteria for accession, paved the way for the

---

[64]   Gerard Quinn, 'The European Union and the Council of Europe on the Issue of Human Rights: Twins Separated at Birth?' (2001) 46 *McGill Law Journal* 849–74.

[65]   An exception to this are the inclusion of 'national minorities' in the International Covenant on Civil and Political Rights (1996) and the non-binding UN General Assembly Declaration on the Rights of Persons Belonging to National or Ethnic, Religious and Linguistic Minorities (adopted by GA Resolution 47/135 of 18 December 1992).

Council of Europe's FCNM in 1995. In turn, the OSCE General Recommendations on the education and linguistic rights of national minorities (1996 and 1998 respectively) and their effective participation in public life (1999) have shaped the Council of Europe's interpretation of the FCNM in its five-year monitoring cycles.

Thus, the norm of national minority protection was anchored in the Council of Europe early on, but it has been shaped by other European institutions and, in particular, by the political changes in Eastern Europe after 1989. Compared to other institutions it was well placed to take on the task of codifying a norm of minority protection – the OSCE is limited to non-binding recommendations, and within the highly integrated legal system of the EU (which cannot afford the automatic opt-out possibility of Council of Europe Conventions) the space for binding agreements is limited, especially as Member State practice varies from the outright denial of the existence of national minorities to highly elaborate mechanisms of accommodation for national diversity. The FCNM explicitly uses the term 'national minority', which remains controversial in international law and politics, and spells out its application in many different spheres of public life. However, it refrains from providing a definition of what constitutes a national minority, thereby indicating the red line of some Council of Europe members.

The EU has used the FCNM as a benchmark of progress in the candidate states. This discrepancy and the fact that the first Copenhagen criterion for accession lists the EU values embodied in Article 6(1) of the Treaty on the European Union – with the notable exception of the minority criterion – gave rise to a discussion about 'double standards'[66] and fed into the reformulation of the EU's values. The Lisbon Treaty and the now legally binding Charter of Fundamental Rights include a reference to 'minorities' and 'national minorities' respectively. Over time, norm coherence has been recalibrated inside the EU and simultaneously makes a step towards inter-institutional norm coherence in Europe. During the accession process the EU's leverage over minority issues – in the absence of EU competences and criteria beyond the norm of anti-discrimination – was reinforced by the expertise and involvement of the OSCE and the Council of Europe. The debate about the scope and effectiveness of EU conditionality is ongoing, but the application of conditionality clearly ends with accession. The leverage of the OSCE and the Council of Europe reaches beyond EU accession, but it is significantly shaped by the politics of EU accession.

---

[66] James Hughes and Gwendolyn Sasse, 'Monitoring the Monitors: EU Enlargement Conditionality and Minority Protection in the Central and East European Countries' (2003) 1 *Journal on Ethnopolitics and Minoritiy Issues in Europe* 1–36; Guido Schwellnus, 'Double Standards? Minority Protection as a Condition for Membership' in Helene Sjursen (ed), *Questioning Enlargement: The EU in search of identity* (London, Routledge, 2006) 186–200.

The restrictive citizenship and language laws in Estonia and Latvia, which excluded a significant proportion of the Russophone population and brought an unprecedented number of stateless residents into the EU, have represented the hardest test for the new European norm on minority protection (in addition to Roma issues). Delayed membership of the Council of Europe and exclusion from the first wave of candidate countries opening accession negotiations with the EU provided important catalysts for a partial rethinking of the legal framework for minority issues in Estonia and Latvia. The OSCE High Commissioner on National Minorites, in particular, provided detailed legal input into the reformulation of the laws.[67] Latvia was the only EU candidate joining the EU in 2004 without having ratified the FCNM. The FCNM was the international document used as a shorthand reference to a commitment to minority protection during the EU accession process. Latvia's post-accession ratification of the FCNM in 2005 demonstrates that domestic political considerations trump international 'pressure'. The case of Latvia also demonstrates that in the medium- to longer-term *not* having ratified the FCNM can have a greater reputational effect than ratifying it (and adding declarations).[68]

The Council of Europe may have provided normative principles and benchmarks such as the FCNM during the EU accession process, but it was less visible as an institutional actor as such. In the post-accession period, however, it emerges as the main actor following up on the protection of national minorities. It can at best hope to gradually shape engrained structural, attitudinal and behavioural trends. The monitoring tied to the FCNM is very detailed – the Advisory Committee often points to the politicised definition of national minorities – and one monitoring cycle includes several reports by the governments and the Council of Europe, both based on consultation with a wide range of domestic actors. During Latvia's first monitoring cycle the Initial Report on the Implementation of the FCNM by the Republic of Latvia of October 2006 emphasised that it effectively opened the application of the FCNM to legally resident non-citizens who identify with a national minority. With regard to Article 15 of

---

[67] For details on the gradual legal changes and contrasting interpretations of the EU's overall effectiveness in this policy area, see Nida Gelazis, 'Statelessness in the Baltic States: Ramifications for European Citizenship and Social Stratification after EU Enlargement' (2004) 6 *European Journal of Migration and Law* 225–42; Judith Kelley, *Ethnic Politics in Europe: The Power of Norms and Incentives* (Princeton, Princeton University Press, 2004); David Galbreath, *Nation-Building and Minority Politics in Post-Socialist States: Interests, Influence and Identities in Estonia and Latvia* (Stuttgart, Ibidem, 2005); James Hughes, '"Exit" in deeply divided societies: regimes of discrimination in Estonia and Latvia and the potential for Russophone migration' (2005) 43 *Journal of Common Market Studies* 739–62; Gwendolyn Sasse, 'The Politics of Conditionality: The Norm of Minority Protection before and after EU Accession' (2006) 15 *Journal of European Public Policy* 842–60.

[68] See: conventions.coe.int/Treaty/Commun/ListeDeclarations.asp?NT=157&CM=8&DF=06/07/2010&CL=ENG&VL=1.

the FCNM, 'effective participation' of national minorities was discussed as a matter of civil society participation rather than as a characteristic of the political system as a whole.[69] The Opinion of the Advisory Committee (2008) responding to this report and subsequent Latvian government comments are not yet publicly available and the final Advisory Committee's Recommendations are still pending.

PACE provides another forum where unresolved minority issues remain on the agenda after EU accession. In 2005, for example, a critical report by the Council of Europe's Parliamentary Assembly rapporteur György Frunda was discussed. The report, which asked Latvia to drop its FCNM declarations, waive the naturalisation of Soviet-era immigrants, and allow non-citizens to vote, was overruled by the Assembly's Monitoring Committee in November 2005. This decision, taken by majority vote, was unusual, as the Assembly tends to accept a rapporteur's recommendations, but it nevertheless shows that the debate about minority-related issues in PACE is ongoing.

The Council of Europe's Commissioner for Human Rights also follows up on the standards for national minority protection, echoing some of the Advisory Committee's comments during the FCNM monitoring process. Thomas Hammarberg's 2007 report on Estonia notes that

> the number of non-citizens is still high and the risk of alienation is present. There is obviously a connection between citizenship and social inclusion, both perceived and real. Increased importance should be given to awareness-raising measures targeting non-citizens about the possibilities of learning the Estonian language and the benefits associated with it.[70]

He also singled out the 2007 amendments to Estonia's Language Law – which gave language inspectorates extended powers, including the right to recommend the dismissal of employees with insufficient language proficiency or to make people holding language certificates re-sit an exam – among his concerns.

Whilst the EU accession process, with its emphasis on the ratification of the FCNM, paved the way for the Council of Europe's increased role in the post- EU accession period, the OSCE saw its scope for action weakened. The politically-motivated closure of the OSCE missions in Estonia and Latvia in late 2001, aimed at avoiding an anomaly inside the EU, limited the OSCE's scope for action in the Baltic states and contributed to an

---

[69] Report submitted by Latvia, 11 October 2006; see: www.coe.int/t/dghl/monitoring/minorities/3_FCNMdocs/PDF_1st_SR_Latvia_en.pdf.

[70] Commissioner for Human Rights of the Council of Europe, 'Memorandum to the Estonian Government. Assessment of the progress made in implementing the 2004 recommendations of the Commissioner for Human Rights of the Council of Europe', CommDH(2007)12, Strasbourg, 11 July 2007; see: wcd.coe.int/ViewDoc.jsp?id=1163131#P99_4201.

internal crisis of the OSCE as a whole, not least because Russia has been less cooperative in response to the mission closure.[71] The immediate post-Cold War period and the process of EU accession only temporarily empowered the OSCE, particularly through the presence of a proactive High Commissioner on National Minorities, Max van der Stoel, in a context in which detailed legal advice was asked for and encouraged by the EU as the international actor offering the biggest incentive structure.

The norm of national minority protection vividly illustrates the position of the Council of Europe vis-à-vis other international institutions. Its low-key way of operating means that it can easily be overshadowed by other institutions and be reduced to a benchmark reference. In the longer run, however, the Council of Europe has the staying power that other norm-centred institutions lack thanks to a lower degree of politicisation and securitisation. It provides a check on actual practice, most importantly also in the EU Member States. This strength of the Council of Europe is conditioned by a crowded institutional space in Europe with overlapping mandates: these institutional interactions facilitate the Council of Europe's norm entrepreneurship.

III.   CONCLUSION

The Council of Europe's legitimacy as an institution depends on ongoing norm production and enforcement. As the latter is harder to secure with the 'soft' means the Council of Europe has at its disposal, the process of norm development takes on a particular significance. This chapter set out to explain the Council of Europe's widely recognised norm entrepreneurship in a setting that would make it easy for Member States to obstruct the process of norm production. Four explanations have been explored which jointly underpin the Council of Europe's political strength. The focus has been on 'hard' cases of contested norms, the pathways of which could not have been assumed a priori. First, the Council of Europe's institutional structure and modus operandi are sufficiently flexible to respond to political changes or challenges. Secondly, this structure enables it to adjust its normative remit through institutional innovations (eg the introduction of a guest status and a quick procedure for full membership in Eastern Europe, or Protocol 14-Bis to manage Russia's veto over ECtHR reform). Thirdly, the Council of Europe actively creates norm coherence, even in the cases of a norm reversal (abolition of the death penalty), a widening and partial redefinition of a norm (multiple citizenship) and a push to give a controversial norm more weight (prevention of statelessness). Fourthly, its

[71] Hughes, '"Exit" in deeply divided societies', above n 67.

interactions with other European institutions reveal it to be prone to be temporarily overshadowed in a crowded institutional space with overlapping mandates, but also to have the institutional muscle to prevail in the longer run. This chapter has demonstrated that the Council of Europe is well equipped for norm production and adaptation over time. Indeed, paradoxically, some of the most often cited weaknesses of the Council of Europe as a norm enforcer underpin its strength as Europe's primary norm entrepreneur.

Part Four

Europe Below the State

8

Recognition as Domination: Constitutionalism, Reciprocity and the Problem of Singularity

HANS LINDAHL*

I. INTRODUCTION

PLURALITY HAS ALREADY been subordinated to unity when one asks how constitutionalism could regulate the process whereby minority groups raise claims to cultural recognition. For the reference to a group as a minority group in quest of cultural recognition takes for granted that, although not (yet) fully recognised as such, the group is nonetheless already part of a collective under a shared constitution. Despite its insistence on diversity, unity is the alpha and the omega of a politics of recognition: its 'alpha' in the form of a pre-given unity in the absence of which minority demands of recognition would not be intelligible as such; its 'omega' in the form of a more inclusive unity that emerges, if things go well, from struggles for recognition.

My aim in this chapter is to critically scrutinise this interpretation of the 'tension' – if 'tension' is at all the proper term – between legal unity and political plurality that emerges with group claims to cultural distinctness. My approach deliberately takes a step back from the contemporary framing of the 'multiculturalism debate'. Instead of taking this frame for granted, and engaging in the vast discussion about different forms of minority 'recognition' and minority-rights, whether extant or desirable, I will probe one of the frame's key features: reciprocity. My central question is this: to what extent does the normative idea of reciprocity or mutual

* Professor, Tilburg University. I appreciate helpful remarks by Ailsa Henderson, Chris Himsworth, Neil Walker and other participants at the Constitutional Mosaic Seminar in Edinburgh; by Gareth Davies, Geoffrey Gordon, Bart van Klink, Irena Rosenthal, Wouter Veraart, Wouter Werner and Bertjan Wolthuis, during a research seminar at the Free University in Amsterdam; and by David Janssens and Bart van Leeuwen.

recognition between equal – but different – groups under a single constitution succeed in reconciling political plurality and legal unity in the face of strong group claims to cultural distinctness?

The rest of this chapter falls into three parts. Section II peruses the models of politico-legal reciprocity at the basis of what Charles Taylor calls a 'politics of equal dignity' and a 'politics of difference', with special attention to what might be dubbed a 'genealogy' of politico-legal reciprocity. Section III carries forward the analysis of reciprocity by exploring the Canadian Supreme Court's well-known *Quebec Secession Reference*. In particular, it examines the reasoning whereby a constitutional court, when granting recognition to group claims to cultural distinctness, takes for granted that such claims are only legitimate if they are constitutional claims, hence the manifestation of a prior, more fundamental political reciprocity. Section IV concludes by exploring whether and how constitutionalism could deal with group claims to distinctness, cultural or otherwise, that resist inclusion within a circle of politico-legal reciprocity. Dealing with such claims, or so I argue, requires a form of political negotiation that partially suspends the normal constitutional regimentation of reciprocity – 'para-constitutionalism', as I will call it. The negotiation of withdrawal by a Member State from the EU, as stipulated in the Treaty of Lisbon, goes part of the way in capturing the spirit of this form of political negotiation.

II.   LIBERALISM AND THE GENEALOGY OF RECIPROCITY

In an essay that foreshadows many of the themes of multinational democracy covered in his contribution to this volume (chapter nine), Ferran Requejo notes that the notion of a demos remains an unresolved problem for most liberal theories of democracy.

> We know that in the empirical world, the demos of democratic systems has not usually been established using the procedural rules of liberal democracies, but through a historical process full of wars, conquests, annexations, exterminations, or marginalizations of whole peoples.

He immediately adds that 'these are far from being sound bases for liberal democratic legitimization'.[1] Requejo's assertions raise two questions which allow me to introduce the general theme of this chapter. First, what is, for liberalism, the 'sound basis' for democratic legitimisation? Secondly, is this basis itself 'sound', and hence itself beyond normative question?

---

[1]   F Requejo, 'Federalism and the Quality of Democracy in Multinational Contexts' in U Amoretti and N Bermeo (eds), *Federalism and Territorial Cleavages* (Baltimore MD, Johns Hopkins University, 2004) 263.

Requejo's normative explorations of multinational democracies draw on the two forms of liberalism sketched by Taylor in his well-known essay on the politics of recognition. For the one, there is the liberalism that focuses on a 'politics of equal dignity', in which 'what is established is meant to be universally the same, an identical basket of rights and immunities'; for the other, there is the liberalism that promotes a 'politics of difference', in which 'what we are asked to recognize is the unique identity of this individual or group, their distinctness from everyone else'.[2] Walzer, in his commentary to Taylor's essay, refers to these two forms of recognition in liberal politics as, respectively, 'Liberalism 1' and 'Liberalism 2'.[3] Whereas authors such as Rawls and Habermas are, arguably, champions of Liberalism 1, the votaries of Liberalism 2 include theorists such as Taylor, Kymlicka and Tully. Instead of taking sides in this debate, what interests me is identifying and critically scrutinising what *joins* the parties in strife, ie the shared presupposition that remains beyond the pale of discussion, such that both camps can view themselves as different manifestations of liberalism. This shared presupposition is the normative principle of *reciprocity*. The differences between these authors concern how reciprocity should be conceptualised and how it can be institutionalised; but liberalism, whatever its modulations, is propelled by the idea that a polity is well ordered to the extent that it actualises relations of political and legal reciprocity among its citizens.

The idea that reciprocity is constitutive for politics and law holds explicit and undisputed sway in 'Liberalism 1'. Consider, first, its characterisation in 'The Idea of Public Reason Revisited', an essay which Rawls viewed as the best presentation of his ideas on public reason and political liberalism. At the very beginning of the essay, Rawls yokes 'constitutional democracy', the 'criterion of reciprocity' and the 'idea of public reason'. And he goes ahead to argue that

> the idea of political legitimacy based on the criterion of reciprocity says: our exercise of political power is proper only when we sincerely believe that the reasons we would offer for our political actions – were we to state them as government officials – are sufficient, and we also reasonably think that other citizens might also reasonably accept these reasons.[4]

Distinct from reasons, in the plural, which are linked to a manifold of conflicting reasonable comprehensive doctrines, the rationality of public reason, in the singular, turns on the preparedness of citizens to subordinate their debate about a just society to the criterion of reciprocity itself.

---

[2] C Taylor, 'The Politics of Recognition' in A Gutmann (ed), *Multiculturalism: Examining the Politics of Recognition* (Princeton NJ, Princeton University Press, 1994) 38.

[3] M Walzer, 'Comment' in Gutmann, *Multiculturalism*, above n 2, 99.

[4] J Rawls, *Political Liberalism*, expanded edition (New York, Columbia University Press, 2005 [1993]) 446–47.

Moreover, public reason so defined reveals a two-way correlation between constitutionalism and democracy. On the one hand, a constitution provides the legal framework within which citizens engage in public reason, that is, engage in democratic deliberation subject to the criterion of reciprocity. On the other hand, democratic deliberation between citizens subject to the criterion of reciprocity is oriented primarily to issues of constitutional essentials and matters of basic justice.[5]

But how far can public reason go in subordinating its own conditions of possibility to the exercise of public reason – in particular the criterion of reciprocity itself? Closer consideration shows that Rawls does not – and arguably *cannot* – bring what renders reciprocity between citizens possible within the cincture of public reason. As Rawls notes, the 'fundamental political relationship of citizenship', without which there could be no reciprocity, 'is a relation of citizens within the basic structure of society, a structure we enter only by birth and exit only by death'.[6] This passage harks back to the crucial assumption that inaugurates *Political Liberalism*: 'I assume that the basic structure is that of a closed society: that is, that we are to regard it as self-contained and as having no relations with other societies'.[7] In his later work, Rawls jettisons this limitation, turning to consider just relations between peoples. This allows him to argue that 'the criterion of reciprocity applies to the Law of Peoples in the same way it does to the principles of justice for a constitutional regime'.[8] But, in either case, what remains beyond the criterion of reciprocity is the *closure* which, determining who counts as a citizen and who does not, gives rise to a polity; hence what gives rise to the exercise of public reason in the first place. This is no mere oversight that Rawls can redress if he is to hold on to the veil of ignorance: reciprocity as deliberation between *citizens* presupposes a closure that by definition cannot itself be the outcome of reciprocal deliberation between citizens. Notice that the prior closure does not only concern who counts as a citizen. In effect, the initial boundaries that determine what counts, in Rawls's terms, as 'fair terms of cooperation' and 'reasonable conceptions of justice' are not and cannot themselves be the outcome of deliberation guided by the principle of reciprocity; to the contrary, a non-deliberative closure must already have taken place to get deliberation going.

---

[5] *ibid*, 442.

[6] *ibid*, 445.

[7] *ibid*, 12. An identical assumption inaugurates his *Theory of Justice*: 'I shall be satisfied if it is possible to formulate a reasonable conception of justice for the basic structure of society conceived for the time being as a closed system isolated from other societies'. J Rawls, *A Theory of Justice* (Cambridge MA, Belknap Press, 1971) 8.

[8] J Rawls, *The Law of Peoples* (Cambridge MA, Harvard University Press, 2002 [1999]) 35.

If reciprocity, to borrow Requejo's formulation, is the 'sound basis' for democratic legitimisation, then reciprocity itself, as conceived by Rawls, has a less than 'sound basis'. In other words, the problem is not, as Requejo puts it, that 'in the empirical world, the demos of democratic systems has not usually been established using the procedural rules of liberal democracies'; it is that the procedural rules of liberal democracies, as described by Rawls, presuppose acts of seizing the initiative that cannot be fully integrated within the constitutional order these acts contribute to creating.

Jürgen Habermas's defence of Liberalism 1 by way of a discourse theory of practical reason fares no better in this respect. The opening passage of his essay, 'Struggles for Recognition in the Democratic Constitutional State', neatly ties together the concept of a modern constitution and the principle of reciprocity:

> Modern constitutions owe their existence to a conception found in modern natural law according to which citizens come together voluntarily to form a legal community of free and equal consociates. The constitution puts into effect precisely those rights that those individuals must grant one another if they want to order their life together legitimately by means of positive law.[9]

Habermas is concerned to show, against Taylor's vindication of a politics of recognition oriented to the constitutional protection of distinct communities, that a 'universalistic' understanding of modern constitutions is up to the normative task of protecting the individuals that are the subjects of rights, whilst also accommodating the struggles for recognition in which the articulation of collective identities takes place. The specifics of his debate with Taylor need not detain us. What interests me in Habermas's interpretation of reciprocity, as was already the case in my perusal of Rawls, is whether and how he deals with what might be called a 'genealogy' of reciprocity.

Habermas's aforementioned essay barely discusses this issue. It is only broached obliquely and in passing, when he asserts that 'a constitution can be thought of as an historical project that each generation of citizens continues to pursue'.[10] He goes ahead to argue that the 'struggle over the interpretation and satisfaction of historically unredeemed claims is a struggle for legitimate rights in which collective actors are once again involved, combating a lack of respect for their dignity'.[11] See here a compact formulation of the equi-primordiality of constitutionalism and democracy: the struggle for recognition concerning collective experiences

---

[9] J Habermas, 'Struggles for Recognition in the Democratic Constitutional State' in Gutmann, *Multiculturalism: Examining the Politics of Recognition*, above n 2, 107.

[10] *ibid.*

[11] *ibid*, 108.

of violated integrity takes place *within* a constitutional cadre and *remains* within it, to the extent that the struggle, if it is to be legitimate, aims to transform the constitution. Group demands of cultural recognition must be formulated as *constitutional claims*; that is, as claims seeking to realise the promise of politico-legal reciprocity lodged in the constitution.

In a later essay, Habermas articulates more fully what he means by referring to the constitution as 'an historical project'. By delving into this issue, Habermas attempts to defuse an objection that threatens to bring to naught his thesis about the equi-primordiality of democracy and the rule of law. Michelman has shown with regard to the enactment of a polity's first constitution that, in Habermas's words, '[t]he constitutional assembly cannot itself vouch for the legitimacy of the rules according to which it was constituted. The chain never terminates, and the democratic process is caught in a circular self-constitution that leads to an infinite regress'.[12] Although Habermas acknowledges the gravity of the problem by referring to the foundation of a constitutional democracy as a 'groundless discursive self-constitution', he argues that it is possible to break out of this circularity provided one focuses on the 'future-oriented character, or openness, of the democratic constitution'.[13] In brief,

> whoever bases her judgment today on the normative expectation of complete inclusion and mutual recognition, as well as on the expectation of equal opportunities for utilizing equal rights, must assume that she can find these standards by reasonably appropriating the constitution and its history of interpretation.[14]

But this surely begs the question: the problem is not merely how to achieve a greater inclusiveness to accommodate those who are subject to a form of exclusion at the foundation of the polity to which they belong. The more fundamental problem is rather that, more or less against their will, a variable range of individuals and groups may have been *included* in the first place; that, despite their opposition, they are deemed to *belong* to the polity. Why should they or those who later rally to their cause at all 'have the *task* of actualizing the still-untapped normative substance of the system

---

[12] J Habermas, 'Constitutional Democracy: A Paradoxical Union of Contradictory Principles?' (2001) 29 *Political Theory* 766, 774. Michelman by no means stands alone here. Hans Kelsen had already discussed this problem in all its acuteness some 70 years earlier. For an analysis of Kelsen's attempt to solve the problem, see my papers 'Dialectic and Revolution: Confronting Kelsen and Gadamer on Legal Interpretation' (2003) 24 *Cardozo Law Review* 769 and 'Constituent Power and Reflexive Identity: Towards an Ontology of Collective Selfhood' in M Loughlin and N Walker (eds), *The Paradox of Constitutionalism* (Oxford, Oxford University Press, 2007).

[13] Habermas, 'Constitutional Democracy', above n 12, 774.

[14] *ibid*, 775.

of rights laid down in the original document of the constitution'? (emphasis added)[15] Why should they have to view themselves at all as 'participants [who] must be able to recognize the project as *the same* throughout history and to judge it from *the same* perspective'?[16] Here, then, is the fraught political dilemma confronting those individuals or groups who were included in the collective against their will, a dilemma we will encounter repeatedly in the following Section when considering the Québécois separatists and members of aboriginal peoples in Canada. On the one hand, they can raise a constitutional claim that, if successful, allows them to obtain political and legal recognition for their cultural distinctness. But if they set foot down this path, they effectively identify themselves as participants in a project with which they do not want to be associated, and hence as a minority group engaged in relations of reciprocity within a broader community. On the other hand, if they oppose their own inclusion, refusing to appeal to the constitution's 'still-untapped' normative possibilities of inclusiveness, they expose themselves to the charge that their acts of contestation need not be accepted as such or even listened to because they are not, to borrow and emphasise Habermas's phrase, '*reasonably* appropriating the constitution and its history of interpretation'. So if they choose this second path, their acts of resistance are vulnerable to censure for being non-reciprocal acts, acts that fall prey to a performative contradiction – *the* cardinal sin of reason.[17] This dilemma surfaces time and again, during the later career of the polity, with regard to all those members of groups who view their inclusion in the polity as the continuation of a prior annexation.

---

[15] *ibid*, 774.

[16] *ibid*, 775.

[17] Anthony Laden's insightful and refined defence of a politics of identity in the framework of a theory of deliberative liberalism also fails to address this difficulty. In particular, Laden endorses a wide reading of the 'circle of reasonable pluralism' with a view to allowing 'people to invoke features of their nonpolitical identities in public reason arguments, and thus call attention to and resist deliberative liberalism's unintended assimilationist pressures'. See A Laden, *Reasonably Radical: Deliberative Liberalism and the Politics of Identity* (Ithaca NY, Cornell University Press, 2001) 162. But, he adds, a theory of deliberative liberalism in particular, and political theory in general, need not – and cannot – concern itself with those citizens who reject 'the necessity of adopting this shared project of together working out legitimate political principles' (*ibid*). For, to the extent that such individuals 'fall outside even this wider circle of reasonableness', they raise a question 'for which I doubt philosophy is the appropriate tool' (*ibid*, 163 fn 6). Indeed, they have placed themselves beyond the pale of reason, the traditional bailiwick of philosophical thinking in general, and political philosophy in particular. Yet is it simply 'unreasonable' or the manifestation of 'anarchy' (*ibid*, 169 fn 19) when those who were included in the polity against their will, or later generations that take up their cause, denounce the alleged 'necessity of adopting this shared project of working out legitimate political principles'? This problem points to what I take to be the fundamental difficulty confronting Laden's philosophical project as a whole: the conditions that govern the genesis of politico-legal reciprocity definitively preclude Laden's strategic move to separate political and non-political elements of personal identity in terms of the distinction between, respectively, its 'formal' and 'substantive' features.

To repeat my earlier thesis, the problem is not, as Requejo would have it, that 'in the empirical world, the demos of democratic systems has not usually been established using the procedural rules of liberal democracies'; it is that the procedural rules of liberal democracies, as articulated and justified by Habermas, presuppose prior acts of inclusion and exclusion that resist legitimation within the constitutional order which these acts contribute to creating. The acts of seizing the initiative to found political and legal reciprocity by way of constitution-making provide a less than 'sound basis' for what liberalism – or at least Liberalism 1 – views as the 'sound basis' of democratic legitimation: the principle of reciprocity.

What about the 'politics of difference' at the heart of Liberalism 2? Here again, reciprocity is the characteristic feature of a 'politics of difference', albeit that reciprocity unfolds through a process different to that in a 'politics of equal dignity'. The basic model of this form of recognition is provided by Hegel's famous discussion of the dialectic of the master and the slave. As Taylor puts it, '[t]he struggle for recognition can find only one satisfactory solution, and that is a regime of reciprocal recognition among equals'.[18] Importantly, Taylor notes that even though there are significant differences between Rousseau's and Hegel's approaches to recognition and reciprocity, Hegel concurs with Rousseau's insight that a regime of reciprocal recognition takes place within 'a society with a common purpose'.[19] This point is important because what is at stake is the *dialectical* structure of recognition: if the struggle for recognition is sparked by the negativity which accompanies a situation experienced as one of inequality, that is, as the absence of mutual recognition, this struggle takes place against the background of *a more fundamental mutual reciprocity that the parties must already have acknowledged*, even if only implicitly, if they are at all to engage in a struggle the stake of which is reaching mutual recognition. Honneth makes this point deftly:

> [I]f the social meaning of the conflict can only be adequately understood by ascribing to both parties knowledge of their dependence on the other, then the antagonized subjects cannot be conceived as isolated beings acting only egocentrically. Rather, in their own action orientation, both subjects have already positively taken the other into account, before they become engaged in hostilities. Both must, in fact, already have accepted the other in advance as a partner to interaction upon whom they are willing to allow their own activity to be dependent.[20]

---

[18]   Taylor, 'The Politics of Recognition', above n 2, 50. For a recent systematic study of recognition in Hegel's *Phenomenology of Spirit*, see P Cobben, 'Anerkennung als moralische Freiheit' (2009) 112 *Philosophische Jahrbuch* 42.

[19]   Taylor, 'The Politics of Recognition', above n 2.

[20]   A Honneth, *The Struggle for Recognition: The Moral Grammar of Social Conflicts*, trans J Anderson (Cambridge, Polity Press, 1995) 45.

To be sure, Honneth's analysis in this passage focuses on the mutual dependence between two individuals, rather than on the more general structure of social conflict mediated by law. No less importantly, it has been perceptively noted that Honneth's theory of recognition requires considerable expansion to account for the recognition of cultural minorities in modern democratic states, as his account focuses primarily on formal recognition between individuals.[21] But what interests me here is the basic structure of interdependence articulated in the final sentence of this quotation, which can be extrapolated and generalised without great difficulty by a theory of constitutionalism that seeks to give normative, conceptual and institutional shape to a 'politics of difference' sensitive to group claims to distinctiveness. Indeed, such a theory of constitutionalism postulates (i) a prior set of values, interests and purposes that must be assumed as shared by all political actors, and which any group that strives to gain cultural recognition must embrace if its claim is to enjoy the patina of legitimacy; (ii) a shared procedural framework, set out in the constitution, which governs the terms in which the struggle takes place and is settled; and (iii) a redefinition of the content of (i), if all goes well, as a result of constitutional struggle in conformity with (ii).

Notice that the aim of the struggle for recognition, in this understanding of a 'politics of difference', is to seek the constitutional affirmation of cultural distinctiveness within a broader collective. At stake is not relinquishing the group's identity but rather showing, first, how and why it ought to be affirmed in its *particularity* in relation to the general values, interests and purposes of the collective, and, secondly, why such particularity is the expression of equality, rather than of inequality.[22] Hence if a group's claim to identity is to be taken seriously by the other groups that partake of the collective, then it must appeal to – and aim to transform the meaning of – the values, interests and purposes the group *already* shares with those groups. The group must be able to present its identity as a particular manifestation of a general, more capacious collective identity. Thus the struggle for cultural recognition, on this reading of a 'politics of difference', has the form of a dialectic of the general and the particular, such that an initial situation of non-reciprocity – where non-reciprocity denotes a yet-to-be-recognised claim to particularity – yields to a novel

---

[21] See B van Leeuwen, 'A Formal Recognition of Social Attachments: Expanding Axel Honneth's Theory of Recognition' (2007) 2 *Inquiry* 180. See also the chapter on multiculturalism in W Kymlicka, *Contemporary Political Philosophy* (Oxford, Oxford University Press, 2002) 327–76.

[22] Iris Marion Young also makes this point, when defending democratic cultural pluralism: 'In this vision the good society does not eliminate or transcend group difference. Rather, there is equality among socially and culturally differentiated groups, who mutually respect one another and affirm one another in their differences'. See IM Young, *Justice and the Politics of Difference* (Princeton NJ, Princeton University Press, 1990) 163.

state of reciprocity or mutual recognition between equal – but different – groups. Legitimate struggles for differentiation are, in this understanding of a politics of difference, struggles for *internal* differentiation, regardless of whether what is at stake is 'accommodation-rights' or 'self-government rights'.[23] Precisely for this reason, Requejo insists that the task of constitutional thinking about federalism is 'practical and constitutional accommodation for multinational polities in which diverse processes of nation building share *the same* arena', and that plural federalism aims 'more at *maintaining the unity* of multinational societies already in existence than at paving the way for new ones to develop' (emphasis added).[24]

Although the theory of constitutionalism that emerges from this dialectical reading of the principle of reciprocity is powerful and persuasive in a number of ways, a nagging question remains: can it elude the problem that the emergence of political reciprocity is never simply the outcome of reciprocity? Can it simply be taken for granted that group claims to cultural distinctiveness must, as Honneth claims, 'in fact, already have accepted the other [groups] in advance as [partners] to interaction upon whom they are willing to allow their own activity to be dependent'? With a view to plumbing the implications of these questions I will now turn to examine what has been widely acclaimed as one of the most striking and daring judicial examples of a recognition-based theory of constitutionalism: the Canadian Supreme Court's *Quebec Secession Reference*.[25]

III.   'RECONCIL[ING] UNITY AND DIVERSITY'

The Supreme Court's reference has been the object of extended attention, and it is by no means my intention here to review that literature.[26] Instead, I will cull only those aspects of the Court's reasoning that are germane to the theme of reciprocity and its genealogy. My analysis proceeds in three

---

[23]   Will Kymlicka, *Politics in the Vernacular: Nationalism, Multiculturalism and Citizenship* (Oxford, Oxford University Press, 2001) 152–76.
[24]   Requejo, 'Federalism and the Quality of Democracy in Multinational Contexts', above n 1, 266, 269.
[25]   The Canadian Supreme Court's reference, *Reference re Secession of Quebec*, [1998] 2 SCR 217. Citations refer, in the footnotes below, to the paragraphs of the Reference.
[26]   See, amongst others, J Tully, 'Introduction' in A-G Gagnon and J Tully (eds), *Multinational Democracies* (Cambridge, Cambridge University Press, 2001); S Choudhry and R Howse, 'Constitutional Theory and the Quebec Secession Reference' (2000) 12 *Canadian Journal of Law and Jurisprudence* 143; D Schneiderman (ed), *The Quebec Decision* (Toronto, Lorimer, 1999); J-F Gaudrealt-Desbiens, 'Underlying principles and the migration of reasoning templates: A trans-systemic reading of the *Quebec Secession Reference*' in S Choudhry (ed), *The Migration of Constitutional Ideas* (Cambridge, Cambridge University Press, 2006).

steps. Initially, it canvasses the Court's defence of the principle of reciprocity as concerns the negotiation of constitutional amendments. Subsequently, it critically explores the genealogy of the Canadian federation, and therewith of politico-legal reciprocity, as sketched by the Court. Finally, it returns to consider how the genealogical problems circumvented by the Court reappear in its vindication of reciprocity, and the implications that follow therefrom for its argument as a whole.

A.   An Unilateral Right to Secession?

The central question the Court was called on to consider in this reference was 'whether Quebec has a right to *unilateral* secession'.[27] The Court rejects such a right. Although the Court does not say so explicitly, it effectively contends that a putative right to unilateral secession is an oxymoron. To invoke a *right*, whatever its nature, is to presuppose relations of political and legal reciprocity with those who must honour the right, or so the Court argues; yet the very idea of *unilateral* secession is incompatible with the reciprocity that must have been presupposed in the act of claiming a *right* to secession. These are, to be sure, but the bare bones of the argument, and it pays to examine in somewhat greater detail how the Court fleshes out its position.

In what amounts to an invocation of the equi-primordiality of constitutionalism and democracy, the Court kicks off its reasoning by asserting that 'in our constitutional tradition, legality and legitimacy are linked'.[28] Indeed, the Court argues that there is a constitutive circularity – in the positive sense of the term – governing the relation between constitutionalism and democracy. The first arc of the circularity concerns the constitution as the framework for political deliberation:

> Democracy in any real sense of the word cannot exist without the rule of law. It is the law that creates the framework within which the 'sovereign will' is to be ascertained and implemented. To be accorded legitimacy, democratic institutions must rest, ultimately, on a legal foundation.[29]

And it adds: 'Constitutionalism facilitates – indeed, makes possible – a democratic political system by creating an orderly framework within which people may make political decisions'.[30] Conversely, and this is the second arc of the circularity, the constitution does not merely regulate political decision-making; it is also, at least in some cases, itself the object of

---

[27]   *Reference re Secession of Quebec*, [1998] 2 SCR 217, §149.
[28]   *ibid*, §33.
[29]   *ibid*, §67.
[30]   *ibid*, §78.

political decision-making. 'A system of government cannot survive through adherence to the law alone. A political system must also possess legitimacy, and in our political culture, that requires an interaction between the rule of law and the democratic principle'.[31] In line with this general principle it asserts that 'constitutional rules are themselves amenable to amendment, but only through a process of negotiation which ensures that there is an opportunity for the constitutionally defined rights of all the parties to be respected and reconciled'.[32]

The equi-primordiality between constitutionalism and democracy retains all its vigour in a federal structure of government. For the one, and this is the first arc,

> [t]he Constitution binds all governments, both federal and provincial, including the executive branch ... They may not transgress its provisions: indeed, their sole claim to exercise lawful authority rests in the powers allocated to them under the Constitution, and can come from no other source.[33]

So, a resounding yea to federalism in the form of a system of government that 'enable[s] citizens to participate concurrently in different collectivities and to pursue goals at both a provincial and a federal level'.[34] But – and this should greatly temper the enthusiasm of legal pluralists – the Court makes no bones about the fact that federalism, so conceived, is a way of institutionalising a *single* legal order: 'there is ... one law for all'.[35] Its guarantor, that is, the guarantor of plurality *within* legal unity, is, predictably, the Supreme Court itself. For the other, and here is the second arc, initiatives by any of the provinces to secede or otherwise transform the terms of Confederation 'would give rise to a reciprocal obligation on all parties to Confederation to negotiate constitutional changes'.[36] And in a decisive passage the Court argues that a province that would claim a *right* to secede or to modify the terms of Confederation, without discharging its obligation to negotiate with the other interested parties as established by the Constitution, effectively engages in a performative contradiction. Indeed, a province that invokes a unilateral right both affirms and denies a 'reciprocal obligation'. In the Court's parlance,

> [r]efusal of a party to conduct negotiations in a manner consistent with constitutional principles and values would put at serious risk the legitimacy of that party's assertion of its rights, and perhaps the negotiation process as a whole. Those who quite legitimately insist upon the importance of upholding the

---

[31]   *ibid*, §78.
[32]   *ibid*, §76.
[33]   *ibid*, §72.
[34]   *ibid*, §66.
[35]   *ibid*, §71.
[36]   *ibid*, §88.

rule of law cannot at the same time be oblivious to the need to act in conformity with constitutional principles and values.[37]

B. Seizing the 'Initiative'

Obviously, the equi-primordiality of constitutionalism and democracy presupposes the foundation of Canada as a federal state. That all parties to the federal state are bound by the 'reciprocal obligation' to both negotiate *under* the Constitution and *about* their constitutional arrangements requires that a constitution has been put in place, to begin with. In other words, it presupposes a 'sound basis' for politico-legal reciprocity, as per the Constitution. What, to use its own phrasing, are 'the principles that underlie the legitimacy of the Constitution itself'?[38]

These are 'democracy and self-government', that is, the principle of popular sovereignty: 'the Constitution is the expression of the sovereignty of the people of Canada'.[39] Importantly, the Court argues, popular sovereignty does not mean that a province can appeal to this principle to secede unilaterally from the federation. For, it avers,

[c]onstitutional government is necessarily predicated on the idea that the political representatives of the people of a province have the capacity and the power to commit the province to be bound into the future by the constitutional rules being adopted. These rules are 'binding' not in the sense of frustrating the will of a majority of a province, but as defining the majority which must be consulted in order to alter the fundamental balances of political power (including the spheres of autonomy guaranteed by the principle of federalism).[40]

That majority, to which the representatives of Quebec agreed when negotiating Confederation, is the majority of the Canadian people. In the result the Court asserts that the foundational acts of constitution-making amount to a mutual promise, whereby its parties commit to acting together into the future with a view to promoting their joint interest. The nature of that mutual promise lies beyond doubt: 'the vision of those who brought about Confederation was to create a unified country, not a loose alliance of autonomous provinces'.[41] So legal reciprocity between the parties to the Canadian federation, as institutionalised in the Constitution, does no more than give legal form to a more primordial form of reciprocity, namely, the political reciprocity which arose as a result of the mutual promise at the origin of Confederation. Because the original promise was one in which

---

[37] *ibid*, §95.
[38] *ibid*, §75.
[39] *ibid*, §85.
[40] *ibid*, §76.
[41] *ibid*, §96.

interested parties participated, and because Confederation was subsequently extended to *all* interested parties, none of the provinces can secede unilaterally without breaching the rights of those 'linguistic and cultural minorities, including aboriginal peoples ... who look to the Constitution of Canada for the protection of their rights'.[42] The Court later reiterates this point when emphasising the importance of the constitutional rights of aboriginal peoples living in the province of Quebec, in the event of a unilateral secession by the province.

But *was* there an original mutual promise which gave rise to Confederation, and which provides a 'sound basis' for 'reciprocal obligations' under the Constitution? The Court's answer to this question is, in fact, the linchpin of *Quebec*: 'Confederation was an initiative of elected representatives of the people then living in the colonies scattered across part of what is now Canada. It was not initiated by Imperial *fiat*'.[43] To be sure, protracted negotiations were necessary between those representatives before they could compact the Confederation. But the mutual promise whereby the delegates enacted the Confederation was itself a representational act. As such, it was an *authorised* initiative and, by extension, an *authorised* mutual promise. Consequently, the initiative to found a Confederation was a *legal* initiative, not a *fiat* – Imperial or otherwise – that would have contaminated the legality and legitimacy of the acts leading to Confederation under a constitution. No less importantly, although the delegates were deemed to represent a *differentiated* unity when founding the federation, they represented, first and foremost, a differentiated *unity* – a 'unified country', to repeat the Court's turn of phrase. This double reality of diversity within a more fundamental unity undergirds the Constitution; the latter, if imperfectly, represents that reality.

> Federalism was a legal response to the *underlying* political and cultural realities that existed at Confederation and continue to exist today. At Confederation, political leaders told their respective communities that the Canadian union would be able to reconcile diversity with unity (emphasis added).[44]

Hence the Court's reconstruction of the foundation of the Canadian federation *presupposes* the 'underlying' mutuality and unity of 'the people then living in the colonies scattered across part of what is now Canada' as the basis of the 'reciprocal obligations' which their representatives laid down in the Constitution. Paradoxically, the Court holds that the foundation of the Canadian federation through the enactment of its first constitution actually comes second; indeed, the act of constitution-making that galvanises legal reciprocity refers back to a prior – the first – foundational

---

[42] *ibid*, §96.
[43] *ibid*, §34.
[44] *ibid*, §43.

moment of political reciprocity, which the Court presupposes without justifying. What the Court has to say about why the framers did not explicitly incorporate these principles into the Constitution Act 1867, also holds for the Court itself: 'the representative and democratic nature of our political institutions was simply assumed'.[45]

In short, by arguing that the initiative to found the Canadian federation was taken by representatives of 'the people then living in the colonies scattered across part of what is now Canada', the Court can elude – and elide – a thorny problem confronting 'Liberalism 1' and 'Liberalism 2': the emergence of politico-legal reciprocity itself. The problem is intimated when the Court acknowledges – as acknowledge it must – that the Canadian federation was born from an *initiative*. In effect, can we at all make sense of an 'initiative' without introducing an element of unilaterality into the relevant act? To a lesser or greater extent, the initiative to found a polity is always seized. Can it be seriously argued – not least in light of the acts of conquest that remain beyond the compass of the Court's historical reconstruction – that the initiative to found the Canadian federation was merely a representational act, an act mandated by a manifold of individuals who, as Honneth puts it, 'have accepted the other[s] in advance as [partners] to interaction upon whom they are willing to allow their own activity to be dependent'?[46]

C. Three Problems

If not, then at least three problems undermine the rest of the Court's argument. First, if the Court argues that there is no unilateral right to secession, because this amounts to an oxymoron, can this argument not be turned against the Canadian Constitution itself? Indeed, do rights and 'reciprocal obligations' under the Constitution not lead back to a foundational act which, to the extent that it is unilateral, is incapable of generating rights and 'reciprocal obligations'?

This problem crops up in the Court's consideration of the principle of effectivity and de facto secession. The Court acknowledges that the province of Quebec could in fact secede from the Canadian federation, and that it might be able to invoke the principle of effectivity in international

---

[45] *ibid*, §62.
[46] For interpretations of the emergence of the Canadian confederation that differ starkly from that espoused by the Canadian Supreme Court see, amongst others, M Chevrier, 'La genèse de l'idée fédérale chez les pères fondateurs américains et canadiens' in A-G Gagnon (ed), *Le fédéralisme canadien contemporain: fondements, traditions, institutions* (Montréal, Presses de l'Université de Montréal, 2006); S Kelly, *La petite loterie. Comment la Couronne a obtenu la collaboration du Canada français après 1837* (Québec, Boréal, 1997); M Bellavance, *Le Québec et la Confédération : un choix libre? Le Clergé et la Constitution de 1867* (Québec, Septentrion, 1992).

law when seeking recognition for itself as an independent polity. But, the Court hastens to add, this does not mean that unilateral secession enjoys the status of a legal right.

> The principle of effectivity operates very differently. It proclaims that an illegal act may eventually acquire legal status if, as a matter of empirical fact, it is recognized on the international plane. Our law has long recognized that through a combination of acquiescence and prescription, an illegal act may at some later point be accorded some form of legal status. In the law of property, for example, it is well known that a squatter on land may ultimately become the owner if the true owner sleeps on his or her right to repossess the land. In this way, a change in the factual circumstances may subsequently be reflected in a change of legal status. It is, however, quite another matter to suggest that a subsequent condonation of an initially illegal act retroactively creates a legal right to engage in the act in the first place.[47]

Notice how those individuals and groups included against their will in the Confederation can turn the Court's argument against it. In effect, to the extent that the Court, in its historical reconstruction, asserts that the initiative to found the Canadian federation was a representational act, does it not gloss over what they view as the *unilaterality* of this act, namely that their having become members of the federation is 'a matter of empirical fact' rather than of right? Yet more pointedly, does not the Court's qualification of the initiative as authorised entail, from their point of view, a 'subsequent condonation of an initially illegal act [whereby the Court] retroactively creates a legal right to engage in the act in the first place'? By the same token, if those individuals, or those who later took up their cause, were to attempt to found an independent polity, they would *not* want to view their act as 'secession', normatively speaking. Instead, they would see it as the 'act of a true owner [who claims] his or her right to repossess the land' against those who have forcibly occupied it. As they know all too well, describing their act as secession – other than in the sense that they are exiting a larger collective of which they partake as 'a matter of empirical fact' – makes it easier for the occupier to invoke 'reciprocal obligations' in a way that deflects attention from the 'initially illegal act' that gave rise to the polity.

The second difficulty is a corollary of the first: can the Court simply brush off as 'unsound' the argument that 'the same popular sovereignty that originally led to the present Constitution must ... also permit the people in their exercise of popular sovereignty to secede by majority vote alone'?[48] Can the Court really claim that 'our national existence [is] seamless in so many aspects'[49]? It is significant, in this respect, that the

---

[47]   *Reference re Secession of Quebec*, [1998] 2 SCR 217, §146.
[48]   *ibid*, §75.
[49]   *ibid*, §96.

Court invokes the constitutional rights enjoyed by the aboriginal peoples living in the province of Quebec. By calling attention to their rights, the Court seeks to undermine the argument that 'the people' of Quebec is a homogeneous group that engages in an act of self-determination. In other words, it contests that such an act could be the legal expression of a prior, more fundamental political reciprocity. And it was indeed the case that secession from Canada was rejected by many among the members of the aboriginal peoples living in the province of Quebec, who invoked rights granted to them under the Canadian Constitution when opposing unilateral secession. The question, however, is whether the Court itself does not engage in the kind of inclusive claim with regard to aboriginals that it aims to debunk as illegitimate when advanced by the would-be Québécois separatists:

> Consistent with this long tradition of respect for minorities, which is at least as old as Canada itself, the framers of the *Constitution Act, 1982,* included in s. 35 explicit protection for existing aboriginal and treaty rights ... The 'promise' of s. 35 ... recognized not only the ancient occupation of land by aboriginal peoples, but their contribution to the building of Canada, and the special commitments made to them by successive governments.[50]

In effect, the first sentence seems to beg the question: Canada emerges as a federal polity when the aboriginal peoples and other groups *become* minorities therein. Not only is the exercise of power under the single Constitution of Canada bound to honour the long tradition of respect for minorities but, conversely, constitutional powers are duty bound to (respectfully) treat aboriginal peoples as *minorities* with a view to ensuring that 'there is ... one law for all'. This is the political upshot of a recognition-based theory of constitutionalism, which views differentiation as *internal* differentiation. The dialectic of particularity and generality animating a Canadian 'politics of difference' has, as its dark side, another, considerably less benevolent meaning: recognising the *particularity* of aboriginal peoples as distinct minority groups serves to celebrate and consolidate the *generality* of the Canadian federation of which they are deemed to partake.

For those members of aboriginal peoples that view the foundation of the Canadian federation as an unilateral act of occupation, as the annexation of their ancestral lands, the oh so gracious and munificent constitutional acknowledgment of their peoples' 'contribution to the building of Canada' is no doubt a particularly invidious way of both securing and concealing alien rule. Indeed, the political and legal reciprocity that a Canadian 'politics of recognition' has on offer is what they shun. For them, *recognition is domination*. Hence the 'promise' contained in section 35 of

[50] *ibid,* §82.

the Constitutional Act 1982 confronts those individuals with the fraught dilemma anticipated in Section II. Instead of resolving the dilemma, the perspective of secession by the province of Quebec only serves to exacerbate it. On the one hand, it seems prudent for them to invoke rights under the Canadian Constitution as a way of parrying yet a greater evil. But, on the other hand, their strategic invocation of constitutional rights comes at a high price: it renders it difficult, if not impossible, for them to continue claiming that they have been illegitimately annexed by Canada, without falling prey to the charge that they engage in a performative contradiction. The constitutional recognition of diversity – as concerns the distinctness of the majority group in Quebec, and the distinctness of aboriginal groups vis-à-vis the majority group in Quebec – becomes the vehicle for celebrating the unity of the Canadian federation – 'seamless in so many aspects'.

The third difficulty concerns, finally, the Court's own authority to issue a reference about the unilateral secession of Quebec. In his submission the amicus curiae had called into question whether, in delivering a reference on the issue, the Court was not encroaching on democratic decision-making by the people of Quebec. The Court flatly rejected this preliminary objection, stating that

> the questions posed in this Reference do not ask the Court to usurp any democratic decision that the people of Quebec may be called on to make. The questions posed by the Governor in Council, as we interpret them, are strictly limited to aspects of the legal framework in which that democratic decision is to be taken.[51]

The Court added that insofar as '[i]n the present reference the questions may clearly be interpreted as directed to legal issues ... the Court is in a position to answer them'.[52] This means, concretely, that whilst the Court acknowledges that it has nothing to say about a political decision by the people of Quebec concerning their desire to secede from Canada, it does have the competence and the authority bestowed on it – the point bears repeating – by the people of Quebec itself, to determine whether the people's decision is the exercise of a *right* to self-determination. The Court has a ready answer to the objection that its assessment of this question would be ultra vires, insofar as such assessment falls under the competence of authorities of international law. In effect, the question whether international law gives Quebec the right to effect the unilateral secession of the province from Canada 'is not an abstract question of "pure" international law but seeks to determine the legal rights and obligations of the National

---

[51] *ibid*, §27.
[52] *ibid*, §28.

Assembly, legislature or government of Quebec, institutions that clearly exist as part of the Canadian legal order'.[53]

We need not rehash the Court's argument that the invocation of an unilateral right to secede under the Canadian Constitution amounts to a performative contradiction. What interests me now is the Court's appraisal of the three circumstances, at international law, that justify unilateral secession. The first concerns peoples under colonial rule, which the Court dismisses out of hand: 'the right of colonial peoples to exercise their right to self-determination by breaking away from "imperial" power is now undisputed, but is irrelevant to this Reference'.[54] Yet the Court itself obliquely – and no doubt inadvertently – calls into question its summary dismissal of 'imperial' power when it extols the continuity of the rule of law so important to the federation's success in reconciling diversity with unity:

> Despite its federal structure, the new Dominion was to have 'a Constitution similar in Principle to that of the United Kingdom' (*Constitution Act, 1867*, preamble). Allowing for the obvious differences between the governance of Canada and the United Kingdom, it was nevertheless thought important to thus emphasize the continuity of constitutional principles, including democratic institutions and the rule of law; and the continuity of the exercise of sovereign power transferred from Westminster to the federal and provincial capitals of Canada. [§44]

Is not the continuity leading from the British Empire to the emergence of the Canadian federation precisely what the separatists both expose and seek to disassociate themselves from? And whilst many members of the aboriginal peoples in Quebec would strenuously oppose secession, does this mean that they have ceased to view the Canadian federation and its recognition of their status as a culturally distinct minority group as a continuation of 'imperial power'? Most fundamentally: does not the Court effectively become both party and judge to the conflict?

The second circumstance in which unilateral secession is justified 'is where a people is subject to alien subjugation, domination or exploitation outside a colonial context', ie to alien rule.[55] Remarkably, the Court contents itself with simply citing the passages of the *Declaration on Friendly Relations*, which contain the apposite circumstance. And it later returns to this circumstance, tersely stating that it arises 'where a people is oppressed, as for example under foreign military occupation'.[56] What the Court omits, however, is to establish, by even exiguous analysis, why this second criterion does not apply to the case at hand. The reason for this

[53] *ibid*, §23.
[54] *ibid*, §132.
[55] *ibid*, §133.
[56] *ibid*, §138.

omission is that, as is surely patent to all who can see, Quebec is part of the Canadian federation, and hence by definition it is *not* subject to alien rule – nor, a fortiori to, say, 'foreign military occupation'. But, from the perspective of would-be Québécois separatists, this is surely to beg the question: the people of Quebec aspire to secede unilaterally from Canada because they view themselves as subject to alien rule. From their perspective, it is not necessarily specious or frivolous to assert that the bases of the Canadian armed forces stationed in Quebec constitute 'foreign military occupation'. Again the troubling question emerges: does not the Court's claim that it can deliver an authoritative judgment about a right to self-determination render it party and judge at the same time?

The third circumstance arises 'where a definable group is denied meaningful access to government to pursue their political, economic, social and cultural development'.[57] This circumstance received short shrift from the Court, which argued that it was 'manifestly' not at hand with respect to Quebec. The denial of a 'meaningful' exercise of internal self-determination amounts to its 'somehow being totally frustrated'.[58] Notice how the Court's latter formulation of this criterion whittles down the scope of its initial formulation in such a way that not even Quebecers, it would seem, could claim that their development has been meaningfully thwarted without opening themselves up to (international) derision. Moreover, the Court notes, Quebecers have enjoyed ample and repeated participation in the government of Canada. By participating in the national government, they not only represent the people of Quebec but represent it as part of the people of Canada. Yet what the would-be separatists impugn is not that their representatives should be more assertive in defending the interests of Quebec in the national government but rather that they are their representatives *at all*: 'not in our name'. Have the dice not already been loaded when the Court affirms that constitutional practice grants the people of Quebec a meaningful exercise of their *internal* right to self-determination, ie a right within the Canadian federation? The disquieting question surfaces yet again: does the Court not play the double role of party and judge when it concludes that,

> to reflect the phraseology of the international documents that address the right to self-determination of peoples, Canada is a 'sovereign and independent state conducting itself in compliance with the principle of equal rights and self-determination of peoples and thus possessed of a government representing the whole people belonging to the territory without distinction'?[59]

---

[57] *ibid*, §138.
[58] *ibid*, §135.
[59] *ibid*, §136.

For the decisive problem arising from Québécois contestation is not how their cultural distinctness could obtain constitutional recognition, such that the Court and the other federal authorities could be reasonably held to represent them as a particular group partaking of 'the whole people'; it is that the Québécois separatists reject being represented as part of 'the whole [Canadian] people'.

In short, the Québécois denunciation of recognition under the Canadian Constitution evinces a concept of difference that resists neutralisation and pacification through the 'politics of difference' advocated by a recognition-based theory of constitutionalism. At stake is a difference – a claim to group distinctness, cultural or otherwise – that is not merely a manifestation of particularity within a more encompassing generality, whether realised or realisable, but rather of *singularity*; that is, a form of difference that obdurately resists inclusion in a given circle of politico-legal reciprocity. Nietzsche formulated this radical concept of difference in the *Twilight of the Idols*: '"Equality for equals and inequality for unequals" – that would be the true voice of justice: and, what follows from it, "Never make equal what is unequal"'.[60] I propose to define a normative theory of law and politics as 'monistic', not because it promotes the unity of a politico-legal order, but because it does so in a way that belies or downplays the problem of singularity. On this reading, a recognition-based theory of constitutionalism is the most powerful and refined vindication of political and legal monism available in our day.

IV. PARA-CONSTITUTIONALISM AND SINGULARITY

The foregoing analysis suggests that it is necessary to reconsider the kinds of problems that confront constitutionalism when engaging with group claims to distinctness, cultural or otherwise. In effect, there is broad agreement in the literature that the task of a theory of constitutionalism, in the face of such claims, is to secure the political and legal conditions for *non-assimilative inclusion*. In other words, it is generally assumed that the vocation of constitutionalism, when dealing with group claims to (cultural) distinctness, is to promote political 'stability' in a way that steers clear of the Scylla of 'exclusion' and the Charybdis of 'assimilation'.[61] To the extent that assimilation is a form of exclusion – the exclusion of what the members of a group value as rendering it distinct – non-assimilative

---

[60] F Nietzsche, *Twilight of the Idols and the Anti-Christ*, trans RJ Hollingdale (London, Penguin, 1990) 113.

[61] Laden correctly identifies exclusion, assimilation and stability as the three key issues of a politics of identity in the framework of liberal constitutionalism. See Laden, *Reasonably Radical*, above n 17, chs 6–8.

inclusion amounts to non-exclusive inclusiveness, that is, inclusive inclusiveness – 'hyper inclusiveness', as one might also put it.

There is a great deal to be said for the desideratum of inclusiveness, and I by no means aim to deprecate or minimise its importance. Instead, the main thrust of this chapter has been to show that, whatever their merits, liberal theories of constitutionalism share a structural blind spot when attempting to deal with group claims to (cultural) distinctness. Indeed, they are impervious to situations in which *inclusion is the problem signalled by those claims, not its solution*. To reiterate an earlier insight, liberal theories of constitutionalism deal with such claims as *normative* claims to the extent that the latter can be viewed as claims to reciprocity, ie to (cultural) particularity within (political) generality. As a votary of 'deep diversity' puts it, liberal theories of constitutionalism postulate 'that all members of the society will have one identity that they share, and that can thus be the basis of their unification into a single (albeit diverse and heterogeneous) society'.[62] While my purpose is not to defenestrate unity – which is the twin sister of inclusiveness – I do want to oppose the monism of liberal constitutionalism by highlighting the ambiguity of both desiderata. For, on a liberal reading of constitutionalism, if the majority of the collective is prepared to grant full constitutional recognition to a group's cultural particularity, thereby securing the continued unity and stability of the polity, then further insistence by this minority group that it wants out forfeits all *normative* significance and can be opprobriated, by the majority, as 'anarchy' (Laden).

Singularity is not particularity, however. The singular, as exemplified by the claims of the Québécois secessionists, denotes a form of distinctness that is recalcitrant to inclusion within a given circle of politico-legal reciprocity. Accordingly, 'reconciling unity with diversity' and promoting non-assimilative inclusiveness does not exhaust the theory and practice of constitutionalism, for there are group claims to (cultural) distinctness which cannot be accommodated on their own terms within the unity of a politico-legal order. Crucially, given that the genesis of political community always depends, to a lesser or greater extent, on unilateral acts – on 'initiatives', as the Canadian Supreme Court puts it – that get politico-legal reciprocity going, those claims cannot simply be written off as 'unreasonable' or 'anarchic', other than at the price of concealing the an-archic

---

[62]   Laden, *Reasonably Radical*, above n 17, 169. Iris Marion Young also endorses plurality within unity when asserting that 'radical democratic pluralism acknowledges and affirms the public and political significance of social group differences as a means of ensuring the participation and inclusion of everyone in social and political institutions'. Young, *Justice and the Politics of Difference*, above n 22, 168. Notice that her reading of 'radical democratic plurality' would accommodate difference within the circle of politico-legal reciprocity; as a result, it subordinates difference to identity: a politics of difference, in her usage of the term, is the preferred vehicle of a politics of identity.

origins of political community.[63] More precisely, singularity attests to a moment of 'an-archy' – of 'a-legality' – that inhabits all and sundry politico-legal orders.[64] In the same way that the initiatives that give rise to a polity, differentiating it from what become its others, can never be fully included within its legal order, so also there are subsequent claims to difference that resist inclusion within this order – on principle, and not merely in fact. As such, these claims are the manifestation of irreconcilable – and in this sense radical – difference. The stalemate that arises between, on the one hand, the Canadian rebuke that the Quebecer secessionists fall prey to a performative contradiction, and, on the other, the Québécois objection that Canadians beg the question when they demand that Québec present its claim as a constitutional claim, is exemplary for the strong form of *political plurality* proper to radical difference. What goes under the name of 'secessionist' movements is but one instance of radical difference; although perhaps it would be more correct to say that radical difference confronts every polity with multifarious figures of secessionist aspirations, whether tumultuous or halcyon, heeded or ignored.

So the fundamental and most general question that arises as a result of our critical scrutiny of *Quebec* and recognition-based theories of constitutionalism is the following: how – if at all – can constitutionalism deal with singularity? Can constitutionalism respond to radical difference in a way that does not reduce it to a claim concerning *internal* differentiation? Is there a way of responding to singularity that does not collapse responsiveness into recognition? If, finally, reciprocity proves insufficient as a normative principle in the face of singularity, what understanding of normativity would such responsiveness enjoin?

These questions are particularly pressing as concerns secession because the nascent polity perforce emerges through acts that are themselves more or less unilateral, thereby reproducing, at least latently, the problem of unwanted inclusion that spawned secession in the first place. This was clearly the case with those aboriginal peoples who rejected becoming part of an independent Quebec.

I do not think there is any way for constitutionalism to respond *directly* to singularity, that is, to deal with radical claims to cultural distinctness in

---

[63] Significantly, although Sunstein vigorously opposes the constitutional entrenchment of a right to secession in democracies, arguing that it undermines the 'ordinary work' of politics indispensable to collective self-government, he does acknowledge the difficulties of democratic constitutionalism in dealing normatively with group claims to secession when the group has been unilaterally incorporated into the collective. The question that Sunstein leaves unanswered is what normative sense can be made of collective *self*-government in such cases. See C Sunstein, 'Constitutionalism and Secession' (1991) 58 *University of Chicago Law Review* 633, especially 661–63.

[64] See my article, 'A-Legality: Postnationalism and the Question of Legal Boundaries' (2010) 1 *Modern Law Review* 30.

a way that entirely circumvents demands of reciprocity. Yet it seems to me that the more or less unilateral origin of polities both spawns the possibility of singularity *and* offers the key to how constitutionalism might be able to deal with it. For if the more or less unilateral inception of a polity catches up with it in the form of group claims to unilateral secession, is it not possible for the polity to respond, when the concrete circumstances so demand, by a novel unilateral act which suspends, *albeit partially*, the constitutional regimentation of reciprocity with a view to initiating political negotiations with those who want out? The suspension of the constitutional regimentation of reciprocity would mean, in such cases, that the negotiation of exit would not be subordinated to the rules governing constitutional amendment, including rules about the majority that must assent to secession by a minority group. For these rules, and the reference to 'majority' and 'minority' groups, presuppose the reciprocity under a constitution that is rejected by one of the negotiating parties. Such political negotiations would inaugurate what might be called a phase of 'para-constitutionalism', that is, a negotiation about the conditions of exit in the form of a *double asymmetry* that arises as a result of the partial suspension of the constitutional regimentation of reciprocity between the negotiating parties.

These are, to be sure, but preliminary and highly sketchy considerations, which require ulterior elaboration. But it seems to me that this interpretation of para-constitutionalism can claim at least initial empirical plausibility in light of the Final Provisions of the Treaty of Lisbon, which set out the procedure for the withdrawal of Member States from the EU. Any Member State is now permitted under Article 49A of the Treaty of European Union to 'withdraw from the Union in accordance with its own constitutional requirements'. Once a state notified the EU of its decision to withdraw, it shall negotiate with the EU the terms of its withdrawal and it future relationship therewith. In the event that negotiations do not prosper, the Treaties cease to apply to the state two years after the notification of withdrawal.

Neil Walker refers to this norm as laying down a 'hybrid' measure in that,

> while it provides a mechanism by which the Member States retain a unilateral right to withdraw, this is subject to a suspension of at least two years during which a negotiated settlement must be sought between the withdrawing party and the European Council.[65]

---

[65] N Walker, 'The Migration of constitutional ideas and the migration of *the* constitutional idea: the case of the EU' in S Choudhry, *The Migration of Constitutional Ideas*, above n 26, 340.

And he adds that this measure distinguishes withdrawal from the EU from either simple withdrawal by a state from an international organisation, on the one hand, or secession of a sub-unit from a federal polity, on the other.[66] Whilst the Member State and the EU are to negotiate the terms of the member state's withdrawal, the ordinary rules for the amendment of the Treaty are not applicable, not only because the Member State may withdraw on the basis of its 'own constitutional requirements', rather than on the basis of criteria established by the Treaty of European Union, but also because its withdrawal is not subordinated to the agreement of the European Council, acting on behalf of the remaining Member States. Other than the mutual obligation to negotiate a settlement during a period of two years, the constitutional regimentation of reciprocity has been suspended, as attested to by the fact that 'the Member State shall neither participate in the discussion of the European Council or Council or in decisions concerning it' nor is bound by the qualified majority decisions taken by the EU. There are, of course, significant differences between the withdrawal of states from the EU and the specific kinds of problems posed by the possible secession of the province of Quebec from Canada. But the draft Article 49A of the Treaty of European Union may well capture the spirit of what I have called 'para-constitutionalism', that is, that a form of constitutionalism that seeks to respond – albeit indirectly – to group claims to singularity, cultural or otherwise.

[66] *ibid.*

9

Liberal Democracy's Timber *is Still Too Straight: The Case of Political Models for Coexistence in Composite States**

FERRAN REQUEJO[1]

I. INTRODUCTION

THIS PAPER ANALYSES the difficulties that traditional liberal democracy experiences when it attempts to achieve an adequate political accommodation of the diverse values, interests and identities that exist in contexts of national pluralism (plurinational states). First, I analyse two theoretical distortions associated with the Western tradition which are present in the majority of the legitimising concepts of the liberal tradition: the fallacy of abstraction and the difficulties that it encounters when attempting to find a suitable way to deal with pluralism in the political theories that stem from the Enlightenment. Secondly, after mentioning the three classic solutions for accommodating plurinational societies – federalism, consociationalism and secession – I analyse the suitability of the first of these to achieve the recognition and political accommodation of national pluralism by means of a number of conclusions drawn from analyses of comparative politics in federations and in a number of regional states. The conclusion is that these two basic objectives can only be achieved, in federal terms, through the *plurinational federalism* model or

* 'Alus so krummen Holze, als woraus des Mensch gemacht ist, kann nichts ganz Gerades gezimmert werden' ('Out of the crooked timber of humanity, no straight thing was ever made'). Isaiah Berlin uses in *The Crooked Timber of Humanity* this classic quotation of Kant's (*Idee su einer allgemeinen Geschichte in weltbürgerlicher Absicht*, 1784) as a starting point for his critique of the Platonic and positivist foundations of Western thought and of the Utopian propositions sometimes associated with them.
[1] Pompeu Fabra University, Barcelona.

the *partnership* model (in combination, or not, with institutions and consociational processes that regulate the possible secession of minority nations).

II.   THE CONCEPTUAL AND NORMATIVE TIMBERS OF POLITICAL LIBERALISM IN RELATION TO THE PLURALISM OF PRESENT-DAY SOCIETIES

Every political tradition creates its own legitimising language, its own concepts, its own objectives and its own values. The history of political liberalism – from its beginnings in the seventeenth century until now – can be presented as a history of the increasing recognition and institutionalisation of a number of specific demands for impartiality by different (social, economic, cultural, national, etc) sectors of modern and contemporary societies. It is often pointed out that the abstract and supposedly universalist language that underlies the presentation of the values of liberty, equality and pluralism of political liberalism has, in practice, contrasted with the exclusion of many 'voices' with regard to the institutional regulation of the specific liberties, equalities and pluralisms of contemporary states. This was the case – and in some contexts continues to be so – of those who do not own property; of women; of indigenous peoples; of racial, national, ethnic and linguistic minorities, etc. Despite everything that political liberalism represented as an emancipative political movement in comparison with the traditional institutions of the *ancien régime* (rights charters, the principle of representation, the principle of legality, competitive elections, constitutionalism and procedures of the rule of law, separation of powers, parliamentarianism, etc), we know that most liberals of the eighteenth and nineteenth centuries were opposed to the regulation of rights of democratic participation such as universal suffrage or the right of association. These rights, whose presence in modern-day democracies is now taken for granted, had to be wrested from early liberalism and constitutionalism after decades of social conflict, above all with the political organisations of the working classes. Later, following the constitutionally recognised 'liberal and democratic waves of democracy' of the second half of the twentieth century, social notions of equality and equity would be transformed, especially after the constitutional inclusion of a 'third wave' of social rights, which formed the base of the welfare states created at the end of the Second World War.

Nowadays, we could say that liberal democracies and international society are faced with a new emancipative element, but this time the legal contrasts are not of a social but of a cultural and national nature. In recent years, the idea has slowly been growing that, if we wish to proceed towards liberal democracies of greater moral and institutional quality, the values of liberty, equality and political pluralism must also be taken into account from the perspective of national and cultural differences. Today we know that the rights of the first three waves – liberal, democratic and social – do not by themselves guarantee the implementation of these values in the cultural and national sphere. In other words, the idea has gradually been gaining ground that state uniformism – implicit in the traditional liberal-democratic (and social) conceptions of equality of citizenship or popular sovereignty – is an enemy of liberty, equality and pluralism in the cultural and national spheres. Moreover, the idea that it is advisable to foster more morally refined and institutionally complex versions of liberal democracies in order to accommodate their diverse types of internal pluralism has also received increased support.

Thus, a value such as equality is no longer exclusively contrasted, in conceptual terms, with political and social *inequality*, but also with cultural and national *difference*. This is linked with a whole collective dimension that cannot be reduced to the individualist, universalist and statist approach of traditional democratic liberalism and constitutionalism. This latter approach still predominates in the values and legitimising discourse of a great many of the political actors of contemporary democracies (governments, parliaments, parties, etc) – both in the sphere of the classic right and the left – as well as in the majority of the variations of liberal and republican theories of democracy. The repercussions of the *cultural and national turn* of the foundations of democratic legitimacy are not limited to the sphere of Western democracies, but also influence the normativity that should rule in an international society. The most significant empirical cases are those related to minority nations, to national minorities, to indigenous peoples and to transnational immigration.[2] All these cases pose specific questions regarding recognition and political accommodation in contemporary democracies (such as group rights, self-government, the defence of particular cultural values, presence in the international sphere, etc). It could be said that we are currently facing a new aspect of political equity which is fundamental in order to progress towards democracies of greater 'ethical' quality, but for which the traditional theories of democracy, liberalism and constitutionalism lack a suitable response. In other words, the idea is gaining ground that uniformism and limited traditional liberal individualism are the enemies of key dimensions of equality, liberty and pluralism. Thus, the quest for suitable

---

[2] The notion of 'minority nations' is used here as the equivalent to that of 'stateless nations' commonly used in the analytical literature on nationalism. However, in this chapter I do not include the case of 'national minorities', which are collectives that live in a different state from that in which the majority of people of the same national group reside (eg, the case of the Hungarian minority in Romania, the Russian minority in Lithuania, etc). Minority nations and national minorities differ both from a descriptive analytical perspective and from a normative perspective.

forms of cosmopolitanism and universalism involves establishing a broad recognition and political accommodation, in terms of equity, of the national and cultural voices that are excluded, marginalised or downgraded in liberal democracies.

In recent years there has been much debate about the cultural 'limits' of a liberal and democratic society. This debate is making it easier to understand liberal and democratic traditions themselves – their limits and possibilities – in terms of theory and institutional practice. It is also facilitating a better understanding and practical expression of the values of these traditions – the regulation of different types of pluralism in civic and political liberties and in different types of equalities. There are many possible forms of democracy and it seems obvious that it is advisable to modulate universalism according to the specific characteristics of empirical contexts. If not, the pompous, ostensible discourse about 'individual rights' and 'universalism' will obscure democracies that are heavily biased in favour of the particularisms of the majority. These are likely to be democracies that are poorly established in normative terms, and even more poorly implemented institutionally. In Kant and Berlin's terms, they will be democracies that are too 'straight' to adequately regulate the human complexity of the different kinds of pluralism which coexist within them.

A.   Do we Interpret Political and Social Reality Correctly? Two Analytical Distortions

The classical Greeks condensed the different characteristics of human beings in the myth of Prometheus and Zeus, depicted in Plato's *Protagoras* dialogue.[3] The gods gave the brothers Prometheus and Epimetheus the task of distributing abilities among the animals and human beings so that they could improve their lives. Epimetheus asked to be allowed to carry out this distribution. To some he gave strength, to others speed or wings with which to flee, in such a way that no species ran the risk of being wiped out. When he had distributed all the abilities, human beings had yet to receive theirs and this was the day that the gods' assignment expired. Prometheus, in his haste to find some form of protection for the human species, stole fire and professional wisdom from Hephaestus and Athena (for which he was subsequently punished). Humans thus possessed these abilities, but still lacked the 'political science' of coexistence, as this belonged to Zeus. Humans perfected their technologies, but fought among themselves whenever they met. Fearing that the human species would die out, Zeus sent Hermes to 'take morality and justice to humans, so that there would be order in the towns'.

---

[3]   Plato, *Protagoras* 320d–322d.

Judging from the development of humanity, it would appear that, regarding the amounts of each type of knowledge distributed, Prometheus was significantly more generous than Zeus. We are better at technology than at politics and justice. This myth illustrates very well that we humans are prone to act hastily and to improvise. Nowadays, we know this to be true due to studies on the evolution of life on the planet. Evolution is not based on a plan; it is the selection of a set of chance improvisations which have turned out to be adaptive. But what in Western culture appears to have been difficult to assimilate since Plato's time is that the thing that most *distinguishes* us from other species – language and technology – does not coincide with that which most *characterises* us as a species in evolution.

On the other hand, we know that political ideologies, when they are adopted unilaterally, distort reality. But together with these ideological distortions are others of which we are less aware: those associated with how we think; how we use language when we attempt to analyse and intervene in the world. Let us consider two of them.

The first is the tendency to use extremely abstract categories in order to include the maximum number of cases of reality. In some way this is inevitable. Naming something involves creating an abstraction. But at times we lean towards what we might call the *fallacy of abstraction*: believing that we understand a phenomenon better the more abstract is the language we use to describe it, explain it or transform it. And what often occurs is exactly the opposite: the more abstract the language, the poorer and further away it is from the empirical cases to which it is attempting to refer.[4]

The second is the tendency of Western thought to deal inadequately with pluralism. Today we recognise that (social, cultural, national, linguistic, religious, ideological, etc) pluralism is not only an insurmountable fact, but also an essential value. We know that when faced with any given situation there is not only one way to act correctly in moral terms; and it is also commonly agreed that there is not merely a single appropriate political decision in a specific moment or context. There are almost always several options which are equally reasonable. But in the history of Western philosophy a different approach has been taken. We have thought more in 'monist' than in 'pluralist' terms. Hannah Arendt and Isaiah Berlin pointed out that a lack of pluralism has run through Western thought since Plato.

---

[4] Hegel knew a lot about this. See GWF Hegel, *Philosophy of Right* [1843], sections 142, 182. Some Marxists, for example, are prone to this kind of distortion by abstraction when, by means of a small number of categories – 'class struggle', 'economic base', etc – they attempt to 'explain' everything from the empire of the Sumerians to the anti-colonial revolutions of the 20th century. This type of theoretical tendency has also been very common in the legitimising language of political liberalism since its beginnings.

And despite the fact that we recognise the existence and/or advisability of comparable value pluralism and lifestyles in contemporary societies, we often persist in believing that there is only one correct practical answer and that all the others are wrong.

Abstract and monist distortions are present in the majority of classic political conceptions. These distortions contribute to the fact that the world of theories of justice and democracy continues to be too 'straight', when the timber of humanity and societies is not. This question has caused and still causes both ethical injustices and institutional dysfunctions in liberal democracies. This is somewhat surprising with regard to a large part of the liberal-democratic tradition, since one of its strong points is the defence of pluralism, now understood as a value worth defending, rather than a mere fact with which it is necessary to coexist in the least harmful way possible.

However much it is repeated, it will never be possible to stress sufficiently the historic change which this tradition has meant for the ethical and functional improvement of the political organisation of a large part of humanity. Nevertheless, we know that this is a process that also displays a number of its own theoretical shadows and practical totalitarian versions. One of the keys to better thought and action lies in achieving a critical control over that pair of distortions – abstraction and monism – that dwell in our discourses. Doing so is not always easy; it requires intellectual effort and empirical sensitivity, but is necessary in order to refine both our analytical capabilities and our moral and political actions. Let us now look at some conceptual elements in which these theoretical distortions are realised and which have an influence on the revision of democratic liberalism in societies characterised by a significant degree of national pluralism.

B.   Twelve Elements for a Political and Moral Refinement of Plurinational Liberal Democracies

1. In general terms, two intellectual attitudes are necessary in order to approach the subject of national pluralism (and multiculturalism): to approach it as a practical problem, the aim of which is to avoid conflicts in the least traumatic and costly way possible (the pragmatic approach); and to approach it as a question of 'justice' in the relations between permanent majorities and minorities in democracies which require correct solutions (the moral approach). A mixture of both approaches is commonly in use in practical politics. Whilst the former is part of the political negotiation between actors, the latter is present in the discourse of these actors' legitimising processes. In plurinational societies, differences are apparent between national collectives regarding the parameters of national and

cultural justice (unlike the intra-communitarian parameters with regard to socio-economic distributive justice – which are also plural, albeit more uniform, between national collectives).[5]

2. We know that the vast majority of human beings are culturally rooted, and it could be said that all cultures have value and that, in principle, all deserve to be respected. This does not imply that they cannot be compared in specific areas, that they are all equivalent and equally successful in these areas, that everything is morally acceptable, that there are no mutual influences, or that elements of several cultures cannot be shared, nor that one is unable to disengage oneself from one's original culture.

3. Today, cultural and national liberty is an essential value for the democratic quality of a society. It is a kind of liberty – one of the human rights – that is crucial for an individual's development and self-esteem and that, like all the other normative objectives of democracies, is limited by other values and other democratic liberties.[6] One of the conclusions of the debate in recent years is, as aforementioned, that cultural and national liberty is not ensured through the mere application of the civil, participatory and social rights usually included in liberal-democratic constitutions at the beginning of the twenty-first century.

4. In the academic world it seems to be generally accepted that cultural and national issues are not simply 'social causes'. The sphere of 'cultural and national justice' is different from the sphere of 'socio-economic justice'. It is true that there are sometimes interrelationships between these two spheres of justice, but the phenomena associated with each one of them are different. These phenomena include different values, objectives, actors, institutions, practices and also different policies. Some institutions and policies may improve the latter sphere while hardly having any effect on the former – and vice versa. This shows the impossibility of equating the paradigm of equality (or of redistribution in socio-economic terms) with the paradigm of difference (or of recognition in national and cultural

[5] For typologies of different phenomena associated with 'multiculturality' and its conceptual, normative and institutional differences, see W Kymlicka and W Norman, *Citizenship in Diverse Societies* (Oxford, Oxford University Press, 2000); F Requejo, *Multinational Federalism and Value Pluralism* (London and New York, Routledge, 2005) ch 3. See also B Parekh, *Rethinking Multiculturalism* (London, Macmillan, 2000).

[6] Human Development Report, United Nations, 2004. This report suggests five elements that contribute to better quality democracies: (i) multiculturalism – assuring the participation of marginalised cultural groups (electoral reforms; federalism with asymmetric features); (ii) policies that ensure religious freedom (including festivals, food and dress customs, etc); (iii) policies of legal pluralism (a more controversial issue that would in any case imply respect for the limits mentioned above); (iv) linguistic policies (some democratic states are still monolingual with regard to their institutions and symbols despite their internal multilingualism); and (v) socio-economic policies (minimum salaries, education, health).

terms).[7] Both kinds of consideration are part of a more inclusive vision of 'justice' in contexts of national pluralism.

5. Traditional theories of democracy – both in their more liberal and more republican versions – usually refer implicitly to concepts, values and experiences in societies which were originally much simpler than their modern-day counterparts. Nowadays there is a 'new agenda' of issues that can no longer be reduced to the central concepts and legitimising language of traditional liberal and republican approaches – individual rights, absence of discrimination before the law, citizenship and popular sovereignty, the public virtues of the republican tradition, etc. Demands for recognition and political and constitutional accommodation of minority nations have found a place on the political agenda, and liberal democracies must find a response to them. Despite their differences, what these distinct cases have in common is the desire to maintain and reinforce a set of specific national characteristics in an increasingly globalised world. This is something that the habitual institutions, processes and policies of current liberal democracies fail to adequately guarantee.

6. Traditional political conceptions have tended to treat the internal national and cultural differences of democracies which did not coincide with those of the majority society as 'particularist deviations'. Too often the practical response of many liberal democracies has been to promote the cultural and national assimilation of minorities in order to achieve their 'political integration'. The practical consequence has been the subsumption and marginalisation of the internal national and cultural minorities of the state in the name of universalist versions of 'freedom of citizenship', 'popular sovereignty' (of the state) or even of 'non-discrimination' (by majorities with regard to the claims of minorities). Practically speaking, these versions have behaved in a highly inegalitarian, discriminatory and biased way in favour of the *particular* characteristics of the culturally and nationally hegemonic or majority groups of the state (which do not always coincide with the groups or sectors which are hegemonic in the socio-economic sphere). It is possible to detect the presence of a uniformising form of statism, in national and cultural terms, which is the practical 'hidden element' of traditional democratic liberalism in the regulation of the rights and duties of the 'citizenry'. In reality, all states, including liberal-democratic ones, have been and continue to be agents of nationalism and nationalisation.

7. Traditional theories of democracy lack a theory of the *demos*. They offer no normative responses to questions such as: 'who should constitute the demos of a democracy?'; 'is there, or should there be, single *demos* for

---

[7] A contrast which is at the heart of current theories of liberal democracy is manifested in the approaches which have come to be called 'Liberalism 1' and 'Liberalism 2'.

each democracy?'; 'which collectivity represents solidarity?'. Moreover, these theories have not developed a theory of legitimate borders. Furthermore, there are conceptual limits to the interpretation of legitimising values even on the part of current liberal-democratic theories that are highly elaborate in other aspects (Rawls, Habermas) when they attempt to deal with the demands for recognition and political accommodation of movements for national and cultural pluralism of a territorial nature.[8]

8. The idea that the democratic state is a culturally 'neutral' entity is a liberal myth that few defend today, not even the majority of liberal authors situated within traditional liberalism, whose theoretical approach could be described as individualist, universalist and statist. All states impose cultural and linguistic features on their citizens. Liberal-democratic states are no exception. In clear contrast with the versions that still defend a kind of laissez-faire approach to cultural matters, or the alleged moral superiority or modernity of values of the majority, experience shows that the state has not been, nor is, nor can ever be, 'neutral' in cultural terms, and that there is no moral superiority whatever in having a greater amount of collective decision-making power.

9. Processes of state-building and nation-building do not coincide. Nowadays, national identities have shown themselves to be long-lasting and increasingly important – in contrast to some liberal and socialist approaches which, since the nineteenth century, have treated these identities as a passing, decadent phenomenon. Both state-building and nation-building processes have conditioned the evolution of federalism.[9]

10. In plurinational societies there will always be values, interests and identities of, at least partially, a competitive nature. It would appear to be counter-productive from a practical perspective, as well as useless from a theoretical one, to attempt to adopt a different approach to the issue through concepts like the existence of an allegedly 'post-nationalist' political stage or of a kind of 'constitutional patriotism' linked only with liberal-democratic values which ignore individuals' national and cultural

---

[8] Theories of socio-economic justice (Rawls) take for granted that equality of citizenship in a just society is not problematic, when constitutional issues in plurinational societies question that very premise. It is not very reasonable to presuppose that 'justice', understood in the restricted sense which it has in the socio-economic sphere, is the first and only virtue of democratic institutions. Normative pluralism includes a (sometimes radical) plurality not only of conflicting values, virtues and interests, but also of identities (consider, for example, the normative and institutional issues involved in the normative debate on the right of secession in plurinational contexts). No theory of justice is capable of including – let alone synthesising – all the components of this agonistic pluralism of values/virtues, interests and identities. Even Berlin failed to go far enough in this area. I have dealt with the unsuitability of the approaches of socio-economic justice and traditional theories of democracy with regard to this type of issue, in Requejo, *Multinational Federalism*, above n 5, ch 1.

[9] For an analysis of 'the two concealments' that both processes have represented for the evolution of contemporary federalism, see Requejo, *Multinational Federalism*, above n 5, ch 3.

characteristics. These attempts are poorly equipped in empirical terms and, in practice, usually act as legitimising elements for the status quo.[10]

11. It is obvious that individual and collective 'identities' are not a fixed reality, but construct themselves and change over time. However, most of the collective elements that constitute the basic features of individual identity are given to us. In other words, we do not choose them. The belief that we are 'autonomous individuals' who choose our (national, ethnic, linguistic, religious, etc) identities is, to a great extent, another of the myths of traditional liberalism. These elements are not normally chosen; any choices we make are based on them.[11]

12. The political contexts in which individuals are socialised are often the result of historical processes that include both peaceful and violent elements – wars of annexation, exterminations, mass deportations, etc – which are sometimes at the root of modern-day struggles for the recognition and self-government of minority nations (and of some national minorities). In the majority of these analytical elements it is possible to verify the presence of the two theoretical distortions mentioned above – the fallacy of abstraction and the inability to deal adequately with pluralism. These distortions have direct repercussions for the quality of our democracies, above all in the current conditions of increasing pluralism and globalisation.

As a result, the construction of increasingly refined liberal democracies in terms of *cultural and national pluralism* is one of the biggest challenges of the normative and institutional revision of contemporary democratic systems. Some of the questions to be answered would be: 'what implications does the regulation of national pluralism have in the sphere of symbols, institutions and self-government?'; 'how should classic notions like representation, participation, citizenship and popular sovereignty be understood and defined in plurinational and increasingly globalised contexts?'; and 'what does accepting national pluralism mean in international society?'.

---

[10] See F Requejo, 'Multinational (not "postnational") Federalism' in R Maiz and F Requejo (eds), *Democracy, Nationalism and Multiculturalism* (London and New York, Routledge, 2005) 96–107.

[11] M Walzer has correctly stressed three 'exaggerations' associated with political liberalism: the elective subject, deliberation and the use of reason in politics. See M Walzer, *Vernunft, Politik und Leidenschaft* (Frankfurt-am-Main, Fischer Taschenbuch Verlag, 1999).

III.   CLASSIC LIBERAL-DEMOCRATIC SOLUTIONS FOR ADDRESSING
'SOCIAL' DIVERSITY

It would appear that the first condition for solving a problem is to try to define or describe it correctly; and defining and describing a problem correctly involves establishing at least three aspects. First is knowing how to identify what the basic issue is, identifying the decisive question that needs to be considered. Secondly, defining a problem also involves knowing how to describe it with the maximum precision possible. This implies both a careful conceptual treatment and the inclusion of elements of a historical nature and the most important empirical data related to the problem. Thirdly, defining a problem is knowing where one has to look to find possible solutions, both in the sphere of political theory and in that of comparative politics. In other words, when we have a question and do not know where to go to find the answers, this normally means that from an epistemological perspective we are not on the right track.

One of the most important questions with regard to the case of plurinational democracies is the recognition and political accommodation of the national pluralism of these democracies. Obviously, in addition to this question there are probably a whole series of aspects which are interrelated with it: economic development; inequalities of income; multi-culturality; and integration in supra-state organisations, such as the European Union; etc. But it is methodologically improper to mix all these elements from the outset. In this case, the key point is to establish not how the *demos* becomes *kratos* – this would be the traditional vision of democracy – but how the different national *demoi* which coexist within the same democracy are politically and constitutionally recognised and accommodated in terms of equality (between the national majorities and minorities) in the *kratos* of the polity. This involves dealing with and introducing aspects of both a 'democratic' nature – participation between majorities and minorities in the 'shared governments of the democracy' – and, above all, of a 'liberal' nature – the protection and development of minority nations confronting the 'tyranny of the (national) majority', both in the internal sphere of this democracy and in the international sphere. It is, therefore, a matter of establishing the 'checks and balances' in a collective dimension which have received little or no attention from traditional political conceptions, but which constitute specific dimensions of core questions of liberal political theory, such as the 'negative theory' of the 'tyranny of the majority'.

Whatever the most suitable liberal-democratic solution or solutions may be will obviously depend, among other things, on the context of each specific case (its history, international situation, types of actors, political culture, etc). But it seems to be clear that in contexts of national pluralism it is necessary to establish a much more refined interpretation than that offered by the basic values of traditional liberal-democratic constitutionalism: liberty, equality, individual dignity and pluralism. This complexity demands theories that are more sensitive and modulated to the variations of empirical reality when one attempts to clearly identify its basic legitimising values. Moreover, it demands, above all, practical, institutional and procedural solutions that are much more suitable for the type of pluralism that one wishes to accommodate. At the beginning of the twenty-first century, the recognition and political accommodation of plurinational democracies continue to be two aspects of the liberal-democratic agenda that have yet to be satisfactorily resolved.

The three 'classic' institutional responses for societies with a strong component of national diversity have been:

1. Federalism (in a wide sense, including federations, associated states, federacies,[12] confederations and regional states);
2. The institutions and processes of a 'consociational' nature (between the majorities and permanent national minorities). One can find examples of these institutions and processes in the democracies of Switzerland and Belgium, in both cases in conjunction with federal solutions; and
3. Secession.

Having pointed out some elements of political theory in the first section, let us now look at some elements offered by comparative politics with regard to federalism. The generic question is whether federalism offers a suitable framework for establishing the recognition and accommodation of plurinational democracies and, if so, which federal models are most suitable and which are not.

Broadly speaking, in studies of federalism – without referring strictly to cases of national diversity – comparative political analyses commonly point out the existence of several *federal models*.[13] To synthesise:

[12] A federacy is a political arrangement where a large unit is linked to a smaller unit or units, but the smaller unit retains much power and has a minimum role in the government of the larger one, and where the relationship can be dissolved only by mutual agreement (Examples: Denmark–Faröe islands; USA–Puerto Rico).

[13] In the discussion that follows we will distinguish, as is usual in the specialised literature on the subject, between *federalism* as a normative notion that can be applied to different federal institutional models, and *federations* (one of those institutional models which in turn contains a series of variants). See R Watts, *Comparing Federal Systems* (Montreal and Kingston, McGill-Queen's University Press, 1999).

Table 1: Some examples of *federal agreements* in contemporary democracies

Regional States	Symmetrical Federations	Asymmetrical Federal Agreements			Confederations
		Asymmetrical Federations	Federacies	Associated States	
Italy	South-Africa	Belgium	Denmark – Faröe Islands	France – Monaco	Commonwealth of Independent States
Portugal	Germany	Canada		India – Bhutan	
Spain*	Argentina	India	Finland – Aaland Islands	Italy – San Marino	Caribbean Community
UK	Australia	Malaysia			
	Austria		UK – Jersey	Netherlands – Antilles	
	Brazil		United States – Puerto Rico	New Zealand – Cook Islands	
	United States				
	Mexico				
	Switzerland			Switzerland – Liechten-stein	
*with some federal trends					

F. Requejo, Multinational Federalism and Value Pluralism, Routledge, London-New York 2005.
(Own elaboration from Watts 1999 and Elazar 1991)

Furthermore, among the conclusions of an exhaustive comparative empirical study into federal democracies – using variables situated on four analytical axes and a variety of indicators applied to 19 cases (federations and a number of regional states)[14] – it is worth pointing out:

1. The existence of a 'federal deficit' of an institutional nature in plurinational federations. In other words, somewhat paradoxically, uninational federations display, as a whole, greater institutional federal logic – albeit in extremely varying degrees – than plurinational federations do. This characteristic is independent of the greater or lesser degree of political decentralisation in both types of federation. The figure below summarises this question:

[14] The four analytical axes are: (i) uninational-plurinational federations; (ii) the degree of institutional federalism; (iii) the degree of political decentralisation; and (iv) the presence or absence of constitutional asymmetries. Each of these axes is broken down into several indicators. See F Requejo, 'Federalism and Democracy. The Case of Minority Nations: a Federalist Deficit' in M Burgess and A Gagnon (eds), *Federal Democracies* (London, Routledge, 2010) 275–98.

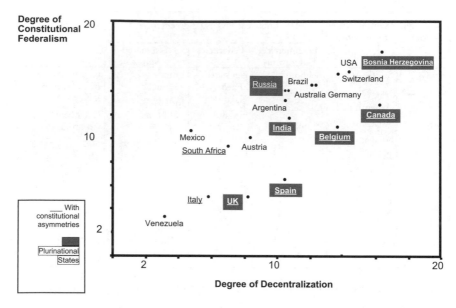

2. Only a few plurinational federations (eg Russia, Ethiopia) establish an explicit constitutional recognition of their internal national pluralism – and also, rather paradoxically, this is not true for those which possess a greater degree of stability and democratic quality. In the other cases, however, this recognition is non-existent or much less explicit in their constitutional regulations, even when the degree of decentralisation of some federations is high in comparative terms.

3. In more predictable terms, there is a greater presence of elements of de jure asymmetry in plurinational federations than in uninational federations. In some of the former there are also pressures working in favour of the symmetry of the system. This occurs, above all, when the number of sub-units is not small (empirically, at least nine sub-units in the sample, whereas such pressures are not present when the number of sub-units is less than four). This is the case for Canada, India, Russia, Ethiopia and Spain, in contrast with Belgium, the United Kingdom and Bosnia-Herzegovina.[15] It is an open question whether

---

[15] When the number of territorial entities of a plurinational state is high, it seems inevitable that simultaneous, albeit contradictory, pressures will emerge, in favour of a more symmetrical or more asymmetrical system. For the Canadian case, see *Asymmetry Series* (IIGR, Queen's University, since 2005), especially G Laforest, 'The Historical and Legal Origins of Asymmetrical Federalism in Canada's Founding Debates: A Brief Interpretative Note', *Asymmetry Series* 2005 (8). The well-known West Lothian Question (participation/inhibition of the representatives of territories endowed with asymmetrical regulations in their

the unwillingness of some federations and plurinational regional states to introduce more asymmetrical regulations will or will not reinforce territorial tensions and secessionist movements in the future.

4. The coexistence in plurinational federations of several processes of nation-building which are partially competitive situates the issue of the construction of a 'federal trust' in different terms to the simpler case of uninational federations. In this case, achieving this trust seems to require two institutional factors: (i) the existence of procedures and rules that allow minority nations to participate in the 'shared government' of the federation (or the regional state) whilst maintaining their singular character – specific presence in the lower chamber, bilateral intergovernmental relations, participation in consociational state institutions, etc; and (ii) the existence of procedures and rules that protect the recognition and self-government of minority nations from the actions of the majorities – powers of veto in the lower chamber; 'alarm bell' procedures; opting in and opting out procedures – which do not require constitutional reforms, appointment of magistrates to the supreme or constitutional courts, or specific participation in processes of constitutional reform.[16]

5. The predominant conception in federations is that the 'right to self-determination' is reserved for the federation. However, this is a conception that some federations have recently questioned. Examples include the case of the famous opinion of the Canadian Supreme Court in the *Secession Reference* (1998); and the regulations introduced into the constitution of Ethiopia – which include the right of self-determination in the preamble and the right of secession in the article for the constituent nations and peoples. Other, more specific cases are the federation of St Kitts & Nevis, or the case of the right of secession

central institutions depending on the nature of the decision to be taken), does not appear to provoke too many problems in the majority of countries (except in the case of the United Kingdom), due to the fact that the true political level of the asymmetries is not very high, and most of the powers are concurrent. For a general overview of constitutional de jure asymmetries, see R Watts, 'A Comparative Perspective on Asymmetry in Federations', *Asymmetry Series* 2005 (4).

[16] It could be said that an additional factor for the construction of federal trust in plurinational democracies is the existence of a 'federal political culture' and of a 'plurinational political culture' in the polity as a whole. The former appears to arise in those democracies with a lengthy history of federal institutional links. The latter, which is more difficult to achieve as it clashes with the inherent nation-building process present in almost all states (whether they are federal or not), appears to arise in those states which were established more as a 'union' – a more pluralist concept – of different entities than as a 'unit' – which is a more monist concept. The acceptance of a process of secession, for example, of one of the sub-state entities appears to be more accepted in the United Kingdom and Canada, which are plurinational states with a common past in the British Empire, than in other contexts. Here we are dealing with a kind of political culture which does not seem to be linked to the federal character of the state. These two questions will, however, require a detailed analysis of specific indicators.

already exercised and approved in 2006 by the old federation of Serbia-Montenegro. In the normative debate of recent years regarding the advisability or the legitimacy of such regulations, moral, strategic and functional reasons have been put forward to oppose the introduction of a right of secession. Some of these reasons have a certain amount of plausibility, particularly in some contexts. However, there seems to be no definitive argument against the introduction of such a right when the rules that regulate it prevent its strategic use by elites of the minorities. The twenty-first Century may be witness to political movements in favour of the 'right to decide' by citizens of minority nations; that is, movements in favour of regarding minority national *demoi* as polities that wish to preserve as much collective negative liberty as possible in an increasingly globalised world.[17]

In previous works I have analysed the practical impossibility of establishing a 'just and stable' regulation of plurinational democracies through (i) federations or regional states that regulate a uniform and symmetrical territorial division of powers; and (ii) composite states which do not establish an explicit recognition of national pluralism and a wide territorial division of powers (political decentralisation) in the internal and international spheres. When different processes of nation-building converge, together with a diversity of values, interests and identities on the part of the different collective actors, federal theory based on Madison's approach is further away from the solution than that which is based on Althussius's approach.[18] Here, the solutions, although it cannot be said that they should be of a strictly pragmatic nature or that they should necessarily reflect normative *modus vivendi* approaches, should include strong components of contextual pragmatism when establishing specific rules for the recognition and self-government of minorities and their participation in any model of 'shared government'.

Thus, in addition to the first and second classic solutions mentioned above (of a consociational nature and secession), in order to proceed towards a recognition and political accommodation of plurinational societies, within the third type of classic solutions – that of the generic group of federalism – there appear to be only two models able to satisfactorily regulate national pluralism: the plurinational federalism model and the partnership model – which latter model includes the cases of associated states, federacies and confederations. Both models can be combined with elements from the other two solutions – consociationalism (Belgium) and

---

[17]   Federal practice and theory would be advised to pay more attention to these movements than they have done in the past.
[18]   See D Karmis and W Norman, *Theories of Federalism: A Reader* (New York, Palgrave Macmillan, 2005). See also T Hueglin, 'Federalism at the Crossroads: Old Meanings, New Significance' (2003) 2 *Canadian Journal of Political Science* 36.

the constitutional regulation of secession (Canada) – but, these options apart, it does not seem possible to regulate the two fundamental questions posed by national pluralism: the recognition and political accommodation of this form of pluralism.

Broadly speaking, the model that I have described as plurinational federalism involves the inclusion of three normative conditions applied to a group of five spheres – the symbolic/linguistic sphere, the institutional sphere, the sphere relating to powers, the economic/fiscal sphere, and the international sphere.[19] The aim is to achieve a 'friendly federal state'; that is, a federal state that is friendly to the minority nations (and vice versa) and which permits a satisfactory and stable regulation of national pluralism for this type of polity. Empirically speaking, however, there is evidence of the existence of territorial tensions in all cases which are close to the plurinational federalism model. There is clear resistance on the part of different actors to the implementation of a plurinational form of institutional federalism, associated with the nation-building and state-building processes of democratic states (although there is a whole range of responses in comparative politics both with regard to recognition and self-government).

Alternatively, the partnership models make it possible to achieve a number of confederal agreements with the state in specific areas (defence, passports, a number of issues relating to foreign policy and the tax system, etc) whilst maintaining, in other areas, a form of self-government that, unlike the model of plurinational federalism, is not limited by the juridical rules of the state. The empirical regulation of this kind of agreement follows the guidelines of comparative politics established in some associated states or in the federacies. Taking into account that these latter types of agreement are usually found in the case of islands and their relations with a much larger geographic and demographic unit, however, we may note that their practical effectiveness for mainland plurinational states appears to be limited to cases where the units to be federated have this kind of relation *inter se*. This is despite the fact that from a logical perspective nothing prevents the establishment of agreements of these types for other sorts of plurinational states as well.

It is an open empirical question whether the twenty-first Century will or will not be a period which sees the consolidation of political movements of the minority nations of plurinational democracies in pursuit of recognition and political accommodation, whether this may be through their accommodation in plurinational federal states, through processes of partnership,

---

[19] I deal with this point in more detail in F Requejo, *Multinational Federalism*, above n 5, ch 4.

or, where none of these options is possible, through secession; in other words, through the stable regulation of self-determination in interdependence.[20]

Traditional federalism and democratic liberalism display, together with emancipative and functional 'lights', a series of 'shadows' that make them excessively 'straight' traditions to be adapted to the more pluralist and complex timber of plurinational democracies. The ethical and functional improvement of both traditions would permit a development of the values of the political Enlightenment that is much more suitable for the pluralism of plurinational democracies. At the beginning of this century, neither liberal democracy nor federalism had reached the end of the story. On the contrary, they are now immersed in a new phase of improvement based on their modulation with respect to contemporary empirical societies.

IV.   CONCLUSION

We have analysed in this chapter some of the normative and institutional elements which make it difficult for the liberal and federal traditions to achieve an effective realisation of the values of liberty, equality and pluralism in plurinational democracies. After pointing out two theoretical distortions of the political theories that have their starting point in the Enlightenment– the fallacy of abstraction and a flawed approach to pluralism – we have described a set of 12 conceptual and normative elements which exemplify these two distortions in the context of plurinational democracies. Following Kant and Berlin, we have said that traditional liberalism and federalism are too 'straight' to adapt to the more pluralist and complex nature of plurinational societies. Subsequently, after mentioning the classic solutions for articulating social diversity – federalism, consociationalism and secession – we have pointed out that only two 'federal models' seem capable of providing an adequate framework for establishing a satisfactory recognition and political accommodation of national pluralism for this kind of democracy. These are plurinational federalism and partnership (in combination, or not, with consociational institutions and processes which regulate the possible secession of minority

---

[20] In fact, what the Opinion of the Canadian Supreme Court establishes is first, that there is a right to self-determination which should in principle be resolved in 'federal' terms and, secondly, that in plurinational democracies, secession is a question of majorities that is not limited to or at the expense of certain constitutional rules when specific rules of 'clarity' are complied with in the construction process of these majorities. See A Gagnon and J Tully (eds), *Multinational Democracies* (Cambridge, Cambridge University Press, 2001); U Amoretti and N Bermeo (eds), *Federalism and Territorial Cleavages* (Baltimore, Johns Hopkins University Press, 2004); and A Gagnon, M Montserrat and F Rocher (eds), *The conditions of diversity in multinational democracies* (Montreal, Institute for Research on Public Policy, 2003).

nations). Empirically, however, these models are difficult to implement, even in purely pragmatic terms. In the plurinational societies at the beginning of the twenty-first century, federal scepticism, one might say, begins at home.

Part Five

Europe and the World

10

The Constitutionalisation of International Organisations

ANNE PETERS*

I. CONCEPTS AND PROBLÉMATIQUE

AMIDST THE GLOBAL process of the constitutionalisation of international law, a sectoral constitutionalisation of special regimes is taking place. The term 'constitutionalisation' is used here as a shorthand term both for the emergence of constitutional law within a given legal order and for the spread of constitutionalism. The concept of 'constitutionalism' is more than the term 'constitution' loaded with material content: '[c]onstitutionalism does not refer simply to having a constitution, but to having a particular kind of constitution, however difficult it may be to specify its contents'.[1] Put differently: constitutionalism relates not just to the concept of constitution but to a specific conception of constitution. Constitutionalism asks for a 'constitutionalist' constitution, enshrining the rule of law, checks and balances, human rights protection, and possibly also democracy.

The concept of constitutionalisation as employed here implies that such a constitutionalist constitution can come into being in a process extended through time. Constitutionalisation also implies that a legal text (or

* Professor of Public International Law and Constitutional Law, University of Basel.

[1] G Casper, 'Constitutionalism' in LW Levy, KL Karst and DJ Mahoney (eds), *Encyclopedia of the American Constitution* vol 2 (New York, Macmillan, 1986) 473, 474. JHH Weiler and M Wind have pointed out 'that there is a difference between constitution and constitutionalism. Constitutionalism ... embodies the values, often non-stated, which underlie the material and institutional provisions in a specific constitution. At this level, separating constitution from constitutionalism would allow us to claim, rightly or wrongly, for example, that the Italian and German constitutions, whilst very different in their material and institutional provisions, share a similar constitutionalism vindicating certain neo-Kantian humanistic values, combined with the notion of the *Rechtsstaat*' (JHH Weiler and M Wind, 'Introduction' in Weiler and Wind (eds), *European Constitutionalism beyond the State* (Cambridge, Cambridge University Press, 2003) 1, 3). See extensively on the 'divorce' of constitution and constitutionalism O Beaud, 'Constitution et constitutionnalisme' in P Raynaud and S Rials (eds), *Dictionnaire de philosophie politique* (2003) 133, 136–42.

various legal texts) can acquire (or eventually lose) constitutional and constitutionalist properties in a positive feedback process. A text can be more (or less) constitution-like and more or less constitutionalist. It may be, in short, a constitution-in-the-making. So global constitutionalisation is a catchword for the continuing, but not linear, process of the gradual emergence and deliberate creation of constitutional and constitutionalist elements in the international legal order by political and judicial actors, bolstered by an academic discourse in which these elements are identified and developed further.[2]

This chapter deals with the sectoral constitutionalisation of international organisations.[3] By sectoral constitutionalisation of international organisations, I appreciate the emergence of constitutional and even constitutionalist elements within the primary and secondary law of the organisation. The constitutionalist approach to certain international organisations does not only consider those organisations to possess a constitution, but to possess a *constitutionalist* constitution-in-the-making. This approach seeks to identify and to advocate the application of constitutionalist principles, such as the rule of law, checks and balances, human rights protection, and possibly also democracy, in the law of international organisations. Because constitutionalism asks for a constitution that satisfies constitutionalist standards, the debate on the constitutionalisation of international organisations stimulates the revelation of legitimacy deficits of the organisations, and may provide a tool-box for improvements.[4]

Sectoral constitutionalisation is one aspect of a presumable broader process of global constitutionalisation that can be quite easily pinpointed and described, because it is firmly rooted in the case law. Almost all international courts' and tribunals' decisions that deploy a constitutional or even constitutionalist vocabulary concern international organisations.

---

[2] Constitutionalisation is multi-factorial. The emerging constitutional and constitutionalist profile of the international order might be well developed in one or more areas or even special branches of law, but underdeveloped in others. The process of global constitutionalisation is not all-encompassing. It is contingent and path-dependent. Patterns of co-existence and cooperation persist even in a generally more constitutionalised world order. Moreover, constitutionalisation is accompanied and even hampered or undone by antagonist, anti-constitutional trends in contemporary international relations, such as the fragmentation of international law, the predominance of one superpower, the privatisation of international law, and the revival of the (sovereign) state, as manifested in the recent financial crisis. See in detail on some anti-constitutionalist trends, A Peters, 'Compensatory Constitutionalism: The Function and Potential of Fundamental International Norms and Structures' (2006) 19 *Leiden Journal of International Law* 579, 602–05.

[3] It develops further ideas first published in A Peters, 'The Members of the Constitutional Community' in J Klabbers, A Peters and G Ulfstein, *The Constitutionalization of International Law* (Oxford, Oxford University Press, 2009) 153, 201–19.

[4] See on this issue also JM Coicaud, 'Conclusion: International Organizations, the Evolution of International Politics, and Legitimacy' in JM Coicaud and V Heiskanen (eds), *The Legitimacy of International Organizations* (Tokyo, New York, Paris, United Nations University Press, 2001) 519–52.

Related, but distinct, themes of the constitutionalisation of international law, broadly conceived, include the constitutionalisation of special branches of law populated by numerous organisations and treaty regimes, such as international environmental law,[5] the reading of the UN Charter as the Constitution *of the world* (not only of the United Nations as an organisation),[6] and the depiction of the European Convention on Human Rights (ECHR) as the Constitution of Europe.[7] I do not espouse these claims, because I think that much of what belongs to the body of global or regional constitutional law is not codified in the respective conventions. The UN Charter says almost nothing about human rights, to name only one typical ingredient of global constitutional law, and the ECHR, conversely, deals only with human rights.

By contrast, sectoral constitutionalisation of the respective organisations seems most visible in the evolution of EU law[8] and World Trade Organization (WTO) law.[9] The following sections seek to highlight and to compare the most important features of these constitutionalisation processes, incorporating other international organisations such as the United Nations and the International Labour Organization within its frame of analysis. The chapter finds that the legal evolution so far identified as (sectoral) constitutionalisation is quite uneven and lacunary. Most conspicuously, any development of democratic structures within international organisations is largely missing. The chapter makes suggestions for democratisation and concludes that the sectoral constitutionalisation of international organisations forms part of a broader, global, multi-level process.

[5] See sceptically D Bodansky, 'Is there an International Environmental Constitution?' (2009) 16 *Indiana Journal of Global Legal Studies* 565–84.

[6] B Fassbender, 'The United Nations Charter as Constitution of the International Community' (1998) 36 *Columbia Journal of Transnational Law* 529–619. Note that Fassbender seeks to reconcile his conception with that of a more inclusive global constitutional process, and considers the Charter as one part of that ongoing process (*ibid*, 616–17).

[7] *Loizidou v Turkey* (preliminary exceptions) (1995) Series A 310, 23 March 1995, para 75: The ECHR as a 'constitutional instrument of the European public order (ordre public)'. See already *Ireland v United Kingdom* (Application No 5310/71) ECHR 18 January 1978, para 239: 'Unlike international treaties of the classic kind, the Convention comprises more than mere reciprocal engagements between contracting States. It creates, over and above a network of mutual, bilateral undertakings, objective obligations which, in the words of the Preamble, benefit from a "collective enforcement"'. But see EA Alkema, 'The European Convention as a Constitution and its Court as a Constitutional Court' in P Mahoney, F Matscher, H Petzold and L Wildhaber (eds), *Protecting Human Rights: The European Perspective: Mélanges à la mémoire de Rolv Ryyssdal* (Köln, Carl Heymans, 2000) 41–63, concluding that the Convention's framework is not a constitution.

[8] See A Peters, *Elemente einer Theorie der Verfassung Europas* (Berlin, Duncker & Humblot, 2001).

[9] See DZ Cass, *Constitutionalization of the WTO* (Oxford, Oxford University Press, 2005).

II.   HYBRIDITY: TREATY-CONSTITUTIONS

The constitutionalist approach moves significantly beyond the older view that the founding Acts of international organisations are constitutions. Several founding Acts even carry the official title 'constitution'.[10] Similarly, scholars have long used the term. For instance, long before the creation of the WTO, John Jackson had contemplated the 'constitutional structure of a possible international trade institution'.[11] This vocabulary is in line with the International Court of Justice (ICJ)'s view that '[f]rom a formal standpoint, the constituent instruments of international organizations are multilateral treaties ... their character ... is conventional and at the same time institutional'.[12] In the same sense, the European Court of Justice (ECJ) argued that the EC Treaty, although it had been concluded in the form of an international agreement, represented the constitutional charter of a legal community.[13] In these judicial awards, the founding documents of international organisations are conceived as having a hybrid character as treaty-constitutions. Doctrinally, this characterisation built on the French and Italian institutionalist theory of the mid-twentieth century.[14] In practice, the hybridity was made explicit for the first time in the official title of an organisation's founding Act in the 'Treaty Establishing a

---

[10]   'Constitution of the United Nations Educational, Scientific and Cultural Organization' (adopted 16 November 1945, entered into force 4 November 1946) 4 UNTS 275; 'Constitution of the World Health Organization' (adopted 22 July 1946, entered into force 7 April 1948) 14 UNTS 185; 'Constitution of the International Labour Organization' (adopted 9 October 1946, entered into force 20 April 1948) 38 UNTS 3; 'Constitution of the Food and Agricultural Organization of the United Nations' (adopted and entered into force 16 October 1945) (1946–47) UNYB 693; 'Constitution of the International Telecommunication Union' (adopted 22 December 1992, entered into force 1 July 1994) 1825 UNTS 3.

[11]   JH Jackson, 'The Constitutional Structure of a Possible International Trade Institution' in *World Trade and the Law of GATT* (Indianapolis, Bobbs Merrill, 1969) ch 304, 780–85.

[12]   *Legality of the Use by a State of Nuclear Weapons in Armed Conflict* (Advisory Opinion), [1996] ICJ Rep 66, para 19.

[13]   Opinion 1/91, *Draft Agreement relating to the creation of the European Economic Area*, [1991] ECR I-6079, 6102, para 21.

[14]   'Sous ce profil, l'acte institutif d'une Organisation déterminée est bien un traité international, fondé, en tant que tel, sur la volonté des contractants et donc soumis, au moment de sa formation, à leur volonté, mais il est par ailleurs destiné à devenir la constitution, c'est-à-dire l'acte de fondation de l'Organisation, auquel celle-ci se rattache tout au long de son existence. On pourrait dire, par conséquent, que l'acte institutif revêt *la forme du pacte, mais possède la substance de la constitution: né sur la base d'une convention, il dépasse, avec le temps, son origine formelle, jusqu'à devenir une constitution* de durée indéterminée dont le développement déborde le cadre à l'intérieur duquel elle avait été initialement conçue' (emphasis added): R Monaco, 'Le caractère constitutionnel des actes institutifs d'organisations internationales' in *Mélanges offerts à Charles Rousseau, La communauté internationale* (Paris, Pédone, 1974) 154.

Constitution for Europe' of 2004.[15] By contrast, hybridity has been denied with regard to the WTO Agreement by the Appellate Body.[16]

That controversial understanding of an international organisation's founding document as a hybrid treaty-constitution did not rely on any material, value-loaded (constitutionalist) principles, but merely on the fact that the founding treaties established institutional structures, delineated the competences of the organisation, and defined the terms of membership. The doctrinal merit of this understanding of the law of international organisations was to overcome the outdated dichotomy between contract or treaty (as a 'horizontal' *inter partes* legal act) and constitution (as a 'vertical' *erga omnes* legal act).[17] But the institutional-constitutional topos did not introduce a *constitutionalist* approach, as defined above, to the law of international organisations.

III. THE AUTONOMY OF INTERNATIONAL ORGANISATIONS

The 'autonomy' of an organisation's legal order is a central theme in the debate on sectoral constitutionalisation. Without making this explicit, the discussants seem to consider the 'autonomy' of an entity as a corollary of its possession of a constitution. The ICJ explained the constitutional status of the World Health Organization (WHO) Charter by saying that this Charter creates a legal subject, the WHO, 'endowed with a certain autonomy'.[18] Likewise, the ECJ judgment in *Van Gend en Loos*, the point of departure for the constitutionalisation of the European Union, held that 'the Community constitutes a new legal order of international law'.[19] In EU legal scholarship, the expression 'new legal order' was quickly understood as 'autonomous legal order'. In the Grand Chamber's *Kadi* judgment, the focus on 'autonomy', going hand in hand with the assertion

---

[15] Treaty Establishing a Constitution for Europe, Rome, 29 October 2004 [2004] OJ C310/1.

[16] *Japan – Taxes on Alcoholic Beverages*, Appellate Body (4 October 1996) WT/DS8/AB/R, WT/DS 10/AB/R, WT/DS11/AB/R, p 15: 'The WTO Agreement is a treaty – the international equivalent of a contract. It is self-evident that in an exercise of their sovereignty, and in pursuit of their own respective national interests, the Members of the WTO have made a bargain. In exchange for benefits they expect to derive as Members of the WTO, they have agreed to exercise their sovereignty according to the committment they have made in the WTO Agreement'.

[17] See on this dichotomy and its relevance for the debate on the legal nature of the EU Treaties, A Peters, 'The Constitutionalization of the European Union – Without the Constitutional Treaty' in SP Riekmann and W Wessels (eds), *The Making of a European Constitution* (Wiesbaden, VS Verlag für Sozialwissenschaften, 2006) 35–67.

[18] *Legality of the Use by a State of Nuclear Weapons in Armed Conflict* (Advisory Opinion), [1996] ICJ Rep 66, para 19.

[19] Case 26/62, *Van Gend en Loos v Nederlandse Administratie der Belastingen*, [1963] ECR 1, 3 (under II.B).

of the EU's constitutional order,[20] was an important discursive building block in the argument that the European courts must fully scrutinise the conformity of regulations which implement the United Nations' targeted sanctions with European fundamental rights, even if a court's annulment of a regulation on the ground of its unconstitutionality inevitably leads to the European Union falling short of compliance with Security Council resolutions.

A.   The Many Meanings of 'Autonomy'

The idea of autonomy has been used notably in the EU context, first, to demonstrate (erroneously in my view) a categorical distinction between EU law and public international law; ultimately, in order to preclude the Member States' power to decide for themselves how to incorporate and rank EU law in relation to the domestic legal order, as they do with public international law.

Secondly, 'autonomy' may denote the originality and non-derivability of the organisation's law – its 'autonomous' basis of validity.

Thirdly, and in practical terms most importantly, 'autonomy' refers to the ongoing relationship between the organisation and its Member States. In this third meaning, the greater or lesser 'autonomy' of an organisation can be diagnosed by looking at various aspects: the conferral of broad competences to an organisation and a looser application of the principle of speciality and of the prohibition of ultra vires acts denotes more autonomy, as does majority voting. On the other hand, easy exit options for Member States seem to suggest a lower degree of organisational autonomy.

Where 'autonomy' in this last sense of practical independence is concerned, concentration on the classical international organisations alone would give a distorted picture. These are far outnumbered by 'secondary' international organisations, agencies and various kinds of complex institutions which have not been created directly by states, but by international organisations (or by states and organisations), either through treaties, through resolutions, or hybrid instruments.[21] Here the states have lost control to a significant degree, and the entities' will does not simply

---

[20] Joined Cases C-420/05 P and C-415/05 P, *Kadi and Al Barakaat International Foundation v European Council and European Commission*, judgment of the Grand Chamber, 3 September 2008, [2008] ECR I-6351, paras 281–2, 316, 326.

[21] See C Shanks, HK Jacobson and JH Kaplan, 'Inertia and Change in the Constellation of International Governmental Organizations, 1981–1992' (1996) 50 *International Organization* 593–627, esp 594 with data.

express the sum of the Member States' positions. The traditional image of the states as masters of the treaties is inadequate to describe that complex reality.[22]

In the special case of the EU, typical structural features that are considered indicators of the organisation's constitutionalisation – such as the direct effect of many provisions of the primary and secondary EU law, the fact that Member States need not transpose and are even prohibited from specifically transposing certain types of secondary law into their domestic law, and, finally, the supremacy of EU law over the domestic law of the Member States – emphasise the EU's 'autonomy' in the sense of practical independence. These structural features are largely absent in the law of other international organisations.

Fourthly, autonomy is associated with judicial *Kompetenz-Kompetenz*. In this regard, it matters for the WTO, for example, that, despite the important legalisation of the dispute settlement mechanism, a key element of judicial or interpretative autonomy is absent: neither the WTO itself nor non-governmental parties can act as independent monitors of compliance – unlike the situation in the EU with the Commission acting as guardian of the treaties.

B.   Revision Procedures and Autonomy

Often, the procedures for revising an organisation's founding treaty are considered the litmus test for the constitutionalisation of its respective treaty regime. Indeed, sophisticated amendment procedures may be a way of entrenching the constituent treaty and thereby conferring on it the status of 'higher' law. However, the procedures for amending the charters of international organisations are normally less burdensome than ordinary international law-making. Amendments sometimes require less than unanimous consent or need only majority ratification to enter into force for all parties. A different aspect of amendment procedures is that amendments often require the participation of the organs of the organisation itself. This is a typical feature of federalist amendment procedures.

Another issue is that ordinary treaties can, under customary law, be revised informally at any time, even if the treaty stipulates a special procedure for revision. The reason is that the contracting parties can always agree to informally abolish those procedures.[23] But if the founding document of an organisation is said to be a constitution, it may only be

---

[22]   C Martini, 'States' Control over New International Organization' (2006) 6 *The Global Jurist Advances* 1–25.
[23]   cf Art 39 Vienna Convention on the Law of Treaties, Vienna (adopted 23 May 1969, entered into force 27 January 1980) 1155 UNTS 331.

amended according to the procedures prescribed in that very document. The circumvention of the written amendment procedures by reliance on a subsequent new consensual decision of the Member States to leave aside those procedures is not permitted in a constitutionalist perspective. The reason is that constitutions are imbued with the principles of legal security and clarity and are therefore hostile towards unwritten and necessarily imprecise customary law.[24] But the deepest reason for the importance attached to revision procedures is the putative link to 'autonomy'. Under the premise that a constitution is characterised by 'autonomy' from its creators, the power to amend a constitution should not lie with the founders (the *pouvoir constituant*), but is a prerogative of the *pouvoir constitué* (the organisation itself). However, in all three international organisations whose constitutionalisation is discussed most vividly, the amendment procedures display only a small degree of autonomy from the state founders.[25]

C.　Autonomy as a Proxy for Sovereignty and a Trigger for Constitutionalist Demands

So what significance does 'autonomy' exactly have for the constitutionalisation of an international organisation? In the usual debates as summarised above, and without openly admitting and perhaps without even realising it, observers deploy 'autonomy' as a proxy for the sovereignty of the organisation. The question of the organisation's autonomy is just a different way of asking: who is the 'master' of the organisation's law? The organisation itself and its institutions, or the Member States? Just like sovereignty, autonomy can be conceived as a graduated or as an all-or-nothing concept. Espousing the graduated view, I find that in terms of autonomy the EU is strongly constitutionalised, whereas the WTO and the UN enjoy a limited degree of autonomy.

However, I think that the postulated link between autonomy and constitutionalisation should be reconsidered. In the traditional discourse, autonomy is considered as a precondition of constitutionalisation. The underlying premise is that only sovereign entities can possess a constitution. By contrast, I submit that autonomy is not a conceptual prerequisite for having a constitution, but should trigger the normative

---

[24] Fassbender, 'UN Charter as Constitution', above n 6, 600.
[25] See for the EU, Art 48 of the EU Treaty, and for the WTO, Art X of the WTO Agreement. Under Arts 108–109 of the UN Charter, amendments can come into force for all Member States after ratification of two thirds of the Member States, including the P5.

quest for accountability and thus for constitutionalisation: the more autonomous is an international organisation, the more it *needs* to be constitutionalised.

IV. CONSTITUTIONAL PRINCIPLES CONTAINING MEMBER STATES

One indicator and promoter of sectoral constitutionalisation might be the endorsement of constitutional rights and principles such as human rights, the rule of law, democracy and solidarity in the law of international organisations. However – and this is important – in the founding treaties of the most important organisations these principles are typically addressed not to the organisations themselves, but exclusively or primarily to the Member States. For example, the UN Charter states that it is the purpose of the United Nations to promote human rights (in Article 2(3) of the UN Charter), and thus in its Member States. In a similar fashion, the prohibition on the use of force and the conferral of a quasi-monopoly on the Security Council to authorise military action works to contain Member States, not the United Nations itself.

In the European Union, the basic freedoms (free movement of goods, workers, services, residence and capital) which limit Member States' regulation are likewise principles which limit Member States' policies, and are increasingly depicted as 'fundamental rights' of the citizens.[26] The International Labour Organization can also be said to be constitutionalised along these lines. The ILO Declaration on Fundamental Principles and Rights at Work of 1998 declares that 'all members, even if they have not ratified' the Conventions adopted by the ILO

> have an obligation arising from the very fact of membership in the organization, to respect, promote, and realize, in good faith and in accordance with the Constitution, the principles concerning the fundamental rights which are the subject of those Conventions.[27]

The declaration thus seeks to contain and bind Member States against or at least independent of their concrete acceptance of specific conventional rules, merely by appealing to the members' subjection to the ILO Constitution.[28]

---

[26] cf (sceptically) T Kingreen, *Die Struktur der Grundfreiheiten des Europäischen Gemeinschaftsrechts* (Berlin, Duncker & Humblot, 1999).

[27] ILO, Declaration on Fundamental Principles and Rights at Work, 86th Session, Geneva, June 1998, Art 2.

[28] See for a trenchant critique of this approach P Alston, '"Core Labour Standards" and the Transformation of the International Labour Rights Regime' (2004) 15 *European Journal of International Law* 457–521.

The most widely discussed case of constitutionalisation in the form of containing and constraining Member States is the WTO. Historically, the General Agreement on Tariffs and Trade (GATT) was established on the ground that policies made in one country often adversely affect people in other countries, who in the absence of any institutional framework have no ability to influence those policies. GATT sought to provide a forum in which one member would challenge the protectionist policies of another member.[29] Such protectionist policies are widely seen to result from an undue influence of rent-seeking groups whose lobbying is apt to flaw the domestic democratic processes. Against this background, the WTO's core function is to neutralise the domestic power of protectionist interests, and thereby the WTO members have enabled themselves to overcome domestic political process deficiencies.[30] This is a typically constitutional function, which is in the domestic realm served by fundamental rights guarantees and by judicial protection by constitutional courts.

In the current WTO, the traditional trade law principles of most-favoured nation and national treatment operate against state failure in the form of protectionism. These principles are constitutive of the system of multi-layered governance and thus may be considered as supplying the constitutional principles of the trading system. They contain and constrain the WTO members and are increasingly viewed as two facets of a constitutional principle of non-discrimination ultimately benefiting the ordinary citizens (importers, exporters, producers, consumers, tax-payers).[31] Likewise, the transparency obligations imposed on the WTO members by provisions such as Article X of GATT and Articles III and VI of the General Agreement on Trade in Services (GATS) seek to prevent illegitimate protectionism and to that extent also serve a constitutional function.[32]

Moreover, WTO constitutionalists have highlighted the need to integrate human rights concerns into world trade law, not only through the interpretation of existing agreements, but also through the building of new common institutions.[33] In fact, a constitutionalist approach is apt to

---

[29]   PM Gerhart, 'The WTO and Participatory Democracy: The Historical Evidence' (2004) 37 *Vanderbilt Journal of Transnational Law* 897, 933.

[30]   JO McGinnis and ML Movsesian, 'The World Trade Constitution' (2000) 114 *Harvard Law Review* 521.

[31]   See E-U Petersmann, 'Multilevel Judicial Governance of International Trade Requires a Common Conception of Rule of Law and Justice' (2007) 10 *Journal of International Economic Law* 529, 533: 'the WTO guarantees of freedom, non-discrimination and rule of law – by enhancing individual liberty, non-discriminatory treatment, economic welfare, and poverty reduction across frontiers – reflect, albeit imperfectly, basic principles of justice'.

[32]   P Delimatsis, *International Trade in Services and Domestic Regulations: Necessity, Transparency, and Regulatory Diversity* (Oxford, Oxford University Press, 2007).

[33]   T Cottier, 'Trade and Human Rights: A Relationship to Discover' (2002) 5 *Journal of International Economic Law* 111.

provide a vocabulary, a theory, and institutional building blocks to satisfy the quest for coherence among trade law and human rights law, and thereby to strengthen members' human rights obligations. Proponents suggest endorsing a general maxim of interpretation of the GATT obligations of WTO members (and the relevant exception clauses) in the light of human rights guarantees.[34]

The rights-based constitutionalist reading of WTO law has (to some extent erroneously) been perceived as narrow. It has been criticised for marginalising social rights and environmental principles and for focusing on economic and property rights. Early constitutionalist scholarship was therefore criticised as masking a radically economically libertarian free-trade agenda. In fact, the old GATT law did neglect social and environmental issues, and was geared towards negative integration by eliminating trade barriers. Today, the Agreement on Trade Related Aspects of Intellectual Property Rights (TRIPS), Article VI of GATS, the Technical Barriers to Trade (TBT) and the Sanitary and Phytosanitary (SPS) Agreements, the Antidumping Agreement, and Agreement on Agriculture all seek to realise positive integration through common standards for members, even if only very few of those standards relate to the environment, and hardly any to social aspects.

In defence of WTO constitutionalism, it can be claimed that the constitutionalist reading of WTO law precisely supports the quest for the adoption of such social and environmental standards binding members. Moreover, trade liberalisation normally triggers a demand for positive integration. However, the WTO, as opposed to the EU, currently lacks the institutions and means to complement the ongoing negative with positive integration.[35] In addition, a large part of the membership opposes the WTO having any social agenda. And unlike the EU, the WTO does not have decision-making structures that easily allow for a variable geometry. To conclude, the 'constitutional' WTO principles addressed to the WTO members are incomplete.

Further constitutionalisation of the WTO in terms of constitutional principles addressed to members could be realised by rectifying the libertarian bias of the nascent WTO constitution. This could be done by strengthening the legal relevance of non-trade issues such as environmental and social concerns. The constitutional principle of solidarity could be implemented by promoting liberalisation in sectors in which poor countries can compete.

---

[34] E-U Petersmann, 'Time for a United Nations "Global Compact" for Integrating Human Rights into the Law of Worldwide Organizations: Lessons from European Integration' (2002) 13 *European Journal of International Law* 621, 645–46.

[35] R Howse and K Nicolaidis, 'Enhancing WTO Legitimacy: Constitutionalization or Global Subsidiarity' (2003) 16 *Governance* 73, 84–85.

Procedurally, the constitutional constraints on Member States of international organisations could be strengthened by granting private actors access to dispute settlement mechanisms and courts, as will be discussed in Section VIII below.

V.   LEGAL ACCOUNTABILITY OF INTERNATIONAL ORGANISATIONS TOWARDS CITIZENS

Constitutionalised international organisations must be accountable. In a constitutionalist framework there is both legal accountability (mainly through judicial review) and political accountability (through the democratic process). The key question, however, is: what is the proper forum for accountability?

A.   Towards Member States

In the traditional view, international organisations are accountable to their Member States. One problem in this context is that in some organisations, Member States have no equal rights and therefore no equal means by which to hold the organisation to account.[36] A related problem is that even organisations whose members have formally equal voting rights practise informal decision-making (eg in the notorious WTO 'green rooms'), which effectively marginalises or excludes less powerful states.

In this traditional perspective, the main accountability problem of international organisations is the 'runaway', or '*Zauberlehrling*' phenomenon; that is the danger that an organisation escapes control by the Member States and acquires too much institutional and bureaucratic independence. This can happen on account of 'mission creep' (dynamic expansion of competencies) or over-long chains of responsibility. A slightly different problem is that of potential capture (eg by 'global capital' in the case of the World Bank), which also distances the organisation from its rightful 'stakeholders'.

In order to improve accountability, the International Law Association's (ILA) report on the accountability of international organisations recommends a host of rules and practices of a constitutionalist nature, such as

---

[36] The most conspicuous examples are the veto-power of the five permanent UN Security Council members and the weighting of votes in the Bretton Woods Institutions.

participatory and reasoned decision-making processes, transparency, institutional balance, procedural regularity and impartiality.[37] Empirical researchers have investigated to what extent international organisations fulfill these and other accountability requirements. Contrary to popular opinion, international organisations are relatively accountable in comparison to transnational corporations and non-governmental organisations (NGOs).[38] Knowledge about the structure and the functioning of accountability principles, as available in constitutional scholarship and practice, can contribute to further operationalise that accountability.

B. Towards Citizens

In a constitutionalist perspective, the ultimate accountability forum for international organisations should be the (global) citizens, not states. In doctrinal terms, the constitutionalist claim is that individuals should be full and active legal subjects of the relevant organisation's legal order.

It is therefore significant that the ECJ in its seminal judgment *Van Gend en Loos* stated that the 'subjects' of the European Community legal order 'comprise not only member states but also their nationals'.[39] By contrast, a WTO panel considered individuals as merely passive beneficiaries of the WTO legal order, and not as subjects: it first stated that

> it would be entirely wrong to consider that the position of individuals is of no relevance to the GATT/WTO legal matrix. Many of the benefits to Members ... depend on the activity of individual economic operators in the national and global market places ... indeed one of the primary objects of the GATT/WTO as a whole, is to produce certain market conditions which would allow this activity to flourish.

But then the panel deliberately distinguished the WTO regime from the EU and the *Van Gend en Loos* conception by highlighting that 'the GATT/WTO did *not* create a new legal order the subjects of which comprise both contracting parties or members and their nationals' (emphasis added).[40]

This panel report thus reflects the traditional position that citizens are represented by their nation states, and should therefore be entirely 'mediated' by their states in international organisations. But that position is – in the eyes of constitutionalists – flawed. As far as political accountability (ie

---

[37] International Law Association, 'First Report on the Accountability of International Organizations', Report of the 71st conference held in Berlin, 16–21 August 2004.

[38] H Kovach, C Nelligan and S Burall, 'The Global Accountability Report: Power without Accountability?' (London, One World Trust, 2003) 31–32, on the basis of a case study of selected international organisations.

[39] Case 26/62, *Van Gend en Loos* [1963] ECR 1, 3 under II.B.

[40] *United States – Section 301–310 of the Trade Act of 1974*, Panel Report (27 January 2000) WT/DS152/R, not appealed, paras 7.73 and 7.72.

the democratic aspect) is concerned, the lines of accountability to the citizens are too long and indirect to allow for effective accountability. Moreover, many Member States of international organisations are not internally democratic, and can therefore not rightfully claim to act for their citizens. As far as legal (notably judicial) accountability is concerned, the incapacity of individuals to institute judicial or administrative proceedings against organisations renders them hostage to their nation states' considerations of high politics.

To secure the legal accountability of international organisations towards citizens, organisations should be subject to the rule of law and bound to respect human rights, as will be discussed in the next Section.[41]

VI.   THE RULE OF LAW AND HUMAN RIGHTS RESPONSIBILITIES OF INTERNATIONAL ORGANISATIONS

The classic theme of constitutionalism is to contain political power. Constitutionalism thus requires that international organisations themselves are subject to the rule of law, and that their powers are bound by legal principles. It is therefore important from a constitutionalist perspective that the internal law of international organisations forms a hierarchy: all acts adopted by the organisations, including all secondary law, must be in conformity with the primary law, the founding Act. Because the principles laid down in the founding Act thus perform a containing function, that document works as a constitution, and the internal hierarchy of the law of the international organisations can count as a feature of sectoral constitutionalisation.[42]

Another constitutional issue arising in the increased activity of international organisations is delegation. With regard to enforcement measures under Article 42 of the UN Charter, for example, there is a tension between safeguarding central oversight and ultimate responsibility on the one hand, and the practical necessity of employing the military apparatus of the UN Member States on the other. The legal tool to deal with this tension between centralisation and decentralisation is the doctrine of delegation. Constitutionalist reflections on the requirements for a proper delegation of competences, as elaborated in the nation state context, can be employed as a source of inspiration to define limits of delegation and resolve questions

[41] In addition, political (as opposed to legal) accountability of international organisations towards citizens would have to be realised through democratic law-making in which citizens participate at least indirectly. See on this issue below Section X, and A Peters, 'Dual Democracy' in J Klabbers, A Peters and G Ulfstein, *The Constitutionalization of International Law* (Oxford, Oxford University Press, 2009) 263–341.
[42] cf F Seyersted, *Common Law of International Organizations* (Leiden, Martinus Nijhoff, 2008) 72–77.

of the attribution of responsibility. Therefore, the doctrine of delegation has an important 'constitutional function' in the law of international organisations.[43]

To be effective, the constitutional limits to the activity of an international organisation must be enforceable. The acts of the organisation itself must be subject to judicial or to a functionally similar review which examines whether the constitutional principles are observed and ensures that the constitutional limits are respected by the organisation itself. This review would, in short, be a constitutional review, and it could be performed either by international or domestic courts.[44]

Currently, only the EU possesses this – in my view – crucial constitutionalist feature. The European courts are competent to control the legality of the acts of the organs and institutions themselves. The ECJ judgment *Les Verts* of 1986 highlighted the constitutional significance of this type of judicial control. Here the question was whether acts of the European Parliament could be attacked in an annulment procedure, although the respective treaty provision did not mention these acts. By pointing out that the European Community is a 'legal community' whose Treaty is a 'constitutional charter', the Court was able to argue that neither the acts of the Member States nor those of the institutions could escape judicial control. It could therefore draw the conclusion that parliamentary acts deploying legal effects must be subject to judicial review even without an explicit treaty basis.[45]

An important issue in this context is whether international organisations must not only respect legality in general, but, more specifically, human rights, which form the core of modern constitutional law. So far the founding documents of the most powerful international organisations do not explicitly state that the organisations themselves must respect human rights. Fully-fledged human rights guarantees against EU acts have been granted only gradually, in a dialectical process triggered through opposition by the Member States. Still, the criticism has been made that the ECJ's human rights protection is rather weak, that it gives too much weight to the interests of European integration and that it too generously allows human rights restrictions on that ground.[46]

[43] R Kolb, *Ius contra bellum: le droit international relatif au maintien de la paix*, 2nd edn (Basel, Helbing Lichtenhahn, 2009) 128–41, 137.

[44] On the specific issue of triggering such judicial review by private individuals, see Section VIII below.

[45] Case 294/83, *Parti Ecologiste 'Les Verts' v European Parliament* [1986] ECR 1339, para 23.

[46] See further the chapters by Douglas-Scott and Williams in the present volume (chs 5 and 4).

A parallel process has been set in motion with regard to the UN Security Council. A milestone in this regard is the *Tadic* judgment of the International Criminal Tribunal for the Former Yugoslavia (ICTY). The argument of Tadic, the appellant, had been that the Tribunal was illegal or not duly created by law, because it had been established only by a Security Council resolution and not by an international treaty. In order to reject the interlocutory appeal on jurisdiction, the Appeals Chamber resorted to constitutional arguments. In a section of the judgment entitled 'Question of constitutionality', the Chamber examined whether Chapter VII (notably Article 39) of the UN Charter, could form a legal basis of the Tribunal. It emphasised that the Security Council is subject to the principle of legality, and is not a purely political organ. It is not 'legibus absolutus'.[47] However, the legal (or constitutional) limits of Security Council action are barely enforceable, and no judicial action is available against the Council as such. The constitutional limits identified in *Tadic* thus remain largely virtual. This problem has gained salience with the Security Council's comprehensive sanctions against Iraq since 1991 and its more recent targeted sanctions against individuals, which notably risk violating social rights, procedural rights and property. As was the case in the evolution of the EU, the threat of non-compliance by outside courts might push the United Nations to clearly subject the Security Council itself to human rights standards, to increase the level of human rights protection, and to create an institution to monitor compliance.

In the WTO, this dimension of sectoral constitutionalisation is completely absent. Although it could be argued that certain WTO policies potentially, even if only indirectly, affect or even infringe social or indigenous rights, especially in developing countries, these policies are not subject to any human rights review. The relevant standards are not agreed upon, nor are monitoring bodies available. The WTO dispute settlement bodies have no jurisdiction over the WTO institutions themselves. This difference between the (quasi-) compulsory jurisdiction of the WTO dispute settlement mechanism and the EU courts is crucial from a constitutionalist perspective. The constitutionalist agenda requires that judicial review against all international institutions itself must be made available to individuals.

To conclude, the EU is a constitutional and constitutionalist system on the ground that individuals enjoy constitutional protection against the organisation itself, and are empowered to enforce that protection. By contrast, individuals are not yet sufficiently empowered vis-à-vis the UN or

---

[47] Case No IT-94-1-AR72, *Prosecutor v Dusko Tadic, Decision on the Defence Motion for Interlocutory Appeal on Jurisdiction*, ICTY Appeals Chamber of 2 October 1995, paras 26–28.

the WTO to warrant the claim that these two organisations have been constitutionalised along the same lines.

VII.   (JUDICIAL) CONSTITUTIONALISATION OF AND THROUGH ADJUDICATION

The constitutionalisation debate on the WTO concentrates on the judiciali-sation of dispute settlement. In the EU debate, the compulsory and extensive jurisdiction of the European courts as a driver of constitutionali-sation is also at the centre of interest. By contrast, the United Nations has not been analysed through this lens at all.

A kind of institutional constitutionalisation lies in the EU's fully-fledged compulsory judicial system and in the WTO's quasi-compulsory and quasi-judicial proceedings, which lead to judgment-like reports. A different facet of constitutionalisation relates to process and substance of adjudica-tion. Specifically for the WTO, it has been argued that the case law of the panels and the Appellate Body 'is beginning to display some characteristics ordinarily associated with constitutional case-law'.[48] Initially, the role of the panels and the Appellate Body corresponded to a contractual setting in which the institutions mechanically examined whether state conduct was in compliance with the agreements. By distinction, considerations of vertical separation and balance of powers, which have shaped domestic standards of review, were not overtly present in the context of the WTO.[49] Later, the dispute settlement institutions indeed borrowed constitutional doctrines, such as a proportionality analysis.[50] They have taken into consideration non-trade issues such as human rights and environmental protection and have applied the constitutional technique of balancing to determine which of the conflicting interests should prevail in the concrete case. Arguably, the conceptual development of a more constitutional framework would provide room for more nuanced and multi-layered standard-of-review

---

[48] DZ Cass, 'The Constitutionalization of International Trade Law: Judicial Norm-Generation as the Engine of Constitutionalization' (2001) 13 *European Journal of International Law* 39, 42. Cass distanced herself from this statement in her later book (Cass, *Constitutionalization of the WTO*, above n 9).

[49] M Oesch, *Standards of Review on WTO Dispute Resolution* (Oxford, Oxford University Press, 2003) 29, 241–42.

[50] See for a balancing approach to the 'necessity'-requirement of Art XX(d) of GATT, which grants an a priori equal rank to the conflicting objecives: *Korea – Measures Affecting Imports of Fresh, Chilled and Frozen Beef*, Appellate Body (11 December 2000), WT/DS161/AB/R, WT/DS169/AB/R, para 162: 'The more vital or important those common interests or values are, the easier it would be to accept as "necessary" a measure designed as an enforcement instrument'. See also A Stone Sweet and J Mathews, 'Proportionality Balancing and Global Constitutionalism' (2008) 47 *Columbia Journal of Transnational Law* 72–164.

principles.[51] This has been called 'constitutionalism in a modest sense', 'an attitude and a framework capable of reasonably balancing and weighing different, equally legitimate and democratically defined basic values and policy goals'.[52]

But that vision of WTO constitutionalism is under heavy critique. A first objection is that by taking the principle of trade liberalisation as a constitutional norm, the trade-off between the obligation to liberalise and the protection of non-trade concerns inevitably ends in a preference for free trade. Competing values enter into the picture only as narrow and carefully policed exceptions, and the onus is on the party which invokes the exception, according to the critique.[53] However, an important strand of WTO constitutionalism seeks precisely to counter this order of priorities. In that perspective, the competing values are not just exceptions to trade liberalisation, but are provisions to protect legitimate policy goals, which form an integral part of a well-balanced multilateral trading system and which should be acknowledged to have the same status as other constitutional principles.

A further criticisim is that the celebration of balancing as constitutionalisation risks falsely dignifying the judicial balancing process, instead of admitting its political character. When a WTO panel invalidates an environmental protection scheme, constitutionalists tend to view this as the enforcement of the higher (namely constitutional) law (of free trade). In reality, however, according to the critique, such invalidation is a political decision of the panel which is presumptively illegitimate because it replaces the policy balancing of domestic democratic institutions with the panel's own policy.

This objection brings us to the heart of the matter. The entire process of sectoral constitutionalisation has so far been adjudicative rather than deliberative. Notably the WTO's capacity for legislative response to judicial constitutional engineering is muted, not least by the current WTO practice for decision- and rule-making which relies on the consensus principle.[54]

[51]   Oesch, *Standards of Review*, above n 49, 243.
[52]   T Cottier, 'Limits to International Trade: The Constitutional Challenge' in The American Society of International Law (ed), *International Law in Ferment: A New Vision for Theory and Practice*, Proceedings of the 94th Annual Meeting (Washington DC, 5–8 April 2000) 221.
[53]   Howse and Nicolaidis, 'Enhancing WTO Legitimacy', above n 35, 75.
[54]   Agreement establishing the World Trade Organization (WTO Agreement), Marrakesh, 15 April 1994, fn 1. Although Art IX of the WTO Agreement foresees majority voting if a consensus is not reached (with decisions to be adopted upon a simple majority of the votes cast), such voting does not happen.

This again fuels the fundamental objection against the constitutionalist reading of international law, namely that this reading condones an impoverished, legalist (judicially-made), apolitical conception of a constitution. A balance of powers should be established by improving the possibility of a 'legislative response' to adjudication. This can be done only by streamlining the current decision-making procedures within international organisations, including the introduction of majority voting.[55] With specific regard to the WTO, a stronger law-making branch is needed to bring about positive integration, which is not yet engrained in the WTO treaties and which can therefore not be effected by the judiciary alone. Effective international legislation is needed to counter the problem of a presumably illegitimate government of judges.

VIII. ACCESS OF PRIVATE ACTORS TO COURTS

Access of private actors to dispute settlement and courts constitutes constitutionalisation on different grounds. First and most importantly, individual claims *against the organisation itself* constitute a kind of constitutional complaint controlling the organisation. Secondly, private action in two functionally equivalent venues, the organisations' controlling bodies and domestic courts, might bring *Member States* to comply with the rules and principles of an international organisation, thereby subjecting those Member States to the 'constitutional' limitations imposed by the organisations. Thirdly, constitutionalisation lies in the fact that the capability of self-interested natural persons to enforce international rules before international or domestic courts empowers individuals and elevates them to the quality of an active subject of the relevant regime's legal order.

A. 'Constitutional' Complaints by Individuals against International Organisations

Judicial or quasi-judicial review securing the legal accountability of organisations not only to their Member States, but to individuals, is currently available only in the EU. Under limited conditions individual persons can institute judicial action before the European courts and can claim the illegality of European institutions' activity.[56] It would significantly increase the accountability of other international organisations, eg the United

---

[55] See for the democratic problems of majority voting Peters, 'Dual Democracy', above n 41, 283–84, 335–36.
[56] Art 263(4) TFEU.

Nations, if individuals could trigger judicial review of the organisation's acts.[57] Along these lines, the ILA report on the accountability of international organisations considered the possibility of remedial action against international organisations by private persons. However, the report assumed that remedies can only originate from contractual or tortious acts of the organisation.[58] Specifically, it did not envisage a constitutional – notably human rights – responsibility of international organisations. I submit that a constitutionalist sensibility would broaden the approach here. From a constitutionalist perspective, international organisations should also be held accountable towards individuals for administrative and constitutional illegality. The creation of judicial actions for individuals on these grounds would constitute a significant step of further constitutionalisation.

B.   Direct Individual Access to the Organisations' Courts and Tribunals for Enforcing Member State Compliance

By granting individuals access to the courts or tribunals of an international organisation, Member States' compliance with the law of the organisation could be better enforced. So far, however, in no international organisation are individuals empowered to institute judicial proceedings before the organisation's bodies to that end – not even in the EU.

In the WTO, traders have no official access to the dispute settlement body. They cannot institute a proceeding against a WTO member. Such direct access of private (business) parties to the WTO dispute settlement institutions with a view to triggering a proceeding against a WTO member has been proposed as a means to liberate business actors from the tutelage of their governments, which are often reluctant to institute WTO proceedings against other members. The governmental choice whether to bring or not to bring a particular WTO case to the dispute settlement forum is often not guided by the importance and merit of the issue, but is instead influenced by diplomatic considerations as to the general relations with another country, by a desire to maintain a legal question undecided, or by the lobbying power (or weakness) of a particular industrial sector. These policy considerations are neglectful of the rule of law, and they lead to unequal treatment of business actors. The privatisation of WTO dispute settlement would remedy these problems and better respect the rule of law and equal protection. Because self-interested commercial actors have a

---

[57] See, for practical suggestions to realise judicial actions of individuals against international organisations, K Wellens, *Remedies against International Organizations* (Cambridge, Cambridge University Press, 2004) 255–61.

[58] International Law Association, 'First Report on the Accountability of International Organizations', Report of the 71st conference held in Berlin, 16–21 August 2004, 38.

strong incentive to sue, it would, moreover, strengthen the GATT by reducing under-enforcement. It would, in addition, bring relief to governments through the avoidance of political tensions.

But such privatisation may go too far. The regulation of trade flows is intrinsically dualist, concerning both public and private interests. The public interest is all the more important because of the foreclosure of the military option. This means that economic and trade regulation is nowadays the main foreign policy instrument of governments. There is therefore a vital societal interest in transparency and publicity of the WTO proceedings.

On the other hand, the acknowledgement of private stakes leads governments litigating before the WTO dispute settlement institutions to seek counsel from the interested business actors, and to protect business secrecy through the non-disclosure of confidential business information.[59]

The duality of interests should be more clearly acknowledged and regulated under due consideration for the public and private concerns at stake, bearing in mind that these concerns need not coincide, but may be in conflict. The appropriate constitutional design of WTO dispute settlement, therefore, seems not to require its complete removal from governmental control. Rather, it involves upholding the system as an essentially inter-state one whilst greatly increasing and formalising the participatory opportunities of private actors.

In conclusion, Member State containment through individual enforcement action in international fora is nowhere in sight, and is perhaps not even desirable. This means that further constitutionalisation along this vector is not unequivocally recommended, but needs further reflection.

C. Direct Application of the Law of the Organisation by Domestic Courts

The functionally equivalent route to individual access to the organisation's dispute settlement mechanism in order to enforce Member State compliance is the direct application of the organisation's rules by national courts. Direct applicability serves to contain Member States. When private actors invoke an international organisation's norm which prohibits certain domestic (eg protectionist) policies, and when the national judiciary declares illegal the relevant domestic act for violation of that international norm, domestic law is deprived of effect by virtue of the organisation's law, and the Member State is thus checked.

---

[59] *Canada – Measures Affecting the Export of Civilian Aircraft*, WTO Panel (14 April 1999) WT/DS70, para 9.68 and *Canada – Measures Affecting the Export of Civilian Aircraft*, Appellate Body (2 August 1999) WT/DS70/AB/R, paras 141 *et seq.*

So far, direct effect is acknowledged by national courts mainly for human rights treaties, and the possibility of direct effect is also accepted with regard to EU primary and secondary law.[60]

By contrast, the direct effect of GATT provisions has been rejected by most domestic courts, the European courts[61] and the WTO dispute settlement institution itself.[62] One argument against the direct application of suitable WTO rules is that this risks giving undue power to domestic courts, to the detriment of the members' political branches. Also, for so long as WTO law has not fully integrated legitimate policy concerns besides trade liberalisation, the 'unfiltered' application of WTO law by domestic courts may threaten those policy concerns.[63]

On the other hand, the constitutionalist agenda encourages a more ready acceptance of the direct effect of suitable provisions of WTO law, because direct effect would enable the domestic judiciary to check Member States' executives, which would otherwise enjoy unfettered discretion in applying rules specifically designed to restrain those very actors. This is the classic theme of constitutionalism, which seeks to contain political power in order to safeguard the autonomy of the individual. From a constitutionalist perspective, the enactment of a WTO norm that would define the criteria of direct applicability, clarify who is entitled to invoke direct effect, and explicitly allow the direct effect of WTO provisions satisfying the established criteria might be a good idea. Provisions which are suited to direct effect are in essence those provisions whose concretisation can, under a theory of delegation informed by the rule of law, be legitimately delegated to a judge.[64] But because the application of those WTO norms by domestic courts bears the risk of divergent case law, the admission of direct effect would ideally have to be accompanied by a system of referral to the international adjudicative organs for preliminary rulings in order to harmonise the interpretation of WTO law. Moreover, the development of WTO law by domestic judges, triggered by private claimants, would have

---

[60]   Case 6/64, *Costa v Ente Nazionale Energie Elettrica (ENEL)* [1964] ECR 585.

[61]   Case C-149/96, *Portuguese Republic v Council of the European Union* [1999] ECR I-8395, paras 34–52; Case C-377/02, *Léon Van Parys NV v Belgisch Interventie-en Restitutiebureau* [2005] ECR I-1465, paras 38–54; Case T-174/00, *Biret International SA v Council of the European Union* (Court of First Instance), [2002] ECR II-17, para 62.

[62]   *United States – Section 301–310 of the Trade Act of 1974*, WTO Panel (27 January 2000) WT/DS152/R, not appealed, para 7.72: 'Neither the GATT nor the WTO has so far been interpreted by GATT/WTO institutions as a legal order producing direct effect [ie as creating enforceable rights and obligations for individuals]'. It would be better to speak of an 'indirect effect' of GATT (para 7.78).

[63]   T Cottier, 'A Theory of Direct Effect in Global Law' in A von Bogdandy, PC Mavroidis and Y Mény (eds), *European Integration and International Co-ordination: Studies in Transnational Economic Law in Honour of Claus-Dieter Ehlermann* (The Hague, London, New York, Kluwer Law International, 2002) 99, 114–15.

[64]   *ibid*, 118–19.

to be accompanied (and eventually corrected) by WTO rule-making processes in which those private actors could also participate.

In conclusion, constitutionalisation along the lines of enforcing Member State compliance through domestic courts presently obtains only with regard to the human rights treaty regimes and the European Union, but not in respect of other international organisations. It demands careful, further consideration as a constitutionalisation strategy.

IX. THE CONSTITUTIONALISATION OF ORGANISATIONS AS JUDICIAL
SELF-EMPOWERMENT

The suspicion of a *gouvernement des juges* is confirmed by the insight that all international courts and tribunals, be it the International Court of Justice, the ICTY, the European Court of Human Rights or the ECJ, have employed constitutional and constitutionalist arguments only in one context, namely that of judicial control or review. In every single case, the underlying issue was the power and the autonomy of the respective court. Each time, the result of the constitutionalist reading of the treaty at issue was to preserve, defend, confirm, or even enlarge the competence of the court. Whether self-empowerment was the hidden agenda of the courts or only a side-effect, it was always the outcome.

The most obvious example of this is the ECJ. Already the *Les Verts* judgment had the consequence of enlarging the competences of the Court by submitting acts of the European Parliament to judicial control, although the Treaty at that time did not include these acts.[65] Also in the opinion on the European Economic Area (EEA),[66] the competences of the ECJ were at issue. In the first version of the EEA Treaty, to be concluded between the EC and third party states, it was foreseen that the ECJ should be accompanied by a new EEA Court. This scheme would have threatened the autonomy and the monopoly of the ECJ as the ultimate interpreter of the Community legal order. It looks as though the Court invoked the constitutional character of the EC Treaty in order to preserve its monopoly. Finally, the ECJ's opinion on the accession of the EC to the ECHR was along the same lines. Here the Court found that the European Community was not competent to accede to the ECHR, because the general clause of Article 352 of the Treaty on the Function of the European Union (then Article 235, later Article 308, of the EC Treaty) did not provide a sufficient legal basis. The reason why the general clause was not deemed sufficient

[65] Case 294/83, *Parti Ecologiste 'Les Verts' v European Parliament* [1986] ECR 1339, para 23.
[66] Opinion 1/91, *Draft Agreement relating to the creation of the European Economic Area* [1991] ECR I-6079, 6102, para 21.

was that the accession to the ECHR would 'engender a substantial change of the current regime ... because it would imply the insertion of the Community in a distinct institutional system'. Such a move would – according to the ECJ – 'involve a constitutional dimension', which would not be covered by the former Article 235 of the EC Treaty.[67] The entry into a distinct institutional system meant, in effect, the submission of the ECJ to the ECHR, or at least that the ECJ be forced to cooperate in some formalised way with the institutions of the ECHR. Faced with these prospects, the ECJ characterised the issue as one of constitutional change which could not be effected without an explicit treaty basis, and so had to be relinquished, thus saving the 'autonomy' of the ECJ in the interim.

For many academics and judges, the characterisation of a treaty as a constitution has a practical consequence for its interpretation.[68] The International Court of Justice and the European Court of Human Rights concluded that *because* of a given treaty's constitutional quality (in these cases the WHO Charter and the ECHR respectively), the appropriate method of interpretation was teleological and dynamic rather than historical and static.[69] The underlying assertion is that the teleological interpretation is the quintessential method of constitutional interpretation. But this view is not generally shared. For example, a core methodological principle of Swiss courts is the 'unity of methods of interpretation' for the judicial interpretation of laws and of the Swiss Constitution.[70] A particular and distinct method of interpretation for the Constitution is explicitly rejected in Swiss law. So the idea that constitutions must be interpreted teleologically requires a justification which would have to rely on particular features of constitutional texts, such as on their typical open-endedness.[71] The appropriate method of interpretation cannot be simply deduced from the characterisation of a text as a constitution, as the European Court of Human Rights and the International Court of Justice did. The consequence or side-effect of the courts' resort to teleological interpretation was, of course, to grant the interpreting institution itself more leeway, and thus to increase its political and institutional standing. So again one witnesses an instance of judicial self-empowerment.

---

[67] Opinion 2/94 of 28 March 1996, *Accession by the Community to the Europrean Convention for the Protection of Human Rights and Fundamental Freedoms*, [1996] ECR I-1759, paras 34–35.

[68] See notably T Sato, *Evolving Constitutions of International Organizations: A Critical Analysis of the Interpretative Framework of the Constituent Instruments of International Organizations* (The Hague, Kluwer Law International, 1996) esp 229–32.

[69] *Legality of the Use by a State of Nuclear Weapons in Armed Conflict* (Advisory Opinion), [1996] ICJ Rep 66, para 19; *Loizidou v Turkey* (preliminary exceptions) ECHR (1995) Series A 310, para 71.

[70] Swiss Federal Tribunal, see only BGE 116a I a 359 E 5c (1990), BGE 131 I 174 E 4.1. (2005).

[71] See in this sense Fassbender, 'United Nations Charter', above n 6, 595–98.

The *Tadic* judgment of the ICTY Appeals Chamber also dealt with the competence of the Tribunal. Besides confirming that a Security Council Resolution was a sufficient legal basis for the ICTY, the *Tadic* Chamber approached the question from a human rights perspective. Every person is entitled to access to a court which has been established by law (see, for example, Article 14 of the International Covenant on Civil and Political Rights or Article 6 of the ECHR). These provisions relate to domestic courts and are addressed to national legislators. The new move of the *Tadic* judgment was to apply the underlying principle also to an international tribunal. In that situation, the legal basis can obviously not be a parliamentary law. The *Tadic* Chamber deemed it sufficient that the international tribunal is 'in accordance with the rule of law', and named the relevant requirements, such as guarantees of equity and impartiality. It concluded that these conditions were met in the case of the ICTY.[72] Consequently, the Tribunal was lawful and competent. Again, a judicial institution here raised the constitutional sceptre to confirm its own jurisdiction and so to defend and even enlarge its political station. However, this strategy is not improper, given the fact that judicial review is a core quest of constitutionalism.

X. DEMOCRATISATION OF INTERNATIONAL ORGANISATIONS

The judge-made and rather rights-focused process of sectoral constitutionalisation has so far not contained a strong democratic element. But the democratisation of international organisations is exceedingly difficult.[73]

A. Engaging National Parliaments

Subtle and not over-ambitious methods of engaging the UN with national parliaments have been suggested by the Cardoso Report of 2004.[74] The expert report recommended a four-pronged strategy for the democratisation of the United Nations: take UN issues to national parliaments more systematically; ensure that parliamentarians coming to UN events have

---

[72] Case No IT-94–1-AR72, *Prosecutor v Dusko Tadic, Decision on the Defence Motion for Interlocutory Appeal on Jurisdiction*, ICTY Appeals Chamber of 2 October 1995, paras 45–47.
[73] See for the problems of democracy on the global level Peters, 'Dual Democracy', above n 41, 263–341.
[74] Report of the Panel of Eminent Persons on United Nations – Civil Society Relations (Cardoso Report), 7 June 2004, proposals 13–18 and Part VI, 'Engaging with elected representatives' (national parliaments), notably by an elected representatives liaison unit (paras 101–52, also in executive summary pp 10 and 19–20).

more strategic roles at those events; link parliaments themselves with international deliberative processes; and provide an institutional home in the UN for engaging parliamentarians.[75] To that end, the Cardoso Report suggested two novel institutions.

First, 'global public policy committees' should be created within the UN, as a global equivalent to national parliamentary standing committees. Such committees should comprise up to 30 parliamentarians (from the relevant national functional parliamentary committees) and be regionally representative. An initial approach might be to invite countries serving on the General Committee of the General Assembly to participate. The function of the global public policy committees would be to forward policy proposals and scrutinise progress on past agreements. They would submit reports to the Secretary-General. This could incrementally lead to globally representative committees on all global priorities, with the right to submit policy recommendations and progress audits to the UN and to Member States.

Additionally, the Secretary-General should form a small, elected representatives' liaison unit (akin to the existing non-governmental liaison service), whose function would be to inform members of national parliaments and to suggest topics for parliamentary debate.[76]

The Cardoso Report proposals were modest and reasonable. Unfortunately, they were not adopted by the General Assembly. In its debate on the Cardoso Report, the Assembly did not discuss in any detail liaison with national parliaments and approached the issue of civil society participation very cautiously, emphasising the inter-governmental nature of the United Nations.[77]

B.   Participatory Democracy: Involvement of Interest Groups

One strategy would be to involve interest groups, notably professional associations in the organisation's decision-making processes. This model

---

[75]   Cardoso Report, 2004, para 102.

[76]   Moreover, the Cardoso Report asked the UN to routinely encourage national parliaments to hold debates on major matters coming up in the UN, and to make the relevant documents available to the parliaments. In that way, national parliaments could debate General Assembly issues in advance, the General Assembly might take note, and this would widen the policy options (proposal 13). Also, Member States should more regularly include members of parliament in their delegations to major UN meetings, while taking care to avoid compromising the independence of parliamentarians (proposal 14).

[77]   General Assembly Plenary Debates of 4 and 5 October 2004 (press releases GA/10268 and GA/10270).

reflects a concept of participatory democracy rather than 'formal' electoral democracy. It has been endorsed for the European Union by Article 11(1)–(3) of the 2007 EU Treaty.[78]

A *'représentation professionelle internationale'*, covering employers and employees, the agricultural sector, the liberal professions and other groups had already been recommended by Georges Scelle in 1927 for the democratisation of the League of Nations as a more realistic alternative to a world parliament. Scelle placed great emphasis on the possibility of the expression of diverse interests and the development of a global public opinion through this process.[79] He thus foreshadowed participatory and deliberative democracy in a world organisation.

A representation of professional interest groups has been realised in the International Labour Organization. However, ILO tripartism has so far not been an encouraging example which would recommend itself to other international organisations. In its law-making body, the international labour conference, each Member State of the organisation is represented by a delegation consisting of two government delegates, an employer delegate, a worker delegate, and their respective advisers. The ILO has been fairly successful in adopting global labour standards. The labour conventions have to be formally ratified by governments, and Member States are obliged to undertake ratification within 18 months and to report back to the Director-General in the case of non-ratification.[80] However, although – or perhaps precisely because – the norms have been produced in participation with non-state actors who have not only a voice, but a vote, in that process, the ratification status of many ILO conventions remains woefully low.[81] ILO-type powers for interest group representatives should therefore not be introduced to the decision-making bodies of other international organisations.

[78] Art 11 TEU: '(1) The institutions shall, by appropriate means, give citizens and representative associations the opportunity to make known and publicly exchange their views in all areas of Union action. (2) The institutions shall maintain an open, transparent and regular dialogue with representative associations and civil society. (3) The European Commission shall carry out broad consultations with parties concerned in order to ensure that the Union's actions are coherent and transparent'. (Art 11(4) concerns the citizens' initiative).

[79] G Scelle, *Une crise de la société des nations* (Paris, Presses universitaires de France, 1927) 142–46, 157.

[80] Article 19(5) ILO Constitution, 38 UNTS 3.

[81] See for the ratification status of the ILO conventions: www.ilo.org/ilolex/english/newratframeE.htm. See in more detail on the problems of tripartism in a globalised world F Maupain, 'L'OIT, la justice sociale et la mondialisation' (1999) 278 *Recueil des Cours* 201, 331–86.

C.   Democratisation of State Assemblies in International Organisations

A yet different strategy would be to bring citizens' weight to bear within the existing state assemblies, notably within the UN General Assembly. To this end, the Member State delegates, who are now appointed by governments, could be in part directly elected (eg one out of the five delegates to the UN General Assembly). It could be made a condition that the national parliamentary opposition is also represented. The size of Member States' delegations could be differentiated, or Member States' votes could be weighted according to a composite index which includes population (and possibly also national income). Alternatively, the voting scheme could strike a middle ground between state equality and citizens' equality, such as the double majority in the EU Council.[82] Such devices are not only familiar in international organisations, but are also used in domestic constitutional law for the composition of the second parliamentary chamber in some federations (such as for the German *Bundesrat*).

D.   Expanding and Invigorating Parliamentary Assemblies in International Organisations

Finally, the most powerful organisations, such as the United Nations, the Bretton Woods Institutions and the World Trade Organization, where parliamentary assemblies are conspicuously absent, could be parliamentarised. For example, proposals to create a Parliamentary Assembly in the WTO have been sponsored by the Inter-Parliamentary Union (IPU) and the European Parliament, but have been opposed by the United States and many developing countries.[83]

(i)   *Parliamentary Assemblies in Current International Law*

Parliamentary assemblies exist in currently 45 international organisations in all world regions, and there is also the Inter-Parliamentary Union. The European Parliament forms an exception. It is directly elected by the EU citizens, and it has legislative and other powers that have been continuously strengthened in the course of the reforms of the founding treaties.

---

[82] Art 238 Treaty on the Functioning of the European Union (TFEU) of 13 December 2007 ([2008] OJ C115/47) (Art 205(1) and (2) TEC).

[83] See the parliamentary conference on the WTO convened by EU Parliament and IPU calling for a parliamentary dimension to the WTO (final declaration of 18 February 2003). See also G Shaffer, 'Parliamentary Oversight of WTO-Rulemaking? The Political, Normative, and Practical Contexts' (2004) 7 *Journal of International Economic* 629–54; E Mann, 'Parliamentary Dimensions in the WTO – More than Just a Vision?' (2004) 7 *Journal of International Economic Law* 659–65.

With the Lisbon amendment, the European Parliament has become a co-legislator in most fields of EU legislation,[84] elects the Commission President, votes on the appointment of the entire Commission[85] and establishes the annual EU budget.[86]

All other existing assemblies under the law as it stands are not parliaments in a constitutionalist sense, because their members are not directly elected by citizens, they do not have law-making and budgetary powers, and they do not elect the organisation's 'executive'. They have memberships ranging from 27 (in the East African Assembly) to 2,000 parliamentarians or former members of national parliaments. They are normally not composed according to the scheme 'one state, one vote', but in consideration of the population sizes of their Member States.

The most powerful – or least powerless – assembly (leaving aside the European Parliament) is the Assembly of the Council of Europe.[87] The Hague Congress of 1948 had demanded, 'as a matter of real urgency, the convening of a European Assembly' designed 'to stimulate and give expression to a European public opinion'.[88] The Statute of the Council of Europe named this body the 'Consultative Assembly', but the assembly has called itself the 'Parliamentary Assembly' since 1974. After the end of the Cold War, the assembly began to influence the policy of admission of new Member States to the Council of Europe from Eastern and Central Europe and to perform an assessment of the internal political and legal system of candidate states. The Assembly thus benefitted from the transition period to increase its political weight in the institutional balance, although its formal competencies were not extended. This power gain was probably facilitated by the existence of relatively clear legal standards for membership to the Council of Europe, and by the strong incentive for (Eastern) European states to accede to the organisation. Any new parliamentary assembly, for example in the WTO, might acquire an equally assertive role if accession conditions and incentives were similarly clear.

---

[84] Art 294 TFEU.
[85] Art 17(7) TEU in the version of the Lisbon Treaty.
[86] Art 314 TFEU.
[87] Arts 22–35 Statute of the Council of Europe of 23 October 1954.
[88] Political Resolution at the Congress of Europe, The Hague (7–10 May 1948), leading to the foundation of the Council of Europe, para 8 (a). Resolutions, London and Paris: International Committee of the Movements for European Unity (no date), at 5–7, available via www.ena.lu).

(ii)   A Parliamentary Assembly in the United Nations?

With regard to the United Nations, the idea of a Global Parliamentary Assembly has been supported by the European Parliament,[89] by the Parliamentary Assembly of the Council of Europe[90] and by the civil society organisations' Millennium Forum.[91] In 2007, a civil society network of NGOs, parliamentarians, activists and academics, among them former UN Secretary-General Boutros-Ghali,[92] launched the Campaign for a United Nations Parliamentary Assembly of around 800 delegates.

Such a UN Parliamentary Assembly could be established as a subsidiary organ to the General Assembly by a decision of the General Assembly under Article 22 of the UN Charter, and would require no amendment to the Charter.[93] Deputies would be either members of national parliaments (dual mandate) or would be specifically elected by the parliaments. The number of deputies would be roughly proportionate to the population of the UN Member States, with minority protection for small states.[94] Once in place, the Parliamentary Assembly could, on the basis of the implied power doctrine, arguably even develop proposals for direct elections by the world's citizens.[95]

The creation of an additional UN Parliamentary Assembly alongside the General Assembly would be in institutional terms more incisive than the Cardoso Report proposals. The model of two assemblies in the UN has a federalist ring. In a global federalist scheme, the General Assembly as the Member States' chamber would become a 'second' chamber.

The UN Parliamentary Assembly would in the foreseeable future not acquire the traditional parliamentary competences of law-making, creation and control of the government. A competence to enact binding decisions or

---

[89]   The EP invited the UN Secretary-General and the UN's political bodies, to extend cooperation with the EU Council and Commission to the European Parliament by jointly launching 'a network of parliamentarians' (Resolution on the Relations between the EU and the UN (2003/2049 (INI)) of 29 January 2004, para 39).

[90]   Recommendation 1476 (2000) of 27 September 2000 of the Parliamentary Assembly of the Council of Europe, 'encourages the UN to start developing, in close co-operation with the Inter-Parliamentary Union, a parliamentary dimension' (para 13).

[91]   'We the Peoples Millennium Forum Declaration and Agenda for Action, Strengthening the UN for the 21st Century' of 26 May 2000, Part F, para 6: The Forum urges the UN to consider the creation of a consultative parliamentary assembly (UN Doc A/54/959, at 16).

[92]   Campaign for the Establishment of a United Nations Parliamentary Assembly, www.unpacampaign.org/. A list of signatures is available on the website.

[93]   The formal status as a subsidiary organ would not adequately reflect the Assembly's political and symbolical significance, but seems the only realistically attainable one.

[94]   For instance, in a total assembly of 560 members, China would have 31 seats, countries up to one million inhabitants would have one seat; D Archibugi, 'From the United Nations to Cosmopolitan Democracy' in D Archibugi and David Held (eds), *Cosmopolitan Democracy: An Agenda for a New World Order* (Cambridge, Polity Press, 1995) 121, 142.

[95]   An example for such an evolution is the EU Parliament, which was initially composed of parliamentarians and only in a second stage based on direct elections.

to adopt treaties is currently even denied to the states' chamber, the General Assembly, and seems out of the question for a new Parliamentary Assembly. In addition, the ILO scheme for the adoption of binding instruments with votes of non-state delegates functions badly. Even if the Security Council was conceived as an analogy to a UN Government, this 'Government' is – under the law as it stands – not elected and is unaccountable to either the General Assembly or any potential UN Parliamentary Assembly.

The creation of an elected and accountable Security Council therefore seems out of reach, as does parliamentary control in the form of a motion of censure. The UN Parliamentary Assembly might, alternatively, share budgetary power with the General Assembly.[96] This seems to be a classical parliamentary power. But the analogy is misleading as long as the budget rules are not radically changed. Because – under the law as it stands – the UN budget is comparatively small, as the regular budget does not cover important positions, notably peace keeping forces, and because the organisation depends on the fragile 'payment morals' of the Member States, the General Assembly (and any potential UN Parliamentary Assembly) lacks the political power associated with budgetary control in democratic states. Potential functions of the Parliamentary Assembly could neverthless consist in the following: it would be consulted by the General Assembly and by other UN organs; major draft resolutions would be read before they were voted on by the General Assembly; the Parliamentary Assembly would convey opinions and have a procedure for questioning the principal organs; it could request that policies adopted by the General Assembly be extended or amended; and it could propose new policies.[97] The greatest short-term potential of a UN Parliamentary Assembly lies in the parliamentary function of socialisation and mediation and in the strengthening of national parliaments as described above. The Parliamentary Assembly would inform national parliaments about UN and global policies and vice versa. To that end, delegates of the UN Parliamentary Assembly should have access to Security Council meetings and to inter-governmental conferences.

Even with such limited powers, an additional UN Parliamentary Assembly would be more democratic than the current UN General Assembly for three basic reasons. First, the parliamentarians are closer to the citizens than the members of the executive and diplomats who represent the Member States in the UN General Assembly. Secondly, population size would be taken into account in fixing the number of delegates per state. Thirdly, the delegates to the UN Parliamentary Assembly would reflect the

---

[96] Art 17 UN Charter.
[97] E Childers and B Urquhart, *Renewing the United Nations System* (Uppsala, Dag Hammarskjöld Foundation, 1994) 179.

political composition of the national parliaments and include members of the opposition. The initially merely consultative competences of the Assembly would – as opposed to law-making competences – exactly reflect the idea of a citizens' *voice* (not vote) on a global level.

(iii)   The Democratic Added Value of Parliamentary Assemblies

The pivotal question is whether the establishment of new parliamentary assemblies and the strengthening the powers of existing ones is a viable strategy to democratise international organisations.[98] One objection is that this strategy overstates the significance of parliaments for democracy. Due to email and internet, with their networking options for active citizens, and due to dependency on experts, parliaments may be in decline. Also, the limited political impact of existing parliamentary assemblies counsels against undue expectations. Another shortcoming is that citizens whose states do not have a parliament, or whose parliament does not emerge from free and fair elections, will not be truly represented in the orgnisations' parliamentary assemblies.

If new assemblies, such as to the UN and the WTO, were modelled on existing ones, which under current law cannot directly influence the organisations' decision-making processes, they would not produce a tangible democratic output. But even merely consultative assemblies perform the typical mediating function of parliaments, create transparency and organise interests. Due to their 'parliamentary' quality, even purely consultative assemblies can open public debates or make public statements for which diplomats are not prepared, they can pave the way for negotiations (or disturb them) and they can promote a political dialogue at the level of parliaments, political parties and civil society. For example, during the Iraq crisis of 2003, transnational interests were articulated in the NATO Parliamentary Assembly and the Parliamentary Assembly of the Western European Union.

Moreover, even consultative parliamentary assemblies may strengthen the role of national parliaments in foreign policy. This depends on good communication between parliamentary assemblies and national parliaments. Another condition of success is that national parliaments must have competencies in foreign politics, or must at least be able to influence policies through their spending power. The impact of parliamentary assemblies makes a difference especially in the field of security policy, because this domain is traditionally closest to domestic parliaments. Here

---

[98] Sceptically, S Marschall, *Transnationale Repräsentation in Parlamentarischen Versammlungen* (Baden-Baden, Nomos, 2005) 334.

parliamentary assemblies can frustrate the two-level games of governmental representative and prevent scapegoating by providing information on the various national and international actors and their political positions. The dual mandate of parliamentarians (who are at the same time members of their national parliaments and of the international assembly) is important here, because it creates a specific 'two-level capacity' which can compensate for the absent formal powers of the assembly. Overall, even consultative parliamentary assemblies can contribute to the democratisation of international organisations in this indirect way via national parliaments. In conclusion, the establishment of parliamentary assemblies in the Bretton Woods Institutions, the UN and the WTO seems worth trying as a first and relatively modest building block of the democratisation of international organisations.

XI. SECTORAL CONSTITUTIONALISATION AS PART OF GLOBAL MULTI-LEVEL CONSTITUTIONALISATION

Sectoral constitutionalisation as analysed and developed in this chapter raises the spectre of fragmentation. When different organisations have their own constitution, how can they still be members of a global constitutional order? I submit that the various processes of constitutionalisation on different levels are not mutually exclusive. Global constitutionalism is pluralist, and it relates to multi-level governance. It implies nested constitutional orders. This is no anomaly, given the fact that within a constitutional state, sub units (such as states within federal states, or local communities) have their own constitutions. From that perspective, it can be easily accepted that the members of a global constitutional order, notably nation states and international organisations, may have their own sectoral constitutions. The result is multi-level constitutionalism.

The very idea of multiple and multi-level constitutionalism implicitly gives up the claim to totality raised by proponents of a more traditional notion of constitution. I submit in response that this claim can in any event no longer be satisfied under conditions of globalisation. Even state constitutions do not govern or regulate all acts of governance which produce effects on their citizens or within their territorial borders. Totality is no longer a relevant quality of constitutions, if ever it was.

11

The European Union in the Global Constitutional Mosaic

JAN KLABBERS*

I. INTRODUCTION

I F THE NOTION of a constitutional world order is taken seriously, its underlying constitution would probably be expected to have a few provisions on some of the staples of constitutionalism.[1] One might expect a global constitutional order to have, for instance, a basic notion of democracy and political participation, in order to do justice to the label 'constitutional'. After all, a typical function of constitutions, and thus of constitutional thought, is to define membership of the relevant political community, and regulate how significant policy decisions are made. One might, likewise, expect some basic rules about how the law should be made and the judiciary organised, for again, those are typically functions performed by modern constitutions. And one might legitimately expect that basic community values (whatever these values may be) are somehow given protection: again, many modern constitutions do so by providing for a catalogue of human rights.[2]

The above would seem to be among the skeleton expectations of any constitutional setting, including the global constitutional setting. In addition, one might expect some statements on how the rules of the system

---

* Professor of International Law, University of Helsinki, and Director of the Academy of Finland Centre of Excellence in Global Governance Research. At the time of writing he was one of the inaugural fellows at the Straus Institute for the Advanced Study of Law and Justice, New York University.

[1] I do not claim here that such an order actually exists; my more modest claim is that if there is – or would be – a global constitutional order, it can – or could – legitimately be expected to somehow address some or all of the issues mentioned in the opening paragraphs.

[2] See generally Jan Klabbers, Anne Peters and Geir Ulfstein, *The Constitutionalization of International Law* (Oxford, Oxford University Press, 2009).

relate to each other: borrowing Hart's terms,[3] one might expect a global constitutional order to contain secondary rules concerning the interactions and relations between and among primary rules, in much the same way as domestic constitutions often contain rules about how formal legislation relates to governmental decrees or municipal ordinances or, in federal systems, state law.

In this chapter I will focus on such secondary rules: the rules regulating conflict between treaties, in particular with reference to the European Union. The underlying idea is to explore to what extent EU law and global law (ie international law, for present purposes[4]) are singing from the same hymn sheet or, more academically put, to explore the question to what extent the EU legal order, as exemplified in its rules governing the EU's external relations, is open to contact with international law, or whether it is closed to such contacts. If the latter is the case, as I think and will demonstrate it is, then a global constitutional mosaic is difficult to imagine in any practically meaningful sense, regardless of whether the international legal order itself is characterised as constitutional. As a result, perhaps the best one can hope for is a sense of responsibility (openness, humility, intellectual honesty) on the part of those involved in interpreting and applying the various legal regimes: here I will appeal to virtue ethics as a source of inspiration. Before going there, however, it may be useful to sketch the international legal background: the rules on treaty conflict.

II.   TREATY CONFLICT

International law does have rules on how other rules relate to each other, albeit in fairly limited measure; most visible and prominent are the rules relating to treaty conflict.[5] It is perhaps useful to spell out that these rules are more or less unique: there are few rules, if any, relating to conflict

---

[3]   This harks back to Herbert LA Hart, *The Concept of Law* (Oxford, Clarendon Press, 1961).

[4]   It is not uncommon to conceptualise global law (or world law) as coming closer to what earlier generations described as transnational law, as something of a third way between domestic law and international law. This transnational law would relate to norms which do not apply merely within or between states, but rather norms applicable to transboundary relations involving both state and non-state actors: human rights, *lex mercatoria*, rules governing international business transactions, etc. The *locus classicus* is Philip C Jessup, *Transnational Law* (New Haven, Yale University Press, 1956).

[5]   Useful recent studies include Guyora Binder, *Treaty Conflict and Political Contradiction: The Dialectic of Duplicity* (New York, Praeger, 1988); Jan Mus, *Verdragsconflicten voor de nederlandse rechter* (Zwolle, Tjeenk Willink, 1996); Joost Pauwelyn, *Conflict of Norms in Public International Law: How WTO Law Relates to Other Rules of International Law* (Cambridge, Cambridge University Press, 2003); Seyed Ali Sadat-Akhavi, *Methods of Resolving Conflicts between Treaties* (Leiden, Brill, 2003); Rüdiger Wolfrum and Nele Matz,

between customary international norms,[6] nor are there any very precise rules relating to conflicts between treaty rules and international customary rules,[7] or between treaty rules and general principles of law. But having said this, there are some rules relating to treaty conflicts.

One of these is Article 103 of the UN Charter: following the precedent of the League of Nations, which introduced the supremacy clause to international law,[8] obligations under the Charter shall prevail over any other obligations under public international law. Whilst the precise scope of this provision is subject to some debate, it is nonetheless clear that it serves to a large extent to make the exercise of collective security under UN auspices possible: states cannot escape from implementing sanctions by reference to other existing legal obligations towards the sanctioned state.[9]

The general provision on treaty conflict in international law is to be found in Article 30 of the Vienna Convention on the Law of Treaties (VCLT), which specifies that when treaties are concluded at different moments in time but between identical parties, the later in time shall prevail.[10] The underlying rationale is that the later in time (between the same parties) will provide the most accurate and up-to-date reflection of those parties' political desires and intentions, and will therefore be conducive to international order and stability. Put differently, trying to get states to adhere to treaty obligations they no longer support might put too much stress on the international legal order.[11]

Still, it was not a foregone conclusion that the Vienna Convention should come to embody the *lex posterior* maxim: a strong case can be built that this allows states to depart from earlier fundamental norms, as Sir

---

Conflicts in International Environmental Law (Berlin, Springer, 2003); and Martti Koskenniemi, 'Fragmentation of International Law: Difficulties Arising from the Diversification and Expansion of International Law'. Report of the Study Group of the International Law Commission (Helsinki, Erik Castrén Institute, 2007).

[6] Typically, conflict between customary norms is often 'reasoned away' on the basis that if one customary norm conflicts with an earlier one, the earlier one can no longer meaningfully be said to exist. While there is some truth in this, it may dissipate when the norm conflict involves different parties: *A* may have a conflict between an obligation under customary international law to *B* which does not chime with a different customary obligation towards *C*.

[7] Moreover, there may be issues involved in the development of customary law based on (but diverging from) treaty obligations.

[8] Article 20 of the Covenant; for a documentary history, see CA Kluyver (ed), *Documents on the League of Nations* (Leiden, Sijthoff, 1920). The term supremacy clause is used here for ease of reference; it may be doubted whether Article 20 Covenant (or Article 103 UN, for that matter) can properly be deemed supremacy clauses.

[9] A good discussion is Rain Liivoja, 'The Scope of the Supremacy Clause of the United Nations Charter' (2008) 57 *International and Comparative Law Quarterly* 583–612.

[10] Useful on questions of drafting is Sir Ian Sinclair, *The Vienna Convention on the Law of Treaties*, 2nd edn (Manchester, Manchester University Press, 1984).

[11] The classic doctrinal defence is Charles Rousseau, 'De la compatibilité des normes juridiques contradictoires dans l'ordre international' (1932) 39 *Revue Générale de Droit International Public* 133–92.

Hersch Lauterpacht noted in his first report as Special Rapporteur on the Law of Treaties.[12] Following the *lex posterior* rule, states can agree to outlaw torture, but later conclude an agreement allowing for torture. If all parties agree, the later agreement prevails, and this, needless to say, will not necessarily be conducive to peace and stability.

To some extent, this state of affairs may be mitigated by the concept of *jus cogens*: peremptory norms, once established, cannot be cast aside by a mere ordinary agreement – torture, once prohibited as a *jus cogens* norm, cannot be set aside by a later treaty. This, however elegant theoretically, might be difficult to maintain as a practical matter. If all parties agree that torture is allowable under certain circumstances, then either the torture prohibition loses its *jus cogens* character or (more likely perhaps, in practice) the new exception becomes part of the rule, and thus perfectly plausible. *Jus cogens* norms, notwithstanding their quasi-constitutional nature, are defenceless in the face of widespread political agreement.

Still, the more urgent practical legal issue arising from Article 30 of the VCLT is a different one, for Article 30 does not properly address the situation involving a conflict of treaty obligations between non-identical parties. If states *A* and *B* conclude a treaty, and *A* later concludes one with *C* which cannot be reconciled with its treaty with *B*, then Article 30 offers little solace. The reason for this is that as dogmatic matter, a treaty is *res inter alios acta* – a thing between the parties which, as a matter of principle, cannot be deemed to radiate outside its own circle of parties. This is one of the fundamental assumptions underlying the Vienna Convention. In the example, *B* has no connection to the treaty between *A* and *C*, and likewise, *C* has no connection to the *A-B* treaty. As a result, the application of a single rule is simply not possible. The *lex posterior* rule would be vulnerable to *B*'s critique that *A* and *C* cannot undermine *B*'s legal position. Likewise, the *lex prior* rule does the same in reverse, allowing *C* to argue that its legal position is independent of any arrangement that may exist between *A* and *B*. And the *lex specialis* rule will typically give rise to disputes over which of the treaties would be the special one, and which would be general.[13] And even when that is settled,

---

[12] See Hersch Lauterpacht, 'Report on the Law of Treaties' (1953) II *Yearbook of the International Law Commission* 90–166.

[13] In order to establish which one is special, does one look at the issue area? Does one look at the circle of parties? And how do considerations of morality come in? Surely, when a bilateral extradition treaty conflicts with a human rights treaty, the *lex specialis* rule might suggest that the extradition treaty ought to be given preference – but as an ethical matter such a position might be difficult to defend, and it is probably no coincidence that Dutch judges have invariably favoured application of the human rights treaty in such circumstances. See Mus, *Verdragsconflicten*. A summary version in English is Jan Mus, 'Conflicts between Treaties in International Law' (1998) 45 *Netherlands International Law Review* 208–32.

the losing state can still point out that it should not be victimised by the desire of other states to create a special regime.[14]

At this point, it may be useful to draw attention to the distinction between bilateral and multilateral treaties, because there is a curious paradox at work with regard to that distinction. With bilateral treaties, things are easy as long as they concern treaties between identical parties. Here, Article 30 of the VCLT works, and even if it did not, Article 59 of the VLCT might step in, providing as it does that an earlier treaty may be cast aside by a later one. Yet, there is no way out when non-identical parties are concerned; at best, the party which has created the conflicting obligations (state *A*, in our example) will have to choose which treaty to favour, and compensate the losing party. In good German, this is known as *Das Prinzip der politischen Entscheidung* (the principle of political decision), a phrase likely coined by Manfred Zuleeg.[15]

Yet, with multilateral treaties, the situation is to some extent the reverse. Whilst here, too, problems are manageable when identical parties are concerned, the more likely scenario will be one involving non-identical parties. Under such a scenario, the favoured solution is to have the later treaty apply to those parties that accept it, whereas the rest will continue to apply the older one. This sounds neat, and might actually work under two conditions.

First, as the title of Article 30 of the VCLT suggests, it might work if the treaties concerned address the same subject-matter. In such a case, the treaty is not likely to involve conflicting values, but will rather set a coordination problem and these, by their very nature, may be easier to solve than clashes between values.[16] It is no doubt for this reason that the Vienna Convention would, at first sight, seem to limit the scope of Article 30 to treaties dealing with the same subject-matter, judging by the title of Article 30.[17] Upon reflection, though, it seems unlikely that the drafters of the Vienna Convention could have intended not to address the more difficult cases of treaties involving different subject-matter, and there is no evidence in the Vienna Convention of a conscious intention to leave the issue un-addressed.[18]

---

[14] The *lex specialis* rule would seem to have little or no application in connection with bilateral treaties, precisely for this reason. A useful discussion of its application is Anja Lindroos, 'Addressing Norm Conflicts in a Fragmented Legal System: The Doctrine of *Lex Specialis*' (2005) 74 *Nordic Journal of International Law* 27–66.

[15] See Manfred Zuleeg, 'Vertragskonkurrenz im Völkerrecht. Teil I: Verträge zwischen souveränen Staaten' (1977) 20 *German Yearbook of International Law* 246–76.

[16] For elaboration see Jan Klabbers, *Treaty Conflict and the European Union* (Cambridge, Cambridge University Press, 2008).

[17] For an argument to this effect, see Christopher J Borgen, 'Resolving Treaty Conflicts' (2005) 37 *George Washington International Law Review* 573–648.

[18] For a discussion of the preparatory works on this point, see Klabbers, *Treaty Conflict*, above n 16, 85–86.

There is a second element required before resorting to the solution of applying the later treaty between willing parties whilst leaving the earlier one in place between reluctant partners, and that is that the treaty must allow itself to be bilateralised, so as to create distinct bilateral relationships between dyads of parties. A good example of such a treaty would be a multilateral extradition treaty: since extradition is principally a bilateral matter, a request by A to B will typically create a bilateral relationship, even if the underlying legal regime is concluded in multilateral fashion. It is different though, typically with human rights treaties, treaties establishing international organisations, and (some) environmental treaties. These tend to create common regimes, which cannot be subdivided into dyads of bilateral relations. It makes little sense to say that the UN Charter creates bilateral relations between The Netherlands and Belgium, The Netherlands and Norway, The Netherlands and Brazil, etc, and it makes even less sense to claim as much with respect to human rights treaties. With environmental treaties, perhaps bilateralisation is an option; one can conceive of emissions trading regimes, for instance, as fundamentally bilateral in nature, even if based on multilateral regimes. *Mutatis mutandis*, much the same can apply to trade agreements: these can be multilateral in nature, but can also be bilateralised.[19]

In many cases, however, neither of these two conditions applies and if so, it can only mean that under Article 30 of the VCLT the treaty conflict cannot be resolved. In those cases, then, nothing remains but the application of Zuleeg's *Prinzip der Politischen Entscheidung*: the state concerned will have to choose which treaty to honour, and compensate the party losing out. That is not necessarily a bad thing, as it opens up a space for debate and deliberation as to which solution might be most proper, but it does mean that certainty and predictability are cast aside. Moreover, precisely in the context of non-bilateralisable treaties, compensation of those losing out may not be the most practical or realistic option.

III.   THE EU RULES IN BRIEF OUTLINE

If the general rules of the Vienna Convention do not offer much guidance, there is always the possibility in international law that its decentralised regimes take care of things. Nothing bars states establishing a regime to create their own norms as to what to do if and when their regime ends up in conflict with norms emanating from elsewhere. To some extent this is

---

[19]   For a suggestion that WTO obligations are bilateral in nature, see Joost Pauwelyn, 'A Typology of Multilateral Treaty Obligations: Are WTO Obligations Bilateral or Collective in Nature?' (2003) 14 *European Journal of International Law* 907–51.

true of the European Union, which has its own sets of rules to address treaty conflict in a variety of settings.

Analytically, it might be useful to note that EC law (broadly conceived[20]) deals with various different circumstances. The most well-known setting (and the only one which is explicitly addressed in the EC treaty itself) relates to the protection of treaties entered into by the EC Member States before the creation of the EC or before they joined the EC (these will be referred to as 'anterior treaties').[21] In addition, there is some case law (but no explicit provision) on what may be called 'posterior treaties', ie treaties concluded by Member States (either with each other or with third parties) after the entry into force of the EC treaty or, as the case may be, after they joined the EC.[22] Thirdly, there is case law on the relationship between EC law and general international law. Fourthly, there are good reasons to single out the relationship between EC law and the UN Charter; and fifthly, there are good reasons to do the same with respect to the relationship between EC law and the European Convention on Human Rights (ECHR). The UN Charter is sometimes deemed to be the constitution of the international community[23] and, moreover, does have its own provision on conflicting obligations in the form of Article 103; hence, this may be expected to influence the relationship between EC and UN law. Something similar may apply to the ECHR, which is also sometimes deemed to be constitutional in nature (at least in accordance with the case law of its own judicial body, the European Court of Human Rights).[24]

An important point to note before digging deeper, however, is that much of the relevant law stems from the European Court of Justice (ECJ). The EC Treaty itself offers only the contribution of Article 351 TFEU (ex Art 307 EC), and this, arguably, is also dominated by the particular way in which the ECJ has addressed the issue. Hence, much of the law on the relationship between international law and EC law is judge-made law. And all of it, by and large, is dominated by a single theme: the ECJ is more

---

[20] In what follows, I will ignore the distinction between the EU and the EC and will treat the terms as synonymous, except in those instances where the distinction is legally relevant.

[21] An excellent treatment is to be found in Panos Koutrakos, *EU International Relations Law* (Oxford, Hart Publishing, 2006) 301–28.

[22] This has received scant treatment in the literature. One of the rare exceptions is Bruno de Witte, 'Old-fashioned Flexibility: International Agreements between Member States of the European Union' in Grainne de Burca and Joanne Scott (eds), *Constitutional Change in the EU: From Uniformity to Flexibility?* (Oxford, Hart Publishing, 2000) 31–58.

[23] For a sustained argument to this effect, see Bardo Fassbender, *The United Nations Charter as the Constitution of the International Community* (Leiden, Martinus Nijhoff, 2009).

[24] See *Loizidou v Turkey*, judgment of 23 February 1995, para 75: the Convention is 'a constitutional instrument of European public order'. Interestingly, when citing this passage, a former president of the Strasbourg Court sometimes omits the term 'constitutional'. See Luzius Wildhaber, 'The European Convention on Human Rights and International Law' (2007) 56 *International and Comparative Law Quarterly* 217–32.

interested in guaranteeing the unity of EU law than it is in upholding the international legal order. As far as constitutional mosaics go, then, the position of the EU in the international legal order is determined by the ECJ and on the ECJ's terms.

The above proposition can be illustrated with the help of four fairly recent sets of decisions. In the spring of 2009, the ECJ rendered judgment in two cases involving bilateral investment treaties (BITs) concluded by individual Member States with third parties before having joined the EU, with a third case still pending.[25] In 2002, it rendered judgments in a number of cases involving air traffic agreements with a single third party, the United States. In 2000, in *Schmidberger*, it spelled out the connection with human rights law, which has obvious ramifications for the place of the ECHR in the EU legal order. And in September 2008 it presented its judgment in the already infamous *Kadi* case. All these sets of decisions illustrate the same tendency – and many more could have been used.[26]

At issue in the *BIT* cases was the conclusion of a number of bilateral investment treaties between Sweden and Austria respectively, and a number of third states.[27] These treaties, all concluded before Swedish and Austrian accession to the EU, included a provision guaranteeing the unimpeded movement of currency between the EU Member State and the third party concerned. The Commission felt that this was now incompatible with certain obligations under the EC Treaty that allow for the imposition of obstacles to currency movements with third parties as an instrument of Community policy, for example, to implement UN sanctions. As a result, the Commission started legal proceedings against both Sweden and Austria, suggesting that these two Member States had failed to fulfill their obligations under EC law by not taking appropriate steps to eliminate such incompatibilities.

The Member States concerned responded that until such Community measures were actually taken, no incompatibility could be demonstrated, and so the provisions on free currency movement between the Member States and the relevant third parties were saved by the general protection of anterior treaties under Article 351(1) TFEU; at best, the Commission was acting on an assumption. Moreover, under international law it would be possible to rapidly re-negotiate the investment treaty if necessary, or even suspend its operation under appeal to the *rebus sic stantibus* rule: this rule allows for suspension upon a radical change of circumstances.

---

[25]   This is Case C-118/07 *Commission v Finland* [2009] ECR I-10889. Advocate-General Sharpston delivered her opinion on 10 September 2009 and found that Finland had failed to fulfill its obligations under Article 351 TFEU.

[26]   See generally Klabbers, *Treaty Conflict*, above n 16.

[27]   See case C-205/06 *Commission v Austria*, [2009] ECR I-1301, judgment of 3 March 2009; Case C-249/06 *Commission v Sweden*, [2009] ECR I-1335, judgment of 3 March 2009.

The ECJ, however, would have none of it.[28] It held that currency restrictions, by their very nature, must be applied immediately, leaving no time for re-negotiation. Moreover, and not without irony, it held that the operation of international law mechanisms such as the *rebus sic stantibus* rule was 'too uncertain in its effects' to be of much help.[29] Most surprisingly, the ECJ seemed to hold that since such treaties have been concluded by several Member States, and since, under Article 351(2) TFEU, they must assist each other with a view to eliminating incompatibilities, the initiation of legal proceedings by the Commission helps 'facilitate mutual assistance' and the 'adoption of a common attitude'.[30] This, however, is hardly a plausible legal ground on which to base the finding of a violation, and seems to be mainly used by the Court to justify its addressing the case in the absence of an actual violation: the creation of Community solidarity makes it imperative that the Member States eliminate any incompatibilities with Community law from their existing agreements.

In the so-called *Open Skies* cases,[31] the Commission brought proceedings against eight Member States of the EU for having concluded air traffic agreements with the United States (and later a ninth case was brought[32]). At the heart of the cases was the fate of new versions of treaties that had been in force for quite some time, some going back to the 1940s.[33] The Court held that since some provisions of those treaties could be incompatible with EC law, the Member States concerned had failed to fulfill their obligations under EC law. Most typically, they had failed to comply with secondary legislation; it was left unclear whether they had actually been in violation of Article 351 TFEU, or whether Article 351 applied at all to begin with.

---

[28] Although in the case concerning Austria it was willing to acknowledge that insertion of a clause granting Community supremacy in future investment treaties might suffice. See *Commission v Austria*, paras 41–42.

[29] See *Commission v Sweden*, above n 27, para 41. The irony resides in the circumstance that the ECJ itself may well be the only court in the world which has ever allowed an appeal to the *rebus* rule to justify a treaty suspension, when it was invoked by the EC Council to justify a suspension of a free trade agreement with Yugoslavia. The case concerned is Case C-162/96, *Racke v Hauptzollamt Mainz*; for commentary see Jan Klabbers, case-note (1999) 36 *Common Market Law Review* 179–89.

[30] *Commission v Sweden (BIT)*, above n 27, para 44.

[31] See Cases C-466/98 *Commission v United Kingdom*, [2002] ECR I-9427; C-467/98 *Commission v Denmark*, [2002] ECR I-9519; C-468/98, *Commission v Sweden*, [2002] ECR I-9575; C-469/98 *Commission v Finland*, [2002] ECR I-9627; C-471/98 *Commission v Belgium*, [2002] ECR I-9681; C-472/98 *Commission v Luxembourg*, [2002] ECR I-9741; C-475/98 *Commission v Austria*, [2002] ECR I-9797; and C-476/98 *Commission v Germany* [2002] ECR I-9855.

[32] Case C-523/04, *Commission v Netherlands*, [2007] ECR I-3267.

[33] The United States-Denmark Treaty, eg, had first been concluded in 1944.

The *Open Skies* cases raise a number of fundamental issues. First, they raise the issue of powers: who is actually competent to conclude air traffic agreements? Throughout the proceedings the Commission suggested that the competence rested with the EC, but did not always invoke the same grounds. At one point it claimed an explicit air traffic power. It also claimed, at times, an implied power (indeed, it invoked several versions, arguing that the EC had competence on the basis of the doctrine set out in *Opinion 1/76*,[34] but also on the basis of the doctrine set out in the *ERTA* case[35]), and in the end, the Court seemed to suggest that the fuzzy notion of *Gemeinschaftstreue* (Community fidelity) had a role to play here. Hence, the one provision of primary EC law the Member States were considered to have violated was the principle of solidarity which, properly speaking, embodies a good faith obligation not to interfere with the operation of EC law. It remains an open question, however, to what extent good faith alone can create obligations where none would otherwise exist, yet the Court seemed to construe a Community power (and therewith Member State pre-emption) on precisely this basis.

Second, the time of conclusion of treaties played an important, if inconclusive, role. For the application of Article 351 TFEU, it would be relevant to decide whether the treaties at issue merely contained cosmetic amendments to anterior treaties, or whether they were to be regarded as new, and thereby posterior treaties left unprotected under Article 351 TFEU. Advocate-General Tizzano – wisely perhaps – decided not to decide the issue, and instead to break down the treaties into their various provisions, leading to the conclusion that even if the treaties generally could, hypothetically, be seen as anterior, nonetheless the same could not apply to the amendments; hence, amendments could not benefit from the protection offered to anterior agreements. The Court adopted a somewhat stricter approach, suggesting that even the non-amended clauses had been confirmed during renegotiations and could thus be considered to fall outside the scope of Article 351.[36] In one case, moreover, it added that since the parties indicated that the new version was 'replacing' the old agreement, Article 351 could not be made to apply.[37] Hence, as in the *BIT* cases, the Court did little to protect the international treaties at issue; in fact, going through the cases, the reader might not even realise that there were valid obligations under international law at stake. The Court's

---

[34] Opinion 1/76 of the Court of Justice, *Draft Agreement establishing a European laying-up fund for inland waterway vessels*, opinion of 26 April 1977.

[35] Case 22/70, *Re The European Road Transport Agreement (ERTA), Commission v Council* [1971] ECR 263.

[36] See, eg, Case C-467/98 *Commission v Denmark*, above n 31.

[37] See Case C-466/98 *Commission v United Kingdom*, above n 31.

knee-jerk reflex at the first sign of a possible risk to Community law is to circle the wagons and protect the internal legal order against outsiders.

This holds true even in respect of human rights, even though human rights have become incorporated in the EU legal order by means of the Treaty establishing the EU. The issue in the 2000 *Schmidberger* case[38] was whether Austria had violated its obligations under Community law when allowing a group of demonstrators to block a mountain pass. Mr Schmidberger, a transporter, claimed that this violated the free movement of goods; the counter-argument rested on freedom of assembly and expression. The Court, in the end, agreed with Austria that nothing wrongful had taken place, but the interesting thing is how the court conceptualised the relationship between the market freedoms and fundamental human rights. The Court held that in the EU legal order those market freedoms reign supreme, but that sometimes an exception must be made for the sake of human rights protection.[39] What is noteworthy is that the Court did not place emphasis on the ECHR, much less on its possibly constitutional role. Instead, assisted by the reference to human rights in Article 6 of the EU Treaty, it confirmed that human rights are part of the EU legal order and, armed therewith the Court could afford not to look outside that legal order. Had it looked outside and had it shown greater empathy with the ECHR, it might have been persuaded to reconceptualise the very relationship between human rights and market freedoms.

Still, the most well-known illustration of the Court's tendency to build a protective wall around the Community legal order is by now its decision in *Kadi*, in September 2008.[40] Mr Kadi was placed on a UN-blacklist under apparent suspicion of somehow aiding and abetting suspected terrorists.[41] The EU imported the underlying Security Council resolution lock, stock and barrel in a few EU instruments. Mr Kadi, unable to appeal against the Security Council decision, went to the ECJ (having first gone to the Court of First Instance) suggesting that certain of his human rights had been violated in the process, in particular his due process rights, his right of access to justice and the right to enjoy his property without disturbance. In other words, the case addressed (in the Court's construction) a conflict between the obligations of the EU Member States to give effect to Security

---

[38] See Case C-1127/00, *Schmidberger v Austria* [2003] ECR I-5659.

[39] If this sounds less than spectacular, try and imagine how a human rights tribunal would have conceptualised the relationship between market freedoms and human rights. And then try and imagine how often a human rights court would hold that freedom of expression and assembly should give way to the free movement of goods.

[40] See case C-402/05 P, *Kadi v Council and Commission*, [2008] ECR I-6351, judgment of 3 September 2008.

[41] For useful background, see Per Cramér, 'Recent Swedish Experiences with Targeted UN Sanctions: The Erosion of Trust in the Security Council' in Erika de Wet and André Nollkaemper (eds), *Review of the Security Council by Member States* (Antwerp, Intersentia, 2003) 85–104.

Council resolutions, and the obligation of the EU institutions, when legislating, to do so in accordance with fundamental human rights to the extent that these are part of the EU legal order. The Court decided firmly to ignore the former and emphasise the latter: EU legislation, even if implementing Security Council resolutions, cannot transgress the EU's human rights catalogue. Whether this results in undermining the authority of the Security Council (which, it should be remembered, is supposed to be supreme by virtue of Article 103 of the UN Charter) is irrelevant, as the Court says it can only apply EC law.[42] Hence, once again, international law is relegated to the backseat.

Technically such positions as offered by the ECJ are defensible under EC law itself even if not, perhaps, in such an unequivocal a manner as is sometimes suggested.[43] Under international law, however, there is some difficulty in accepting the proposition that international law can simply be ignored or cast aside. Generally, states cannot invoke their domestic legal obligations as an excuse for failing to live up to treaty commitments; this is one obvious implication of the *pacta sunt servanda* maxim, and has found recognition in Article 27 of the Vienna Convention on the Law of Treaties. It is not immediately self-evident if states cannot use internal rules, why would it be different for as tight-knit an organisation as the EU? Indeed, its secondary law (regulations and decisions in particular) is to be considered as domestic law within its 27 Member States; the only thing non-domestic about regulations and decisions is their sources.

If the ECJ's position were put in terms of constitutionalism, the following picture would emerge. In a situation in which the global constitutional order conflicts with its own local constitutional order, the ECJ invariably protects its own brand of constitutionalism. It does so by building a wall around the EU legal order,[44] which signifies that somehow the local order is deemed to be superior and, what is more, is deemed to be in need of protection. The ECJ does so when regular international law is at

---

[42]   Additionally, there is the circumstance that the EU itself is not a member of the UN, and thus, technically, not bound by any Security Council resolution – its individual Member States are. Still, this argument would be a double-edged sword as the Union, despite not being bound, does implement Security Council resolutions, almost as if it is bound by them.

[43]   On the jurisdiction of the ECJ to only apply EC law, see Klabbers, *Treaty Conflict*, above n 16, 142–45.

[44]   It already did so in the first case involving Article 351 TFEU, in the early 1960s, and could do so back then due to the precise circumstances of the case, with Italy aiming to escape from EC law by reference to an earlier treaty (GATT) to which all EC Member States were parties. The Court had to construe a distinction between the rights of third parties under such treaties, and the position of Community Member States; it is this distinction that has come to dominate the case law, even in circumstances less favourable to this construction. The case concerned is Case 10/61, *Commission v Italy* [1961] ECR 1. For further discussion and analysis, see Klabbers, *Treaty Conflict*, above n 16, 120–25.

stake, as the *BIT* and *Open Skies* cases illustrate. This would be problematic enough in light of the injunction generally accepted under international law that domestic law cannot be invoked as a justification for failing to respect treaty commitments.[45] The Court goes further, however, and extends its protection in cases which emphatically involve a larger constitutional order: the global order of the UN, and the pan-European order of the European Convention on Human Rights.

<h2 style="text-align:center">IV.   CONSEQUENCES</h2>

As noted, the attitude of the ECJ towards international law, as exemplified most of all by the *Kadi* decision, has two consequences for constitutionalism. First, it may be argued that it denies global constitutionalism. By isolating the EU from general international law, and perhaps in particular by ignoring the authority of the UN Security Council, the ECJ's approach emphasises that global constitutionalism, in any meaningful sense, is still a remote prospect. Secondly, the ECJ arguably does so by upgrading European constitutionalism: EU legislative acts are to be tested against the EU human rights catalogue, which suggests a strongly constitutionalist element within the EC legal order. The point to note though is that this is limited to the EU human rights catalogue; other human rights catalogues have great difficulty entering the EU legal order and being embraced by the ECJ, as the *Schmidberger* case suggests.[46]

If it is correct to suggest that the ECJ puts a premium on local, European constitutionalism, the next question to consider is whether this also inaugurates a constitutional pluralism. The underlying idea would be that if everyone has their own constitutional house in order, the larger, overarching global constitutional house is not required. That is, needless to say, a tricky claim to make, if only for empirical reasons. After all, the chance of all political entities getting their own houses in order seems fairly remote; it is precisely this circumstance that gives rise to calls for 'compensatory constitutionalism'.[47]

On a deeper level though, a model of constitutional pluralism along these lines (with every state or region having its own constitutionalism in place) is eventually little else but classical dualism in a Westphalian world

---

[45] This presupposes, of course, that EC law can be equated with domestic law. I will briefly discuss this below.

[46] For critical discussion of the position of human rights in the EU, see Paivi Leino-Sandberg, 'Particularity as Universality: The Politics of Human Rights in the European Union' (Doctoral dissertation, University of Helsinki, 2005).

[47] See, eg, Anne Peters, 'Compensatory Constitutionalism: The Function and Potential of Fundamental International Norms and Structures' (2006) 19 *Leiden Journal of International Law* 579–610.

order. Whilst the political scientist can be excused for claiming that Westphalia is, too, somehow a constitutional order,[48] a broader and more substantive notion of global constitutionalism (such as the one hinted at in the opening paragraph of this chapter) would beg to differ. And when people speak of constitutional pluralism, they usually do have something else in mind: not just the co-existence, peaceful or otherwise, of sovereign equals, but a deeper, 'thicker' form of constitutionalism, adorned by a sense of community based on shared values.

In recent scholarship, Andrew Hurrell represents a fascinating approach and perhaps comes closest to a Westphalian model. He is by no means ready to do away with sovereign statehood, and sees much that is commendable in the Westphalian model, but even so he remains mindful of its drawbacks, in particular its lack of justice. Hurrell argues that a return to yesteryear's Westphalian world is impossible and would be undesirable at any rate, if only because the Westphalian model does little to achieve justice on the global level.[49]

If the Westphalian model of sovereign but equal states is one way to conceptualise pluralism, the term pluralism is more commonly used in relation to describing ways to accommodate the co-existence of different levels or modes of political organisation. A leading exponent thereof is James Tully, for whom the core of pluralism is precisely the absence of a single final source.[50] Neil Walker, moreover, taps into this idea and expands it, suggesting that constitutional pluralism also plays out on the epistemological level. There simply cannot be a single fount of wisdom, and thus there is not much point in trying.[51] Philosophically, these are attractive positions, but they do require open-mindedness and, more to the point perhaps, retaining an open attitude to norms coming from the outside. This now is what the ECJ does not do, as the above cases suggest.[52]

Intriguingly, and closely mirroring the ECJ's attitude, the US Supreme Court has adopted a similar approach to international law in recent case

---

[48] Classic is Hedley Bull, *The Anarchical Society: A Study of Order in World Politics* (Houndmills, MacMillan, 1977).

[49] See Andrew Hurrell, *On Global Order: Power, Values, and the Constitution of International Society* (Oxford, Oxford University Press, 2007).

[50] See James Tully, *Strange Multiplicity: Constitutionalism in an Age of Diversity* (Cambridge, Cambridge University Press, 1995).

[51] See Neil Walker, 'The Idea of Constitutional Pluralism' (2002) 65 *Modern Law Review* 317–59.

[52] Moreover, as Amartya Sen has pointed out, it may be incompatible with very basic methodologies involved in doing justice: adopting an outside perspective, if only to prevent parochialist group-think, is an integral part of Sen's idea of justice. See Amartya Sen, *The Idea of Justice* (Cambridge, Massachusetts, Harvard University Press, 2009).

law, most prominently perhaps in *Medellin*.[53] In this case, the Supreme Court held that while the Vienna Convention on Consular Relations creates binding obligations for the US on the international level, the United States is not bound by any interpretations of that Convention, not even interpretations stemming from the International Court of Justice. Hence, much like the ECJ's approach, the US Supreme Court is reluctant to allow international law into the local legal order.

All this raises two related issues. A first question is why the ECJ seeks refuge in parochialism or, more charitably put, local constitutionalism. Why is it that the ECJ (as well as the US Supreme Court) closes the European legal order off from the influence of international law? The answer will necessarily remain speculative, but may well have something to do with a perceived lack of legitimacy on the part of international law.[54] The Security Council, receiving the brunt of the ECJ's attack in *Kadi*, is mostly seen as an international body which may possess some legitimacy in respect of its core task (maintaining peace and security), but quite possibly a lot less when it comes to engaging in quasi-legislative activities. Part of the puzzle at issue in *Kadi* may reside in the awkward circumstance that the Security Council was never meant to legislate and thus any legislative attempt in which it engages is bound to meet with some suspicion.

There may be other, competing or (more likely perhaps) complementary explanations, for on one level, at least, it is far too facile to claim that international law, including international human rights law, might not be legitimate enough. After all, international law comes into existence by means of the consensual activities of states. Hence, to the extent that those participating in the making of international law possess some measure of legitimate authority and follow international law's and their own domestic procedures for treaty-making with a measure of seriousness, the result need not necessarily lack legitimacy – or, at the very least, the legitimacy of many manifestations of international law cannot be considered hampered by the absence of procedural or input legitimacy.[55] Claiming that individual manifestations of international law (particular treaties, particular customary rules) lack legitimacy and therefore should not reign supreme or should perhaps even be guarded against, reeks of rationalisation.

What may be the case, however – and curiously enough – is that international law as a whole is seen as illegitimate. The somewhat clumsy

[53] See *José Ernesto Medellin v Texas*, US Supreme Court, decision of 30 April 2007, Docket # 06–984. Pre-dating this decision, the doctrinal position is well represented in Mark L Movsesian, 'Judging International Judgments' (2007) 48 *Virginia Journal of International Law* 65–118.

[54] For such an argument, see Jed Rubenfeld, 'Unilateralism and Constitutionalism' (2004) 79 *New York University Law Review* 1971–2028.

[55] Useful on the various forms of legitimacy is Fritz W Scharpf, *Governing in Europe: Effective and Democratic?* (Oxford, Oxford University Press, 1999).

distinction made by the US Supreme Court in *Medellin* – distinguishing between the binding effect of a treaty provision and the binding effect of an authoritative interpretation of that same provision – would seem to point in this direction. Even if there is nothing wrong with the treaty per se, so the argument could go, nonetheless international tribunals and other authoritative interpreters are beyond democratic control, and since treaties only acquire meaning through the process of interpretation, it follows that a distinction between treaty provision and its interpretation is relevant: the treaty itself can boast democratic legitimacy, but its interpretation may lack democratic legitimacy. Much the same argument (if not in exactly the same terms) has always influenced the case law of the ECJ involving the General Agreement on Tariffs and Trade (GATT) – and has never really been cast aside by the transformation of GATT into the World Trade Organisation (WTO), despite attempts in the literature[56] to claim that with the creation of the WTO's dispute settlement mechanism, it could no longer be suggested that the panels could decide as they saw politically fit: for the evolution from a diplomatic into a more judicial process has failed to impress the ECJ.[57]

There is a second issue raised by the reluctance to embrace a form of pluralism, and that resides in the (perhaps curious) move by international lawyers to adopt a constitutionalist vocabulary. Among the hotter themes for international legal scholarship (if not international legal practice) in recent years has been the discussion about the possible constitutionalisation of international law.[58] On one level, surely, this aims at identifying a higher authority, exemplifying the age-old dream of a single and peaceful global order under international law.[59] Whilst this may be radical within the four corners of international legal argument, it is not all that radical in that it stays within those four corners. Here then, international law takes on constitutionalist dimensions, thereby entering into a form of normative competition with local constitutional orders, and thus raising the spectre of a loss of legitimate authority. It may be precisely this constitutionalisation of the international legal order about which the courts in *Kadi* and *Medellin* seem to be worried.

But there is a second version of constitutionalism at work that, more interestingly perhaps, seems to be born out of a certain disappointment

---

[56]   See, eg, Joanne Scott, 'The GATT and Community Law: Rethinking the Regulatory Gap' in Jo Shaw and Gillian More (eds), *New Legal Dynamics of European Union* (Oxford, Oxford University Press, 1995) 147–64.

[57]   See more generally also Jan Klabbers, 'International Law in Community Law: The Law and Politics of Direct Effect' (2002) 21 *Yearbook of European Law* 263–98.

[58]   For a general overview, see Klabbers, Peters and Ulfstein, *The Constitutionalization*.

[59]   This would apply to Fassbender, *The United Nations Charter*, and also to Erika de Wet, 'The International Constitutional Order' (2006) 55 *International and Comparative Law Quarterly* 51–76.

with international law and its possibilities – and also its limitations. Here then, it is not so much about imagining or re-imagining an international legal constitutional order with a specific treaty such as the UN Charter at the top of the *Stufenbau*; instead it is more about changing the vocabulary altogether. This may seem like the classic move of yesteryear, infusing international law with constitutional-sounding notions (*jus cogens, erga omnes*), but that is not what it is: it is not about retaining and refining or strengthening international law – instead, this position owes more to a certain *tristesse*, a melancholy assessment of the lost promise of international law. International law has failed to live up to its promise, prompting a mildly disillusioned departure for greener fields. If the vocabulary of international law cannot tame the beast of politics, then perhaps the vocabulary should be dropped and replaced by the promise of a constitutionalist vocabulary.

Perhaps most interesting is that some of Martti Koskenniemi's more recent work can be read in this light.[60] Where the optimist, liberal strand of constitutionalism thinks in terms of law reigning supreme over politics, for Koskenniemi taming the beast of politics means channelling it, rather than discarding it. If *The Gentle Civilizer of Nations* already bore witness to a certain *ennui* with the discipline of international law at large,[61] some of his more recent writings shun the vocabulary of international law altogether and adopt something of a constitutional vocabulary. Yet, Koskenniemi does so with a twist: his interest resides in the constitutionalist mind-set, not in constitutionalist sets of norms.[62] It resides, in the words of *The Gentle Civilizer*, in a culture of formalism,[63] not for the sake of formalism, but for the sake of the possibility of a substantively just world order, to be arrived at – or aspired to, as it necessarily remains beyond full

---

[60] This is all the more interesting in that contemporary philosophers seem to have embraced the international law vocabulary in its more liberal guises, precisely when international lawyers are looking elsewhere. This applies to John Rawls, *The Law of Peoples* (Cambridge, Massachusetts, Harvard University Press, 1999), as well as to Jurgen Habermas, *The Divided West*, trans C Cronin (Cambridge, Polity, 2006). The latter, intriguingly and somewhat counter-intuitively, comes close to adopting Fassbender's distinctly liberal brand of constitutionalist international legal thought.

[61] See Martti Koskenniemi, *The Gentle Civilizer of Nations: The Rise and Fall of International Law 1870–1960* (Cambridge, Cambridge University Press, 2001).

[62] See Martti Koskenniemi, 'Constitutionalism as Mindset: Reflections on Kantian Themes about International Law and Globalization' (2007) 8 *Theoretical Inquiries in Law* 9–38. Elsewhere Koskenniemi posits international law as 'a kind of secular faith': see Martti Koskenniemi, 'The Fate of Public International Law: Between Technique and Politics' (2007) 70 *Modern Law Review* 1–30, 30.

[63] The way I read this is by emphasising the term 'culture' rather than the particular historical record of 'formality' in international law, thereby avoiding throwing the baby out with the bathwater: what is relevant here is the attitude of those making and applying international law.

realisation[64] – on the basis of honest and open discussion. It involves a refusal to give in to the classic political temptation that the ends always justify the means. This even takes on dimensions that are beyond law altogether, putting faith in the redeeming qualities (dare one say virtues?) of the individuals who end up working with international law.

V.   THE MOVE TO VIRTUE

Perhaps the move towards some attention being paid to the virtues of the individuals involved in making and applying international law, as exemplified by Koskenniemi's work, is inevitable.[65] Legal rules have been shown to be both over-inclusive and under-inclusive,[66] and tend to be defenceless in the face of political agreement. This applies not just to rules generally, but also to rules of a constitutional nature.[67] In such a setting, if it is indeed the case that not too much can be expected from reliance on rules alone, it stands to reason that attention shifts to processes of interpretation and application,[68] and thereby inevitably also to the characteristic traits of the individuals who are charged with the responsibility of interpreting and applying legal texts.[69]

What, then, does all this mean for the global constitutional mosaic? If states (or entities such as the EU) are reluctant to have international legal norms enter their internal order, perhaps the global constitutional mosaic can only be rescued by a sense of humility on the part of those who are given the task of protecting their own constitutions. Political leaders as well as judges (and Advocates-General) may be expected to have a sense of respect not only for their own precedents and traditions, but also for what goes on elsewhere. They may be expected to have some integrity in coming

[64]   This must be so in the sense that justice will always have to be contextual and thus can never be fully laid down in a single set of rules. To some extent, justice will always remain an abstract ideal.

[65]   Recent expositions of virtue ethics include Philippa Foot, *Virtues and Vices and Other Essays in Moral Philosophy*, 2nd edn (Oxford, Oxford University Press, 2002) and Rosalind Hursthouse, *On Virtue Ethics* (Oxford, Oxford University Press, 1999). A useful collection of essays is Roger Crisp and Michael Slote (eds), *Virtue Ethics* (Oxford, Oxford University Press, 1997).

[66]   For one classic formulation, see Frederick Schauer, *Playing by the Rules: A Philosophical Examination of Rule-based Decision-making in Law and in Life* (Oxford, Clarendon Press, 1991).

[67]   See Jan Klabbers, 'Constitutionalism Lite' (2004) 1 *International Organizations Law Review* 31–58.

[68]   See eg Jan Klabbers, 'On Rationalism in Politics: Interpretation of Treaties and the World Trade Organization' (2005) 74 *Nordic Journal of International Law* 405–28.

[69]   See Jan Klabbers, 'Virtuous Interpretation' in Malgosia Fitzmaurice and Panos Merkouris (eds), *Treaty Interpretation and the Vienna Convention on the Law of Treaties: Thirty Years On* (Leiden, Martinus Nijhoff, 2010) 17–37.

to decisions and candour in the presentation of arguments grounding those decisions; they may be expected to accept the possibility of disagreement, and be humble about their own claims of truth. As Jeff Powell put it in the context of the US Supreme Court, 'we must act on the presumption that what fundamentally unites us is not agreement – or coercion – but a willingness to listen to the other even when we disagree strongly and on grounds of high principle'.[70]

In the end, then, this boils down to advocating not so much hard-core constitutionalism, but rather a thinner version of constitutionalism or, perhaps, a 'virtue jurisprudence':[71] an attitude on the part of the courts displaying some of the classic virtues and having an open mind. The European Union's place in the global constitutional mosaic cannot be determined with the help of a clear and simple rule, but needs a receptive attitude on the part of the EU courts. The tendency to fence off the internal legal order, however understandable that might be from the perspective of the EU legal order, is bound to be counter-productive, if only because the classic argument that EU law needs protection in order to grow can no longer be credibly justified. After an existence of more than 60 years, surely the claim that the EU legal order is a fragile youngster which needs to be protected against its parent (ie international law)[72] seems less than fully plausible.

The larger argument, however, is that constitutionalism in one part of the world may come at the expense of constitutionalism elsewhere, and in particular, at the expense of constitutionalism in the overarching global order. Even if a local constitutionalism could be defended on its own terms, it should not result in an erosion of the global or pan-European constitutional orders; yet, arguably, this is precisely what cases such as *Kadi* and *Schmidberger* result in. From this perspective, there is something to be said for the controversial decision of the European Court of Human Rights in *Behrami* and *Saramati*, where the Strasbourg Court paid due deference to the role of the Security Council in the maintenance of international peace and security.[73] It held that the behaviour of international forces in Kosovo was attributable to the UN, and that the Court was unable to review UN

---

[70] See H Jefferson Powell, *Constitutional Conscience: The Moral Dimension of Judicial Decision* (Chicago IL, University of Chicago Press, 2008) 101.

[71] See Lawrence B Solum, 'Virtue Jurisprudence: A Virtue-Centred Theory of Judging' (2003) 34 *Metaphilosophy* 178–213, and the penetrating critique by RA Duff, 'The Limits of Virtue Jurisprudence' (2003) 34 *Metaphilosophy* 214–24.

[72] This narrative is most overtly produced in Christiaan Timmermans, 'The EU and Public International Law' (1999) 4 *European Foreign Affairs Review* 181–94. Note, incidentally, that the analogy is one of domestic abuse: child needs to be protected against parent. One can only marvel at the Freudian implications of such a portrayal, and what it will do for global constitutionalism.

[73] See *Behrami and Behrami v France*; *Saramati v France, Germany and Norway*, Grand Chamber, admissibility decision of 2 May 2007 (2007) 45 EHRR SE10.

activities, as the UN is not a party to the ECHR. Whilst it may be claimed that the Strasbourg Court decided the way it did mainly so as to prevent its having to say anything at all (hardly an exercise of the virtues), and whilst the case has been less than warmly received by the human rights community, nonetheless it does have the merit of respecting the position of the United Nations in the global constitutional mosaic.

All this is not to say that constitutionalism should shed all its ambitions. Nor is it meant to suggest that virtue ethics or virtue jurisprudence are the panacea to all evils; surely, any attempt at introducing virtue ethics into international law will necessarily have to be complementary to a more deontological approach, not a substitute thereof.[74] But it is to say, as Ivor Jennings already recognised in the midst of a world war, that 'the psychology of government is more important than the forms of government'.[75] Rules, whether constitutional or not, and no matter how detailed or open-ended, can never decide the conditions of their own application. This is still dependent on human agency; hence, the qualities of human agents do have a role to play, also in the global constitutional mosaic.

VI.   CONCLUSION

This chapter has discussed the position of the EU in the world from the rather peculiar perspective of a possible global constitutional order. Whether such an order can actually be said to exist is not all that relevant – the present exercise is a thought-experiment more than anything else. As such an experiment, it leads to the conclusion that the fencing off of the EU legal order, defended within the EU on constitutionalist grounds (it would, after all, follow from respect for the founding treaties, for the autonomy of the Community legal order, and from the human rights catalogue which forms part of that legal order), may not be all that easy to reconcile with more global strands of constitutionalism. In order to mitigate the tension between the two, this chapter suggests – without having worked out all the details – the incorporation of some form of virtue ethics into international law. Faced with competing claims of authority, the best one can hope for is not a single rule which could possibly decide all cases: the indeterminacy of the Vienna Convention on the Law of Treaties when dealing with treaty conflict strongly suggests that no one-size-fits-all provisions can be found –

---

[74] For further elaboration, see Jan Klabbers, 'Autonomy, Constitutionalism, and Virtue in International Institutional Law' in Richard Collins and Nigel D White (eds), *International Organizations and the Idea of Autonomy* (London, Routledge, forthcoming 2011).

[75] See Sir W Ivor Jennings, *The Law and the Constitution*, 3rd edn (London, University of London Press, 1943) xxxi.

if such a provision would be desirable to begin with. What may just be workable, though, is an appeal to the virtues of honesty, humility and seeing the bigger picture: if those who are charged with interpreting and applying the law refuse to give in to partisan concerns and the sort of knee-jerk reflexes that would see them protect their own little parish at all costs, then maybe, just maybe, a global constitutionalism can be reconciled with different localised manifestations of constitutionalism. And only in such circumstances would it be appropriate to speak of a global constitutional mosaic.

Part Six

Other Case Studies

12

European Criminal Law Under the Developing Constitutional Setting of the European Union

I. INTRODUCTION

I HAVE A simple claim. The criminal law angle is helpful for a general analysis and understanding of the European Union as a polity and for understanding the challenges the EU is facing, whilst at the same time new developments in criminal law call for rethinking the constitutionality and reshaping the constitutional frames within which transnational criminal law is nurtured on our continent. There is nothing very surprising about this claim, but I wish to substantiate it more thoroughly than I have done before[1] and show that this is a useful point of entry to the debate about the current state and stage of the development of European constitutionalism.

I do not look at the emergence of what could be called an EU criminal legal order from the usual, rather positivist perspective, but wish to discuss the developments and problems from the point of view of its legitimacy conditions and a 'thick' conception of justification. Such an analysis of the emergence of the EU criminal legal order will inevitably require that the constitutional context of this development be taken into account. Both criminal law and constitutionalism are intimately related to the values of the legal and political community. In a sense they *are* these fundamental values.

---

* Centre of Excellence in Foundations of European Law and Polity, University of Helsinki.
[1] Cf K Nuotio, 'On the Significance of Criminal Justice for a Europe "United in Diversity"' in K Nuotio (ed), *Europe in Search of 'Meaning and Purpose* (Helsinki, Forum Iuris, 2004) 171–210; K Nuotio, 'Criminal Law of a Transnational Polity' in H Müller-Dietz, E Müller and K-L Kunz (eds), *Festschrift Heike Jung* (Baden-Baden, Nomos, 2007) 685–98.

This is thus a sort of mutual interdependence thesis. The criminal law dimension may shed new light upon issues such as the democratic deficit and rights deficit, because it leads us to think about the question of how and why democracy matters and how and why rights matter, as they obviously do. Rethinking the constitutional dimension becomes increasingly important as the EU starts to address this kind of security-related policy issue. We see in the developing EU constitutionalism an expression of the fact that legal integration touches on increasingly sensitive issues that the Member States have so far sought to keep out of the core areas of the legal integration process at the same time as they have increasingly extended their forms of cooperation. The history of unease in the constitutional positioning of the Area of Freedom, Security and Justice (AFSJ) illustrates such contradictory tendencies. The European constitutional framework needs to be adjusted and stretched in order to fit the phenomena of the AFSJ.[2] The present thesis does not include any simple claim about lines of causation or forces behind these twin developments in the fields of criminal law and constitutionalism. The most we can say at the moment is that they are interrelated. Obviously, the explanatory factors should be sought from both external and internal sources.

Interestingly, both criminal law and constitutionalism sit uncomfortably in the EU setting. Miguel Maduro has spoken of an existential crisis of the European Constitution,[3] which at least partly explains and justifies the search for constitutional reform in the EU setting. The Lisbon Treaty is both a product of and an answer to this crisis. This treaty will not end the existential crisis, but rather reframes it. It will also reframe the constitutional setting of European criminal law and bring the criminal law issues closer to the core of European constitutionalism by abolishing the wall, or the veil, between the different pillars of integration almost entirely, but will thereby bring new challenges to the European Constitution. Valsamis Mitsilegas speaks about the ongoing transformation of criminal law in an 'area' of freedom, security and justice, the full impact of which is not yet obvious.[4]

The point is also that criminal law may be regarded as an expression of a culture capable of indicating many things in its surroundings. Criminal law is a rich vocabulary, and the recognition or mis-recognition of this richness is one of the challenges to our understanding of its relationship to

---

[2] See the various observations about the underlying unresolved tensions in the constitutional foundations of the AFSJ in N Walker, 'In Search of the Area of Freedom, Security and Justice: A Constitutional Odyssey' in Walker (ed), *Europe's Area of Freedom, Security and Justice* (Oxford, Oxford University Press, 2004) 3–37.

[3] M Maduro, 'Europe and the Constitution: What if this is as good as it gets?' in JHH Weiler and M Wind (eds), *European Constitutionalism Beyond the State* (Cambridge, Cambridge University Press, 2003) 76–100.

[4] V Mitsilegas, *EU Criminal Law* (Oxford, Hart Publishing, 2009) 323–24.

the wider constitutional landscape. Is criminal law qualitatively distinct; does it require full-blown recognition as such, or can it be reduced to one instance of a general sanctioning mechanism? Should cooperation in criminal law matters even *count* as criminal law, and if not, what is it? The legal order of the European Union deals increasingly with matters of criminal law, but there are always question marks.

This potential richness is one of the reasons criminal law becomes so important and interesting when a transnational setting is involved. The European legal order also includes national legal orders and, especially in fields such as criminal law, we will be able to see the tensions and tendencies that form this multi-dimensional order, that bring coherence to it, and that perhaps also show ideological and other disparities and ruptures. A minimum harmonisation of some fragments of the penal law at the European level will inevitably continue and even fuel divergent tendencies, leading to problems of coherence within the larger frames of the European legal order. Fragmentation also has many faces, as it presents itself differently at the European level compared to the Member State. We have fragmentation that is due to the fragmented nature of policies and legal instruments, and we have fragmentation that has to do with diverging understandings and underlying rationalities.

We also have counter-tendencies of striving towards increased coherence. Legislative fragmentation might look different to fragmentation perceived from the point of view of European or national courts. According to one view, European criminal law should be understood as a kind of common law, with a particular emphasis on the role of the European Court of Justice (ECJ) in its development.[5] One feature of the dynamics of convergence and divergence is to be found in constitutional challenges to the European legal instruments and to the implementing legislation.[6] In a sense, the struggle for coherence and unity is a very general characteristic of law, and clearly the process of maturing something like European criminal law requires progress in this respect as well.[7]

In the following, I will try to develop the claim about the mutual dependence of the constitutional and criminal law developments, and so contribute to two discussions that tend to run in isolation from one another. The theorists of constitutionalism seldom pay attention to the substantive issues, such as those of criminal law, that the EU as a polity is supposed to be dealing with, whereas scholars of European criminal law

---

[5] A Klip, *European Criminal Law* (Antwerp, Intersentia, 2009) 10.

[6] E Guild (ed), *Constitutional Challenges to the European Arrest Warrant* (Nijmegen, Wolf Legal Publishers, 2006); E Guild and L Marin (eds), *Still not resolved? Constitutional issues of the European Arrest Warrant* (Nijmegen, Wolf Legal Publishers, 2009).

[7] See the helpful discussions in S Prechal and B van Roermund (eds), *The Coherence of EU Law: The Search for Unity in Divergent Concepts* (Oxford, Oxford University Press, 2008).

seldom engage in deeper studies as regards the interplay between the constitutional schemes and the content of the penal law. That this connection remains under-theorised renders the development of new thinking very timely in an era marked by much new practice.[8] A legitimacy perspective is especially promising as a way of forging this connection, as this has been so important in the general theorising of European legal developments and the European political culture.[9]

The concept of legitimacy obviously has many meanings. It could refer to the rationality of a legal system, its moral contents, its empirical acceptance, the ethical qualities of a legal system, its political procedures, and so forth. I will deploy the term broadly, as I see several dimensions of a legitimacy analysis as mutually connected. The following will attempt to bring at least some conceptual clarity to the use of the term.

II.   THE SPECIFICITY OF CRIMINAL LAW

Criminal law could be characterised as having a very special character, which comes from the moral dilemma it has to face. Whilst the state prohibits certain forms of behaviour and labels them as offences, as bad and wrongful, at the same it threatens the perpetrators with something equally bad, a punishment. In order to be able to defend this state practice, one has to produce specific justifications that accord penal law its legitimacy.

The quest for legitimacy thus stems from the moral dilemma, which is not that easily resolved. The history of criminal law theorising is full of efforts to discuss these issues, but the answers are far from fully convincing. Retribution theories suffer from emptiness with regard to broader social purposes, whereas prevention theories suffer from the utilitarian disease of treating the person to be punished as an object, and even as a tool.

What this means is that the legitimacy of the state having a penal law and enforcing it by punishing members of the polity is in any case disputed and weak. This weakness requires the attention of several fundamental principles in order to preserve at least some of the legitimacy of penal law. It is probably the case that no other field of law faces such a pressing dilemma in establishing its first premises.

---

[8] One important effort is L Gröning, *EU, staten och rätten att straffa: Problem och principer för EU:s straffrättsliga lagstiftning* (Lund University doctoral thesis, Santérus, 2008).

[9] See, eg, JHH Weiler, *The Constitution of Europe: 'Do the Clothes have an Emperor?' and other Essays on European integration* (Cambridge, Cambridge University Press, 1999).

The legitimacy conditions of the penal law are, then, partly built into rules and principles of the criminal law itself, and partly located in the larger setting accounting for the legitimacy of law more generally.[10] The principles marking the specific character of criminal law are all expressions of the fundamental moral dilemma mentioned earlier. It is neither possible nor necessary here to go into details of all these principles, but something must be said. *The principle of individual guilt* says that only those who exercise the agency we associate with human beings may commit crimes and that the attribution of penal liability always needs to based on a wrongful act that the individual person can be blamed for. Strict liability, therefore, is not compatible with the principle of guilt. *The principle of legality* requires that all wrongful acts which count as offences must already be substantially defined in law at the time of the commission of the action. Further, guilt must be proven in a fair trial *beyond reasonable doubt.*

The *ultima ratio* principle (the last resort principle) requires that criminalisation may be resorted to only when there is no other way for society to deal with the problem.[11] The *ultima ratio* principle expresses the specific character of criminal law in that criminalisation of a type of conduct subjects it to very specific treatment in our legal system. It quite simply makes a difference when we are talking about statutory offences compared to administrative sanctions, for instance. Criminal law uses a very elaborate, morally-laden vocabulary. The *ultima ratio* can be understood as a particular form of subsidiarity: try everything else first. The *ultima ratio* principle is thus actually a version of the well-known subsidiarity principle. All this is not to say, however, that the *ultima ratio* principle has been a powerful weapon against the recent flood of new criminalisations.[12]

Finally, *human dignity and act-proportionality shall be respected*, so that the punishments may not be cruel or humiliating or too severe. Just as only a certain quality of conduct should be criminalised, so too punishment should be attuned to qualitative differences within the category of criminal conduct.

All these principles mark a certain culture of criminal law that should be cherished in order to preserve the moral nature of the whole enterprise. Taking a certain issue to the table as a penal issue brings it simultaneously

---

[10] On the need to preserve the *Rechtsstaatlichkeit* of criminal law, see K Nuotio, 'The Ethics of Criminal Justice' in P Wahlgren (ed), *Criminal Law, Scandinavian Studies in Law*, vol 54 (Stockholm Institute for Scandinavian Law, 2009) 63–76.

[11] See, eg, P Minkkinen, '"If Taken In Earnest": Criminal Law Doctrine and the Last Resort' (2006) 45(5) *The Howard Journal of Criminal Justice* 521–36.

[12] D Husak, 'The Criminal Law as Last Resort' (2004) 24(2) *Oxford Journal of Legal Studies* 207–35.

into this circle of penal law which has a very special character. Criminalising a form of conduct by a legislative decision, or abolishing a criminal offence by statute, offer the clearest examples of how this borderline frequently shifts in one direction or the other. The history of criminal law, legally speaking, is very much the history of development of these ideas, which mark the specificity of criminal law.

As Wolfgang Frisch put it,

> [i]f the Europe of today shares in some sense a common basis in criminal law, if there are commonly European principles and institutions, this is mostly due to the philosophical reflections on the matters of criminal law. The differences, in turn, can be found in areas where the philosophical reflections have not led to clear insights – leaving room for pragmatics, tradition, and other things.[13]

The philosophy of the Enlightenment has been influential both as regards the development of principles of criminal law and as regards the development of constitutional doctrines and principles more generally. It is no surprise that this link can be found, since we see immediately that many of the criminal law principles mentioned above, if not themselves directly constitutional legal principles, then at least are located in close proximity to the latter. The principles of legality and proportionality are certainly general constitutional principles, and the criminal law context mainly just adds an extra layer of strictness and emphasis to them. Human dignity is a constitutional principle par excellence, but the criminal law context is crucial for it. The *ultima ratio* principle, for instance, really marks the distinction between penal law and other laws by requiring every effort to be made not to resort to it in the first place. The principle of individual guilt is a criminal law principle, but non-observance of it would severely risk citizens' enjoyment of their constitutional rights and liberties more generally, because a penal liability could strike them unexpectedly and unfairly.

All these principles have been developed over the years as a response to challenges and criticisms, thus contributing to solving the problems of the legitimacy of criminal law and state punishment. As all these principles are also apt to be compromised in actual political dealings with and development of the criminal law, accordingly the legitimacy of criminal law may vary considerably. In one legal order, the problems may focus on one aspect, whereas in another the problems lie elsewhere. We could say that a full set of criminal law principles enables at least some sort of normative assessment of the legitimacy of the penal order. Certainly, someone might challenge this whole idea and say that such a thing does not exist, and that

---

[13] W Frisch, 'Einheit und Vielfalt des Strafrechts in Europa: Wirkungen und Grenzen der Strafrechtsphilosophie' in K Nuotio (ed), *Festschrift in Honour of Raimo Lahti*, (Helsinki, Forum Iuris, University of Helsinki, 2007) 7–23, 8 (trans KN).

either all criminal law is just plainly wrong, or, conversely, it faces no specific problems of legitimacy beyond those that affect other areas of law. I can only hope to have convinced the reader that if we wish to engage in a legitimacy analysis, we must put aside these threshold reservations and take the first and necessary step of identifying the basic criminal law principles.

If I am right in my analysis, many well-respected states would patently face at least some problems when measured against such yardsticks. This would be true even for some states of generally high constitutional standards. I will not go into the details of why this is so here, only pointing out that cherishing a highly principled penal law culture is often or at least sometimes at odds with the workings of democracy. Popular opinion can easily be mobilised against principles with which particular politicians and political parties disagree, and the general public does not always perceive the need to guard the principles of good criminal law administration. National policies differ to a great extent; much more, in fact, than do the levels of criminality. The more penal law issues become politicised, the more we tend to see erosion of the traditional principles. This is not, of course, to deny that a certain transformation and development not only of penal law, but of these principles themselves, is necessary when societies develop and must face up to and respond to new social problems.

We should also take notice of one specific criminal law mechanism, namely, that of codification. The principle of legality is important in criminal law, and partly for this reason most European legal systems have a long history of codifying their penal laws. The work of codification makes it possible to further underline the common principles that all offences may share. Modern penal codes often include a general part. The history of codification, then, tells us about a certain documentation and 'positivisation' – the becoming black-letter law – of the principles of criminal law.

We should always bear in mind that the Council of Europe has been a very significant forum for European states in developing their cooperation in criminal matters. The Council has developed a rich arsenal of conventions addressing a variety of issues. These include conventions introducing obligations to criminalise certain forms of behaviour as well as those organising mutual assistance, and similar issues. In the Council of Europe setting, the general aims of the organisation also colour these enterprises. The Council of Europe and the EU now have a great deal of overlapping regulation, and the two systems are developing in parallel. Formally, cooperation in the framework of the Council of Europe is different mainly because it follows the models and legal instruments provided by public international law. Both organisations have been prolific in drafting measures for combating terrorism by means of criminal law, for example.

The maturation of a criminal legal order presupposes that the law is normatively embedded in the constitution of the polity. In a favourable situation, the basic commitments of the criminal law are reflected in constitutional values and principles, and this applies as much to the supranational as to the national level. For example, the development of European criminal law through the case law of the ECJ is significant for understanding the broader jurisprudential logic of this European development. The ECJ, interestingly, operates with a dual function. It decides cases brought before it, but also acts as a sort of constitutional court in that it actively interprets the norms of European law, and underlines some norms as fundamental as part of this interpretive activity. As concerns criminal law, the principle of legality was recognised as a general principle of European law as early as 1984 in *Regina v Kent Kirk*.[14] According to the ECJ, the principle that penal provisions may not have retroactive effect 'takes its place among the general principles of law whose observance is ensured by the court of justice'.[15] We could also refer to the fundamental role of the *ne bis in idem* principle of Article 54 of the Convention implementing the Schengen Agreement (CISA) as interpreted in a long list of ECJ judgments, and the importance of the *ne bis in idem* principle is further stressed by its inclusion as Article 50 in the Charter of the Fundamental Rights of the European Union. In the literature, further-more, the principle of proportionality has been referred to as having a constitutional status in EU law – a status again nurtured by the ECJ, and also further confirmed by Article 49 of the Charter.[16]

In the pre-Lisbon setting, the applicability of principles of First Pillar EC law in matters concerning the Third Pillar EU criminal law has not always been clear. Post-Lisbon, with the formal ending of the three pillar structure, the ECJ will certainly continue extending the role of the EC legal principles to cover the whole of the EU law. The strengthening of the role of human rights in the EU context will further support this development. As concerns the pre-Lisbon setting, the *Pupino* decision[17] deserves special mention. In that case, the ECJ extended the duty of loyal cooperation to cover Title VI of the Treaty on European Union, thus abandoning the view that frame-work decisions are in this regard very different from EC law directives. The ECJ thereby introduced the obligation for a national judge to interpret national laws in the light of the wording and purpose of the framework decision.[18]

Let us return for now to the development of criminal law principles in the original context of the state. Traditionally, criminal law has been

---

[14]   Case C-63/83 *R v Kirk* [1984] ECR 2689.
[15]   *ibid*, para 2.
[16]   T Tridimas, *The General Principles of EU Law*, 2nd edn (Oxford, Oxford EC Library, 2006) 174–75.
[17]   Case C-105/03 *Criminal proceedings against Pupino* [2005] ECR I-5285, Judgment of 16 June 2005.
[18]   *ibid*.

developed and handled at the state level. Criminal law has been one of the markers of the state itself, as the holder of penal law authority and the monopoly of the use of force. The state has acquired a distinctive significance in this picture because only the state has been able to provide safeguards for the individual. The attainment of the monopoly over the authorised use of force has required the state to take over this function and to bring rival institutions, such as the church, under the broader purview of the state's jurisdiction.

A democratic *Rechtsstaat* is in one sense the culmination of this trend, incorporating protective schemes concerning the rights of the individual vis-à-vis the state and also enabling democratic procedures, thus allowing the voice of the people to be heard in the political process. The private sphere also enjoys adequate protection, as individual autonomy remains the ultimate source of state authority. This is sometimes called the 'co-originality' of the two sides of human autonomy – public and private. The democratic *Rechtsstaat* is an ideal type of state, which would effectively build its criminal law and policy on the cultural premises sketched out above. It may be politically geared towards achieving various goals, but even as an instrument it preserves much of its specific nature.[19]

If we look at the matter in long historical terms, this view as to the specificities of the principles of criminal law was probably first developed even before the full-blown realisation of a democratic *Rechtsstaat*. At that earlier juncture, the recognition of these specificities was rather a product of criminal science and the broader Enlightenment critique of arbitrary power. The maturing constitutional development has meant that the criminal law and the constitution, as parts of the legal order, have ultimately grown to share more of the same value basis, notwithstanding the differences that we observe at the surface level. The criminal law is a much more elaborate and concrete part of the legal order, and for that reason also provides vital material for comparative analysis.

The conjunction of constitutional developments with criminal law developments has some important implications. Disruption of the legitimacy of criminal law could easily have a negative impact on the system of rights more generally. The political process, which constantly feeds the broader legal system with pressures to respond to societal needs, also exercises pressure on the criminal law and its guiding principles. Mireille

---

[19]   See, eg, the discussion in R Nickel, 'Private and Public Autonomy Revisited: Habermas' Concept of Co-originality in Times of Globalization and the Militant Security State' in M Loughlin and Neil Walker (eds), *The Paradox of Constitutionalism: Constituent Power and Constitutional Form* (Oxford, Oxford University Press, 2007) 147–67.

Delmas-Marty, for example, has stressed the importance of human rights as the underlying basis of value needed for backing up harmonisation or unification in criminal law.[20]

Including a temporal dimension in our scrutiny, we could say that many more recent legal developments can in some sense be regarded as an erosion of classical criminal law principles. The sphere of criminal law has grown to cover economic and organisational or systemic activities more intensively than ever; new liability structures have been developed; the occurrence of actual harm is no longer always necessary for penal liability. Crime is today a much more complex social construct than it used to be. All this does not necessarily challenge the fundamental legitimacy of criminal law, but it certainly demonstrates the flexibility of criminal law under circumstances of rapid social change.

Following Habermas (and Kant), Kaarlo Tuori emphasises that we should distinguish between the ethical and moral in speaking about law-making procedures. This distinction is useful here. Ethics here involves a specific conception of good that the political system of a community tries to define in its everyday working and struggles. Morality concerns principles of justice and means, in turn, the general and abstract moral principles. Society defines itself, its values and preferences, by applying and nuancing the broadly morally justifiable procedures for doing so. The ethical discourses need to be tracked by moral discourses in order to guarantee that the outcomes of the ethical discourses do not violate the moral principles of justice.[21] In this sense criminal law, too, when transformed through the political processes of a modern or late-modern society, is an expression of the society's view of itself, and in a way inevitably includes both ethical and moral questions that in a sense always precede the juridical discourse.

The actual criminal law is one of the markers of a good and decent polity. Issues of criminal law also require special treatment in their political handling. Following Habermas and Tuori, I would stress the need to adopt a 'we-perspective' in the elaboration and evaluation of proposed legal regulations. The political argument should be structured accordingly. The we-perspective is normatively binding in the sense that even the affected groups and persons, as well as the potential perpetrator, need to be addressed and involved in this debate. The arguments need to be generalised in order to overcome the limited perspective of individual and private

---

[20] M Delmas-Marty, *Towards a truly common law: Europe as a Laboratory for Legal Pluralism* (Cambridge, Cambridge University Press, 2002).
[21] K Tuori, *Critical Legal Positivism* (Aldershot, Ashgate, 2002) 94–100.

interests. Legislation includes and expresses a collective identity and can be regarded as a reflexive expression of the legal and political community.[22]

Criminal law requires that normative moral-ethical language should be adopted at the stage of political debate. The previous remarks on the potential risks of democratic processes could be related to these ideas. Too often criminal policy issues are approached offensively, in terms of 'fight' and 'combat', as if the 'enemy' were external rather than internal, as if the targeted group were not moved by reasons and were not part of the legal and political community as well. In democratic theory, deliberative persuasion-based models express an inclusive approach to the distribution of roles within a legal and political community better than do the interest-aggregative and preference-counting models. This does not mean that a consensus perspective should generally be adopted. However, what I would like to stress here is the basic form of a sound political argument.[23]

Offensive and aggressive views on crime and criminality may be based on various other reasons as well. In the EU context, considerations of economic rationality could lead to an exaggeration of the risks of criminality, because the market presuppositions about human behaviour read facts differently from the criminological literature. Indeed, economic rationality perhaps may not see any ethical point of view at all, just technical problems to be solved by imposing sanctions and offering incentives.

If we look at the current criminal policy battles in multicultural societies, the we-perspective forces a move beyond our 'own' narrow cultural community, which might be based on strong shared values. In a sense, it forces a move from ethics to universal morals. Unless the whole political community can share such strong values, the criminal law should not be used to enforce them. In multicultural matters, such as blasphemy laws or regulating the circumcision of boys, more often than not the only wise solution is to withdraw these issues from the criminal law sphere, because of the lack of ethical consensus in the political community on the issue.

III. EUROPEAN UNION CRIMINAL LAW

We should now return to the European Union and the particular challenges criminal law raises in this context. Since Maastricht, the EU has dealt with criminal law issues in its Third Pillar law – originally under the label of

---

[22] Hans Lindahl has gone down this road in his discussion of the connection between democracy and *Rechtsstaat*: see H Lindahl, 'Constituent Power and Reflexive Identity: Towards an Ontology of Collective Selfhood' in Loughlin and Walker, *The Paradox of Constitutionalism*, above n 19, 9–24.

[23] See the critical remarks on deliberative democracy, J Waldron, *Law and Disagreement* (Oxford, Oxford University Press, 1999) 91–93.

Justice and Home Affairs. During the Maastricht era the Third Pillar was still largely intergovernmental and thus belonged mainly to international law. At this time, cooperation in substantive criminal law issues was in its infancy, and the instruments used were conventions and joint actions. Conventions were used, for example, in the areas of fraud against the EU and corruption.[24]

Since the Treaty of Amsterdam, much has changed. The Union's objectives post-Amsterdam included a commitment

> to provide citizens with a high level of safety within an area of freedom, security and justice by developing common action among the Member States in the fields of police and judicial cooperation in criminal matters and by preventing and combating racism and xenophobia.[25]

> That objective shall be achieved by preventing and combating crime, organised or otherwise, in particular terrorism, trafficking in persons and offences against children, illicit drug trafficking and illicit arms trafficking, corruption and fraud, through ... [inter alia] approximation, where necessary, of rules on criminal matters in the Member States.[26]

Article 31(1)(e), in turn, provides for common action in judicial cooperation with a view to

> progressively adopting measures establishing minimum rules relating to the constituent elements of criminal acts and to penalties in the fields of organised crime, terrorism and illicit drug trafficking.

Article 34 includes the particular rules concerning the legal instruments available to achieve these common ends, such as the framework decision.

The post-Amsterdam EU criminal law is already more difficult to place in a general category. The Treaty provisions give a relatively clear and ambitious view of the purposes of cooperation, yet the decision-making procedure is still based on unanimity. The intergovernmental European Council rather than the supranational Commission acts as the key legislative body. And whilst framework decisions for the approximation of law are binding upon the Member States as to the result to be achieved directly upon their being concluded, they lack direct effect. Since the role of the Parliament and the ECJ are more marginal than in the Community pillar, the Member States' representatives acting together in the Council have clearly remained the main power centre – the Union legislator, supported

---

[24] Convention on the Protection of the European Communities' Financial Interests ([1995] OJ C316/03 27 November 1995); Convention on the Fight against Corruption involving officials of the European Communities or officials of Member States of the European Union ([1997] OJ C195/01, 25 June 1997).

[25] Art 29, Treaty on European Union.

[26] *ibid.*

by the Commission and, of course, backed up by the whole apparatus preparing the decision-making of the Council at working group levels and upper levels.

It is a commonplace that the Amsterdam Treaty model was not an entirely happy solution, and almost immediately thereafter other larger processes got underway which were partly related to the problems caused by the uncertain progress in the Third Pillar legal setting. Third Pillar law was still mainly viewed under the profile of 'complementary measures', thus reflecting practical needs for common action that had their ultimate source in the economic integration process itself. In addition to that, new issues were raised, such as action against the sexual abuse of children, and environmental crimes, and perhaps also racism. Many of these new 'regulatory problems' were not just practical matters for enhanced cooperation that needed a back-up from the European institutions, but were also very much symbols that were extremely important for the self-image of the polity. The political process which had been created could be used for new policies alongside the old economically-sourced ones, as long as every state agreed. There were signs of progress in developing a polity, because these policies had become pan-European issues. The introduction of European citizenship both contributed to this emphasis and could draw on it.

From the point of view of the interests of ordinary *European* citizens, many limitations of the EU competences seemed irrational, which led to active testing of these limits. It had become clear from this new perspective that national differences remained much too large to allow for a uniform European standard to be developed over a more broadly-defined range of criminal policy. One of the documents that reflects this novel perspective is the 2004 Green Paper on the approximation, mutual recognition and enforcement of criminal sanctions in the EU.[27] The approximation of penalties Europe-wide would have helped give 'the general public a shared sense of justice',[28] which was regarded as one of the conditions for establishing the Area of Freedom, Security and Justice. The Member States were not willing to take these steps, however.

Referring back to what was said earlier, the progress on Third Pillar law symbolised a certain rather minimal but still significant shared view of the central problems of criminal law. As so often, the same phenomenon could be looked at from various angles and always be perceived differently. The fight against terrorism, which so dominated the political scene just a few years ago, was not just about harmonising legislation, creating new legal institutions and mobilising the national police forces and prosecutors and

---

[27] Green Paper on the approximation, mutual recognition and enforcement of criminal sanctions in the European Union, Brussels 30 April 2004, COM(2004) 334 final.
[28] *ibid*, 9.

courts to work better together, but was also a symbol of sufficient value consensus to make the *common* political processing of these matters possible in the first place. We should of course not be naïve and see all this *only* as a maturing of general thinking, but in the political and legal structures of the EU, practical and symbolic considerations became closely linked. Many things suddenly became possible which had not been possible before.

Almost from the start of the Amsterdam period, it was clear that the Union needed to rethink its general political and legal framework. The agenda was growing beyond the existing political structures and a political reform of the constitutional framework seemed inevitable. The more inclusive decision-making procedures of the 'constitutional convention' method of law-making were first applied in drafting the Charter of Fundamental Rights for the European Union. In the preamble to the Charter we read, inter alia, that

> the Union is founded on the indivisible, universal values of human dignity, freedom, equality and solidarity; it is based on the principles of democracy and the rule of law. It places the individual at the heart of its activities, by establishing the citizenship of the Union and by creating an area of freedom, security and justice.

The Charter is an impressive commitment to constitutional values and, had it been formally equipped with legally-binding status, it would most certainly be relevant as regards the legitimacy of the various pieces of secondary legislation adopted under the Third Pillar. With the ratification of the Lisbon Treaty, this finally is the case.

Following the Charter, the second constitutionalising effort was the equally famous, and equally contested one of reforming the entire Treaty framework by introducing a new structure under which Third Pillar procedures and Third Pillar competences would have undergone fundamental revision. Certainly, narrowly practical considerations also called for revision (such as that the Council under successive enlargements consisting of 15, then 25, and then 27 members, no longer reaches unanimous decisions easily), but broader political-theoretical reasons were weighty as well. One of these was that the involvement of the democratic institution of parliaments, both European and national, should be increased. The Treaty reform effort, of course, has had its ebbs and flows. The original Constitutional Treaty under which these reforms were mooted, and which like the Charter used the convention method of deliberation, was defeated in 2005, and its successor, the Lisbon Treaty, containing substantially the same reform provisions, was not finally ratified until 2009.

Armed with this contextual understanding, we should now return to our basic question: is the European Union well-equipped to deal with criminal law issues without the risk that it and its general constitutional framework becomes a problem as concerns the legitimacy of the European criminal legal order? Is the EU prepared to take into account the ethical-political dimension of criminal law?

There is no doubt that criminal law may develop beyond the national level, as we know from international treaty law, the law on international core crimes and from the workings of the international criminal courts. The European way to proceed is mainly to approximate legislation. This is what has happened so far: the list of framework decisions having provisions of a substantive penal law character already exceeds 10 in number. According to the treaty provisions, only 'minimum rules relating to the constituent elements of criminal acts and to penalties' should be provided. The provisions of many framework decisions are, however, quite detailed, so one could ask whether this is still minimum harmonisation.

One obvious problem has been that the ECJ has only had restricted powers to control the validity of framework decisions. Under the constitutional setting of Amsterdam, the ECJ has also been unwilling to annul framework decisions for reasons other than that a particular framework decision has violated a Community competence.

The EU constitutional setting would perhaps not be such a large issue from the penal law point of view if the substantive issues had not been and did not continue to be so exceptional and difficult to handle. We have seen measures taken against terrorism, organised crime, drug trafficking, trafficking of human beings, child pornography, etc. The European Union has not always generated these common policy issues simply internally, but has also channelled international efforts regionally, as in the case of international terrorism, for instance.

How can the EU deal with these issues in a balanced way, taking all relevant aspects into account, and formulate good penal policy? There are many answers to these questions, none of them obvious. We could of course assume that the Member States continue to make the *real* criminal policy when negotiating the instruments and when implementing the common measures nationally. The Member States will certainly try to do that and are often in a practical position to exert significant influence. But, as experience has shown, implementing EU measures is, from the point of view of domestic policy, quite a different type of activity from other legal reforms. Quite clearly the penal policy debate is completely differently structured when the national parliament already faces binding obligations in dealing with the issue.

One way to think about all of this is to start from the premise that the substantive criminal policy is still primarily a matter for the Member States. The principle of subsidiarity has been invoked in order for this to happen. The common policy areas are always marked in one way or another by the need to address a problem in common at some very general level, and this also applies here. The basic approach has been agreed at the treaty level, and the ECJ has further elaborated on restricting principles, such as proportionality and legality.

The problem still is that the EU framework decisions lead to modifications of national penal systems which are not only of technical quality, but which entail substantial value-based changes. National political processes can hardly take full responsibility for the outcome. Part of the political responsibility requires to be borne at the European level.

In terms of my legitimacy analysis, the legitimacy of criminal law is a graduated affair. The quality of democratic and constitutional processes is crucial for reaching a high level of legitimacy. This would sometimes also be the easiest way to increase the legitimacy of the system. Under current circumstances, the matter of how far and how deeply national parliaments are involved in the preparation of European instruments depends mainly on national constitutional structures. The involvement of a national parliament in the first cycle – the preparation stage – is important and would increase the legitimacy of the procedure. The national parliament would mediate the voice of its people in the process, and the unanimity principle has until now ensured that it would be heard at the centre (but only if the national constitution allows for this).

The graduated quality of legitimacy – and its gradual realisation – is also demonstrated in other variable features. The more technical issues do not require as much debate and reasoning as do the substantive issues. Minimum harmonisation requires less legitimacy than does full unification. This can readily be confirmed by thinking about the theoretical possibility of passing a European penal code through a (what used to be First Pillar) regulation. That way we would have abandoned the oft-criticised minimum-harmonisation approach, and changed it into something quite different – a European code equipped with directly applicable provisions.[29] Nevertheless, in one sense such an idea could seem natural, because in the course of history, codification has been one of the ways to reduce complexity in penal law matters. The modern era has been marked by massive codification processes. The treaty establishing the International Criminal Court, for instance, can also be seen as a codification of the substance of international criminal law, albeit only for the purposes of defining the competence of the International Criminal Court itself.

A penal code should, of course, only cover those areas that fall within shared competence or within an exclusive Community competence. The

---

[29] Art 325 of the new Lisbon-derived Treaty on the Functioning of the European Union no longer excludes the possibility of resorting to criminal law measures, which might open up the way towards fully European, transnational criminal law provisions, where the protection of EU's financial interests is concerned. This matter is connected with the issue of possibly developing the powers of Eurojust under the Lisbon Treaty.

main reason why this is quite unthinkable in today's world is that the political and constitutional structures of the EU are just not able to handle this sort of process. The necessary deliberative processes would have to enable the adoption of a European ethical we-perspective and combine it with the criminal law's many abstract and universal moral principles. The cultural preconditions of this are simply unavailable.

The legitimacy of EU criminal law is heavily dependent on the availability of adequate constitutional processes pitched at a more modest level. In a sense, even today, the treaty framework with its constitutional contents bridges the two levels of criminal law, the European and the national, bringing them into contact with one another.

IV.   CONSTITUTIONAL PLURALISM

In fact, the legitimacy issues of criminal law strongly suggest some sort of constitutional pluralism as the best way to increase and safeguard the legitimacy of criminal law.[30] We could even speak of a criminal law pluralism, which in some sense reproduces structures similar to constitutional pluralism. Transnational criminal law can no longer be denied existence, whilst at the same time not being the whole story. The Lisbon model goes a long way down this path. The diversity of legal systems with their distinct legal traditions is being raised as a value in itself,[31] which marks both the relative existence and the lack of deep shared ethical convictions of a type that would render European politics possible, and at the same time highlights the need to preserve the legal fundamentals of all Member States.

The European Parliament will henceforth be better included in the processes at the European level, and some of the checks and controls also involve Member State parliaments.[32] The powers of the ECJ will be extended, which will strengthen the role of the European judiciary. The Charter has become binding law.[33] The Commission as well as other Member States have been entrusted with the power to use infringement proceedings against individual Member States failing to implement the

---

[30] See the general analysis in M Maduro, 'Contrapunctual Law: Europe's Constitutional Pluralism in Action' in N Walker (ed), *Sovereignty in Transition: Essays in European Law* (Oxford, Hart Publishing, 2003) 501–37.
[31] Art 67, para 1 TFEU.
[32] Eg Art 69 TFEU.
[33] Art 6, para 1 TEU.

agreed measures accordingly.[34] The national judiciary will also have an increased role in that all Member States would have to allow preliminary rulings in this area.[35]

The introduction of the emergency brake allows for the case in which, during the negotiation process, a national parliament regards the provisions introduced in a proposed measure as running against the fundamental legal principles of that state's legal order.[36] This mechanism is highly pertinent from the point of view of safeguarding the legitimacy of national penal systems in particular and national legal orders more generally, because this entails a sort of veto right to stop the proceedings and refer the case for further scrutiny. Such a procedure is valuable because it will enable Member States to normatively censure the measures which are on the table according to their own important preferences, among them those elements constituting the legitimacy of their own domestic legal systems. It should also be remembered that the coherence of a penal system is an important independent value, which should not be endangered. The existence of such a procedure to contest a measure on such grounds is likely to strengthen the observance of such values during the negotiations. All this will indirectly enhance the legitimacy of the instruments adopted when viewed from the perspective of the national legal orders.

The perspective of national legal orders is, however, no longer enough, as a European perspective also needs to be provided. The European legal order consists not only of norms that are part of the Union legal order in a strict sense – mainly by having been adopted following distinct European procedures – but also of norms implementing these at a national level. The protective schemes upholding the legitimacy of a criminal legal order have to be present at both of these levels, the European and the national. For example, the main point in the complex and now famous *Kadi* decision[37] was that the EU must be able to review its own legal instruments judicially from the point of view of adequate protection of the fundamental right, even where the Union is under a binding obligation of public international law to introduce a specific legal instrument.

Fundamental rights and human rights are crucial from the point of view of the legitimacy of criminal law norms. In order not to risk their legitimacy, these rights should be accorded a strong position. This would have an impact on the legitimacy issue both directly and indirectly. These norms need to be legally effective in order to trump other norms and to guide legal interpretation.

---

[34]   Arts 258–60 TFEU.
[35]   Art 267 TFEU.
[36]   Art 82, para 3 TFEU.
[37]   Joined cases C-402/05 P *Kadi v Council and Commission* and C-415/05 P *Al Barakaat International Foundation v Council and Commission* [2008] ECR I-6351.

The other source of normative censure and support may be found in the general principles of the EC/EU, which could start giving support to the legitimacy of penal law measures. In Kaarlo Tuori's terms, we might speak about a qualitative shift leading to the strengthening of the EU legal order's ability to check its own legal quality, which could be regarded as a sign of the maturity of the EU legal order.[38]

The diffuse nature of European criminal law is also manifested in the fact that national courts actually do most of the work. They apply the national provisions, but they also act as European courts. And it is these courts which in the last instance decide on the concrete principles of European law. What we see now is a growing interest in and significance for national courts in Europe generally, as these courts communicate with each other more than ever before, and refer not only to the case law of the ECJ, but also to other relevant European courts.[39]

V.   THE NEED TO MOVE FORWARD IN CRIMINAL POLICY

It has been clear since the Amsterdam era that cooperation in criminal law is a high priority for the EU. A lack of European rules was deeply felt, which finally led first to the approval of the Amsterdam model in general terms and later to an increasingly active use of the newly-agreed competence. The first years of the new millennium were marked by the active negotiation and conclusion of legal instruments, such that both the Member States and European actors have now accumulated important experience of what this all means in practice.

From the point of view of legitimacy, things have gone a rather strange way, in the reverse order. The Lisbon model tries to introduce a more legitimate framework for drafting what is basically the law that already exists, at least insofar as we are referring to substantive criminal law rather than procedural law, mutual recognition instruments or police cooperation. The Third Pillar *acquis* has been produced under politically favourable circumstances, with strong strategic support from both the European Council and the Commission, but also under circumstances in which the legitimacy of the instruments has not been much debated as part of these procedures themselves.

The practical necessity to take further steps has been part of the experience. Preparations for the enlargement of 2004 further underlined the need for action. Fighting terrorism and organised crime became a high

---

[38]   See the discussion in K Tuori, *Critical Legal Positivism*, above n 21, 205–09.
[39]   For example, the Nordic Supreme Courts have started to add links to each other's case law on their web pages. The web page of the European Criminal Law Academic Network ECLAN includes information on both European and national cases.

priority for well-known practical and political reasons. The EU could not fail – and could not be seen to fail – to address some of the most threatening phenomena of our time. For some reason, after getting most of the *acquis* in place, the momentum disappeared. The framework decision concerning the rights of the accused has long been in draft form, but does not seem to move forward. It is a major concern that we get the substantive rules first, whilst procedural guarantees lag behind. The political priorities of the Stockholm Programme (2010–14), adopted in December 2009,[40] include the challenge of ensuring respect for fundamental freedoms and integrity whilst guaranteeing security in Europe. The need to improve policy coherence and the need to comprehensively address the challenges the area is facing are stressed. The full implementation of current instruments is a priority, rather than the introduction of new instruments.

The future, post-Lisbon, era will have to readdress the Amsterdam products and see how they should be redrafted. So far it is hard to say what will happen. The Lisbon transition rules[41] entail a promise that all Third Pillar framework decisions must be renegotiated, because they only continue to be valid for five years following the coming into force of the Lisbon Treaty. The new legislative procedure will, however, be rather different. Now that qualified majority voting will be applied, the national parliaments could intervene, and the ECJ could now also become more active in seeing that all EU legal principles are being met. We might therefore see more framework decisions being quashed or challenged, or this may turn out to be a chimera, where nobody dares to care any longer, because if there were problems for the national legal order in the first round, the damage may already be done. The logic of penal law reform is that you seldom take steps back. The development of EU law more generally, moreover, has also been marked throughout the years by a pragmatic interest in moving forward in what is being regarded as furthering legal and other forms of integration. Not even Third Pillar law is an exception to that.

The strategically remorseless commitment to progress has long been part of the project, at least since the Tampere European Council in 1999. The European Council will continue to be the strategic power centre in the Lisbon system as well, and even more so. The European Council has become a full EU body, reinforcing this centrality.[42] It will also have to resolve the disputes raised by national parliaments.

---

[40]   EU OJ C115/1.
[41]   Protocol No 36 to the TFEU, on transitional provisions.
[42]   Art 68 TFEU.

This strength of the European Council reminds us of the fact that criminal law and other AFSJ matters are close to national sovereignty. The principle of mutual recognition goes well together with the wish not to give away real powers in this sector, but rather to act collaboratively. The principle of mutual recognition combined with the minimum harmonisation approach, 'when necessary', opens the door to indirect policy-making via harmonisation. The increased role of the European Parliament and other transnational actors counterbalances this state-centralism and allows the regime to be brought under the common umbrella of EU law. The Stockholm programme also indicates that the European Council is strongly committed to introducing full legal protection schemes to the AFSJ setting. The document demonstrates a consciousness that in this area the balance between rights and security needs to be rethought in order to improve the legal quality of the common rules. In one sense, the legal criteria and the legal principles themselves are regarded as the true guarantees of legal protection. This is certainly very interesting with regard to the legitimacy analysis.

Where democratic legitimacy remains rather weak, the quality of law itself may become the vehicle of legitimacy. It could somehow act as a surrogate for democracy. In thinking about the legitimacy of European criminal law, one should take into account these specific constitutional features and not try to measure the law directly by the usual yardsticks. There is certainly much room for further crystallisation of European criminal law as a legal order as the process of its formation continues.

VI.   TOWARDS EUROPEAN CRIMINAL LAW

The question that remains to be answered is whether Europe can fix the problems of legitimacy concerning criminal law issues that it itself reflects. Is there a chance that something qualitatively and normatively defensible might develop out of this massive product of law-building and polity-building? Is there a future for a truly transnational criminal law, or should we understand this part of the EU legal order as a form of background common law?

I believe that an analysis of the legitimacy of EU criminal law is the first step towards assessing this. This analysis needs to take into account the special nature of criminal law as expressed in criminal law principles and other principles and practices accounting for the legitimacy of criminal law in any possible setting. My view is that an output-legitimacy, which would measure itself solely in terms of lives saved and harm prevented, is far from being enough here. We need a normative analysis which has to be stretched over the entire project.[43] This analysis would be well advised not to understand legitimacy in an all-or-nothing fashion, but as a relational and gradual concept. The need for legitimacy grows greater the more we enter substantive criminal policy issues and beyond the mere coordination of legislative action.

Such an analysis would also lead us to think about the mutual interdependence between criminal law and constitutional procedures and guarantees. The deepest question concerns the ability of the European Union to develop political structures capable of handling sensitive value-issues. Criminal law is replete with values and ideologies, which are hard to avoid wherever and however the field is addressed.

The model of constitutional pluralism seems at least to be a temporary solution, building on the division of labour that involves both the ECJ (and of course the national courts as well) and the parliaments (national and European) having the functions of checking the proposed legal instruments and ensuring that they meet all normative criteria which are part of the system. In this way, a legal culture could develop that could meet certain legitimacy requirements when regarded from both standpoints, the European and the national.

In fact, the challenge that the EU is facing is qualitatively new. It concerns the 'taming' of politics in a special transnational setting, and introducing reason. The criminal law context renders this effort a risky one, because the stakes are very high. Should the European project not succeed, the national legal orders would mainly bear the costs, and criminal laws with diminished legitimacy would be a high cost, even for short-term gains.

There are some signs of a growing awareness of these problems. We cannot deny that the EU framework has had difficulty in addressing matters of criminal law. After all, these matters have not been directly addressed from the ordinary perspective of criminal policy, but from that of creating a transnational legal and judicial area by means of enhanced cooperation. Interestingly, the procedural approach – that of working through the principle of mutual recognition instead of directly addressing these matters from the point of view of substantial harmonisation – has proved to generate constitutional problems just as much as substantial

---

[43] One of the critical voices, Winfried Hassemer, has encouraged researchers to focus first on issues of European criminal procedure instead of only looking at the substantive criminal law issues. The reasons are manifold. Among them is the great practical relevance of the procedural rules as well as the close connection between them and the rules of constitutional law. See W Hassemer, 'Ein Strafrecht für Europa' in W Hassemer, *Strafrecht: Sein Selbstverständnis, seine Welt* (Berlin, BWV, 2008) 204–18.

harmonisation has done. It seems that enhanced horizontal legal cooperation has been the true engine of European developments, which has also
meant a qualitative leap in integration compared with the approach of the
Council of Europe.[44]

The mutual relations between the principles of mutual recognition and
substantial harmonisation add an important aspect to the entire enterprise
of building up a European Area of Freedom, Security and Justice as well as
adding a further level of complexity to this development. In my view, the
implications of building on the mutual recognition principle should be
studied theoretically. The main reason why this principle is so radical is
that it allows a European system to be generated without detailed
knowledge in advance of what will happen. The philosophy of mutual
recognition is important, as this principle obviously creates new links and
commonalities between parts of the system, despite its character as a
formal principle and allowing for differences to be maintained. The mutual
recognition instruments also differ as to their nature. Some are instruments
for efficient cross-border enforcement, whereas others concern taking
foreign criminal judgments into account in a substantial sense in national
proceedings, for instance, though without introducing any direct harmonising effect whatsoever.[45]

Concerning discussions of the role of substantial harmonisation of
criminal law, one of the most valuable and penetrating statements is found
in Advocate-General Mazak's opinion delivered on 28 June 2007 in the
case concerning the Framework Decision on Ship-Source Pollution.[46] The
Advocate-General highlighted the specific character of criminal law, going
well beyond a mere sanctioning mechanism. In his words, criminal law

> stands out from other areas of law. Availing itself of the most severe and most
> dissuasive tool of social control – punishments – it delineates the outer limits of
> acceptable behaviour and in that way protects the values held dearest by the
> community at large. As an expression essentially of the common will, criminal
> penalties reflect particular social disapproval and are in that respect of a
> qualitatively different nature as compared with other punishments such as
> administrative sanctions.[47]

---

[44] Cf M Fichera, *The Implementation of the European Arrest Warrant in the European Union: Law, Policy and Practice* (Antwerp, Intersentia, 2011).

[45] Council Framework Decision 2008/675/JHA of 24 July 2008 on taking account of convictions in the Member States of the European Union in the course of new criminal proceedings [2008] OJ L220/32.

[46] Case C-440/05 *Commission v Council*, [2007] ECR I-9097.

[47] *ibid*, para 67.

Criminal law 'largely mirrors the particular cultural, moral, financial and other attitudes of a community and is especially sensitive to societal developments'.[48]

Mazak points out that there is 'no uniform concept of the notion of criminal law and the Member States may have very different ideas when it comes to identifying in closer detail the purposes which it should serve and the effects it may have'.[49] He further stresses that 'in accordance with the principle of subsidiarity, the Member States are as a rule better placed than the Community to "translate" the concept of "effective, proportionate and dissuasive criminal penalties" into their respective legal systems and societal context'.[50]

He also points out that it would be problematic to recognise the Community's criminal law competence only 'as a single aspect of the Community policy concerned – whilst at the same time its implications have to be accommodated by the criminal law of the Member States, which is normally perceived as forming a distinct body of law'.

A similar struggle with the concept of criminal law in an EU setting can be observed in the domestic setting. In its *Lisbon* judgment,[51] the German Federal Constitutional Court likewise emphasised the particular nature of criminal law:

> To what extent and in what areas a polity uses exactly the means of criminal law as an instrument of social control is a fundamental decision. By criminal law, a legal community gives itself a code of conduct that is anchored in its values, whose violation is, according to the shared convictions on law, regarded as so grievous and unacceptable for social existence in the community that it requires punishment.[52]

> Due to the fact that democratic self-determination is affected in an especially sensitive manner by provisions of criminal law and law of criminal procedure, the corresponding foundations of competence in the Treaties must be interpreted strictly – on no account extensively – and their use requires particular justification. The core content of criminal law does not serve as a technical instrument for effectuating international cooperation but stands for the particularly sensitive democratic decision on the minimum standard according to legal ethics. This is explicitly recognised by the Treaty of Lisbon where it equips the newly established competences in the administration of criminal law with a so-called emergency brake which permits a member of the Council, which is

---

[48] *ibid*, para 68.
[49] *ibid*, para 69.
[50] *ibid*, para 108.
[51] BVerfG, 2 BvE 2/08, judgment of 30 June 2009, Absatz-Nr (1–421).
[52] *ibid*, para 355.

ultimately responsible to its parliament, to prevent directives with relevance to criminal law at least for its own country, invoking 'fundamental aspects of its criminal justice system'.[53] [54]

This decision elaborates on several aspects relevant to the mutual interdependencies of criminal law and constitutional law. An example is the criminal law principle of guilt.[55] The German Federal Constitutional Court holds that the EU criminal law competence must be interpreted narrowly and consistently with the constitutionally protected specificities of criminal law. According to that Court, 'The principle of guilt forms part of the constitutional identity which is inalienable due to Article 79.3 of the Basic Law and which is also protected against encroachment by supranational public authority'.[56]

The FCC went so far as to say that from the perspective of German constitutional law, the democratic legitimisation via national parliaments can only be guaranteed by the German representative on the Council exercising the Member State's rights, and this on the instruction of the German *Bundestag* and *Bundesrat*. The FCC generally criticised the line of thought that European law could gain its legitimacy directly by means of democratic processes at the European level.

In my view, the FCC decision deserves merit in that it seeks to recognise the full significance of the legal norms strongly expressing and affecting the self-image of the polity. Criminal law is a good candidate for such a reading. One should add, however, that a 'traditional' view of criminal law does not automatically have to carry with it a traditional view of democratic legitimacy. In my view, we should not tie these two together as the FCC did. Otherwise we remain trapped in the old views about criminal law only belonging to the domain of national legal orders, and we fail to appreciate the nuances concerning increased democratic legitimacy at the European level.

Neither should we forget that the Lisbon framework strengthens the observance of the subsidiarity and proportionality principles, both of which will be controlled by national parliaments. The developing network of legal and political controls, some national and some transnational, will in the long run shape the developing European criminal law.

Thus, the European criminal law as an order is in the process of being created. It will emerge out of these tensions, challenges and disputes. As the political programme develops, the legal quality will also develop. The constitutional development will start framing this development more actively than it has so far. The constitutional developments could be

---

[53]   Article 83.3, TFEU.
[54]   Lisbon judgment, above n 51, para 358.
[55]   *ibid*, para 365.
[56]   *ibid*, para 365.

regarded only as reactive – as a resistant force. But I do not wish to put it so crudely or one-sidedly. The constitutional debates are also part of the (re)formation of the political culture, including those aspects relevant to criminal law. We cannot see clearly into the future, but we see today that European criminal law is still very much in the making, and that it will have broader implications for European law and Europe as a polity in general.

The Hague Programme of 2004 had already underlined the need for strengthening mutual trust through progressively developing a European judicial culture of cooperation in both civil and criminal matters.[57] The subsequent Stockholm Programme[58] restates the call to develop a European judicial culture. It calls for better legislation and addresses horizontal problems of fragmentation and overlaps concerning lack of coherence between various legal instruments.[59] Going further than the Hague Programme, it introduces the idea that the core criminalisation principles, such as the *ultima ratio* principle, will be applicable to actual criminal law matters. A degree of concern for the coherence of the European legal instruments has equally been voiced. It remains to be seen how 'thick' a criminal law concept is actually constructed with a view to developing a European judicial culture. Certainly, this judicial culture needs to be carefully analysed, as it could mean something very different from the national context. In a sense, such a project still must presuppose developing a European legal culture, because a European judicial culture without a legal culture would be strangely superficial and devoid of content. It is in the area of legal culture, more broadly conceived, that we see the true dynamics of the process of the maturation of European criminal law.

The complexities of the formation of European criminal law are many, as the ever stronger emphasis on the mutual recognition principle reflects the view that the diversity of European national traditions is a fact to be recognised and respected rather than simply a problem to be remedied. European criminal law is emerging and maturing within these tensions. The first weak expressions of European criminal law that started to become visible 10 or 15 years ago have now taken a much clearer shape. The order that is developing is something *sui generis*. The more we see of it, the more convinced we are of this fact. Introducing criminal law into European law requires rethinking European law. There is nothing about criminal law itself that would prohibit it from being developed in the direction of transnational law. Yet criminal law carries certain heightened

---

[57] The Hague Programme: *Strengthening Freedom, Security and Justice in the European Union*, Presidency Conclusions, Brussels, 4–5 December 2004.
[58] EU OJ C115/1, 11.
[59] *Ibid*, 4–6.

expectations of legitimacy within itself, and for this reason it is not easily raised to the level of transnational law.

The development of theoretical models for understanding how European criminal law develops faces similar issues to those relating to constitutional developments and constitutionality. European criminal law is a story about developing transnational law that has not cut its ties with the Members States' legal orders; quite the contrary. It is about reorganising, about borrowing, about referring back, about seeking to recognise law as it is. Europe needs constitutionality in order to produce criminal law in a legitimate fashion. But equally European criminal law may test the limits of European constitutionality, and itself contribute to European constitutionality by means of the contestation it produces and addresses.

13

The Constitutional Function of Labour Law in the European Union

RUTH DUKES*

I. INTRODUCTION

T HE STORY OF the development of the labour law of the European Union is well known and often told.[1] As originally constituted in the Treaty of Rome, the European Economic Community had no legislative competence over labour and other social matters. The guiding principle was that the intergovernmental institutions of the Community should bear responsibility for the creation and maintenance of a common market in goods and services; responsibility for the maintenance and improvement of social standards – of living and working conditions – should remain firmly in the hands of the Member States. In time, this principle proved unworkable. A first challenge arose by reason of a growing cognisance within the Community of the potential benefits of Community involvement in social policy. By endowing the Community with a 'human face', a European social policy could provide legitimacy for EEC economic activities; it could help to turn the common market into 'a genuine Community', capable of '[commanding] the loyalties of its citizens, strong enough to resist the centrifugal forces of nationalism and sectional pressures'.[2] With such considerations in mind, efforts were made from the early 1970s to involve the EEC in the promotion of improved

* School of Law, University of Glasgow. I am very grateful to Richard Hyman and Adam Tomkins for comments on an earlier draft.

[1] eg HG Mosley, 'The Social Dimension of European Integration' (1990) 129 *International Labour Review* 147; C Barnard, 'EC "Social" Policy' in P Craig and G de Burca (eds), *The Evolution of EU Law* (Oxford, Oxford University Press, 1999); J Kenner, *EU Employment Law* (Oxford, Hart Publishing, 2003).

[2] M Shanks, 'The Social Policy of the European Communities' (1977) 14 *Common Market Law Review* 373, 378.

standards of living and working. At the same time, a second challenge emerged to the Member State reservation of responsibility for social policy, as the enforcement of the law of the common market threatened to restrict the freedom of Member States to regulate social matters as they saw fit. In particular, national labour laws or social standards might constitute unlawful barriers to Community market freedoms, or distortions of competition. Since the 1990s, concern regarding the potential consequences of this second challenge has grown. On the one hand, the accession to the EU of former Communist states has accentuated the already existing problems associated with disparities in labour costs and labour standards between Member States. On the other, it has become increasingly clear that, despite expanded legislative competence, the upward harmonisation of labour laws across Member States is no longer a policy objective of the Community. Since the Treaty of Maastricht, social policy initiatives have tended to emphasise the importance of the principle of subsidiarity, and to introduce 'soft' law rather than hard law measures.

My aim in this chapter is to revisit this narrative from a perspective which understands labour law principally in terms of its constitutional function.[3] In a collection of essays on the 'constitutional mosaic' of transnational Europe, this perspective is particularly useful, since it directs us to consider both the ways in which labour laws are constrained by the broader constitutional context in which they operate, and the ways in which labour laws serve in the EU (as in its Member States) to perform the constitutional task of establishing a particular economic and social order. More specifically, the idea of the constitutional function of labour law directs us to the question of whether and, if so how, labour laws have been adopted with the intention of addressing certain problems associated with the Constitution of the EU: for example, widely-held perceptions that the EU is fundamentally undemocratic; that its 'unbalanced' Constitution furthers the interests of capital at the expense of the interests of citizens.

Insofar as space allows, the discussion contained in the present chapter is aimed at attempting an answer to this last question. In the first part of the chapter, I explain what is meant by the constitutional function of labour law. I then consider the ways in which the Constitution and labour laws of the EU have been shaped by the goal of market integration, constraining both the ability of Member States to maintain social and labour standards, and the ability of trade unions to influence decision-making by way of autonomous collective bargaining. Finally, I examine two attempts to use labour law to address the problem of the unbalanced EU Constitution: the social dialogue, and the protection of labour rights as fundamental rights

---

[3] For an analysis motivated by a similar aim, see F Rödl, 'The Labour Constitution' in A von Bogdandy and J Bast (eds), *Principles of European Constitutional Law*, 2nd edn (Oxford, Hart Publishing, 2010).

within the 1989 and 2000 Charters – including, in the context of the 2000 Charter, the intriguing possibilities opened up by the EU's complementary move of promising accession to the European Convention on Human Rights (ECHR), the separate framework of transnational European human rights protection supplied under the aegis of the Council of Europe. I conclude that the unbalanced EU Constitution is unlikely to be righted through either of these initiatives since they are themselves crucially constrained by the constitutional context in which they operate: the multi-level division of authority between the EU and the Member States; and the constitutional priority of the economic freedoms.

II. THE CONSTITUTIONAL FUNCTION OF LABOUR LAW

Over the past decade or so, reference has been made with increasing frequency to the potential benefits of constitutionalising labour rights and social rights, of entrenching certain rights as fundamental at the national and transnational level. The argument has been advanced that if labour rights are universally recognised as fundamental human rights, they might act as a defence against the pernicious consequences of globalisation: the dismantling of labour standards and worker protections at national level in the name of improved economic flexibility and competitiveness in the global marketplace. As I have discussed elsewhere, the term 'constitutionalisation', used in application to labour law, has an older and rather different meaning.[4] At the end of the nineteenth century and during the earlier part of the twentieth century, the idea of the industrial, or economic, constitution was used to support arguments in favour of collective bargaining, and the democratisation of work and production through the collective participation of labour in management. In their book *Industrial Democracy*, Sidney and Beatrice Webb used the idea of an industrial constitution to emphasise the role that law could play in limiting the power wielded by employers over workers. Likening that power to the power of a king over his subjects, the legal recognition of collective bargaining and the gradual elaboration of a labour code were said by the Webbs to signify the concession of a 'Magna Carta' to the entire wage-earning class.[5] Twenty years later, the terms 'industrial constitution' and 'labour constitution' were developed by the German labour lawyer Hugo Sinzheimer in contribution to the debates surrounding the establishment of

[4] R Dukes, 'Constitutionalising Employment Relations: Sinzheimer, Kahn-Freund and the Role of Labour Law' (2008) 35 *Journal of Law and Society* 341.
[5] S and B Webb, *Industrial Democracy*, vol 2 (London, Longman, 1897) 840–42.

a new social democratic German state at the end of the First World War.[6] Again, the idea of a constitution was invoked with reference to the function of labour law – facilitating the participation of collectivised labour in the management of the economy – and not to signify that labour rights would be protected as fundamental within the Weimar Constitution. Again, the process of constitutionalising the economy was understood to be fundamental to the creation of a truly democratic state.

In more contemporary discussions of the meaning and aims of labour law, this notion of its *constitutional* function has tended to be overlooked. For the most part, scholars have focused more narrowly on the imbalance of bargaining power in employment relations as the paradigm which gives coherence and purpose to labour law. In recent years, some have sought to position themselves *against* the 'inequality of bargaining power' paradigm, arguing that it no longer fits the realities of modes and relations of production under globalisation; that, in any case, it is futile in these times of increased economic competitiveness to remain tied to a notion of labour law as state intervention to impose fair terms and conditions of employment.[7] More realistic and more useful, in the opinion of some, are conceptions of labour law which work with and not against the logic of global markets: labour law as regulating for competitiveness or flexibility; labour law as increasing access to labour markets.[8]

It is undoubtedly the case that the globalisation of capital and the liberalisation of markets in goods and services have wrought significant changes on work and working relationships. In the context of efforts to make sense of these changes and to consider the question of what labour law is, or ought to be, under conditions of globalisation, the idea of the constitutional function of labour law seems to me to have continued value as an analytical tool (I refer to the 'constitutional function' rather than the 'constitutionalisation' of labour law or labour rights, since my concern is not exclusively with the entrenchment of labour rights as fundamental rights). Thinking about labour law in terms of its constitutional function emphasises the importance of giving consideration to labour law's contribution to the constitutional task of establishing a particular economic and social order. It reminds us that the regulation of working relationships cannot usefully be considered in isolation from the broader constitutional context. Against those who argue for a labour law shaped to answer the need for ever greater flexibility and competitiveness, the idea of the

[6] For references see Dukes, 'Constitutionalising Employment Relations', above n 4, 345–52.
[7] eg P Davies and M Freedland, *Towards a Flexible Labour Market* (Oxford, Oxford University Press, 1997) especially ch 5.
[8] H Collins, 'Regulating Employment for Competitiveness' (2001) 30 *Industrial Law Journal* 17.

constitutional function of labour law directs us to focus on the role that labour law ought to play in constituting labour as something other than a commodity.[9] And it reminds us that notwithstanding globalisation there are choices to be made in what is rigid and what is flexible:[10] choices that might involve the entrenchment of certain rights and standards, the creation of legal frameworks allowing for processes of negotiation, the establishment of the contextual conditions – in the sense of fundamental commitments, principles, procedural guarantees etc – that configure the space for possible negotiation. In short, thinking about labour law in terms of its constitutional function allows us to maintain a critical edge, to resist the logic of the market where that logic causes harm, and to focus instead on conceptions of the role and aims of labour law which take the humanity of the worker as the first reference point.

In the EU, as in the Member States, the adoption of labour legislation has been informed by a variety of policy objectives. Sometimes the intention has been to improve the rights of workers, sometimes to further the goal of market integration, and sometimes to improve the performance of the European economy.[11] Ever since the first Community Social Action Programme of 1974, an important motivation for the adoption of labour laws has been the wish to provide the single market project with greater legitimacy: to demonstrate, in a way that was immediately apparent, the potential benefits of the project for the working people of the Member States, and to strengthen the Union's claim to democracy by improving rights to worker participation in decision-making within companies and within Community institutions. In recent years, such efforts have been discussed in connection with the postulated 'European Social Model': a model, according to the European Council, which is based on 'good economic performance, a high level of social protection and education and social dialogue'.[12] Reviewing the history of the EU, it is clear that labour law initiatives have formed the core of efforts to build up the 'social' aspect of the Union. But the question remains: to what extent has that body of law contributed, in fact, to the creation of a legal and political system deserving of the label 'European Social Model'?

In what follows, my approach to this question is informed by conceptions of the constitutional function of labour law developed in the context

---

[9] International Labour Organisation, *Declaration of Philadelphia*, adopted 10 May 1944 at the 26th Conference of the ILO, article 1.

[10] R Hyman, 'Flexible Rigidities: A Model for Social Europe?' in LE Alonso and M Martínez (eds), *Employment Relations in a Changing Society: Assessing the Post-Fordist Paradigm* (London, Palgrave Macmillan, 2006) 215.

[11] P Syrpis, *EU Intervention in Domestic Labour Law* (Oxford, Oxford University Press, 2007).

[12] Barcelona European Council, Presidency Conclusions, 15 and 16 March 2002, SN 100/1/02.

of the nation state; by the idea of labour law as a means of 'constitution-alising' or democratising national economies through the institution of systems of worker participation. Does the constitutional framework of the EU guarantee or recognise a role for labour in shaping European policies and legislation? Does that framework otherwise encourage, or obstruct, or constrain, the efforts of labour to represent its interests within a variety of contexts: policy-making and legislation at European and Member State level; decision-making within companies and workplaces? Does the frame-work make any alternative provision for the democratisation of the economic sphere? That said, the approach is also sensitive to the constitu-tional particularities of the EU. Clearly the labour law of the EU cannot properly be understood without reference to the constitutional division of labour between the EU and the Member States in respect of social policy matters. Nor can it properly be understood without considering the ways in which EU and Member State laws interact with, and are constrained by, different treaty aims, and in particular the fundamental aim of market integration. With these points in mind, I turn now to examine the founding Treaties of the European Communities, and the subsequent development of the EU Constitution.

III. THE UNBALANCED CONSTITUTION

In the Treaties of Rome of 1957, very little provision was made for trade union involvement in either the Economic or the Atomic Energy Community. Trade unions and other interest groups were excluded from the purely intergovernmental negotiations to establish the Communities and, under early drafts of the Treaties, were given no rights whatsoever to be represented within Community institutions. After much union lobbying, provision was made for the creation of an Economic and Social Committee (ESC), consisting of representatives of trade unions, industry and other interest groups, with responsibility for advising the Commissions and Councils on specified matters. This was a relatively weak body, with no power to draw up its own budget or to create its own rules of procedure, no power of initiative, and no right to offer advice unless called upon to do so by the Council or Commission. Nonetheless, it was only through representation on the ESC that the right of trade unions to participate in Community decision-making was acknowledged in the Treaties of Rome. This contrasted quite starkly with the case of the European Coal and Steel Community (ECSC) some years before. In the negotiation of the constitu-tive Treaty of Paris of 1951, trade unionists participated directly, acting together with government ministers, industrialists and academics as part of the national delegations to the Paris Summit. Under the terms of that

Treaty, trade unions were represented within and vis-a-vis the ECSC institutions, enjoying rights to be consulted, to make suggestions and remarks of their own and to raise claims before the European Court of Justice (ECJ).[13]

The different treatment of the trade unions in 1951 and 1957 can be explained, at least in part, by reference to the different nature of the projects involved; in particular, to the markedly more intergovernmental, as opposed to supranational, nature of the common market project.[14] In the case of the ECSC, the aim was to create a supranational means of regulating production in the coal and steel industries. At the urging of Jean Monnet and Robert Schuman, there was acceptance across the Member States of the need to cede power to a supranational body (the High Authority) to govern the ECSC, and of the importance of securing the cooperation and expertise of trade unions and other interest groups. By the time of the negotiation of the Rome Treaties, the Member States were more reticent to cede power to the supranational level. Though it grew, like the ECSC, out of federal sentiments, the EEC was shaped more significantly by Erhardian economic liberalism than by plans for a United Europe.[15] Like the West German *soziale Marktwirtschaft*, the Constitution of the EEC fitted rather well with ordo-liberal prescriptions for a law-based order committed to guaranteeing economic freedoms, and for a market sphere insulated from social and political considerations.[16] In the context of the EEC, of course, the 'social market economy' had a split-level structure: supranational institutions were assigned the task of ensuring economic rationality and a system of undistorted competition, and national institutions the task of pursuing redistributive (social) policies.[17] In such a Community, the case for the integration of trade unions and other interest groups in decision-making procedures was not obvious. If decision-making in social policy matters was to remain in the hands of the Member States, then it was within the Member States, primarily, that trade unions would be able to pursue their interests. If Community decisions were conditional on the agreement of an intergovernmental Council, then unions and other interest groups would anyway be able to exert an influence on such decisions from within the Member States, through established channels.

---

[13] C Beever, *European Unity and the Trade Union Movements* (Leiden, Sythoff, 1960); M Bouvard, *Labor Movements in the Common Market Countries* (New York, Praeger, 1972).

[14] E Haas, *The Uniting of Europe: Political, Social And Economic Forces 1950–1957* (Stanford, Stanford University Press, 1968 [1958]).

[15] Ludwig Erhard was Minister of the Economy in Germany from 1949 until 1963, and Chancellor from 1963 until 1966.

[16] Key works of the 'Ordo-Kreis' are translated in A Peacock and H Willgerodt (eds), *German Neo-Liberals and the Social Market Economy* (London, Macmillan, 1989).

[17] C Joerges, 'What is Left of the European Economic Constitution?' EUI Working Paper LAW No 2004/13, 14–17.

That was the theory at least, developed by the Ohlin and Spaak committees, and reflected in the terms of the Treaty of Rome.[18] In practice, it was not terribly long before the wisdom of a strict division between the regulation of the common market at Community level and the regulation of social policy at Member State level was placed in doubt. In the context of efforts to find a new impetus for European integration following the policy stalemate of the 1960s, and in the aftermath of the Paris Spring, arguments were increasingly made in favour of Community involvement in social matters as a means of legitimating the economic policies associated with the establishment of the common market.[19] On the back of a Social Action Programme of 1974, a swathe of social legislation was adopted, aimed at the upward harmonisation of certain labour standards.[20] In respect of the role and status of trade unions in the Community, two goals were proclaimed in the Action Programme: that of furthering the democratisation of European workplaces; and that of strengthening the involvement of management and labour in Community decision-making. In directives dealing with collective redundancies and the transfer of businesses, first steps were taken towards Community regulation of worker participation in managerial decision-making, with the creation of employee rights to information and consultation.[21] In respect of Community decision-making, meanwhile, efforts were made to construct a kind of European-level corporatism, involving representatives of capital and labour in a variety of bipartite and tripartite committees and discussions.[22]

Insofar as they signalled the beginnings of a rejection of the economic argument upon which the Treaty of Rome had been based – that social improvements would result more or less automatically from the removal of barriers to trade, the resulting growth of productivity, and the consequent enhancement of social conditions by Member States – these developments

---

[18] Both the Ohlin Report and the Spaak Report envisage an important role for trade unions, working within Member States to ensure improved standards of living and working. The Ohlin Report is summarised at (1956) 74 *International Labour Review* 99. Part I of the Spaak Report is published in English in PEP, *Planning*, No 405 (1956). The role of trade unions is referred to at (1956) 74 *International Labour Review* 99, 112 and at PEP, *Planning*, No 405 (1956) 235.

[19] Shanks, *The Social Policy of the European Communities*, above n 2.

[20] *EC Bulletin*, no 10, 1974.

[21] European Commission Green Paper, 'Employee Participation and Company Structure' (1975), 9–10; See also 'Multi-national undertakings and the Community' (*EC Bulletin* Supp 15/73). See also Council Directive 75/129/EEC of 17 February 1975 on the approximation of the laws of the Member States relating to collective redundancies [1975] OJ L48/29, and Council Directive 77/187/EEC of 14 February 1977 on the approximation of the laws of the Member States relating to the safeguarding of employees' rights in the event of transfers of undertakings, businesses or parts of businesses [1977] OJ L61/26.

[22] W Streeck and PC Schmitter, 'From National Corporatism to Transnational Pluralism: Organised Interests in the Single European Market' in W Streeck (ed), *Social Institutions and Economic Performance* (London, Sage, 1992) 200.

were highly significant. In terms of any meaningful adjustment of the constitutional framework of the Community, however, their influence was rather limited. The Social Action Programme did not amend the Treaty, or otherwise extend the legislative competence of the Community, nor did it relax the requirement for unanimity in the Council of Ministers for the adoption of legislation. Reflecting the need to be politically acceptable to all, the directives passed in the 1970s were thus quite restricted in terms of subject-matter, dealing chiefly with health and safety and sex discrimination. The Euro-corporatism project ended in failure in 1978, when the European Trade Union Confederation (ETUC) withdrew its support in protest at the lack of any meaningful progress. Notwithstanding the efforts of the Commission and the Council, then, the original ascription of responsibility for the maintenance of social standards to the individual Member States remained essentially unchallenged.

Although it went largely unrecognised at the time, a potentially more serious threat to the constitutional division of labour between an Economic Community responsible for the market and Member States responsible for social matters emerged during the 1970s from an alternative and most unexpected source, namely the interpretation of EEC law by the ECJ. As a result of the development by the Court of the doctrine of direct effect and the doctrine of the supremacy of Community law, the possibility arose that the capacity of the Member States to improve social standards might be *restricted*, rather than facilitated, by the enforcement of market-creating economic policies at supranational level.[23] Taken together, the combined effect of the two doctrines was that Community law figured as a form of higher law within the Member States: as a set of norms which national institutions were powerless to amend or overrule, but obliged to enforce. Because the Community was an *Economic* Community, because its laws were directed for the most part at the creation of a common market, what the doctrine of direct effect and the doctrine of the supremacy of Community law entailed was the elevation of the *law of the common market* to a form of higher law – the institution of a constitutional prioritisation of economic aims above other aims.[24]

It was in this constitutional context that the implications for labour law of the 1992 project to complete the single market had to be understood. As provided for in the Single European Act of 1986, it was clear that the completion of the internal market might entail the dismantling of a whole range of national labour laws as barriers to the free movement of goods,

---

[23] JHH Weiler, 'A Quiet Revolution: "The European Court and its Interlocutors"' (1994) 26 *Comparative Political Studies* 510.

[24] F Scharpf, 'Negative Integration and Positive Integration in the Political Economy of European Welfare States' in G Marks, FW Scharpf, PC Schmitter and W Streeck (eds), *Governance in the European Union* (London, Sage, 1996).

capital and services, or as contrary to European competition law. If, for example, a national law which prevented shops from opening on Sundays were found to conflict with EEC legislation protecting freedom of movement of goods, the latter would prevail and the national law would require to be disapplied.[25] The economic aim of creating a single market for goods would trump the social aim of ensuring a fixed weekly rest day for affected workers. If a national law which permitted the monopolisation of the provision of dock-work services were found to conflict with EEC legislation preventing abuse of a dominant market position, then, again, the latter would prevail and the national law would require to be disapplied.[26] The economic aim of ensuring the efficient functioning of the internal market for services would trump the social aim of protecting workers from the evils of casual work. Clearly a lot would depend on the ECJ's interpretation of EC law: its interpretation of what it understood to constitute a barrier to the freedom of movement of goods, services and capital; and its interpretation of the circumstances in which such barriers could be justified. But the danger existed that, as a result of the enforcement of European economic laws, the ability of nation states to improve or maintain social standards would be restricted. At the same time as the capacity of nation states to protect social standards was threatened, moreover, the ability of the EEC to guarantee equivalent standards remained limited. In addition to the difficulties involved in securing agreement for social legislation in the Council of Ministers, differences in the traditions and institutions of Member States created very significant barriers to the development of unitary European models of social welfare, health insurance and labour law.[27] For these reasons, it was highly unlikely that any levelling down of social standards at national level occasioned by the completion of the common market would be compensated by a process of re-regulation at the European level. By reason of the institutional set up of the EEC, and the nature of its Constitution as interpreted by the ECJ, the fact of the matter was that the creation of the common market looked set to involve the institution of a kind of 'competency gap', with neither the Community nor the Member States freely able to maintain or improve social standards.[28]

From the time of the Single European Act, steps were taken to ease the adoption by the Community of legislation regulating labour and social policy matters. Under the terms of that Act, the rule requiring unanimity in

---

[25] P Davies, 'Market Integration and Social Policy in the Court of Justice' (1995) 24 *Industrial Law Journal* 49.

[26] Case C-179/90 *Merci convenzionali porto di Genova SpA v Siderurgica Gabrielli SpA* [1991] ECR I-5889.

[27] Scharpf, 'Negative Integration', above n 24, 19, 32.

[28] *ibid*, 15.

Council was relaxed in respect of measures intended to improve health and safety at work. At the same time, the Commission under Jacques Delors sought to encourage management and labour to develop something akin to European-level collective bargaining, meeting to discuss policy and to negotiate joint statements or agreements.[29] From the point of view of Delors, the initiative was bound up with the advocacy of a 'European social space' as an adjunct to completion of the single market. The hope was that bipartite discussions might develop in time into negotiations capable of resulting in substantial 'contractual' collective agreements; that, in this manner, difficulties associated with fostering unanimity in the Council could be circumvented.[30] In 1989, the notion of a European social space took a more concrete form with the adoption of the Community Charter of Fundamental Social Rights – a 'bill of rights' type document, proclaiming a variety of labour and social rights including freedom of association, collective bargaining and collective action. Of itself, the Community Charter was not legally binding, but it was closely followed by a second Action Programme of legislative proposals and a second wave of labour law directives.[31] In 1992, a new 'Social Chapter' introduced by the Treaty of Maastricht further extended the power of the Community to adopt directives in the field of social policy, allowing the Council to act by qualified majority voting in respect of a much wider variety of subject-matter. Again, the extension of legislative competence was accompanied by measures to encourage trade unions and management to themselves enter into negotiations with a view to reaching agreements. The right of the 'social partners' to reach contractually-binding agreements, and to have these implemented either by way of collective agreements within Member States, or by Directive adopted by the Council, was now guaranteed in the Social Chapter. And the involvement of the social partners in Community social policy and legislation was formalised by way of a legal obligation on the Commission to consult the partners in a two-stage process: on legislative proposals; and, if action was to be taken on those proposals, on the content of the legislation.

Significant though the 1992 developments were, it is important to note that they did not herald a renewed push to harmonise labour law at the European level. As will be discussed in more detail below, the extension of the legislative competence of the Community was undertaken in connection with the formalisation of the social dialogue, and not primarily in order to facilitate the adoption by the Community of new labour

---

[29] H Northrup, D Campbell and B Slowinski, 'Multinational union-management consultation in Europe: Resurgence in the 1980s?' (1988) 127 *International Labour Review* 525.

[30] G Ross, *Jacques Delors and European Integration* (Cambridge, Polity Press, 1995) 45.

[31] Dealing with, inter alia, health and safety, pregnant workers, working time and posted workers.

legislation. From 1992 there was a marked move away from policies of harmonisation in the social and labour fields.[32] There was a move away, too, from the use of centrally-issued legislation to achieve social and labour policy goals, and an emphasis instead on soft law methods and the principle of subsidiarity.[33] The context for these changes was shaped significantly by the expansion of the European Union towards the East. In terms of the labour policies of the Union, this brought with it a number of barriers to the goal of upward harmonisation of labour standards, not least disparities in wage costs and labour standards between the old Member States and the new accession states: what Brian Bercusson called the 'elephant lurking in the European social model'.[34] In a single market, these disparities raised real concerns in the old Member States about social dumping and the creation of downward pressure on existing social protections. As expansion proceeded, the question of the preparedness of the Court of Justice to confirm the constitutional priority of free trade laws at the cost of national labour protections raised its ugly head again, with augmented significance. In four landmark decisions of 2007 and 2008, *Laval, Viking, Rüffert* and *Luxembourg*, the Court answered this question with a resounding 'yes'.[35] Fears of social dumping and downward harmonisation notwithstanding, freedom of establishment and freedom to provide services would be upheld at the cost of national labour laws.

In the *Laval* and *Viking* decisions, the national labour laws at stake were laws protecting freedom of association. The principal question at issue for the ECJ was whether such laws could constitute unlawful barriers to the exercise of freedom to supply services and freedom of establishment. Having proclaimed freedom of association to be a fundamental right within the EU, the Court went on to rule that Treaty provisions protecting freedom to supply services and freedom of establishment could apply horizontally to the actions of trade unions. Accordingly, it was not the Member State legislation but the industrial action itself which was regarded as constituting a barrier to the economic freedoms.[36] When the Court came to address the possibility that the barriers might be justified, and therefore lawful, it was with reference to the industrial action that the questions of aims and proportionality were assessed. By finding that

---

[32] Cf Commission, 'Medium-Term Social Action Programme 1995–97' COM(95) 134, 2; Commission Green Paper 2006 COM(2006) 708.

[33] W Streeck, 'Neo-Voluntarism: a New European Social Policy Regime?' (1995) 1 *European Law Journal* 31.

[34] B Bercusson, 'The Trade Union Movement and the European Union: Judgment Day' (2007) 13 *European Law Journal* 279, 305.

[35] Case C-341/05 *Laval v Svenska Byggnadsarbetareförbundet* [2007] ECR I-11767; Case C-438/05 *International Transport Workers' Union v Viking* [2007] ECR I-10779; Case-346/06 *Rüffert v Land Niedersachsen* [2008] ECR I-1989; Case C-319/06 *Commission v Luxembourg* [2008] ECR I-4323.

[36] Compare Case-112/00 *Schmidberger v Austria* [2003] ECR I-5659.

Articles 43 and 49 of the Treaty applied to the actions of the trade unions, the Court assigned itself jurisdiction to scrutinise the aims of the trade unions in taking industrial action and the means employed by them. Moreover, the approach taken to the questions of justification and proportionality was in these cases very narrow. In *Laval*, the Court tied the question of the legitimacy of the trade union's aims directly to its interpretation of the Posted Workers' Directive.[37] Since the terms of the collective agreement which the trade union wished the employer to sign went beyond the minimum necessary to protect posted workers, as defined by the Directive, the trade union's actions could not be justified.[38] In *Viking*, the decision turned on the fact that the employer had given an assurance that the terms and conditions of *current* employees would not be affected by the re-flagging of a ship in Estonia. The Court affirmed that the right to take action for the protection of workers was a legitimate interest. Since current workers would not be affected, however, the trade union could not be said to be pursuing that interest in this case. The Court also objected to the fact that the trade union's action had been successful. '[T]o the extent that [the trade union's] policy results in shipowners being *prevented* from registering their vessels in a State ... the restrictions on freedom of establishment resulting from such action *cannot* be objectively justified' (emphasis added).[39] The more successful the industrial action, it seems, the more difficult it will be to establish proportionality.[40]

Whilst this is not the place to consider the *Laval* and *Viking* decisions in any detail, emphasis might be given, in conclusion of this part of the chapter, to the implications of the decisions for the protection of labour rights within the EU. Together with questions of pay, the right of association and the right to strike continue to be explicitly excluded from the legislative competence of the Community.[41] Presumably the intention behind this exclusion was to affirm the right of Member States to protect freedom of association in domestic law in accordance with individual traditions and systems of industrial relations. As a result of the rulings of the ECJ, however, the capacity of Member States to protect trade union rights has been significantly restricted.[42] At the same time, the capacity of trade unions to participate effectively in the regulation of employment

---

[37] Dir 96/71/EC of the European Parliament and of the Council of 16 December 1996 concerning the posting of workers in the framework of the provision of services [1996] OJ L18/1.

[38] *Laval*, above n 35, paras 106–111.

[39] *Viking*, above n 35, para 88.

[40] ACL Davies, 'One Step Forward, Two Steps Back?' (2008) 37 *Industrial Law Journal* 126.

[41] Article 137(5) TEC.

[42] J Malmberg and T Sigeman, 'Industrial Actions and EU Economic Freedoms' (2008) 45 *Common Market Law Review* 1115.

relations, through processes of autonomous collective bargaining, has also been restricted. With its *Laval* and *Viking* decisions, the ECJ has done much to affirm the view that European integration entails the creation of a competency gap, with neither the EU nor the Member States freely able to maintain social and labour standards.[43] By proclaiming freedom of association to be a fundamental right, only to subject that right to a test of compatibility with market freedoms, the Court has raised significant doubts regarding the democratic nature of the EU.[44]

IV.   SOCIAL DIALOGUE

Fraught with ambiguity – does it refer to a type of collective bargaining, a form of corporatism, a method of legislation? – the term 'social dialogue' is used within the EU to refer to European-level negotiations between representatives of trade unions and representatives of employers. As sketched above, the formalisation of such arrangements in 1992 represented the culmination of a series of efforts to involve representatives of trade unions and management in social policy and legislation, through the institution of European-level collective negotiations. Both the corporatist experiments of the 1970s and the bipartite talks of the mid-1980s had ended with little to show for them by way of agreements or joint action.[45] The framing of the social dialogue within the Maastricht Treaty was intended to change that; to ensure its effectiveness in furthering economic and social reform. Since 1992, it has been given a prominent place in EU pronouncements regarding social policy, the European social model, and even the democratic legitimacy of the EU.[46] A closer examination of the social dialogue – its historical development, its outputs, and the nature and motivations of the social partners – places the validity of these pronouncements in doubt.

Dating back to the 1970s, efforts to encourage negotiations between trade unions and employers were hindered by the constitutional framework within which the parties met and negotiated.[47] Before Maastricht, the starting point for any negotiation between management and labour was a Community without social policy and legislation, without specific legislative competence in the field of social policy, and with a legislative

---

[43]   Resolution of the Executive Committee of the ETUC, 4 March 2008.

[44]   A Supiot, 'Europe Won Over to the Communist Market Economy' (July 2008) *Notre Europe*.

[45]   Northrup, Campbell and Slowinski, 'Multi-national union-management consultation', above n 29, 538.

[46]   Eg Commission Communication on the European Social Dialogue, COM(2002) 341.

[47]   Streeck and Schmitter, 'From National Corporatism', above n 22, 204–07.

process that required unanimity in the Council of Ministers for the adoption of legislation. In order to further the interests of workers by means of new initiatives or new legislation, the representatives of labour faced a formidable set of hurdles. In order to further the interests of business, the representatives of management had merely to maintain the status quo. From the viewpoint of business, essentially hostile to the development of supranational social policy, there was no incentive to engage in productive centralised negotiations with labour.[48] Where labour representatives sought the agreement of management to social policy proposals, management could simply refuse to negotiate. Where a Commission proposal was on the table, management could lobby within Member States to ensure that at least one state exercised its right of veto.

A second barrier to effective negotiations between management and labour arose by reason of the nature of the 'social partners' at European level. On the trade union side, the representative was the ETUC, created in 1973. In terms of its membership, this was a very large and comprehensive body, open to the affiliation of all national peak organisations and European industrial committees.[49] Despite its size, however, it remained essentially a Brussels lobbyist.[50] Financially, it was very weak.[51] Organisationally, it lacked authority to take decisions on behalf of its members, so that it could act only by fostering agreement among affiliates with very diverse traditions and interests. Within national peak organisations, the tendency was still to prioritise national interests, and to pursue these either at the national level or through intergovernmental channels. Despite all efforts to reach agreements, then, any joint platforms adopted by the ETUC tended to be deliberately vague, declaring general aims only.[52] As for BusinessEurope, the peak organisation of business, it too was small in terms of size and budget, and it too lacked authority to take decisions on behalf of members.[53] By reason of the technical, legal, linguistic and financial resources of its members, however, it was in a much stronger

[48] Z Tyszkiewicz, 'European Social Policy – Striking the Right Balance' (Winter 1989) *European Affairs*.

[49] BC Roberts and B Liebhaberg, 'The European Trade Union Confederation: Influence of Regionalism, Détente and Multinationals' (1976) XIV *British Journal of Industrial Relations* 261, 264–6.

[50] J Dolvik and J Visser, 'ETUC and European Social Partnership: a Third Turning-Point?' in H Compston and J Greenwood (eds), *Social Partnership in the European Union* (Basingstoke, Palgrave, 2001) 16.

[51] A Martin and G Ross, 'In the Line of Fire: the Europeanization of Labour Representation' in A Martin and G Ross (eds), *The Brave New World of European Labor: European Trade Unions at the Millenium* (New York, Berghahn Books, 1999) 322.

[52] Streeck and Schmitter, 'From National Corporatism', above n 22, 205.

[53] Known until 2007 as the *Union of Industrial and Employers' Confederations of Europe* (UNICE). For simplicity, 'BusinessEurope' is used throughout, even when referring to earlier periods.

bargaining position than the ETUC.[54] Of course, BusinessEurope also drew strength from the fact that its intention was to block, rather than shape, social policy initiatives. Threatening a boycott of talks in the mid-1980s, for example, it was able to insist on a Commission guarantee that any agreement which might result would *not* be used as a basis for Commission legislative proposals.[55] Viewed in this light, even the inability of Business Europe to bargain on behalf of members amounted to a strength.[56]

Recognising the existence of such barriers to a successful dialogue, the Commission eventually developed a more strategic approach to the promotion of participation. From 1988, it took steps to bolster the ETUC, and to create an incentive for employers to engage more fully in participatory initiatives.[57] In addition to taking time to convince reluctant union groups and individuals of the benefits of participation, the Commission began to provide the ETUC with financial support to the value of several million Euros per year. In respect of BusinessEurope, it adopted a stance of 'negotiate or we will legislate': if BusinessEurope refused to participate in negotiations with labour, the Commission would come forward with legislative proposals of its own.[58] With the extension of qualified majority voting to social matters on the horizon, this threat was sufficient to secure the involvement of BusinessEurope in the negotiation of an agreement with the ETUC and CEEP (the representative of public sector employers[59]) on the formalisation of the social dialogue in October 1991. The terms of this agreement were then used as the template for the relevant provisions of the Maastricht Social Chapter.

As a means of providing management with an incentive to participate in negotiations, the 'negotiate or we will legislate' threat left a lot to be desired. From the viewpoint of management, the incentive offered was the incentive to negotiate an agreement that was more attractive, or less burdensome, than any legislation that might be approved by the Council of Ministers. Rather than setting a floor of legislative standards, in other words, Community legislation had come to represent a potential *ceiling* of standards, above which agreement would not be reached. Furthermore, the creation of such an incentive shed doubt on the autonomy of the social dialogue: the likelihood was that management would only be motivated to negotiate in respect of matters already regarded by the Commission as the

[54]   Martin and Ross, 'In the Line of Fire', above n 51, 324.
[55]   P Teague, 'The Social Dimension to the 1992 Project' (1989) 27 *British Journal of Industrial Relations* 310, 318.
[56]   Martin and Ross, 'In the Line of Fire', above n 51, 324.
[57]   *ibid*, 324–27.
[58]   Dolvik and Visser, 'ETUC and European Social Partnership', above n 50, 21–22.
[59]   European Centre of Employers and Enterprises providing Public Services.

potential subject of legislation.[60] The ETUC, of course, was anything but independent of the Commission, relying on it almost wholly for financial support.[61]

In the years since 1992, the outputs of the social dialogue have tended to confirm doubts regarding its effectiveness. Only seven trans-sectoral agreements have been reached by the social partners. Of these, the first three (dealing with parental leave (1995), part-time work (1997) and fixed-term work (1999)) were each initiated by Commission consultation and implemented by way of Council Directive.[62] Whilst important symbolically as the first fruits of the social dialogue, the three agreements were so meagre in terms of substantive provisions, that a number of ETUC affiliates wished union support for them to be withdrawn.[63] Under pressure from these affiliates, the ETUC agreed in 1999 that it should review experience to date and evaluate the conditions under which social dialogue negotiations should be preferred to legislation initiated by the Commission. Since that time, the social partners have begun to issue periodic 'joint work programmes' signalling their intention to set their own policy agenda, rather than simply responding to Commission initiatives. Three further trans-sectoral agreements, dealing with telework (2002), work-related stress (2004) and harassment and violence at work (2007), have been reached, each making provision for 'autonomous' implementation by the social partners within the Member States.[64] At sectoral level, too, relations between European industrial committees and management representatives have developed such that a small number of collective agreements has been concluded. Initially, these were closely related to the Community's regulatory framework and were implemented by way of Council Directive but more recently, sectoral agreements have been reached which are to be implemented autonomously in the Member States.[65]

Writing at the end of the last century, it was difficult to argue that the social dialogue was anything other than a tool of regulation, championed by the Commission as a means of circumventing difficulties otherwise

[60] The general secretary of Business Europe expressed the attitude of management as follows: 'If employers were unhappy about [potential Commission proposals], they had only one remedy; to secure the option to step in and negotiate as reasonable a deal as they could with ETUC'. Cited in Dolvik and Visser, 'ETUC and European Social Partnership', above n 50, 22.

[61] Martin and Ross, 'In the Line of Fire', above n 51, 355–57.

[62] As at 25 August 2009: www.etuc.org/r/615. One further agreement was reached to revise the parental leave agreement of 1995.

[63] Dolvik and Visser, 'ETUC and European Social Partnership', above n 50, 27–29.

[64] www.etuc.org/r/615.

[65] S Smismans, 'The European Social Dialogue between Constitutional and Labour Law' (2007) 32 *European Law Review* 1.

associated with the Community's legislative process.[66] Since then there have been some small signs that the social dialogue might develop along more autonomous lines. Significant doubts remain, however, regarding the capacity of the 'social partners' within Member States to implement autonomous agreements effectively at Member State level.[67] Such doubts have increased following enlargement to the East and the accession of countries with little tradition of collective bargaining.[68] Doubts have been raised, too, regarding the extent to which 'autonomous' social partner agreements are truly the result of independent initiatives of the social partners: both the telework and the work-related stress agreements, for example, were signed under the threat of Commission legislation.[69] Finally, attention has been drawn to the ways in which the potential for autonomous action has been limited by the introduction of European Monetary Union (EMU), and the likely increase of competition for jobs between workers in different regions and companies.[70]

In light of such considerations, even those who attempt a more positive assessment of the social dialogue remain wary of predicting too rosy a future: '[T]o what extent the trade unions will prove capable of transforming the hitherto rather toothless European mode of social partnership ... remains to be seen'.[71] Others are much more damning. Corinne Gobin, for example, has drawn attention to the importance of the idea of consensus in shaping the social dialogue, and the consequent closing down of areas of conflict.[72] She reminds us that in the context of the EU's unbalanced Constitution, an increase in the autonomy of the social dialogue is not necessarily to be welcomed: the removal of the threat of Community legislation leaves the employers, again, without an incentive to negotiate. The ETUC, meanwhile, has little choice but to negotiate, being reliant on Commission support and on institutional recognition of the importance of its role. If the ETUC wishes the social dialogue to persist, confirming its status as a key European player, then it must ensure that agreements continue to be reached. If the employers are unwilling to compromise, then

---

[66] A Lo Faro, *Regulating Social Europe: Reality and Myth of Collective Bargaining in the EC Legal Order* (Oxford, Hart Publishing, 2000); N Bernard, 'Legitimising EU Law: Is the Social Dialogue the Way Forward?' in J Shaw (ed), *Social Law and Policy in an Evolving European Union* (Oxford, Hart Publishing, 2000).

[67] W Wedderburn, 'Inderogability, Collective Agreements and Community Law' (1992) 21 *Industrial Law Journal* 245.

[68] A Branch, 'The Evolution of the European Social Dialogue Towards Greater Autonomy: Challenger and Potential Benefits' (2005) 21 *International Journal of Comparative Labour Law and Industrial Relations* 342.

[69] Smismans, 'European Social Dialogue', above n 65, 346.

[70] Martin and Ross, 'In the Line of Fire', above n 51, 345–48.

[71] Dolvik and Visser, 'ETUC and European Social Partnership', above n 50, 34.

[72] C Gobin and A Dufresne, 'The impossibility of the right to strike at a European Union level', presented to the *European Consortium for Political Research*, September 2009.

agreement will mean little more that union acceptance of the employers' point of view. Gobin concludes by characterising the social dialogue as a mechanism for teaching trade unions to adjust to the hard laws of the market: to accept 'the employers' neo-liberal positions'.[73]

V.   LABOUR RIGHTS AS CONSTITUTIONAL RIGHTS?

The first Community charter of fundamental rights, of 1989, grew out of the Single European Act and the threat to the maintenance of social standards at Member State level posed by the project to complete the single market. Acting on a recommendation of the ESC in 1987, the Commission issued proposals, which were amended and then agreed in December 1989 by 11 of the 12 Member States (the UK opting out). The final version of the Charter was rather less radical than originally intended. According to the Commission's proposals, the aim had been to create a Charter which would provide a concrete foundation for a European social state, guaranteeing to all 'citizens' a wide catalogue of social rights extending beyond even those protected in the Council of Europe's Social Charter.[74] As agreed by 11 of the 12, the Charter was far narrower than this in substance, dealing only with the social rights of *workers* and not those of *citizens*. Nor was it legally binding on the institutions of the Community or the Member States: in the words of the Commission, it 'merely *state[d]* and *note[d]* the rights which were the subject of deliberations' (emphasis added).[75] Finally, the possibility of adopting directives in implementation of the Charter was limited by exactly those constraints which hindered the adoption of any other social or labour legislation: the lack of specific legislative competences, and the requirement for unanimity in the Council. In the final reckoning, the term 'Charter of Fundamental Social Rights' was something of a misnomer: at best, it was rather 'a reference point for a step-by-step programme of limited workers' rights tied to internal market goals'.[76]

Given the shortcomings of the 1989 Charter, renewed attempts were made in the 1990s to create a more substantial and legally-binding bill of rights. In 1996 and again in 1999, committees of experts recommended that a catalogue of fundamental rights – civil and political, and social and economic – be incorporated into the EC Treaty, such that all European citizens could refer to those rights and assert them in courts of law. The

[73]   *ibid*; C Gobin, *L'Europe syndicale: entre désir et réalité* (Brussels, Labor, 1997) 116.
[74]   COM(89) 248, discussed in S Leibfried and P Pierson, 'Prospects for Social Europe' (1992) 20 *Politics & Society* 333.
[75]   COM(92) 562.
[76]   J Kenner, *EU Employment Law* (Oxford, Hart Publishing, 2003).

final text of the EU Charter of Fundamental Rights was published in
October 2000. Again, the end result was less transformative than many
had hoped.[77] Rather than being incorporated into the Treaty of Nice, the
Charter was only 'solemnly proclaimed' by the heads of state and
government, the European Parliament and Commission. As such, it was
not legally binding. In terms of substance, the final text was limited by a
decision of the Cologne European Council that it should be declarative of
existing rights only, and should not guarantee any new rights. For the
avoidance of doubt, this was emphasised in the Preamble of the Charter,
and in the body of the text.[78] Though, on the face of it, the Charter
protected rights such as freedom of association, and collective bargaining
and collective action, this did *not* signal an extension of Community
legislative competence in these areas: the explicit exclusion of these rights
from Community competence remained unaffected.[79] Moreover, many of
the labour rights declared within the Charter were hedged around with
qualifications to the point where they were arguably empty of substance.
Under Article 27, for example, workers were to be guaranteed rights to
information and consultation, 'under the conditions provided for by
Community law and national laws and practices'. What was this intended
to mean, other than that workers were to be guaranteed those rights which
they were already guaranteed? Given such limitations, it seemed fair to
conclude in 2002 that the new Charter was best regarded as a statement of
policy or set of guiding principles only, and not as a new basis for
legislative action or litigation.[80]

Under the Treaty of Lisbon, the 2000 Charter of Fundamental Rights
will become legally binding on the institutions of the European Union, and
on the Member States 'when they are implementing Union law'.[81] Important, perhaps, symbolically, the impact of this development on the constitutional framework of the EU seems unlikely to be very great.[82] Since none
of the qualifications built into the Charter are to be removed, it will remain
declarative of existing rights only. In fact, it will be emphasised again in the

[77] B Hepple, 'The EU Charter of Fundamental Rights' (2001) 30 *Industrial Law Journal*
225.
[78] Preamble: 'This Charter reaffirms ... rights'. Article 51(2): 'This Charter does not
establish any new power or task for the Community or the Union'.
[79] Art 137(5) TEC.
[80] B Hepple, 'Enforcement: the law and politics of cooperation and compliance' in Hepple
(ed), *Social and Labour Rights in a Global Context* (Cambridge, Cambridge University Press,
2002) 243.
[81] Art 6(1) TEU; Art 51 EU Charter. The earlier EU institutional strategy was for the
Charter to become law as part of the EU's Constitutional Treaty, but with the abandonment
of that Treaty in the wake of the ratification crisis of 2005, the Charter, and indeed most of
the other provisions of the original Constitutional Treaty, were allocated a new legislative
home in the Treaty of Lisbon.
[82] P Syrpis, 'The Treaty of Lisbon: Much Ado... But About What?' (2008) 37 *Industrial
Law Journal* 219.

Treaty of European Union that Charter provisions, 'shall not extend in any way the competences of the Union'.[83] Neither will the weakness of the Charter as a source of free-standing, justiciable rights be addressed by the move to make it legally binding. Experience of the approach taken by the ECJ to date in assessing the weight of Charter rights reveals both a willingness on the part of the Court to declare certain rights to be fundamental, having reference to the Charter, and a tendency to undermine such rights by judging them constitutionally posterior to market freedoms. In *Laval* and *Viking*, as we have seen, freedom of association was recognised by the Court to be a fundamental right, but was nonetheless scrutinised for compatibility with the employers' freedom of establishment and freedom to provide services. The exercise of the 'fundamental right' was judged to constitute a barrier to the exercise of the economic freedoms and was subjected to a strict application of the proportionality test. In the course of the judgments, even the most fundamental of values, human dignity, was said by the Court to require to be reconciled with the economic rights protected under the EC Treaty.[84] The value of fundamental rights in the eyes of the Court was clear: all must yield to the exercise of the constitutionally prior market freedoms.[85]

In terms of the constitutional protection of labour rights within the EU, a second and potentially more significant change effected by the Treaty of Lisbon is the enactment of an undertaking to accede to the European Convention on Human Rights (ECHR).[86] As yet, the exact form that accession will take is unknown; however, it seems likely that, as a result, EU institutions will be subject to the direct jurisdiction of the European Court of Human Rights (ECtHR).[87] If this is so, one important consequence would be what Phil Syrpis has called the 'reversal of the proportionality principle'.[88] Instead of beginning with the question of whether the exercise of labour rights constitute barriers to market freedoms, the ECtHR would take the labour rights themselves as the starting point, requiring any breaches of those rights to be justified in accordance with the terms of the ECHR. The potential significance of this reversal becomes even clearer when we consider the recent approach of the ECtHR to interpreting and guaranteeing labour rights. At the same time as the ECJ has shown itself willing to 'balance' away rights to freedom of association protected at Member State level, the ECtHR has taken an increasingly expansive approach to the interpretation of such rights as protected by

---

[83] Art 6(1) TEU.
[84] *Viking*, above n 35, para 46; *Laval*, above n 35, para 94.
[85] Supiot, 'Europe Won Over', above n 44.
[86] Art 6(2) TEU, as amended by Treaty of Lisbon.
[87] Syrpis, 'The Treaty of Lisbon', above n 82, 233.
[88] *ibid*, 234.

Article 11 of the ECHR. Overruling earlier decisions that the Article 11 guarantee of freedom of association did *not* protect collective rights such as collective bargaining or industrial action, the ECtHR held in 2008 and 2009 that it did exactly that.[89] Moreover, in reaching these conclusions, the Court declared itself bound to have reference to sources of international law other than the ECHR when interpreting Convention rights.[90] In particular, it referred to the labour standards and rights protected by the International Labour Organisation (ILO) and the Council of Europe's own European Social Charter, using these sources as a guide to help it decide not only which rights were protected under Article 11, but also the substance and nature of those rights, and the boundaries of legitimate restrictions of those rights for the purposes of Article 11(2).[91]

The decisions of the ECtHR have been greeted with much enthusiasm.[92] Alain Supiot, for example, has spoken of the prospect of the ECtHR assuming a new role within the EU as a 'guardian of fundamental social rights': 'Social Europe will cease to be an empty term on the day when a special jurisdiction is created to lead the mission of ensuring that the objectives of social justice are fulfilled'.[93] Is this enthusiasm well founded? Is it right to suggest that the solution to the problem of the unbalanced Constitution lies here, with the protection of the human rights of citizens by the ECtHR? Can we detect, in the willingness of that Court to have reference to ILO and ESC standards when interpreting Convention rights, the possibility of the gradual entrenchment of a variety of labour and social rights such that would herald the emergence of a new and fundamentally different European Constitution? Might the ETUC develop a more meaningful role for itself within such a reconfigured Constitution, acting not as a trade union in the traditional sense, but in the manner of a social activist group, as a 'promoter of human rights, democracy and social justice'?[94]

A labour law perspective would urge caution in assessing these possibilities. For all that the ECtHR has taken an expansive approach to the interpretation of Convention rights in recent years, it remains the case that the rights protected within the Convention are civil and political, rather than social. With the best will in the world, there is only so much that the Court can do to safeguard labour and other social rights. It must also be borne in mind that the expansive approach of the Court follows decades of decisions which involved a prioritisation of individual over

---

[89] *Demir and Baykara v Turkey* (2009) 48 EHRR 54; *Enerji Yapi-Yol Sen v Turkey* (Application No 68959/01), 21 April 2009.

[90] *Demir*, paras 66–8, 85–6, 146.

[91] *Demir*, paras 154, 147, 165.

[92] KD Ewing and J Hendy, 'The Implications of *Demir and Baykara*' (2010) 39(1) *Industrial Law Journal* 2.

[93] A Supiot, 'A Sense of Measure' (2010) 19 *Social & Legal Studies* 217.

[94] Dolvik and Visser, *ETUC and European Social Partnership*, above n 50, 36.

collective interests such that it was very difficult to conceive of the Convention as a useful source of labour rights.[95] Whether the recent case law will prove to herald a lasting change of approach remains to be seen. Similarly, the matter of the ECtHR's willingness to overrule decisions of the ECJ is placed in doubt when we consider the deference shown by the ECtHR to the ECJ in past cases.[96] In light of these considerations, it remains far from clear that accession to the ECHR will bring about fundamental change.

VI.   CONCLUSION

In this chapter, I have addressed the subject of the labour law of the European Union as a matter of constitutional law. I have focused on the use of labour law within the EU to serve a legitimising or constitutional function, addressing criticisms that the Constitution is unbalanced in favour of the interests of capital, or that the EU is undemocratic. With an eye to conceptions of the constitutional function of labour law developed in the context of the nation state, I looked first at the participation of organised labour in EU legislation and policy-making as a means of strengthening the EU's claim to democracy. I then looked at the protection of labour rights as fundamental rights within the EU Constitution, assessing the likelihood that a variety of labour and social rights might be entrenched in a way that would herald the emergence of a new, more balanced, European Constitution.

My investigation of the social dialogue highlighted a number of respects in which the effectiveness of labour/management negotiations in the EU has been limited by the constitutional context in which they proceed. First, the constitutional preservation of Member State competence over social policy and legislation has hindered the development of effective interest representation at the European level, reinforcing notions of national interest, and tying trade unions and other interest groups to the *national* level as the dominant site of political decision-making. Attempts by the Commission to bolster the strength of the ETUC, so that it might nonetheless become an effective 'social partner' left the organisation compromised by its reliance on financial support from the Commission, and institutional recognition of its role. Caught in the trap of the 'elitist embrace', the ETUC's capacity to act in furtherance of its members' interests at times conflicted with its wish to cooperate with institutional

---

[95]   KD Ewing, 'Constitutional Reform and Human Rights: Unfinished Business?' (2001) 5 *Edinburgh Law Review* 297.

[96]   Syrpis, 'The Treaty of Lisbon', above n 82, 234.

decision-making processes and policies in order to reinforce its position of influence.[97] The representatives of the employers, meanwhile, have drawn strength from the fact that their interests lie with maintaining the status quo of an underdeveloped European social policy. The constitutional framework of the EU is weighted in favour of inaction in the social field. Even the threat of Commission legislation, used several times in the 1990s to encourage the employers to negotiate, is now rarely employed. Understood in the light of these constraints, the social dialogue appeared in a rather less positive light: the subordination of direct government intervention through regulation to a process of formalised, 'neo-voluntarist' consensus-building, and thus, the victory of economic liberalism over 'economic democracy'.[98]

My investigation of the protection of labour rights within the Charters of 1989 and 2000 raised the question of the meaning of 'fundamental rights' within the EU Constitution. On the evidence of the ECJ's decisions in the *Laval* and *Viking* cases, it seemed clear that elevation to the status of 'fundamental' would not protect labour rights from being judicially dismantled as unlawful barriers to the constitutionally prior market freedoms. Of itself, the conferral of legal status on the 2000 Charter seemed unlikely to compel a change in the approach of the ECJ. Potentially more significant, at least in that respect, was the undertaking in the Treaty of Lisbon for the EU to accede to the ECHR. But this, too, was judged unlikely to have a wider transformative effect on the EU Constitution. In addition to more general arguments about the limitations of 'bill of rights' type litigation as a means of effecting constitutional change (which space did not permit me to rehearse),[99] this verdict was informed by certain characteristics of the ECHR: by its civil and political rights composition; and by doubts regarding the long-term reliability of the judicial 'entrenchment' of labour rights in the face of an ECJ which thought otherwise. What might we conclude other than that fundamental rights initiatives, like the social dialogue, are after all incapable of addressing the 'fatal flaw' of the EU Constitution: the constitutional prioritisation in the Treaty of Rome of economic above social aims? Conceived as a potential antidote to the flaw, and to the 'competency gap' that resulted from it, each of the initiatives has been constrained in its operation by those aspects of the Constitution which it was intended to address.

[97] R Hyman, 'Trade Unions and the Politics of the European Social Model' (2005) 26 *Economic and Industrial Democracy* 9, 27.

[98] Streeck, 'Neo-Voluntarism', above n 33.

[99] H Arthurs, 'Constitutionalism – An Idea Whose Time Has Come… And Gone?' (2008) 75 *Amicus Curiae* 3.

Bibliography

ALONSO, LE and MARTÍNEZ, M (eds), *Employment Relations in a Changing Society: Assessing the Post-Fordist Paradigm* (London, Palgrave Macmillan, 2006)

ALSTON, P and DE SCHUTTER, O (eds), *Monitoring Fundamental Rights in the European Union* (Oxford, Hart Publishing, 2005)

ALSTON, P, '"Core Labour Standards" and the Transformation of the International Labour Rights Regime' (2004) 15 *European Journal of International Law* 457

AMORETTI, U and BERMEO, N, (eds), *Federalism and Territorial Cleavages* (Baltimore, Johns Hopkins University Press, 2004)

ARCHIBUGI, D and HELD, D (eds), *Cosmopolitan Democracy: An Agenda for a New World Order* (Cambridge, Polity Press, 1995)

ARENDT, H, *Origins of Totalitarianism*, new ed edn (New York, Harcourt Brace Jovanovich, 1973)

——, *On Revolution* (London, Penguin, 1990)

ARTHURS, H, 'Constitutionalism – An Idea Whose Time Has Come ... And Gone?' (2008) 75 *Amicus Curiae* 3

AVBELJ, M, 'The EU and the Many Faces of Legal Pluralism: Toward a Coherent or Uniform EU Legal Order?' (2006) 2 *Croatian Yearbook of European Law and Policy* 377

BALDACCINI, A, GUILD, E and TONER, H (eds), *Whose Freedom, Security and Justice: EU Immigration and Asylum Law and Policy* (Oxford, Hart Publishing, 2007)

BANKOWSKI, Z and SCOTT, A, *The European Union and its Order* (Oxford, Blackwell, 1999)

BARBER, N, 'Legal Pluralism and the European Union' (2006) *European Law Journal* 306

BARNARD, C and ODUDU, O (eds), *The Outer Limits of EU Law*, (Oxford, Hart Publishing, 2009)

BAUBÖCK, R, PERCHINIG, B and SIEVERS, W (eds), *Citizenship Policies in the New Europe*, 2nd edn (Amsterdam, Amsterdam University Press, 2009)

BEAUD, O, *Constitution et constitutionnalisme*, in *Dictionnaire de philosophie politique* (P Raynaud and S Rials eds, 2003) 133

BEDAU, HA, 'On Civil Disobedience' (1961) *Journal of Philosophy* 653

—— (ed), *Civil Disobedience in Focus* (London and New York, Routledge, 1991)

BEDDARD, P, *Human Rights and Europe*, 3rd edn (Cambridge, Cambridge University Press, 1993) 5

BEEVER, C, *European Unity and the Trade Union Movements* (Leiden, Sythoff, 1960)

BELLAMY, R, 'Legitimizing the Euro-'polity' and its 'Regime: The Normative Turn in EU Studies' (2003) 2(7) *European Journal of Political Theory* 7
——, Political Constitutionalism: *A Republican Defence of the Constitutionality of Democracy* (Cambridge, Cambridge University Press, 2007)
BELLAMY, R and CASTIGLIONE, D, 'Building the Union: The Nature of Sovereignty in the Political Architecture of Europe' (1997) 16(4) *Law and Philosophy* 421
BELLAVANCE, M, *Le Québec et la Confédération : un choix libre? Le Clergé et la Constitution de 1867* (Québec, Septentrion, 1992)
BESSON, S, 'European Legal Pluralism after Kadi' (2009) 5(2) *European Constitutional Law Review* 237
BERCUSSON, B, 'The Trade Union Movement and the European Union: Judgment Day' (2007) 13 *European Law Journal* 279
BESSON, S, 'Gender Discrimination under EU and ECHR Law: Never Shall the Twain Meet?' (2008) *Human Rights Law Review* 647
BINDER, G, *Treaty Conflict and Political Contradiction: The Dialectic of Duplicity* (New York, Praeger, 1988)
BODANSKY, D, 'Is there an International Environmental Constitution?' (2009) 16 *Indiana Journal of Global Legal Studies* 565
VON BOGDANDY, A, 'The European Union as a Human Rights Organization? Human Rights and the Core of the European Union' (2000) 37 *Common Market Law Review* 1307
——, 'The European Union as a Supranational Federation: A Conceptual Attempt in the Light of the Amsterdam Treaty' (2000) 6 *Columbia Journal of European Law* 27
VON BOGDANDY, A, MAVROIDIS, PC, and MÉNY, Y (eds), *European Integration and International Co-ordination: Studies in Transnational Economic Law in Honour of Claus-Dieter Ehlermann* (The Hague, Kluwer Law International, 2002)
VON BOGDANDY, A and BAST, J (eds), *Principles of European Constitutional Law*, 2nd edn (Oxford, Hart Publishing, 2009)
BOHM, D, *On Dialogue* (London and New York, Routledge, 2004)
BOLJKA, U, *The Unfinished Business of the Fifth Enlargement Countries. Country Report: Slovenia* (Sofia, Open Society Institute, European Policies Initiative, 2009)
BORGEN, CJ, 'Resolving Treaty Conflicts' (2005) 37 *George Washington International Law Review* 573
BOUVARD, M, *Labor Movements in the Common Market Countries* (New York, Praeger, 1972)
BRADLEY, A and EWING, K, *Constitutional and Administrative Law*, 14th edn (Harlow, Pearson, 2007)
BRANCH, A, 'The Evolution of the European Social Dialogue Towards Greater Autonomy: Challenger and Potential Benefits' (2005) 21 *International Journal of Comparative Labour Law and Industrial Relations* 342
BROWNLIE, I, *Principles of Public International Law* (Oxford, Oxford University Press, 2008)
BRUBAKER, R, 'Citizenship Struggles in Soviet Successor States' (1992) 26 *International Migration Review* 269
BULL, A, *The Anarchical Society: A Study of Order in World Politics* (Houndmills, MacMillan, 1977)

DE BURCA, G, 'The EU, the European Court of Justice and the International Legal Order after Kadi' (2009) 1(51) *Harvard International Law Journal*.

DE BURCA, G and SCOTT, J (eds), *Constitutional Change in the EU: From Uniformity to Flexibility?* (Oxford, Hart Publishing, 2000) 31

BURGESS, M and GAGNON, A, *Federal Democracies* (London, Routledge, forthcoming 2010)

BURKE, E, *Reflections on the Revolution in France* (London, Penguin, 1969)

BURKOV, A, 'Ratification of Protocol 14 to the Convention on Human Rights', *EU-Russia Centre*, 26th February 2010

CAPPELLETTI, M, SECCOMBE, M and WEILER, JHH, *Integration through Law: Europe and the American Federal Experience* (Berlin and New York, Walter de Gruyter, 1985–1988)

CASPER, G, *Constitutionalism*, in *Encyclopedia of the American Constitution*, vol 2 (LW Levy, KL Karst and DJ Mahoney eds, 1986)

CASS, DZ, 'The Constitutionalization of International Trade Law: Judicial Norm-Generation as the Engine of Constitutionalization' (2001) 13 *European Journal of International Law* 39

——, *Constitutionalization of the WTO* (Oxford, Oxford University Press, 2005)

CHECKEL, J, 'Why Comply? Social Learning and European Identity Change' (2001) 55 *International Organization* 553

CHILDERS, E and URQUHART, B, *Renewing the United Nations System* (Uppsala, Dag Hammarskjöld Foundation, 1994)

CHOUDHRY, S (ed), *The Migration of Constitutional Ideas* (Cambridge, Cambridge University Press, 2006)

CHOUDHRY, S and HOWSE, R, 'Constitutional Theory and the Quebec Secession Reference' (2000) 12 *Canadian Journal of Law and Jurisprudence* 143

CHRISTODOULIDIS, E, 'Constitutional Irresolution: Law and the Framing of Civil Society' (2003) 9(4) *European Law Journal* 401

COBBEN, P, 'Anerkennung als moralische Freiheit' (2009) 112 *Philosophische Jahrbuch* 42

COHEN, J and SABEL, C, 'Directly-Deliberative Polyarchy' (1997) 3 *European Law Journal* 313

COICAUD, JM and HEISKANEN, V (eds), *The Legitimacy of International Organizations* (Tokyo, New York, Paris, United Nations University Press, 2001)

COLLINS, H, 'Regulating Employment for Competitiveness' (2001) 30 *Industrial Law Journal* 17

COLLINS, R and WHITE, ND (eds), *International Organizations and the Idea of Autonomy* (London, Routledge, forthcoming 2010)

COMPSTON, H and GREENWOOD, J (eds), *Social Partnership in the European Union* (Basingstoke, Palgrave, 2001) 16

CONSTANTINESCO, L-J, 'La spécificité du Droit communautaire' (1966) *Revue trimestrielle du droit européen* 15

COTTIER, T, 'Trade and Human Rights: A Relationship to Discover' (2002) 5 *Journal of International Economic Law* 111

COX, A, *The Court and the Constitution* (Boston, Houghton Mifflin, 1987)

CRAIG, P, 'Sovereignty of the United Kingdom Parliament after Factortame' (1991) 11 *Yearbook of European Law* 221

CRAIG, P and DE BURCA, G (eds), *The Evolution of EU Law* (Oxford, Oxford University Press, 1999)

VAN CREVELD, M, *The Rise and Decline of the State* (Cambridge, Cambridge University Press, 1999)

CRISP, R and SLOTE, M (eds), *Virtue Ethics* (Oxford, Oxford University Press, 1997)

CRUZ, JB, 'Europa invertebrada: una conversación con Ortega' (2006) *Revista de Occidente* 129

——, 'The Changing Constitutional Role of the European Court of Justice' (2006) 34 *International Journal of Legal Information* 223

——, 'The Legacy of the Maastricht-Urteil and the Pluralist Movement' (2008) *European Law Journal* 289

——, 'What's Left of the Charter? Reflections on Law and Political Mythology' (2008) *Maastricht Journal of European and Comparative Law* 65

CRUZ, JB and MONTERO, CC (eds), *European Integration from Rome to Berlin, 1957–2007: History, Law and Politics* (Brussels, Peter Lang, 2009)

DAVIES, ACL, 'One Step Forward, Two Steps Back?' (2008) 37 *Industrial Law Journal* 126

DAVIES, G, '"Any Place I Hang My Hat?" or: Residence is the New Nationality' (2005) 11 *European Law Journal* 43

DAVIES, P, 'Market Integration and Social Policy in the Court of Justice' (1995) 24 *Industrial Law Journal* 49

DAVIES, P and FREEDLAND, M, *Towards a Flexible Labour Market* (Oxford, Oxford University Press, 1997)

DEIGHTON, A, 'Writing Europe into the World', Paper given at the European Studies Centre at St Antony's College, University of Oxford, 4th February 2010

DELANTY, G, 'Peripheries and borders in a post-western Europe', *Eurozine*, 20th December 2007

DELIMATSIS, P, *International Trade in Services and Domestic Regulations: Necessity, Transparency, and Regulatory Diversity* (Oxford, Oxford University Press, 2007)

DELMAS-MARTY, M, *Towards a Truly Common Law: Europe as a Laboratory for Legal Pluralism* (Cambridge, Cambridge University Press, 2002)

——, *Towards a truly common law: Europe as a Laboratory for Legal Pluralism* (Cambridge, Cambridge University Press, 2002)

DEMBOUR, M-B, *Who Believes in Human Rights? Reflections on the European Convention* (Cambridge, Cambridge University Press, 2006)

DENNING, Lord, *Introduction to the European Court of Justice: Judges or Policy Makers?* (London, Bruges Group, 1990)

DERRIDA, J, *The Other Heading: Reflections on Today's Europe* (Bloomington, Indiana University Press, 1992)

DIEZ, T, 'The Paradoxes of Europe's Borders' (2006) 4 *Comparative European Politics* 235

DIKA, M, HELTON, A and OMEJEC, J (eds) 'The Citizenship Status of Citizens of the Former SFR Yugoslavia After its Dissolution' (1998) 3 *Croatian Critical Law Review*, nos 1–2

DOWRICK, F, 'A Model of the European Communities' Legal System' (1983) 3 *Yearbook of European Law* 169

DRZEMCZEWSKI, A, 'The Internal Organisation of the European Court of Human Rights' (2000) *European Human Rights Law Review* 233

DRZEMCZEWSKI, P, 'The Council of Europe's Position with Respect to the EU Charter of Fundamental Rights' (2001) 22 *Human Rights Law Journal* 31

DUBOUT, E and TOUZÉ, S (eds), *Les droits fondamentaux: charnières entre ordres et systèmes juridiques* (Paris, Pedone, 2010)

DUFF, RA, 'The Limits of Virtue Jurisprudence' (2003) 34 *Metaphilosophy* 214

DUKES, R, 'Constitutionalising Employment Relations: Sinzheimer, Kahn-Freund and the Role of Labour Law' (2008) 35 *Journal of Law and Society* 341

DUNOFF, J and TRACTMAN, J (eds), *Ruling the World? Constitutionalism, International Law and Global Governance* (Cambridge, Cambridge University Press, 2009)

DZANKIC, J, *Transformations of Citizenship in Montenegro: A Context-generated Evolution of Citizenship Policies* CITSEE Working Paper 2010/03

EWING, KD, 'Constitutional Reform and Human Rights: Unfinished Business?' (2001) 5 *Edinburgh Law Review* 297

FARO, AL, *Regulating Social Europe: Reality and Myth of Collective Bargaining in the EC Legal Order* (Oxford, Hart Publishing, 2000)

FASSBENDER, B, 'The United Nations Charter as Constitution of the International Community' (1998) 36 *Columbia Journal of Transnational Law* 529

——, *The United Nations Charter as the Constitution of the International Community* (Leiden, Martinus Nijhoff, 2009)

FICHERA, M, *The Implementation of the European Arrest Warrant in the European Union: Law, Policy and Practice* (unpublished, doctoral thesis, University of Edinburgh, 2009)

FINNEMORE, M and SIKKINK, K, 'International Norm Dynamics and Political Change' (1998) *International Organization* 52, 887

FITZMAURICE, M and MERKOURIS, P (eds), *Treaty Interpretation and the Vienna Convention on the Law of Treaties: Thirty Years On* (Leiden, Martinus Nijhoff, 2010)

FLAHERTY, J, 'The Autonomy of the Political' (Unpublished PhD Thesis, Massachusetts Institute of Technology, 2003) 7

FOOT, P, *Virtues and Vices and Other Essays in Moral Philosophy*, 2nd edn (Oxford, Oxford University Press, 2002)

FOX, J, 'Unpacking "Transnational Citizenship"' (2005) 8 *Annual Review of Political Science* 171

FREYBURG, T and RICHTER, S, 'National Identity Matters: the Limited Impact of EU Political Conditionality in the Western Balkans' (2010) 17 *Journal of European Public Policy* 263

GAGNON, A-G (ed), *Le fédéralisme canadien contemporain: fondements, traditions, institutions* (Montréal, Presses de l'Université de Montréal, 2006)

GAGNON, A-G and TULLY, J (eds), *Multinational Democracies* (Cambridge, Cambridge University Press, 2001)

GAGNON, A-G, Montserrat, M and Rocher, F (eds), *The Conditions of Diversity in Multinational Democracies* (Montreal, Institute for Research on Public Policy, 2003)

GALBREATH, D, *Nation-Building and Minority Politics in Post-Socialist States: Interests, Influence and Identities in Estonia and Latvia* (Stuttgart, Ibidem, 2005)

GARLICKI, L, 'Cooperation of Courts: The Role of Supranational Jurisdictions in Europe' (2008) *International Journal of Constitutional Law* 6

GEARTY,C, 'The European Court of Human Rights and the Protection of Civil Liberties: An Overview' (1993) 52 *Cambridge Law Journal* 89

——, *Can human rights survive* (Cambridge, Cambridge University Press, 2006)

GELAZIS, N, 'Statelessness in the Baltic States: Ramifications for European Citizenship and Social Stratification after EU Enlargement' (2004) *European Journal of Migration and Law* 6, 225

GERHART, PM, 'The WTO and Participatory Democracy: The Historical Evidence' (2004) 37 *Vanderbilt Journal of Transnational Law* 897

GLENCROSS, A, 'Altiero Spinelli and the Idea of the US Constitution as a Model for Europe: The Promises and Pitfalls of an Analogy' (2009) 47(2) *Journal of Common Market Studies* 287

GOBIN, C, *L'Europe syndicale: entre désir et réalité* (Brussels, Labor, 1997) 116

GOLDSWORTHY, J, *The Sovereignty of Parliament* (Oxford, Oxford University Press, 1999)

GREER, S, *The European Convention on Human Rights* (New York, Cambridge University Press, 2006)

——, *The European Convention on Human Rights: Achievements, Problems, and Prospects* (Cambridge, Cambridge University Press, 2006)

GRIFFIN, J, *On Human Rights* (Oxford, Oxford University Press, 2008)

GRIMM, D, 'Does Europe Need a Constitution?' (1995) 1(3) *European Law Journal* 282

——, 'Integration by Constitution' (2005) 3(2–3) *International Journal of Constitutional Law* 193

GRÖNING, L, *EU, staten och rätten att straffa: Problem och principer för EU:s straffrättsliga lagstiftning* (Lund University doctoral thesis, Santérus, 2008)

GUILD, E (ed), *Constitutional Challenges to the European Arrest Warrant* (Nijmegen, Wolf Legal Publishers, 2006)

GUILD, E, GROENENDIJK, K and CARRERA, S (eds), *Illiberal Liberal States: Immigration, Citizenship and Integration in the EU* (Farnham, Ashgate, 2009)

GUTMANN, A (ed), *Multiculturalism: Examining the Politics of Recognition* (Princeton, Princeton University Press, 1994)

HAAS, E, *The Uniting of Europe* (London, Stevens & Sons, 1958)

——, *The Uniting of Europe: Political, Social And Economic Forces 1950–1957* (Stanford, Stanford University Press, 1958, 1968)

HABERMAS, J, *Between Facts and Norms* (Cambridge, MA, MIT Press, 1996)

——, 'Constitutional Democracy: A Paradoxical Union of Contradictory Principles?' (2001) 29 *Political Theory* 766

——, *The Divided West*, translation (Cambridge, Polity, 2006)

HALTERN, U, 'Pathos and Patina: the Failure and Promise of Constitutionalism in the European Imagination' (2003) 9 *European Law Journal* 14

HANSEN, R, 'The Poverty of Postnationalism: Citizenship, Immigration, and the New Europe' (2009) 38 *Theory and Society* 1

HARDT, M and NEGRI, A, *Empire* (Cambridge, MA, Harvard University Press, 2000)

HART, HLA, *The Concept of Law* (Oxford, Clarendon Press, 1961/1994)

HASSEMER, W, *Strafrecht: Sein Selbstverständnis, seine Welt* (Berlin, BWV, 2008)

HELD, D, *Democracy and the Global Order* (Cambridge, Polity, 1995)

HELFER, L, 'Redesigning the ECHR: Embeddedness as a Deep Structural Principle of the European Human Rights Regime' (2008) 19 *European Journal of International Law* 125

HENNETTE-VAUCHEZ, S, 'Divided in Diversity: National Legal Scholarship(s) and the European Convention of Human Rights' EUI-RSCAS Research Paper 2008/39

HEPPLE, B, 'The EU Charter of Fundamental Rights' (2001) 30 *Industrial Law Journal* 225

—— (ed), *Social and Labour Rights in a Global Context* (Cambridge, Cambridge University Press, 2002)

HOBBES, T, *Leviathan* [1951], Richard Tuck (ed) (Cambridge, Cambridge University Press, 1996)

——, *On the Citizen* [1641], Richard Tuck and Michael Silverthorne (eds) (Cambridge, Cambridge University Press, 1998)

HONNETH, A, *The Struggle for Recognition: The Moral Grammar of Social Conflicts*, trans J Anderson (Cambridge, Polity Press, 1995)

HOOGHE, L and MARKS, G, *Multi-level Governance and European Integration* (Lanham, Rowman and Littlefield, 2001)

HOWSE, R and NICOLAIDIS, K, 'Enhancing WTO Legitimacy: Constitutionalisation or Global Subsidiarity' (2003) 16 *Governance* 73

HUEGLIN, T, 'Federalism at the Crossroads: Old Meanings, New Significance' (2003) 2 *Canadian Journal of Political Science* 36

HUGHES, J, '"Exit" in Deeply Divided Societies: Regimes of Discrimination in Estonia and Latvia and the Potential for Russophone Migration' (2005) *Journal of Common Market Studies* 43, 739

HUGHES, J and SASSE, G, 'Monitoring the Monitors: EU Enlargement Conditionality and Minority Protection in the Central and East European Countries' (2003) *Journal on Ethnopolitics and Minority Issues in Europe* 1, 1

HULS, N, Adams, M and Bomhoff, J (eds), *The Legitimacy of Highest Courts' Rulings – Judicial Deliberations and Beyond* (The Hague, TMC Asser Press, 2009)

HURRELL, A, *On Global Order: Power, Values, and the Constitution of International Society* (Oxford, Oxford University Press, 2007)

HURSTHOUSE, R, *On Virtue Ethics* (Oxford, Oxford University Press, 1999)

HUSAK, D, 'The Criminal Law as Last Resort' (2004) 24 (2) *Oxford Journal of Legal Studies* 207

HYMAN, R, 'Trade Unions and the Politics of the European Social Model' (2005) 26 *Economic and Industrial Democracy* 9

IKENBERRY, J and KUPCHAN, C, 'Socialization and Hegemonic Power' (1990) *International Organization* 44, 283

IMERI, S (ed), *Rule of Law in the Countries of the Former SFR Yugoslavia and Albania: Between Theory and Practice* (Gostivar, Association for Democratic Initiatives, 2006)

JACKSON, JH, *World Trade Law and the Law of GATT* (Indianapolis, Bobbs Merrill, 1969)

JALUŠIC, V and DEDIC, J, '(The) Erasure – Mass Human Rights Violation and Denial of Responsibility: The Case of Independent Slovenia' (2008) 9 *Human Rights Review* 9

JANIS, M, 'Russia and the Legality of Strasbourg Law' (1997) 1 *European Journal of International Law* 93

JANO, D, 'How Legacies of the Past and Weakness of the State Brought Violent Dissolution and Disorder to the Western Balkan States' (July 2009) 14 *Journal of Peace, Conflict and Development*

JENNINGS, WI, *The Law and the Constitution*, 3rd edn (London, University of London Press, 1943)

JENSEN, OB and RICHARDSON, T, *Making European Space* (London, Routledge, 2004)

JESSUP, PC, *Transnational Law* (New Haven, Yale University Press, 1956)

JOERGES, C, *'What is Left of the European Economic Constitution?'* EUI Working Paper Law No 2004/13, 14–17

JOERGES, C and GHALEIGH, NS (eds) *Darker Legacies of Law in Europe: The Shadow of National Socialism and Fascism Over Europe and Its Legal Traditions* (Oxford and Portland, Oregon, Hart Publishing, 2003)

JOERGES, C and NEYERS, J, *'Deliberative Supranationalism Revisited'*, EUI Working Paper Law No 2006/20

JOERGES, C, Inher-Johanne, S and Tuebner, G (eds), *Transnational Governance and Constitutionalism* (Oxford, Hart Publishing, 2004)

JONES, ML, 'The Legal Nature of the European Community: A Jurisprudential Model Using Hart's Model of Law and Legal System' (1984) 17 *Cornell International Law Journal* 1

JOPPKE, C, 'Transformation of Citizenship: Status, Rights, Identity' (2007) 11 *Citizenship Studies* 37

——, 'The Vulnerability of Non-citizens' (2009) 39 *Perspectives on Europe* 18

KAHN, J, 'Russian Compliance with Articles Five & Six of the European Convention of Human Rights as a Barometer of Legal Reform & Human Rights in Russia' (2002) 35 *University of Michigan Journal of Law Reform* 641

KALYVAS, A, 'Popular Sovereignty, Democracy, and the Constituent Power' (2005) 12:2 *Constellations* 223

KARMIS, D and NORMAN, W, *Theories of Federalism: A Reader*, (New York, Palgrave Macmillan, 2005)

KEANE, J (ed), *Civil Society and the State* (London, Verso, 1988)

KELLEY, J, *Ethnic Politics in Europe: The Power of Norms and Incentives* (Princeton, Princeton University Press, 2004)

KELLY, S, *La petite loterie. Comment la Couronne a obtenu la collaboration du Canada français après 1837* (Québec, Boréal, 1997)

KELSEN, H, *General Theory of Law and State* (Cambridge, MA: Harvard University Press, 1946)

——, *Reine Rechtslehre* (Vienna, Österreichische Staatsdruckerei, 1992)

KENNER, J, *EU Employment Law* (Oxford, Hart Publishing, 2003)

KINGREEN, T, *Die Struktur der Grundfreiheiten des Europäischen Gemeinschaftsrechts* (Berlin, Duncker & Humblot, 1999)

KINGSBURY, B, 'The Concept of 'Law' in Global Administrative Law' (2009) 20:1 *European Journal of International Law* 23–57

KINGSBURY ET AL, 'The Emergence of Global Administrative Law' (2005) 68 *Law and Contemporary Problems* 15

KIRCHHOF, P, 'The Balance of Powers between National and European Institutions' (1999) 5 *European Law Journal* 225

KLABBERS, J, 'International Law in Community Law: The Law and Politics of Direct Effect' (2002) 21 *Yearbook of European Law* 263

——, 'Constitutionalism Lite' (2004) 1 *International Organizations Law Review* 31

——, 'On Rationalism in Politics: Interpretation of Treaties and the World Trade Organization' (2005) 74 *Nordic Journal of International Law* 405

——, *Treaty Conflict and the European Union* (Cambridge, Cambridge University Press, 2008)

KLABBERS, J, Peters, A and Ulfstein, G, *The Constitutionalization of International Law* (Oxford, Oxford University Press, 2009)

KLIP, A, *European Criminal Law* (Antwerp, Intersentia, 2009)

KLUYVER, CA (ed), *Documents on the League of Nations* (Leiden, Sijthoff, 1920)

KOLB, R, *Ius contra bellum: le droit international relatif au maintien de la paix*, 2nd edn (Basel, Helbing Lichtenhahn, 2009)

KOMÁREK, J and AVBELJ, M (eds), *Constitutional Pluralism in the European Union and Beyond* (forthcoming, 2011)

KOSKENNIEMI, M, *The Gentle Civilizer of Nations: The Rise and Fall of International Law 1870–1960* (Cambridge, Cambridge University Press, 2001)

——, 'Constitutionalism as Mindset: Reflections on Kantian Themes about International Law and Globalization' (2007) 8 *Theoretical Inquiries in Law* 9

——, 'The Fate of Public International Law: Between Technique and Politics' (2007) 70 *Modern Law Review* 1

——, *Fragmentation of International Law: Difficulties Arising from the Diversification and Expansion of International Law. Report of the Study Group of the International Law Commission* (Helsinki, Erik Castrén Institute, 2007)

KOSTOVICOVA, D and BOJICIC-DZELILOVIC, V (eds), *Persistent State Weakness in the Global Age* (Aldershot, Ashgate, 2009)

KOUTRAKOS, P, *EU International Relations Law* (Oxford, Hart Publishing, 2006)

KOVACH, H, Nelligan, C and Burall, S, *The Global Accountability Report: Power without Accountability?* (London, One World Trust, 2003)

KRASNIQI, G, *The Challenge of Building an Independent Citizenship Regime in a Partially Recognised State: The Case of Kosovo*, CITSEE Working Paper 2010/04

KRISCH, N, 'The Open Architecture of European Human Rights Law' (2008) *Modern Law Review* 183

KUMM, M, 'The Jurisprudence of Constitutional Conflict: Constitutional Supremacy in Europe before and after the Constitutional Treaty' (2005) 11(3) *European Law Journal* 299

KUMM, M and COMELLA, VF, 'The Primacy Clause of the Constitutional Treaty and the Future of Constitutional Conflict in the European Union' (2005) *International Journal of Constitutional Law* 473

KYMLICKA, W, *Politics in the Vernacular: Nationalism, Multiculturalism and Citizenship* (Oxford, Oxford University Press, 2001)
——, *Contemporary Political Philosophy* (Oxford, Oxford University Press, 2002) 327
KYMLICKA, W and NORMAN, W, *Citizenship in Diverse Societies* (Oxford, Oxford University Press, 2000)
LADEN, A, *Reasonably Radical: Deliberative Liberalism and the Politics of Identity* (Ithaca, Cornell University Press, 2001)
LAUTERPACHT, H, 'Report on the Law of Treaties' (1953/II) *Yearbook of the International Law Commission*, 90
VAN LEEUWEN, B, 'A Formal Recognition of Social Attachments: Expanding Axel Honneth's Theory of Recognition' (2007) 2 *Inquiry* 180
LEIBFRIED, S and PIERSON, P, 'Prospects for Social Europe' (1992) 20 *Politics & Society* 333
LEINO-SANDBERG, P, *Particularity as Universality: The Politics of Human Rights in the European Union* (University of Helsinki, doctoral dissertation, 2005)
LESTER OF HERNE HILL, LORD, 'Universality Versus Subsidiarity: A Reply' (1998) *European Human Rights Law Review* 73
LIEBICH, A and BAUBÖCK, R (eds), *Is there (still) an East-West divide in the conception of citizenship in Europe?*, RSCAS Working Paper 2010/19
LIIVOJA, R, 'The Scope of the Supremacy Clause of the United Nations Charter' (2008) 57 *International and Comparative Law Quarterly* 583
LINDAHL, H, 'Acquiring a Community: The Acquis and the Institution of European Legal Order' (2003) 9(4) *European Law Journal* 433
——, 'Dialectic and Revolution: Confronting Kelsen and Gadamer on Legal Interpretation' (2003) 24 *Cardozo Law Review* 769
——, 'Sovereignty and Representation in the EU' in Walker (ed), *Sovereignty in Transition*, 92 (Oxford, Hart Publishing, 2003)
——, 'A-Legality: Postnationalism and the Question of Legal Boundaries' (2010) 1 *Modern Law Review* 30
LINDROOS, A, 'Addressing Norm Conflicts in a Fragmented Legal System: The Doctrine of Lex Specialis' (2005) 74 *Nordic Journal of International Law* 27
LOUGHLIN, M, *The Idea of Public Law* (Oxford, Oxford University Press, 2003)
LOUGHLIN, M and WALKER, N (eds), *The Paradox of Constitutionalism* (Oxford, Oxford University Press, 2007)
LUBAN, D, 'Just War and Human Rights' (1980) 9:2 *Philosophy and Public Affairs* 160
LUCAS, M (ed), *The CSCE in the 1990s: Constructing European Security and Cooperation* (Baden-Baden, Nomos, 1993)
MAC AMHLAIGH, C, 'Revolt by Referendum? In search of a European Constitutional Narrative' (2009) 15(4) *European Law Journal* 552
MACCORMICK, N, 'Beyond the Sovereign State' (1993) 56 *Modern Law Review* 1
——, 'The Maastricht-Urteil: Sovereignty Now' (1995) 1 *European Law Journal* 259
——, *Questioning Sovereignty: Law, State and Nation in the European Commonwealth* (Oxford, Oxford University Press, 1999)
MADURO, M, *We the Court* (Oxford, Hart Publishing, 1998)

——, 'The Importance of Being Called a Constitution: Constitutional Authority and the Authority of Constitutionalism' (2005) 3 *International Journal of Constitutional Law* 373

MADURO, M and AZOULAI, L, *The Past and Future of EU Law: Revisiting the Classics on the 50ᵗʰ Anniversary of the Rome Treaty* (Oxford, Hart Publishing, 2010)

MAHONEY, P, 'New Challenges for the European Court of Human Rights Resulting from the Expanding Caseload and Membership' (2002) 21 *Pennsylvania State International Law Review* 101

MAHONEY, P, Matscher, F, Petzold, H and Wildhaber, L (eds), *Protecting Human Rights: The European Perspective: Mélanges à la mémoire de Rolv Ryyssdal* (Köln, Carl Heymans, 2000)

DE MAISTRE, J-M, *Œuvres*, edited by Pierre Glaudes (Paris, Laffont, 2007)

MAIZ, R and REQUEJO, F (eds), *Democracy, Nationalism and Multiculturalism* (London and New York, Routledge, 2005)

MAJONE, G, *The Dilemmas of European Integration* (Oxford, Oxford University Press, 2005)

MALMBERG, J and SIGEMAN, T, 'Industrial Actions and EU Economic Freedoms' (2008) 45 *Common Market Law Review* 1115

MANCINI, F, 'The Making of a Constitution for Europe' (1989) 26 *Common Market Law Review* 595

MANN, E, 'Parliamentary Dimensions in the WTO – More than Just a Vision?' (2004) 7 *Journal of International Economic Law* 659

MANNERS, I, 'Normative Power Europe: A Contradiction in Terms?' (2002) *Journal of Common Market Studies* 40, 245

MARKS, G, *et al* (eds) *Governance in the European Union* (London, Sage, 1996)

MARSCHALL, S, *Transnationale Repräsentation in Parlamentarischen Versammlungen* (Baden-Baden, Nomos, 2005)

MARTIN, A and ROSS, G (eds) *The Brave New World of European Labor: European Trade Unions at the Millenium* (New York, Berghahn Books, 1999) 322

MARTIN, SJ, *The Biochemistry of Viruses* (Cambridge, Cambridge University Press, 1978)

MARTINEZ, H, 'The Legislative Role of the Security Council in its fight against Terrorism: Legal, Political and Practical Limits' (2008) 57 *International and Comparative Law Quarterly* 333

MARTINI, C, 'States' Control over New International Organization' (2006) 6 *The Global Jurist Advances* 1

MAUPAIN, F, 'L'OIT, la justice sociale et la mondialisation' (1999) 278 *Recueil des Cours* 201

McGINNIS, JO and MOVSESIAN, ML, 'The World Trade Constitution' (2000) 114 *Harvard Law Review* 521

McILWAIN, C, *Constitutionalism: Ancient and Modern*, (Indianapolis, Liberty, 1975)

MILLER, M, 'Dual Citizenship: A European Norm?' (1989) *International Migration Review*, 23, 948

MILWARD, AS, *The European Rescue of the Nation-State*, 2nd edn (London, Routledge, 2000)

MINKKINEN, P, '"If Taken In Earnest": Criminal Law Doctrine and the Last Resort' (2006) 45 (5) *The Howard Journal of Criminal Justice* 521

MITSILEGAS, V, *EU Criminal Law* (Oxford, Hart Publishing, 2009)

MONTESQUIEU, BARON DE, *The Spirit of the Laws* [1748], Anne Cohler, Basia Miller & Harold Stone (eds), (Cambridge, Cambridge University Press, 1989)

MOORE, SF, 'Law and Social Change: The Semi-Autonomous Social Field as an Appropriate Subject of Study'(1972/1973) 7 *Law and Society Review* 720

MORAVCSIK, A, *The Choice For Europe: Social Purpose And State Power From Messina To Maastricht* (Ithaca, Cornell University Press, 1998)

——, 'In Defence of Democratic Deficit: Reassessing Legitimacy in the EU' (2002) 40 (4) *Journal of Common Market Studies* 603

——, 'What Can we Learn from the Collapse of the European Constitutional Project?' (2006) *Politische Vierteiljahresschrift* 47:2

MOSLEY, HG, 'The Social Dimension of European Integration' (1990) 129 *International Labour Review* 147

MOVSESIAN, ML, 'Judging International Judgments' (2007) 48 *Virginia Journal of International Law* 65

MOWBRAY, A, 'Crisis Measures of Institutional Reform for the European Court of Human Rights' (2009) *Human Rights Law Review* 9, 647

MÜLLER-DIETZ, H, Müller, E and Kunz, K-L (eds), *Festschrift Heike Jung* (Baden-Baden, Nomos, 2007)

MUS, J, *Verdragsconflicten voor de nederlandse rechter* (Zwolle, Tjeenk Willink, 1996)

——, 'Conflicts between Treaties in International Law' (1998) 45 *Netherlands International Law Review* 208

NADELMANN, E, 'Global Prohibition Regimes: The Evolution of Norms in International Society' (1990) *International Organization* 44, 479

NAIPAUL, VS, *An Area of Darkness* (London, Picador, 2002)

NEUMAYER, E, 'Unequal Access to Foreign Spaces: How States use Visa Restrictions to Regulate Mobility in a Globalized World' (2006) *Transactions of the Institute of British Geographers* 72

NIETZSCHE, F, *Twilight of the Idols and the Anti-Christ*, trans R J Hollingdale (London, Penguin, 1990)

NORTHRUP, H, CAMPBELL, D and SLOWINSKI, B, 'Multinational Union-management Consultation in Europe: Resurgence in the 1980s?' (1988) 127 *International Labour Review* 525

NOUTCHEVA, G, 'Fake, Partial and Imposed Compliance: the Limits of the EU's Normative Power in the Western Balkans' (2009) 16 *Journal of European Public Policy* 1065

NUOTIO, K (ed), *Europe in Search of 'Meaning and Purpose'* (Helsinki, Forum Iuris, 2004)

—— (ed), *Festschrift in Honour of Raimo Lahti*, trans K Nuotio (Helsinki, Forum Iuris, University of Helsinki, 2007)

OAKESHOTT, M, *On Human Conduct*, (Oxford, Clarendon, 1975)

OESCH, M, *Standards of Review on WTO Dispute Resolution* (Oxford, Oxford University Press, 2003)

OUTHWAITE, W, *European Society* (Cambridge, Polity Press, 2008)

PAMUK, O, *The Black Book* (London, Faber & Faber, 2006)

PAREKH, B, *Rethinking Multiculturalism* (London, Macmillan, 2000)

PAUWELYN, J, 'A Typology of Multilateral Treaty Obligations: Are WTO Obligations Bilateral or Collective in Nature?' (2003) 14 *European Journal of International Law* 907

——, *Conflict of Norms in Public International Law: How WTO Law Relates to Other Rules of International Law* (Cambridge, Cambridge University Press, 2003)

PEACOCK, A and WILLGERODT, H (eds) *German Neo-Liberals and the Social Market Economy* (London, Macmillan, 1989)

PERNICE, I, 'Multilevel constitutionalism in the European Union' (2002) 27 *European Law Review* 511

——, 'The Treaty of Lisbon: Multilevel Constitutionalism in Action' (2009) 2/09 *Walter Hallestein Institut Working Paper*

PERNICE, I and TANCHEV, E (eds), *Ceci n'est pas une Constitution – Constitutionalisation without a Constitution?* (Baden-Baden, Nomos, 2009)

PESCATORE, P, *Le droit de l'intégration* (Leiden, Sijthoff, 1972)

PETERS, A, 'Compensatory Constitutionalism: The Function and Potential of Fundamental International Norms and Structures' (2006) 19 *Leiden Journal of International Law* 579

——, *Elemente einer Theorie der Verfassung Europas* (Berlin, Duncker & Humblot, 2001)

PETERSMANN, E-U, 'Time for a United Nations "Global Compact" for Integrating Human Rights into the Law of Worldwide Organizations: Lessons from European Integration' (2002) 13 *European Journal of International Law* 621

——, 'Multilevel Judicial Governance of International Trade Requires a Common Conception of Rule of Law and Justice' (2007) 10 *Journal of International Economic Law* 529

PETTIT, P, *Republicanism: A Theory of Freedom and Government*, (Oxford, Oxford University Press, 1999)

POCOCK, JGA, *The Machiavellian Moment: Florentine Political Thought and the Atlantic Republican Tradition*, rev edn (Princeton, Princeton University Press, 2003)

POGGE, T, *World Poverty and Human Rights: Cosmopolitan Responsibilities and Reform* (Cambridge, Polity, 2002)

POSPISIL, LJ, *Anthropology of Law – A Comparative Theory* (New York, Harper & Row Publishers, 1971)

POWELL, HJ, *Constitutional Conscience: The Moral Dimension of Judicial Decision* (Chicago, University of Chicago Press, 2008)

PRECHAL, S, van Roermund, B (eds), *The Coherence of EU Law: The Search for Unity in Divergent Concepts* (Oxford, Oxford University Press, 2008)

QUINN, G, 'The European Union and the Council of Europe on the Issue of Human Rights: Twins Separated at Birth?' (2001) *McGill Law Journal* 46, 849

RAWLS, J, *A Theory of Justice* (Cambridge, Massachusetts, Belknap Press, 1971)

——, 'The idea of an overlapping consensus' (1987) *Oxford Journal of Legal Studies* 1

——, *The Law of Peoples* (Cambridge, Massachusetts, Harvard University Press, 2002 [1999])

——, *Political Liberalism*, expanded edition (New York, Columbia University Press, 2005 [1993])

RAZ, J, 'On the Authority and Interpretation of Constitutions: Some Preliminaries' (2001) 2 *Anuario de Derechos Humanos, Nueva Epoca*

REQUEJO, F, *Multinational Federalism and Value Pluralism* (London and New York, Routledge, 2005)

RICHMOND, C, 'Preserving the Identity Crisis: Autonomy, System and Sovereignty in European Law' (1997) 16(4) *Law and Philosophy* 337

RIEKMANN, SP and WESSELS, W (eds), *The Making of a European Constitution* (Wiesbaden, VS Verlag für Sozialwissenschaften, 2006)

RITTBERGER, V (ed), *Regime Theory and International Relations* (Oxford, Clarendon Press, 1995)

ROBERTS, BC and LIEBHABERG, B, 'The European Trade Union Confederation: Influence of Regionalism, Détente and Multinationals' (1976) XIV *British Journal of Industrial Relations* 261

ROSE, G, *The Broken Middle* (Oxford, Blackwell, 1992)

——, *Jacques Delors and European Integration* (Cambridge, Polity Press, 1995)

ROTH, K, 'Defending Economic, Social and Cultural Rights' (2004) 26 *Human Rights Quarterly* 63

ROUSSEAU, C, 'De la compatibilité des norms juridiques contradictoires dans l'ordre international' (1932) 39 *Revue Générale de Droit International Public* 133

ROUSSEAU, J-J, *The Social Contract* [1762] (Oxford, Oxford University Press, 1994)

ROYER, A, *The Council of Europe* (Strasbourg, Council of Europe, 2010)

RUBENFELD, J, 'Unilateralism and Constitutionalism' (2004) 79 *New York University Law Review* 1971

RYSSDAL, R, 'On the road to a European constitutional Court' (1991) *Recueil des cours de l'Académie de droit européen* 3

SADAT-AKHAVI, SA, *Methods of Resolving Conflicts between Treaties* (Leiden, Brill, 2003)

SADURSKI, W, 'Partnering with Strasbourg: Constitutionalization of the European Court of Human Rights, the Accession of Central and East European States to the Council of Europe, and the Idea of Pilot Judgments' (2009) 9 (3) *Human Rights Law Review* 397

SARAJLIC, E, *The Bosnian Triangle: Ethnicity, Politics and Citizenship*, CITSEE Working Paper 2010/06

SASSE, G, 'The Politics of Conditionality: The Norm of Minority Protection before and after EU Accession' (2006) *Journal of European Public Policy* 15, 842

SATO, T, *Evolving Constitutions of International Organizations: A Critical Analysis of the Interpretative Framework of the Constituent Instruments of International Organizations* (The Hague, Kluwer law International, 1996)

SAURUGGER, S, 'The Social Construction of the Participatory Turn: The Emergence of a Norm in the European Union' (2010) *European Journal of Political Research* 49, 471

SCELLE, G, *Une crise de la société des nations* (Paris, Presses universitaires de France, 1927)

SCHÄRER, R, 'The Council of Europe and the Reduction of Statelessness' (2006) *Refugee Survey Quarterly* 25, 33

SCHARPF, FW, *Governing in Europe: Effective and Democratic?* (Oxford, Oxford University Press, 1999)

SCHAUER, F, *Playing by the Rules: A Philosophical Examination of Rule-based Decision-making in Law and in Life* (Oxford, Clarendon Press, 1991)

SCHMITT, C, *Political Theology* (Chicago, 2005)

SCHNEIDERMAN, D (ed), *The Quebec Decision* (Toronto, Lorimer, 1999)

SEN, A, *The Idea of Justice* (Cambridge, Massachusetts, Harvard University Press, 2009)

SEYERSTED, F, *Common Law of International Organizations* (Leiden, Martinus Nijhoff, 2008)

SHAFFER, G, 'Parliamentary Oversight of WTO-Rulemaking? The Political, Normative, and Practical Contexts' (2004) 7 *Journal of International Economic* 629

SHANKS, M, 'The Social Policy of the European Communities' (1977) 14 *Common Market Law Review* 373

SHANKS, C, JACOBSON, HK and KAPLAN, JH, 'Inertia and Change in the Constellation of International Governmental Organizations, 1981–1992' (1996) 50 *International Organization* 593

SHAW, J, 'European Union Legal Studies in Crisis? Towards a New Dynamic' (1996) 16 *Oxford Journal of Legal Studies* 231

——, 'Postnational Constitutionalism in the European Union' (1999) 6:4 *Journal of European Public Policy* 579

——, 'Process, Responsibility and Inclusion in EU Constitutionalism' (2003) 9(1) *European Law Journal* 45

—— (ed), *Social Law and Policy in an Evolving European Union* (Oxford, Hart Publishing, 2000)

SHAW, J and MORE, G (eds), *New Legal Dynamics of European Union* (Oxford, Oxford University Press, 1995) 147

SHEVEL, O, 'The Politics of Citizenship Policy in New States' (2009) 41 *Comparative Politics* 273

SHUTE, S and HURLEY, S (eds) *On Human Rights: The Oxford Amnesty Lectures 1993* (Oxford, Oxford University Press, 1993)

SIKKINK, K, 'Transnational Politics, International Relations Theory, and Human Rights' (1998) *PS: Political Science and Politics* 31

SILBER, L and LITTLE, A, *The Death of Yugoslavia*, rev edn, (London, Penguin Books / BBC Books, 1996)

SIMPSON, AWB, *Human Rights and the End of Empire: Britain and the Genesis of the European Convention* (Oxford, Oxford University Press, 2001)

SINCLAIR, I, *The Vienna Convention on the Law of Treaties*, 2nd edn (Manchester, Manchester University Press, 1984)

SJURSEN, H (ed), *Questioning Enlargement: The EU in Search of Identity* (London, Routledge, 2006)

SMISMANS, S, 'The European Social Dialogue between Constitutional and Labour Law' (2007) 32 *European Law Review* 1

SOLUM, LB, 'Virtue Jurisprudence: A Virtue-Centred Theory of Judging' (2003) 34 *Metaphilosophy* 178

SOMEK, A, 'Postconstitutional Treaty' (2007) 8:12 *German Law Journal* 1121

DE SOUSA SANTOS, B, *Towards a New Legal Common Sense* (Cambridge, Cambridge University Press, 2002)

SOYSAL, Y, *Limits of Citizenship. Migrants and Postnational Membership in Europe* (Chicago and London, University of Chicago Press, 1994)

SPASKOVSKA, L, *Macedonia's Nationals, Minorities and Refugees in the Post-Communist Labyrinths of Citizenship*, CITSEE Working Paper 2010/05

STEIN, E, 'Lawyers, Judges and the Making of a Transnational Constitution' (1981) 75 *American Journal of International Law* 1

ŠTIKS, I, 'Nationality and Citizenship in the Former Yugoslavia: From Disintegration to European Integration' (2006) 6 *Southeast European and Black Sea Studies* 483

——, *A Laboratory of Citizenship: Nations and Citizenship in the Former Yugoslavia and its Successor States*, PhD Dissertation, Northwestern University (June 2009)/Sciences Po, Paris (March 2009)

——, *A Laboratory of Citizenship: Shifting Conceptions of Citizenship in Yugoslavia and its Successor States,* CITSEE Working Paper 2010/2

——, '"The Berlin Wall Crumbled Down upon Our Heads!": 1989 and Violence in the Former Socialist Multinational Federations' (2010) 24 *Global Society* 91

STREECK, W, '*Neo-Voluntarism: a New European Social Policy Regime?*' (1995) *European Law Journal* 31

—— (ed), *Social Institutions and Economic Performance* (London, Sage, 1992)

SUNSTEIN, C, 'Constitutionalism and Secession' (1991) 58 *University of Chicago Law Review* 633

——, 'Social Norms and Social Roles' in Cass Sunstein (ed), *Free Markets and Social Justice* (New York, Oxford University Press, 1997)

SUPIOT, A, 'Europe Won Over to the Communist Market Economy' (July 2008) *Notre Europe* www. globallabour.info/en/2008/07/europe_won_over_to_the_communi.html

SWEET, AS and MATHEWS, J, 'Proportionality Balancing and Global Constitutionalism' (2008) 47 *Columbia Journal of Transnational Law* 72

SYRPIS, P, *EU Intervention in Domestic Labour Law* (Oxford, Oxford University Press, 2007)

——, 'The Treaty of Lisbon: Much Ado . . . But About What?' (2008) 37 *Industrial Law Journal* 219

TAYLOR, C, *Multiculturalism and the Politics of Recognition* (Princeton, Princeton University Press, 1994)

TEAGUE, P, 'The Social Dimension to the 1992 Project' (1989) 27 *British Journal of Industrial Relations* 310

THORNHILL, C, 'Towards a Historical Sociology of Constitutional Legitimacy' (2008) 37 *Theory and Society* 161

THYM, D, 'In the Name of Sovereign Statehood: A Critical Introduction to the Lisbon Judgment of the German Constitutional Court' (2009) 46 *Common Market Law Review* 1795

TIMMERMANS, C, 'The EU and Public International Law' (1999) 4 *European Foreign Affairs Review* 181

TOMKINS, A, *Our Republican Constitution* (Oxford, Hart Publishing, 2005)

TRIDIMAS, T and GUTIERREZ-FONS, J, 'EU Law, International Law, and Economic Sanctions against Terrorism: The Judiciary in Distress?' (2009) 32 *Fordham International Law Journal* 660

TRIDIMAS, T, *The General Principles of EU Law,* 2nd edn (Oxford, Oxford EC Library, 2006)

TULLY, J, *Strange Multiplicity: Constitutionalism in an Age of Diversity* (Cambridge, Cambridge University Press, 1995)

——, 'The Unfreedom of the Moderns in Comparison to Their Ideals of Constitutional Democracy' (2002) 65 *Modern Law Review* 204

——, *Public Philosophy in a New Key,* 2 Vols, (Cambridge, Cambridge University Press, 2009)

TUORI, K, *Critical Legal Positivism* (Aldershot, Ashgate, 2002)

TYSZKIEWICZ, Z, 'European Social Policy – Striking the Right Balance', *European Affairs* (Winter 1989) 70

ULLMAN, W, 'The Development of the Medieval Idea of Sovereignty' (1949) 64 *English Historical Review* 1

VERDERY, K, 'Transnationalism, Nationalism, Citizenship and Property: Eastern Europe since 1989' (1998) 25 *American Ethnologist* 291

DE VILLE, J, 'Sovereignty without sovereignty: Derrida's Declarations of Independence' (2008) 19 *Law and Critique* 87

WADE, W, 'Sovereignty – Revolution or Evolution?' (1996) 112 *Law Quarterly Review* 568

WAHLGREN, P (ed), *Criminal Law, Scandinavian Studies in Law,* Vol 54 (Stockholm Institute for Scandinavian Law, 2009)

WALDRON, J, *Law and Disagreement* (Oxford, Oxford University Press, 1999)

WALKER, N, *'Fundamental Law'* in *Stair Memorial Encyclopedia of the Laws of Scotland (Re-issue 4)* (Butterworths Law, 2001) Volume on Constitutional Law, 29–82

——, 'The Idea of Constitutional Pluralism' (2002) 65 (3) *Modern Law Review* 317

——, 'A Constitutional Reckoning' (2006) 13(2) *Constellations* 140

——, 'Big "C" or small "c"' (2006) 12:1 *European Law Journal* 12

——, 'Beyond Boundary Disputes and Basic Grids: Mapping the Global Disorder of Normative Orders' (2008) 6 *International Journal of Constitutional Law* 375

——, 'Not the European Constitution' (2008) 15(1) *Maastricht Journal of European and Comparative Law*

——, 'Taking Constitutionalism Beyond the State' (2008) *Political Studies* 56, 525

—— (ed), *Sovereignty in Transition* (Oxford, Hart Publishing, 2003)

—— (ed), *Europe's Area of Freedom, Security and Justice* (Oxford, Oxford University Press, 2004)

WALL, I, 'On Pain and the Sense of Human Rights' (2008) 29 *Australian Feminist Law Journal* 53

WALZER, M, *Vernunft, Politik und Leidenschaft* (Frankfurt-am-Main, Fischer Taschenbuch Verlag, 1999)

WATTS, R, *Comparing Federal Systems* (Montreal and Kingston, McGill-Queen's University Press, 1999)

WEBB, B and WEBB, S, *Industrial Democracy,* vol 2 (London, Longman, 1897)

WEBER, M, *On Law in Economy and Society,* (Cambridge, Massachusetts, Harvard University Press, 1954)

WEDDERBURN, W, 'Inderogability, Collective Agreements and Community Law' (1992) 21 *Industrial Law Journal* 245

WEILER, JHH, 'The Community System: The Dual Character of Supranationalism' (1981) 1 *Year Book of European Law* 268
——, 'The Transformation of Europe' (1991) 100 *Yale Law Journal* 2403
——, 'A Quiet Revolution: "The European Court and its Interlocutors"' (1994) 26 *Comparative Political Studies* 510
——, 'Does Europe Need a Constitution? Demos, Telos and the German Maastricht Decision' (1995) 1(3) *European Law Journal* 219
——, *The Constitution of Europe: 'Do the Clothes have an Emperor?' and other Essays on European integration* (Cambridge, Cambridge University Press, 1999)
WEILER, JHH and WIND, M, *European Constitutionalism Beyond the State* (Cambridge, Cambridge University Press, 2003)
WELLENS, K, *Remedies against International Organizations* (Cambridge, Cambridge University Press, 2004)
WERNER, W and DE WILDE, J, 'The Endurance of Sovereignty' (2001) 7(3) *European Journal of International Relations* 283
DE WET, E, 'The International Constitutional Order' (2006) 55 *International and Comparative Law Quarterly* 51
DE WET, E and NOLLKAEMPER, A (eds), *Review of the Security Council by Member States* (Antwerp, Intersentia, 2003)
WEYLAND, I, 'The Application of Kelsen's Theory of the Legal System to European Community Law – The Supremacy Puzzle Resolved' (2002) 21 *Law and Philosophy* 1
WILDHABER, L, 'A Constitutional Future for the European Court of Human Rights?' (2002) 23 *Human Rights Law Journal* 161
——, 'The European Convention on Human Rights and International Law' (2007) 56 *International and Comparative Law Quarterly* 217
WILKINSON, M, 'Civil Society and the Re-imagination of European Constitutionalism' (2003) 9:4 *European Law Journal* 451
WILLIAMS, A, *EU Human Rights Policies: A Study in Irony* (Oxford, Oxford University Press, 2004)
——, 'Human Rights and Law: Between Sufferance and Insufferability' (2007) 122 *Law Quarterly Review* 132
——, 'Taking Values Seriously: Towards a Philosophy of EU Law' (2009) 29:3 *Oxford Journal of Legal Studies* 549
——, *The Ethos of Europe* (Cambridge, Cambridge University Press, 2010)
WIND, M and WEILER, JHH (eds), *European Constitutionalism Beyond the State* (Cambridge, Cambridge University Press, 2003)
WITTGENSTEIN, L (translated by Pears, D and McGuinness, B), *Tractatus Logico-Philosophicus*, 2nd edn (London, Routledge, 2001)
WOLFRUM, R and MATZ, N, *Conflicts in International Environmental Law* (Berlin, Springer, 2003)
WOODS, K, 'Suffering, Sympathy, and (Environmental) Security: Reassessing Rorty's Contribution to Human Rights Theory' (2009) 15:1 *Res Publica* 1356
WOUTERS, J, Nollkaemper, A and de Wet, E (eds), *The Europeanisation of Public International Law: The Status of Public International Law in the EU and its Member States* (The Hague, TMC Asser Press, 2008)

YOUNG, IM, *Justice and the Politics of Difference* (Princeton, Princeton University Press, 1990)

ZIELONKA, J, *Europa as Empire* (Oxford, Oxford University Press, 2007)

ZULEEG, M, 'Vertragskonkurrenz im Völkerrecht. Teil I: Verträge zwischen souveränen Staaten' (1977) 20 *German Yearbook of International Law* 246

Index